Lecture Notes in Computer Science 5922

Commenced Publication in 1973
Founding and Former Series Editors:
Gerhard Goos, Juris Hartmanis, and Jan van Leeuwen

Editorial Board

Bimal Roy   Nicolas Sendrier (Eds.)

Progress in Cryptology - INDOCRYPT 2009

10th International Conference on Cryptology in India
New Delhi, India, December 13-16, 2009
Proceedings

 Springer

Volume Editors

Bimal Roy
Indian Statistical Institute, Applied Statistics Unit
203 B.T. Road, Kolkata 700108, India
E-mail: bimal@isical.ac.in

Nicolas Sendrier
Centre de Recherche INRIA Paris-Rocquencourt, Projet-Team SECRET
B.P. 105, 78153 Le Chesnay Cedex, France
E-mail: Nicolas.Sendrier@inria.fr

Library of Congress Control Number: 2009939328

CR Subject Classification (1998): E.3, C.2, D.4.6, K.6.5, G.2

LNCS Sublibrary: SL 4 – Security and Cryptology

ISSN   0302-9743
ISBN-10   3-642-10627-7 Springer Berlin Heidelberg New York
ISBN-13   978-3-642-10627-9 Springer Berlin Heidelberg New York

springer.com

© Springer-Verlag Berlin Heidelberg 2009
Printed in Germany

Typesetting: Camera-ready by author, data conversion by Scientific Publishing Services, Chennai, India
Printed on acid-free paper   SPIN: 12802036   06/3180   5 4 3 2 1 0

Message from the General Chair

Starting with organizing the first International Conference on Cryptology in India (INDOCRYPT) in 2000, Cryptology Research Society of India (CRSI) has been spearheading these conferences in India every year in December at different places within the country. This year, the tenth conference in this series - INDOCRYPT 2009 was held in Delhi. The event was organized jointly by Scientific Analysis Group (SAG), Defense Research and Development Organization (DRDO) and Delhi University (DU) under the aegis of CRSI.

As is apparent, INDOCRYPT has been emerging as a powerful forum for researchers to interact, share their thoughts and their work with others for the overall growth of cryptology research in the world, more specifically in India. The overwhelming response in quality submissions to the conference and transparent open review mechanism helped in keeping the standards high and also in inducing researchers to participate in the conference and take up serious interest in the subject and R&D in this area. The response from within the country as well as from abroad was overwhelming, even from those participants who did not have contributory papers.

The complete INDOCRYPT 2009 event spanned over four days from 13 to 16 December 2009. The very first day was totally dedicated to two tutorials, whereas the main conference was held on the remaining three days with three invited talks and presentation of 20 papers. The tutorials were delivered by two eminent speakers—Willi Meier and Nicolas Sendrier provided insight of the subject to young researchers and also stimulated the thinking of others. The three invited talks were delivered by Dan Bernstein, Marc Girault and Thomas Johansson. I am thankful to all these speakers.

A conference of this kind would not have been possible to organize without full support from different people across different committees. While all logistic and general organizational aspects were looked after by the Organizing Committee teams, the coordination and selection of technical papers required dedicated and time-bound efforts by the Program Chairs. I am thankful to Nicolas Sendrier and Bimal Roy for their efforts in bringing out such an excellent technical program for the participants.

I am indebted to my fellow Organizing Chairs, Neelima Gupta (DU) and S.S. Bedi (SAG), and all other members of the organizing team from SAG and DU, who worked hard in making all the arrangements. Special thanks are due to the Organizing Secretary, S.K. Pal, for working tirelessly, shoulder to shoulder with volunteers and other team members from SAG and DU to make the stay of participants comfortable and the event enjoyable.

I express my heartfelt thanks to DRDO and DU for supporting us in all possible manners and also to MCIT (DIT), MSRI, BEL and ITI for sponsoring the event.

Last but not the least, I extend my sincere thanks to all those who contributed to INDOCRYPT 2009 and especially to the lucky ones who are now "authors" in this prestigious LNCS series of conference proceedings.

December 2009   P.K. Saxena

Message from the Technical Program Chairs

We are glad to present the proceedings of the 10th International Conference on Cryptology, INDOCRYPT 2009. This annual event started off nine years ago in the year 2000 by the Cryptology Research Society of India and has gradually matured into one of the topmost international cryptology conferences. This year we received 104 proposals of contributed talks from all over the world. After a rigorous review process, the Program Committee selected 28 papers out of those submissions. Each paper was thoroughly examined by several independent experts from the Program Committee or from the scientific community. The papers along with the reviews were then scrutinized by the Program Committee members during a discussion phase. We would like to thank the authors of all the papers for submitting their quality research work to the conference. Special thanks go to the Program Committee members and to the external reviewers for the time and energy they spent throughout the selection process so as to offer a conference and a volume of high scientific quality.

In addition to the contributed talks, we were fortunate to hear several keynote speakers who presented two very instructive tutorials:

Willi Meier	Analysis of Certain Stream Ciphers and Hash Functions
Nicolas Sendrier	The Design of Code-Based Cryptosystems

There were also three insightful survey talks:

Daniel J. Bernstein	High-speed Cryptography
Marc Girault	Cryptology and Elliptic Curves: A 25-Year Love (?) Story
Thomas Johansson	Coding Theory as a Tool in Cryptology

Finally, let us say that we are greatly indebted to Matthieu Finasz for setting up and running the submission and review server and for his help in the handling of the camera-ready versions of the published papers. We wish you a pleasant reading.

December 2009

Bimal K. Roy
Nicolas Sendrier

Organization

General Chair

P.K. Saxena   SAG, Delhi, India

Program Chairs

Bimal Roy   ISI Kolkata, India
Nicolas Sendrier   INRIA, France

Organizing Chairs

Neelima Gupta   Delhi University, India
S.S. Bedi   SAG, Delhi, India

Organizing Secretary

Saibal K. Pal   SAG, Delhi, India

Organizing Committee

S.K. Muttoo   Delhi University, India
Meena Kumari   SAG, Delhi, India
Shrikant   JCB, Delhi, India
Naveen Kumar   Delhi University, India
N. Rajesh Pillai   SAG, Delhi, India
Sarvjeet Kaur   SAG, Delhi, India
Rajeev Thaman   SAG, Delhi, India
P.D. Sharma   Delhi University, India
S.K. Azad   Delhi University, India
Noopur Shrotriya   SAG, Delhi, India
Sanchit Gupta   SAG, Delhi, India
Sandhya Khurana   Delhi University, India
Rahul Johari   Delhi University, India
Ajay Shrivastava   SAG, Delhi, India

Program Committee

Gildas Avoine	Université catholique de Louvain, Belgium
Thierry Berger	Université de Limoges, France
Raghav Bhaskar	Microsoft Research Bangalore, India
Johannes Buchmann	Technische Universität Darmstadt, Germany
Sanjay Burman	CAIR Bangalore, India
Sanjit Chatterjee	University of Waterloo, Canada
Cusheng Ding	Hong Kong University of Science and Technology, China
Jintai Ding	University of Cincinnati, USA
Orr Dunkelman	École Normale Supérieure, France
Bao Feng	Institute for Infocomm Research, Singapore
Matthieu Finiasz	ENSTA, France
Pierrick Gaudry	LORIA, France
Guang Gong	University of Waterloo, Canada
Neelima Gupta	University of Delhi, India
Tor Helleseth	University of Bergen, Norway
Seokhie Hong	Korea University, Korea
Pascal Junod	University of Applied Sciences Western Switzerland, Switzerland
Jens-Peter Kaps	George Mason University, USA
Andrew Klapper	University of Kentucky, USA
Tanja Lange	Technische Universiteit Eindhoven, The Netherlands
Subhamoy Maitra	ISI Kolkata, India
Keith Martin	Royal Holloway, University of London, UK
Alfred Menezes	University of Waterloo, Canada
Marine Minier	INSA de Lyon, France
S.K. Muttoo	University of Delhi, India
Mridul Nandi	NIST, USA
Kaisa Nyberg	Helsinki University of Technology, Finland
Tatsuaki Okamoto	NTT Corporation, Japan
Dingyi Pei	Guangzhou University, China
Josef Pieprzyk	Macquarie University, Australia
C. Pandu Rangan	IIT Chennai, India
Vincent Rijmen	K.U. Leuven, Belgium and Graz University of Technology, Austria
Matt Robshaw	Orange Labs, France
Dipanwita RoyChaudhury	IIT Kharagpur, India
Kouichi Sakurai	Kyushu University, Japan
Palash Sarkar	ISI Kolkata, India
P.K. Saxena	SAG, Delhi, India
Jean-Pierre Tillich	INRIA, France
C.E. Veni Madhavan	IISC Bangalore, India

Additional Referees

Avishek Adhikari
Carlos Aguilar Melchor
François Arnault
Daniel J. Bernstein
Rishiraj Bhattacharyya
Jaydeb Bhowmik
Anne Canteaut
Yaniv Carmeli
Donghoon Chang
Qi Chen
Joo Yeon Cho
Abhijit Das
Sharmila Deva Selvi
Yusong Du
Xinxin Fan
Georg Fuchsbauer
Sugata Gangopadhyay
Indivar Gupta

Mohammad Hassanzadeh
Michael Hojsik
Honggang Hu
Thomas Icart
Ellen Jochemz
Ramakanth Kavuluru
John Kelsey
Eike Kiltz
Ki Tak Kim
S. Kiyomoyo
Meena Kumari
Yann Laigle-Chapuy
Cédric Lauradoux
Gaëtan Leurent
Zhijun Li
Alexander May
Seyed Mehdi
S.P. Mishra

Saibal K. Pal
Arpita Patra
Goutam Paul
Kun Peng
Ludovic Perret
N.R. Pillai
Benjamin Pousse
Padmanabhan Raman
Sumanta Sarkar
Berry Schoenmakers
Peter Schwabe
Yannick Seurin
Thomas Shrimpton
Damien Stehlé
C. Su
V. Suresh
Kumar Swamy H.V.
Damien Vergnaud

Table of Contents

Hash Functions

Number Theoretic Cryptology

Lightweight Cryptology

Signature Protocols

Multiparty Computation

Secure Parameters for SWIFFT

Johannes Buchmann and Richard Lindner

Technische Universität Darmstadt, Department of Computer Science
Hochschulstraße 10, 64289 Darmstadt, Germany
{buchmann,rlindner}@cdc.informatik.tu-darmstadt.de

Abstract. The SWIFFT compression functions, proposed by Lyuba-shevsky *et al.* at FSE 2008, are very efficient instantiations of general-ized compact knapsacks for a specific set of parameters. They have the property that, *asymptotically*, finding collisions for a randomly chosen compression function implies being able to solve computationally hard ideal lattice problems in the *worst-case*.

We present three results. First, we present new average-case problems, which may be used for all lattice schemes whose security is proven with the worst-case to average-case reduction in either general or ideal lattices. The new average-case problems require less description bits, resulting in improved keysize and speed for these schemes. Second, we propose a pa-rameter generation algorithm for SWIFFT where the main parameter n can be any integer in the image of Euler's totient function, and not nec-essarily a power of 2 as before. Third, we give experimental evidence that finding *pseudo-collisions*[1] for SWIFFT is as hard as breaking a 68-bit symmetric cipher according to the well-known heuristic by Lenstra and Verheul. We also recommend conservative parameters corresponding to a 127-bit symmetric cipher.

Keywords: post-quantum cryptography, hash functions, lattices.

1 Introduction

Collision-resistant hash functions play a key role in the IT world. They are an important part of digital signatures as well as authentication protocols.

Despite their fundamental importance, several established hash designs have turned out to be insecure, for example MD5 and SHA-1 [24,6]. To avoid this lack of security in a central place for the future, we need efficient hash functions with strong security guarantees.

One such hash function with an intriguing design is SWIFFTX [2]. In contrast to all other practical hash functions, including all SHA-3 candidates, it remains the only hash function, where the most prominent security property, namely collision-resistance relies solely on the hardness of a well studied mathematical problem. This guarantee on the collision-resistance of SWIFFTX is a feature

---

[1] These pseudo-collisions were named by the SWIFFT authors and are not related to the usual pseudo-collisions as defined in e.g. the Handbook of Applied Cryptography.

B. Roy and N. Sendrier (Eds.): INDOCRYPT 2009, LNCS 5922, pp. 1–17, 2009.

derived directly from SWIFFT [17], the internal compression function, which has the same guarantee.

SWIFFTX was part of a hash design competition by the National Institute for Standards and Technology (NIST). It did not survive the competition, and we suspect this is due to inefficiency, with the main bottleneck being SWIFFT.

Our paper has three contributions. First, we show that SWIFFT is even less efficient than asserted by the authors, because their security analysis against lattice-based attacks is too optimistic. We will show that sublattice attacks are possible and analyze the implications on practical parameters.

Second, we present a variant of SWIFFT that is more efficient, since its collision-resistance can be reduced from a new average-case problem which requires less description bits, but can still be used to solve the same worst-case problems that were used before. This improvement to space and time requirements applies universally to all lattice-schemes based on worst-case problems via Ajtai's reduction (e.g. [10,9,17,16,25]).

Third, we present the smallest parameter set for SWIFFT which gives 100-bit symmetric security according to the heuristic by Lenstra and Verheul [14], it does in fact give 127-bit.

The paper is organized as follows. Section 2 deals with basics about lattices. Section 3 introduces the new average-case problems and reductions from SIS. Section 4 describes the SWIFFT compression function family. Section 5 presents the parameter generation algorithm and Section 6 discusses SWIFFT's security.

2   Preliminaries

A lattice Λ is a discrete, additive subgroup of $\mathbb{R}^n$. It can always be described as $\Lambda = \{\sum_{i=1}^{d} x_i \mathbf{b}_i \mid x_i \in \mathbb{Z}\}$, where $\mathbf{b}_1, \ldots, \mathbf{b}_d \in \mathbb{R}^n$ are linearly independent. The matrix $\mathbf{B} = [\mathbf{b}_1, \ldots, \mathbf{b}_d]$ is a *basis* of Λ and we write $\Lambda = \Lambda(\mathbf{B})$. The number of vectors in the basis is the dimension of the lattice.

For each basis $\mathbf{B}$ there is a decomposition $\mathbf{B} = \mathbf{B}^* \mu$, where $\mathbf{B}^*$ is orthogonal and μ is upper triangular. The decomposition is uniquely defined by these rules

$$\mu_{j,i} = \langle \mathbf{b}_i, \mathbf{b}_j^* \rangle / \|\mathbf{b}_j^*\|^2, \quad \mathbf{b}_i = \mu_{1,i} \mathbf{b}_1^* + \cdots + \mu_{i-1,i} \mathbf{b}_{i-1}^* + \mathbf{b}_i^*, \quad 1 \leq j \leq i \leq n.$$

It can be computed efficiently with the Gram-Schmidt process and $\mathbf{B}^*$ is the *Gram-Schmidt Orthogonalization* (GSO) of $\mathbf{B}$.

Conforming with notations in previous works, we will write vectors and matrices in boldface. Special tuples of vectors will be denoted with a hat (for an example see Section 4). The residue class ring $\mathbb{Z}/\langle q \rangle$ is denoted $\mathbb{Z}_q$.

3   Two Average-Case Problems

In this section we present a new average-case problem SIS'. We show that the average-case *small integer solution* problem (SIS) reduces to SIS'. So, SIS' can be used, for example, to solve worst-case problems that reduce to SIS without any loss in the parameters. The advantage is that SIS' requires $n^2 \log(q)$ less random bits. A similar construction is possible for the average-case problem LWE and has indeed been suggested (without naming it or proving reductions) by Regev and Micciancio in [18].

All cryptographic schemes, whose security relies on SIS, can switch to SIS' resulting in a scheme with smaller keys, which is also slightly faster (due to the structure of SIS'). This includes *all* systems based on worst-case lattice problems via Ajtai's reduction [1] or the adaptions thereof (e.g. [10,9]).

We will also show that the same idea can be adapted to the IdealSIS problem, which is SIS restricted to the class of ideal lattices. The number of description bits we save in this case is $n \log(q)$. So, *all* schemes based on worst-case problems in ideal lattices via the reduction of Lyubashevsky and Micciancio [16] can benefit from using IdealSIS' (e.g. [17,16,25,23]). How these improvements apply to SWIFFT may be seen in Section 4.1.

The technical difference is that SIS chooses a somewhat random basis for a random lattice, whereas SIS' chooses only a random lattice and takes the basis in Hermite normal form. This is analogous to using the standard form for linear codes in coding theory.

Definition 1 (SIS). *Given integers n, m, q, a matrix $\mathbf{A} \in \mathbb{Z}_q^{n \times m}$, and a real β, the small integer solution problem (in the ℓ_r norm) is to find a nonzero vector $\mathbf{z} \in \mathbb{Z}^m \setminus \{\mathbf{0}\}$ such that*

$$\mathbf{z} \in \Lambda_q^\perp(\mathbf{A}) = \{\mathbf{z} \in \mathbb{Z}^m \mid \mathbf{A}\mathbf{z} = \mathbf{0} \pmod{q}\} \qquad and \qquad \|\mathbf{z}\|_r \leq \beta.$$

We will now define two probability ensembles over SIS instances and show that these are essentially equivalent.

Definition 2. *For any functions $q(n), m(n), \beta(n)$ let*

$$SIS_{q(n),m(n),\beta(n)} = \{(q(n), U(\mathbb{Z}_{q(n)}^{n \times m(n)}), \beta(n))\}_n$$

be the probability ensemble over SIS instances $(q(n), \mathbf{A}, \beta(n))$, where $\mathbf{A}$ is chosen uniformly at random from all $n \times m(n)$ integer matrices modulo $q(n)$. Alternatively let

$$SIS'_{q(n),m(n),\beta(n)} = \{(q(n), [\mathbf{I}_n, U(\mathbb{Z}_{q(n)}^{n \times (m(n)-n)})], \beta(n))\}_n$$

be the probability ensemble over SIS instances $(q(n), \mathbf{A}, \beta(n))$, where $\mathbf{A}$ is an n-dimensional identity matrix concatenated with a matrix chosen uniformly at random from all $n \times (m(n) - n)$ integer matrices modulo $q(n)$.

Theorem 1. *Let $n, q(n) \geq 2, m(n) \geq (1+\epsilon)n$ be positive integers, and $\beta(n) > 0$ be a positive real, then $SIS_{q,m,\beta}$ reduces to $SIS'_{q,m,\beta}$. Here, $\epsilon > 0$ is some real number independent of n.*

The proof is given in Appendix A.

In the remainder of the section we will adept Theorem 1 to the case of ideal lattices. Throughout this part, let ζ_n be a sequence of algebraic integers, such that the ring $R_n = \mathbb{Z}[\zeta_n]$ is a $\mathbb{Z}$-module of rank n, i.e. $R_n \cong \mathbb{Z}^n$ as an additive group. Since $R_n = [1, \zeta_n, \ldots, \zeta_n^{n-1}]\mathbb{Z}^n$, we can use any ℓ_r norm on ring elements, by transforming them to integral coefficient vectors of this power basis. In order to apply ℓ_r norms on tuples of ring elements, we take the norm of the vector consisting of the norms of each element, so for $\widehat{\mathbf{z}} \in R_n^m$ we have $\|\widehat{\mathbf{z}}\|_r = \|(\|\mathbf{z}_1\|_r, \ldots, \|\mathbf{z}_m\|_r)\|_r$. We use the shorthand $R_{n,q} = R_n/\langle q \rangle = \mathbb{Z}_q[\zeta_n]$.

Definition 3 (IdealSIS). *Given integers n, m, q, a tuple $\widehat{\mathbf{a}} = [\mathbf{a}_1, \ldots, \mathbf{a}_m] \in R_{n,q}^m$, and a real β, the* ideal shortest vector problem *(in the ℓ_r norm) is to find a nonzero vector $\widehat{\mathbf{z}} = [\mathbf{z}_1, \ldots, \mathbf{z}_m] \in R_n^m \setminus \{\mathbf{0}\}$, such that*

$$\widehat{\mathbf{z}} \in \Lambda_q^\perp(\widehat{\mathbf{a}}) = \{\widehat{\mathbf{z}} \in R_n^m \mid \sum_{i=1}^m \mathbf{a}_i \mathbf{z}_i = \mathbf{0} \pmod{q}\} \qquad and \qquad \|\widehat{\mathbf{z}}\|_r \le \beta.$$

Analogous to the case of general lattices, we have two probability ensembles.

Definition 4. *For any functions $q(n), m(n), \beta(n)$ let*

$$IdealSIS_{q(n),m(n),\beta(n)} = \{(q(n), U(R_{n,q(n)}^{m(n)}), \beta(n))\}_n$$

be the probability ensemble over IdealSIS instances $(q(n), \widehat{\mathbf{a}}, \beta(n))$, where $\widehat{\mathbf{a}}$ is chosen uniformly at random from all $m(n)$ tuples of ring elements modulo $q(n)$. Alternatively let

$$IdealSIS'_{q(n),m(n),\beta(n)} = \{(q(n), [\mathbf{1}, U(R_{n,q(n)}^{m(n)-1})], \beta(n))\}_n$$

be the probability ensemble over IdealSIS instances $(q(n), \widehat{\mathbf{a}}, \beta(n))$, where $\widehat{\mathbf{a}}$ is a 1 concatenated with a tuple chosen uniformly at random from all $(m(n) - 1)$ tuples of ring elements modulo $q(n)$.

Theorem 2. *Let $n, m(n) \in \Omega(\log(n))$ be positive integers, $q(n) \in \omega(n)$ be prime, and $\beta(n) > 0$ be real, then $IdealSIS_{q,m,\beta}$ reduces to $IdealSIS'_{q,m,\beta}$.*

The proof is similar to the one before and can be found in Appendix B.

4   SWIFFT Compression Functions

The SWIFFT compression function family was proposed by Lyubashevsky *et al.* at FSE 2008 [17]. They showed that for one set of parameters, its efficiency is comparable to SHA-2, while its collision resistance is asymptotically based on *worst-case* computational problems in ideal lattices.

Specifically, for a set of integer parameters (n, m, p), in their case $(64, 16, 257)$, they use the polynomial $f(x) = x^n + 1$, the ring $R_{p,n} = \mathbb{Z}_p[x]/\langle f \rangle$, and the subset $D_n = \{0,1\}[x]/\langle f \rangle$ to define the family

$$\mathcal{H}_{n,m,p} = \left\{ h_{\widehat{\mathbf{a}}} \colon D_n^m \ni \widehat{\mathbf{x}} \longmapsto \sum_{i=1}^m \mathbf{a}_i \mathbf{x}_i \pmod{p} \,\middle|\, (\mathbf{a}_1, \ldots, \mathbf{a}_m) = \widehat{\mathbf{a}} \in R_{p,n}^m \right\}.$$

These functions can be computed efficiently. Let $\omega_0, \ldots, \omega_{n-1}$ be the roots of f in $\mathbb{Z}_p$ in any order, and $\mathbf{V}$ be the Vandermonde matrix generated by them

$$\mathbf{V} = \begin{pmatrix} 1 & \omega_0 & \cdots & \omega_0^{n-1} \\ \vdots & \vdots & & \vdots \\ 1 & \omega_{n-1} & \cdots & \omega_{n-1}^{n-1} \end{pmatrix}.$$

Applying the *Fast Fourier Transform* over $\mathbb{Z}_p$ to SWIFFT we get

$$\mathbf{z} \equiv \sum_{i=0}^{m-1} \mathbf{a}_i \mathbf{x}_i \bmod f \equiv \mathbf{V}^{-1} \left(\sum_{i=0}^{m-1} \mathbf{V}\mathbf{a}_i \odot \mathbf{V}\mathbf{x}_i \right) \pmod{p}, \qquad (1)$$

where $\odot$ is the pointwise multiplication in $\mathbb{Z}_p^n$. Since $\mathbf{V}$ is invertible, we may use $\mathbf{z}' = \mathbf{V}\mathbf{z}$ as hash, instead of $\mathbf{z}$. Since the compression function key $\widehat{\mathbf{a}}$ is fixed, we may precompute $\mathbf{a}_i' = \mathbf{V}\mathbf{a}_i$ for all i. So evaluating the compression function amounts to computing all n components of $\mathbf{z}'$ with

$$z_j' = \sum_{i=0}^{m-1} a_{i,j}' \, x_{i,j}' \bmod p, \qquad\qquad x_{i,j}' = \sum_{l=0}^{n-1} \omega_j^l \, x_{i,l} \bmod p.$$

Due to the form of f we can set $\omega_j \leftarrow \omega^{2j+1}$ for any element ω of order $2n$ in $\mathbb{Z}_p$. We insert the parameters and split up the indices $j = j_0 + 8j_1$ and $l = l_0 + 8l_1$.

$$x_{i,j_0+8j_1}' = \sum_{l_0=0}^{7} \sum_{l_1=0}^{7} \omega^{(l_0+8l_1)(2(j_0+8j_1)+1)} \, x_{i,l_0+8l_1} \bmod p$$

$$= \sum_{l_0=0}^{7} \omega^{16l_0 j_1} \cdot \underbrace{\omega^{l_0(2j_0+1)}}_{m_{l_0,j_0}} \cdot \underbrace{\sum_{l_1=0}^{7} \omega^{8l_1(2j_0+1)} \, x_{i,l_0+8l_1}}_{t_{l_0,j_0}} \bmod p \qquad (2)$$

The quantities t_{l_0,j_0} for all 2^8 possible x_{i,l_0+8l_1} and m_{l_0,j_0} can be precomputed. The SWIFFT authors recommend using $\omega = 42$, because then $\omega^{16} \bmod p = 4$, so some multiplications in the last expression can be realized with bit-shifts. A single $\mathbf{x}_i'$, i.e. the last expression for all j, can then be evaluated with a total of 64 multiplications, $8 \cdot 24$ additions/subtractions using an FFT network. The total number of operations (ignoring index-calculations and modular reduction) for the standard SWIFFT parameters is

$$\underbrace{16 \cdot 64}_{\text{computing } x_{i,j}'} + \underbrace{16 \cdot 64}_{\text{all } a_{i,j}' \cdot x_{i,j}'} = 2048 \text{ multiplications}$$

$$\underbrace{16 \cdot 8 \cdot 24}_{\text{computing } x_{i,j}'} + \underbrace{16 \cdot 64 - 1}_{\text{summing } a_{i,j}' \cdot x_{i,j}'} = 4095 \text{ additions/subtractions}$$

Lyubashevsky and Micciancio showed in [15] that *asymptotically* these compression functions are collision resistant, as long as standard lattice problems in lattices corresponding to ideals of $\mathbb{Z}[x]/\langle f \rangle$ are hard in the *worst-case*. The arguments given later by Peikert and Rosen in [19] can also be adapted to prove collision resistance of SWIFFT with a *tighter* connection to the same worst-case problem.

4.1   More Parameters

Let $k > 0$ be some integer, p be prime and $n = \varphi(k)$, where φ is Euler's totient function. Furthermore, let f be the kth cyclotomic polynomial, which is monic, irreducible over the integers, and has degree equal to n. Using the same structures as above, i.e. the ring $R_{p,n} = \mathbb{Z}_p[x]/\langle f \rangle$, and subset $D_n = \{0,1\}[x]/\langle f \rangle$ with this new f, we can construct the same compression function family as above and the asymptotic security argument given in [19,15] still holds. In order to apply FFT as before, we need to ensure that elements of order k exist in $\mathbb{Z}_p$. This is guaranteed whenever $k \mid (p-1)$.

Optimizations similar to the ones available for SWIFFT in this more general setting are still an area of investigation. We show how this can be done specifically for the parameters we recommend in Section 5.1.

For arbitrary parameters, we found that using additions in a logarithmic table instead of multiplications in $\mathbb{Z}_p$ is comparable in speed to the normal multiplication and special bit shifting reduction modulo 257 used in SWIFFT.

Another very general optimization follows from the observations given in Section 3. Using functions from the set

$$\mathcal{H}'_{n,m,p} = \left\{ h_{\widehat{\mathbf{a}}} \colon D_n^m \ni \widehat{\mathbf{x}} \longmapsto \mathbf{x}_1 + \sum_{i=1}^{m-1} \mathbf{a}_i \mathbf{x}_{i+1} \pmod{p} \;\middle|\; (\mathbf{a}_1, \ldots, \mathbf{a}_{m-1}) = \widehat{\mathbf{a}} \in R_{p,n}^{m-1} \right\}.$$

results in a slightly more efficient scheme, which uses less memory. Recall that all entries in $\widehat{\mathbf{a}}'$ can be precomputed in practice and having one of them equal $\mathbf{1}$ saves some multiplications during evaluation depending on the implementation. In Equation (1), if we would computed $\mathbf{z}$ instead of $\mathbf{z}'$ the speed-up is $1/m$. For $m = 16$ this is $\approx 6\%$ and it may be further increased with the sliding window method used for NTRU [3]. However, at the moment it is more efficient to compute $\mathbf{z}'$. In this case we save n multiplications, which is about 1% of all operations for standard SWIFFT parameters.

We believe that optimizations are easiest to find in the cases where k is prime or a power of two. Focusing on these two special cases, we can already see much more variety in the choice of parameters. See Table 1 for comparison of parameters where n is between 64 and 128.

4.2   SWIFFT Lattice

Let $\widehat{\mathbf{a}} \in R_{p,n}$. Consider the function $h_{\widehat{\mathbf{a}}} \in \mathcal{H}_{n,m,p}$ and extended the domain to $R_n = \mathbb{Z}[x]/\langle f \rangle$. The coefficient vectors of *periods* of this function form the set

$$\Lambda_p^\perp(\widehat{\mathbf{a}}) = \left\{ (x_1, \ldots, x_{nm}) \in \mathbb{Z}^{nm} \;\middle|\; h_{\widehat{\mathbf{a}}}\left(\sum_{i=0}^{n-1} x_{i+1} x^i, \ldots, \sum_{i=0}^{n-1} x_{m(i+1)} x^i \right) = \mathbf{0} \right\}.$$

This is a lattice of dimension nm, since the extended $h_{\hat{a}}$ is R_n-linear. A basis for this lattice can be found efficiently using a method described by Buchmann et $al.$ [4]. Collisions in the original (unextended) function $h_{\hat{a}}$ correspond exactly to vectors in this lattice with ℓ_∞-norm bounded by 1. Therefore we refer to these lattices as SWIFFT lattices.

A *pseudo-collision* is a vector in this lattice with Euclidean norm less than $\sqrt{nm}$, i.e. all vectors in the smallest ball containing all collisions. So every collision is a pseudo-collision, but not vice versa.

5   Parameter Generation

We now describe an algorithm for generating parameter sets (n, m, p) for the SWIFFT compression function families in Section 4. For the polynomial f we will use the kth cyclotomic polynomial, such that $n = \varphi(k)$. If multiple polynomials are possible, we choose the one, where the resulting bitlength of the output is shorter, i.e. the one with smaller p. For example, if $n + 1$ is prime, we will use the polynomial $f(x) = x^n + x^{n-1} + \cdots + 1$, and if n is a power of two, we will use the polynomial $f(x) = x^n + 1$.

Input: Integer n, s.t. $n = \varphi(k), k > 0$
Output: Parameters (n, m, p)

$l \leftarrow 1$
$p \leftarrow k + 1$
while *not isPrime(p)* **do**
     $l \leftarrow l + 1$
     $p \leftarrow l \cdot k + 1$
end
$m \leftarrow \lceil 1.99 \cdot \log_2(p) \rceil$

Algorithm 1. Parameter generation for $n = \varphi(k), k > 0$.

For each set of parameters, we may additionally compute the output bitlength $out = n(\lfloor \log_2(p) \rfloor + 1)$, the compression rate $cr = m/\log_2(p)$, the Hermite factor δ required for finding pseudo-collisions, and the minimal dimension d where we can expect to find pseudo-collisions. These values are listed in Table 1.

The two latter values δ and d are computed in the following fashion. Consider the function $len(d) = p^{n/d}\delta^d$. According to an analysis by Gama and Nguyen [8][2] this is the Euclidean size of the smallest vector we are likely to find when reducing a sublattice with dimension d of any SWIFFT lattice $\Lambda_p^\perp(\hat{a})$. Micciancio and Regev observed in [18] that this function takes its minimal value

$$len(d_{min}) = \delta^{2\sqrt{n \log(p)/\log(\delta)}} \qquad \text{for} \qquad d_{min} = \sqrt{n \log(p)/\log(\delta)}.$$

[2] Their experiments were performed on random lattices following a different distribution, but experimentally their results apply here as well.

Table 1. Parameters for $64 \leq n \leq 128$, k prime or a power of two

k	n	m	p	out	cr	δ	d
128	64	16	257	513	1.999	1.0084	206
67	66	17	269	529	2.106	1.0084	211
71	70	19	569	631	2.076	1.0073	248
73	72	17	293	577	2.074	1.0077	231
79	78	17	317	625	2.046	1.0072	251
83	82	15	167	575	2.032	1.0075	237
89	88	15	179	617	2.004	1.0071	255
97	96	18	389	769	2.092	1.0061	308
101	100	19	607	901	2.055	1.0056	340
103	102	19	619	919	2.049	1.0055	348
107	106	19	643	955	2.037	1.0053	361
109	108	21	1091	1081	2.081	1.0049	392
113	112	16	227	785	2.044	1.0058	325
127	126	18	509	1009	2.002	1.0047	408
256	128	16	257	1025	1.999	1.0051	373

A pseudo-collision is a vector in $\Lambda_p^{\perp}(\hat{\mathbf{a}})$ with Euclidean norm $\sqrt{nm}$. In order to find such a vector, we need a δ, s.t. $len(d_{min}) = \sqrt{nm}$. We say this is the Hermite factor required for finding pseudo-collisions, and the corresponding d_{min} is the minimal dimension, where we can expect to find a pseudo-collision. Note that these minimal dimensions, which we will work in are about 5 *times* smaller than the corresponding dimensions of the SWIFFT lattices. To give an intuition, Gama and Nguyen state that the best lattice reduction algorithms known today can achieve a Hermite factor of roughly $\delta = 1.01$ in high dimension within acceptable time.

5.1   Recommended Parameters

We will give arguments in Section 6.2 that parameters with $d \geq 260$ correspond to SWIFFT instances, where finding pseudo-collisions is at least as hard as breaking a 100-bit symmetric cipher. The smallest such parameters in Table 1 are $(n, m, p) = (96, 18, 389)$. Finding pseudo-collisions for these parameters is as hard as breaking a 127-bit symmetric cipher. Concerning all other known attacks, these parameters are more secure than $(64, 16, 257)$.

Note that most of the efficiency improvements we outlined in Section 5 for the original SWIFFT function can be adapted to this setting. Recall Equation 2, since $k = 97$ is prime we can set $\omega_j \leftarrow \omega^{j+1}$ for any element ω of order k in $\mathbb{Z}_p$. We recommend to split up the indices $l = l_0 + 8l_1$, where $0 \leq l_0 \leq 7, 0 \leq l_1 \leq 11$, j similar and use $\omega = 275$, and since multiplying with $\omega^8 = 16$ can then be realized with bit-shifts. Corresponding to Equation 2 we get

$$x'_{i,j_0+8j_1} = \sum_{l_0=0}^{7} \omega^{8l_0 j_1} \cdot \underbrace{\omega^{l_0(j_0+1)}}_{m_{l_0,j_0}} \cdot \underbrace{\sum_{l_1=0}^{11} \omega^{l_1(8j_0+64j_1+8)} x_{i,l_0+8l_1}}_{t_{l_0,j_0,j_1}} \mod p.$$

Note that the precomputed t part depends on j_1 now, and needs to be available for 2^{12} possible $x_{i,l}$. So this part will need $12 \cdot 2^4 = 192$ times the space it did before. Doing the same reasoning as before, the number of operations is:

$$\underbrace{18 \cdot 64}_{\text{computing } x'_{i,j}} + \underbrace{18 \cdot 96}_{\text{all } a'_{i,j} \cdot x'_{i,j}} = 2880 \ (+40\%) \text{ multiplications}$$

$$\underbrace{18 \cdot 12 \cdot 24}_{\text{computing } x'_{i,j}} + \underbrace{18 \cdot 96 - 1}_{\text{summing } a'_{i,j} \cdot x'_{i,j}} = 6911 \ (+68\%) \text{ additions/subtractions.}$$

6 Security Analysis

The collision resistance of SWIFFT has the desirable property of being reducible from a worst-case computational problem. In particular, this means an algorithm which breaks random instances of SWIFFT compression functions with main parameter n can also be used to find short nonzero vectors in *all* ideals of the ring $\mathbb{Z}[x]/\langle x^n + 1 \rangle$. Finding such vectors is assumed to be infeasible for large n. However, for the current parameter, $n = 64$, exhaustive search algorithms find these short vectors in less than one hour. In the lattice challenge [4] open for all enthusiasts similar problems have been solved[3] up to $n = 108$. Gama and Nguyen even state that finding the *shortest* vector in n-dimensional lattices for $n \leq 70$ should be considered easy [8]. So the resulting lower bound on the attacker's runtime is insignificant. However, attacking not the underlying worst-case problem, but a concrete SWIFFT instance is much harder.

We will analyze the *practical* security of SWIFFT. As we have seen in Section 4.2, collisions in the SWIFFT compression functions naturally correspond to vectors with ℓ_∞-norm bounded by 1 in certain lattices. These may be recovered with lattice basis reduction algorithms. Since these algorithms are highly optimized to find small vectors in the Euclidean norm, it is reasonable to analyze the computational problem of finding pseudo-collisions instead of collisions. These are vectors in the *smallest ball* which contains all vectors corresponding to collisions, so an algorithm which minimizes the Euclidean norm cannot distinguish between the two. In this section, we give experimental evidence that according to a well-known heuristic by Lenstra and Verheul [14], finding pseudo-collisions is comparable to breaking a 68-bit symmetric cipher. In comparison, all other attacks analyzed by the SWIFFT authors take 2^{106} operations and almost as much space.

In their original proposal of SWIFFT, Lyubashevsky *et al.* provide a first analysis of all standard attacks. When it comes to attacks using lattice reduction however they state that the dimension 1024 of SWIFFT lattices is too big for current algorithms. We start by showing that reducing sublattices of dimension 251, which corresponds to $m = 4$, is sufficient to find pseudo-collisions and

---

[3] See http://www.latticechallenge.org

dimension 325 ($m = 5$) is sufficient for collisions and beyond this point as Micciancio and Regev observe in [18] "the problem [SVP] cannot become harder by increasing m". This means if we find a pseudo-collision in dimension 251, we can pad it with zeroes to obtain a pseudo-collision for SWIFFT. In practice, even dimension $d = 205$ is sufficient to find pseudo-collisions (cf. Table 1). In particular this means SWIFFTX, where internally SWIFFT is used with $m = 32$ is not more secure.

6.1   Existence of (Pseudo-)Collisions in d-Dimensional Sublattices

The method we have given in Section 5 for choosing the dimension of the sublattice we attack with lattice-basis reduction algorithms is a heuristic, because it is based on extensive experiments by Gama and Nguyen. We will now give a related result independent of experiments but dependent on the construction of SWIFFT lattices and other lattices of the form $\{\mathbf{v} \in \mathbb{Z}^d : \mathbf{Av} \equiv \mathbf{0} \pmod{p}\}$, where $\mathbf{A}$ is some integral matrix. These lattices are widely used in practice for constructing provably secure cryptosystems (see e.g. [9,16,20]) and they originate from Ajtai's work [1].

Let $h_{\widehat{\mathbf{a}}}$ be a random SWIFFT compression function with parameters (n, m, p). The range of this function has size $|R| = p^n$. We change the domain of $h_{\widehat{\mathbf{a}}}$ to all vectors in a d-dimensional subspace of $\mathbb{Z}^{nm}$ that have Euclidean norm less than $r = \sqrt{nm}/2$. The size of this space can be very well approximated by the volume of a d-dimensional ball with radius r, i.e. $|D| \approx r^d \pi^{d/2} / \Gamma(d/2 + 1)$.

Now any collision in the modified $h_{\widehat{\mathbf{a}}}$ corresponds to a pseudo-collision of the corresponding SWIFFT function by the triangle inequality. These collisions exist for certain by the pigeonhole principle for all $d \geq 251$. So the dimension $d = 205$ suggested by the heuristic looks too optimistic, but remember that this argument only gives an upper bound on the required d and doesn't take into account the randomness in the choice of $\widehat{\mathbf{a}}$.

The situation for proper collisions is similar. Here, we shrink the input to all vectors in a d-dimensional subspace that have coefficients in $\{0,1\}$. The size of this input space is $|D| = 2^d$. Again, collisions exist by the pigeonhole principle for all $d \geq 513$.

A different analysis is possible here, which takes into account the randomness of $\widehat{\mathbf{a}}$ and reveals that proper collisions exist for all $d \geq 325$ (see Appendix C).

6.2   Experiments

For our experiments we chose the sublattice dimension where lattice basis reduction algorithms like LLL/BKZ behave optimal in practice (see Section 5). We then proceeded to compare the following lattice basis reduction algorithms to see which performs best in practice on the lattices in our experiment. BKZ as implemented in version 5.5.1 of the "Number Theory Library" (NTL) by Shoup [22], Primal-Dual (PD) as implemented by Filipović and Koy, and finally RSR as implemented by Ludwig. Both latter algorithms are available on request from

Table 2. Parameters used for our experiments

n	m	p	δ	d
64	16	29	1.0140	125
64	16	33	1.0135	130
64	16	37	1.0131	134
64	16	41	1.0127	138
64	16	45	1.0124	141
64	16	49	1.0121	144
64	16	53	1.0119	147
64	16	57	1.0117	150
64	16	61	1.0115	152

the authors[4]. It became apparent that Primal-Dual runs much slower than both competitors, so for the main experiment we omitted it.

For our experiments, we fixed $n = 64$, $m = 16$ to their standard values and chose the third parameter p variable. This results in a steady decrease in the Hermite factor and increase in the dimension required to find pseudo-collisions (see Table 2). We found that for smaller values of p, corresponding to smaller values of d, pseudo-collisions were found too fast to make sensible measurements.

For each of these 9 parameter sets, we created 10 random SWIFFT lattices using the PRNG, which is part of NTL. We then proceeded to break all instances with the NTL floating-point variant of BKZ (bkzfp), by increasing the BKZ parameter β until a pseudo-collision was found and recording the total time taken in each case. We also broke all instances with a floating-point variant of Schnorr's random sampling reduction (RSR) algorithm [21] (rsrfp) implemented by Ludwig [5] using the parameters $\delta = 0.9, u = 22$ and again increasing β until a pseudo-collision was found.

In all cases, we computed the average runtime of both algorithms and plotted the base two log of this value relative to the dimension d. We also plotted a conservative extrapolation (assuming linear growth in logscale) for the average runtime of both algorithms (see Figure 1). The same growth assumption has often been made when analyzing NTRU lattices [11].

All our experiments were run on a single 2.3 GHz AMD Opteron processor. According to the predictions of Lenstra and Verheul [14] the computational hardness of a problem solved after t seconds on such a machine is comparable to breaking a k-bit symmetric cipher, where

$$k = \log_2(t) + \log_2(2300) - \log_2(60 \cdot 60 \cdot 24 \cdot 365.25) - \log_2(5 \cdot 10^5) + 56.$$

Using the data in Figure 1, we can compute the security level k corresponding to the average runtime of each algorithm relative to the dimension d for each parameter set.

---

[4] PD, Bartol Filipović, `bartol.filipovic@sit.fraunhofer.de`
PSR, Christoph Ludwig, `cludwig@cdc.informatik.tu-darmstadt.de`

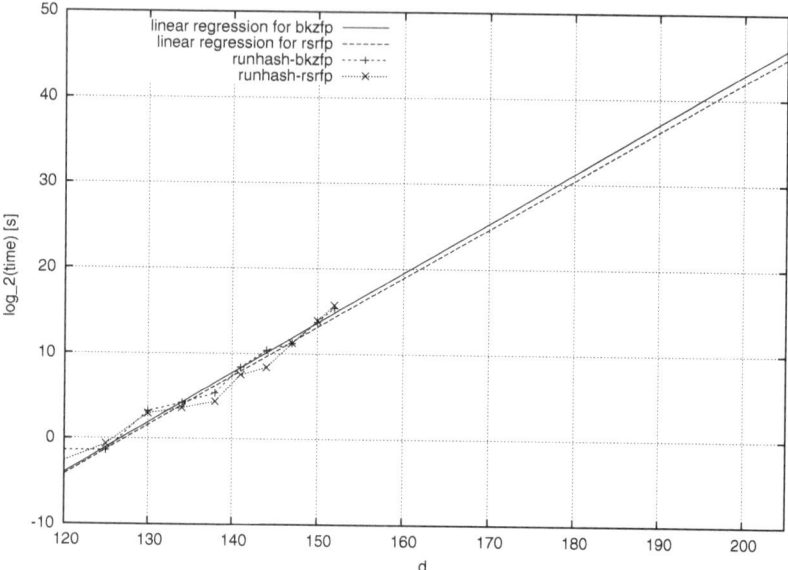

Fig. 1. Average runtimes of our experiments

The rightmost side of Figure 1 corresponds to $p = 257$, i.e. a *real* SWIFFT lattice. The extrapolated symmetric bit security for finding pseudo-collisions on these lattices is $k = 68.202$. Any parameter set, where $d \geq 260$ would correspond to a cipher with symmetric bit-security at least 100 according to our extrapolation. Parameters realizing this paradigm are given in Section 5.1.

Some further speculations about the relevance of Hybrid Lattice Reduction as introduced by Howgrave-Graham [12] in 2007 can be found in Appendix D.

Acknowledgments

We would like to thank Chris Peikert and Alon Rosen for helpful advice and encouragement. We also want to thank Bartol Filipović, Henrik Koy and Christoph Ludwig for letting us use their lattice reduction code. Finally, we thank Markus Rückert and Michael Schneider for their patience and unbounded cooperation.

References

1. Ajtai, M.: Generating hard instances of lattice problems (extended abstract). In: Proceedings of the Annual Symposium on the Theory of Computing (STOC) 1996, pp. 99–108. ACM Press, New York (1996)
2. Arbitman, Y., Dogon, G., Lyubashevsky, V., Micciancio, D., Peikert, C., Rosen, A.: SWIFFTX: A proposal for the SHA-3 standard (2008),
   http://www.eecs.harvard.edu/~alon/PAPERS/lattices/swifftx.pdf

3. Buchmann, J., Döring, M., Lindner, R.: Efficiency improvement for NTRU. In: Alkassar, A., Siekmann, J. (eds.) SICHERHEIT 2008. Lecture Notes in Informatics, vol. 128, pp. 79–94. Bonner Köllen Verlag (2008)
4. Buchmann, J., Lindner, R., Rückert, M.: Explicit hard instances of the shortest vector problem. In: Buchmann, J., Ding, J. (eds.) PQCrypto 2008. LNCS, vol. 5299, pp. 79–94. Springer, Heidelberg (2008)
5. Buchmann, J., Ludwig, C.: Practical lattice basis sampling reduction. In: Hess, F., Pauli, S., Pohst, M.E. (eds.) ANTS 2006. LNCS, vol. 4076, pp. 222–237. Springer, Heidelberg (2006)
6. De Cannière, C., Mendel, F., Rechberger, C.: Collisions for 70-step sha-1: On the full cost of collision search. In: Adams, C.M., Miri, A., Wiener, M.J. (eds.) SAC 2007. LNCS, vol. 4876, pp. 56–73. Springer, Heidelberg (2007)
7. Coppersmith, D., Shamir, A.: Lattice attacks on NTRU. In: Fumy, W. (ed.) EUROCRYPT 1997. LNCS, vol. 1233, pp. 52–61. Springer, Heidelberg (1997)
8. Gama, N., Nguyen, P.Q.: Predicting lattice reduction. In: Smart, N.P. (ed.) EUROCRYPT 2008. LNCS, vol. 4965, pp. 31–51. Springer, Heidelberg (2008)
9. Gentry, C., Peikert, C., Vaikuntanathan, V.: Trapdoors for hard lattices and new cryptographic constructions. In: Proceedings of the Annual Symposium on the Theory of Computing (STOC) 2008, pp. 197–206. ACM Press, New York (2008)
10. Goldreich, O., Goldwasser, S., Halevi, S.: Collision-free hashing from lattice problems. Electronic Colloquium on Computational Complexity (ECCC) 3(42) (1996)
11. Hirschhorn, P., Hoffstein, J., Howgrave-Graham, N., Whyte, W.: Choosing NTRU parameters in light of combined lattice reduction and MITM approaches (will be published at ACNS) (2009), http://www.ntru.com/cryptolab/pdf/params.pdf
12. Howgrave-Graham, N.: A hybrid lattice-reduction and meet-in-the-middle attack against ntru. In: Menezes, A. (ed.) CRYPTO 2007. LNCS, vol. 4622, pp. 150–169. Springer, Heidelberg (2007)
13. Howgrave-Graham, N., Silverman, J.H., Whyte, W.: A meet-in-the-middle attack on an NTRU private key, http://www.ntru.com/cryptolab/tech_notes.htm#004
14. Lenstra, A.K., Verheul, E.R.: Selecting cryptographic key sizes. J. Cryptology 14(4), 255–293 (2001)
15. Lyubashevsky, V., Micciancio, D.: Generalized compact knapsacks are collision resistant. In: Bugliesi, M., Preneel, B., Sassone, V., Wegener, I. (eds.) ICALP 2006. LNCS, vol. 4052, pp. 144–155. Springer, Heidelberg (2006)
16. Lyubashevsky, V., Micciancio, D.: Asymptotically efficient lattice-based digital signatures. In: Canetti, R. (ed.) TCC 2008. LNCS, vol. 4948, pp. 37–54. Springer, Heidelberg (2008)
17. Lyubashevsky, V., Micciancio, D., Peikert, C., Rosen, A.: SWIFFT: A modest proposal for FFT hashing. In: Nyberg, K. (ed.) FSE 2008. LNCS, vol. 5086, pp. 54–72. Springer, Heidelberg (2008)
18. Micciancio, D., Regev, O.: Lattice-based Cryptography. In: Post Quantum Cryptography. Springer, Heidelberg (2009)
19. Peikert, C., Rosen, A.: Efficient collision-resistant hashing from worst-case assumptions on cyclic lattices. In: Halevi, S., Rabin, T. (eds.) TCC 2006. LNCS, vol. 3876, pp. 145–166. Springer, Heidelberg (2006)
20. Regev, O.: On lattices, learning with errors, random linear codes, and cryptography. In: Gabow, H.N., Fagin, R. (eds.) STOC, pp. 84–93. ACM, New York (2005)
21. Schnorr, C.-P.: Lattice reduction by random sampling and birthday methods. In: Alt, H., Habib, M. (eds.) STACS 2003. LNCS, vol. 2607, pp. 145–156. Springer, Heidelberg (2003)

22. Shoup, V.: Number theory library (NTL) for C++, http://www.shoup.net/ntl/
23. Stehlé, D., Steinfeld, R., Tanaka, K., Xagawa, K.: Efficient public key encryption based on ideal lattices. Technical Report 285, Cryptology ePrint Archive (2009)
24. Stevens, M., Lenstra, A.K., de Weger, B.: Chosen-prefix collisions for MD5 and colliding X.509 certificates for different identities. In: Naor, M. (ed.) EUROCRYPT 2007. LNCS, vol. 4515, pp. 1–22. Springer, Heidelberg (2007)
25. Xagawa, K., Tanaka, K.: A compact signature scheme with ideal lattice. In: Asian Assiciation for Algorithms and Computation (AAAC) (2008)

A   SIS Reduces to SIS'

Theorem 3. *Let $n, q(n) \geq 2, m(n) \geq (1+\epsilon)n$ be positive integers, and $\beta(n) > 0$ be a positive real, then $SIS_{q(n),m(n),\beta(n)}$ reduces to $SIS'_{q(n),m(n),\beta(n)}$. Here, $\epsilon > 0$ is some real number independent of n.*

Proof. Given an instance of SIS $(q(n), \mathbf{A}, \beta(n))$, let E be the event, that there are n column vectors in $\mathbf{A}$ which are linearly independent mod $q(n)$.

Assuming E holds, there is a permutation matrix $\mathbf{P} \in \{0,1\}^{m(n) \times m(n)}$, such that $\mathbf{AP} = [\mathbf{A}', \mathbf{A}'']$ and $\mathbf{A}'$ is invertible mod $q(n)$. We let the SIS' oracle solve the instance $(q(n), [\mathbf{I}_n, \mathbf{A}'^{-1}\mathbf{A}''], \beta(n))$. This instance is distributed according to SIS', when the matrix $\mathbf{A}'^{-1}\mathbf{A}''$ is distributed according to $U(\mathbb{Z}_{q(n)}^{n \times (m(n)-n)})$. This is the case, since $\mathbf{A}''$ was distributed this way and $\mathbf{A}'^{-1}$ is invertible mod $q(n)$, so it is a permutation on the vectors $\mathbb{Z}_{q(n)}^n$ which does not effect the uniform distribution. From the SIS' oracle, we obtain a solution $\mathbf{z}$. The vector $\mathbf{Pz}$ solves our SIS instance because

$$0 = [\mathbf{I}_n, \mathbf{A}'^{-1}\mathbf{A}'']\mathbf{z} = [\mathbf{A}', \mathbf{A}'']\mathbf{z} = \mathbf{APz} \quad (\text{mod } q).$$

We will show that the probability of E not occurring is negligible. For brevity, we will write q, m instead of $q(n), m(n)$ for the remaining part. The number of matrices $\mathbf{A}$ with n linearly independent columns is equal to the number of matrices with n linearly independent rows. For E to occur, the first row may be anything but the zero-row giving $(q^m - 1)$ possibilities, the second row, can be all but multiples of the first giving $(q^m - q)$ possibilities and so on. The total number of matrices is q^{nm}, so we get

$$\Pr[\text{not } E] = 1 - q^{-nm} \prod_{i=0}^{n-1} (q^m - q^i) = 1 - \prod_{i=0}^{n-1} (1 - q^{i-m}).$$

Let $c = -2\ln(1/2)$, we bound the probability

$$1 - \prod_{i=0}^{n-1}(1 - q^{i-m}) = 1 - \exp((-1)^2 \ln(\prod_{i=0}^{n-1}(1 - q^{i-m})))$$

$$\overset{(1)}{\leq} \sum_{i=0}^{n-1} -\ln(1 - q^{i-m}) \overset{(2)}{\leq} c\,q^{-m} \sum_{i=0}^{n-1} q^i$$

$$= c(q^n - 1)/(q^m(q-1)) \leq c/q^{m-n} \overset{(3)}{\leq} c/2^{\epsilon n}.$$

Inequality (1) holds, because for all real x, $1 - \exp(-x) \leq x$. Similarly, inequality (2) holds because for all $0 \leq x \leq 1/2$ we have $-\ln(1-x) \leq cx$. Finally, inequality (3) follows from the conditions stated in the theorem. The resulting function is negligible which completes the proof.   □

B   IdealSIS Reduces to IdealSIS'

Theorem 4. *Let $n, m(n) \in \Omega(\log(n))$ be positive integers, $q(n) \in \omega(n)$ be prime, and $\beta(n) > 0$ be real, then $IdealSIS_{q,m,\beta}$ reduces to $IdealSIS'_{q,m,\beta}$.*

Proof. Given an instance of IdealSIS $(q(n), \hat{\mathbf{a}}, \beta(n))$, let E be the event, that there is an index i, such that $\mathbf{a}' = \mathbf{a}_i$ is invertible mod $q(n)$.

Assuming E holds, there is a permutation $\mathbf{P} \in \{0,1\}^{m(n) \times m(n)}$, such that $\hat{\mathbf{a}}\mathbf{P} = [\mathbf{a}', \hat{\mathbf{a}}'']$ and $\mathbf{a}'$ is invertible mod $q(n)$. We let the IdealSIS' oracle solve the instance $(q(n), [\mathbf{1}, \mathbf{a}'^{-1}\hat{\mathbf{a}}''], \beta(n))$. This instance is distributed according to IdealSIS', when the tuple $\mathbf{a}'^{-1}\hat{\mathbf{a}}''$ is distributed according to $U(R_{n,q}^{m(n)-1})$. This is the case, since $\hat{\mathbf{a}}''$ was distributed this way and $\mathbf{a}'^{-1}$ is invertible mod $q(n)$, so it is a permutation on the elements $R_{n,q(n)}$ which does not effect the uniform distribution. From the IdealSIS' oracle, we obtain a solution $\hat{\mathbf{z}}$. The vector $\mathbf{P}\hat{\mathbf{z}}$ solves our IdealSIS instance.

$$0 = [\mathbf{1}, \mathbf{a}'^{-1}\hat{\mathbf{a}}'']\hat{\mathbf{z}} = [\mathbf{a}', \hat{\mathbf{a}}'']\hat{\mathbf{z}} = \hat{\mathbf{a}}\mathbf{P}\hat{\mathbf{z}} \pmod{q}.$$

We will show that the probability of E not occurring is negligible. For brevity, we will write q, m instead of $q(n), m(n)$ for the remaining part. Let f be the minimal polynomial of ζ_n, and $f_1, \ldots, f_k$ be the irreducible factors of f over $\mathbb{Z}_q$. Since q is prime, for any invertible element in $\mathbf{a} \in R_{n,q}$, it is necessary and sufficient that $\mathbf{a} \bmod f_i \neq \mathbf{0}$. So, the number of invertible elements is $|R_{n,q}^*| = \prod_{i=1}^{k}(q^{\deg(f_i)} - 1)$. The total number of ring elements is $|R_{n,q}| = q^n$. For E to occur, only one of the m ring elements must be invertible, so we get

$$\Pr[\text{not } E] = (1 - q^{-n}\prod_{i=1}^{k}(q^{\deg(f_i)} - 1))^m = (1 - \prod_{i=1}^{k}(1 - q^{-\deg(f_i)}))^m$$

Let $c = -2\ln(1/2)$, we bound $(\Pr[\text{not } E])^{1/m}$

$$1 - \prod_{i=1}^{k}(1 - q^{-\deg(f_i)}) \overset{(1)}{\leq} \sum_{i=1}^{k} -\ln(1 - q^{-\deg(f_i)}) \overset{(2)}{\leq} c\sum_{i=1}^{k} q^{-\deg(f_i)}$$

$$= ck/q \leq cn/q \overset{(3)}{\in} 1/\omega(1).$$

Inequality (1) holds, because for all real x, $1 - \exp(-x) \leq x$. Similarly, inequality (2) holds because for all $0 \leq x \leq 1/2$ we have $-\ln(1-x) \leq cx$. Finally, (3) follows from the conditions stated in the theorem. Since $m(n) \in \Omega(\log(n))$, $\Pr[\text{not } E]$ is negligible.   □

C   Existence of Collisions in d-Dimensional Sublattices

This section represents an analysis of the probability of the existence of collisions in a SWIFFT instance. This is similar the analyses found in Section 6.1. Unlike before however, we now take into account the randomness of the hash-function key $\hat{\mathbf{a}}$.

For simplicity, we deal with the case, that the key defining the hash-function (written as a matrix) $\mathbf{A}$ is unstructured and chosen completely at random. An adaption to the case of skew-circulant keys (used in SWIFFT) yields similar results. The following Lemma gives the probability that a randomly chosen SWI-FFT instance has *no collisions*.

Lemma 1. *Let* $T = \{0, \pm 1\}^d \setminus \{\mathbf{0}\}$ *and* $\mathbf{A} \in \mathbb{Z}_q^{n \times d}$ *be chosen uniformly at random, then* $\Pr[\ \forall \mathbf{v} \in T, \mathbf{A}\mathbf{v} \bmod q \neq \mathbf{0}] = \prod_{i=0}^{d-1} \max\{q^n - 3^i, 0\}$.

Proof. Consider the columns of $\mathbf{A}$ being drawn consecutively. We count the number of cases where the condition we check for holds. Certainly the condition is true iff the first drawn column is non-zero, giving $(q^n - 1)$ positive cases. Let the fist column we drew be $\mathbf{a}_1$. For the condition to remain true, the second column must not be in the set $\{0, \pm 1\}\mathbf{a}_1$, giving $(q^n - 3)$ positive cases. Similarly, the third column must not be in $\{0, \pm 1\}\mathbf{a}_1 + \{0, \pm 1\}\mathbf{a}_2$, which yields $q^n - 3^2$ positive cases. An induction on d validates the given formula.   □

Some exemplary probabilities for the existence of SWIFFT collisions in a given sublattice dimension d are:

d	273	$\cdots$	299	$\cdots$	325
Pr	2^{-80}		2^{-39}		1

D   Hybrid Lattice Reduction

There is a *strong* similarity between NTRU lattices and SWIFFT lattices which we will make explicit. According to the most recent NTRU flavor [11], an NTRU trapdoor one-way function family is described by the parameters

$$(q^{NTRU}, p^{NTRU}, N^{NTRU}, d_f^{NTRU}, d_g^{NTRU}, d_r^{NTRU}).$$

These relate to SWIFFT families in the following way. Choose $n = N^{NTRU}, m = 2, p = q^{NTRU}$. Use the polynomial $f(x) = x^n - 1$ for the ring $R_{p,n}$. Let $\mathcal{T}_d$ be the set of trinary polynomials of degree $n - 1$ with $d + 1$ entries equal to 1 and d entries equal to -1. In the NTRU setting, we choose our hash-keys (a_1, a_2) not uniformly from $R_{p,n}^2$ but rather from $(1 + p^{NTRU} \mathcal{T}_{d_f^{NTRU}}) \times \mathcal{T}_{d_g^{NTRU}}$ which are the NTRU secret key spaces.

The strong limitation on the choice of keys allows the trapdoor to work. The use of a reducible polynomial does not guarantee collision resistance anymore [15], but one-wayness is sufficient for NTRUs security. In summation, the step from NTRU to SWIFFT is exchanging a huge $N^{NTRU} = 401, q^{NTRU} = 2048$ with $n = 64, p = 257$ but in turn increase m from 2 to 16. This seems risky because as we mentioned at the beginning of this section, the problem cannot become harder by increasing m beyond some unknown threshold which is at most 8. This upper bound for the threshold given by the dimension d of a sublattice in which short enough lattice vectors must exist (see Section 6.1).

The strongest attack on NTRU lattices is a hybrid method presented at CRYPTO 2007 by Howgrave-Graham [12]. It combines both Meet-in-the-middle (MITM) attacks by Odlyzko [13] and lattice reduction attacks by Coppersmith and Shamir [7]. In our brief summary of the attack we describe three distinct phases.

1. Reduce the public NTRU lattice and save the result in **B**.
2. Reduce the maximal *sublattice* of **B**, which satisfies the geometric series assumption (GSA), i.e. for which the $\|\mathbf{b}_i^*\|$ descend linearly in logscale.
3. Let k be the last index of a length contributing vector in $\mathbf{B}^*$, meaning $\|\mathbf{b}_i^*\| \approx 0$ for all $i > k$. Howgrave-Graham introduced a modification of Babai's Nearest Plane algorithm that allows us to perform a MITM attack on the final $\dim(\mathbf{B}) - k$ entries of the secret keys.

Phases 1–2 ensure that $\|\mathbf{b}_k^*\|$ is as big as possible. This allows Babai's original algorithm, and the modification to better approximate CVP in the lattice spanned by the first k basis vectors.

Stated in this form the same algorithm can be used to search for collisions (not pseudo-collisions) in SWIFFT lattices. However, preliminary experiments show that this methodology is not helpful. At the end of phase 2 we find that $k \approx 128$. Obviously, even if the CVP oracle works perfectly we would still have to do a MITM attack on the last $\dim(\mathbf{B}) - k \approx 896$ entries. This is too much to be practical.

We are currently working on a generalization of the attack, where step 2 is iterated for $m - 1$ different overlapping parts of the basis, namely

$$[\mathbf{b}_1, \ldots, \mathbf{b}_{2n}], [\mathbf{b}_{n+1}, \ldots, \mathbf{b}_{3n}], \ldots, [\mathbf{b}_{(m-2)n+1}, \ldots, \mathbf{b}_{mn}].$$

This modification is only sensible for SWIFFT and not NTRU. It should bring k closer to $\dim(\mathbf{B})$ possibly at the expense of CVP approximation quality. It remains to be seen if this is a good strategy.

FSBday:

Implementing Wagner's Generalized Birthday Attack against the SHA-3* Round-1 Candidate FSB

Daniel J. Bernstein[1], Tanja Lange[2], Ruben Niederhagen[3], Christiane Peters[2], and Peter Schwabe[2,**]

[1] Department of Computer Science
University of Illinois at Chicago, Chicago, IL 60607-7045, USA
djb@cr.yp.to
[2] Department of Mathematics and Computer Science
Technische Universiteit Eindhoven, P.O. Box 513, 5600 MB Eindhoven, Netherlands
tanja@hyperelliptic.org, c.p.peters@tue.nl, peter@cryptojedi.org
[3] Lehrstuhl für Betriebssysteme, RWTH Aachen University
Kopernikusstr. 16, 52056 Aachen, Germany
ruben@polycephaly.org

Abstract. This paper applies generalized birthday attacks to the FSB compression function, and shows how to adapt the attacks so that they run in far less memory. In particular, this paper presents details of a parallel implementation attacking FSB_{48}, a scaled-down version of FSB proposed by the FSB submitters. The implementation runs on a cluster of 8 PCs, each with only 8GB of RAM and 700GB of disk. This situation is very interesting for estimating the security of systems against distributed attacks using contributed off-the-shelf PCs.

Keywords: SHA-3, Birthday, FSB – Wagner, not much Memory.

1 Introduction

The hash function FSB [2] uses a compression function based on error-correcting codes. This paper describes, analyzes, and optimizes a parallelized generalized birthday attack against the FSB compression function.

This paper focuses on a reduced-size version FSB_{48} which was suggested as a training case by the designers of FSB. The attack against FSB_{48} has been implemented and carried out successfully, confirming our performance analysis. Our results allow us to accurately estimate how expensive a similar attack would be for full-size FSB.

---

* SHA-2 will soon retire; see [10].

** This work was supported by the National Science Foundation under grant ITR-0716498, by the European Commission under Contract ICT-2007-216499 CACE, and by the European Commission under Contract ICT-2007-216646 ECRYPT II. Permanent ID of this document: ded1984108ff55330edb8631e7bc410c. Date: 2009.10.02.

B. Roy and N. Sendrier (Eds.): INDOCRYPT 2009, LNCS 5922, pp. 18–38, 2009.
© Springer-Verlag Berlin Heidelberg 2009

A straightforward implementation of Wagner's generalized birthday attack [12] would need 20 TB of storage. However, we are running the attack on 8 nodes of the Coding and Cryptography Computer Cluster (CCCC) at Technische Universiteit Eindhoven, which has a total hard-disk space of only 5.5 TB. We detail how we deal with this restricted background storage, by applying and generalizing ideas described by Bernstein in [6] and compressing partial results. We also explain the algorithmic measures we took to make the attack run as fast as possible, carefully balancing our code to use available RAM, network throughput, hard-disk throughput and computing power.

We are to the best of our knowledge the first to give a detailed description of a full implementation of a generalized birthday attack. We have placed all code described in this paper into the public domain to maximize reusability of our results. The code can be found at `http://www.polycephaly.org/fsbday`.

Hash-function design. This paper achieves new speed records for generalized birthday attacks, and in particular for generalized birthday attacks against the FSB *compression* function. However, generalized birthday attacks are still much more expensive than generic attacks against the FSB *hash* function. "Generic attacks" are attacks that work against any hash function with the same output length.

The FSB designers chose the size of the FSB compression function so that a particular lower bound on the cost of generalized birthday attacks would be safely above the cost of generic attacks. Our results should not be taken as any indication of a security problem in FSB; the actual cost of generalized birthday attacks is very far above the lower bound stated by the FSB designers. It appears that the FSB compression function was designed too conservatively, with an unnecessarily large output length.

FSB was one of the 64 hash functions submitted to NIST's SHA-3 competition, and one of the 51 hash functions selected for the first round. However, FSB was significantly slower than most submissions, and was not one of the 14 hash functions selected for the second round. It would be interesting to explore smaller and thus faster FSB variants that remain secure against generalized birthday attacks.

Organization of the paper. In Section 2 we give a short introduction to Wagner's generalized birthday attack and Bernstein's adaptation of this attack to storage-restricted environments. Section 3 describes the FSB hash function to the extent necessary to understand our attack methodology. In Section 4 we describe our attack strategy which has to match the restricted hard-disk space of our computer cluster. Section 5 details the measures we applied to make the attack run as efficiently as possible dealing with the bottlenecks mentioned before. We evaluate the overall cost of our attack in Section 6, and give cost estimates for a similar attack against full-size FSB in Section 7.

Naming conventions. Throughout the paper we will denote list j on level i as $L_{i,j}$. For both, levels and lists we start counting at zero.

Logarithms denoted as lg are logarithms to the base 2.

Additions of list elements or constants used in the algorithm are additions modulo 2.

In units such as GB, TB, PB and EB we will always assume base 1024 instead of 1000. In particular we give 700 GB as the size of a hard disk advertised as 750 GB.

2   Wagner's Generalized Birthday Attack

The generalized birthday problem, given 2^{i-1} lists containing B-bit strings, is to find 2^{i-1} elements — exactly one in each list — whose xor equals 0.

The special case $i = 2$ is the classic birthday problem: given two lists containing B-bit strings, find two elements — exactly one in each list — whose xor equals 0. In other words, find an element of the first list that equals an element of the second list.

This section describes a solution to the generalized birthday problem due to Wagner [12]. Wagner also considered generalizations to operations other than xor, and to the case of k lists when k is not a power of 2.

2.1   The Tree Algorithm

Wagner's algorithm builds a binary tree as described in this subsection starting from the input lists $L_{0,0}, L_{0,1}, \ldots, L_{0,2^{i-1}-1}$ (see Figure 4.1). The speed and success probability of the algorithm are analyzed under the assumption that each list contains $2^{B/i}$ elements chosen uniformly at random.

On level 0 take the first two lists $L_{0,0}$ and $L_{0,1}$ and compare their list elements on their least significant B/i bits. Given that each list contains about $2^{B/i}$ elements we can expect $2^{B/i}$ pairs of elements which are equal on those least significant B/i bits. We take the xor of both elements on all their B bits and put the xor into a new list $L_{1,0}$. Similarly compare the other lists — always two at a time — and look for elements matching on their least significant B/i bits which are xored and put into new lists. This process of *merging* yields 2^{i-2} lists containing each about $2^{B/i}$ elements which are zero on their least significant B/i bits. This completes level 0.

On level 1 take the first two lists $L_{1,0}$ and $L_{1,1}$ which are the results of merging the lists $L_{0,0}$ and $L_{0,1}$ as well as $L_{0,2}$ and $L_{0,3}$ from level 0. Compare the elements of $L_{1,0}$ and $L_{1,1}$ on their least significant $2B/i$ bits. As a result of the xoring in the previous level, the last B/i bits are already known to be 0, so it suffices to compare the next B/i bits. Since each list on level 1 contains about $2^{B/i}$ elements we again can expect about $2^{B/i}$ elements matching on B/i bits. We build the xor of each pair of matching elements and put it into a new list $L_{2,0}$. Similarly compare the remaining lists on level 1.

Continue in the same way until level $i - 2$. On each level j we consider the elements on their least significant $(j+1)B/i$ bits of which jB/i bits are known to be zero as a result of the previous merge. On level $i-2$ we get two lists containing about $2^{B/i}$ elements. The least significant $(i-2)B/i$ bits of each element in both lists are zero. Comparing the elements of both lists on their $2B/i$ remaining bits gives 1 expected match, i.e., one xor equal to zero. Since each element is the xor of elements from the previous steps this final xor is the xor of 2^{i-1} elements from the original lists and thus a solution to the generalized birthday problem.

2.2   Wagner in Memory-Restricted Environments

A 2007 paper [6] by Bernstein includes two techniques to mount Wagner's attack on computers which do not have enough memory to hold all list entries. Various special cases of the same techniques also appear in a 2005 paper [4] by Augot, Finiasz, and Sendrier and in a 2009 paper [9] by Minder and Sinclair.

Clamping through precomputation. Suppose that there is space for lists of size only 2^b with $b < B/i$. Bernstein suggests to generate $2^{b \cdot (B-ib)}$ entries and only consider those of which the least significant $B - ib$ bits are zero.

We generalize this idea as follows: The least significant $B - ib$ bits can have an arbitrary value, this *clamping value* does not even have to be the same on all lists as long as the *sum* of all clamping values is zero. This will be important if an attack does not produce a collision. We then can simply restart the attack with different clamping values.

Clamping through precomputation may be limited by the maximal number of entries we can generate per list. Furthermore, halving the available storage space increases the precomputation time by a factor of 2^i.

Note that clamping some bits through precomputation might be a good idea even if enough memory is available as we can reduce the amount of data in later steps and thus make those steps more efficient.

After the precomputation step we apply Wagner's tree algorithm to lists containing bit strings of length B' where B' equals B minus the number of clamped bits. For performance evaluation we will only consider lists on level 0 *after* clamping through precomputation and then use B instead of B' for the number of bits in these entries.

Repeating the attack. Another way to mount Wagner's attack in memory-restricted environments is to carry out the whole computation with smaller lists leaving some bits at the end "uncontrolled". We then can deal with the lower success probability by repeatedly running the attack with different clamping values.

In the context of clamping through precomputation we can simply vary the clamping values used during precomputation. If for some reason we cannot clamp any bits through precomputation we can apply the same idea of changing clamping values in an arbitrary merge step of the tree algorithm. Note that any solution to the generalized birthday problem can be found by some choice of clamping values.

Expected number of runs. Wagner's algorithm, without clamping through precomputation, produces an expected number of exactly one collision. However this does not mean that running the algorithm necessarily produces a collision.

In general, the expected number of runs of Wagner's attack is a function of the number of remaining bits in the entries of the two input lists of the last merge step and the number of elements in these lists.

Assume that b bits are clamped on each level and that lists have length 2^b. Then the probability to have at least one collision after running the attack once is

$$P_{\text{success}} = 1 - \left(\frac{2^{B-(i-2)b} - 1}{2^{B-(i-2)b}}\right)^{2^{2b}},$$

and the expected number of runs $E(R)$ is

$$E(R) = \frac{1}{P_{\text{success}}}. \tag{2.1}$$

For larger values of $B - ib$ the expected number of runs is about 2^{B-ib}. We model the total time for the attack t_W as being linear in the amount of data on level 0, i.e.,

$$t_W \in \Theta\left(2^{i-1} 2^{B-ib} 2^b\right). \tag{2.2}$$

Here 2^{i-1} is the number of lists, 2^{B-ib} is approximately the number of runs, and 2^b is the number of entries per list. Observe that this formula will usually underestimate the real time of the attack by assuming that all computations on subsequent levels are together still linear in the time required for computations on level 0.

Using Pollard iteration. If because of memory restrictions the number of uncontrolled bits is high, it may be more efficient to use a variant of Wagner's attack that uses Pollard iteration [8, Chapter 3, exercises 6 and 7].

Assume that $L_0 = L_1$, $L_2 = L_3$, etc., and that combinations $x_0 + x_1$ with $x_0 = x_1$ are excluded. The output of the generalized birthday attack will then be a collision between two distinct elements of $L_0 + L_2 + \cdots$.

We can instead start with only 2^{i-2} lists $L_0, L_2, \ldots$ and apply the usual Wagner tree algorithm, with a nonzero clamping constant to enforce the condition that $x_0 \neq x_1$. The number of clamped bits before the last merge step is now $(i-3)b$. The last merge step produces 2^{2b} possible values, the smallest of which has an expected number of $2b$ leading zeros, leaving $B - (i-1)b$ uncontrolled.

Think of this computation as a function mapping clamping constants to the final $B - (i-1)b$ uncontrolled bits and apply Pollard iteration to find a collision between the output of two such computations; combination then yields a collision of 2^{i-1} vectors.

As Pollard iteration has square-root running time, the expected number of runs for this variant is $2^{B/2-(i-1)b/2}$, each taking time $2^{i-2}2^b$ (cmp. (2.2)), so the expected running time is

$$t_{PW} \in \Theta\left(2^{i-2} 2^{B/2-(i-1)b/2+b}\right). \tag{2.3}$$

The Pollard variant of the attack becomes more efficient than plain Wagner with repeated runs if $B > (i + 2)b$.

3   The FSB Hash Function

In this section we briefly describe the construction of the FSB hash function. Since we are going to attack the function we omit details which are necessary for implementing the function but do not influence the attack. The second part of this section gives a rough description of how to apply Wagner's generalized birthday attack to find collisions of the compression function of FSB.

3.1   Details of the FSB Hash Function

The Fast Syndrome Based hash function (FSB) was introduced by Augot, Finiasz and Sendrier in 2003. See [3], [4], and [2]. The security of FSB's compression function relies on the difficulty of the "Syndrome Decoding Problem" from coding theory.

The FSB hash function processes a message in three steps: First the message is converted by a so-called domain extender into suitable inputs for the compression function which digests the inputs in the second step. In the third and final step the Whirlpool hash function designed by Barreto and Rijmen [5] is applied to the output of the compression function in order to produce the desired length of output.

Our goal in this paper is to investigate the security of the compression function. We do not describe the domain extender, the conversion of the message to inputs for the compression function, or the last step involving Whirlpool.

The compression function. The main parameters of the compression function are called n, r and w. We consider n strings of length r which are chosen uniformly at random and can be written as an $r \times n$ binary matrix H. Note that the matrix H can be seen as the parity check matrix of a binary linear code. The FSB proposal [2] actually specifies a particular structure of H for efficiency; we do not consider attacks exploiting this structure.

An n-bit string of weight w is called *regular* if there is exactly a single 1 in each interval $[(i-1)\frac{n}{w}, i\frac{n}{w} - 1]_{1 \leq i \leq w}$. We will refer to such an interval as a *block*. The input to the compression function is a regular n-bit string of weight w.

The compression function works as follows. The matrix H is split into w blocks of n/w columns. Each non-zero entry of the input bit string indicates exactly one column in each block. The output of the compression function is an r-bit string which is produced by computing the xor of all the w columns of the matrix H indicated by the input string.

Preimages and collisions. A preimage of an output of length r of one round of the compression function is a regular n-bit string of weight w. A collision occurs if there are $2w$ columns of H — exactly two in each block — which add up to zero.

Finding preimages or collisions means solving two problems coming from coding theory: finding a preimage means solving the Regular Syndrome Decoding problem and finding collisions means solving the so-called 2-regular Null-Syndrome Decoding problem. Both problems were defined and proven to be NP-complete in [4].

Parameters. We follow the notation in [2] and write FSB_{length} for the version of FSB which produces a hash value of length length. Note that the output of the compression function has r bits where r is considerably larger than length.

NIST demands hash lengths of 160, 224, 256, 384, and 512 bits, respectively. Therefore the SHA-3 proposal contains five versions of FSB: FSB_{160}, FSB_{224}, FSB_{256}, FSB_{384}, and FSB_{512}. We list the parameters for those versions in Table 7.1.

The proposal also contains FSB_{48}, which is a reduced-size version of FSB and the main attack target in this paper. The binary matrix H for FSB_{48} has dimension $192 \times 3 \cdot 2^{17}$; i.e., r equals 192 and n is $3 \cdot 2^{17}$. In each round a message chunk is converted into a regular $3 \cdot 2^{17}$-bit string of Hamming weight $w = 24$. The matrix H contains 24 blocks of length 2^{14}. Each 1 in the regular bit string indicates exactly one column in a block of the matrix H. The output of the compression function is the xor of those 24 columns.

A pseudo-random matrix. In our attack against FSB_{48} we consider a pseudo-random matrix H which we constructed as described in [2, Section 1.2.2]: H consists of 2048 submatrices, each of dimension 192×192. For the first submatrix we consider a slightly larger matrix of dimension 197×192. Its first column consists of the first 197 digits of π where each digit is taken modulo 2. The remaining 191 columns of this submatrix are cyclic shifts of the first column. The matrix is then truncated to its first 192 rows which form the first submatrix of H. For the second submatrix we consider digits 198 up to 394 of π. Again we build a 197×192 bit matrix where the first column corresponds to the selected digits (each taken modulo 2) and the remaining columns are cyclic shifts of the first column. Truncating to the first 192 rows yields the second block matrix of H. The remaining submatrices are constructed in the same way.

We emphasize that this is one possible choice for the matrix H. The attack described in our paper does not make use of the structure of this particular matrix. We use this construction in our implementation since it is also contained in the FSB reference implementation submitted to NIST by the FSB designers.

3.2   Attacking the Compression Function of FSB_{48}

Coron and Joux pointed out in [7] that Wagner's generalized birthday attack can be used to find preimages and collisions in the compression function of FSB. The following paragraphs present a slightly streamlined version of the attack of [7] in the case of FSB_{48}.

Determining the number of lists for a Wagner attack on FSB$_{48}$. A collision for FSB$_{48}$ is given by 48 columns of the matrix H which add up to zero; the collision has exactly two columns per block. Each block contains 2^{14} columns and each column is a 192-bit string.

We choose 16 lists to solve this particular 48-sum problem. Each list entry will be the xor of three columns coming from one and a half blocks. This ensures that we do not have any overlaps, i.e., more than two columns coming from one matrix block in the end. We assume that taking sums of the columns of H does not bias the distribution of 192-bit strings. Applying Wagner's attack in a straightforward way means that we need to have at least $2^{\lceil 192/5 \rceil}$ entries per list. By clamping away 39 bits in each step we expect to get at least one collision after one run of the tree algorithm.

Building lists. We build 16 lists containing 192-bit strings each being the xor of three distinct columns of the matrix H. We select each triple of three columns from one and a half blocks of H in the following way:

List $L_{0,0}$ contains the sums of columns i_0, j_0, k_0, where columns i_0 and j_0 come from the first block of 2^{14} columns, and column k_0 is picked from the following block with the restriction that it is taken from the first half of it. Since we cannot have overlapping elements we get about 2^{27} sums of columns i_0 and j_0 coming from the first block. These two columns are then added to all possible columns k_0 coming from the first 2^{13} elements of the second block of the matrix H. In total we get about 2^{40} elements for $L_{0,0}$.

We note that by splitting every second block in half we neglect several solutions of the 48-xor problem. For example, a solution involving two columns from the first half of the second block cannot be found by this algorithm. We justify our choice by noting that fewer lists would nevertheless require more storage and a longer precomputation phase to build the lists.

The second list $L_{0,1}$ contains sums of columns i_1, j_1, k_1, where column i_1 is picked from the second half of the second block of H and j_1 and k_1 come from the third block of 2^{14} columns. This again yields about 2^{40} elements.

Similarly, we construct the lists $L_{0,2}$, $L_{0,3}, \ldots, L_{0,15}$.

For each list we generate more than twice the amount needed for a straightforward attack as explained above. In order to reduce the amount of data for the following steps we note that about $2^{40}/4$ elements are likely to be zero on their least significant two bits. Clamping those two bits away should thus yield a list of 2^{38} bit strings. Note that since we know the least significant two bits of the list elements we can ignore them and regard the list elements as 190-bit strings. Now we expect that a straightforward application of Wagner's attack to 16 lists with about $2^{190/5}$ elements yields a collision after completing the tree algorithm.

Note on complexity in the FSB proposal. The SHA-3 proposal estimates the complexity of Wagner's attack as described above as $2^{r/i}r$ where 2^{i-1} is the number of lists used in the algorithm. This does not take memory into account, and in general is an underestimate of the work required by Wagner's algorithm; i.e., attacks of this type against FSB are more difficult than claimed by the FSB designers.

Note on information-set decoding. The FSB designers say in [2] that Wagner's attack is the fastest known attack for finding preimages, and for finding collisions for small FSB parameters, but that another attack — information-set decoding — is better than Wagner's attack for finding collisions for large FSB parameters.

In general, information-set decoding can be used to find an n-bit string of weight 48 indicating 48 columns of H which add up to zero. Information-set decoding will not take into account that we look for a *regular* n-bit string. The only known way to obtain a regular n-bit string is running the algorithm repeatedly until the output happens to be regular. Thus, the running times given in [2] provide certainly lower bounds for information-set decoding, but in practice they are not likely to hold.

4   Attack Strategy

In this section we will discuss the necessary measures we took to mount the attack on our cluster. We will start with an evaluation of available and required storage.

4.1   How Large Is a List Entry?

The number of bytes required to store one list entry depends on how we represent the entry. We considered four different ways of representing an entry:

Value-only representation. The obvious way of representing a list entry is as a 192-bit string, the xor of columns of the matrix. Bits we already know to be zero of course do not have to be stored, so on each level of the tree the number of bits per entry decreases by the number of bits clamped on the previous level. Ultimately we are not interested in the *value* of the entry — we know already that in a successful attack it will be all-zero at the end — but in the column positions in the matrix that lead to this all-zero value. However, we will show in Section 4.3 that computations only involving the *value* can be useful if the attack has to be run multiple times due to storage restrictions.

Value-and-positions representation. If enough storage is available we can store positions in the matrix alongside the value. Observe that unlike storage requirements for *values* the number of bytes for *positions* increases with increasing levels, and becomes dominant for higher levels.

Compressed positions. Instead of storing full positions we can save storage by only storing, e.g., positions modulo 256. After the attack has successfully finished the full position information can be computed by checking which of the possible positions lead to the appropriate intermediate results on each level.

Dynamic recomputation. If we keep full positions we do not have to store the value at all. Every time we need the value (or parts of it) it can be dynamically recomputed from the positions. In each level the size of a single entry doubles (because the number of positions doubles), the expected number of entries per list remains the same but the number of lists halves, so the total amount of data is the same on each level when using dynamic recomputation. As discussed in Section 3 we have 2^{40} possibilities to choose columns to produce entries of a list, so we can encode the positions on level 0 in 40 bits (5 bytes).

Observe that we can switch between representations during computation if at some level another representation becomes more efficient: We can switch between value-and-position representation to compressed-positions representation and back. We can switch from one of the above to compressed positions and we can switch from any other representation to value-only representation.

4.2   What List Size Can We Handle?

To estimate the storage requirements it is convenient to consider *dynamic recomputation* (storing positions only) because in this case the amount of required storage is constant over all levels and this representation has the smallest memory consumption on level 0.

As described in Section 3.2 we can start with 16 lists of size 2^{38}, each containing bit strings of length $r' = 190$. However, storing 16 lists with 2^{38} entries, each entry encoded in 5 bytes requires 20 TB of storage space.

The computer cluster used for the attack consists of 8 nodes with a storage space of 700 GB each. Hence, we have to adapt our attack to cope with total storage limited to 5.5 TB.

On the first level we have 16 lists and as we need at least 5 bytes per list entry we can handle at most $5.5 \cdot 2^{40}/2^4/5 = 1.1 \times 2^{36}$ entries per list. Some of the disk space is used for the operating system and so a straightforward implementation would use lists of size 2^{36}. First computing one half tree and switching to compressed-positions representation on level 2 would still not allow us to use lists of size 2^{37}.

We can generate at most 2^{40} entries per list so following [6] we could clamp 4 bits during list generation, giving us 2^{36} values for each of the 16 lists. These values have a length of 188 bits represented through 5 bytes holding the positions from the matrix. Clamping 36 bits in each of the 3 steps leaves two lists of length 2^{36} with 80 non-zero bits. According to (2.1) we thus expect to run the attack 256.5 times until we find a collision.

The only way of increasing the list size to 2^{37} and thus reduce the number of runs is to use value-only representation on higher levels.

4.3   The Strategy

The main idea of our attack strategy is to distinguish between the task of finding clamping constants that yield a final collision and the task of actually computing the collision.

Finding appropriate clamping constants. This task does not require storing the positions, since we only need to know whether we find a collision with a particular set of clamping constants; we do not need to know which matrix positions give this collision.

Whenever storing the value needs less space we can thus *compress* entries by switching representation from positions to values. As a side effect this speeds up the computations because less data has to be loaded and stored.

Starting from lists $L_{0,0}, \ldots, L_{0,7}$, each containing 2^{37} entries we first compute list $L_{3,0}$ (see Figure 4.1) on 8 nodes. This list has entries with 78 remaining bits each. As we will describe in Section 5, these entries are presorted on hard disk according to 9 bits that do not have to be stored. Another 3 bits are determined by the node holding the data (see also Section 5) so only 66 bits or 9 bytes of each entry have to be stored, yielding a total storage requirement of 1152 GB versus 5120 GB necessary for storing entries in positions-only representation.

We then continue with the computation of list $L_{2,2}$, which has entries of 115 remaining bits. Again 9 of these bits do not have to be stored due to presorting, 3 are determined by the node, so only 103 bits or 13 bytes have to be stored, yielding a storage requirement of 1664 GB instead of 2560 GB for uncompressed entries.

After these lists have been stored persistently on disk, we proceed with the computation of list $L_{2,3}$, then $L_{3,1}$ and finally check whether $L_{4,0}$ contains at least one element. These computations require another 2560 GB.

Therefore total amount of storage sums up to 1152 GB + 1664 GB + 2560 GB = 5376 GB; obviously all data fits onto the hard disk of the 8 nodes.

If a computation with given clamping constants is not successful, we change clamping constants only for the computation of $L_{2,3}$. The lists $L_{3,0}$ and $L_{2,2}$ do not have to be computed again. All combinations of clamping values for lists $L_{0,12}$ to $L_{0,15}$ summing up to 0 are allowed. Therefore there are a large number of valid clamp-bit combinations.

With 37 bits clamped on every level and 3 clamped through precomputation we are left with 4 uncontrolled bits and therefore, according to (2.1), expect 16.5 runs of this algorithm.

Computing the matrix positions of the collision. In case of success we know which clamping constants we can use and we know which value in the lists $L_{3,0}$ and $L_{3,1}$ yields a final collision. Now we can recompute lists $L_{3,0}$ and $L_{3,1}$ without compression to obtain the positions. For this task we decided to store only positions and use dynamic recomputation. On level 0 and level 1 this is the most space-efficient approach and we do not expect a significant speedup from switching to compressed-positions representation on higher levels. In total one half-tree computation requires 5120 GB of storage, hence, they have to be performed one after the other on 8 nodes.

The (re-)computation of lists $L_{3,0}$ and $L_{3,2}$ is an additional time overhead over doing all computation on list positions in the first place. However, this cost is incurred only once, and is amply compensated for by the reduced data volume in previous steps. See Section 5.2.

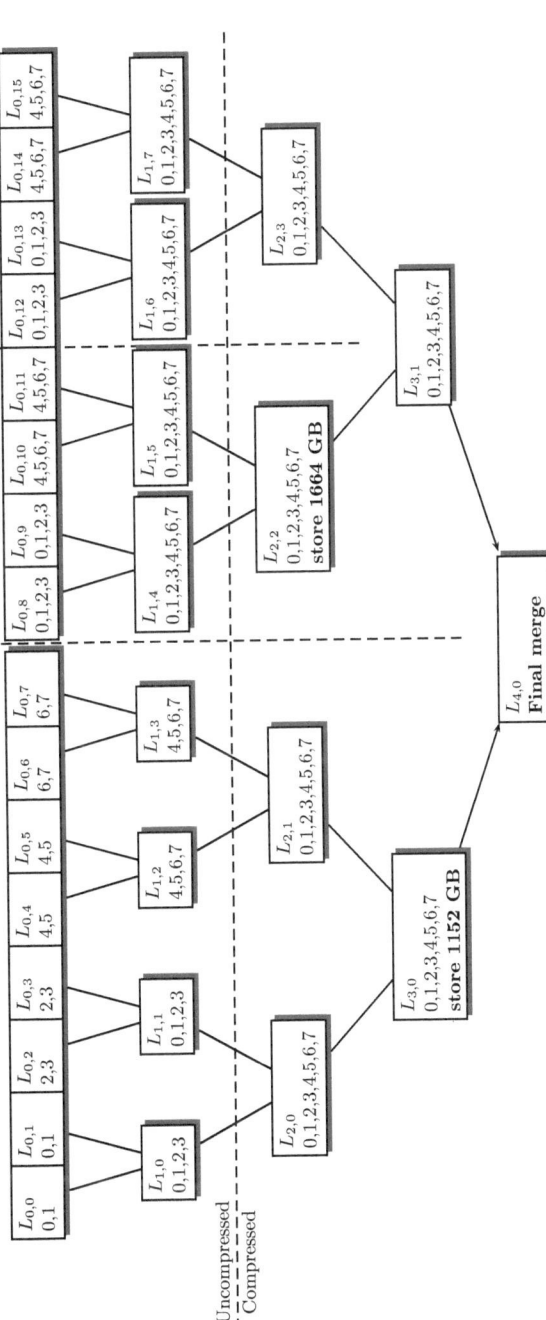

Fig. 4.1. Structure of the attack: in each box the upper line denotes the list, the lower line gives the nodes holding fractions of this list

5   Implementing the Attack

The computation platform for this particular implementation of Wagner's generalized birthday attack on FSB is an eight-node cluster of conventional desktop PCs. Each node has an Intel Core 2 Quad Q6600 CPU with a clock rate of 2.40 GHz and direct fully cached access to 8 GB of RAM. About 700 GB mass storage are provided by a Western Digital SATA hard disk with 20 GB reserved for system and user data. The nodes are connected via switched Gigabit Ethernet using Marvell PCI-E adapter cards.

We chose MPI as communication model for the implementation. This choice has several virtues:

- MPI provides an easy interface to start the application on all nodes and to initialize the communication paths.
- MPI offers synchronous message-based communication primitives.
- MPI is a broadly accepted standard for HPC applications and is provided on a multitude of different platforms.

We decided to use MPICH2 [1] which is an implementation of the MPI 2.0 standard from the University of Chicago. MPICH2 provides an Ethernet-based back end for the communication with remote nodes and a fast shared-memory-based back end for local data exchange.

We implemented two micro-benchmarks to measure hard-disk and network throughput. The results of these benchmarks are shown in Figure 5.1. Note that we measure hard-disk throughput directly on the device, circumventing the filesystem, to reach peak performance of the hard disk. We measured both sequential and randomized access to the disk.

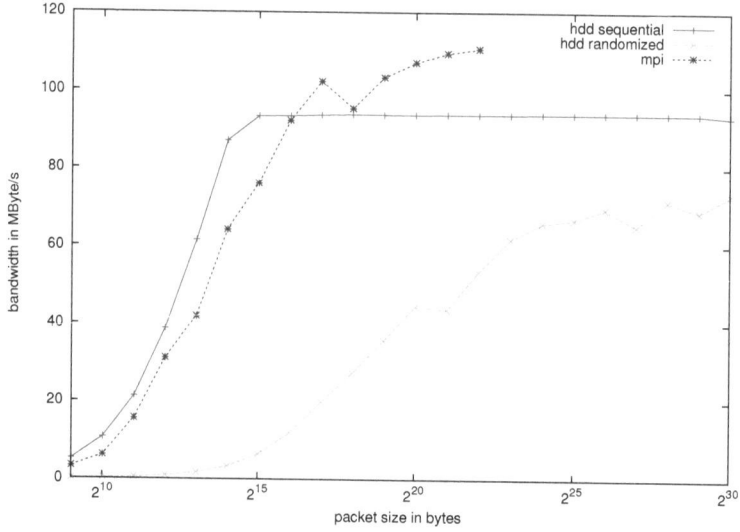

Fig. 5.1. Micro-benchmarks measuring hard-disk and network throughput

The rest of this section explains how we parallelized and streamlined Wagner's attack to make the best of the available hardware.

5.1   Parallelization

Most of the time in the attack is spent on determining the right clamping constants. As described in Section 4 this involves computations of several partial trees, e.g., the computation of $L_{3,0}$ from lists $L_{0,0}, \ldots, L_{0,7}$ (half tree) or the computation of $L_{2,2}$ from lists $L_{0,8}, \ldots, L_{0,11}$ (quarter tree). There are also computations which do not start with lists of level 0; the computation of list $L_{3,1}$ for example is computed from the (previously computed and stored) lists $L_{2,2}$ and $L_{2,3}$.

Lists of level 0 are generated with the current clamping constants. On every level, each list is sorted and afterwards merged with its neighboring list giving the entries for the next level. The sorting and merging is repeated until the final list of the partial tree is computed.

Distributing data over nodes. This algorithm is parallelized by distributing fractions of lists over the nodes in a way that each node can perform sort and merge locally on two lists. On each level of the computation, each node contains fractions of two lists. The lists on level j are split between n nodes according to $\lg(n)$ bits of each value. For example when computing the left half-tree, on level 0, node 0 contains all entries of lists 0 and 1 ending with a zero bit (in the bits not controlled by initial clamping), and node 1 contains all entries of lists 0 and 1 ending with a one bit.

Therefore, from the view of one node, on each level the fractions of both lists are loaded from hard disk, the entries are sorted and the two lists are merged. The newly generated list is split into its fractions and these fractions are sent over the network to their associated nodes. There the data is received and stored onto the hard disk. The continuous dataflow of this implementation is depicted in Figure 5.2.

Presorting into parts. To be able to perform the sort in memory, incoming data is presorted into one of 512 parts according to the 9 least significant bits of the current sort range. This leads to an expected part size for uncompressed entries of 640 MB (0.625 GB) which can be loaded into main memory at once to be sorted further. The benefit of presorting the entries before storing them is:

1. We can sort a whole fraction, that exceeds the size of the memory, by sorting its presorted parts independently.
2. Two adjacent parts of the two lists on one node (with the same presort-bits) can be merged directly after they are sorted.
3. We can save 9 bits when compressing entries to value-only representation.

Merge. The merge is implemented straightforwardly. If blocks of entries in both lists share the same value then all possible combinations are generated: specifically, if a b-bit string appears in the compared positions in c_1 entries in the first list and c_2 entries in the second list then all $c_1 c_2$ xors appear in the output list.

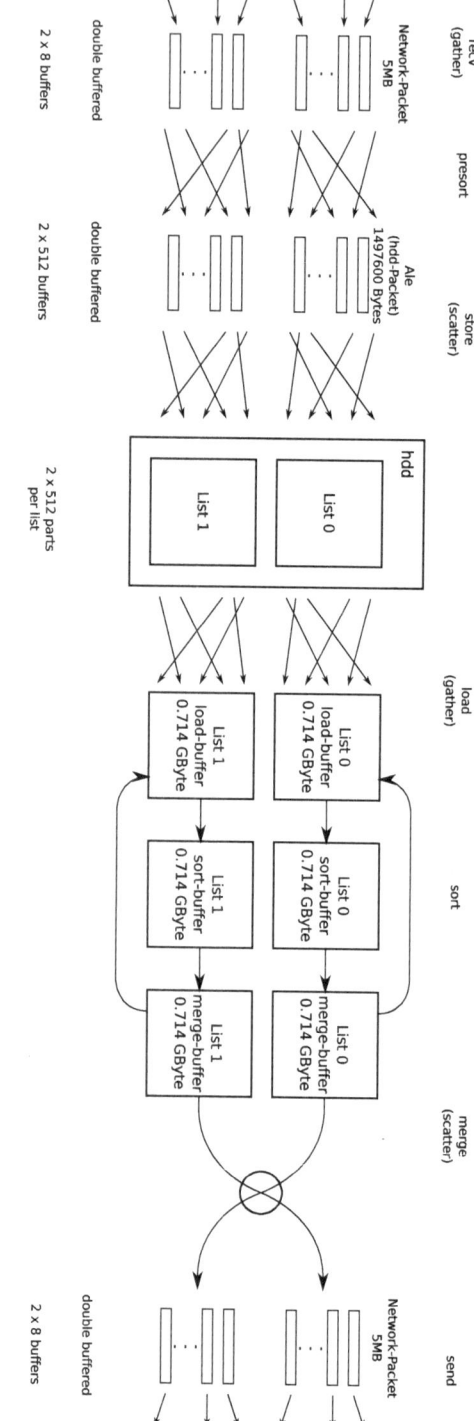

Fig. 5.2. Data flow and buffer sizes during the computation

5.2   Efficient Implementation

Cluster computation imposes three main bottlenecks:

- the computational power and memory latency of the CPUs for computation-intensive applications
- limitations of network throughput and latency for communication-intensive applications
- hard-disk throughput and latency for data-intensive applications

Wagner's algorithm imposes hard load on all of these components: a large amount of data needs to be sorted, merged and distributed over the nodes occupying as much storage as possible. Therefore, demand for optimization is primarily determined by the slowest component in terms of data throughput; latency generally can be hidden by pipelining and data prefetch.

Finding bottlenecks. Our benchmarks show that, for sufficiently large packets, the performance of the system is mainly bottlenecked by hard-disk throughput (cmp. Figure 5.1). Since the throughput of MPI over Gigabit Ethernet is higher than the hard-disk throughput for packet sizes larger than 2^{16} bytes and since the same amount of data has to be sent that needs to be stored, no performance penalty is expected by the network for this size of packets.

Therefore, our first implementation goal was to design an interface to the hard disk that permits maximum hard-disk throughput. The second goal was to optimize the implementation of sort and merge algorithms up to a level where the hard disks are kept busy at peak throughput.

Persistent data storage. Since we do not need any caching-, journaling- or even filing-capabilities of conventional filesystems, we implemented a throughput-optimized filesystem, which we call *AleSystem*. It provides fast and direct access to the hard disk and stores data in portions of *Ales*. Each cluster node has one large unformatted data partition sda1, which is directly opened by the AleSystem using native Linux file I/O. Caching is deactivated by using the open flag O_DIRECT: after data has been written, it is not read for a long time and does not benefit from caching. All administrative information is persistently stored as a file in the native Linux filesystem an mapped into the virtual address space of the process. On sequential access, the throughput of the AleSystem reaches about 90 MB/s which is roughly the maximum that the hard disk permits.

Tasks and threads. Since our cluster nodes are driven by quad-core CPUs, the speed of the computation is primarily based on multi-threaded parallelization. On the one side, the receive-/presort-/store, on the other side, the load-/sort-/merge-/send-tasks are pipelined. We use several threads for sending/receiving data and for running the AleSystem. The core of the implementation is given by five threads which process the main computation. There are two threads which have the task to presort incoming data (one thread for each list). Furthermore, sorting is parallelized with two threads (one thread for each list) and for the merge task we have one more thread.

Memory layout. Given this task distribution, the size of necessary buffers can be defined. The micro-benchmarks show that bigger buffers generally lead to higher throughput. However, the sum of all buffer sizes is limited by the size of the available RAM. For the list parts we need 6 buffers; we need two times 2×8 network buffers for double-buffered send and receive, which results in 32 network buffers. To presort the entries double-buffered into 512 parts of two lists, we need 2048 ales.

When a part is loaded from disk, its ales are treated as a continuous field of entries. Therefore, each ale must be completely filled with entries; no data padding at the end of each ale is allowed. Thus, we must pick a size for the ales which enables the ales to be completely filled independent of the varying size of entries over the whole run of the program. Valid sizes of entries are 5, 10, 20, and 40 bytes when storing positions and 5, 10, 13, and 9 bytes when storing compressed entries. Furthermore, since we access the hard disk using DMA, the size of each ale must be a multiple of 512 bytes. A multiple of a full memory page (4096 bytes) is not mandatory.

For these reasons, the size of one ale must be a multiple of $5 \times 9 \times 13 \times 512$. The size of network packets does not necessarily need to be a multiple of all possible entry sizes; if network packets happen not to be completely filled we merely waste some bytes of bandwidth.

In the worst case, on level 0 one list containing 2^{37} entries is distributed over 2 nodes and presorted into 512 parts; thus the size of each part should be larger than $2^{37}/2/512 \times 5$ bytes $= 640$ MB. The actual size of each part depends on the size of the ales since it must be an integer multiple of the ale size.

Finally, we chose a size of $2^{20} \cdot 5$ bytes $= 5$ MB for the network packets summing up to 160 MB, a size of $5 \times 9 \times 13 \times 512 \times 5 = 1497600$ bytes (about 1.4 MB) for the ales giving a memory demand of 2.9 GB for 2048 ales, and a size of $5 \times 9 \times 13 \times 512 \times 5 \times 512 = 766771200$ bytes (731.25 MB) for the parts summing up to 4.3 GB for 6 parts. Overall our implementation requires about 7.4 GB of RAM leaving enough space for the operating system and additional data as stack and the administrative data for the AleSystem.

Efficiency and further optimizations. Using our rough splitting of tasks to threads, we reach an average CPU usage of about 60% up to 80% peak. Our average hard-disk throughput is about 40 MB/s. The hard-disk micro-benchmark (see Figure 5.1) shows that an average throughput between 45 MB/s and 50 MB/s should be feasible for packet sizes of 1.25 MB. Since sorting is the most complex task, it should be possible to further parallelize sorting to be able to use 100% of the CPU if the hard disk permits higher data transfer. We expect that further parallelization of the sort task would increase CPU data throughput on sort up to about 50 MB/s. That should suffice for maximum hard-disk throughput.

6   Results

We have successfully carried out our FSB$_{48}$ attack. This section presents (1) our estimates, before starting the attack, of the amount of time that the attack would need; (2) measurements of the amount of time actually consumed by the attack; and (3) comments on how different amounts of storage would have changed the attack time.

6.1 Cost Estimates

Step one. As described before the first major step is to compute a set of clamping values which leads to a collision. In this first step entries are stored by positions on level 0 and 1 and from level 2 on list entries consist of values.

Computation of list $L_{3,0}$ takes about 32h and list $L_{2,2}$ about 14h, summing up to 46h. These computations need to be done only once.

The time needed to compute list $L_{2,3}$ is about the same as for $L_{2,2}$ (14h), list $L_{3,1}$ takes about 4h and checking for a collision in lists $L_{3,0}$ and $L_{3,1}$ on level 4 about another 3.5h, summing up to about 21.5h. The expected value of repetitions of these steps is 16.5 and and we thus expected them to take about 355h.

Step two. Finally, computing the matrix positions after finding a collision, requires recomputation with uncompressed lists. We only have to compute the entries of lists $L_{3,0}$ and $L_{3,1}$ until we have found the entry that yields the collision. In the worst case this computation with uncompressed (positions-only) entries takes 33h for each half-tree, summing up to 66h.

Total. Overall we expected to find a collision for the FSB_{48} compression function using our algorithm and cluster in 467h or about 19.5 days.

6.2 Cost Measurements

We ran the code described above on our cluster and were lucky: In step one we found clamping constants after only five iterations (instead of the expected 16.5). In total the first phase of the attack took 5 days, 13 hours and 20 minutes.

Recomputation of the positions in $L_{3,0}$ took 1 day, 8 hours and 22 minutes and recomputation of the positions in $L_{3,1}$ took 1 day, 2 hours and 11 minutes. In total the attack took 7 days, 23 hours and 53 minutes.

Recall that the matrix used in the attack is the pseudo-random matrix defined in Section 3. We found that matrix positions (734, 15006, 20748, 25431, 33115, 46670, 50235, 51099, 70220, 76606, 89523, 90851, 99649, 113400, 118568, 126202, 144768, 146047, 153819, 163606, 168187, 173996, 185420, 191473 198284, 207458, 214106, 223080, 241047, 245456, 247218, 261928, 264386, 273345, 285069, 294658, 304245, 305792, 318044, 327120, 331742, 342519, 344652, 356623, 364676, 368702, 376923, 390678) yield a collision.

6.3 Time-Storage Tradeoffs

As described in Section 4, the main restriction on the attack strategy was the total amount of background storage.

If we had 10496 GB of storage at hand we could have handled lists of size 2^{38}, again using the compression techniques described in Section 4. As described in

Section 4 this would give exactly one expected collision in the last merge step and thus reduce the expected number of required runs to find the right clamping constants from 16.5 to 1.58. With a total storage of 20 TB we could have run a straightforward Wagner attack without compression which would eliminate the need to recompute two half trees at the end.

Increasing the size of the background storage even further would eventually allow to store list entry values alongside the positions and thus eliminate the need for dynamic recomputation. However, the performance of the attack is bottlenecked by hard-disk throughput rather than CPU time so we don't expect any improvement through this measure.

On clusters with even less background storage the computation time will (asymptotically) increase by a factor of 16 with each halving of the storage size. For example a cluster with 2688 GB of storage can only handle lists of size 2^{36}. The attack would then require (expected) 256.5 computations to find appropriate clamping constants.

Of course the time required for one half-tree computation depends on the amount of data. As long as the performance is mainly bottlenecked by hard-disk (or network) throughput the running time is linearly dependent on the amount of data, i.e., a Wagner computation involving 2 half-tree computations with lists of size 2^{38} is about 4.5 times as fast as a Wagner computation involving 18 half-tree computations with lists of size 2^{37}.

7   Scalability Analysis

The attack described in this paper including the variants discussed in Section 6 are much more expensive in terms of time and especially memory than a brute-force attack against the 48-bit hash function FSB_{48}.

This section gives estimates of the power of Wagner's attack against the larger versions of FSB, demonstrating that the FSB design overestimated the power of the attack. Table 7.1 gives the parameters of all FSB hash functions.

A straightforward Wagner attack against FSB_{160} uses 16 lists of size 2^{127} containing elements with 632 bits. The entries of these lists are generated as xors of 10 columns from 5 blocks, yielding 2^{135} possibilities to generate the entries. Precomputation includes clamping of 8 bits. Each entry then requires 135 bits of storage so each list occupies more than 2^{131} bytes. For comparison, the largest currently available storage systems offer a few petabytes (2^{50} bytes) of storage.

To limit the amount of memory we can instead generate, e.g., 32 lists of size 2^{60}, where each list entry is the xor of 5 columns from 2.5 blocks, with 7 bits clamped during precomputation. Each list entry then requires 67 bits of storage.

Clamping 60 bits in each step leaves 273 bits uncontrolled so the Pollard variant of Wagner's algorithm (see Section 2.2) becomes more efficient than the plain attack. This attack generates 16 lists of size 2^{60}, containing entries which are the xor of 5 columns from 5 distinct blocks each. This gives us the possibility to clamp 10 bits through precomputation, leaving $B = 630$ bits for each entry on level 0.

Table 7.1. Parameters of the FSB variants and estimates for the cost of generalized birthday attacks against the compression function. Storage is measured in bytes.

	n	w	r	Number of lists	Size of lists	Bits per entry	Total storage	Time
FSB$_{48}$	3×2^{17}	24	192	16	2^{38}	190	$5 \cdot 2^{42}$	$5 \cdot 2^{42}$
FSB$_{160}$	7×2^{18}	112	896	16	2^{127}	632	$17 \cdot 2^{131}$	$17 \cdot 2^{131}$
				16 (Pollard)	2^{60}	630	$9 \cdot 2^{64}$	$9 \cdot 2^{224}$
FSB$_{224}$	2^{21}	128	1024	16	2^{177}	884	$24 \cdot 2^{181}$	$24 \cdot 2^{181}$
				16 (Pollard)	2^{60}	858	$13 \cdot 2^{64}$	$13 \cdot 2^{343}$
FSB$_{256}$	23×2^{16}	184	1472	16	2^{202}	1010	$27 \cdot 2^{206}$	$27 \cdot 2^{206}$
				16 (Pollard)	2^{60}	972	$14 \cdot 2^{64}$	$14 \cdot 2^{386}$
				32 (Pollard)	2^{56}	1024	$18 \cdot 2^{60}$	$18 \cdot 2^{405}$
FSB$_{384}$	23×2^{16}	184	1472	16	2^{291}	1453	$39 \cdot 2^{295}$	$39 \cdot 2^{295}$
				32 (Pollard)	2^{60}	1467	$9 \cdot 2^{65}$	$18 \cdot 2^{618.5}$
FSB$_{512}$	31×2^{16}	248	1987	16	2^{393}	1962	$53 \cdot 2^{397}$	$53 \cdot 2^{397}$
				32 (Pollard)	2^{60}	1956	$12 \cdot 2^{65}$	$24 \cdot 2^{863}$

The time required by this attack is approximately 2^{224} (see (2.3)). This is substantially faster than a brute-force collision attack on the compression function, but is clearly much slower than a brute-force collision attack on the hash function, and even slower than a brute-force *preimage* attack on the hash function.

Similar statements hold for the other full-size versions of FSB. Table 7.1 gives rough estimates for the time complexity of Wagner's attack without storage restriction and with storage restricted to a few hundred exabytes (2^{60} entries per list). These estimates only consider the number and size of lists being a power of 2 and the number of bits clamped in each level being the same. The estimates ignore the time complexity of precomputation. Time is computed according to (2.2) and (2.3) with the size of level-0 entries (in bytes) as a constant factor.

Although fine-tuning the attacks might give small speedups compared to the estimates, it is clear that the compression function of FSB is oversized, assuming that Wagner's algorithm in a somewhat memory-restricted environment is the most efficient attack strategy.

References

1. MPICH2: High-performance and widely portable MPI,
   http://www.mcs.anl.gov/research/projects/mpich2/ (accessed 08-18-2009)
2. Augot, D., Finiasz, M., Gaborit, P., Manuel, S., Sendrier, N.: SHA-3 Proposal: FSB (2009), http://www-rocq.inria.fr/secret/CBCrypto/index.php?pg=fsb
3. Augot, D., Finiasz, M., Sendrier, N.: A fast provably secure cryptographic hash function (2003), http://eprint.iacr.org/2003/230

4. Augot, D., Finiasz, M., Sendrier, N.: A family of fast syndrome based cryptographic hash functions. In: Dawson, E., Vaudenay, S. (eds.) Mycrypt 2005. LNCS, vol. 3715, pp. 64–83. Springer, Heidelberg (2005)

5. Barreto, P.S.L.M., Rijmen, V.: The WHIRLPOOL Hashing Function, `http://www.larc.usp.br/~pbarreto/WhirlpoolPage.html`

6. Bernstein, D.J.: Better price-performance ratios for generalized birthday attacks. In: Workshop Record of SHARCS '07: Special-purpose Hardware for Attacking Cryptographic Systems (2007), `http://cr.yp.to/papers.html#genbday`

7. Coron, J.-S., Joux, A.: Cryptanalysis of a provably secure cryptographic hash function (2004), `http://eprint.iacr.org/2004/013`

8. Knuth, D.E.: The Art of Computer Programming. vol. 2, Seminumerical Algorithms, 3rd edn. Addison-Wesley Publishing Co., Reading (1997)

9. Minder, L., Sinclair, A.: The extended k-tree algorithm. In: Mathieu, C. (ed.) SODA, pp. 586–595. SIAM, Philadelphia (2009)

10. Naehrig, M., Peters, C., Schwabe, P.: SHA-2 will soon retire (to appear), `http://cryptojedi.org/users/peter/index.shtml#retire`

11. Wagner, D.: A generalized birthday problem (extended abstract). In: Yung, M. (ed.) CRYPTO 2002. LNCS, vol. 2442, pp. 288–304. Springer, Heidelberg (2002), See also newer version [12], `http://www.cs.berkeley.edu/~daw/papers/genbday.html`

12. Wagner, D.: A generalized birthday problem (extended abstract) (long version), See also older version [11] (2002), `http://www.cs.berkeley.edu/~daw/papers/genbday.html`

Reusing Static Keys in Key Agreement Protocols

Sanjit Chatterjee[1], Alfred Menezes[2], and Berkant Ustaoglu[3]

[1] Department of Combinatorics & Optimization, University of Waterloo
s2chatte@uwaterloo.ca
[2] Department of Combinatorics & Optimization, University of Waterloo
ajmeneze@uwaterloo.ca
[3] NTT Information Sharing Platform Laboratories, Tokyo, Japan
bustaoglu@cryptolounge.net

Abstract. Contrary to conventional cryptographic wisdom, the NIST SP 800-56A standard explicitly allows the use of a static key pair in more than one of the key establishment protocols described in the standard. In this paper, we give examples of key establishment protocols that are individually secure, but which are insecure when static key pairs are reused in two of the protocols. We also propose an enhancement of the extended Canetti-Krawczyk security model and definition for the situation where static public keys are reused in two or more key agreement protocols.

1 Introduction

Conventional cryptographic practice dictates that keying material should never be used in more than one protocol. For example, Principle 2 of Anderson and Needham's robustness principles for public key protocols [3] advises:

> If possible avoid using the same key for two different purposes (such as signing and decryption)...

Section 13.5.1 of the Handbook of Applied Cryptography [18] states:

> The principle of *key separation* is that keys for different purposes should be cryptographically separated.

Several examples of the pitfalls of reusing keying material can be found in [3] and [18]. Kelsey, Schneier and Wagner [13] introduced the notion of a 'chosen-protocol attack' whereby an attacker designs a new protocol based on an existing protocol in such a way that sharing of keying material between the two protocols renders the existing protocol insecure. More recently, Gligoroski, Andova and Knapskog [11] showed that using a secret key in more than one mode of operation of a block cipher can have an adverse effect on security.

Despite the potential security vulnerabilities, many systems today reuse keying material for different protocols and applications. As mentioned in [13], one of the reasons behind this phenomenon is that certification and maintenance of

B. Roy and N. Sendrier (Eds.): INDOCRYPT 2009, LNCS 5922, pp. 39–56, 2009.

public keys can be a costly process, and therefore it is cost-effective to use the same public key for multiple protocols. Of course, reuse of keying material does not necessarily result in a loss of security. For example, Coron et al. [9] proved that there is no security loss if RSA key pairs are reused in the PSS versions of the RSA signature and encryption schemes. Two examples were provided by Vasco, Hess and Steinwandt [24], who proved that the Pointcheval-Stern [22] and Fujisaki-Okamoto [10] variants of the ElGamal signature and encryption schemes remain secure when key pairs are reused, as do the Boneh-Franklin identity-based encryption scheme [5] and Hess's identity-based signature scheme [12].

The objective of this paper is to investigate the security issues that can arise when static (long-term) asymmetric key pairs are reused in more than one key agreement protocol. Our work is motivated by the NIST SP 800-56A standard for key establishment [23]. This standard specifies several variants of the Diffie-Hellman protocol, including one-pass, two-pass and three-pass versions of the Unified Model (UM) (see [4] and [19]) and MQV [16] key agreement protocols. Section 5.6.4.2 of [23] explicitly allows the reuse of static key pairs:

> A static key pair may be used in more than one key establishment scheme. However, one static public/private key pair **shall not** be used for different purposes (for example, a digital signature key pair is not to be used for key establishment or vice versa) with the following possible exception: when requesting the (initial) certificate for a public static key establishment key, the key establishment private key associated with the public key may be used to sign the certificate request.

The allowance of the reuse of static public keys is somewhat surprising since the UM and MQV protocols are quite different, and also because the protocols have different security attributes. For example, the MQV protocols appear to be resistant to key-compromise impersonation attacks, while the UM protocols are not. Also, the three-pass protocols achieve (full) forward secrecy, the two-pass protocols achieve weak forward secrecy, while the one-pass protocols have neither full nor weak forward secrecy. Thus it is conceivable that reusing static public keys results in a situation where a stronger protocol may inherit the weaknesses of a protocol that was not intended to provide certain security attributes.

The remainder of this paper is organized as follows. In §2 we give three examples of pairs of key agreement protocols where the protocols in each pair are individually secure, but where one protocol in each pair becomes insecure when static public keys are reused for both protocols in that pair. The first example shows that the three-pass UM protocol as described in SP 800-56A [23] can be successfully attacked if parties reuse their static key pairs with the one-pass UM protocol described in [23]. Similarly, the three pass MQV protocol as described in [23] can be successfully attacked if parties reuse their static key pairs with the one-pass MQV protocol. In §3 we describe a 'shared' model — an enhancement of the extended Canetti-Krawczyk security model and associated definition [7,14] that aims to capture the assurances guaranteed by multiple key agreement protocols when each party uses the same static key pair in all the protocols. §4 presents two protocols, which are proven secure in our shared model in [8].

Notation and terminology. Let $\mathcal{G} = \langle g \rangle$ denote a multiplicatively-written cyclic group of prime order q, and let $\mathcal{G}^* = \mathcal{G} \setminus \{1\}$. The *Computational Diffie-Hellman (CDH) assumption* in $\mathcal{G}$ is that computing $\mathrm{CDH}(U, V) = g^{uv}$ is infeasible given $U = g^u$ and $V = g^v$ where $u, v \in_R [1, q-1]$. The *Decisional Diffie-Hellman (DDH) assumption* in $\mathcal{G}$ is that distinguishing DH triples (g^a, g^b, g^{ab}) from random triples (g^a, g^b, g^c) is infeasible. The *Gap Diffie-Hellman (GDH) assumption* in $\mathcal{G}$ is that the CDH assumption holds even when a CDH solver is given a DDH oracle that distinguishes DH triples from random triples.

With the exception of Protocols 1 and 2 in §2.3, all key agreement protocols in this paper are of the Diffie-Hellman variety where the two communicating parties $\hat{A}$ and $\hat{B}$ exchange static public keys. Party $\hat{A}$'s static private key is an integer $a \in_R [1, q-1]$, and her corresponding static public key is $A = g^a$. Similarly, party $\hat{B}$ has a static key pair (b, B), and so on. A certifying authority (CA) issues certificates that binds a party's identifier to its static public key. We do not assume that the CA requires parties to prove possession of their static private keys, but we do insist that the CA verifies that static public keys belong to $\mathcal{G}^*$. See §2.1 for a discussion on the format of certificates in the context of static key reuse. A party $\hat{A}$ called the *initiator* commences the protocol by selecting an ephemeral (one-time) key pair and then sends the ephemeral public key (and possibly other data) to the second party. In our protocols, the ephemeral private key is either a randomly selected integer $x \in [1, q-1]$ or a randomly selected binary string $\tilde{x}$ which is used together with the static private key to derive an integer $x \in [1, q-1]$, and the corresponding ephemeral public key is $X = g^x$. Upon receipt of X, the *responder* $\hat{B}$ selects an ephemeral private key y or $\tilde{y}$ and sends $Y = g^y$ (and possibly other data) to $\hat{A}$; this step is omitted in the one-pass UM protocol of §2.2. The parties may exchange some additional messages, after which they accept a session key. We use $\mathcal{I}$ and $\mathcal{R}$ to denote the constant strings "initiator" and "responder". (The NIST SP 800-56A standard uses the strings "KC_1_U" and "KC_1_V".)

2 Examples

We provide three examples of interference between a pair of key agreement protocols in the situation where parties are allowed to reuse their static keys. Since static keys are assumed to be certified, such reuse needs to take into account certificate format; this issue is discussed in §2.1.

The pair of protocols considered in the first two examples in §2.2 and §2.3 belong to the same family — Unified Model for the former and the so-called Generic 2-pass KEM for the latter. In each case we exploit — albeit in a different manner — their structural similarity together with the fact that the same static key is reused to mount an attack on one protocol based on our knowledge of a session key in the other. Our third example in §2.4, in contrast, does not involve protocols of the same family. They are derived from two existing provably secure protocols to emphasize the danger of static key reuse. The session keys in these two protocols are computed in different fashions and the attack, though active, does not involve any *SessionKeyReveal* query like the other two examples.

2.1   Certificate Format

As already mentioned, a certifying authority (CA) issues certificates binding a user's identifier to its static public key. We consider a scenario where parties are permitted to reuse their static public keys in two key agreement protocols, Π_1 and Π_2. There are essentially two cases depending upon whether the certificate also binds the protocol(s) for which that public key will be used. We emphasize that our attacks are equally valid in both cases. However, a certificate formatted according to Case 2 gives the adversary additional power, namely the ability to replay the certificate, which is not possible in Case 1.

Case 1. The certificate specifies the protocol(s) for which the public key will be used. This can be further sub-divided into two cases as follows.

(a) *Parties obtain a single certificate for each static public key.* For example, if $\hat{A}$ wishes to reuse her static public key A in both Π_1 and Π_2 then this information should be included in $\hat{A}$'s certificate for A. When another party $\hat{B}$ wishes to establish a session key with $\hat{A}$ using Π_1, then he will learn from $\hat{A}$'s certificate that $\hat{A}$ reuses the public key A in Π_2.

(b) *Parties obtain separate certificates for each protocol pertaining to the same static public key.* If $\hat{A}$ wishes to reuse her static public key A in both Π_1 and Π_2 then she obtains two different certificates, where each certificate specifies for which particular protocol A will be used. In this case, when $\hat{B}$ wishes to establish a session key with $\hat{A}$ using Π_1 then he retrieves $\hat{A}$'s certificate for Π_1 and may not be aware that A is being reused in Π_2.

All three examples of protocol interference mentioned in this section work in either of these subcases. In the first two examples both parties have to reuse their static keys in the two protocols. An interesting feature of the third example, which distinguishes it from the other two examples, is that even if only one of the parties reuses its static key amongst the two protocols then that will lead to the compromise of the session key at another party in one of the protocols even though that party does not reuse its static key.

Case 2. The certificate does not specify for which protocol(s) the public key will be used. When $\hat{A}$ obtains a certificate for her public key A then the certificate itself does not contain any information about the protocol(s) for which A will be used. For example, $\hat{A}$ can reuse the public key in both Π_1 and Π_2 or use it only in one protocol. Suppose, $\hat{A}$ reserves the public key A for use in Π_1 only. Since the certificate on A does not bind it to Π_1, an adversary can easily pass it as the public key of $\hat{A}$ in Π_2. In this scenario, the attacks described here work even if *none* of the parties reuse their public key in more than one protocol.

2.2   The One-Pass and Three-Pass Unified Model Protocols

The 'unified model' is a family of two-party Diffie-Hellman key agreement protocols that has been standardized in ANSI X9.42 [1], ANSI X9.63 [2], and NIST
SP 800-56A [23]. In [23], the one-pass protocol is called 'dhHybridOneFlow' when
the underlying group $\mathcal{G}$ is a DSA-type group, and 'One-Pass Unified Model' when
$\mathcal{G}$ is an elliptic curve group. One-pass UM is suitable for applications such as
email, where the intended receiver is not online and therefore unable to con-
tribute an ephemeral key. In [23], the three-pass protocol, which consists of the
two-pass protocol combined with bilateral key confirmation, is called 'dhHybrid1'
when $\mathcal{G}$ is a DSA-type group, and 'Full Unified Model' when $\mathcal{G}$ is an elliptic curve
group.

One-pass UM. The protocol is depicted in Figure 1. Here, keydatalen is an integer that indicates the bitlength of the secret keying material to be generated,
AlgorithmID is a bit string that indicates how the deriving keying material will
be parsed and for which algorithm(s) the derived secret keying material will be
used, and Λ denotes optional public information that can be included in the key
derivation function H. The session key is κ_1.

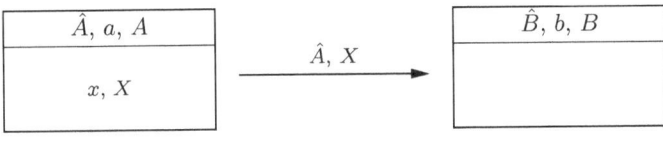

$$\kappa_1 = H(g^{xb}, g^{ab}, \text{keydatalen}, \text{AlgorithmID}, \hat{A}, \hat{B}, \Lambda)$$

Fig. 1. The one-pass UM protocol

Three-pass UM. The protocol is depicted in Figure 2. Here, MAC is a message
authentication code scheme such as HMAC, and Λ_1 and Λ_2 are optional strings.
The session key is κ_2, whereas κ' is an ephemeral secret key used to authenticate
the exchanged ephemeral public keys and the identifiers.

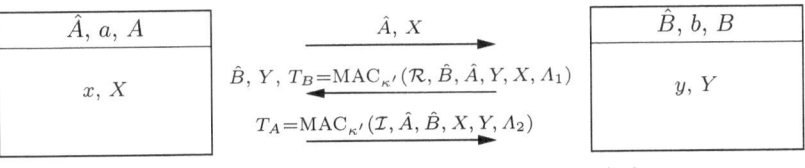

$$(\kappa', \kappa_2) = H(g^{xy}, g^{ab}, \text{keydatalen}, \text{AlgorithmID}, \hat{A}, \hat{B}, \Lambda)$$

Fig. 2. The three-pass UM protocol

The attack. We describe an attack against the three-pass UM protocol in the situation where parties reuse their static keys in the one-pass UM protocol. The attack makes the following plausible assumptions. First, the one-pass protocol is used to derive 256 bits of keying material κ_1, which is then divided into a 128-bit HMAC key κ_m and a 128-bit AES key κ_e; these keys are subsequently used in an application to encrypt and authenticate data. Second, the three-pass protocol uses HMAC with a 128-bit key κ' for key confirmation, and produces a 128-bit AES session key κ_2. Third, both protocols use the same AlgorithmID — this is consistent with the description of the AlgorithmID field in [23, Section 5.8.1] where it is stated:

> For example, AlgorithmID might indicate that bits 1-80 are to be used as an 80-bit HMAC key and that bits 81-208 are to be used as a 128-bit AES key.

Finally, it is assumed that the attacker is able to use a *SessionKeyReveal* query to obtain session keys produced by the one-pass protocol, but is unable to obtain session keys generated by the three-pass protocol; this assumption is reasonable if the one-pass protocol is used in relatively low security applications, whereas the three-pass protocol is reserved for high security applications.[1]

The attack proceeds as follows:

1. The adversary $\mathcal{M}$ initiates a session sid_1 of the three-pass UM protocol at $\hat{A}$ and receives $(\hat{A}, X)$.
2. $\mathcal{M}$ forwards $(\hat{A}, X)$ to $\hat{B}$ in a session sid_2 of the one-pass UM protocol.
3. $\hat{B}$ computes a session key κ_1 following the one-pass UM protocol.
4. $\mathcal{M}$ issues a *SessionKeyReveal* query to session sid_2 at $\hat{B}$ to obtain $\kappa_1 = (\kappa_m, \kappa_e)$.
5. $\mathcal{M}$ sets $Y = B$; note that $\kappa_1 = (\kappa', \kappa_2)$ under our assumptions. $\mathcal{M}$ then computes T_B using κ' and sends $(\hat{B}, Y, T_B)$ to session sid_1 at $\hat{A}$.
6. $\hat{A}$ computes a session key κ_2 following the three-pass UM protocol. Note that $\mathcal{M}$ knows this session key.

We note that such an attack can also be launched on the three-pass MQV protocol as specified in [23] if parties reuse their static keys with the one-pass MQV protocol. Such protocol interference attacks can be prevented by following the general advice given in [13] – each protocol should have its own unique identifier that is included in the cryptographic operations. In the case of the one-pass and three-pass UM protocols, the attack we described can be thwarted by including the protocol identifiers in the optional input Λ to the key derivation function. As a further safeguard against potential interference attacks with other protocols, the protocol identifier can be included in the optional inputs Λ_1 and Λ_2 to the MAC algorithm.

---

[1] A well-designed key agreement protocol should achieve its security goals even if an attacker is able to learn some session keys. This is because a key agreement protocol cannot guarantee that session keys won't be improperly used in an application (e.g., to encrypt messages with a weak symmetric-key encryption scheme, or in applications where expired session keys may not be securely destroyed).

2.3   Generic 2-Pass KEM Protocols

Boyd et al. [6] proposed two generic key agreement protocols based on a pseudo-random function family and an arbitrary identity-based key encapsulation mechanism (IB-KEM) that is secure against chosen-ciphertext attack. Both protocols are proven secure in the Canetti-Krawczyk security model [7], which the authors extend to the identity-based setting. The second protocol provides a stronger security guarantee, namely weak forward secrecy under the DDH assumption. The authors also mention that their protocols can be easily adapted to the PKI setting where the IB-KEM is replaced by a CCA-secure KEM. We show that a modified version of the second protocol can be easily broken if the same static key is reused by the parties amongst the protocols. We emphasize that our attack does not illustrate any weakness in the Boyd et al. protocols which were designed and analyzed for the stand-alone setting.

In the following description $\mathsf{Enc}()$ (resp. $\mathsf{Dec}()$) is the encapsulation (resp. decapsulation) algorithm of the underlying IB-KEM. The function $\mathsf{Exct}_\kappa(\cdot)$ is chosen uniformly at random from a strong (m, ϵ)-strong randomness extractor, while $\mathsf{Expd}_K(\cdot)$ is a pseudorandom function family. See Definitions 2, 3 and 4 in [6] for their exact descriptions. In the protocol descriptions, d_A and d_B denote the private keys of $\hat{A}$ and $\hat{B}$, while pk is the master public key of the Key Generation Center (KGC) of the underlying IB-KEM.

Protocol 1. In Figure 3, the actual order in which the parties $\hat{A}$, $\hat{B}$ exchange their messages is irrelevant. If $\hat{A} < \hat{B}$ under some predetermined lexicographic ordering, then the session identifier is defined as $s = \hat{A}||C_A||\hat{B}||C_B$. We note in passing that this definition of session identifier deviates from that in the original CK model [7]. In particular, the session initiator cannot know in advance the complete session identifier.

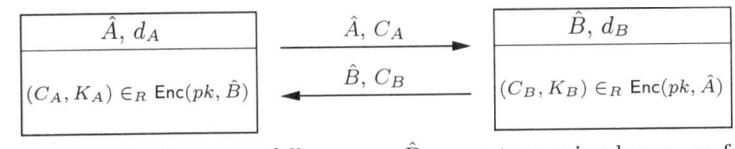

$\hat{A}$ computes session key κ_1 as follows:
1. $K_B = \mathsf{Dec}(pk, d_A, C_B)$
2. $K'_A = \mathsf{Exct}_\kappa(K_A)$
3. $K'_B = \mathsf{Exct}_\kappa(K_B)$
4. $s = \hat{A}||C_A||\hat{B}||C_B$
5. $\kappa_1 = \mathsf{Expd}_{K'_A}(s) \oplus \mathsf{Expd}_{K'_B}(s)$

$\hat{B}$ computes session key κ_1 as follows:
1. $K_A = \mathsf{Dec}(pk, d_B, C_A)$
2. $K'_B = \mathsf{Exct}_\kappa(K_B)$
3. $K'_A = \mathsf{Exct}_\kappa(K_A)$
4. $s = \hat{A}||C_A||\hat{B}||C_B$
5. $\kappa_1 = \mathsf{Expd}_{K'_B}(s) \oplus \mathsf{Expd}_{K'_A}(s)$

Fig. 3. Protocol 1 from [6]

Protocol 2. The description of Protocol 2 in Figure 4 differs slightly from the description in [6] in that session identifiers are defined in a manner analogous to that of Protocol 1. Incidentally, this modified version is identical to an earlier version of Protocol 2 (see the March 1, 2008 version of [6] in the IACR ePrint Archive).

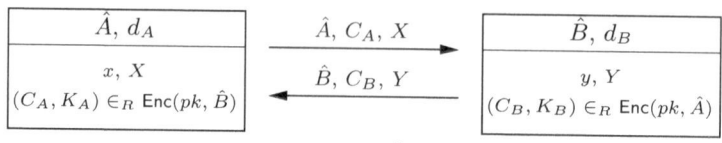

$\hat{A}$ computes session key κ_2 as follows:

1. $K_B = \mathsf{Dec}(pk, d_A, C_B)$
2. $K'_A = \mathsf{Exct}_\kappa(K_A)$
3. $K'_B = \mathsf{Exct}_\kappa(K_B)$
4. $K'_{AB} = \mathsf{Exct}_\kappa(Y^x)$
5. $s = \hat{A}\|C_A\|\hat{B}\|C_B$
6. $\kappa_2 = \mathsf{Expd}_{K'_A}(s) \oplus \mathsf{Expd}_{K'_B}(s) \oplus$
   $\quad \mathsf{Expd}_{K'_{AB}}(s)$

$\hat{B}$ computes session key κ_2 as follows:

1. $K_A = \mathsf{Dec}(pk, d_B, C_A)$
2. $K'_B = \mathsf{Exct}_\kappa(K_B)$
3. $K'_A = \mathsf{Exct}_\kappa(K_A)$
4. $K'_{BA} = \mathsf{Exct}_\kappa(X^y)$
5. $s = \hat{A}\|C_A\|\hat{B}\|C_B$
6. $\kappa_2 = \mathsf{Expd}_{K'_B}(s) \oplus \mathsf{Expd}_{K'_A}(s) \oplus$
   $\quad \mathsf{Expd}_{K'_{BA}}(s)$

Fig. 4. Protocol 2 from [6]

The attack. The following attack can be mounted against Protocol 2 when static keys are reused in both the protocols.

1. The adversary $\mathcal{M}$ initiates a session of Protocol 1 at $\hat{A}$ and receives $(\hat{A}, C_A)$.
2. $\mathcal{M}$ chooses (x, X) and sends $(\hat{A}, C_A, X)$ to $\hat{B}$ in a session of Protocol 2.
3. $\hat{B}$ responds with $(\hat{B}, C_B, Y)$ and accepts a session key κ_2 following Protocol 2.
4. $\mathcal{M}$ forwards $(\hat{B}, C_B)$ to $\hat{A}$ in Protocol 1.
5. $\hat{A}$ computes a session key κ_1 following Protocol 1.
6. $\mathcal{M}$ issues a *SessionKeyReveal* query to $\hat{A}$ to obtain κ_1.
7. $\mathcal{M}$ computes κ_2 given κ_1 and x.

Remark 1. For the above attack to be successful, it is necessary that both parties reuse their static keys (and the same IB-KEM, $\mathsf{Exct}_\kappa(\cdot)$, and $\mathsf{Expd}_K(\cdot)$). In the identity-based setting, the unique identity of a user is treated as her public key and the corresponding private key is derived from this identity string by the KGC. It is natural in such a setting to use the same identity-private key pair for two different key agreement protocols.

Remark 2. The above attack per-se does not work against Protocol 2 as it is described in [6]. However, we would like to note that the (informal) protocol description in [6] is not exactly suitable for analysis in the Canetti-Krawczyk model. If instead we define the session identifier s according to the original Canetti-Krawczyk model, then the security argument remains unaffected in the stand-alone setting and the attack goes through if the static key is reused.

2.4   KEA+h and τ

We provide another example of a pair of protocols where reuse of the static key pair by one of the communicating parties leads to the compromise of a session key of the other communicating party in one of the protocols.

KEA+h. Lauter and Mityagin introduced the authenticated key exchange (AKE) protocol KEA+ in [15] — this is a modification of the KEA protocol introduced earlier by the National Security Agency [21]. They showed that KEA+ achieves, under the GDH and random oracle assumptions, what they call AKE security against a strong adversary along with a form of weak forward secrecy and resistance to key compromise impersonation. Figure 5 depicts a slight modification of the KEA+ protocol, which we call the KEA+h protocol, where the key derivation function is modified by introducing a new hash function H_1. Interested readers are referred to [15] for a description of the original KEA+ and its security argument. We note that it is easy to verify that KEA+h achieves all the security attributes of KEA+.

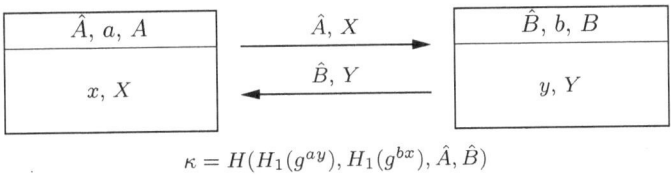

$$\kappa = H(H_1(g^{ay}), H_1(g^{bx}), \hat{A}, \hat{B})$$

Fig. 5. Protocol KEA+h

τ-Protocol. The τ-protocol is a new protocol derived from the μ-protocol (see [20, §3.1]) augmented with key confirmation. It was designed to highlight the problems that can arise from reusing the same static key among different protocols. The τ-protocol is informally presented in Figure 6, and formally given in Appendix A. It uses an MTI/C0-like exchange of messages [17] to confirm the receipt of ephemeral public keys. It can be proven secure in the Canetti-Krawczyk model [7] under the GDH and random oracle assumptions — the proof is straightforward but tedious, and so it is omitted.

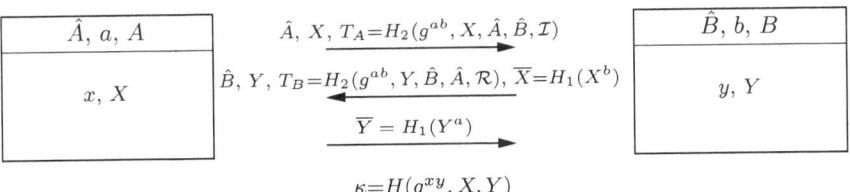

$$\kappa = H(g^{xy}, X, Y)$$

Fig. 6. Protocol τ

The attack. We can mount the following attack against KEA+h when one of the communicating parties (namely $\hat{B}$) shares a static key with the τ protocol.

1. The adversary $\mathcal{M}$ initiates a KEA+h session at $\hat{A}$ with $\hat{B}$ as the peer and obtains the outgoing ephemeral public key X.
2. $\mathcal{M}$ controls a party $\hat{E}$ with static key pair $(e, E = g^e)$ and initiates a τ-session with $\hat{B}$ by sending the message $X, T_E = H_2(B^e, X, \hat{E}, \hat{B}, \mathcal{I})$.

3. $\hat{B}$ responds with $(Y, T_B, H_1(X^b))$ from which $\mathcal{M}$ obtains $H_1(X^b)$.
4. $\mathcal{M}$ selects an ephemeral key pair $(z, Z = g^z)$ and sends $(\hat{B}, Z)$ to $\hat{A}$ in KEA+h.
5. $\hat{A}$ computes the KEA+h session key as $\kappa = H(H_1(Z^a), H_1(B^x), \hat{A}, \hat{B})$.
6. $\mathcal{M}$ computes the same session key as $\kappa = H(H_1(A^z), H_1(X^b), \hat{A}, \hat{B})$.

Note that the attack does not rely on $\hat{A}$ reusing her static public key A in the two protocols even when $\hat{A}$'s certificate for A does bind it to a particular protocol, thus preventing the adversary from passing A as the public key of the other protocol. It suffices that $\hat{B}$ shares his static key between the two protocols to attack a KEA+h session at $\hat{A}$. In fact, it is not difficult to imagine a scenario where $\hat{A}$ uses the KEA+h protocol in a stand-alone setting while $\hat{B}$ uses both KEA+h and τ and moreover reuses his static key in the two protocols. $\hat{A}$ may not even be aware of this reuse on the part of $\hat{B}$ in case $\hat{B}$ uses two separate certificates for KEA+h and τ. Under such a circumstance, $\hat{A}$ will end up getting her session key compromised by just trying to establish a KEA+h session with $\hat{B}$. Also note that adding the protocol identifier as an argument in the key derivation function H for KEA+h is not sufficient to prevent this kind of attack. We will revisit the issue of adding protocol identifiers in the key derivation function as a safeguard against protocol interference attacks in more detail in the next section.

3   Security Model

This section describes a "shared" model and associated security definition that aims to capture the security assurances guaranteed by d distinct key agreement protocols $\Pi_1, \Pi_2, \ldots, \Pi_d$, in the case where each party uses the same static key pair in all the d protocols. The individual protocols are assumed to be of the two-party Diffie-Hellman variety, where the communicating parties $\hat{A}$ and $\hat{B}$ exchange static and ephemeral public keys (and possibly other data) and use the static and ephemeral keying information to derive a session key $\kappa \in \{0,1\}^\lambda$. The model enhances the extended Canetti-Krawczyk model [7,14], and the description closely follows that of [20] in the pre-specified peer model.

Notation. We assume that messages are represented as binary strings. If m is a vector then $\#m$ denotes the number of its components. Two vectors m_1 and m_2 are said to be *matched*, written $m_1 \sim m_2$, if the first $t = \min\{\#m_1, \#m_2\}$ components of the vectors are pairwise equal as binary strings.

Session creation. A party $\hat{A}$ can be activated via an incoming message to create a session. The incoming message has one of the following forms: (i) $(\Pi_i, \hat{A}, \hat{B})$ or (ii) $(\Pi_i, \hat{A}, \hat{B}, In)$, where Π_i identifies which protocol is activated. If $\hat{A}$ was activated with $(\Pi_i, \hat{A}, \hat{B})$ then $\hat{A}$ is the session *initiator*; otherwise $\hat{A}$ is the session *responder*.

Session initiator. If $\hat{A}$ is the session initiator then $\hat{A}$ creates a separate session state where session-specific short-lived data is stored, and prepares a reply Out that includes an ephemeral public key X. The session is labeled *active* and identified via a (temporary and incomplete) session identifier $sid = (\Pi_i, \hat{A}, \hat{B}, \mathcal{I}, Comm)$ where $Comm$ is initialized to Out. The outgoing message is $(\Pi_i, \hat{B}, \hat{A}, Out)$.

Session responder. If $\hat{A}$ is the session responder then $\hat{A}$ creates a separate session state and prepares a reply Out that includes an ephemeral public key X. The session is labeled active and identified via a (temporary and incomplete) session identifier $sid = (\Pi_i, \hat{A}, \hat{B}, \mathcal{R}, Comm)$ where $Comm = (In, Out)$. The outgoing message is $(\Pi_i, \hat{B}, \hat{A}, \mathcal{I}, In, Out)$.

Session update. A party $\hat{A}$ can be activated to update a session via an incoming message of the form $(\Pi_i, \hat{A}, \hat{B}, role, Comm, In)$, where $role \in \{\mathcal{I}, \mathcal{R}\}$. Upon receipt of this message, $\hat{A}$ checks that she owns an active session with identifier $sid = (\Pi_i, \hat{A}, \hat{B}, role, Comm)$; except with negligible probability, $\hat{A}$ can own at most one such session. If no such session exists then the message is rejected, otherwise $\hat{A}$ updates $Comm$ by appending In. The session identifier sid is $(\Pi_i, \hat{A}, \hat{B}, role, Comm)$ where the updated $Comm$ is used. If the protocol requires a response by $\hat{A}$, then $\hat{A}$ prepares the required response Out; the outgoing message is $(\Pi_i, \hat{B}, \hat{A}, role, Comm, Out)$ where $role$ is $\hat{B}$'s role as perceived by $\hat{A}$. The session identifier is further updated by appending Out to $Comm$. If the protocol specifies that no further messages will be received, then the session completes and accepts a session key.

Aborted sessions. A protocol may require parties to perform some checks on incoming messages. For example, a party may be required to perform some form of public key validation or verify a signature. If a party is activated to create a session with an incoming message that does not meet the protocol specifications, then that message is rejected and no session is created. If a party is activated to update an active session with an incoming message that does not meet the protocol specifications, then the party deletes all information specific to that session (including the session state and the session key if it has been computed) and *aborts* the session. Abortion occurs before the session identifier is updated. At any point in time a session is in exactly one of the following states: active, completed, aborted.

Matching sessions. Since ephemeral public keys are selected at random on a per-session basis, session identifiers are unique except with negligible probability. A session sid with identifier $(\Pi_i, \ldots)$ is called a Π_i-*session*. Party $\hat{A}$ is said to be the *owner* of a session $(\Pi_i, \hat{A}, \hat{B}, *, *)$. For a session $(\Pi_i, \hat{A}, \hat{B}, *, *)$ we call $\hat{B}$ the session *peer*; together $\hat{A}$ and $\hat{B}$ are referred to as the *communicating parties*. Let $sid = (\Pi_i, \hat{A}, \hat{B}, role_A, Comm_A)$ be a session owned by $\hat{A}$, where $role_A \in \{\mathcal{I}, \mathcal{R}\}$. A session $sid^* = (\Pi_j, \hat{C}, \hat{D}, role_C, Comm_C)$, where $role_C \in \{\mathcal{I}, \mathcal{R}\}$, is said to be *matching* to sid if $\Pi_i = \Pi_j$, $\hat{A} = \hat{D}$, $\hat{B} = \hat{C}$, $role_A \neq role_C$, and $Comm_A \sim Comm_C$. It can be seen that the session sid, except with negligible probability, can have more than one matching session if and only if $Comm_A$ has exactly one component, i.e., is comprised of a single outgoing message.

Adversary. The adversary $\mathcal{M}$ is modeled as a probabilistic Turing machine and controls *all* communications. Parties submit outgoing messages to $\mathcal{M}$, who makes decisions about their delivery. The adversary presents parties with incoming messages via *Send*(message), thereby controlling the activation of parties. The adversary does not have immediate access to a party's private information, however in order to capture possible leakage of private information $\mathcal{M}$ is allowed to make the following queries:

- *StaticKeyReveal*($\hat{A}$): $\mathcal{M}$ obtains $\hat{A}$'s static private key.
- *EphemeralKeyReveal*(*sid*): $\mathcal{M}$ obtains the ephemeral private key held by session *sid*. We will henceforth assume that $\mathcal{M}$ issues this query only to sessions that hold an ephemeral private key.
- *SessionKeyReveal*(*sid*): If *sid* has completed then $\mathcal{M}$ obtains the session key held by *sid*. We will henceforth assume that $\mathcal{M}$ issues this query only to sessions that have completed.
- *EstablishParty*($\hat{A}, A$): This query allows $\mathcal{M}$ to register an identifier $\hat{A}$ and a static public key A on behalf of a party. The adversary totally controls that party, thus permitting the modeling of attacks by malicious insiders. Parties that were established by $\mathcal{M}$ using *EstablishParty* are called *corrupted* or *adversary controlled*. If a party is not corrupted it is said to be *honest*.

Adversary's goal. To capture indistinguishability $\mathcal{M}$ is allowed to make a special query *Test*(*sid*) to a 'fresh' session *sid*. In response, $\mathcal{M}$ is given with equal probability either the session key held by *sid* or a random key. If $\mathcal{M}$ guesses correctly whether the key is random or not, then the adversary is said to be successful and meet its goal. Note that $\mathcal{M}$ can continue interacting with the parties after issuing the *Test* query, but must ensure that the test session remains fresh throughout $\mathcal{M}$'s experiment.

Definition 1 (Π-fresh). Let *sid* be the identifier of a completed Π-session, owned by an honest party $\hat{A}$ with peer $\hat{B}$, who is also honest. Let sid^* be the identifier of the matching session of *sid*, if the matching session exists. Define *sid* to be Π-*fresh* if none of the following conditions hold:

1. $\mathcal{M}$ issued *SessionKeyReveal*(*sid*) or *SessionKeyReveal*(sid^*) (if sid^* exists).
2. sid^* exists and $\mathcal{M}$ issued one of the following:
   (a) Both *StaticKeyReveal*($\hat{A}$) and *EphemeralKeyReveal*(*sid*).
   (b) Both *StaticKeyReveal*($\hat{B}$) and *EphemeralKeyReveal*(sid^*).
3. sid^* does not exist and $\mathcal{M}$ issued one of the following:
   (a) Both *StaticKeyReveal*($\hat{A}$) and *EphemeralKeyReveal*(*sid*).
   (b) *StaticKeyReveal*($\hat{B}$).

Definition 2. Let $\Pi_1, \Pi_2, \ldots, \Pi_d$ be a collection of d distinct key agreement protocols. The protocol collection is said to be *secure* in the shared model if the following conditions hold:

1. For any $i \in [1, d]$ if two honest parties complete matching Π_i-sessions then, except with negligible probability, they both compute the same session key.
2. For any $i \in [1, d]$ no polynomially bounded adversary $\mathcal{M}$ can distinguish the session key of a fresh Π_i-session from a randomly chosen session key, with probability greater than $\frac{1}{2}$ plus a negligible fraction.

We emphasize that our shared model assumes that *all* parties reuse their static keys in each of the d protocols. If a collection $\Pi_1, \Pi_2, \dots, \Pi_d$ of key agreement protocols is shown to be secure with respect to Definition 2, then each of the protocols Π_i is individually secure in the extended Canetti-Krawczyk model. Moreover, the collection of protocols is also secure in the situation where a subset of parties use their static keys in only one protocol (and do not participate in runs of the other protocols); this was the setting of the attack in §2.4.

4   The NAXOS-C and DHKEA Protocols

The purpose of presenting the NAXOS-C and DHKEA protocols is to demonstrate that the security definition of §3 is useful (and not too restrictive) in the sense that there exist practical protocols that meet the definition under reasonable assumptions. The protocols were designed to allow a straightforward (albeit tedious) reductionist security argument, and have not been optimized.

In the protocol descriptions and the security argument, γ is the security parameter and $H : \{0,1\}^* \to \{0,1\}^\gamma \times \{0,1\}^\gamma$, $H_1 : \{0,1\}^* \to [1, q-1]$ and $H_2 : \{0,1\}^* \to \{0,1\}^{2\gamma}$ are hash functions.

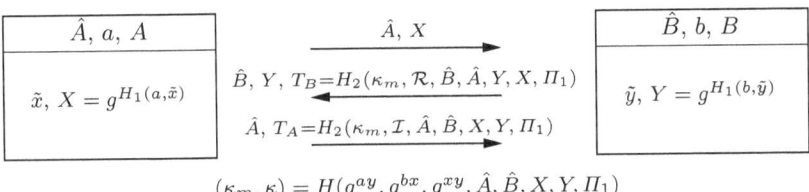

$$(\kappa_m, \kappa) = H(g^{ay}, g^{bx}, g^{xy}, \hat{A}, \hat{B}, X, Y, \Pi_1)$$

Fig. 7. The NAXOS-C protocol

Definition 3 ([20]). The NAXOS-C protocol, identified by Π_1, proceeds as follows (cf. Figure 7):

1. Upon receiving $(\Pi_1, \hat{A}, \hat{B}, \mathcal{I})$, party $\hat{A}$ (the initiator) does the following:
   (a) Select an ephemeral private key $\tilde{x} \in_R \{0,1\}^\gamma$ and compute $X = g^{H_1(a, \tilde{x})}$.
   (b) Initialize the session identifier to $(\Pi_1, \hat{A}, \hat{B}, \mathcal{I}, X)$.
   (c) Send $(\Pi_1, \hat{B}, \hat{A}, \mathcal{R}, X)$ to $\hat{B}$.
2. Upon receiving $(\Pi_1, \hat{B}, \hat{A}, \mathcal{R}, X)$, party $\hat{B}$ (the responder) does the following:
   (a) Verify that $X \in \mathcal{G}^*$.
   (b) Select an ephemeral private key $\tilde{y} \in_R \{0,1\}^\gamma$, and compute $y = H_1(b, \tilde{y})$ and $Y = g^y$.

(c) Compute $\sigma_1 = A^y$, $\sigma_2 = X^b$ and $\sigma_e = X^y$.

(d) Compute $(\kappa_m, \kappa) = H(\sigma_1, \sigma_2, \sigma_e, \hat{A}, \hat{B}, X, Y, \Pi_1)$ and $T_B = H_2(\kappa_m, \mathcal{R}, \hat{B}, \hat{A}, Y, X, \Pi_1)$.

(e) Destroy $\tilde{y}$, y, σ_1, σ_2 and σ_e.

(f) Initialize the session identifier to $(\Pi_1, \hat{B}, \hat{A}, \mathcal{R}, X, Y, T_B)$.

(g) Send $(\Pi_1, \hat{A}, \hat{B}, \mathcal{I}, X, Y, T_B)$ to $\hat{A}$.

3. Upon receiving $(\Pi_1, \hat{A}, \hat{B}, \mathcal{I}, X, Y, T_B)$, party $\hat{A}$ does the following:

  (a) Verify that an active $(\Pi_1, \hat{A}, \hat{B}, \mathcal{I}, X)$ session exists and $Y \in \mathcal{G}^*$.

  (b) Compute $x = H_1(a, \tilde{x})$.

  (c) Compute $\sigma_1 = Y^a$, $\sigma_2 = B^x$ and $\sigma_e = Y^x$.

  (d) Compute $(\kappa_m, \kappa) = H(\sigma_1, \sigma_2, \sigma_e, \hat{A}, \hat{B}, X, Y, \Pi_1)$.

  (e) Destroy $\tilde{x}$, x, σ_1, σ_2 and σ_e.

  (f) Verify that $T_B = H_2(\kappa_m, \mathcal{R}, \hat{B}, \hat{A}, Y, X, \Pi_1)$.

  (g) Compute $T_A = H_2(\kappa_m, \mathcal{I}, \hat{A}, \hat{B}, X, Y, \Pi_1)$.

  (h) Destroy κ_m.

  (i) Send $(\Pi_1, \hat{B}, \hat{A}, \mathcal{R}, X, Y, T_B, T_A)$ to $\hat{B}$.

  (j) Update the session identifier to $(\Pi_1, \hat{A}, \hat{B}, \mathcal{I}, X, Y, T_B, T_A)$ and complete the session by accepting κ as the session key.

4. Upon receiving $(\Pi_1, \hat{B}, \hat{A}, \mathcal{R}, X, Y, T_B, T_A)$, party $\hat{B}$ does the following:

  (a) Verify that an active $(\Pi_1, \hat{B}, \hat{A}, \mathcal{R}, X, Y, T_B)$ session exists.

  (b) Verify that $T_A = H_2(\kappa_m, \mathcal{I}, \hat{A}, \hat{B}, X, Y, \Pi_1)$.

  (c) Destroy κ_m.

  (d) Update the session identifier to $(\Pi_1, \hat{B}, \hat{A}, \mathcal{R}, X, Y, T_B, T_A)$ and complete the session by accepting κ as the session key.

If any of the verifications fail, the party erases *all* session-specific information and marks the session as aborted.

Definition 4 (DHKEA). The DHKEA protocol, identified by Π_2, proceeds as follows (cf. Figure 8):

1. Upon receiving $(\Pi_2, \hat{A}, \hat{B}, \mathcal{I})$, $\hat{A}$ (the initiator) does the following:

  (a) Select an ephemeral private key $\tilde{x} \in_R \{0, 1\}^\gamma$ and compute $X = g^{H_1(a, \tilde{x})}$.

  (b) Initialize the session identifier to $(\Pi_2, \hat{A}, \hat{B}, \mathcal{I}, X)$.

  (c) Send $(\Pi_2, \hat{B}, \hat{A}, \mathcal{R}, X)$ to $\hat{B}$.

2. Upon receiving $(\Pi_2, \hat{B}, \hat{A}, \mathcal{R}, X)$, $\hat{B}$ (the responder) does the following:

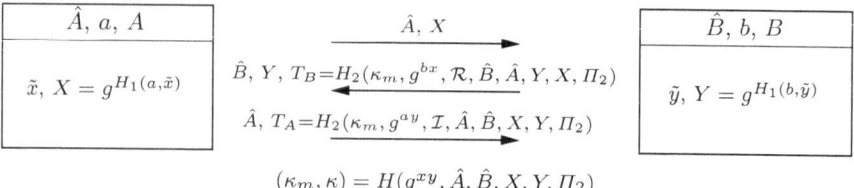

$$(\kappa_m, \kappa) = H(g^{xy}, \hat{A}, \hat{B}, X, Y, \Pi_2)$$

Fig. 8. The DHKEA protocol

(a) Verify that $X \in \mathcal{G}^*$.
(b) Select an ephemeral private key $\tilde{y} \in_R \{0,1\}^\gamma$, and compute $y = H_1(b, \tilde{y})$ and $Y = g^y$.
(c) Compute $\sigma_1 = A^y$, $\sigma_2 = X^b$ and $\sigma_e = X^y$.
(d) Compute $(\kappa_m, \kappa) = H(\sigma_e, \hat{A}, \hat{B}, X, Y, \Pi_2)$ and $T_B = H_2(\kappa_m, \sigma_2, \mathcal{R}, \hat{B}, \hat{A}, Y, X, \Pi_2)$.
(e) Destroy $\tilde{y}$, y, σ_1, σ_2 and σ_e.
(f) Initialize the session identifier to $(\Pi_2, \hat{B}, \hat{A}, \mathcal{R}, X, Y, T_B)$.
(g) Send $(\Pi_2, \hat{A}, \hat{B}, \mathcal{I}, X, Y, T_B)$ to $\hat{A}$.
3. Upon receiving $(\Pi_2, \hat{A}, \hat{B}, \mathcal{I}, X, Y, T_B)$, $\hat{A}$ does the following:
   (a) Verify that an active $(\Pi_2, \hat{A}, \hat{B}, \mathcal{I}, X)$ session exists and $Y \in \mathcal{G}^*$.
   (b) Compute $x = H_1(a, \tilde{x})$.
   (c) Compute $\sigma_1 = Y^a$, $\sigma_2 = B^x$ and $\sigma_e = Y^x$.
   (d) Compute $(\kappa_m, \kappa) = H(\sigma_e, \hat{A}, \hat{B}, X, Y, \Pi_2)$.
   (e) Destroy $\tilde{x}$, x, σ_1, σ_2 and σ_e.
   (f) Verify that $T_B = H_2(\kappa_m, \sigma_2, \mathcal{R}, \hat{B}, \hat{A}, Y, X, \Pi_2)$.
   (g) Compute $T_A = H_2(\kappa_m, \sigma_1, \mathcal{I}, \hat{A}, \hat{B}, X, Y, \Pi_2)$.
   (h) Destroy κ_m.
   (i) Send $(\Pi_2, \hat{B}, \hat{A}, \mathcal{R}, X, Y, T_B, T_A)$ to $\hat{B}$.
   (j) Update the session identifier to $(\Pi_2, \hat{A}, \hat{B}, \mathcal{I}, X, Y, T_B, T_A)$ and complete the session by accepting the session key κ.
4. Upon receiving $(\Pi_2, \hat{B}, \hat{A}, \mathcal{R}, X, Y, T_B, T_A)$, $\hat{B}$ does the following:
   (a) Verify that an active $(\Pi_2, \hat{B}, \hat{A}, \mathcal{R}, X, Y, T_B)$ session exists.
   (b) Verify that $T_A = H_2(\kappa_m, \sigma_1, \mathcal{I}, \hat{A}, \hat{B}, X, Y, \Pi_2)$.
   (c) Destroy κ_m.
   (d) Update the session identifier to $(\Pi_2, \hat{B}, \hat{A}, \mathcal{R}, X, Y, T_B, T_A)$ and complete the session by accepting the session key κ.

If any of the verifications fail, the party erases *all* session-specific information and marks the session as aborted.

A proof of the following can be found in [8].

Theorem 1. *If H, H_1 and H_2 are modeled as random oracles, and $\mathcal{G}$ is a group where the GDH assumption holds, then the pair of protocols (NAXOS-C,DHKEA) is secure in the shared model.*

5 Concluding Remarks

Our shared model assumes that each party has exactly one static key pair, which is reused in all the d key agreement protocols. It would be interesting to consider the more general scenario where each party may have multiple static key pairs, each of which may be reused for a subset of the d protocols. A further refinement of the shared model worthy of study is for the situation in which the protocols have different security attributes, as is the case with one-pass and three-pass protocols.

References

1. ANSI X9.42, Public Key Cryptography for the Financial Services Industry: Agreement of Symmetric Keys Using Discrete Logarithm Cryptography, American National Standards Institute (2003)
2. ANSI X9.63, Public Key Cryptography for the Financial Services Industry: Key Agreement and Key Transport Using Elliptic Curve Cryptography, American National Standards Institute (2001)
3. Anderson, R., Needham, R.: Robustness principles for public key protocols. In: Coppersmith, D. (ed.) CRYPTO 1995. LNCS, vol. 963, pp. 236–247. Springer, Heidelberg (1995)
4. Blake-Wilson, S., Johnson, D., Menezes, A.: Key agreement protocols and their security analysis. In: Darnell, M.J. (ed.) Cryptography and Coding 1997. LNCS, vol. 1355, pp. 30–45. Springer, Heidelberg (1997)
5. Boneh, D., Franklin, M.: Identity-based encryption from the Weil pairing. In: Kilian, J. (ed.) CRYPTO 2001. LNCS, vol. 2139, pp. 213–229. Springer, Heidelberg (2001)
6. Boyd, C., Cliff, Y., Nieto, J., Paterson, K.: Efficient one-round key exchange in the standard model. In: Mu, Y., Susilo, W., Seberry, J. (eds.) ACISP 2008. LNCS, vol. 5107, pp. 69–83. Springer, Heidelberg (2008),
http://eprint.iacr.org/2008/007
7. Canetti, R., Krawczyk, H.: Analysis of key-exchange protocols and their use for building secure channels. In: Pfitzmann, B. (ed.) EUROCRYPT 2001. LNCS, vol. 2045, pp. 453–474. Springer, Heidelberg (2001),
http://eprint.iacr.org/2001/040
8. Chatterjee, S., Menezes, A., Ustaoglu, B.: Reusing static keys in key agreement protools (full version), Technical Report CACR 2009-36,
http://www.cacr.math.uwaterloo.ca/techreports/2009/cacr2009-36.pdf
9. Coron, J., Joye, M., Naccache, D., Paillier, P.: Universal padding schemes for RSA. In: Yung, M. (ed.) CRYPTO 2002. LNCS, vol. 2442, pp. 226–241. Springer, Heidelberg (2002)
10. Fujisaki, E., Okamoto, T.: Secure integration of asymmetric and symmetric encryption schemes. In: Wiener, M. (ed.) CRYPTO 1999. LNCS, vol. 1666, pp. 537–554. Springer, Heidelberg (1999)
11. Gligoroski, D., Andova, S., Knapskog, S.: On the importance of the key separation principle for different modes of operation. In: Chen, L., Mu, Y., Susilo, W. (eds.) ISPEC 2008. LNCS, vol. 4991, pp. 404–418. Springer, Heidelberg (2008)
12. Hess, F.: Efficient identity based signature schemes based on pairings. In: Nyberg, K., Heys, H.M. (eds.) SAC 2002. LNCS, vol. 2595, pp. 310–324. Springer, Heidelberg (2003)
13. Kelsey, J., Schneier, B., Wagner, D.: Protocol interactions and the chosen protocol attack. In: Christianson, B., Lomas, M. (eds.) Security Protocols 1997. LNCS, vol. 1361, pp. 91–104. Springer, Heidelberg (1998)
14. LaMacchia, B., Lauter, K., Mityagin, A.: Stronger security of authenticated key exchange. In: Susilo, W., Liu, J.K., Mu, Y. (eds.) ProvSec 2007. LNCS, vol. 4784, pp. 1–16. Springer, Heidelberg (2007)
15. Lauter, K., Mityagin, A.: Security analysis of KEA authenticated key exchange. In: Yung, M., Dodis, Y., Kiayias, A., Malkin, T.G. (eds.) PKC 2006. LNCS, vol. 3958, pp. 378–394. Springer, Heidelberg (2006)

16. Law, L., Menezes, A., Qu, M., Solinas, J., Vanstone, S.: An efficient protocol for authenticated key agreement. Designs, Codes and Cryptography 28, 119–134 (2003)
17. Matsumoto, T., Takashima, Y., Imai, H.: On seeking smart public-key distribution systems. The Transactions of the IECE of Japan E69, 99–106 (1986)
18. Menezes, A., van Oorschot, P., Vanstone, S.: Handbook of Applied Cryptography. CRC Press, Boca Raton (1997)
19. Menezes, A., Ustaoglu, B.: Security arguments for the UM key agreement protocol in the NIST SP 800-56A standard. In: Proceedings of ASIACCS 2008, pp. 261–270. ACM Press, New York (2008)
20. Menezes, A., Ustaoglu, B.: Comparing the pre- and post-specified peer models for key agreement. In: Mu, Y., Susilo, W., Seberry, J. (eds.) ACISP 2008. LNCS, vol. 5107, pp. 53–68. Springer, Heidelberg (2008)
21. NIST, SKIPJACK and KEA Algorithm Specifications (1998), http://csrc.nist.gov/groups/ST/toolkit/documents/skipjack/skipjack.pdf
22. Pointcheval, D., Stern, J.: Security arguments for digital signatures and blind signatures. Journal of Cryptology 13, 361–396 (2000)
23. SP 800-56A, Special Publication 800-56A, Recommendation for Pair-Wise Key Establishment Schemes Using Discrete Logarithm Cryptography (Revised), National Institute of Standards and Technology (March 2007)
24. Vasco, M., Hess, F., Steinwandt, R.: Combined (identity-based) public key schemes, Cryptology ePrint Archive Report 2008/466, http://eprint.iacr.org/2008/466

A   The τ Protocol

Let γ denote the security parameter. In the protocol description, $H : \{0,1\}^* \to \{0,1\}^\gamma$ and $H_2 : \{0,1\}^* \to \{0,1\}^\gamma$ are hash functions. The full description of the τ protocol is in the original Canetti-Krawczyk model [7] in which a session has identifier $(\hat{A}, \hat{B}, \Psi, role)$, where Ψ is a string that is unique to that session and its matching session.

Definition 5 (τ-protocol). The protocol proceeds as follows:

1. Upon activation $(\hat{A}, \hat{B}, \Psi, \mathcal{I})$, $\hat{A}$ (the initiator) does the following:
   - (a) Create a session with identifier $(\hat{A}, \hat{B}, \Psi, \mathcal{I})$, provided that no session with identifier $(\hat{A}, \hat{B}, \Psi, *)$ exists.
   - (b) Select an ephemeral private key $x \in_R [1, q-1]$ and compute the corresponding ephemeral public key $X = g^x$.
   - (c) Compute $\sigma_s = B^a$ and commitment for X, $T_A = H_2(\sigma_s, \Psi, X, \hat{A}, \hat{B}, \mathcal{I})$.
   - (d) Destroy σ_s and send $(\hat{B}, \hat{A}, \Psi, \mathcal{R}, X, T_A)$ to $\hat{B}$.
2. Upon activation $(\hat{B}, \hat{A}, \Psi, \mathcal{R}, X, T_A)$, $\hat{B}$ (the responder) does the following:
   - (a) Create a session with identifier $(\hat{B}, \hat{A}, \Psi, \mathcal{R})$, provided that no session with identifier $(\hat{B}, \hat{A}, \Psi, *)$ exists.
   - (b) Verify that $X \in \mathcal{G}^*$.
   - (c) Compute $\sigma_s = A^b$ and verify that $T_A = H_2(\sigma_s, \Psi, X, \hat{A}, \hat{B}, \mathcal{I})$.
   - (d) Select an ephemeral private key $y \in_R [1, q-1]$ and compute the corresponding ephemeral public key $Y = g^y$.

(e) Compute commitment for Y, $T_B = H_2(\sigma_s, \Psi, Y, \hat{B}, \hat{A}, \mathcal{R})$ and verification value $\overline{X} = H_1(X^b)$.

(f) Destroy σ_s and send $(\hat{A}, \hat{B}, \Psi, \mathcal{I}, Y, T_B, \overline{X})$ to $\hat{A}$.

3. Upon activation $(\hat{A}, \hat{B}, \Psi, \mathcal{I}, Y, T_B, \overline{X})$, $\hat{A}$ does the following:

(a) Verify that $(\hat{A}, \hat{B}, \Psi, \mathcal{I})$ exists and $Y \in \mathcal{G}^*$.

(b) Compute $\sigma_s = B^a$ and verify that $T_B = H_2(\sigma_s, \Psi, Y, \hat{B}, \hat{A}, \mathcal{R})$.

(c) Verify that $\overline{X} = H_1(B^x)$.

(d) Compute verification value $\overline{Y} = H_1(Y^a)$.

(e) Compute the session key $\kappa = H(Y^x, X, Y)$.

(f) Destroy σ_s and x.

(g) Send $(\hat{B}, \hat{A}, \Psi, \mathcal{R}, \overline{Y})$ to $\hat{B}$.

(h) Complete session $(\hat{A}, \hat{B}, \Psi, \mathcal{I})$ with output $(\hat{A}, \hat{B}, \Psi, \kappa)$.

4. Upon activation $(\hat{B}, \hat{A}, \Psi, \mathcal{R}, \overline{Y})$, $\hat{B}$ does the following:

(a) Verify that $(\hat{B}, \hat{A}, \Psi, \mathcal{R})$ exists and that the session state contains X.

(b) Verify that $\overline{Y} = H_1(A^y)$.

(c) Destroy y.

(d) Compute the session key $\kappa = H(X^y, X, Y)$.

(e) Complete the session $(\hat{B}, \hat{A}, \Psi, \mathcal{R})$ with output $(\hat{B}, \hat{A}, \Psi, \kappa)$.

If any of the verifications fail, the party erases all session-specific information including the corresponding ephemeral private key.

A Study of Two-Party Certificateless Authenticated Key-Agreement Protocols

Colleen Swanson[1] and David Jao[2,*]

[1] David R. Cheriton School of Computer Science
[2] Department of Combinatorics and Optimization
University of Waterloo
Waterloo, Ontario, N2L 3G1, Canada
{c2swanso@cs,djao@math}.uwaterloo.ca

Abstract. We survey the set of all prior two-party certificateless key agreement protocols available in the literature at the time of this work. We find that all of the protocols exhibit vulnerabilities of varying severity, ranging from lack of resistance to leakage of ephemeral keys up to (in one case) a man-in-the-middle attack. Many of the protocols admit key-compromise impersonation attacks despite claiming security against such attacks. In order to describe our results rigorously, we introduce the first known formal security model for two-party authenticated certificateless key agreement protocols. Our model is based on the extended Canetti-Krawczyk model for traditional authenticated key exchange, except that we expand the range of allowable attacks to account for the increased flexibility of the attacker in the certificateless setting.

Keywords: key agreement, certificateless public key cryptography.

1 Introduction

Certificateless public key cryptography was introduced by Al-Riyami and Paterson [1] to serve as a middle ground between traditional public key cryptography based on PKI and the newer notion of identity-based cryptography in which a third party generates users' private keys. In certificateless public key cryptography, a user generates his private key by combining a secret value with a partial private key provided by the Key Generation Center (KGC). Similarly, to generate a public key, the user combines his secret value with public information from the KGC. Unlike in the case of identity-based cryptography, public keys are no longer easily computable by third parties, so they must be made available in some other way, such as via a public directory. However, once made available, the public keys do not need to be validated in any way; the security model for certificateless public key cryptography assumes that an adversary can replace public keys at will. Dent [4] has published a survey of the various certificateless public key encryption schemes that have been published since the introductory work of Al-Riyami and Paterson.

---

* The authors were partially supported by NSERC.

B. Roy and N. Sendrier (Eds.): INDOCRYPT 2009, LNCS 5922, pp. 57–71, 2009.
© Springer-Verlag Berlin Heidelberg 2009

In this work we focus on two-party key agreement schemes in the certificateless setting. In such schemes, two parties can establish a shared secret via a certificateless public key protocol. Work in the area of certificateless key agreement protocols is relatively limited. At the time this work was performed, we were aware of only five such schemes: one from the original Al-Riyami and Paterson paper [1], and four others by Mandt and Tan [11], Wang et al. [18], Shao [14], and Shi and Lee [15]. None of these works define a security model and therefore all of them lack a rigorous proof of security.

The contributions of this article are twofold. In the first part of the paper, we introduce a formal security model for certificateless authenticated key exchange protocols. Our security model is an extended version of the extended Canetti and Krawczyk model [7] for traditional authenticated key exchange. The modifications consist of enhancing the powers of the adversary to take into account the greater capabilities afforded in the certificateless setting. In the second part of the paper, we examine all five extant two-party certificateless authenticated key agreement protocols in the context of our security model. We find that all existing certificateless protocols allow for practical attacks of varying severity, ranging from relatively minor attacks involving leaked ephemeral secrets, up to (in one case) an outright man-in-the-middle attack. These results indicate that more work is required in order to fully realize the benefits of the certificateless paradigm in the context of key agreement.

We remark that, based upon an earlier unpublished version of this work [16], Lippold et al. [9] have published a subsequent security model for certificateless key agreement schemes, as well as a two-party certificateless key agreement scheme which is provably secure in their model (as well as ours). In Section 4 we explain the relationship between our security model and theirs. The provable security of their protocol means that, in a theoretical sense, the question of constructing a provably secure certificateless key agreement scheme in the context of a suitable security model has been settled. However, their protocol is slow, requiring each party to perform 10 pairing operations in order to compute the common key (or 5 at the cost of a stronger assumption). Therefore, it remains an open question whether there exists a provably secure certificateless key agreement protocol having minimal performance penalty compared to the alternatives. We discuss these and other issues in Section 6.

2   Background

We recall the standard terminology of key agreement protocols. A *key establishment protocol* is a protocol in which two or more parties gain access to a shared secret. If the shared secret is a function of information provided by and/or associated with each party (as opposed to the case where only one party is involved in choosing and/or obtaining the secret), we say the protocol is a *key agreement* protocol (KAP). We concern ourselves mainly with the two-party *dynamic* key agreement setting, wherein the established key varies with each execution. We refer to a protocol run as a *session*, and each message transmitted from one party to another as a *flow*. The shared secret resulting from a session is generally called (or used to determine) a *session key*. Protocols generally assume users (or pairs of users) have *long-term keys*, which are static secrets that are usually precomputed and stored securely. These are often used in conjunction with randomized secret input, which we refer to as *ephemeral* or *short-term* keys. Many key agreement protocols also assume the existence of a centralized server, known as a *Key Generation Center (KGC)*. We refer to this entity's secret information as the *master secret key*. We assume that the KGC communicates with users via a secure channel, whereas protocol flows are sent via an open channel. That is, eavesdroppers have no access to KGC/user communication, but can easily read anything sent between protocol participants.

2.1 Bilinear Pairings

All of the protocols that we discuss make use of bilinear pairings. Let q be a prime, G a cyclic additive group of order q generated by P, and G_T a multiplicative group of order q. Let $e\colon G \times G \to G_T$ be an admissible pairing, namely, one where e satisfies the following properties:

1. *Bilinearity*: $\forall P, Q, R \in G$ we have both $e(P + Q, R) = e(P, R)e(Q, R)$ and $e(P, Q + R) = e(P, Q)e(P, R)$.
2. *Non-degeneracy*: For all $P \neq 1_G$, we have $e(P, P) \neq 1_{G_T}$.
3. The pairing is efficiently computable.

The hardness assumption required for the pairing varies depending on the protocol. The survey article of Boyen [3] contains a list of the standard assumptions used in pairing-based protocols.

3 Security Attributes

Authenticated key agreement protocols satisfy the property that an entity is only able to compute a shared secret key if it holds the claimed identity. In particular, key agreement protocols should not allow an adversary to impersonate a user without that user's private key. The following security attributes apply to key agreement protocols in general:

- *Known session key security*: Key agreement protocols should be dynamic: each protocol run should result in a unique session key. An attacker who learns a given number of session keys should not be able to discover other session keys.
- *Forward secrecy*: Given the long-term private keys of one or more users, it is clearly desirable that an attacker not be able to determine previously established session keys. *Perfect forward secrecy* implies an attacker, even armed with all participants' long-term private keys, cannot determine old session keys. *Partial forward secrecy* implies an attacker armed with some, but not all, participants' long-term private keys cannot determine old session keys.

Similarly, *KGC forward secrecy* deals with the case in which the attacker has the master secret key. *Weak perfect forward secrecy* deals with the case where all long-term private keys are known, but the attacker was not actively involved in choosing ephemeral keys during the sessions of interest. It has been shown by Krawczyk [6] that no 2-flow authenticated key agreement protocol can do better than this weaker version of forward secrecy.

- *Unknown key-share security*: It should be impossible to coerce A into thinking he is sharing a key with B, when he is actually sharing a key with another (honest) user C. That is, it should not be possible for A to believe he is sharing a key with $B \neq C$, while C correctly thinks the key is shared with A.

- *Resilience to key-compromise impersonation (KCI)*: If the long-term private key of user A is compromised, the attacker should not be able to impersonate another user B to A. Obviously, if a long-term private key of A is compromised, we wish to replace this key as soon as possible, as the attacker can certainly impersonate A to any other user; this property is nevertheless important in the sense that it minimizes the damage until the user can detect that his key has been compromised.

- *Resistance to leakage of ephemeral keys*: If the attacker has access to the ephemeral keys of a given protocol run, he should be unable to determine the corresponding session key. As argued by Menezes and Ustaoglu [12], adversaries may gain access to this information through a side-channel attack or use of a weak random number generator; alternatively this information might be stored insecurely. We refer to such attacks as *known ephemeral key attacks*.

Additional security requirements arise in the case of certificateless key agreement protocols. Since public keys are not validated as in ID-based schemes or traditional PKI, we must assume that an adversary can replace public keys at will, and this attack must be incorporated into the security model. Now, if a KGC replaces public keys, it will be able to impersonate any user, since it can easily compute the corresponding private key. Thus, for all certificateless schemes, the KGC can launch a man-in-the-middle attack. For this reason, security models for certificateless schemes generally assume that the KGC never replaces public keys. Al-Riyami and Paterson [2] argue that this amounts to roughly the same amount of trust that is invested in a certificate authority (CA) in a traditional PKI. They make the point that, while often not stated explicitly, we usually trust that CAs do not produce certificates binding arbitrary public keys to a given identity. In any case, CL-PKC amounts to less trust than in an ID-based scheme, where the KGC has access to users' private keys by definition.

One way to avoid the issue of the KGC replacing public keys is to bind a user's public and private keys, as noted in Al-Riyami and Paterson [1]. This technique requires the user to send his fixed public key to the KGC, which is then incorporated into the partial private key. The result is that there can be only one working public key per user, so the existence of more than one implies that the KGC created more than one partial private key binding the user to different public keys. In fact, with this binding technique, the partial private keys do not need to be kept secret. The corresponding unique public key was computed with the user's secret value—this value is necessary to compute the full private key and cannot be determined from the exposed partial private key. While this binding technique has certain advantages, it comes at the added cost of reduced flexibility. With the binding technique in place, users must establish their public key before receiving their partial private key from the KGC.

4   Security Model

In this section, we give an extension of the extended Canetti-Krawczyk (eCK) [7] model suitable for the certificateless key agreement setting. In particular, the eCK model (and our model as well) captures all of the basic security attributes mentioned in Section 3.

We note that Al-Riyami and Paterson give a security definition relevant to certificateless encryption in [1,2], but our key agreement model is based on the eCK model and is not the natural extension of their definition to key establishment protocols. The treatment of the long-term secret information of the user is different in Al-Riyami and Paterson's definition, as their adversary is not allowed to know only part of a user's private key, an issue which restricts the treatment of leakage of ephemeral information. In particular, Al-Riyami and Paterson's model does not account for the attacks given in the following section, so this model is not sufficient when we consider several real-world attacks. Nevertheless there are some similarities, and we owe the general adversarial model to Al-Riyami and Paterson: we consider two possible types of adversaries, namely those without the master secret key, who can replace public keys at will, and those with the master secret key, who are not allowed to replace public keys at any time.

Informally, we refer to these types of attackers as either *outside* or *inside* attackers, in the following sense:

- An adversary is an *outside attacker* if the adversary does not have the master secret key; an outside attacker is able to replace public keys of users.
- An adversary is an *inside attacker* if the adversary has access to the master secret key; an inside attacker cannot replace public keys of users.

The formal adversarial model is as follows.

As in the eCK model, we consider a finite set of parties $P_1, P_2, \ldots, P_n$ modeled by probabilistic Turing machines. The adversary, also modeled by a probabilistic Turing machine, controls all communication—parties give outgoing messages to the adversary, who has control over their delivery via the Send query. Parties are activated by Send queries, so the adversary has control over the creation of protocol sessions, which take place within each party. We call the initiator of a session the *owner*, the responder the *peer*, and say both are *partners* of the given session. We define a *conversation* for a given session to be the ordered concatenation of all messages (both incoming and outgoing), and say two sessions s and s' have *matching conversations* if the outgoing messages of one are the incoming messages of the other, and vice versa. In particular, we assume that the public keys of the parties are a part of the message flows.[1]

We borrow the queries EphemeralKeyReveal and SessionKeyReveal from the eCK model. The EphemeralKeyReveal(s) query allows the adversary to obtain the ephemeral private key of the session s; this is not equivalent to issuing the query EphemeralKeyReveal on the session matching to s (if it exists), as only the ephemeral information chosen by the session owner is revealed. The SessionKeyReveal(s) query allows the adversary to obtain the session key for the specified session s (so long as s holds a session key).

In addition to these queries, we allow the adversary the queries RevealMasterKey, ReplacePublicKey, RevealPartialPrivateKey(party), and RevealSecretValue (party). The adversary can gain access to the master secret key via the query RevealMasterKey and replace the public key of a given party via ReplacePublicKey query. Unlike in the eCK model, this does not mean the adversary has control over the party. Instead, it implies that all other parties will use the adversary's version of the party's public key, while the given party will continue to use the correct public key in any calculations.[2] The RevealPartialPrivateKey(party) query gives the adversary access to the given party's partial private key, which is generated from the master secret key. (Note that this command is redundant if the RevealMasterKey query has been issued.) Lastly, the RevealSecretValue(party) query gives the adversary access to the party's chosen secret value (which is used to generate the party's public key). We assume that an adversary cannot issue a RevealSecretValue query against a party which has already received the ReplacePublicKey query.

We consider an adversary-controlled party to be one against which the adversary has issued both the ReplacePublicKey and RevealPartialPrivateKey queries. If the RevealMasterKey query has been issued, any party issued the ReplacePublicKey query is considered to be adversary-controlled; in this way, we capture the intent of the requirement that adversaries holding the master key should not be allowed to replace public keys. In particular, we say a party that is not adversary-controlled is *honest*. Formally, we define a *fresh* session as follows:

Definition 1. Let s be a completed session owned by party P_i with peer P_j, both of whom are honest. Let s^* denote the matching session (if such a session exists). We say s is *fresh* if none of the following conditions hold, where E denotes the adversary:

1. E issues a SessionKeyReveal(s) or SessionKeyReveal(s^*) query (provided s^* exists);

---

[1] The thesis version of this work [16], as pointed out by Lippold et al. [9], did not include public keys in the definition of a matching conversation. This is an oversight in our original model, as it does not allow an adversary to replay conversations with replaced public keys without detection.

[2] In Lippold et al. [9]'s model, the given party will use the replaced public key instead of his chosen key. While their model is strictly stronger than ours because of this, we feel it is a more natural choice to assume that a party knows his own public key.

2. $\mathfrak{s}^*$ exists and E either makes queries:
   (a) both RevealPartialPrivateKey(P_i) and RevealSecretValue(P_i) as well as EphemeralKeyReveal($\mathfrak{s}$) or
   (b) both RevealPartialPrivateKey(P_j) and RevealSecretValue(P_j) as well as EphemeralKeyReveal($\mathfrak{s}^*$);
3. No matching session $\mathfrak{s}^*$ exists and E either makes queries:
   (a) both RevealPartialPrivateKey(P_i) and RevealSecretValue(P_i) as well as EphemeralKeyReveal($\mathfrak{s}$) or
   (b) both RevealPartialPrivateKey(P_j) and RevealSecretValue(P_j).

This definition encompasses both types of adversaries. In the case where the adversary has issued the RevealMasterKey query, he cannot issue replace public key queries without making the involved parties dishonest. Moreover, as this adversary automatically has access to users' partial private keys, he is assumed unable to issue both the RevealSecretValue(P_i) and EphemeralKeyReveal($\mathfrak{s}$) or the RevealSecretValue(P_j) and EphemeralKeyReveal($\mathfrak{s}^*$) queries (provided that $\mathfrak{s}^*$ exists).

As in the eCK model, we allow the adversary E a single Test($\mathfrak{s}$) query, which can be issued at any stage to a completed, fresh session $\mathfrak{s}$. A bit b is then picked at random. If $b = 0$, the test oracle reveals the session key, and if $b = 1$, it generates a random value in the key space. E can continue to issue queries as desired, with the requirement that the test session remain fresh. At any point, the adversary can try to guess b. Let $\text{GoodGuess}^E(k)$ be the event that E correctly guesses b, and $\text{Advantage}^E(k) = \max\left\{0, \left|\Pr[\text{GoodGuess}^E(k)] - \frac{1}{2}\right|\right\}$, where k is a security parameter. We are now ready to formally define our notion of a secure session.

Definition 2. We say a certificateless key establishment protocol is *secure* if the following conditions hold:

1. If honest parties have matching sessions and no ReplacePublicKey queries have been issued, these sessions output the same session key (except with negligible probability).
2. For any polynomial time adversary E, $\text{Advantage}^E(k)$ is negligible.

5 Attacks

In this section we explore several two-party certificateless authenticated key agreement protocols from the literature, as well as one "self-certified" protocol (which on closer analysis actually appears to be certificateless). We first establish notation and give a summary of the protocols in Section 5.1. We then discuss each protocol in detail and present relevant attacks, modeled within the framework given in Section 4. We pay particular attention to the existence of key compromise impersonation attacks and whether or not the protocols have resistance to leakage of ephemeral keys, and in one case we show the protocol to be entirely insecure.

Table 1. Parameters for user i

Scheme	P_i	Q_i	S_i	X_i
AP [1]	$\langle x_i P, x_i P_{\mathrm{KGC}} \rangle$	$h(\mathrm{ID}_i)$	$s Q_i$	$x_i S_i$
MT [10,11]	$x_i P$	$h(\mathrm{ID}_i)$	$s Q_i$	$(s + x_i) Q_i$
WCW [18]	$x_i P$	$h(\mathrm{ID}_i)$	$s Q_i$	$\langle x_i, S_i \rangle$
Shao [14]	$x_i P$	$h'(\mathrm{ID}_i, P_i)$	$s Q_i$	$\langle x_i, S_i \rangle$
SL[15]	$e(P, x_i P)$	$H(\mathrm{ID}_i)$	$\frac{1}{Q_i + s} P$	$x_i S_i$

5.1 Protocol Summaries

In all of the following protocols, the Key Generation Center (KGC) has master secret key $s \in \mathbb{Z}_q^*$ and master public key $P_{\mathrm{KGC}} = sP$. The system parameters $\langle q, G, G_T, e, P, P_{\mathrm{KGC}} \rangle$ are as in Section 2.1. Let $k \in \mathbb{N}$ denote the number of bits in the shared session key. We will need the following hash functions and key derivation functions:

$H \colon \{0,1\}^* \to \mathbb{Z}_q^*$, $H' \colon G_T \to \mathbb{Z}_q^*$, $h \colon \{0,1\}^* \to G$, $h' \colon \{0,1\}^* \times G \to G$, and $h'' \colon G_T \times G \to \{0,1\}^k$, $\mathrm{kdf}_{\mathrm{MT}} \colon G_T \times G \times G \to \{0,1\}^k$, $\mathrm{kdf}_{\mathrm{WCW}} \colon \{0,1\}^* \times \{0,1\}^* \times G_T \times G \times G \to \{0,1\}^*$, $\mathrm{kdf}_{\mathrm{Shao}} \colon G_T \times \{0,1\}^* \times \{0,1\}^* \to \{0,1\}^k$, and $\mathrm{kdf}_{\mathrm{SL}} \colon G_T \to \{0,1\}^k$.

The certificateless protocols we study are given in Tables 1, 2, and 3, and include all certificateless protocols published at the time of our work, namely those of Al-Riyami and Paterson (AP) [1], Mandt and Tan (MT) [10,11], Wang, Cao, and Wang (WCW) [18], Shao [14], and Shi and Li (SL) [15].

In Table 1, we give a summary of user parameters for each of the protocols. For a given user i, we use P_i to denote the public key of i and Q_i to denote the mapping of ID_i into G. Each user has two pieces of secret information, a user-chosen secret value $x_i \in_R \mathbb{Z}_q^*$ and a partial private key $S_i \in G$, provided by the KGC. We use X_i to denote user i's full private key, which is formed from a combination of the user's secret information S_i and x_i.

We give the shared secret and session key computation information in Tables 2 and 3, respectively. For each protocol we have users A and B, with communication consisting of one message flow each. User A picks $a \in_R \mathbb{Z}_q$ and sends T_A to B, and B similarly chooses $b \in_R \mathbb{Z}_q$ and sends T_B to A. Some of the protocols specifically send user public keys as part of the message flows, and some assume the existence of a public directory for this purpose. For ease of representation, we do not specify which. Similarly, we do not include all of the computational checks that users perform during the protocol, but note that each protocol has group membership checks in place to thwart subgroup membership attacks, such as those of Lim and Lee [8], and the AP protocol includes a check to ensure that user public keys are of the correct form.

5.2 Al-Riyami and Paterson (AP) Protocol

As pointed out by Mandt [10], the AP protocol does not have resistance to leakage of ephemeral keys. However, we can easily fix this by computing the

Table 2. Shared secret computation

Scheme	T_i		Shared Secret K
AP [1]	T_A	aP	$e(X_B, T_A)e(X_A, T_B)$
	T_B	bP	$e(Q_B, x_A P_{\mathrm{KGC}})^a e(X_A, T_B)$
MT [11]	T_A	aP	$e(Q_B, P_{\mathrm{KGC}} + P_B)^a e(Q_A, P_{\mathrm{KGC}} + P_A)^b$
	T_B	bP	$e(Q_B, P_{\mathrm{KGC}} + P_B)^a e(X_A, T_B)$
WCW [18]	T_A	aP	$e(Q_A, Q_B)^s$
	T_B	bP	$e(S_A, Q_B)$
Shao [14]	T_A	aP_B	$H'(e(Q_A, Q_B)^s)abP$
	T_B	bP_A	$H'(e(S_A, Q_B))ax_A^{-1} \pmod{q} T_B$
SL [15]	T_A	$a(Q_B + P_{\mathrm{KGC}})$	$P_A^b P_B^a$
	T_B	$b(Q_A + P_{\mathrm{KGC}})$	$e(T_B, X_A)P_B^a$

Table 3. Session key computation. Here K denotes the shared secret from Table 2.

Scheme	Session Key
AP [1]	$h''(K\|abP)$
MT [11]	$\mathrm{kdf}(K\|abP\|x_A x_B P)$
WCW [18]	$\mathrm{kdf}(\mathrm{ID}_A, \mathrm{ID}_B, K, ax_B P, bx_A P)$
Shao [14]	$\mathrm{kdf}(K\|\mathrm{ID}_A\|\mathrm{ID}_B)$
SL [15]	$\mathrm{kdf}(K)$

session key to be $h''(K\|abP\|x_A x_B P)$ instead of $h''(K\|abP)$, modifying h'' as necessary (where Alice computes $x_A(x_B P)$ and Bob computes $x_B(x_A P)$).

Our fix is not quite as strong as we would like, however. In the context of our formal model from Section 4, an outside adversary (one who has not issued the RevealMasterKey query) can still mount an attack on A. He simply issues the ReplacePublicKey query on B and uses the EphemeralKeyReveal query on both the test session and its matching session. The initial vulnerability of the protocol to the leakage of ephemeral keys allows the attacker to compute K. He can compute A's version of $x_A x_B P$ by using his knowledge of the replaced public key. Specifically, suppose he chooses to replace B's public key with $\langle x_B' P, x_B' sP\rangle$ for some $x_B' \in_R \mathbb{Z}_q^*$. Then A will compute $x_A x_B P$ as $x_A(x_B' P) = x_B'(x_A P)$. It is clear that the adversary will be able to distinguish the session key held by A from a randomly chosen element of the keyspace.

5.3   Mandt and Tan (MT) Protocol

The MT protocol [10,11] was designed to satisfy all the security properties of the Al-Riyami and Paterson protocol, as well as the additional property of resistance to leakage of ephemeral keys. Mandt and Tan argue heuristically that the MT protocol has this property, as well as known session key security, weak forward secrecy, and resistance to key compromise impersonation, unknown key share, and key control attacks. We now show that resistance to leakage of ephemeral information does not hold, and that the protocol actually admits both a key compromise impersonation and a known ephemeral key attack. The KCI attack mentioned below was also independently discovered by Xia et al. [19].

Mandt and Tan provide two variations of the basic protocol given above, one in which the protocol participants use separate KGCs and one which provides key confirmation. The former is almost identical to the basic protocol, with the substitution of the different master keys where appropriate. The latter uses a MAC keyed under a value related to that of the session key, i.e., derived using a different key derivation function on the same inputs. Both versions are vulnerable to the attacks outlined below. We have included only the basic version of the protocol as described in [10] to improve readability.

We first show the protocol is vulnerable to a key compromise impersonation attack from an outside attacker. In fact, it suffices for the adversary Eve (E) to know a user's secret value x_i; she does not need the partial private key provided by the KGC. As the flows in the protocol are symmetric, it does not matter whether the adversary attempts to impersonate the initiator or responder of the protocol run. Formally, we describe this attack sequence on a session held by Alice as RevealSecretValue(A) and ReplacePublicKey(B) where no matching session exists, i.e., the adversary uses the Send query to send messages purportedly from B to A.

Assume Eve has access to x_A. She impersonates Bob to Alice by selecting $\beta, b \in \mathbb{Z}_q^*$ and sending $P_B^* = -P_{KGC} + \beta P$ for B's public key and $T_B = bP$ as usual. Since $P_B^* \in G^*$, Alice computes

$$
\begin{aligned}
K &= e(Q_B, P_{KGC} + P_B^*)^a e(X_A, T_B) \\
&= e(Q_B, P_{KGC} - P_{KGC} + \beta P)^a e((s + x_A)Q_A, bP) \\
&= e(Q_B, \beta P)^a e(bQ_A, (s + x_A)P) \\
&= e(\beta Q_B, aP)e(bQ_A, P_{KGC} + P_A).
\end{aligned}
$$

We denote by K_A the value of K computed by Alice above; that is, Alice thinks K_A is the correct value of K. Alice then derives the session key from kdf($K_A \| aT_B \| x_A P_B$).

As Eve chooses both β and b, she can compute K_A and $aT_B = bT_A$. Note that we have not needed knowledge of x_A up to this point. The only reason we need x_A is to compute $x_A P_B$ to input into the kdf, so this term is the only preventative measure against a man-in-the-middle attack similar to the KCI attack above. We see no clever substitution for P_B which allows for both the calculation of $e(Q_B, P_{KGC} + P_B)^a$ and $x_A P_B$, however. The heuristic argument against KCI attacks given in [10] fails to consider the scenario where the public key for B is replaced. The subsequent paper by Mandt and Tan [11] recognizes the possibility of replacing public keys, but still fails to identify the above attack.

Mandt and Tan also claim the protocol has the property of resistance to leakage of ephemeral keys. However, it is an easy matter to mount an outsider man-in-the-middle attack if given a and b. Suppose Eve substitutes $P_A^* = \alpha P$ for P_A and $P_B^* = \beta P$ for P_B in the protocol run, where $\alpha, \beta \in_R \mathbb{Z}_q^*$. From above we have that A and B will compute $K_A = e(Q_B, P_{\text{KGC}} + P_B^*)^a e(Q_A, P_{\text{KGC}} + P_A)^b$ and $K_B = e(Q_B, P_{\text{KGC}} + P_B)^a e(Q_A, P_{\text{KGC}} + P_A^*)^b$, respectively, so Eve will have no problem calculating K_A and K_B if she knows a and b.

Moreover, we have $x_A P_B^* = x_A \beta P = \beta P_A$, so Eve will establish the session key $\text{kdf}(K_A \| a T_B \| x_A P_B^*) = \text{kdf}(K_A \| abP \| \beta P_A)$ with A. Similarly she will establish $\text{kdf}(K_B \| abP \| \alpha P_B)$ as the session key with B. Thus the protocol fails to have resistance to leakage of ephemeral keys against outside attackers. If, on the other hand, the attacker is passive or cannot replace public keys, the protocol remains secure. The variants of the protocol are similarly vulnerable. Note that this is essentially the same attack mentioned in Section 5.2 on the improved version of the Al-Riyami Paterson KAP.

Interestingly, the MT protocol is almost identical to the protocol of Wang and Cao [17]. The main difference between the two protocols is that in the latter, the private keys are bound to the public keys, so the attacks presented above are not possible in an ideal protocol specification of Wang and Cao's protocol, whereas the MT protocol allows adversaries to easily replace public keys. We achieve the same scheme if we apply the binding technique of Al-Riyami and Paterson [1] to Mandt's protocol, although for cheating to be evident, we must require the partial private keys (or users' certificates) to be public.

5.4 Wang et al. (WCW) Protocol

Wang et al. [18] claim the WCW protocol is secure against both man-in-the-middle attacks mounted by the KGC and KCI attacks. Since all certificateless key agreement protocols are vulnerable to a KGC man-in-the-middle attack (if the KGC can replace public keys), the first claim is certainly false. We show the second claim to be false by presenting a KCI-attack below; this attack was also independently discovered by Meng and Futai [13]. We mention that Wang et al. also claim their protocol has known-key security, weak partial and KGC forward secrecy, unknown key-share resistance, and key control.

We observe that use of the static shared secret K prevents the formal attack outlined in Section 5.2, where knowledge of the matching sessions' ephemeral keys and one public key replacement allows a successful attack. This static shared secret implies a successful attacker must have access to at least one of the participating party's partial private keys. However, the protocol does not guard against an adversary who, for a test session $\mathfrak{s}$ with owner A and matching session $\mathfrak{s}^*$, issues the queries RevealPartialPrivateKey(A), EphemeralKeyReveal($\mathfrak{s}$), and EphemeralKeyReveal($\mathfrak{s}^*$). The adversary will be able to compute the session key $\text{kdf}(\text{ID}_A, \text{ID}_B, K, ax_B P, bx_A P)$.

We mount an outsider KCI attack as follows. As with the KCI attack on the Mandt protocol, we can express this attack using the formal terminology of Section 4. The adversary chooses a test session owned by B and takes advantage of the queries Send, RevealPartialPrivateKey(B) and ReplacePublicKey(A). The (informal) details follow.

We assume that Eve is attempting to impersonate Alice to Bob, where Alice is the initiator and Bob is the responder. For such an attack, we would generally assume our attacker Eve has access to all of B's private key, that is, both x_B and S_B. Here we show that it is sufficient for Eve to have S_B.

Eve proceeds by sending $T_A = aP$ as usual (for her own choice of $a \in_R \mathbb{Z}_q^*$). She completes the attack by replacing A's public key entry with $P_A^* = \alpha P$ for some $\alpha \in_R \mathbb{Z}_q^*$.

Note that Eve can easily compute $K = e(S_B, Q_A)$, as she has access to S_B. Recall that B will use $x_B T_A$ and $b P_A^*$ in his computation of the secret key. Since $x_B T_A = a P_B$ and $b P_A^* = b \alpha P = \alpha T_B$, Eve can compute these as well, because a and α were chosen by her, the term P_B is public, and B sends T_B to A during the protocol run. Thus Eve can compute $K_B = \text{kdf}(\text{ID}_A, \text{ID}_B, K, x_B T_A, b P_A^*)$, as desired. It is worth stressing that Eve cannot succeed without knowledge of S_B, as without it she cannot compute K.

5.5   Shao Protocol

The Shao [14] protocol purportedly provides weak forward secrecy, known-key security, and resilience to a "masquerade attack," which refers to KCI attacks where not *all* of the user's private key is compromised. We show that the latter claim is false by providing a KCI attack that only requires the adversary to have access to part of the user's private key. Although Shao claims his protocol is self-certified, the scheme is much closer to a certificateless protocol than Girault's [5] notion of a self-certified key agreement protocol. In contrast to Girault's model, the KGC has partial key escrow (in that it computes the partial private keys) and requires a secure channel between itself and the users. Also, users cannot be sure that they have the correct public key of another party, so the adversarial model is equivalent to that of certificateless schemes.

Moreover, although at first glance it seems that Shao's protocol has applied the binding technique of Al-Riyami and Paterson mentioned in Section 2, given his definition of Q_i for user i, this is not quite the case. The protocol relies in an essential way on the secrecy of the partial private keys; if we make these keys public, the scheme reduces to the basic Diffie-Hellman KAP (with a single extra term $H'(e(S_A, Q_B))$ that anyone can compute).

We observe that this protocol, like that of Section 5.4, does not hold up to the following formal attack. Letting $\mathfrak{s}$ denote the test session with owner A and matching session $\mathfrak{s}^*$, suppose the adversary issues the RevealPartialPrivateKey(A), EphemeralKeyReveal($\mathfrak{s}$), and EphemeralKeyReveal($\mathfrak{s}^*$) queries. The adversary will be able to compute $H'(e(S_A, Q_B))abP$, and hence the session key as well.

Let us now consider Shao's claim that the protocol is secure provided not all of the user's private key (x_i, S_i) is compromised. We show the protocol is in fact vulnerable in the scenario where S_i is known, but x_i and s remain secure.

We launch an outsider key compromise impersonation attack on Alice with the knowledge of S_A, but not x_A, as follows. Since knowing $S_A = s Q_A = s H'(\text{ID}_A, x_A P)$ is not the same as knowing s, replacing public keys is permissible in this scenario. As the protocol messages are symmetric, there is a corresponding attack on Bob, and thus it does not matter whether or not the attacker initiates the protocol run. The formal queries needed for this attack are similar to the KCI attack outlined in Section 5.4, so we do not mention them here.

Our attacker Eve replaces Bob's public key with $P_B^* = \beta P$ for $\beta \in_R \mathbb{Z}_q^*$ of her choosing. She then follows the protocol and sends ID_B and $T_B = bP_A$ for some $b \in_R \mathbb{Z}_q^*$. Alice will then compute Q_B as $Q_B = h'(\mathrm{ID}_B, P_B^*)$, and $H'(e(S_A, Q_B))ax_A^{-1} \pmod{q}$.

Alice calculates the session secret as

$$
\begin{aligned}
K &= H'(e(S_A, Q_B))ax_A^{-1}bP_A \\
&= H'(e(S_A, Q_B))bax_A^{-1}x_A P \\
&= H'(e(S_A, Q_B))baP.
\end{aligned}
$$

We see that Eve can compute $H'(e(S_A, Q_B))b$, as she possesses S_A and chooses b herself. Moreover, since A sends $T_A = a\beta P$ in the first round (and Eve knows β), Eve can compute aP and thus K.

5.6   Shi Li (SL) Protocol

In the SL protocol [15], the session key is derived directly from $P_A^b P_B^a$, so this protocol certainly does not have resistance to leakage of ephemeral keys. The authors claim that this protocol provides implicit key authentication, known session key security, weak partial forward secrecy, key compromise impersonation resistance, and unknown key share resistance. We show the protocol fails to provide implicit key authentication by demonstrating a man-in-the-middle attack by an outside attacker.

Our attacker Eve intercepts Alice's $\langle T_A, P_A \rangle$ and instead sends $\langle T_A^*, P_A^* \rangle$ to Bob. Here $T_A^* = a^*(H(\mathrm{ID}_B)P + P_{\mathrm{KGC}})$ and $P_A^* = e(\alpha(H(\mathrm{ID}_A)P + P_{\mathrm{KGC}}), P)$ for $a^*, \alpha \in_R \mathbb{Z}_q^*$ of Eve's choosing.

Similarly Eve replaces Bob's message $\langle T_B, P_B \rangle$ with $\langle T_B^*, P_B^* \rangle$, where $T_B^* = b^*(H(\mathrm{ID}_A)P + P_{\mathrm{KGC}})$ and $P_B^* = e(\beta(H(\mathrm{ID}_A)P + P_{\mathrm{KGC}}), P)$ for $b^*, \beta \in_R \mathbb{Z}_q^*$ of her choosing.

Notice that $P_A^* \in G_T$, so Bob will compute

$$
\begin{aligned}
K_B &= e(T_A^*, X_B)(P_A^*)^b \\
&= e\left(a^*(H(\mathrm{ID}_B)P + P_{\mathrm{KGC}}), \frac{x_B}{H(\mathrm{ID}_B)+s}P\right) e(\alpha(H(\mathrm{ID}_A)P + P_{\mathrm{KGC}}), P)^b \\
&= e(a^*P, x_B P)e(b(H(\mathrm{ID}_A)P + P_{\mathrm{KGC}}), \alpha P) \\
&= P_B^{a^*} e(T_B, \alpha P).
\end{aligned}
$$

As Eve chooses both a^* and α, she can compute K_B. Similarly, Eve will be able to compute Alice's key $K_A = P_A^{b^*} e(T_A, \beta P)$. We have therefore shown the protocol to be insecure. The corresponding formal attack on the protocol is modeled by picking a test session with owner A and using the ReplacePublicKey(B) and Send queries to alter the messages sent by B to A. As shown above, the adversary will be able to compute the session key. Interestingly, this attack fails if we transform this protocol into a certificate-based protocol, whereby the public keys of users are bound to the corresponding partial private keys and the latter are used as public certificates.

6 Conclusion

Our work demonstrates that all existing CL-KAPs are insecure to some extent in the sense of the security model of Section 4. In our opinion, this model is a natural one, and our findings provide motivation for developing new CL-KAPs meeting this security definition. We remark that, since the initial version of this work [16], new protocols have appeared [13,9] which were designed to address some of the shortcomings of the earlier protocols.

The existence of practical CL-KAPs remains an interesting open question, given that these schemes are designed to avoid both the key escrow problem and the high management costs of certificate distribution, storage, verification, and revocation present in public key infrastructures. These protocols also have the added advantage of flexibility—the user can generate his public key before *or* after receiving his partial private key. Consequently, while applying Al-Riyami and Paterson's binding technique fixes some of the security vulnerabilities mentioned in Section 5, doing so limits the advantages gained by using a certificateless scheme in the first place.

Although Lippold et al. [9] have settled the question of whether a CL-KAP exists that is secure in the extended eCK model given in Section 4 (as well as their strengthened version of this model), the question of whether a computationally practical scheme exists remains. Lippold et al.'s scheme, which is secure given the bilinear and computational Diffie-Hellman assumptions, requires 10 pairing computations per party; even the version relying on the gap bilinear Diffie-Hellman assumption is expensive, requiring 5 pairing computations per party. In addition, the security of their scheme is proven using the random oracle model, so it remains an open question to devise a scheme secure in the standard model.

References

1. Al-Riyami, S.S., Paterson, K.G.: Certificateless public key cryptography. In: Laih, C.-S. (ed.) ASIACRYPT 2003. LNCS, vol. 2894, pp. 452–473. Springer, Heidelberg (2003)
2. Al-Riyami, S.S., Paterson, K.G.: CBE from CLE-PKE: A generic construction and efficient schemes. In: Vaudenay, S. (ed.) PKC 2005. LNCS, vol. 3386, pp. 398–415. Springer, Heidelberg (2005)
3. Boyen, X.: The uber-assumption family – a unified complexity framework for bilinear groups. In: Galbraith, S.D., Paterson, K.G. (eds.) Pairing 2008. LNCS, vol. 5209, pp. 39–56. Springer, Heidelberg (2008)
4. Dent, A.W.: A survey of certificateless encryption schemes and security models. Int. J. Inf. Secur. 7(5), 349–377 (2008)
5. Girault, M.: Self-certified public keys. In: Davies, D.W. (ed.) EUROCRYPT 1991. LNCS, vol. 547, pp. 490–497. Springer, Heidelberg (1991)

6. Krawczyk, H.: HMQV: A high-performance secure Diffie-Hellman protocol. In: Shoup, V. (ed.) CRYPTO 2005. LNCS, vol. 3621, pp. 546–566. Springer, Heidelberg (2005)
7. LaMacchia, B., Lauter, K., Mityagin, A.: Stronger security of authenticated key exchange. In: Susilo, W., Liu, J.K., Mu, Y. (eds.) ProvSec 2007. LNCS, vol. 4784, pp. 1–16. Springer, Heidelberg (2007)
8. Lim, C.H., Lee, P.J.: A key recovery attack on discrete log-based schemes using a prime order subgroup. In: Kaliski Jr., B.S. (ed.) CRYPTO 1997. LNCS, vol. 1294, pp. 249–263. Springer, Heidelberg (1997)
9. Lippold, G., Boyd, C., Nieto, J.G.: Strongly secure certificateless key agreement. In: Shacham, H. (ed.) Pairing 2009. LNCS, vol. 5671, pp. 206–230. Springer, Heidelberg (2009)
10. Mandt, T.K.: Certificateless authenticated two-party key agreement protocols. Master's thesis, Gjøvik University College, Department of Computer Science and Media Technology (2006)
11. Mandt, T.K., Tan, C.H.: Certificateless authenticated two-party key agreement protocols. In: Okada, M., Satoh, I. (eds.) ASIAN 2006. LNCS, vol. 4435, pp. 37–44. Springer, Heidelberg (2008)
12. Menezes, A., Ustaoglu, B.: Security arguments for the UM key agreement protocol in the NIST SP 800-56A standard. In: ASIACCS 2008: Proceedings of the 2008 ACM symposium on Information, computer and communications security, pp. 261–270. ACM, New York (2008)
13. Meng, G., Futai, Z.: Key-compromise impersonation attacks on some certificateless key agreement protocols and two improved protocols. In: International Workshop on Education Technology and Computer Science, vol. 2, pp. 62–66 (2009)
14. Shao, Z.-h.: Efficient authenticated key agreement protocol using self-certified public keys from pairings. Wuhan University Journal of Natural Sciences 10(1), 267–270 (2005)
15. Shi, Y., Li, J.: Two-party authenticated key agreement in certificateless public key cryptography. Wuhan University Journal of Natural Sciences 12(1), 71–74 (2007)
16. Swanson, C.M.: Security in key agreement: Two-party certificateless schemes. Master's thesis, University of Waterloo, Department of Combinatorics and Optimization (2008)
17. Wang, S., Cao, Z.: Escrow-free certificate-based authenticated key agreement protocol from pairings. Wuhan University Journal of Natural Sciences 12(1), 63–66 (2007)
18. Wang, S., Cao, Z., Wang, L.: Efficient certificateless authenticated key agreement protocol from pairings. Wuhan University Journal of Natural Sciences 11(5), 1278–1282 (2006)
19. Xia, L., Wang, S., Shen, J., Xu, G.: Breaking and repairing the certificateless key agreement protocol from ASIAN 2006. In: Okada, M., Satoh, I. (eds.) ASIAN 2006. LNCS, vol. 4435, pp. 562–566. Springer, Heidelberg (2008)

Fault Analysis of Rabbit: Toward a Secret Key Leakage

Alexandre Berzati[1,2], Cécile Canovas-Dumas[1], and Louis Goubin[2]

[1] CEA-LETI/MINATEC, 17 rue des Martyrs, 38054 Grenoble Cedex 9, France
{alexandre.berzati,cecile.canovas}@cea.fr
[2] Versailles Saint-Quentin-en-Yvelines University,
45 Avenue des Etats-Unis, 78035 Versailles Cedex, France
Louis.Goubin@prism.uvsq.fr

Abstract. Although Differential Fault Analysis (DFA) led to powerful applications against public key [15] and secret key [12] cryptosystems, very few works have been published in the area of stream ciphers.

In this paper, we present the first application of DFA to the software eSTREAM candidate Rabbit that leads to a full secret key recovery. We show that by modifying modular additions of the next-state function, 32 faulty outputs are enough for recovering the whole internal state in time $\mathcal{O}\left(2^{34}\right)$ and extracting the secret key. Thus, this work improves the previous fault attack against Rabbit both in terms of computational complexity and fault number.

Keywords: Stream cipher, Rabbit, fault attacks, carry analysis.

1 Introduction

The stream cipher Rabbit has been selected in the final portfolio of the ECRYPT stream cipher project (eSTREAM) [13]. It was first presented at FSE 2003 [14], targeting both hardware and software environments. It has been selected as a software candidate for the third evaluation phase of the project.

Rabbit has a 128-bit key (also supports 80-bit key), 64-bit initialization vector (IV), and 513-bit internal state. Although it has been designed to be faster than commonly used ciphers, the level of security provided by this stream cipher has not been disregarded by the designers. Indeed, they made the efforts of a deep security analysis [13] and published a series of white papers [1,2,3,4,5,6] to prove the robustness of Rabbit to the well-known attacks (*i.e.* algebraic, correlation, guess-and-determine, differential). Until now, only two papers discussing the cryptographic security of Rabbit have been published. Both propose to exploit the bias of the core function "g". In [7], the function "g" was firstly shown to be unbalanced. The resulting distinguishing attack requires the analysis of 2^{247} keystream sub-blocks generated from random keys and IV's, which is higher than the complexity of the key exhaustive search (*i.e.* 2^{128}). The second article provides an improved distinguishing attack based on the use of the Fast Fourier Transform (FFT) for computing the exact Rabbit keystream bias. This

B. Roy and N. Sendrier (Eds.): INDOCRYPT 2009, LNCS 5922, pp. 72–87, 2009.
© Springer-Verlag Berlin Heidelberg 2009

reduces the complexity of the distinguishing attack from $\mathcal{O}\left(2^{247}\right)$ to $\mathcal{O}\left(2^{97.5}\right)$ in the multi-frame extension [7]. Recently, the security of Rabbit in the context of faults has been discussed in [23]. Under a classical fault model, the authors demonstrated that the complete internal state can be recovered from $128 - 256$ faults in $\mathcal{O}\left(2^{38}\right)$ steps. The attack also requires to precompute a table of size $\mathcal{O}\left(2^{41.6}\right)$ bytes. From our knowledge, it was the best known attack against Rabbit.

In this paper, we propose a new method to exploit faults against Rabbit implementations. We show that, if an attacker is able to perturb transiently modular additions in the next-state function, then he can recover the whole internal state and predict the keystream. The analysis can also lead to a full key recovery if the first two iterations of Rabbit are targeted.

We provide evidences that this attack does not only improves the previous result in terms of fault number but in terms of complexity. Indeed, from 32 faults injected according to our model, the attacker is able to recover the whole internal state in time $\mathcal{O}\left(2^{34}\right)$.

After a brief presentation of the Rabbit stream cipher, Sect. 3 provides an overview of previous fault attacks against implementations of stream ciphers. Then, we describe in Sect. 4 the fault model we have chosen and a complete differential analysis of the faulty keystreams. The final part of the paper provides the attack algorithm and an analysis of its performance.

2   The Stream Cipher Rabbit

2.1   Notations

The notations we use in this paper to describe Rabbit are extracted from the original description of the stream cipher presented at FSE 2003 [14].

- $\oplus$ denotes logical XOR,
- $\wedge$ denotes logical AND,
- $\vee$ denotes logical OR,
- $\ll$ and $\gg$ denote respectively left and right logical bit-wise shift,
- $\lll$ and $\ggg$ denote respectively left and right logical bit-wise rotation,
- $A^{[g..h]}$ denotes the part of the vector A from bit g to bit h,
- $A_{[k]}$ denotes the value of A mod k.

2.2   Description of Rabbit

Rabbit is a synchronous stream cipher. It takes as input a 128-bit secret key and a 64-bit public initialization vector (IV). For each iteration, it generates a 128-bit pseudo-random output block. This output block, usually referred as the keystream, is XOR-ed with a plaintext/ciphertext to perform the encryption/decryption.

The internal state of Rabbit is composed of 513 bits:

- Eight 32-bit state variables denoted by $(x_{j,i})_{0 \leq j \leq 7}$ at iteration i,
- Eight 32-bit counters $(c_{j,i})_{0 \leq j \leq 7}$,
- One counter carry bit $\phi_{7,i}$.

At epoch $i = 0$, the state variables and the counters are initialized with the Key Setup and IV Setup schemes. We recall neither Key Setup nor IV Setup schemes since our attack does not rely on the initialization process. Further details are provided in [14,13].

Then, for $i \geq 1$, state variables and counters are updated according to the following schemes. Each iteration produces 128 bits of the keystream.

Next-State Function

$$x_{0,i+1} = g_{0,i} + (g_{7,i} \lll 16) + (g_{6,i} \lll 16)$$
$$x_{1,i+1} = g_{1,i} + (g_{0,i} \lll 8) + g_{7,i}$$
$$x_{2,i+1} = g_{2,i} + (g_{1,i} \lll 16) + (g_{0,i} \lll 16)$$
$$x_{3,i+1} = g_{3,i} + (g_{2,i} \lll 8) + g_{1,i}$$
$$x_{4,i+1} = g_{4,i} + (g_{3,i} \lll 16) + (g_{2,i} \lll 16)$$
$$x_{5,i+1} = g_{5,i} + (g_{4,i} \lll 8) + g_{3,i}$$
$$x_{6,i+1} = g_{6,i} + (g_{5,i} \lll 16) + (g_{4,i} \lll 16)$$
$$x_{7,i+1} = g_{7,i} + (g_{6,i} \lll 8) + g_{5,i}$$

Where $g_{j,i}$ is defined by the following expression:

$$g_{j,i} = (x_{j,i} + c_{j,i+1})^2 \oplus \left((x_{j,i} + c_{j,i+1})^2 \gg 32 \right) \bmod 2^{32} \qquad (1)$$

All additions are performed modulo 2^{32} and squaring modulo 2^{64}.

Counter System

$$c_{0,i+1} = c_{0,i} + a_0 + \phi_{7,i} \bmod 2^{32}, \qquad (2)$$
$$c_{j,i+1} = c_{j,i} + a_j + \phi_{j-1,i+1} \bmod 2^{32}, \text{ for } 0 < j < 8.$$

where the counter carry bit $\phi_{j,i+1}$ is obtained as follows:

$$\phi_{j,i+1} = \begin{cases} 1 & \text{if } c_{0,i} + a_0 + \phi_{7,i} \geq 2^{32} \wedge j = 0, \\ 1 & \text{if } c_{j,i} + a_j + \phi_{j-1,i+1} \geq 2^{32} \wedge j > 0, \\ 0 & \text{otherwise} \end{cases}$$

Furthermore, the constants $(a_j)_{0 \leq j \leq 7}$ are defined as:

- $a_0 = a_3 = a_6 = $ 0x4D34D34D,
- $a_1 = a_4 = a_7 = $ 0xD34D34D3,
- $a_2 = a_5 = $ 0x34D34D34.

Extraction Scheme. For each iteration i of the next-state function, the current output keystream $s_i^{[127..0]}$ is extracted as follows:

$$
\begin{aligned}
s_i^{[15..0]} &= x_{0,i}^{[15..0]} \oplus x_{5,i}^{[31..16]} \\
s_i^{[31..16]} &= x_{0,i}^{[31..16]} \oplus x_{3,i}^{[15..0]} \\
s_i^{[47..32]} &= x_{2,i}^{[15..0]} \oplus x_{7,i}^{[31..16]} \\
s_i^{[63..48]} &= x_{2,i}^{[31..16]} \oplus x_{5,i}^{[15..0]} \\
s_i^{[79..64]} &= x_{4,i}^{[15..0]} \oplus x_{1,i}^{[31..16]} \\
s_i^{[95..80]} &= x_{4,i}^{[31..16]} \oplus x_{7,i}^{[15..0]} \\
s_i^{[111..96]} &= x_{6,i}^{[15..0]} \oplus x_{3,i}^{[31..16]} \\
s_i^{[127..112]} &= x_{6,i}^{[31..16]} \oplus x_{1,i}^{[15..0]}
\end{aligned}
$$

2.3   Previous Work on Rabbit

The stream cipher Rabbit has been designed to be faster than commonly used ciphers and to justify a key size of 128 bits for encrypting up to 2^{64} blocks of plaintext. In a series of white papers [1,2,3,4,5,6] and in [14], the designers gave convincing arguments to claim that Rabbit is resistant against algebraic, correlation, differential, guess-and-determine, and statistical attacks. Particularly, in [13], authors claim that Rabbit is immune to the replacement of all additions performed in the next-state function by XORs (see Sect. 2.2). Indeed, since all possible byte-wise combinations of the output depend on at least four different g-functions, they conclude that "it seems to be impossible to verify a guess of fewer that 128 bits against the output".

In 2007, J-P. Aumasson raised a statistical weakness on Rabbit and more specifically on the core function "g" [7]. Although this function, based on a modular square, was expected to be strongly non-linear, J-P. Aumasson highlighted the non-uniformity of the bit distribution given a random initial state. The complexity of the resulted distinguishing attack is about $\mathcal{O}\left(2^{247}\right)$ which is much bigger than the complexity of a key exhaustive search (*i.e.* 2^{128}). That is why he concluded that the bias of the function "g" does not represent a real threat for Rabbit. Inspired by this work, L. Yi *et al.* used Fast Fourier Transformed (FFT) to compute the exact bias of Rabbit's keystream based on the bias of "g" [28]. That way, the distinguishing attack complexity equals to $\mathcal{O}\left(2^{158}\right)$, which is much closer to the key exhaustive search complexity. Moreover they extended their distinguishing attack to a multi-frame key recovery attack. This evolution has a $\mathcal{O}\left(2^{32}\right)$ memory complexity and $\mathcal{O}\left(2^{97.5}\right)$ time complexity. It is the first known key-recovery attack on Rabbit.

The first paper about the robustness of Rabbit implementations in the context of faults is due to A. Kirkanski and A. M. Youssef at SAC 09 [23]. They showed that by randomly flipping bits of the internal state, an attacker is able to recover the whole internal state from $128 - 256$ faulty keystreams in $\mathcal{O}\left(2^{38}\right)$ steps with a precomputed table of size $\mathcal{O}\left(2^{41.6}\right)$ bytes. Nevertheless, the analysis does not succeed if more than one bit of the internal state is flipped at a time. Furthermore the proposed fault analysis is limited to the recovery of the sole internal state.

In this paper, we propose to improve these results by considering another fault model. This new fault model is inspired by the design change studied in the context of a guess-and-verify attack [13]. Under this model, we prove that an attacker can completely recover the internal state from 32 faulty keystreams and in time $\mathcal{O}\left(2^{34}\right)$. The attack can also lead to a full secret key recovery (see Sec. 4.6).

3   Fault Attacks on Stream Ciphers

At the end of the nineties, a new class of active side channel attack appeared when Bellcore researchers proposed a way for recovering secret data by perturbing the behavior of public key cryptographic algorithms [15]. Then E. Biham and A. Shamir [12] proposed an application to the DES and named this class of attack Differential Fault Analysis (DFA).

Although fault attacks have been shown to be powerful against implementations of both public key [8,27,16] and secret key cryptosystems [12,18,24], few attacks have been published against the implementation of stream ciphers.

J. Hoch and A. Shamir [21] first addressed the issue of injecting fault to perturb the behavior of stream ciphers. They published in [21] a method for exploiting perturbations of LFSR based stream ciphers, and successful applications to LILI-128, SOBER-t32 and RC4. The fault attack against RC4 was later improved by Biham *et al.* [11]. In this paper, they showed how to use faults for setting the internal state of RC4 in an "impossible" state and a way to exploit it. Thus, they improved previous results both in terms of fault number and in terms of complexity. So, they concluded that the simplicity of the design of RC4 makes it weak against fault attacks.

The security against perturbations of the pseudo-random bit generator A5/1 has also been evaluated [20]. This stream cipher used in GSM networks for its cheap and efficient hardware implementation is composed of three LFSRs. The authors suggested to stop one of the shift register from clocking at a given moment and exploit the faulty output. According to this model, the use of faults speeds up the previous resynchronization attack on A5/1 by a factor 100.

A fault attack against Trivium was presented at FSE 2008 [22]. This hardware eSTREAM candidate is based on a 288-bit internal state split into three nonlinear shift registers. The principle of this DFA is to perturb the internal state by flipping one bit at a random position. Then, the attacker obtains a system of equations in the internal state bits and takes advantage of the simplicity of the Trivium non-linear feedback function for solving it. According to this fault model, 43 fault injections (12 in the optimized version) are enough for recovering the secret key and the IV. This attack against Trivium is also the first application of DFA to a non-linear shift register based stream cipher.

A variant of an other eSTREAM finalist, GRAIN-128, has been evaluated in the context of fault attacks [10]. From an average of 24 consecutive bit-flips in the GRAIN-128 LFSR, A. Berzati *et al.* showed that it is possible to recover the secret key in a couple of minutes. Since the best known mathematical attack against GRAIN-128 is the brute force key-search, fault injections dramatically improve the efficiency of the key recovery.

The fault attack against Rabbit presented at SAC 09 [23] and the one proposed in this paper complete the *state-of-the-art* of fault attacks against stream ciphers (see Sect. 2.3).

4 Fault Attack on Rabbit

4.1 Preliminaries

Theorem 1. *If an attacker knows the values of the $(g_{j,i})_{0 \leq j \leq 7}$ for two consecutive iterations i and $i+1$, then he can reduce the number of candidates for the remaining part of the internal state from 2^{256+1} to 80 in average, and predict the keystream.*

Proof. We assume that the attacker knows all the values of $(g_{j,i-1})_{0 \leq j \leq 7}$ and $(g_{j,i})_{0 \leq j \leq 7}$. From these values, he can compute respectively $(x_{j,i})_{0 \leq j \leq 7}$ and $(x_{j,i+1})_{0 \leq j \leq 7}$ by using the relations described in Sect. 2.2.

To completely determine the internal state at iteration $i+1$, the attacker has to find the counter variables $(c_{j,i+1})_{0 \leq j \leq 7}$ and the carry bit $\phi_{7,i+1}$. But, the counters are the input of the function g (see (1)). Although this function is not bijective [7], previous results [28] emphasized by our own experimentation have shown that there are in average only 1.59 possible inputs that map to the same output $g_{i,j}$. Hence, as the attacker already knows all the $(g_{j,i})_{0 \leq j \leq 7}$ and a part of the input $(x_{j,i})_{0 \leq j \leq 7}$, he will find in average 1.59 candidate values for each $c_{j,i+1}$. As a consequence, he will find only $1.59^8 = 40$ candidate values for all the $(c_{j,i+1})_{0 \leq j \leq 7}$ among $2^{8 \cdot 32}$. Then, it remains the carry bit $\phi_{7,i+1}$ that can be found by exhaustive search or by comparing $c_{7,i+1}$ to a_7[1]. Thus the average number of candidates for the remaining part of the keystream is $2 \times 40 = 80$. $\square$

4.2 Motivations

To evaluate the level of security of Rabbit, the designers have considered in [13] a guess-and-verify attack on a weak version of Rabbit. Indeed, they slightly modified the design of Rabbit by replacing all additions performed in the next-state function by XORs (see Sect. 2.2). Under this assumption they showed that this weaker Rabbit was also immune against this kind of attack since all possible bytewise combinations of the output depend on at least four different g-functions. But authors have not considered the security of Rabbit if only one addition is punctually replaced by a XOR. In the following study, we show that this state can be obtained by injecting faults and that it can be exploited to recover the secret key.

---

[1] Indeed, if $c_{7,i+1} < a_7$, it means that a modular reduction occurs in the addition, and then $\phi_{7,i+1} = 1$.

4.3   Fault Model

The principle of our attack is based on the recovery of all the values of $(g_{j,i})_{0 \le j \le 7}$, for two consecutive iterations. Then Theorem 1 is applied to predict the keystream. These values are involved in the next-state function (see Sect. 2.2), as a consequence, we have chosen to perturb the behavior of that specific function.

According to the next-state scheme, the computation of each $x_{j,i+1}$ requires two consecutive modular additions (*i.e.* mod 2^{32}) that involves three values: $g_{j,i}$, $g_{(j+7)_{[8]},i}$ and $g_{(j+6)_{[8]},i}$. In our fault model, we assume that the attacker is able to perturb transiently one of these additions such that it becomes a bit-wise XOR only for the current operation. Indeed, all subsequent additions performed must result *error-free*. As several faults are necessary for recovering the key, the attacker must have the ability to run the stream cipher with the same initialization vector (not necessarily chosen). Like this, the state remains always the same.

Moreover we suppose the attacker can choose the iteration i and the index j of the affected value $x_{j,i+1}$ and which addition will be corrupted. This implies a preliminary fault setup stage. First as the algorithm implementation is software, the operations are executed sequentially and locating the time of the computation of the chosen value $x_{j,i+1}$ is possible. A transient fault generated by power glitches or light stimulation can produce various effects [9,19,26,25]. In our case, the transformation of addition to XOR can occur by two ways:

- Corruption of the carry register: if it is cleared, the addition is equivalent to a binary addition, *i.e.* an exclusive or, if the carry is set to 1, the addition is changed into a binary addition followed by a complement operation.
- Corruption of the processed code: The non volatile memory where the operating code is supposed to be stored can be modified while the reading of the memory is performed. For example, from the instruction set of the 8051 microprocessor, we can see that the code for ADD is 0x20 while it is 0x60 for XRL, so only one bit is distinctive. Let's note that the fetch code can also be corrupted in the cache memory of the internal register of the CPU.

If the attacker has a reference device, he can precompute the different expected bitstreams with a known key and compare the faulty ciphertexts until he obtains the setup corresponding to the fault model.

Otherwise, among the different faulty ciphertexts obtained by the attacker, some of them correspond to our fault model, and some others must be discarded. As our model corresponds to only 32 different faults, the attacker must only obtain 32 different faulty ciphertexts and can thus try the different combinations (see Appendix B).

Depending on the modified addition, the faulty state variable $\hat{x}_{j,i+1}$ can be expressed by:

- If j is even,

$$\hat{x}_{j,i+1} = \begin{cases} \left(g_{j,i} + \left(g_{(j+7)_{[8]},i} \lll 16\right)\right) \oplus \left(g_{(j+6)_{[8]},i} \lll 16\right) \\ \text{or} \left(g_{j,i} \oplus \left(g_{(j+7)_{[8]},i} \lll 16\right)\right) + \left(g_{(j+6)_{[8]},i} \lll 16\right) \end{cases}$$

– Else, if j is odd,

$$\hat{x}_{j,i+1} = \begin{cases} \left(g_{j,i} + \left(g_{(j+7)_{[8]},i} \lll 8\right)\right) \oplus g_{(j+6)_{[8]},i} \\ \text{or } \left(g_{j,i} \oplus \left(g_{(j+7)_{[8]},i} \lll 8\right)\right) + g_{(j+6)_{[8]},i} \end{cases}$$

In Rabbit, the output keystream $s_i^{[127..0]}$ depends on the values of the internal state. Thus, depending on which $\hat{x}_{j,i}$ that is perturbed, the output keystream will be infected as:

– If j is even, then the faulty part of the keystream is $\hat{s}_i^{[(16\cdot(j+2)-1)..(16\cdot j)]}$,
– Else, if j is odd, the faulty parts of the keystream are
  $\hat{s}_i^{[16\cdot((j-2)_{[8]}+1)-1..16\cdot(j-2)_{[8]}]}$ and $\hat{s}_i^{[16\cdot((j+3)_{[8]}+1)-1..16\cdot(j+3)_{[8]}]}$

This effect of the fault is helpful in case of a wrong time location. Indeed by computing $s_i^{[127..0]} \oplus \hat{s}_i^{[127..0]}$ and analyzing the position of non-zero values, one can immediately identify the state variable that has been infected by the fault during its update.

4.4 Fault Analysis

In the previous section, we have detailed the fault model used to perform our attack and the different ways to practice it. In this section, we provide the different steps for exploiting a set of faulty outputs.

Useful Propositions. This section provides some propositions that are used in the following description of our fault attack.

Proposition 1. *For all pairs* $(x, y) \in (\mathbb{Z}/n\mathbb{Z})^2$, *the resulted carry vector of the operation* $x + y \mod 2^n$, *denoted by* $Carry\,(x, y)$, *can be obtained by computing:*

$$Carry\,(x, y) = (x + y) \oplus (x \oplus y) \tag{3}$$

Proof. This is just a rewriting of the additional carry definition.

Proposition 2. *For all pairs* $(x, y) \in (\mathbb{Z}/n\mathbb{Z})^2$, *the i-th carry bit of the operation* $x + y \mod 2^n$, $Carry_i(x, y)$, *can be defined recursively as:*

– For $i = 0$, $Carry_0(x, y) = 0$
– For $i = 1$, $Carry_1(x, y) = x_0 \wedge y_0$
– For $1 < i \leq n$, $Carry_i(x, y) = x_{i-1} \wedge y_{i-1} \vee \left(Carry_{i-1}(x, y) \wedge (x_{i-1} \vee y_{i-1})\right)$

Proof. This is the formula of the additive carry propagation.

Proposition 3. *For all triplets* $(x, y, z) \in (\mathbb{Z}/n\mathbb{Z})^3$, *we have:*

$$(x + y + z) \oplus ((x + y) \oplus z) = Carry\,(x + y, z) \tag{4}$$

Proof. This equality is a direct consequence of Proposition 1.

Proposition 4. *For all triplets* $(x, y, z) \in (\mathbb{Z}/n\mathbb{Z})^3$, *we have:*

$$(x + y + z) \oplus ((x \oplus y) + z) \tag{5}$$
$$= Carry\ (x + y, z) \oplus Carry\ (x \oplus y, z) \oplus Carry\ (x, y)$$

Proof. This is also a consequence of Proposition 1. For a given triplet $(x, y, z) \in (\mathbb{Z}/n\mathbb{Z})^3$, $x + y + z$ can be written as:

$$x + y + z = (x + y) \oplus z \oplus \text{Carry}\ (x + y, z)$$
$$= x \oplus y \oplus \text{Carry}\ (x, y) \oplus$$
$$z \oplus \text{Carry}\ (x + y, z)$$

Moreover, $((x \oplus y) + z) = x \oplus y \oplus z \oplus \text{Carry}\ (x \oplus y, z)$. Finally, we have:

$$(x + y + z) \oplus ((x \oplus y) + z)$$
$$= x \oplus y \oplus z \oplus \text{Carry}\ (x, y) \oplus \text{Carry}\ (x + y, z) \oplus$$
$$x \oplus y \oplus z \oplus \text{Carry}\ (x \oplus y, z)$$
$$= \text{Carry}\ (x + y, z) \oplus \text{Carry}\ (x \oplus y, z) \oplus \text{Carry}\ (x, y)$$

Differential Analysis. Fault attacks are often based on exploiting differences between a correct and a faulty output. Our attack is not different from it. We assume that the attacker is able to access the keystream[2]. Hence to perform the analysis, he differentiates the faulty keystream block with a correct block. In Sect. 4.3, we concluded that a fault injected according to our model only infects 32 bits of the output keystream. As a consequence, the difference is null except for the 32 infected bits:

– If j is even, then

$$s_i^{[(16 \cdot (j+2)-1)..(16 \cdot j)]} \oplus \hat{s}_i^{[(16 \cdot (j+2)-1)..(16 \cdot j)]}$$
$$= x_{j,i}^{[31..0]} \oplus \hat{x}_{j,i}^{[31..0]} \tag{6}$$

and 0 elsewhere,
– Else, if j is odd, then

$$s_i^{[16 \cdot ((j-2)_{[8]}+1)-1..16 \cdot (j-2)_{[8]}]} \oplus \hat{s}_i^{[16 \cdot ((j-2)_{[8]}+1)-1..16 \cdot (j-2)_{[8]}]}$$
$$= x_{j,i}^{[15..0]} \oplus \hat{x}_{j,i}^{[15..0]}, \tag{7}$$
$$s_i^{[16 \cdot ((j+3)_{[8]}+1)-1..16 \cdot (j+3)_{[8]}]} \oplus \hat{s}_i^{[16 \cdot ((j+3)_{[8]}+1)-1..16 \cdot (j+3)_{[8]}]}$$
$$= x_{j,i}^{[31..16]} \oplus \hat{x}_{j,i}^{[31..16]} \tag{8}$$

and 0 elsewhere,

---

[2] The attacker knows a pair plaintext/ciphertext.

Furthermore, depending on the modular addition that has been modified, the difference $x_{j,i}^{[31..0]} \oplus \hat{x}_{j,i}^{[31..0]}$ can be reformulated thanks to Propositions 3 and 4. As an example, we obtain for the perturbation of the second addition:

– If j is even,

$$x_{j,i}^{[31..0]} \oplus \hat{x}_{j,i}^{[31..0]}$$
$$= \text{Carry}\left((g_{j,i-1} + g_{(j+7)_{[8]},i-1} \lll 8), g_{(j+6)_{[8]},i-1}\right) \qquad (9)$$

– Or if j is odd,

$$x_{j,i}^{[31..0]} \oplus \hat{x}_{j,i}^{[31..0]}$$
$$= \text{Carry}\left((g_{j,i-1} + g_{(j+7)_{[8]},i-1} \lll 16), g_{(j+6)_{[8]},i-1} \lll 16\right) \qquad (10)$$

Similar expressions can be obtained if the first addition is perturbed by applying Proposition 4. The complete system of equations obtained after gathering faulty outputs modified at different locations in the next-state function is described in Appendix A. Hence, the differential fault analysis of the faulty output provides a set of particular equations that involves carries from the computation of additions in the next-state function (see Sect. 2.2).

Carry Analysis. The purpose of the attack is to use faults to recover the values of $(g_{j,i})_{0 \le j \le 7}$. Thus, the attacker has modified both first and second modular additions in the next-state function one-by-one at iteration i for all $0 \le j \le 7$. This means that the attacker has to gather $8 + 8 = 16$ faulty keystream blocks modified at the same iteration i. Hence, the attacker can extract a system of equations that involves all the $(g_{j,i})_{0 \le j \le 7}$ (see Appendix A). The number of obtained binary equations is[3] $16 \times 31 = 496$ for $8 \times 32 = 512$ binary unknowns $(g_{j,i})_{0 \le j \le 7}$.

Because of the carry propagation, the degree of multivariate polynomials in the equations increases with the depth of the carry bit to analyze (*i.e.* the degree of the multivariate polynomial obtained by expressing Carry_i is $i + 1$). So, relinearization method like XL algorithm [17] are not relevant. The best way we found to solve this system is performing an exhaustive search on each 8-bit parts of $x_{j,i+1} \oplus \hat{x}_{j,i+1}$ and so, on the 4 resulting sub-equations:

$$x_{j,i+1} \oplus \hat{x}_{j,i+1} \Rightarrow \begin{cases} x_{j,i+1} \oplus \hat{x}_{j,i+1}^{[7..0]} \\ x_{j,i+1} \oplus \hat{x}_{j,i+1}^{[15..8]} \\ x_{j,i+1} \oplus \hat{x}_{j,i+1}^{[23..16]} \\ x_{j,i+1} \oplus \hat{x}_{j,i+1}^{[31..24]} \end{cases} \qquad (11)$$

Depending on the infected modular addition, each 8-bit sub-equation may have two different expressions (see Appendix A) that involves 8 bits of $g_{j,i}, g_{(j+7)_{[8]},i}$,

---

[3] $\forall (x, y) \in \left(\mathbb{Z}/2^{32}\mathbb{Z}\right)^2$, $\text{Carry}_0(x, y) = 0$, so the number of binary equations that results from a carry is 31.

and $g_{(j+6)_{[8]},i}$. As an example, for the expression $x_{0,i+1} \oplus \hat{x}_{0,i+1}^{[7..0]}$, the attacker will simultaneously search $g_{0,i}^{[7..0]}$, $g_{7,i}^{[23..16]}$ and $g_{6,i}^{[23..16]}$ that satisfy:

$$
\begin{cases}
\Delta_1 = \mathrm{Carry}\left(\left(g_{0,i}^{[7..0]} + g_{7,i}^{[23..16]}\right), g_{6,i}^{[23..16]}\right) \\[2mm]
\Delta_2 = \quad \mathrm{Carry}\left(\left(g_{0,i}^{[7..0]} + g_{7,i}^{[23..16]}\right), g_{6,i}^{[23..16]}\right) \\[2mm]
\qquad \oplus\, \mathrm{Carry}\left(\left(g_{0,i}^{[7..0]} \oplus g_{7,i}^{[23..16]}\right), g_{6,i}^{[23..16]}\right) \\[2mm]
\qquad \oplus\, \mathrm{Carry}\left(g_{0,i}^{[7..0]}, g_{7,i}^{[23..16]}\right)
\end{cases}
$$

where Δ_1 and Δ_2 are equal to $x_{0,i+1} \oplus \hat{x}_{0,i+1}^{[7..0]}$ respectively when the second and first modular additions of the next state function are modified. Then, four pairs of equations have to be solved for each $0 \le j \le 7$. So, the obtained system of equations is considered as a 8-bit system of $2 \times 4 \times 8 = 64$ equations of $8 \times 4 = 32$ unknowns, as each $g_{j,i}$ is split in four 8-bit windows.

Solving each 8-bit sub-equation requires to search simultaneously 8 bits of three $g_{j,i}$. Moreover sub-equations from bit 8 to 31, the attacker has to speculate on $\mathrm{Carry}_7(g_{j,i}, g_{(j+7)_{[8]},i})$, $\mathrm{Carry}_{15}(g_{j,i}, g_{(j+7)_{[8]},i})$ and $\mathrm{Carry}_{23}(g_{j,i}, g_{(j+7)_{[8]},i})$ since their values are unknown at the beginning of the search. As a consequence, for each j, the computational complexity equals to $\mathcal{O}\left(4 \times 2^{3\times8+3}\right) = \mathcal{O}\left(2^{29}\right)$. To solve the whole system, the resolution has to be performed for all the eight j. So, the computational complexity of the resolution is $\mathcal{O}\left(2^{32}\right)$.

In order to study the characteristics of the system, and particularly, if the number of solutions for all the $(g_{j,i})_{0 \le j \le 7}$ is bounded, we have randomly generated 20000 possible faulty outputs and counted the number of solutions provided by the system of equations. The experimental results show that the real 32-bit system of equations has an average of $2^{13.72}$ solutions. To recover the whole state of Rabbit, two systems from consecutive iterations have to be solved. Hence, the average number of possible solutions for $(g_{j,i-1})_{0 \le j \le 7}$ and $(g_{j,i})_{0 \le j \le 7}$ is $2^{2\times13.72} = 2^{27.44}$. By combining these results with Theorem 1, the number of possible Rabbit states is the number of $(g_{j,i})_{0 \le j \le 7}$ obtained for two consecutive iterations multiplied by the number of associated $((c_{j,i+1})_{0 \le j \le 7}$ and $\phi_{7,i+1})$ found to complete the internal state: $2^{27.44} \times 80 \approx 2^{34}$.

Finally, for determining the attacked Rabbit state, at iteration $i+1$, among the 2^{34} candidates, the attacker has just to compute the corresponding internal state $\left((x_{j,i+1})_{0 \le j \le 7}, (c_{j,i+1})_{0 \le j \le 7}, \phi_{7,i+1}\right)$, generate the output keystream block for iterations $i+1$ and $i+2$, for each candidate, and compare it to the attacked Rabbit keystream at same iterations.

4.5   Attack Algorithm

Algorithm. Our fault attack against Rabbit can be divided into 5 distinguishable steps that have been presented in previous sections. This paragraph provides a summary that lists these steps:

Step 1: Gather faulty outputs, for iterations i and $i+1$, by perturbing one-by-one, all the sixteen additions of the next-state function. As a consequence, the attacker has to execute (with the same initialization vector) and perturb the Rabbit algorithm according to our model $2 \times 16 = 32$ times,

Step 2: Differentiate the faulty outputs $\hat{s}_i^{[127..0]}$ and $\hat{s}_{i+1}^{[127..0]}$, with correct outputs, $s_i^{[127..0]}$ and $s_{i+1}^{[127..0]}$. Then, check that faults were correctly injected (see Sect. 4.4),

Step 3: Built two systems of equations (see Appendix A) from the difference between faulty and correct outputs at iteration i and $i+1$. Then, recover possible candidates for $(g_{j,i-1})_{0 \leq j \leq 7}$ and $(g_{j,i})_{0 \leq j \leq 7}$. Compute $(x_{j,i})_{0 \leq j \leq 7}$ and $(x_{j,i+1})_{0 \leq j \leq 7}$,

Step 4: Solve $(c_{j,i+1})_{0 \leq j \leq 7}$ and $\phi_{7,i+1}$ from previously recovered $(g_{j,i-1})_{0 \leq j \leq 7}$ and $(g_{j,i})_{0 \leq j \leq 7}$ (see Theorem 1),

Step 5: For each possible Rabbit state candidate at iterations $i+1$, compare the output keystream to the expected one until they are equal. When it is satisfied, the attacker has recovered the whole Rabbit state at iteration $i+1$ and can predict the subsequent keystream blocks.

Complexity. The efficiency of a fault attack is not only based on the fault model but in the number of faults to inject for obtaining secret information. Theoretically, to have an exploitable number of equations and performing the resolution, the attacker has to inject 32 faults that suits the model, at different locations of the next-state function and two consecutive iterations of the algorithm. In practice, the fault number can be more important, depending on its ability for reproducing the attack and the targeted device (see Sect. 4.3).

In terms of computational complexity, the overall complexity of the attack is dominated by the complexity for testing the possible solutions obtained from the differentiation of faulty outputs. So, the computational complexity of our attack is $\mathcal{O}\left(2^{34}\right)$. Moreover, since our analysis does not require any precomputation, the memory complexity of our fault attack is negligible compared to A. Kirkanski and A. M. Youssef proposal [23]. Hence, our new fault attack improves the best known time complexity from 2^{38} to 2^{34} [23] with a negligible memory consumption.

4.6   Extension to a Full Key Recovery

The fault attack against Rabbit presented in this article allows the attacker to recover the whole Rabbit state at a given iteration i. As we previously noticed, it can be used to predict the keystream, but, if i is small enough, the attacker can recover the secret key. According to [28], if $i = 2$ then the attacker can recover the secret key used to generate the keystream in time $\mathcal{O}\left(2^{32}\right)$. To do it, the attacker guesses the values of the missing $\phi_{i,j}$'s to revert the Rabbit next-state function (see Sect. 2.2) and the key setup scheme. More details about the key recovery are provided in [28]. Hence, if $i = 2$ the complexity of this additional step is dominated by the full internal state recovery, and so, the global time complexity of this attack remains $\mathcal{O}\left(2^{34}\right)$.

5   Conclusion

This paper introduces an improved fault attack against implementations of Rabbit. Our theoretical results emphasized by our experimentation show that the fault analysis reduces the best known attack complexity against Rabbit from $\mathcal{O}\left(2^{38}\right)$ to $\mathcal{O}\left(2^{34}\right)$ [23]. This improvement is also effective in terms of memory consumption. Moreover, our attack requires only 32 faulty outputs, and we provide evidence that the fault model is practicable on various devices. The algorithm can be protected against faults by adding redundancy in the next-state function. As our attack only uses an addition corruption, the result of the additions can also be doubled and computed differently. Since this operation is faster than "g" function, this countermeasure does not increase the global complexity of Rabbit.

As a consequence, we can conclude that Differential Fault Analysis is a real threat for Rabbit implementations. Hence, protecting it against DFA is now challenging.

References

1. Cryptico A/S. Algebraic analysis of Rabbit. White paper (2003)
2. Cryptico A/S. Analysis of the key setup function in Rabbit. White paper (2003)
3. Cryptico A/S. Hamming weights of the g-function. White paper (2003)
4. Cryptico A/S. Periodic properties of Rabbit. White paper (2003)
5. Cryptico A/S. Second degree approximations of the g-function. White paper (2003)
6. Cryptico A/S. Security analysis of the IV-setup for Rabbit. White paper (2003)
7. Aumasson, J.P.: On a Bias of Rabbit. In: State of the Art of Stream Ciphers (SASC 2007) (2007)
8. Bao, F., Deng, R.H., Jeng, A., Narasimhalu, A.D., Ngair, T.: Breaking Public Key Cryptosystems on Tamper Resistant Devices in the Presence of Transient Faults. In: Lomas, M., Christianson, B. (eds.) Security Protocols 1997. LNCS, vol. 1361, pp. 115–124. Springer, Heidelberg (1998)
9. Bar-El, H., Choukri, H., Naccache, D., Tunstall, M., Whelan, C.: The Sorcerer's Apprentice Guide to Fault Attacks. Cryptology ePrint Archive, Report 2004/100 (2004)
10. Berzati, A., Canovas, C., Castagnos, G., Debraize, B., Goubin, L., Gouget, A., Paillier, P., Salgado, S.: Fault Analysis of Grain-128. In: IEEE International Workshop on Hardware-Oriented Security and Trust (HOST 2009). IEEE Computer Society, Los Alamitos (2009)
11. Biham, E., Granboulan, L., Nguyen, P.: Impossible Fault Analysis of RC4 and Differential Analysis of RC4. In: Gilbert, H., Handschuh, H. (eds.) FSE 2005. LNCS, vol. 3557, pp. 359–367. Springer, Heidelberg (2005)
12. Biham, E., Shamir, A.: Differential fault analysis of secret key cryptosystems. In: Kaliski Jr., B.S. (ed.) CRYPTO 1997. LNCS, vol. 1294, pp. 513–525. Springer, Heidelberg (1997)
13. Boesgaard, M., Vesterager, M., Christiensen, T., Zenner, E.: The stream cipher Rabbit. eStream Report 2005/024, the ECRYPT stream cipher project (2005)
14. Boesgaard, M., Vesterager, M., Pedersen, T., Christiansen, J., Scavenius, O.: Rabbit: A High-Performance Stream Cipher. In: Johansson, T. (ed.) FSE 2003. LNCS, vol. 2887, pp. 307–329. Springer, Heidelberg (2003)

15. Boneh, D., DeMillo, R.A., Lipton, R.J.: On the Importance of Checking Cryptographic Protocols for Faults. In: Fumy, W. (ed.) EUROCRYPT 1997. LNCS, vol. 1233, pp. 37–51. Springer, Heidelberg (1997)
16. Brier, E., Chevallier-Mames, B., Ciet, M., Clavier, C.: Why One Should Also Secure RSA Public Key Elements. In: Goubin, L., Matsui, M. (eds.) CHES 2006. LNCS, vol. 4249, pp. 324–338. Springer, Heidelberg (2006)
17. Courtois, N., Klimov, A., Patarin, J., Shamir, A.: Efficient Algorithms for Solving Overdefined Systems of Multivariate Polynomial Equations. In: Preneel, B. (ed.) EUROCRYPT 2000. LNCS, vol. 1807, pp. 392–407. Springer, Heidelberg (2000)
18. Dusart, P., Letourneux, G., Vivolo, O.: Differential Fault Analysis on AES. In: Zhou, J., Yung, M., Han, Y. (eds.) ACNS 2003. LNCS, vol. 2846, pp. 293–306. Springer, Heidelberg (2003)
19. Giraud, C.: A survey on fault attacks. In: CARDIS 2004. Smart Card Research and Advanced Applications, vol. IV, pp. 159–176 (2004)
20. Gomulkiewicz, M., Kutilwoski, M., Wlaz, P.: Synchronization Fault Analysis for Breaking A5/1. In: Nikoletseas, S.E. (ed.) WEA 2005. LNCS, vol. 3503, pp. 415–427. Springer, Heidelberg (2005)
21. Hoch, J., Shamir, A.: Fault Analysis of Stream Ciphers. In: Joye, M., Quisquater, J.-J. (eds.) CHES 2004. LNCS, vol. 3156, pp. 240–253. Springer, Heidelberg (2004)
22. Hojsik, M., Rudolf, B.: Differential Fault Analysis of Trivium. In: Nyberg, K. (ed.) FSE 2008. LNCS, vol. 5086, pp. 158–172. Springer, Heidelberg (2008)
23. Kirkanski, A., Youssef, A.M.: Differential Fault Analysis of Rabbit. In: Jacobson, M.J., Rijmen, V., Safavi-Naini, R. (eds.) SAC 2009. LNCS, vol. 5867, pp. 200–217. Springer, Heidelberg (2009)
24. Piret, G., Quisquater, J.-J.: A Differential Fault Attack Technique against SPN Structures, with Application to the AES and KHAZAD. In: Walter, C.D., Koç, Ç.K., Paar, C. (eds.) CHES 2003. LNCS, vol. 2779, pp. 77–88. Springer, Heidelberg (2003)
25. Skorobogatov, S.P.: Optically Enhanced Position-Locked Power Analysis. In: Goubin, L., Matsui, M. (eds.) CHES 2006. LNCS, vol. 4249, pp. 61–75. Springer, Heidelberg (2006)
26. Skorobogatov, S.P., Andersson, R.J.: Optical Fault Induction Attacks. In: Kaliski Jr., B.S., Koç, Ç.K., Paar, C. (eds.) CHES 2002. LNCS, vol. 2523, pp. 2–12. Springer, Heidelberg (2003)
27. Wagner, D.: Cryptanalysis of a provably secure CRT-RSA algorithm. In: Proceedings of the 11th ACM Conference on Computer Security (CCS 2004), pp. 92–97. ACM, New York (2004)
28. Yi, L., Huaxiong, W., Ling, S.: Cryptanalysis of Rabbit. In: Wu, T.-C., Lei, C.-L., Rijmen, V., Lee, D.-T. (eds.) ISC 2008. LNCS, vol. 5222, pp. 204–214. Springer, Heidelberg (2008)

A   System Extracted

We assume that the attacker has injected a fault, at iteration $i+1$, on different modular additions of the next-state function.

A.1   First Set of Equations

By modifying the second addition for all eight equations of the next-state function at iteration $i+1$, computing the difference $s_{i+1} \oplus \hat{s}_{i+1}$ (see Sect. 4.4), and using Proposition 3 the attacker obtains the following set of equations:

$$x_{0,i+1} \oplus \hat{x}_{0,i+1} = \text{Carry}((g_{0,i} + (g_{7,i} \lll 16)),$$
$$(g_{6,i} \lll 16))$$
$$x_{1,i+1} \oplus \hat{x}_{1,i+1} = \text{Carry}\left((g_{1,i} + (g_{0,i} \lll 8)), g_{7,i}\right)$$
$$x_{2,i+1} \oplus \hat{x}_{2,i+1} = \text{Carry}((g_{2,i} + (g_{1,i} \lll 16)),$$
$$(g_{0,i} \lll 16))$$
$$x_{3,i+1} \oplus \hat{x}_{3,i+1} = \text{Carry}\left((g_{3,i} + (g_{2,i} \lll 8)), g_{1,i}\right)$$
$$x_{4,i+1} \oplus \hat{x}_{4,i+1} = \text{Carry}((g_{4,i} + (g_{3,i} \lll 16)),$$
$$(g_{2,i} \lll 16))$$
$$x_{5,i+1} \oplus \hat{x}_{5,i+1} = \text{Carry}\left((g_{5,i} + (g_{4,i} \lll 8)), g_{3,i}\right)$$
$$x_{6,i+1} \oplus \hat{x}_{6,i+1} = \text{Carry}((g_{6,i} + (g_{5,i} \lll 16)),$$
$$(g_{4,i} \lll 16))$$
$$x_{7,i+1} \oplus \hat{x}_{7,i+1} = \text{Carry}\left((g_{7,i} + (g_{6,i} \lll 8)), g_{5,i}\right)$$

A.2   Second Set of Equations

This second set of equations results from the perturbation of all the eight first additions of the next-state function and the application of Proposition 4:

– If j is even, $x_{j,i+1} \oplus \hat{x}_{j,i+1}$ equals to:

$$\text{Carry}((g_{j,i} + (g_{(j+7)_{[8]},i} \lll 16)),$$
$$(g_{(j+6)_{[8]},i} \lll 16))$$
$$\oplus \ \text{Carry}((g_{j,i} \oplus (g_{(j+7)_{[8]},i} \lll 16)),$$
$$(g_{(j+6)_{[8]},i} \lll 16))$$
$$\oplus \ \text{Carry}(g_{j,i}, (g_{(j+7)_{[8]},i} \lll 16))$$

– Else, if j is odd, $x_{j,i+1} \oplus \hat{x}_{j,i+1}$ equals to

$$\text{Carry}\left(\left(g_{j,i} + \left(g_{(j+7)_{[8]},i} \lll 8\right)\right), g_{(j+6)_{[8]}}\right)$$
$$\oplus \ \text{Carry}\left(\left(g_{j,i} \oplus \left(g_{(j+7)_{[8]}} \lll 8\right)\right), g_{(j+6)_{[8]}}\right)$$
$$\oplus \ \text{Carry}\left(g_{j,i}, \left(g_{(j+7)_{[8]}} \lll 8\right)\right)$$

B   Case of Unexploitable Faults

Among the different faulty ciphertexts obtained by the attacker, some of them correspond to our fault model, and some others must be discarded. This case happens when the faults have not been injected according to our model. We have simulated this situation by trying to solve the system of equations with wrong ones. With our detection strategy no 8-uplet for $(g_{j,i})_{0 \leq j \leq 7}$ was found for such wrong systems.

So the attacker has to try to withdraw some equations until the system has solutions. Thus he determines the wrong equations. Once identified, the equations must replaced by other ones obtained from new faults.

On Physical Obfuscation of Cryptographic Algorithms*

Julien Bringer[1], Hervé Chabanne[1,2], and Thomas Icart[1,3]

[1] Sagem Sécurité
[2] Télécom ParisTech
[3] Université du Luxembourg
firstname.name@sagem.com

Abstract. We describe a solution for physically obfuscating the representation of a cipher, to augment chips resistance against physical threats, by combining ideas from masking techniques and Physical Obfuscated Keys (POKs). With embedded chips – like RFID tags – as main motivation, we apply this strategy to the representation of a Linear Feedback Shift Register (LFSR).

The application of this technique to LFSR-based stream ciphers, such as the Self Shrinking Generator, enables to share key materials between several chips within a system while increasing the resistance of the system against compromise of chips. An extension of our ideas to non-linear ciphers is also presented with an illustration onto Trivium.

Keywords: RFID tags, POK, PUF, masking, stream ciphers.

1 Introduction

Physical Obfuscated Keys (POK) [14] are a means to store keys inside an Integrated Circuit (Section 2). Their use is based on the paradigm that an unauthorized access to a value represented by a POK will affect the behavior of this POK and make it non-operational. This way, when an adversary compromises a chip to read a key, he will not be able to use the same POK again. In particular, when different values are represented by the same POK, a compromise at some time will render activation of further values impossible. This type of situation has been considered in [14] with a general line of defense for POKs: split the computations with a key K in two steps, one related to a random key K' and the other one to another key K'' where the pair (K', K'') depends solely on the chip implementing the POK. Doing that, when a chip is tampered with, this will not allow an adversary to recover the key K or to interfere on the value of K contained in another chip. Here the difficulty is to find a way to split the cryptographic computations. This is illustrated with public key encryption schemes based on exponentiation by the key in [14]. [7] describes the modification of an existing protocol relying on an XOR with a key to incorporate POKs' trick.

---

* This work has been partially funded by the ANR T2TIT project.

B. Roy and N. Sendrier (Eds.): INDOCRYPT 2009, LNCS 5922, pp. 88–103, 2009.
© Springer-Verlag Berlin Heidelberg 2009

In the paper, we extend this idea by combining physical obfuscated keys and classical masking techniques, similar to that used to counter Side Channel Analysis (SCA) attacks, to construct physically obfuscated ciphers. Indeed splitting the computation in several steps is essentially the goal of masking techniques or masked logic to thwart SCA attacks (see for instance [29, 3] for masked AND and XOR applied to the AES). And we illustrate here how this strategy can be employed successfully via POKs for obfuscating the secret material of a cipher. Some other related techniques are secret sharing techniques [31].

As a proof-of-concept, we apply this strategy to the general case of linear feedback shift registers (LFSR). LFSRs are easy to design and to implement with low hardware requirements. The operations of a LFSR are deterministic, which means that a polynomial and a state completely determine the next output values. For a system with shared materials between several tags, the use of the same LFSR and initial value, for instance to generate a key stream, would thus face the problem of resistance of tags against compromise: the opening of one tag gives the possibility to know the key stream of other tags. We explain here how to hide the value of the state and the polynomial during the execution by implementing the operations with POKs.

Our main achievement is to show that it is possible to hide their content and their connections by making use of POKs (Section 3). As an immediate application of our proposal, we introduce an implementation of LFSR-based hashing for message authentication [23] (Section 4.1). As LFSR is a very popular primitive in the design of stream-ciphers, we also give examples in this context and explain how POKs can be adapted to handle some small non-linear operations. As a relevant example, we give details of an obfuscated version of the Self-Shrinking Generator [27] (Section 4.2). Finally, we modify further our techniques to be able to protect the Trivium stream-cipher [8] with POKs (Section 4.3). Moreover our strategy is quite general and can be applied to other ciphers.

To conclude, we want to stress the fact that POKs do not make use of memories to store keys and need only few hardware resources to be implemented. They are well-suited for very constrained chips or those only allowing a small amount of their capacity to cryptographic computations. Our constructions show that they can also provide some inherent resistance against tampering. We thus think that RFID tags are targets of choice for implementing the results of our paper.

2   Physically Obfuscated Key

In [14], it is shown how to implement a key with a Physical Unclonable Function (PUF) by applying a fixed hard-wired challenge to the PUF (cf. Appendix A for description of the notion of PUF); this implementation is called a Physically Obfuscated Key (POK). In fact, using different challenges, several POKs can be obtained from one PUF. In the sequel, we refer to a POK as a value, stored in a tag, which is accessible only after the underlying PUF is stimulated; once erased from volatile memory, the value of the key is no longer available.

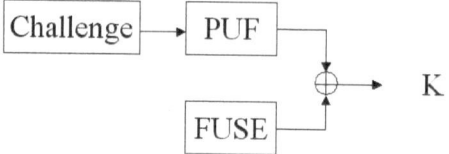

Fig. 1. Example of POK

To be able to set a POK to a chosen value, the output of the PUF – which cannot be chosen – can be combined to some fuse (or any data stored in the EEPROM) via an exclusive-or operation (Figure 1). In the sequel, we assume that any implemented POK is obtained via an I-PUF (cf. Appendix A), which gives us the following property.

Property 1. Any corruption of or intrusion into the chip leads to the end-of-life of the chip: an adversary could not continue to use the chip, particularly he can only obtain information on the content of the memory at this time and could not access the others POKs (if any) implemented in it.

More generally, inside a chip, we say that a primitive is **physically obfuscated** when it is implemented via some POKs so that an adversary could not learn any secret information from an intermediate result obtained by opening the chip.

3 Physically Obfuscated Linear Feedback Shift Register

A linear feedback shift register (LFSR) is a binary shift register where the update of the input bits are made via a linear function of the previous ones. The initial value of a LFSR is called the seed, the current input bits in the register are the current state and the update of the state is the result of the evaluation of a feedback function – represented by a so-called feedback polynomial – corresponding to exclusive-or of some bits at given positions (the connecting taps) of the state.

We consider here a linear feedback shift register (LFSR) of length L with a feedback polynomial $P \in GF(2)[X]$ of degree L. The polynomial is often chosen to be primitive to obtain a LFSR of maximal period $2^L - 1$. This avoids the occurrence of repeating cycle after a short delay. Let $P = \sum_{k=0}^{L} a_k X^k$, let $S^0 = (s_0, \ldots, s_{L-1})$ be the initial state of the LFSR. Then the next state is $S^1 = (s_1, \ldots, s_{L-1}, s_L)$ where s_L is the value $a_0 s_0 \oplus \cdots \oplus a_{L-1} s_{L-1}$, and s_0 is outputted. More generally, S^n denotes the n-th state.

3.1 Obfuscation of Basic Operations

Let $l \geq 1$. For $i \in \{1, 2, 3\}$, let $K[i]$ be a l-bit vector, implemented by two POKs $K[i]'$, $K[i]''$ such that $K[i] = K[i]' \oplus K[i]''$. Let x and y be two l-bit vectors.

Definition 1. *A physically obfuscated XOR, denoted by* $_{PO}XOR$, *corresponds to the computation of a masked XOR of two masked inputs.* $_{PO}XOR_l(x \oplus K[1], y \oplus$

Table 1. $_{\mathsf{PO}}\mathsf{XOR}_l(x \oplus K[1], y \oplus K[2], K[1], K[2], K[3])$ implementation

---

1. Set $z = (x \oplus K[1]) \oplus (y \oplus K[2]) = (x \oplus y) \oplus (K[1] \oplus K[2])$
2. For $i = 1$ to 3 do
    activate $K[i]'$, update $z \leftarrow z \oplus K[i]'$, erase $K[i]'$ from memory
End For
3. For $i = 1$ to 3 do
    activate $K[i]''$, update $z \leftarrow z \oplus K[i]''$, erase $K[i]''$ from memory
End For
4. Output z

$K[2], K[1], K[2], K[3])$ is the computation of $x \oplus y \oplus K[3]$ with the inputs $x \oplus K[1]$ and $y \oplus K[2]$ and is implemented as in Table 1.

It is straightforward to check that $_{\mathsf{PO}}\mathsf{XOR}_l(x \oplus K[1], y \oplus K[2], K[1], K[2], K[3])$ outputs the desired value, $x \oplus y \oplus K[3]$. Moreover, thanks to the POKs Property 1 (see page 90), we ensure the physical obfuscation of the XOR.

Lemma 1. $_{\mathsf{PO}}\mathsf{XOR}$ *is a physically obfuscated primitive.*

Proof. (sketch) The implementation of $_{\mathsf{PO}}\mathsf{XOR}$ does not leak information to an adversary on $x, y, x \oplus y, K[1], K[2]$ or $K[3]$. Indeed, recall that an adversary $\mathcal{A}$ can eavesdrop on the memory only once before destroying the chip. We assume that $\mathcal{A}$ already knows the inputs $x \oplus K[1]$ and $y \oplus K[2]$ and the output $x \oplus y \oplus K[3]$. If he corrupted the chip in step 1, he would learn nothing more. If he corrupted the chip during the step 2, say when $i = 2$, he would learn $K[2]'$ and $(x \oplus y) \oplus (K[1]'' \oplus K[2]'')$. If he corrupted the chip during the step 3, say whence $i = 1$, he would learn $K[1]''$ and $(x \oplus y) \oplus K[2]'' \oplus K[3]'$. In any case, $\mathcal{A}$ does not gain information on the un-masked result $x \oplus y$ or on the un-masked inputs x, y. □

From $_{\mathsf{PO}}\mathsf{XOR}$, we deduce another interesting physically obfuscated operation, $_{\mathsf{PO}}\mathsf{Convert}$, which converts the mask of a physically masked value into another mask. $_{\mathsf{PO}}\mathsf{Convert}_l(x \oplus K[1], K[1], K[3])$ takes as input $x \oplus K[1]$ and outputs $x \oplus K[3]$; it is implemented via $_{\mathsf{PO}}\mathsf{XOR}_l(x \oplus K[1], 0, K[1], 0, K[3])$. And the property of lemma 1 holds.

Let now $K[3]$ be restricted to a 1-bit vector.

Definition 2. *We define the function* $_{\mathsf{SemiPO}}\mathsf{Scalar}$ *as the masked scalar product of a first non-masked input with a second masked input (the term* Semi *underlines this asymmetry).* $_{\mathsf{SemiPO}}\mathsf{Scalar}_l(x, y \oplus K[2], K[2], K[3])$ *is the computation of* $(x \cdot y) \oplus K[3]$ *with the inputs* x *and* $y \oplus K[2]$ *(cf. Table 2).*

As for $_{\mathsf{PO}}\mathsf{XOR}$, this implementation with sequential activation of the POKs implies that $_{\mathsf{SemiPO}}\mathsf{Scalar}$ is physically obfuscated: no information on $y, K[2], K[3]$ or $(x \cdot y)$ are leaked.

Lemma 2. $_{\mathsf{SemiPO}}\mathsf{Scalar}$ *is a physically obfuscated primitive.*

Table 2. SemiPO $\mathsf{Scalar}_l(x, y \oplus K[2], K[2], K[3])$ implementation

1. Set $z = x \cdot (y \oplus K[2])$
2. Activate $K[2]'$, update $z \leftarrow z \oplus (x \cdot K[2]')$, erase $K[2]'$ from memory
3. Activate $K[3]'$, update $z \leftarrow z \oplus K[3]'$, erase $K[3]'$ from memory
4. Activate $K[2]''$, update $z \leftarrow z \oplus (x \cdot K[2]'')$, erase $K[2]''$ from memory
5. Activate $K[3]''$, update $z \leftarrow z \oplus K[3]''$, erase $K[3]''$ from memory
6. Output z

For $l = 1$, SemiPO Scalar corresponds to a AND operator. Here only one input can be masked; for both inputs to be masked, i.e. for a general obfuscated scalar product, we need a slightly more complex implementation as the operations related to the POKs are not linear anymore. This is illustrated on the AND operator in section 4.3.

For all above primitives, note that no mask ($KS[3]$) needs to be applied to the output whence the latter does not need to be protected. In that case, it does not alter the physical obfuscation of the others values (un-masked inputs, $K[1]$ and $K[2]$).

3.2 Obfuscating the Taps

We now represent the operation of the feedback polynomial $P = \sum_{k=0}^{L} a_k X^k$ as a scalar product by its coefficients, $s_{n+L} = S^n \cdot KF$, with $KF = (a_0, \ldots, a_{L-1})$ and $S^n = (s_n, \ldots, s_{n+L-1})$. KF can be seen as a feedback key and for some cryptographic primitives (cf. section 4) we want to thwart an adversary to recover it by opening a tag.

Let KF' be a random L-bit vector and $KF'' = KF \oplus KF'$; we also assume that KF', KF'' are implementing as physically obfuscated keys (POKs). The computation of s_{n+L} is thus seen as

$$s_{n+L} = \mathsf{SemiPO\,Scalar}_L(S^n, 0, KF, 0).$$

In contrast to the general use of SemiPO Scalar in section 3.1, the output is not masked here; only KF is to be kept obfuscated during execution. In addition to the value of s_{n+L}, an adversary who opens a tag during execution only learns information either on KF' or KF'', but not both at the same time, thanks to the POKs property 1. As the separation of KF into $KF' \oplus KF''$ can be made different for each tag, he cannot recover KF from this information.

However from the knowledge of the value of s_{n+L}, he gains some information on KF if he also knows the value of S^n. And from about L values S^{n_i} and s_{n_i+L} obtained by opening as many tags sharing the same KF, it is easy to recover KF by solving a linear system. This issue is addressed in the sequel.

3.3 Towards Obfuscating the Taps and the State Simultaneously

To hide the state during execution of the register, we introduce another key KS, called key state, with the intended goal to manage the state S masked by the key $KS = (KS_0, \ldots, KS_{L-1})$ without letting the state appearing in clear. Here the key KS can be different from one tag to another. It is the state S which may be shared and consequently has to be protected, in particular if the initial state corresponds to a shared key for a set of tags within the system.

Rather than the state S^n, we store the value $M^n = S^n \oplus KS$ and want to update the register directly via the masked state M^n and the feedback key KF. We think again of the $_{\mathsf{SemiPO}}$Scalar solution, but as explained in section 3.1, it is not straightforward to apply it when both inputs are masked. Here, we choose KS such that $KS \cdot KF = 0$ which leads to the simplification $M^n \cdot KF = (S^n \oplus KS) \cdot KF = S^n \cdot KF$. To enable the update of the masked register, we split the key KS into two POKs as in the previous section for KF. Let KS' be a random L-bit vector and $KS'' = KS \oplus KS'$. The operations of the previous section are completed as follows.

After the computation of $s_{n+L} = {}_{\mathsf{SemiPO}}\mathsf{Scalar}_L(M^n, 0, KF, 0)$, the register outputs $m_n = s_n \oplus KS_0$ and the state becomes

$$temp = ((s_{n+1} \oplus KS_1, \ldots, s_{n+L-1} \oplus KS_{L-1}, s_{n+L})).$$

Then, $_{\mathsf{PO}}\mathsf{Convert}_L(temp, K[1], K[3])$ is run to update $temp$ where $K[3] = KS$ and $K[1] = (KS_{1\ldots L-1}\|0)$ the vector resulting from the concatenation of the bits $KS_1, \ldots, KS_{L-1}$ and the bit 0. Subsequently, the register state is updated as $M^{n+1} = temp$ which is equal to $S^{n+1} \oplus KS$.

This doing and thanks to the splitting of the operations with two POKs, the state is not available in clear for an adversary in the second step. Note that the value s_{n+L} is not hidden in the first step. In the next section, we fuse the two previous process to enable obfuscation of this value too.

3.4   Fill in the Gap

Given $2L$ consecutive bits of an outputted stream from an LFSR, it is known that one can reconstruct an LFSR by using the Berlekamp-Massey [26] algorithm which will produce the same stream. It emphasizes the interest to mask any bit of the state whence the tags share the same feedback function and the same initial state. We describe now the whole process which achieves obfuscation of the feedback key and the state, including the new input bits s_{n+L} and the outputted bits.

We assume below that within a tag the LFSR is used as a key stream generator to encrypt a message by xoring it. In the sequel, let x be the current bit to be encrypted and assume that the current masked state is $M^n = S^n \oplus KS = (s_n \oplus KS_0, s_{n+1} \oplus KS_1, \ldots, s_{n+L-1} \oplus KS_{L-1})$. Note that all bits KS_i of KS can be seen as well as a combination of two 1-bit POKs, $KS_i = KS'_i \oplus KS''_i$. The algorithm is split in consecutive steps as detailed in Table 3.

Lemma 3. *The LFSR implementation of Table 3 leads to a physically obfuscated primitive.*

Proof. (sketch) Assume that x is unknown by the adversary then all bit values of the state are always masked along the different steps, either by x, or a bit of

Table 3. A physically obfuscated LFSR implementation

---

1. Set $z = {}_{\mathsf{SemiPO}}\mathsf{Scalar}_L(M^n, 0, KF, KS_{L-1})$.
2. The register outputs $m_n = s_n \oplus KS_0$ and the state becomes $temp = (s_{n+1} \oplus KS_1, \ldots, s_{n+L-1} \oplus KS_{L-1}, z)$ with $z = s_{n+L} \oplus KS_{L-1}$.
3. Then set $y = x \oplus m_n = x \oplus s_n \oplus KS_0$, erase x from memory, and output ${}_{\mathsf{PO}}\mathsf{Convert}_1(y, KS_0, 0)$.
4. Finally, $temp \leftarrow {}_{\mathsf{PO}}\mathsf{Convert}_L(temp, K[1], K[3])$ is run to update the register with $M^{n+1} = temp$ where $K[1] = (KS_{1\ldots L-1}||0)$ and $K[3] = (KS_{0\ldots L-2}||0)$.

KS, KS' or KS''. The important point now is that all these values are different from one tag to another one, this means that even if an adversary succeeds in obtaining N consecutive masked values, say $s_{k+1} \oplus \alpha_{k+1}, \ldots, s_{k+N} \oplus \alpha_{k+N}$ of the state by opening several tags (at least N, as opening a tag implementing a POK implies its end-of-life prematurely), he cannot recover the value of the state thanks to the bitwise independence of the bits $\alpha_{k+1}, \ldots, \alpha_{k+N}$.   □

Corollary 1. *The implementation above without the execution of the step 3 remains physically obfuscated, i.e. the state and the feedback key stay hidden; which implementation we denote by* ${}_{\mathsf{PO}}\mathsf{LFSRupdate}$.

4   Applications

4.1   Krawczyk's MACs and LFSR-Based Hashing

[23] describes an efficient construction for Message Authentication Codes relying on traditional hashing techniques. The basic idea is to use a family H of linear *hash* functions which map $\{0,1\}^m$ to $\{0,1\}^L$ in a balanced way. Interestingly, such hashing family can be constructed as LFSR-based hashing. See Appendix B for a quick description of the MAC mechanism and the related notions.

An efficient solution using multiplication by matrices provided in [23] is to use specific Toeplitz matrices which can be described by a LFSR. Let the LFSR be represented by its feedback polynomial P, a primitive polynomial over $GF(2)$ of degree L, and an initial state $S^0 = (s_0, \ldots, s_{L-1}) \neq 0$. Then $h_{P,S^0} \in H$ is defined by the linear combinations $h_{P,s}(X) = \bigoplus_{j=0}^{m-1} x_j.S^j$ where $X = (x_0, \ldots, x_{m-1})$ and S^j is the j-th state of the LFSR. This leads to an ϵ-balanced family H (see Definition 4 in Appendix B) for at least $\epsilon \leq \frac{m}{2^{L-1}}$ as proved by [23]. Moreover, a hash function h_{P,S^0} is easily implemented as the message authentication can be computed progressively with an accumulator register which is updated after each message bit: the implementation does not depend on the size m of X.

Let $X = (x_0, \ldots, x_{m-1})$ be the message to be authenticated. We can manage the computation of $h_{P,S^0}(x)$ in an obfuscated way thanks to the previous algorithm for LFSR obfuscation. All updates of the LFSR are made thanks to ${}_{\mathsf{PO}}\mathsf{LFSRupdate}$ (modification of the method of section 3.4 where the step 3

Table 4. A physically obfuscated LFSR-based hashing implementation

$counter \leftarrow 0$
$result \leftarrow (0, \ldots, 0)$
For $n = 0$ to $m - 1$ do
    If $(x_j == 1)$ then
        $result \leftarrow result \oplus M^n$
        $counter \leftarrow counter \oplus 1$
    End If
    execute poLFSRupdate() to obtain M^{n+1}
    $n \leftarrow n + 1$
End For
If $(counter == 0)$ then Output $result$
    Else Output poConvert$_L(result, KS, 0)$
End If

is skipped). Let $result$ be the variable which will correspond to the value of $h_{P,S^0}(x)$ at the end of the execution. Starting from the initial masked state $M^0 = S^0 \oplus KS$, we update the register $m - 1$ times and before each clocking, we update the value of $result$. The execution is summarized in Table 4. All computations to obtain h_{P,S^0} are made directly on the masked states and if necessary (when the weight of x is odd) KS is used at the end to unmask the result. Thanks to lemma 1 and corollary 1, we have the following results.

Lemma 4. *The LFSR-based hashing implementation in Table 4 is a physically obfuscated primitive.*

Remark 1. This obfuscation can be for instance applied to the implementation of an authentication protocol which makes use of LFSR-based hashing. It would be a way to answer the possible weakness of use of LFSR in RFID tags as underlined in [13] where the LFSR feedback polynomial is assumed to be known as soon it is the same in all tags. With our obfuscation technique this is not anymore the case.

4.2   Self-shrinking Generator

The self-shrinking generator (SSG) [27] consists of one LFSR combined with a so-called shrinking function. Let KF be the feedback function of the LFSR and $S^0 = (s_0, \ldots, s_{L-1})$ be its initial state. The shrinking function $f : GF(2) \times GF(2) \rightarrow GF(2) \cup \{\epsilon\}$ is defined as follows: for $(x, y) \in GF(2) \times GF(2)$, $f(x, y) = y$ if $x = 1$, $f(x, y) = \epsilon$ if $x = 0$, which could be interpreted as $f(0, y)$ outputs nothing. Hence a given output stream $s_0, \ldots, s_{2N}$ of length $2N$ from the LFSR is split in N couples and the shrinking function acts on each of them to output at the end the bitstream $f(s_0, s_1) \ldots f(s_{2N-1}, s_{2N})$ of length $\leq N$. As empty output may appear, the exact length is in fact hard to know in advance.

The solutions described in section 3 can be applied to the LFSR of the self-shrinking generator, thus protecting the state and the feedback function[1] against an intrusive adversary. Nevertheless, one constraint arises with the use of the shrinking function on the output bits: the value of the output bit in the algorithm of section 3.4 can not be masked anymore by x in order to be able to compare it with 0 or 1, which leads to a potential source of leakage. We have to distinguish two situations:

- The tags share at most one of the following data – feedback key or (exclusive) initial state, which means that the opening of different tags will not give enough information to recover the shared data.
- The tags share both data, feedback key and initial state, and in that case, the leakage of the output bit can afford to an adversary the possibility to reconstruct the LFSR via Berlekamp-Massey, by opening many tags. To avoid this, we suggest below a small modification of the SSG.

Masked SSG. We consider the algorithm $_{PO}$LFSRupdate of section 3.4 for the execution of the LFSR assuming that it outputs the value $m_n = s_n \oplus KS_0$. We operate two bits by two bits for the shrinking function. I.e. we use the output bits $m_n = s_n \oplus KS_0$ and $m_{n+1} = s_{n+1} \oplus KS_0$.

Let x be the current bit to be encrypted, i.e. to be xored with the keystream generated by the SSG. In our modification the shrinking check $s_n == 1$ is replaced by the check $s_n \oplus KS_0 == 1$ (cf. Table 5). Note that this modification does not change the standard analysis of SSG as KS_0 is a constant.

Table 5. A physically obfuscated SSG implementation

While $m_n \neq 1$
      execute $_{PO}$LFSRupdate() twice to output two new bits (m_n, m_{n+1}) (where $n \leftarrow n + 2$)
End While
Set $y = x \oplus m_{n+1}$
Output $_{PO}$Convert$_1(y, KS_0, 0)$ (i.e. $x \oplus s_{n+1}$).

Lemma 5. *The above implementation of our modification of the SSG is physically obfuscated.*

Remark 2. All LFSR-based stream ciphers are possible targets for our obfuscation method as soon as operations remain linear. For instance, it can be adapted for the shrinking generator [10] or for some generalizations of the self-shrinking generator [24, 25]. LFSR-based stream ciphers with irregular clocking are also good targets. These include as examples the Alternating Step Generator [18],

---

[1] Note that for analysis of the SSG security, it is generally assumed that the feedback polynomial is known; here we consider the case where the system may try to hide it too.

A5/1 [4], or W7 [33]. To activate the clocking of some registers, clocking bits at fixed position are used. If all initial data (states and feedback polynomials) are not shared between several tags then those bits may be managed unmasked (in some cases) to check whether a register might clock (e.g. for A5/1 this check is made by a majority vote between the values of 3 bits coming from the 3 registers of the cipher). If all data are shared, then to avoid the risk of compromise we can modify slightly the scheme by checking the clocking condition directly on the masked bits.

4.3   Trivium

Trivium [8, 9] is a stream cipher which has been elected as one of the three hardware oriented stream ciphers of the eStream project portfolio (http://www. ecrypt.eu.org/stream/). This is thus natural to consider it as a possible cipher for implementation into tags. Technically, it is not a linear LFSR-based stream cipher, but its structure remains quite simple and the small number of non-linear operations enables us to adapt our obfuscation technique.

Trivium is roughly a concatenation of 3 registers which are updated via quadratic feedback functions. It contains a 288-bit internal state $(s_0, \ldots, s_{287})$ and once initialized, the key stream generation of a bit y and the update of the state follow the algorithm in Table 6 (where $\otimes$ stands for a product of bits, i.e. a AND). Here, the feedback function is fixed, so we do not need to mask the feedback key KF in the same way as in section 3.2 but to simplify the analysis we can keep the method described in section 3.4 as a baseline. The method is similar for handling all the linear computations above. The only specificity concerns the steps (5), (6), (7) where a general obfuscated AND is needed.

AND obfuscation. Here we focus on an AND of two bits (this is easily generalizable to l-bit vectors). For $i \in \{1, 2, 3\}$, let $K[i]$ be a binary value, implemented by two POKs $K[i]'$, $K[i]''$ such that $K[i] = K[i]' \oplus K[i]''$. Compare to the XOR,

Table 6. Trivium key stream generation

$$
\begin{aligned}
t_1 &\leftarrow s_{65} \oplus s_{92} & (1)\\
t_2 &\leftarrow s_{161} \oplus s_{176} & (2)\\
t_3 &\leftarrow s_{242} \oplus s_{287} & (3)\\
y &\leftarrow t_1 \oplus t_2 \oplus t_3 & (4)\\
t_1 &\leftarrow t_1 \oplus (s_{90} \otimes s_{91}) \oplus s_{170} & (5)\\
t_2 &\leftarrow t_2 \oplus (s_{174} \otimes s_{175}) \oplus s_{263} & (6)\\
t_3 &\leftarrow t_3 \oplus (s_{285} \otimes s_{286}) \oplus s_{68} & (7)\\
(s_0', s_1', \ldots, s_{92}') &\leftarrow (t_3, s_0, \ldots, s_{91}) & (8)\\
(s_{93}', s_{94}', \ldots, s_{176}') &\leftarrow (t_1, s_{93}, \ldots, s_{175}) & (9)\\
(s_{177}', s_{178}', \ldots, s_{287}') &\leftarrow (t_2, s_{177}, \ldots, s_{286}) & (10)
\end{aligned}
$$

we also introduce a couple of POKs $K[4]'$, $K[4]''$. Also let x and y be two binary values.

Definition 3. *A physically obfuscated AND, denoted by* poAND, *corresponds to the computation of a masked AND of two masked bits.* poAND$(x \oplus K[1], y \oplus K[2], K[1], K[2], K[3], K[4])$ *is the computation of* $(x \otimes y) \oplus K[3]$ *with the inputs* $x \oplus K[1]$ *and* $y \oplus K[2]$ *and is implemented as in Table 7.*

The implementation is based on the following relation:

$$x \otimes y = \Big((x \oplus K[1]) \otimes (y \oplus K[2]) \Big) \oplus \Big(K[1] \otimes (y \oplus K[2]) \Big)$$
$$\oplus \Big((x \oplus K[1]) \otimes K[2] \Big) \oplus \Big(K[1] \otimes K[2] \Big)$$

Table 7. poAND$(x \oplus K[1], y \oplus K[2], K[1], K[2], K[3], K[4])$ implementation

1. Set $z = ((x \oplus K[1]) \otimes (y \oplus K[2]))$
2. $z \leftarrow z \oplus {}_{\mathsf{SemiPO}}\mathsf{Scalar}_1(x \oplus K[1], 0, K[2], 0) \oplus {}_{\mathsf{SemiPO}}\mathsf{Scalar}_1(y \oplus K[2], 0, K[1], 0)$
3. $z \leftarrow {}_{\mathsf{PO}}\mathsf{Convert}_1(z, 0, K[3])$
4. Activate $K[1]'$ and $K[2]'$, update $z \leftarrow z \oplus (K[1]' \otimes K[2]')$
5. Erase $K[1]'$ and $K[2]'$ from memory
6. Activate $K[1]''$ and $K[2]''$, update $z \leftarrow z \oplus (K[1]'' \otimes K[2]'')$
7. Activate $K[4]', K[4]''$, set $temp_1 = K[4]' \oplus K[1]''$ and $temp_2 = K[4]'' \oplus K[2]''$
8. Erase $K[1]'', K[2]'', K[4]'$ and $K[4]''$ from memory
9. Activate $K[1]', K[2]'$, update $temp_1 \leftarrow temp_1 \otimes K[2]'$, $temp_2 \leftarrow temp_2 \otimes K[1]'$
10. Update $z \leftarrow z \oplus temp_1 \oplus temp_2$, erase $temp_1, temp_2$ from memory
11. Activate $K[4]', K[4]''$, update $z \leftarrow z \oplus (K[4]' \otimes K[2]') \oplus (K[4]'' \otimes K[1]')$
12. Erase $K[4]', K[4]'', K[1]'$ and $K[2]'$ from memory
13. Output z

The steps 4 to 12 are used to compute $K[1] \otimes K[2]$ as the XOR of $K[1]' \otimes K[2]'$, $K[1]' \otimes K[2]''$, $K[1]'' \otimes K[2]'$ and $K[1]'' \otimes K[2]''$.

Lemma 6. poAND *is a physically obfuscated primitive.*

With this additional physically obfuscated primitive, it becomes possible to obfuscate non linear stream-ciphers such as Trivium.

Whole Description of Trivium Obfuscation. As in section 3.4, we assume that the current masked state is $M = (s_0, \ldots, s_{287}) \oplus (KS_0, \ldots, KS_{287})$ where the key state KS is computed thanks to the two POKs KS' and KS''.

Let x be the current bit to be encrypted, the obfuscated key stream generation is made as follows.

– Set $t_1' = M_{65} \oplus M_{92}$,
– $t_2' \leftarrow M_{161} \oplus M_{176}$,

- $t_3' \leftarrow M_{242} \oplus M_{287}$,
- set $y = t_1' \oplus t_2' \oplus t_3'$, $y \leftarrow y \oplus x$ and erase x from memory.
- Output $_{PO}\mathsf{Convert}_1(y, KS_{65} \oplus KS_{92} \oplus KS_{161} \oplus KS_{176} \oplus KS_{242} \oplus KS_{287}, 0)$.

At this stage the encrypted version of x has been obtained correctly.

- Update $t_1' = t_1' \oplus M_{170}$, $t_2' = t_2' \oplus M_{263}$, $t_3' = t_3' \oplus M_{68}$.
- Update $t_1' = t_1' \oplus {}_{PO}\mathsf{AND}(M_{90}, M_{91}, KS_{90}, KS_{91}, KS_{93}, K[4])$
- Update $t_2' = t_2' \oplus {}_{PO}\mathsf{AND}(M_{174}, M_{175}, KS_{174}, KS_{175}, KS_{177}, K[4])$
- Update $t_3' = t_3' \oplus {}_{PO}\mathsf{AND}(M_{285}, M_{286}, KS_{285}, KS_{286}, KS_0, K[4])$

where KS_{93}, KS_{177} and KS_0 corresponds to the bits of KS whose indexes are the future positions of t_1', t_2', t_3' for the register updating) and with $K[4]$ corresponding to a couple of two POKs as in Table 7.

- Update $t_1' = {}_{PO}\mathsf{Convert}_1(t_1', KS_{170} \oplus KS_{65} \oplus KS_{92} \oplus KS_{93}, KS_{93})$
- Update $t_2' = {}_{PO}\mathsf{Convert}_1(t_2', KS_{177} \oplus KS_{263} \oplus KS_{161} \oplus KS_{176}, KS_{177})$
- Update $t_3' = {}_{PO}\mathsf{Convert}_1(t_3', KS_0 \oplus KS_{68} \oplus KS_{242} \oplus KS_{287}, KS_0)$

At this stage, this leads to the equality between t_1' and $s_{65} \oplus s_{92} \oplus s_{170} \oplus (s_{90} \otimes s_{91}) \oplus KS_{93}$, i.e. the value of t_1 at the original step (9) xored with KS_{93} (similar for t_2', t_3' with the values $t_2 \oplus KS_{177}$ and $t_3 \oplus KS_0$). To finish the register updating, we run these last operations.

- Compute M' as
  $(M_0', M_1', \ldots, M_{92}') \leftarrow (t_3', M_0, \ldots, M_{91})$,
  $(M_{93}', M_{94}', \ldots, M_{176}') \leftarrow (t_1', M_{93}, \ldots, M_{175})$,
  $(M_{177}', M_{178}', \ldots, M_{287}') \leftarrow (t_2', M_{177}, \ldots, M_{286})$
- Then update M' with
  $_{PO}\mathsf{Convert}\Big(M', (0, KS_0, \ldots, KS_{91}, 0, KS_{93}, \ldots, KS_{175}, 0, KS_{177}, \ldots, KS_{286}),$
  $(0, KS_1, \ldots, KS_{92}, 0, KS_{94}, \ldots, KS_{176}, 0, KS_{178}, \ldots, KS_{287})\Big)$

This leads to the update version of the state register obfuscated by KS.

Lemma 7. *This implementation of the key stream generation of Trivium is physically obfuscated.*

5   Conclusion

We describe in this paper physical obfuscation of binary operations (XOR, AND, Scalar Product) with a study of their applications to stream ciphers. As these binary operations enable any boolean operations to be computed, our ideas are useful for other kind of cryptographic primitives which use basic operations and where increasing resistance of tags against compromise is required. For instance, the HB-related RFID protocols (HB [21], HB+ [22] and modified version [6, 12, 16, 28, 30, 5]) are good targets for our obfuscation techniques which can be seen as a enhancement of [20, 19] where PUF are introduced. Other RFID protocols based on binary operations can be improved as well, e.g. the scheme [11]. Efficient hash functions such as [2, 1] are also of interest.

Further works would include the analysis of the implementation overhead to achieve such physical resistance. In many settings, one chooses connection polynomials for LFSRs such that their Hamming weight is small. This lowers the cost of computing the state change. But the obfuscation technique essentially randomizes the state change. The expected Hamming weight of the masked connection polynomial is then half the length of the LFSR.

Acknowledgements. The authors thank the referees for their helpful comments.

References

1. Bertoni, G., Daemen, J., Peeters, M., Van Assche, G.: Keccak specifications. Submission to NIST (2008)
2. Bertoni, G., Daemen, J., Assche, G.V., Peeters, M.: Radiogatún, a belt-and-mill hash function. NIST - Second Cryptographic Hash Workshop, August 24-25 (2006)
3. Blömer, J., Guajardo, J., Krummel, V.: Provably secure masking of AES. In: Handschuh, H., Hasan, M.A. (eds.) SAC 2004. LNCS, vol. 3357, pp. 69–83. Springer, Heidelberg (2004)
4. Briceno, M., Goldberg, I., Wagner, D.: A pedagogical implementation of A5/1 (1999), http://jya.com/a51-pi.htm
5. Bringer, J., Chabanne, H.: Trusted-HB: A low-cost version of HB$^+$ secure against man-in-the-middle attacks. IEEE Transactions on Information Theory 54(9), 4339–4342 (2008)
6. Bringer, J., Chabanne, H., Dottax, E.: HB^{++}: a lightweight authentication protocol secure against some attacks. In: SecPerU, pp. 28–33. IEEE Computer Society, Los Alamitos (2006)
7. Bringer, J., Chabanne, H., Icart, T.: Improved privacy of the tree-based hash protocols using physically unclonable function. In: Ostrovsky, R., De Prisco, R., Visconti, I. (eds.) SCN 2008. LNCS, vol. 5229, pp. 77–91. Springer, Heidelberg (2008)
8. De Cannière, C., Preneel, B.: Trivium specifications. eSTREAM, ECRYPT Stream Cipher Project (2005)
9. De Cannière, C., Preneel, B.: Trivium - a stream cipher construction inspired by block cipher design principles. In: eSTREAM, ECRYPT Stream Cipher Project (2006)
10. Coppersmith, D., Krawczyk, H., Mansour, Y.: The shrinking generator. In: Stinson, D.R. (ed.) CRYPTO 1993. LNCS, vol. 773, pp. 22–39. Springer, Heidelberg (1994)
11. Dolev, S., Kopeetsky, M., Shamir, A.: RFID authentication efficient proactive information security within computational security. Technical Report 08-2007, Department of Computer Science, Ben-Gurion University (July 2007)
12. Duc, D.N., Kim, K.: Securing HB+ against GRS man-in-the-middle attack. In: Proceedings of the Symposium on Cryptography and Information Security (SCIS 2007) (2007)
13. Frumkin, D., Shamir, A.: Un-trusted-HB: Security vulnerabilities of trusted-HB. Cryptology ePrint Archive, Report 2009/044 (2009), http://eprint.iacr.org/
14. Gassend, B.: Physical random functions. Master's thesis, Computation Structures Group, Computer Science and Artificial Intelligence Laboratory. MIT (2003)

15. Gassend, B., Clarke, D.E., van Dijk, M., Devadas, S.: Silicon physical random functions. In: Atluri, V. (ed.) ACM Conference on Computer and Communications Security, pp. 148–160. ACM, New York (2002)

16. Gilbert, H., Robshaw, M., Seurin, Y.: HB#: Increasing the security and efficiency of HB$^+$. In: Smart, N.P. (ed.) EUROCRYPT 2008. LNCS, vol. 4965, pp. 361–378. Springer, Heidelberg (2008)

17. Guajardo, J., Kumar, S.S., Schrijen, G.J., Tuyls, P.: FPGA Intrinsic PUFs and Their Use for IP Protection. In: Paillier, P., Verbauwhede, I. (eds.) CHES 2007. LNCS, vol. 4727, pp. 63–80. Springer, Heidelberg (2007)

18. Günther, C.G.: Alternating step generators controlled by de bruijn sequences. In: Price, W.L., Chaum, D. (eds.) EUROCRYPT 1987. LNCS, vol. 304, pp. 5–14. Springer, Heidelberg (1988)

19. Hammouri, G., Öztürk, E., Birand, B., Sunar, B.: Unclonable lightweight authentication scheme. In: Chen, L., Ryan, M.D., Wang, G. (eds.) ICICS 2008. LNCS, vol. 5308, pp. 33–48. Springer, Heidelberg (2008)

20. Hammouri, G., Sunar, B.: Puf-hb: A tamper-resilient hb based authentication protocol. In: Bellovin, S.M., Gennaro, R., Keromytis, A.D., Yung, M. (eds.) ACNS 2008. LNCS, vol. 5037, pp. 346–365. Springer, Heidelberg (2008)

21. Hopper, N.J., Blum, M.: Secure human identification protocols. In: Boyd, C. (ed.) ASIACRYPT 2001. LNCS, vol. 2248, pp. 52–66. Springer, Heidelberg (2001)

22. Juels, A., Weis, S.A.: Authenticating pervasive devices with human protocols. In: Shoup, V. (ed.) CRYPTO 2005. LNCS, vol. 3621, pp. 293–308. Springer, Heidelberg (2005)

23. Krawczyk, H.: LFSR-based Hashing and Authentication. In: Desmedt, Y.G. (ed.) CRYPTO 1994. LNCS, vol. 839, pp. 129–139. Springer, Heidelberg (1994)

24. Lee, D.H., Park, J.H., Han, J.W.: Security analysis of a variant of self-shrinking generator. IEICE Transactions 91-A(7), 1824–1827 (2008)

25. Lihua, D., Yupu, H.: Weak generalized self-shrinking generators. Journal of Systems Engineering and Electronics 18(2), 407–411 (2007)

26. MacWilliams, F., Sloane, N.: The theory of error-correcting codes, ch. 9. North-Holland, Amsterdam (1977)

27. Meier, W., Staffelbach, O.: The self-shrinking generator. In: De Santis, A. (ed.) EUROCRYPT 1994. LNCS, vol. 950, pp. 205–214. Springer, Heidelberg (1995)

28. Munilla, J., Peinado, A.: HB-MP: A further step in the HB-family of lightweight authentication protocols. Computer Networks 51(9), 2262–2267 (2007)

29. Oswald, E., Mangard, S., Pramstaller, N., Rijmen, V.: A side-channel analysis resistant description of the AES S-box. In: Gilbert, H., Handschuh, H. (eds.) FSE 2005. LNCS, vol. 3557, pp. 413–423. Springer, Heidelberg (2005)

30. Piramuthu, S., Tu, Y.-J.: Modified HB authentication protocol. In: Western European Workshop on Research in Cryptology, WEWoRC (2007)

31. Shamir, A.: How to share a secret. ACM Commun. 22(11), 612–613 (1979)

32. Suh, G.E., Devadas, S.: Physical unclonable functions for device authentication and secret key generation. In: DAC, pp. 9–14. IEEE, Los Alamitos (2007)

33. Thomas, S., Anthony, D., Berson, T., Gong, G.: The W7 stream cipher algorithm. Internet Draft, April 2002 (2002)

34. Tuyls, P., Batina, L.: RFID-tags for anti-counterfeiting. In: Pointcheval, D. (ed.) CT-RSA 2006. LNCS, vol. 3860, pp. 115–131. Springer, Heidelberg (2006)

A   Physical Unclonable Function

Gassend in [14] introduces the concept of Physical Unclonable Function (PUF): a function that maps challenges (stimuli) to responses, that is embodied by a physical device, and that has the following properties:

1. easy to evaluate,
2. hard to characterize, from physical observation or from chosen challenge-response pairs,
3. hard to reproduce.

For a given challenge, a PUF always gives the same answer. The hardness of characterization and reproduction means that it is impossible to reproduce or to characterize the PUF thanks to a reasonable amount of resources (time, money, . . .). PUF can thus be viewed as pseudo-random function (note however that they can be limited in the number of possible challenge-response pairs as explained in [17]) where the randomness is insured thanks to physical properties.

[34] defines an Integrated Physical Unclonable Function (I-PUF) as a PUF with the additional interesting properties listed below:

1. The I-PUF is inseparably bound to a chip. This means that any attempt to remove the PUF from the chip leads to the destruction of the PUF and of the chip.
2. It is impossible to tamper with the communication (measurement data) between the chip and the PUF.
3. The output of the PUF is inaccessible to an attacker.

These properties ensure the impossibility to analyze physically a PUF without changing its output. Hence, physical attacks corrupt the PUF and the chip leaving the attacker without any information about the PUF. Particularly, volatile memory cannot be read out without destroying the I-PUF. Silicon PUF have been already described in [15] and can be taken as relevant examples of I-PUF, they are based on delay comparison among signals running through random wires. Moreover, they only require a few resources to be implemented. A practical example of implementation is described in [32]. The final output of a PUF should not contain any errors, whatever the external conditions are. This problem is generally handle thanks to error correcting techniques (cf. [34]).

B   Krawczyk's MACs

The MAC mechanism described by [23] works as follows.

If two parties share a common key consisting of a particular function $h \in H$ and a random pad e of length L, then the MAC of a message X is computed as $t = h(X) \oplus e$. To break the authentication, an adversary should find X' and t' such that $t' = h(X) \oplus e$. For this, h and e must remain secret.

Definition 4. *A family H of hash functions is said ϵ-balanced (or ϵ-almost universal) if: $\forall X \in \{0,1\}^m, X \neq 0, c \in \{0,1\}^L, \Pr[h \in H, h(X) = c] \leq \epsilon$.*

[23] proves the property below.

Proposition 1. *If H is a family of linear hash functions and if H is ϵ-balanced then the probability of success of an adversary is lower than ϵ.*
The scheme is then said ϵ-secure.

Following the principle of a one-time pad, the same h can be reused but e must be a random pad different each time.

Cache Timing Attacks on Clefia

Chester Rebeiro[1], Debdeep Mukhopadhyay[1], Junko Takahashi[2],
and Toshinori Fukunaga[2]

[1] Dept. of Computer Science and Engineering
Indian Institute of Technology Kharagpur, India
{chester,debdeep}@cse.iitkgp.ernet.in
[2] NTT Information Sharing Platform Laboratories
Nippon Telegraph and Telephone Corporation, Japan
{takahashi.junko,fukunaga.toshinori}@lab.ntt.co.jp

Abstract. The paper discusses the performance of cache timing attacks
on Clefia, which is based on the generalized Feistel structure and implemented using small tables. We mention the difficulties on mounting a
timing based cache attack on the cipher, and then explain why a cache
attack is still possible. To the best of our knowledge, no reported work
on cache attacks target ciphers which are implemented with small tables.
Our attack uses the fact that parallelization and pipelining of memory
accesses can only be done within a single round of a cipher, but not
across rounds. Our findings show that 121 bits of the 128 bit key can be
revealed in $2^{26.64}$ Clefia encryptions on an Intel Core 2 Duo machine.

1 Introduction

The biggest threat to crypto systems is from information leaking through side
channels such as power, radiation, timing, etc. A class of side channel attacks
that makes use of information leakages due to the processor's cache memory is
called cache attacks. Cache memory is a small high speed memory that stores
recently used data and instructions. The time required to access data present in
the cache (*cache hit*) is much lesser than when the data is not present in cache
(*cache miss*). This differential timing between a hit and a miss is used in cache
attacks.

The idea of using the nonuniform memory access timings to launch attacks
on crypto systems was first proposed by Kelsey et. al.[11]. A model for such
attacks based on the cipher's structure was then formulated and simulated by
Page in [16]. The first successful cache attack was demonstrated by Tsunoo et.
al. on Misty1 [19]. They then extended the attack to DES and 3-DES[18]. *AES*
was the next target with cache attacks by Bernstein [3] and Osvik [15]. Since
then there have been several works that have analyzed, enhanced, and provided
countermeasures for these attacks.

All cache attacks can be categorized into three classes: cache trace attacks,
cache access attacks, and cache timing attacks. *Trace attacks* [1,4,9] require detailed profiling of cache access patterns during encryption. Traces are generally

B. Roy and N. Sendrier (Eds.): INDOCRYPT 2009, LNCS 5922, pp. 104–118, 2009.

obtained from power measurements and require sophisticated measuring equipment. *Access driven attacks* such as [13,15] rely on spy processes to gain information about the cache access pattern of the cipher. *Timing attacks* [3,5,14,18,19] on the other hand just require knowledge of the overall execution time of the cipher. This timing information can be easily captured, even over a network, thus resulting in remote attacks [2,6].

As on date, the only block ciphers that have been attacked by the cache are Misty1, DES, 3-DES, and AES. Little work has been done on cache attacks for other block ciphers. In this paper we present a cache timing attack on Sony's block cipher Clefia [17], which is used for copyright protection and authentication. Clefia has a generalized Feistel structure in which 64 bits of the first set of round keys are ex-ored with whitening keys. In order to break the cipher, it is essential to separate these round keys from the whitening keys. This is not straight forward. In our attack on Clefia, we show how 57 out of the 64 bits of the round keys can be extracted from the whitening keys.

All cache timing attacks published so far are based on the large table assumption, where the cipher's execution time is proportional to the number of misses during encryption[11,18]. This assumption does not hold for ciphers implemented with small tables, as at every encryption the entire table gets loaded into cache. This makes the number of misses a constant. This limitation was stated in [18], where larger than required DES tables were used to obtain results. In this paper we show how cipher implementations, such as Clefia, which use small tables, can be still attacked on microprocessors that support parallel and overlapped memory accesses and out-of-order execution. These memory access features are present in most modern day microprocessors as they increase execution performance. Our attack is based on the fact that these memory access features are effective only within a round of the cipher, while memory accesses across rounds cannot be accelerated due of data dependencies.

The paper is organized as follows : the next section is the related work. Section 3 discusses the difficulties in attacking Clefia compared to other ciphers, in particular AES. Section 4 analyzes the processor features which could cause cache attacks on ciphers that are implemented with small tables. Section 5 describes our attack on Clefia. Section 6 presents experimental results while the final section is the conclusion.

2   Related Work

In this section an overview of three main cache attack methodologies is given. These attacks form the base on which several other attacks on AES were devised.

The first practical cache attack was on DES[18] where ex-or of the round keys were deduced from the encryption timing. The analysis was done by correlating the number of misses with the encryption time. To obtain this correlation, the authors used large tables of 256 bytes instead of standard 64 byte DES tables. In addition, the small number of look-ups (16 per table) per encryption, and the small cache line of the experimental machine (Pentium III, with 32 bytes cache line) were critical to make the required deductions. Our attack on the other hand uses an implementation[1] of Clefia with 256 byte tables, and is implemented on a processor with 64 byte cache line. Thus the table is much smaller than in [18] considering the cache size. Moreover, 72 look-ups are done on each table during a single encryption. These factors result in a high probability that the entire table is loaded into cache at every encryption, thus making the number of cache misses a constant and independent of the inputs. In contrast in [18], the probability that the entire table loads into the cache during an encryption is lesser thus the number of misses are not a constant and have a strong correlation with the encryption.

In [15], the attacker loads an array into cache before the start of encryption. Immediately after the encryption, the array elements evicted from the cache is determined thus revealing the cache access patterns for the encryption. The attack will fail on ciphers implemented with small tables because all array data will be evicted from the cache at every encryption, thus leaking no patterns in the cache access.

The attack by Bernstein [3] was the first timing attack on AES. It requires the attacker to have access to an exact replica of the machine running the cryptographic algorithm. There are two phases in the attack. In the first phase, a template [7] is created by profiling the execution time for each byte of the known key. In the second phase, the attacker determines the execution time profile for bytes of the unknown key. A set of candidates for the unknown key are obtained by a statistical correlation between the two profiles. Performing brute force search through every possible combination of candidate keys reveals the unknown key. On cipher implementations which use small tables, the number of cache misses is a constant, therefore there is small variations in execution time. A straight forward implementation of [3] is unable to capture such small execution time variations, therefore it has to be modified to suit ciphers with small table implementations.

2.1   The Clefia Structure

Clefia is a 128 bit block cipher with a generalized Feistel structure. The specification [17] defines three key lengths of 128, 192, and 256 bits. For brevity, this paper considers 128 bit keys though the results are valid for the other key sizes too. The structure of Clefia is shown in Figure 1. The input has 16 bytes, P_0 to P_{15}, grouped into four 4 byte words. There are 18 rounds, and in each round, the first and third words are fed into nonlinear functions $F0$ and $F1$ respectively. The output of $F0$ and $F1$, collectively known as F functions, are ex-ored with the second and fourth words. Additionally, the second and fourth words are also whitened at the beginning and end of the encryption.

The non-linearity in the F functions are created by two sboxes $S0$ and $S1$. These sboxes are in the form of 256 byte look-up tables, and are invoked twice in each F function, making a total of eight table look-ups per round and 144

---

[1] The reference implementation *(http://www.sony.net/Products/cryptography/clefia)*

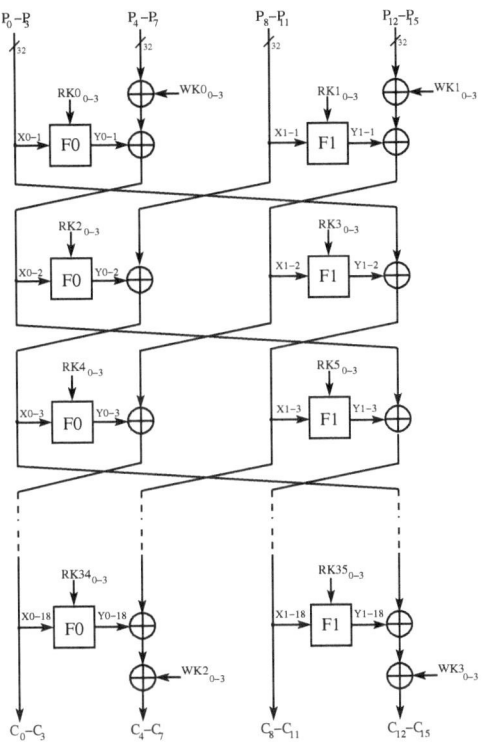

Fig. 1. Structure of Clefia

($= 8*18$) look-ups per encryption. Equations for functions $F0$ and $F1$ are shown in Equation 1.

$$\mathbf{F0}: \{y_0, y_1, y_2, y_3\} = (S0[x_0 \oplus k_0], S1[x_1 \oplus k_1], S0[x_2 \oplus k_2], S1[x_3 \oplus k_3]) \cdot M0$$
$$\mathbf{F1}: \{y_0, y_1, y_2, y_3\} = (S1[x_0 \oplus k_0], S0[x_1 \oplus k_1], S1[x_2 \oplus k_2], S0[x_3 \oplus k_3]) \cdot M1$$
$$(1)$$

The F functions take 4 input bytes, x_0, x_1, x_2, and x_3, and 4 round keys, k_0, k_1, k_2, and k_3. After the sbox look-ups, the bytes are diffused by multiplying them with (4×4) matrices $M0$ and $M1$ respectively. The $M0$ and $M1$ matrices are defined as follows:

$$M0 = \begin{pmatrix} 1 & 2 & 4 & 6 \\ 2 & 1 & 6 & 4 \\ 4 & 6 & 1 & 2 \\ 6 & 4 & 2 & 1 \end{pmatrix} \qquad M1 = \begin{pmatrix} 1 & 8 & 2 & A \\ 8 & 1 & A & 2 \\ 2 & A & 1 & 8 \\ A & 2 & 8 & 1 \end{pmatrix} \qquad (2)$$

The Clefia encryption requires 4 whitening keys WK_0, WK_1, WK_2, and WK_3, and 36 round keys $RK_0, \cdots, RK_{35}$. Key expansion is a two step process. First a 128 bit intermediate key L is generated from the secret key K, using a GFN

function [17]. From this the round keys and whitening keys are generated as shown below.

> *Step 1:* $WK_0|WK_1|WK_2|WK_3 \leftarrow K$
> *Step 2:* For $i \leftarrow 0$ to 8
> $\quad T \leftarrow L \oplus (CON_{24+4i}|CON_{24+4i+1}|CON_{24+4i+2}|CON_{24+4i+3})$
> $\quad L \leftarrow \Sigma(L)$
> $\quad$ if i is odd: $T \leftarrow T \oplus K$
> $\quad RK4i|RK4i+1|RK4i+2|RK4i+3 \leftarrow T$

The function Σ, known as the *double swap* function, rearranges the bits of L as shown in Equation 3.

$$\Sigma(L) \leftarrow L_{(7\cdots63)}|L_{(121\cdots127)}|L_{(0\cdots6)}|L_{(64\cdots120)} \qquad (3)$$

From the structure of Clefia it is obvious that the knowledge of any set of 4 round keys $(RK4i, RK4i+1, RK4i+2, RK4i+3)$, where $i \bmod 2 = 0$, is sufficient to revert the key expansion process to obtain the secret key. In the attack on Clefia described in this paper, round keys $RK0$, $RK1$, $RK2$, and $RK3$ are determined from which L is computed. K can then be obtained from L by the inverse GFN function.

3   Complications in Cache Attacks on Clefia

In this section we justify why attacking Clefia using the cache is more difficult than attacking AES using similar techniques.

3.1   Small Tables

Conventionally, execution time for a block cipher encryption (T) was said to depend on the number of cache hits (n_h) and misses (n_m) as shown in Equation 4. T_h and T_m are the data access time when there is a hit and miss respectively, while k is a constant.

$$T = n_h T_h + n_m T_m + k \qquad (4)$$

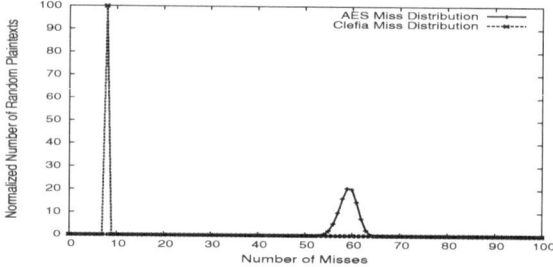

Fig. 2. Distribution of Number of Misses for AES and Clefia

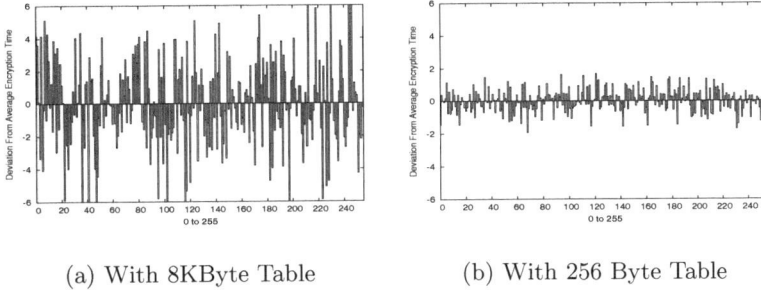

(a) With 8KByte Table   (b) With 256 Byte Table

Fig. 3. Timing Profiles for $RK0_0$ of Clefia

Generally $T_h << T_m$, leading Kelsey et. al. to make the prophecy that attacks based on cache hit ratio are possible on ciphers which use large look-up tables[11]. This prophecy has come true, for example in AES implementations that use five 1024 byte tables. However in Clefia, the two tables used in the reference implementation are much smaller with just 256 bytes each. On most modern systems which have 64 byte cache lines, each Clefia table requires just 4 cache lines. The implication of this can be seen in Figure 2, which shows the distribution of the average number of misses for OpenSSL's AES and the reference implementation of Clefia. The y axis has the number of plaintexts taken(normalized to 100). Both experiments were simulated with 65536 plaintexts and a 64 byte cache line. AES shows a normal distribution for the number of misses, while Clefia has a single spike at 8 misses. The result of the constant misses is that the variation in execution time is small. Figures 3(a) and 3(b) show deviations from average encryption time (as was done in [3]) for the first byte of $RK0$ for Clefia. Figure 3(a) was taken by padding each element of the sbox with 31 bytes, thus having a huge table of $8KBytes$. Figure 3(b) is for the standard sized table of 256 bytes. The figures clearly show that for large tables the deviation from average encryption time is much more significant than that for small tables. This makes most cache attacks that were successful on AES fail on Clefia with its sbox implemented as it is. In Section 4 we provide an intuition on why cache timing attacks still work on ciphers with small tables. In Section 5 we present a modification of Bernstein's cache timing attack [3] that is successful on Clefia.

3.2 Extraction of Round Keys $RK2$ and $RK3$

For cache timing attacks to work, one or more structures such as that in Figure 4 should be present in the cipher [20]. Figure 4 shows two accesses to the same sbox table with indices $(in_0 \oplus k_0)$ and $(in_1 \oplus k_1)$, where $in0$ and $in1$ are the inputs and k_0 and k_1 are the key. Cache hits occur when $(in_1 \oplus k_1)$ fall in the same cache line as $(in_0 \oplus k_0)$, in all other cases cache misses occur. To gain information about the key, the attacker should be able to control in_0 and in_1.

---

[1] http://www.sony.net/Products/cryptography/clefia/

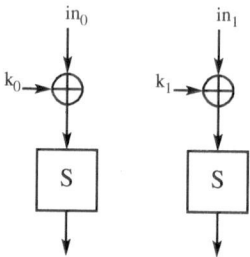

Fig. 4. Simple Sbox Look-up Structure

This is possible only in the first few rounds of the cipher. In AES for example, most cache timing attacks target the first round where 16 bytes of key are ex-ored with the plaintext in a manner similar to Figure 4.

In Clefia, determination of $RK2$ and $RK3$ is not trivial, because the input to the F functions in round 2 not only depend on the plaintext $P_4 \cdots P_7$ and $P_{11} \cdots P_{15}$ (Figure 1), but also on the outputs of the first round F functions and the whitening keys WK_0 and WK_1 respectively. Moreover, even if the effect of the F functions is nullified, it is still impossible to extract $RK2$ and $RK3$ from $RK2 \oplus WK0$ and $RK3 \oplus WK1$ respectively. In our attack we show how the whole of $RK2$ and 25 bits of $RK3$ are obtained by taking advantage of the key expansion algorithm of Clefia.

4   Cache Attacks on Small Table Cipher Implementations

The biggest design challenge for cache memory with respect to cache reads is to reduce the miss penalty. There are several techniques which are supported by today's microprocessors in order to reduce the miss penalty. Most important of them are speculative loading, out-of-order loading, prefetching, parallelization, and overlapping[10]. *Speculative loading* enables data to be loaded into the processor before preceding branches are resolved. For a block cipher, speculative loading has no effect on the execution time. *Prefetching* is done when the processor detects a sequence of memory accesses in a specific order. This again has no effect on block ciphers because the key dependent load operations are random in nature.

With *out-of-order* loading, the microprocessor can access memory in a sequence not strictly specified by the program. Additionally cache misses can be handled out of order. In block ciphers, outputs from one round are used in the next, while operations within a round can in general be made independent of each other. This implies that memory accesses within a round can be done out of order, while accesses in adjacent rounds have to follow the sequence. For example, consider the memory access dependency diagram for the first four rounds of Clefia (Figure 5). Each circle specifies a memory access, while each row specifies a round. It may be noted that the table accesses in function F0 (or F1) in the second or third round cannot be done before the accesses to F0 (or F1) of

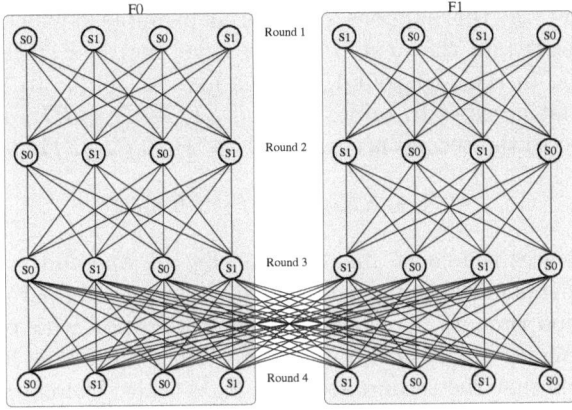

Fig. 5. Memory Access Dependency Diagram for First 4 Rounds of Clefia

the previous round is completed. Moreover, the fourth round memory accesses cannot be done until the third round is completed. However, the 8 look-ups in any particular round can be done out of order.

By *parallelization*, the microprocessor will be able to perform multiple loads, and even service multiple misses simultaneously. For example, Intel Core 2 is capable of handling two cache misses simultaneously. That is, two cache lines can be loaded into the $L1$ cache in parallel [8]. *Overlapping* of memory reads allows pipelining of reads so that on an average, back-to-back memory accesses are completed faster than scattered accesses. During a back-to-back access, only the first read will have to wait for the whole cache miss duration ([10], Section 8.5.4).

Parallelization and overlapping have an effect on the encryption time of a block cipher. Two misses that happen in the same round completes faster compared to when the two misses are in different rounds. This is because misses that occur in the same round can be parallelized while misses in different rounds cannot be due to dependencies of data.

From the above discussions it can be concluded that the encryption time not only depends on the number of hits and misses but also on the distribution of misses across the rounds. It is now left to be shown that the distribution of the misses depend on the key.

To do this, let n_h and n_m be the number of hits and misses during a Clefia encryption. Because of the small tables, it can be safely assumed that the whole table gets loaded into cache at each encryption. Due to the 8 cache lines (assuming 64 byte cache line) required to hold the two 256 byte Clefia tables, the expected value for n_m is 8, which matches with the observed value (Figure 2). These 8 cache misses are distributed across the rounds with most cache misses occurring in the first round, and least cache misses occurring in the final round. We found experimentally that *the number of cache misses in the first round is correlated to the encryption time, with encryptions having maximum number of first round misses take least encryption time.*

To understand why this happens, consider an example in which the first round has 3 cache misses and the next 5 rounds have one miss each. All the other accesses are hits. In the first round, 2 cache misses are due to the compulsory misses in the first accesses to tables $S0$ and $S1$, ie. $P_0 \oplus RK_0$ and $P_1 \oplus RK_1$. The third is due to the second access in $S0$, ie. $P_2 \oplus RK_2$. Therefore,

$$< P_0 \oplus RK_0 > \neq < P_2 \oplus RK_2 > \tag{5}$$

where $<>$ indicates the cache line accessed by the operand. The three cache misses are independent of each other and can be serviced in parallel resulting in a total encryption time T_a. Consider another encryption with encryption time T_b having two misses in the first round and the next 6 rounds having one miss each. This means that the second access in S_0 is a hit. Therefore,

$$< P_0 \oplus RK_0 > = < P_2 \oplus RK_2 > \tag{6}$$

The misses in the 6 rounds cannot be parallelized, as a result $T_b > T_a$. This shows that although the number of misses are equal, the distribution of misses across rounds leak information about the key.

5   The Attack

The proposed attack has four steps. The first is the determination of round keys $RK0$ and $RK1$. Then $RK2 \oplus WK0$ and $RK3 \oplus WK1$ is found. Using this information $RK4$ and $RK5$ are determined. Exploiting the key expansion algorithm the whole of $RK2$ and 25 bits of $RK3$ can be computed from $RK4$ and $RK5$. With the knowledge of $RK0$, $RK1$, $RK2$, $RK3$, it is trivial to obtain the secret key. Our attack follows the method of Bernstein's, which was demonstrated on AES[3]. The original attack however fails for Clefia because the variations in encryption time for Clefia (Figure 3(b)) is significantly lesser than that in AES. It was therefore required to modify Bernstein's attack in order to increase the accuracy of the timing profile.

5.1   Modifications of Bernstein's Attack

In [3], Bernstein observed that the indices to the sbox in the first round is the ex-or of the plaintext byte with the corresponding key byte: $x_i = p_i \oplus k_i$. Additionally, the entire encryption time depends on whether other first round table accesses, $x_j = p_j \oplus k_j$, cause cache hits with x_i. This observation is used to build a timing profile for key byte k_i by varying p_i. The average time required for each p_i is obtained from several encryptions done with *all* other plaintext bytes varying randomly.

We modify Bernstein's technique based on the fact that in the first round, the timing profile for k_i can be affected only by those plaintexts which access the same table as x_i. That is, if x_i and x_j access different tables, then p_j has no affect on the timing profile of k_i. However cache accesses in tables other than the table used by k_i cause unrequired deviations in the encryption time. This increases the error in the profile for k_i. Therefore, while taking the timing profile for k_i, it is sufficient to vary only those bytes of plaintext which use the same sbox as k_i. This results in more accurate timing profiles.

Another modification to improve the accuracy is in the timing measurement. Bernstein used the *rdtsc* instruction to make the time measurements. However this is known to have errors in measurement due to the out-of-order execution in the pipeline. In our timing measurement, the *cpuid* instruction is invoked before the *rdtsc* to flush the pipeline thus reducing errors[12].

5.2   Determining $RK0$ and $RK1$

In the first round, each sbox $S0$ and $S1$ is accessed four times; twice inside each function $F0$ and $F1$ (Equation 1). The indices to the tables are solely determined by the plaintext and the round keys $RK0$ and $RK1$ as shown in Equation 7. Ix_{Sy}^z is the index of the zth access to sbox Sy in round x.

$$
\begin{aligned}
I1_{S0}^0 &= P_0 \oplus RK0_0 & I1_{S1}^0 &= P_1 \oplus RK0_1 \\
I1_{S0}^1 &= P_2 \oplus RK0_2 & I1_{S1}^1 &= P_3 \oplus RK0_3 \\
I1_{S0}^2 &= P_9 \oplus RK1_1 & I1_{S1}^2 &= P_8 \oplus RK1_0 \\
I1_{S0}^3 &= P_{11} \oplus RK1_3 & I1_{S1}^3 &= P_{10} \oplus RK1_2
\end{aligned}
\tag{7}
$$

Round keys $RK0$ and $RK1$ can be easily determined by correlating the timing profiles for a known $RK0$ and $RK1$ with the unknown $RK0$ and $RK1$.

5.3   Determining $RK2 \oplus WK0$ and $RK3 \oplus WK1$

Indices to the table accesses in function $F0$ in round 2 are shown in Equation 8. In the equations $P_{(q,r,s,t)} = P_q|P_r|P_s|P_t$.

$$
\begin{aligned}
I2_{S0}^0 &= P_4 \oplus RK2_0 \oplus WK0_0 \oplus F0(P_{(0,1,2,3)}, RK0)_0 \\
I2_{S1}^0 &= P_5 \oplus RK2_1 \oplus WK0_1 \oplus F0(P_{(0,1,2,3)}, RK0)_1 \\
I2_{S0}^1 &= P_6 \oplus RK2_2 \oplus WK0_2 \oplus F0(P_{(0,1,2,3)}, RK0)_2 \\
I2_{S1}^1 &= P_7 \oplus RK2_3 \oplus WK0_3 \oplus F0(P_{(0,1,2,3)}, RK0)_3
\end{aligned}
\tag{8}
$$

In order to obtain $RK2 \oplus WK0$, a structure similar to Figure 4 is essential. However, as seen in Equation 8, an additional term $F0$ is present. In order to get the required results, this term has to be cancelled. This is done by taking timing profiles for a known $RK2 \oplus WK0$ keeping $P_{(0,1,2,3)}$ constant, and using the $RK0$ determined in the first step of the attack. The timing profiles for the unknown $RK2 \oplus WK0$ is then taken maintaining the same constants. Correlating the two timing profile will cancel out the effect of the first round $F0$ revealing $RK2 \oplus WK0$.

The indices to the table look-ups in function $F1$ in the second round is given by Equation 9. $RK3 \oplus WK1$ can be derived in a manner similar to $RK2 \oplus WK0$ by taking timing profiles keeping $P_{(8,9,10,11)}$ constant, and using the predetermined value of $RK1$.

$$I2^2_{S1} = P_{12} \oplus RK3_0 \oplus WK1_0 \oplus F1(P_{(8,9,10,11)}, RK1)_0$$
$$I2^2_{S0} = P_{13} \oplus RK3_1 \oplus WK1_1 \oplus F1(P_{(8,9,10,11)}, RK1)_1$$
$$I2^3_{S1} = P_{14} \oplus RK3_2 \oplus WK1_2 \oplus F1(P_{(8,9,10,11)}, RK1)_2$$
$$I2^3_{S0} = P_{15} \oplus RK3_3 \oplus WK1_3 \oplus F1(P_{(8,9,10,11)}, RK1)_3$$

(9)

5.4 Determining $RK4$ and $RK5$

From the Clefia structure (Figure 1), it can be noted that the input to the third round $F0$ function, X0-3, is $(Y0-2 \oplus P_{(8,9,10,11)})$. The value of Y0-2 can be computed for a given plaintext from the values of $RK0$ and $WK0 \oplus RK2$ that were determined in the previous steps of the attack. If $P_{(8,9,10,11)}$ are kept constant, then we have a structure similar to Figure 4, with Y0-2 as the input and $RK4$ as the key. Thus a correlation of a known $RK4$ with the unknown $RK4$ will give the desired result.

In a similar manner $RK5$ can be determined by keeping $P_{(0,1,2,3)}$ constant and obtaining the timing profile for $RK5$ with respect to Y1-2.

5.5 Computing $RK2$ and $RK3$

In the key expansion algorithm, if $i = 0$ then $T = RK_0|RK_1|RK_2|RK_3$, and

$$T = L \oplus (CON_{24}|CON_{25}|CON_{26}|CON_{27})$$

64 bits of the key dependent constant L can be computed using the values of RK_0 and RK_1, which were determined in the first stage of the attack.

$$(L_0|L_1) = (RK_0|RK_1) \oplus (CON_{24}|CON_{25}) \tag{10}$$

The double swap operation on L places 57 known bits of L in the lower bit positions. Let the new L after double swap be denoted by L'.

$$L'_{(0\cdots56)} = L_{(7\cdots63)} \tag{11}$$

Again, in the key expansion algorithm, if $i = 1$, then $T = RK_4|RK_5|RK_6|RK_7$. This is represented in equation form as

$$T = L' \oplus (CON_{28}|CON_{29}|CON_{30}|CON_{31}) \oplus (WK_0|WK_1|WK_2|WK_3) \tag{12}$$

Therefore,

$$WK0|WK1_{(0\cdots24)} = L'(0\cdots56) \oplus (CON_{28}|CON_{29(0\cdots25)}) \oplus (RK_4|RK_5) \tag{13}$$

Thus it is possible to ascertain $WK0$ and 25 bits of $WK1$. $WK0 \oplus RK2$ and $WK1 \oplus RK3$ have been determined in the second step of the attack. With the knowledge of $WK0$ and $WK1_{0\cdots24}$ the whole of $RK2$ and 25 bits of $RK3$ can be determined.

6   Results

A $3GHz$ Intel Core 2 Duo processor with processor number $E8400$ and specification number $SLB9J$ was used for the attack. The processor had $32MB$ L1 data cache, configured in 8 way associativity and 64 bytes in each cache line. Sony's reference code for Clefia was attacked using a non networked implementation as was done in [12]. Moreover an assumption was made that each encryption starts with a clean cache.

In order that the correct key appears with sufficiently good correlation, a minimum of 2^{21} samples needs to be taken. However for Clefia, the result of a step in the attack depends on the correctness of the previous steps, therefore the timing profiles need to be strongly correlated. In our experiments we built timing profiles using 2^{24} samples for the known key and 2^{22} samples for the unknown key, this most often resulted in the right key having a correlation value at least twice that of any other key. The complexity for obtaining all the keys $RK0$, $RK1$, $RK2 \oplus WK0$, $RK3 \oplus WK1$, $RK4$, and $RK5$ required $2^{26.64}$ encryptions. In addition to this, 2^7 possible options for $RK3$ are to be explored, as 25 out of 32 bits of $RK3$ were discovered.

Consider the Clefia key : *12 11 20 09 24 d6 8f a4 fa 45 89 13 7f 0c 26 09.* Table 1 shows the top 5 correlation results for each round key along with their correlation value within braces. It can be seen that the correct result is strongly correlated compared to other keys and can easily be distinguished. This shows that cache timing attacks are possible even on cipher implementations that use small tables. This contradicts the popular belief that only cipher implementations with large table are vulnerable to cache attacks [11,18].

Table 1. Correlation Results for the Attacked Key

Key Byte	Correct Key	Obtained Correlation results (with correlation value)
$RK0_0$	0a	**0a***(884.6)*, 6b*(469.7)*, 5f*(368.3)*, 20*(357.3)*, ef*(263.7)* ...
$RK0_1$	96	**96***(1853.4)*, 7b*(438.0)*, bc*(437.5)*, 4a*(366.7)*, ee*(361.8)* ...
$RK0_2$	c1	**c1***(1942.1)*, 93*(672.7)*, 98*(598.3)*, f9*(573.2)*, 24*(559.5)* ...
$RK0_3$	68	**68***(1680.3)*, 23*(415.9)*, 9e*(414.1)*, 6e*(398.9)*, 99*(375.9)* ...
$RK1_0$	ac	**ac***(4077.6)*, c1*(853.4)*, 11*(843.5)*, 7c*(650.9)*, 71*(639.2)* ...
$RK1_1$	b0	**b0***(3089.8)*, 73*(740.8)*, 07*(716.7)*, f7*(677.1)*, 01*(658.1)* ...
$RK1_2$	7a	**7a***(5721.0)*, 0a*(1539.1)*, 08*(1230.2)*, 6f*(967.8)*, 05*(931.3)* ...
$RK1_3$	79	**79***(5361.6)*, fb*(1202.0)*, 2b*(1196.0)*, 9a*(1106.6)*, 07*(1007.9)* ...
$RK2_0 \oplus WK0_0$	6e	**6e***(4194.0)*, f9*(1526.2)*, 07*(1491.3)*, 96*(1257.9)*, 2f*(1194.3)* ...
$RK2_1 \oplus WK0_1$	b1	**b1***(4344.0)*, 39*(1197.5)*, 59*(1056.8)*, ad*(980.9)*, f9*(926.9)* ...
$RK2_2 \oplus WK0_2$	9f	**9f***(2662.0)*, d4*(1327.9)*, 68*(1071.1)*, 1b*(1056.2)*, 89*(1000.0)* ...
$RK2_3 \oplus WK0_3$	61	**61***(6840.2)*, 0a*(1783.8)*, 97*(1587.3)*, 8c*(1555.8)*, 87*(1491.4)* ...
$RK3_0 \oplus WK1_0$	c3	**c3***(21042.8)*, 38*(4644.1)*, ea*(4429.9)*, d3*(3999.8)*, 01*(3995.1)* ...
$RK3_1 \oplus WK1_1$	85	**85***(34258.3)*, 7d*(8695.1)*, 83*(8576.9)*, 3a*(8401.3)*, ec*(8318.5)* ...
$RK3_2 \oplus WK1_2$	2c	**2c***(37773.2)*, 3c*(7131.3)*, 28*(6804.1)*, 05*(6263.3)*, b5*(5906.3)* ...
$RK3_3 \oplus WK1_3$	4d	**4d***(37267.7)*, f2*(9903.8)*, 33*(9625.5)*, 24*(8613.2)*, cf*(8595.4)* ...
$RK4_0$	3f	**3f***(1321.7)*, 5e*(535.2)*, 39*(328.4)*, 83*(302.9)*, 04*(276.8)* ...
$RK4_1$	df	**df***(2066.6)*, e6*(510.7)*, 69*(463.6)*, ad*(441.4)*, 5a*(399.3)* ...
$RK4_2$	d7	**d7***(1367.1)*, 09*(331.8)*, b5*(322.7)*, be*(319.7)*, 39*(313.6)* ...
$RK4_3$	5f	**5f***(1530.7)*, cb*(409.6)*, ae*(392.4)*, 1e*(373.3)*, ee*(365.7)* ...
$RK5_0$	66	**66***(5056.0)*, 4e*(938.3)*, 01*(924.7)*, b6*(886.9)*, 05*(870.5)* ...
$RK5_1$	97	**97***(3577.9)*, e4*(795.5)*, 54*(794.1)*, 42*(674.6)*, 4a*(633.2)* ...
$RK5_2$	2d	**2d***(6248.1)*, 5f*(1313.0)*, 5d*(1274.5)*, b3*(1180.1)*, 38*(1134.4)* ...
$RK5_3$	4e	**4e***(6405.4)*, cc*(1363.7)*, 8d*(1173.4)*, ff*(1147.6)*, 1a*(1140.9)* ...

7 Conclusion

The paper presents a cache timing attack on the Clefia cipher, which is designed by Sony Corporation. Contrary to the belief that ciphers implemented with smaller tables are more resistant against cache timing attacks, we show that they still leak information about the key, and can be attacked with the same complexity required for a cipher implemented with large tables. Detailed analysis and experimentation have been performed on an Intel Core 2 Duo processor to establish that the Clefia key can be revealed using $2^{26.64}$ encryptions.

References

1. Aciiçmez, O., Koç, Ç.K.: Trace-Driven Cache Attacks on AES (Short Paper). In: Ning, P., Qing, S., Li, N. (eds.) ICICS 2006. LNCS, vol. 4307, pp. 112–121. Springer, Heidelberg (2006)
2. Aciiçmez, O., Schindler, W., Koç, Ç.K.: Cache Based Remote Timing Attack on the AES. In: Abe, M. (ed.) CT-RSA 2007. LNCS, vol. 4377, pp. 271–286. Springer, Heidelberg (2006)
3. Bernstein, D.J.: Cache-timing attacks on AES. Technical report (2005)
4. Bertoni, G., Zaccaria, V., Breveglieri, L., Monchiero, M., Palermo, G.: AES Power Attack Based on Induced Cache Miss and Countermeasure. In: ITCC, vol. (1), pp. 586–591. IEEE Computer Society, Los Alamitos (2005)
5. Bonneau, J., Mironov, I.: Cache-Collision Timing Attacks Against AES. In: Goubin, L., Matsui, M. (eds.) CHES 2006. LNCS, vol. 4249, pp. 201–215. Springer, Heidelberg (2006)
6. Brumley, D., Boneh, D.: Remote timing attacks are practical. Computer Networks 48(5), 701–716 (2005)
7. Chari, S., Rao, J.R., Rohatgi, P.: Template attacks. In: Kaliski Jr., B.S., Koç, Ç.K., Paar, C. (eds.) CHES 2002. LNCS, vol. 2523, pp. 13–28. Springer, Heidelberg (2003)
8. Fog, A.: The Microarchitecture of Intel and AMD CPU's, An Optimization Guide for Assembly Programmers and Compiler Makers (2009)
9. Fournier, J.J.A., Tunstall, M.: Cache Based Power Analysis Attacks on AES. In: Batten, L.M., Safavi-Naini, R. (eds.) ACISP 2006. LNCS, vol. 4058, pp. 17–28. Springer, Heidelberg (2006)
10. Intel Corporation. Intel 64 and IA-32 Architectures Optimization Reference Manual (2009)
11. Kelsey, J., Schneier, B., Wagner, D., Hall, C.: Side Channel Cryptanalysis of Product Ciphers. J. Comput. Secur. 8(2,3), 141–158 (2000)
12. Neve, M.: Cache-based Vulnerabilities and SPAM Analysis. PhD thesis, Thesis in Applied Science, UCL (2006)
13. Neve, M., Seifert, J.-P.: Advances on Access-Driven Cache Attacks on AES. In: Biham, E., Youssef, A.M. (eds.) SAC 2006. LNCS, vol. 4356, pp. 147–162. Springer, Heidelberg (2007)

14. Neve, M., Seifert, J.-P., Wang, Z.: A Refined Look at Bernstein's AES Side-Channel Analysis. In: Lin, F.-C., Lee, D.-T., Lin, B.-S., Shieh, S., Jajodia, S. (eds.) ASI-ACCS, p. 369. ACM, New York (2006)
15. Osvik, D.A., Shamir, A., Tromer, E.: Cache attacks and countermeasures: The case of aes. In: Pointcheval, D. (ed.) CT-RSA 2006. LNCS, vol. 3860, pp. 1–20. Springer, Heidelberg (2006)
16. Page, D.: Theoretical Use of Cache Memory as a Cryptanalytic Side-Channel (2002)
17. Sony Corporation. The 128-bit Blockcipher CLEFIA: Algorithm Specification (2007)
18. Tsunoo, Y., Saito, T., Suzaki, T., Shigeri, M., Miyauchi, H.: Cryptanalysis of DES Implemented on Computers with Cache. In: Walter, C.D., Koç, Ç.K., Paar, C. (eds.) CHES 2003. LNCS, vol. 2779, pp. 62–76. Springer, Heidelberg (2003)
19. Tsunoo, Y., Tsujihara, E., Minematsu, K., Miyauchi, H.: Cryptanalysis of Block Ciphers Implemented on Computers with Cache. In: International Symposium on Information Theory and Its Applications, pp. 803–806 (2002)
20. Tsunoo, Y., Tsujihara, E., Shigeri, M., Kubo, H., Minematsu, K.: Improving Cache Attacks by Considering Cipher Structure. Int. J. Inf. Sec. 5(3), 166–176 (2006)

Appendix

Experimental Setup

In order to test our results, we used a $3GHz$ Intel Core 2 Duo platform with $32KB$ L1 cache, $1GB$ RAM running Linux (Ubuntu 8.04). The code was compiled with $gcc - 4.2.4$ with the $O3$ optimization enabled.

In the first phase, data was collected for the known key. This took around 1300 seconds with each step requiring 2^{24} iterations. The second phase, which is the actual attack on the unknown key, was done with randomly generated secret keys. 1000 tests were done with different random keys. Data collection for each test took 312.5 seconds on an average with a standard deviation of 4.01 seconds. Table 2 shows few of the sample keys which were attacked, along with the time required.

In the 1000 tests that were conducted, in more than half of the cases all the 16 bytes of the key were successfully obtained. For the remaining cases, there were error in mostly 1 byte and in few cases in 2 bytes.

Table 2. Sample Timing for Determining Unknown Keys

Random Key	Running Time (seconds)
48 61 44 66 26 21 12 47 47 53 56 91 31 75 27 16	314.7
35 31 28 74 94 57 50 57 82 28 99 37 87 01 49 21	309.3
49 85 50 32 61 14 79 09 53 19 13 92 20 67 35 26	310.6
53 68 46 82 72 48 72 03 86 87 44 18 37 41 83 74	318.4
42 89 94 63 15 24 77 22 04 56 82 02 21 04 92 20	310.7
05 98 65 05 11 60 68 27 06 03 19 07 41 17 93 03	310.0
56 43 17 14 80 14 35 89 92 92 20 43 21 50 54 91	308.8
28 67 10 98 19 58 40 19 64 78 39 09 11 45 59 58	309.6
03 48 04 68 40 79 59 37 70 32 61 02 38 94 44 68	318.3
69 43 65 74 38 40 62 87 15 91 29 57 54 72 02 12	310.8
⋮	⋮

Software Oriented Stream Ciphers Based upon FCSRs in Diversified Mode[*]

Thierry P. Berger[1], Marine Minier[2], and Benjamin Pousse[1]

[1] XLIM (UMR CNRS 6172), Université de Limoges
23 avenue Albert Thomas, 87060 Limoges Cedex - France
thierry.berger@unilim.fr, benjamin.pousse@xlim.fr
[2] Lyon University - CITI Laboratory - INSA de Lyon
6, avenue des arts, 69621 Villeurbanne Cedex - France
marine.minier@insa-lyon.fr

Abstract. Feedback with Carry Shift Registers (FCSRs) are a promising alternative to LFSRs for the design of stream ciphers. Most of the FCSR-based stream ciphers use a Galois representation. In this case, the control of a single bit leads to the control of the feedback values. This particular property was exploited to break most of the existing proposals. Recently, a new representation for FCSR automata was presented. This representation is a generalization of both Galois and Fibonacci representations. In this representation any cell can be used for a feedback for any other cell. With a good choice for the parameters, those new FCSR automatas are resistant to the previous attacks and the internal diffusion is significantly improved. Using this approach, a new hardware oriented version of F-FCSR has been recently proposed.

In this paper, we propose a new design for FCSRs suitable for software applications. Using this approach, we present a new version of X-FCSR-128 suitable for software applications which is really efficient in software.

Keywords: stream cipher, FCSRs, software design, cryptanalysis.

Introduction

Whereas a LFSR performs x-or additions, a FCSR performs additions with carries leading to a non-linear transition function. Any cell of the main register of such automaton computes the 2-adic expansion of some 2-adic rational number p/q. This can be used to prove several interesting properties such as proven period, non-degenerated states, good statistical properties [14,18,12]. The high non-linearity of the FCSR transition function provides an intrinsic resistance to algebraic attacks and seems to prevent correlation attacks. There exists a hardware efficient family of stream ciphers based on FCSRs: the filtered FCSR or F-FCSR [3,1,4,6]. In these ciphers, the internal state of the FCSR is filtered by a linear function to provide from 1 to 16 output bits at each iteration. There

---

[*] This work was partially supported by the French National Agency of Research: ANR-06-SETI-013.

B. Roy and N. Sendrier (Eds.): INDOCRYPT 2009, LNCS 5922, pp. 119–135, 2009.
© Springer-Verlag Berlin Heidelberg 2009

exists also a software version of FCSR-based stream cipher: the X-FCSR family, which uses an extraction function based on block cipher design [5].

FCSRs are usually represented using either the Fibonacci representation or the Galois one [13]. In the Fibonacci representation, all the feedback bits influence a single cell. In the Galois mode, a single feedback bit influences all the carry cells. As noticed in [11], the Fibonacci mode is not suitable for cryptographic applications since most of cells have a linear transition function. The Galois mode has a quadratic transition function which seems better for cryptographic applications. However, and as noticed in [16], due to the dependency between the carries and the single feedback bit, a Galois FCSR could be easily linearized during some clocks. This weakness that happens with a non-negligible probability, leads to LFSRization of FCSRs and to powerful attacks against all the versions of stream ciphers based on FCSRs [28].

In [2], Arnault et al. have responded to this attack by introducing a new FCSR representation called ring representation. In this case, any cell can be used as a feedback bit for any other cell. The attacks introduced in [16,28] are thus totally discarded when this new mode is used. Many other advantages have also appeared with this new representation if the automaton is well-chosen. For hardware implementations, the new representation leads to a better path in the circuit (equal to 1) and a better fan-out (equal to 2). The circuit is naturally more resistant to side-channel attacks, and the diffusion of differences is quicker in the circuit. This leads to new versions of F-FCSR stream ciphers designed for hardware applications.

In this paper, we are interested in software applications. In Section 1 we introduce the ring representation for FCSR, and give a particular realization suitable for software utilization. This realization uses a specific circuit which acts essentially on 32-bits words. An equivalent design can naturally be constructed for 64-bits architectures. As an application in Section 2, we present a new version of X-FCSR-128 efficient in software.

1   FCSR Automata in Ring Representation

A FCSR as defined in [14,18] is composed of a binary main register and of a carry register but contrary to LFSRs the performed operations are no more x-ors over $\mathbb{F}_2$ but additions with carry in the set of 2-adic integers $\mathbb{Z}_2$ (i.e. the set of power series: $\sum_{i=0}^{\infty} s_i 2^i$, $s_i \in \{0,1\}$). Note that each cell of the main register produces a sequence $S = (s_n)_{n \in \mathbb{N}}$ that is eventually periodic if and only if there exist two numbers p and q in $\mathbb{Z}$, q odd, such that $s = p/q$. This sequence is strictly periodic if and only if $pq \leq 0$ and $|p| \leq |q|$. The period of S is the order of 2 modulo q, i.e., the smallest integer P such that $2^P \equiv 1 \pmod{q}$. The period satisfies $P \leq |q| - 1$. If q is prime and if $P = |q| - 1$, the sequence S is called an ℓ-sequence. ℓ-sequences have many proved properties that could be compared to the ones of m-sequences: known period, good statistical properties, fast generation, etc.

Usually, FCSRs are represented using Galois or Fibonacci representations. In this section, we generalize this approach via matrix definition. Those results hold also for LFSRs where in this last case all the operations are x-ors over $\mathbb{F}_2$ and no more additions with carry in the set $\mathbb{Z}_2$.

1.1 Diversified FCSR Automata

The following definition is an extension of the one given in [2] and introduces the update function of an FCSR via a matrix definition.

Definition 1. *A (diversified or ring) FCSR is an automaton composed of a main shift register of n binary cells $m = (m_0, \ldots, m_{n-1})$, and a carry register of n integer cells $c = (c_0, \ldots, c_{n-1})$. It is updated using the following relations:*

$$\begin{cases} m(t+1) = Tm(t) + c(t) \mod 2 \\ c(t+1) = Tm(t) + c(t) \div 2 \end{cases} \tag{1}$$

where T is a $n \times n$ matrix with coefficients 0 or 1 in $\mathbb{Z}$, called transition matrix. Note that $\div 2$ is the traditional expression: $X \div 2 = \frac{X - (X \mod 2)}{2}$.

The main property of such automaton is the following:

Theorem 1 ([2] Theorem 1). *The series $M_i(t)$ observed in the cells of the main register are 2-adic expansion of p_i/q with $p_i \in \mathbb{Z}$ and with $q = \det(I - 2T)$.*

The T transition matrix completely defines the ring FCSR as shown in Theorem 1, the only common element for all ring FCSRs is the over-diagonal full of 1 (to guarantee the shifted elementary structure) whereas some other 1s appear in the rest of the matrix as shown below:

$$\begin{pmatrix} * & 1 & & & & \\ & * & 1 & & (*) & \\ & & * & 1 & & \\ & & & \ddots & \ddots & \\ & (*) & & & * & 1 \\ 1 & & & & & * \end{pmatrix}$$

The Galois and Fibonacci representations are special cases of ring FCSR with the following respective transition matrices T_G and T_F:

$$T_G = \begin{pmatrix} d_0 & 1 & & & & \\ d_1 & 0 & 1 & & (0) & \\ d_2 & & 0 & 1 & & \\ \vdots & & & \ddots & \ddots & \\ d_{n-2} & (0) & & & 0 & 1 \\ 1 & & & & & 0 \end{pmatrix} \qquad T_F = \begin{pmatrix} 0 & 1 & & & & \\ & 0 & 1 & & (0) & \\ & & 0 & 1 & & \\ & (0) & & \ddots & \ddots & \\ & & & & 0 & 1 \\ 1 & d_{n-2} & \ldots & d_2 & d_1 & d_0 \end{pmatrix}$$

where $(d_0, \ldots, d_{n-1})$ is the binary representation of $d = (1 + |q|)/2$ and represents all the non null carry bits.

1.2 Main Advantages of Diversified FCSRs

The diversified FCSRs have many advantages detailed below (the reader can refer to [2] for more details).

- Any cell can be used for a feedback for any other cell. Under the condition that the FCSR automaton is sufficiently diversified, this property ensures a full resistance to the recent attacks on previous FCSR stream ciphers [16]. Sufficiently diversified means that there are a significant number of rows and columns with more than one 1.
- The critical path (i.e. a shorter longest path) of the corresponding hardware circuit is given by the row a_i of the matrix T with the largest number of 1. It is equal to
  $\max(\lceil \log_2(w_H(a_i)) \rceil)$.
- the fan-out is given by the column b_i with the largest number of 1. This is the number of 1 of this column. By limiting the number of 1 per row and per column, it is possible to design ring FCSR with a critical path of 1 and a fan-out of 2.
- The diffusion of differences is generally quicker than for the Galois or Fibonacci representations. It could be computed as the diameter Di of the graph associated to the transition matrix T. Typically this value is close to $n/4$ instead of n in the Galois or Fibonacci cases.

However, for a given connection integer q, to build a good transition matrix T and thus a good diversified FCSR seems to be really difficult. The authors of [2] obtained good diversified FCSRs trying randomly many T matrix under the following constraints: the ring structure, a critical path of 1, a fan-out of 2, a small diameter, and a connecting integer q such that the automaton generates maximal ℓ-sequences (see [2] for more details).

1.3 Design of a Diversified FCSR for Software Applications

The question is now how to find a way to build a software oriented FCSR. First, let us introduce previous works done for the LFSR case to optimize software performances.

LFSR case. The LFSR case has been widely studied in the literature especially for pseudo random number generation. A LFSR is simply an automaton composed of a main register with n binary cells $m = (m_0, \ldots, m_{n-1})$ with an update function that could be written with our generalized representation $m(t+1) = Tm(t)$ over $\mathbb{F}_2$ where T is a $n \times n$ matrix over $\mathbb{F}_2$. As previously studied for the FCSR case, T could be a random matrix or could be written to lead to a Galois or a Fibonacci representation.

Firstly, the Generalized Feedback Shift Registers were introduced in [19] to increase the throughput. The main idea here was to parallelize w Fibonacci LFSRs. More formally, the corresponding matrix of such a construction is:

$$T = \begin{pmatrix} 0 & I_w & & & & \\ & 0 & I_w & & (0) & \\ & & 0 & I_w & & \\ & (0) & & \ddots & & \ddots \\ & & & & 0 & I_w \\ I_w & a_{n-2}I_w & \ldots & a_2I_w & a_1I_w & a_0I_w \end{pmatrix}$$

where I_w represents the $w \times w$ identity matrix over $\mathbb{F}_2$ and where the a_i for i in $[0, .., n-2]$ are binary coefficients. The T matrix could be seen at bit level but also at w-bits word level, each bit of the w-bits word is in fact one bit of the internal state of one Fibonacci LFSR among the w LFSRs.

In [27], Roggeman applied the previous definition to LFSRs to obtain the Generalized Linear Feedback Shift Registers but in this case the matrix T is always defined at bit level. In 1992, Matsumoto in [21] generalized this last approach considering no more LFSR at bit level but at vector bit level (called word). This representation is called Twisted Generalized Feedback Shift Register whereas the same kind of architecture was also described in [22] and called the Mersenne Twister. In those approaches, the considered LFSRs are in Fibonacci mode seen at word level with a unique linear feedback. The corresponding matrices are of the form:

$$T = \begin{pmatrix} 0 & I_w & & & \\ & 0 & I_w & (0) & \\ & & 0 & I_w & \\ & (0) & & \ddots & \ddots \\ & & & 0 & I_w \\ A & & I_w & & 0 \end{pmatrix}$$

where I_w represents the $w \times w$ identity matrix and where A is a $w \times w$ binary matrix. In this case, the matrix is defined over $\mathbb{F}_2$ but could also be seen at w-bits word level. This is the first generalization of LFSR specially designed for software applications due to the word oriented structure.

The last generalization was introduced in 1995 in [23] with the Multiple-Recursive Matrix Method and used in the Xorshift Generators described in [20]. In this case, the used LFSRs are in Fibonacci mode with several linear feedbacks. The matrix representation is:

$$T = \begin{pmatrix} 0 & I_w & & & & \\ & 0 & I_w & & (0) & \\ & & 0 & I_w & & \\ & (0) & & \ddots & & \ddots \\ & & & & 0 & I_w \\ A_1 & A_2 & A_3 & \ldots & A_{r-2} & A_{r-1} & A_r \end{pmatrix}$$

where I_w is the identity matrix and where the matrices A_i are software efficient transformations such as right or left shifts at word level or word rotation. The main advantage of this representation is its word-oriented software efficiency but it also preserves all the good LFSRs properties if the underlying polynomial is primitive. As for the FCSR case and as shown in [20], this polynomial could be directly computed using the matrix representation: $P(X) = \det(I - XT)$. Indeed, the word oriented representation does not change the intrinsic LFSRs properties.

First, applying our ring representation to word oriented LFSR case leads to ring LFSRs with high diffusion efficient for software applications. However, our main goal consists in considering the same kind of representations but no more for LFSRs but for FCSRs to improve usual software performances of FCSRs and to guarantee a non-linear update function.

FCSR case. We could directly apply the results of the previous subsection to build software efficient ring FCSRs working on $\mathbb{Z}_2$ instead of $\mathbb{F}_2$. Those FCSRs would be completely determined by the choice of the matrix T. The willing size of words k is determined by software constraints and could be equal to 8, 16, 32 or 64 bits according the targeted architecture. As seen in the LFSR case, the ring structure of the transition matrix T need to be defined in a "word-ring" way. We consider a FCSR and its associated transition matrix defined on k-bits word. In this case, the main register of the FCSR could be seen as r k-bits words $M_0, ..., M_{r-1}$ with feedback words $C_0, \cdots, C_{r-1}$, the $r \times r$ matrix T represents the new word oriented structure:

$$
\begin{pmatrix}
I_k & & R_0 & & \\
R_1 & I_k & & (0) & \\
 & I_k & R_2 & & \\
 & (0) & & \ddots & \\
 & & R_{r-2} & & I_k \\
I_k & R_{r-1} & & &
\end{pmatrix}
$$

where I_k denotes the identity matrix of binary size $k \times k$ at word level whereas the R_i represent particular word oriented operations on k-bits words such as shifts or rotations for software efficiency.

As noticed in [24] and in [20] for the LFSR case, the simplest operations that could be easily represented at word level are right and left shift and rotations. Following this approach, the FCSR chosen in the stream cipher described in this paper follows this rule. More precisely, if left and right shift are used at word level, they could be represented by the following matrices SL and SR for a k-bits word:

$$
\begin{cases}
SL \cdot (x_0, \cdots, x_{k-1})^t = (x_1, \cdots, x_{k-1}, 0)^t \\
SR \cdot (x_0, \cdots, x_{k-1})^t = (0, x_0, x_1, \cdots, x_{k-2})^t
\end{cases}
$$

whereas the rotations could be represented by the following matrices RL and RR at bit level:

$$
\begin{cases}
RL \cdot (x_0, \cdots, x_{k-1})^t = (x_{k-1}, x_0, x_1, \cdots, x_{k-2})^t \\
RR \cdot (x_0, \cdots, x_{k-1})^t = (x_1, \cdots, x_{k-1}, x_0)^t
\end{cases}
$$

In this case, the R_i parameters of the matrix T are equal to SL^a, SR^b, RL^c or RR^d where a, b, c and d represent the desired shifts or rotations. Thus for example, the following matrix T for $k = 8$ bits word

$$T = \begin{pmatrix} 0 & I & SR^4 & 0 & 0 \\ 0 & 0 & I & 0 & 0 \\ 0 & 0 & 0 & I & 0 \\ 0 & 0 & 0 & SL^1 & I \\ I & SL^2 & 0 & 0 & 0 \end{pmatrix}$$

completely defines the associated FCSR represented in Figure 1 with $n = 40$ and $k = 8$.

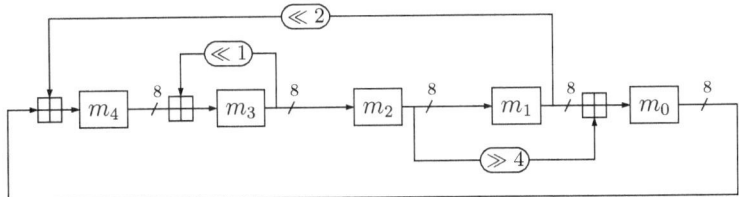

Fig. 1. A diversified FCSR with efficient software design

The corresponding q value could be directly computed using the formula given in Theorem 1 and is equal to -1375125994241. This number is prime but has not a maximal order. Thus the corresponding FCSR does not produce ℓ-sequences, but is efficient in software due to the word oriented structure.

Software performances of word ring FCSRs. Word ring FCSRs are of course more efficient than classical ring FCSRs. More precisely, when clocking a classical ring FCSR, a vector containing the feedback values is built. Each feedback is computed in this case applying a mask and shifting the vector until the correct bit places. Once done, the content of the main register is shifted using rotations with carries. Then, the additions with carries are performed. For a word ring FCSR, feedbacks are computed first. This step is faster than for classical ring FCSRs due to the use of shifts and rotations. Then, the content of the main register is shifted at word level using only memory copies. And the last step is the same: additions with carries.

Of course, the first and the second steps are more efficient when word ring FCSRs are used. The gain between the two structures is about 200 cycles/clock for a 256-bits ring FCSR (25 cycles for clocking one time a word ring FCSR whereas one clock requires 221 cycles for a classical ring FCSR). It is directly linked with the first step that requires about twice as many operations for a classical ring FCSR.

We are thus particularly interested in using the word ring FCSR for designing a stream cipher efficient in software. In [2], the proposed versions of F-FCSR using classical ring FCSR have been specially design for hardware purpose. Using the software efficient ring representation previously presented, it is really easy to directly adapt the F-FCSR construction for software applications. This construction called F-FCSR-32 supports key of length 128 bits and an IV with the same length. It is composed of a 256-bits word ring FCSR (composed of 16 32-bits words for the main register and also for the carry register) described in Figure 2 in Appendix B. This FCSR is built on the elementary operations "shifts" and "rotations". F-FCSR-32 outputs 32 bits (a word) at each clock using the following linear extraction function:

$$Output_{32}(t) = M_1(t) \oplus (M_2(t) >>> 3) \oplus (M_4(t) >>> 5) \oplus (M_5(t) >>> 7)$$
$$\oplus (M_6(t) >>> 11) \oplus (M_7(t) >>> 13) \oplus (M_8(t) >>> 17)$$
$$\oplus (M_9(t) >>> 19) \oplus (M_{10}(t) >>> 23)$$

where $(M_0(t), \cdots, M_{15}(t))$ represents the 16 32-bits words of the main register. We do not detail here the key and IV injection that are very simple and could be easily deduced from [2]. We have integrated F-FCSR-32 to the eSTREAM benchmark suite ([10]) and have obtained the results summed up in Table 1 when comparing F-FCSR-32 with the AES in counter mode and with F-FCSR-16 v3 (see [2]) that uses a classical ring FCSR. As anyone can notice, the gain between F-FCSR-32 and F-FCSR-16 is rather important due to the dedicated design of F-FCSR-32.

Table 1. Performances computed using the eSTREAM benchmark suite

Algorithm	Keystream speed	cycles/byte 40 bytes	576 bytes	1500 bytes	cycles/key Key setup	cycles/IV IV setup
F-FCSR-32	11.92	104.23	18.05	14.63	13.42	3717.39
AES-CTR (128)	12.4	18.27	12.64	12.52	336.54	16.73
F-FCSR-16 v3	130.81	1682.56	243.12	170.56	43.44	61719.00

2   Design of X-FCSR-128 v.2

In [28], Paul Stankovski, Martin Hell and Thomas Johansson presented an efficient attack against X-FCSR-256. This attack is less efficient against X-FCSR-128 even if its theoretical bound is under the exhaustive key search (see [5] for the specifications of the various versions of X-FCSRs). Those two attacks are based on the same principles that the one described in [16] and always exploit the dependencies between the feedback bit and all the other carries bits leading to LFSRization of FCSRs. In this section, a new version of X-FCSR-128 is proposed that completely discards the previous attacks using always a well-chosen ring FCSR.

As done for the other X-FCSR versions, the design exploits particular operations (S-boxes and linear operations) coming from the block cipher world to improve the efficiency of the structure as done in the previous version of X-FCSR-128. X-FCSR takes a 128-bit length secret key K and a public initialization vector IV of bitlength ranging from 64 and 128 as inputs and outputs 128 bits at each clock. The X-FCSR primitive is composed of one FCSR of bitlength 512 seen as 16 32-bits words.

2.1 FCSR Choice

The core of the design is composed of one single ring FCSR of length $n = 512$ bits acting on 32-bits words. It can be represented at word level with the 16×16 transition matrix T given in Figure 2 in Appendix B.

   This ring FCSR has been randomly chosen using algorithm 1 described in Appendix A. It verifies the following condition: $\log_2(q) \geq n$, $q = \det(I - 2T)$ is prime, the order of 2 modulo q is equal to $|q| - 1$ and is maximal to ensure that the outputs are composed of ℓ-sequences. Moreover, q has been chosen such that the diameter Di is sufficiently small to ensure a quick diffusion. The q value is given in Appendix B.

   At time t, we denote by $M(t) = (M_0(t), \cdots, M_{15}(t))$ the content of the main register composed of 16 32-bits words and by $C(t) = (C_0(t), \cdots, C_{15}(t))$ the content of the carry register.

2.2 Extraction Function

The extraction function is constituted of a function $Round_{128}$ (already used for X-FCSR-128 v1) working on 128-bit input/output words, and a memory of 16 128-bit words which stores the output of $Round_{128}$ that will be used 16 iterations later. More formally, the full extraction function works as follows:

- compute the 128-bit word $Y(t) = (Y_0(t)|| \cdots ||Y_3(t))$ with:

$$Y_0(t) = M_0(t) \oplus (M_4(t) >>> 11) \oplus (M_8(t) >>> 19) \oplus (M_{12}(t) >>> 23)$$
$$Y_1(t) = M_1(t) \oplus (M_5(t) >>> 11) \oplus (M_9(t) >>> 19) \oplus (M_{13}(t) >>> 23)$$
$$Y_2(t) = M_2(t) \oplus (M_6(t) >>> 11) \oplus (M_{10}(t) >>> 19) \oplus (M_{14}(t) >>> 23)$$
$$Y_3(t) = M_3(t) \oplus (M_7(t) >>> 11) \oplus (M_{11}(t) >>> 19) \oplus (M_{15}(t) >>> 23)$$

- Thus, compute $Z(t) = Round_{128}(Y(t))$.
- Store $Z(t)$ in memory (keep it during 16 iterations).
- Output the 128-bit word $Output_{128}(t) = Y(t) \oplus Z(t - 16)$.

$Round_{128}$ (already described in [5]) is a one-round function from $\{0, 1\}^{128}$ into itself: $Round_{128}(a) = Mix_{128}(SR_{128}(SL_{128}(a)))$. If the 128-bit word a is represented at byte level by a 4×4 matrix M where each byte is represented by the word $a_{i,j}$ with $0 \leq i, j \leq 3$, then the function $Round_{128}$ works as follows:

- $SL_{128}()$ is a S-box layer applied at byte level: each byte $a_{i,j}$ is transformed into an other byte $b_{i,j}$ with $b_{i,j} = S(a_{i,j})$ where S is the S-box given in Appendix C chosen for its good properties (see Appendix C for the details).
- The $SR_{128}()$ operation corresponds with the AES ShiftRows() operation.

– the $Mix_{128}()$ operation is the one used in [15] computed using the operations over $GF(2)$. More precisely for each column of a, we compute $\forall j, 0 \leq j \leq 3$:

$$
Mix_{128}
\begin{pmatrix}
a_{0,j} \\
a_{1,j} \\
a_{2,j} \\
a_{3,j}
\end{pmatrix}
=
\begin{pmatrix}
a_{3,j} \oplus a_{0,j} \oplus a_{1,j} \\
a_{0,j} \oplus a_{1,j} \oplus a_{2,j} \\
a_{1,j} \oplus a_{2,j} \oplus a_{3,j} \\
a_{2,j} \oplus a_{3,j} \oplus a_{0,j}
\end{pmatrix}.
$$

Even if this function is not fully optimal for a diffusion purpose, its branch number is however equal to 4 and its computation is significantly faster than the MixColumns of the AES: Mix_{128} can be computed with only six 32-bit bitwise XORs.

2.3 Key and IV Injection

As shown in [2], using a ring FCSR leads to a new problem: we can not ensure the entropy of the automaton. In the case of F-FCSR with Galois or Fibonacci structure, zeroing the content of the carry register prevents collisions (i.e. one point of the states graph with two preimages) and warrants a constant entropy. This is no more the case for ring FCSRs because no more structure exists in the adjacency matrix of T. In this last case, an attacker could search direct collisions and time memory data trade-off attacks for collisions search built upon entropy loss. As noticed in [2], the first attack becomes an instance of the subset sum problem, with a complexity equals to $2^{n/2}$ (if the carries are zeroes) or $2^{3n/2}$ (in the general case). With $n = 512$, this attack is more expensive than the exhaustive search for a 128-bit key. For the second attack and as noticed in [2] and in [26], considering that the key and IV setup are random function, the induced entropy loss is about 1 bit, so considering an initial entropy equal to n bits, the entropy after the key and IV setup is close to $n - 1$ bits. Thus, with $n = 512$, this attack is discarded.

Thus, under all those conditions, we have decided to build the key and IV setup as previously done for X-FCSR-128 v1 and as previously done in [7]. We have split the initialization process into two steps to speed up the IV injection:

– The key schedule, which processes the secret key but does not depend on the IV.
– The IV injection, which uses the output of the key schedule and the IV.

This initializes the stream cipher internal state. Then, the IV setup for a fixed key is less expensive than a complete key setup, improving the common design since changing the IV is more frequent than changing the secret key.

Key schedule. The key setup process used here corresponds to a classical key schedule of a block cipher and is inspired by the one of the DES due to its good resistance against related key attacks [9] and against related key rectangle attacks [17]. The key expansion produces 25×128-bit subkeys denoted $K_0, \cdots, K_{24}$. It works as follow:

- the subkey K_0 is deduced from the master key: $K_0 = (Round_{128}(K))_{<<<23}$ where $_{<<<j}$ denotes a 128-bit left rotation of j positions.
- then K_i is deduced from K_{i-1}: $K_i = Round_{128}((K_{i-1})_{<<<j})$ where $j = 23$ if $i \equiv 3 \bmod 4$ and $j = 11$ otherwise.

IV injection. If necessary the IV is extended to a 128-bit word by adding leading zeros. Then, this value is considered as a plaintext that is first enciphered 12 times using the $Round_{128}$ function and then xored with the subkey of the round K_j. More precisely, the process is the following if we denote by V_i the ciphertext after the round i:

$$V_0 = IV \oplus K_0; \qquad \text{for } i \text{ from 1 to 24 do } V_i = Round_{128}(V_{i-1}) \oplus K_i.$$

Then, the values V_{12}, V_{16} V_{20} and V_{24} are used to initialize the main register of the FCSR as follows: $M(0) = (V_{12}||V_{20}, V_{16}||V_{24})$ whereas the carry register is initialized to zero. The FCSR is then clocked 16 times to fill the sixteen memory registers of the extraction function.

2.4   Security

Design rational of X-FCSR-128. In [8], the authors prove that the key and IV setup (parametrized by the key K) of an IV-dependent stream cipher must be a pseudo-random function to obtain a sufficient security level. We have tried to achieve this goal designing our key and IV setup as a block cipher using the round function $Round_{128}$. Under those conditions, the secret key of the cipher cannot be easily recovered from the initial state of the generator. Once the initial state is recovered, the attacker is only able to generate the output sequence for a particular key and a given IV. Moreover, the use of the new ring FCSR construction leads to some possible collisions after the key and IV setup due to a loose of entropy. In X-FCSR-128v.2, to find a collision becomes as difficult as a block cipher cryptanalysis (i.e. inverting a block cipher without knowing the key).

The use of an FCSR in the ring mode prevents the attack described in [16] and [11] to happen: the LFSRization of Galois FCSRs is no more possible as previously described.

The round function $Round_{128}$ has been chosen for its good diffusion and non-linear properties. The use of 16 memory registers is a good compromise between a better security and a limited performance cost and introduces high non-linearity in the outputs. Even if there exists dependencies between $Y(t)$ and $Y(t-16)$, it is computationally infeasible to determine the values of the main registers at time $t + 16$ from the values at time t using the transition function.

Resistance against known attacks. The good statistical properties (period, balanced sequences and so on) of our constructions are provided by the 2-adic properties.

We do not discuss here resistance against traditional attacks such as guess and determine attacks, algebraic attacks, etc. Some details about this can be found in [4]. Resistance against TMDTO attacks was considered in Section 2.3. As noticed in [2], recent attacks against FCSRs and F-FCSRs described in [16] and [11] are also discarded. More precisely, the attack of [16,28] against F-FCSR using Galois representation exploits the control of the feedback bit over all the other feedbacks. This relation is no more true in the case of a ring FCSR: the linear behavior is observed with probability about 2^{-t} during t clocks for a Galois FCSR whereas it becomes $2^{-t \cdot k}$ for k feedbacks for a ring FCSR. Moreover, the attack described in [11] could only be applied when a Fibonacci FCSR is used. Moreover, correlation and fast correlation attacks are also really difficult to mount due to the inherent non-linearity of a ring FCSR and due to the design of the *Round* function.

To sum up all the previous analyses, the ring representation prevents all the previous known attacks from happening because previous dependencies that produce weaknesses for Fibonacci and Galois modes do no more occur due to the intrinsic new definition of ring FCSRs. More precisely, in the ring case, the dependencies are no more localized at special places but are completely distributed through all the cells leading to a better non-linear behavior. We think that traditional attacks against stream cipher that exploit linear relations built upon the transition function are not realistic in our case. Thus, wanting to cryptanalyse ring FCSRs leads to create new attacks exploiting other sorts of relations.

2.5   Performances

We have integrated the X-FCSR-128 v2 stream cipher to the eSTREAM benchmark suite ([10]). We gather the results in Table 2 comparing the different stream ciphers based on FCSRs with the AES in counter mode and the software oriented stream ciphers of eSTREAM. The gain provided by word ring FCSR design (X-FCSR-128 v2 and F-FCSR-32) is important when comparing with F-FCSR-16 v3 that uses a classical ring FCSR. X-FCSR-128 v2 has really good performances compared with the AES-CTR and is also the fastest stream cipher based on FCSRs for software applications.

Table 2. Performances computed using the eSTREAM benchmark suite

		cycles/byte			cycles/key	cycles/IV
Algorithm	Keystream speed	40 bytes	576 bytes	1500 bytes	Key setup	IV setup
Rabbit	2.35	17.94	3.06	2.81	412.04	347.57
HC-128	2.38	502.69	36.84	15.70	54.40	19851.28
Salsa 20/12	2.56	12.67	2.80	3.02	27.27	16.47
Sosemanuk	3.43	25.16	6.07	5.08	793.65	651.30
X-FCSR-128 v2	7.54	114.70	16.16	11.59	1478.94	3968.20
X-FCSR-128 v1	11.21	78.37	15.61	15.17	1256.70	2954.88
F-FCSR-32	11.92	104.23	18.05	14.63	13.42	3717.39
AES-CTR (128)	12.4	18.27	12.64	12.52	336.54	16.73
F-FCSR-16 v3	130.81	1682.56	243.12	170.56	43.44	61719.00

3   Conclusion

We have proposed in this paper a new stream cipher construction based upon ring FCSR designed for software applications. The new ring FCSR representation was introduced in [2] and prevent all the previous known attacks against FCSRs and F-FCSRs to happen due to a reduced dependency between particular bits (the feedback one and the carries). Moreover, software efficiency is reached due to the use of a new word oriented representation of FCSRs leading to really simple and efficient implementations. As shown in the performances results presented along this paper, the software performances of the new stream ciphers are really good.

References

1. Arnault, F., Berger, T.P., Lauradoux, C.: The FCSR: primitive specification and supporting documentation. In: ECRYPT - Network of Excellence in Cryptology, Call for stream Cipher Primitives (2005), http://www.ecrypt.eu.org/stream/
2. Arnault, F., Berger, T.P., Lauradoux, C., Minier, M., Pousse, B.: A new approach for FCSRs. In: Jacobson Jr., M.J., Rijmen, V., Safavi-Naini, R. (eds.) SAC 2009. LNCS, vol. 5867, pp. 433–448. Springer, Heidelberg (2009), http://eprint.iacr.org/2009/167
3. Arnault, F., Berger, T.P.: F-FCSR: Design of a new class of stream ciphers. In: Gilbert, H., Handschuh, H. (eds.) FSE 2005. LNCS, vol. 3557, pp. 83–97. Springer, Heidelberg (2005)
4. Arnault, F., Berger, T.P., Lauradoux, C.: Update on F-FCSR Stream Cipher. In: ECRYPT - Network of Excellence in Cryptology, Call for stream Cipher Primitives - Phase 2 (2006), http://www.ecrypt.eu.org/stream/
5. Arnault, F., Berger, T.P., Lauradoux, C., Minier, M.: X-FCSR - a new software oriented stream cipher based upon FCSRs. In: Srinathan, K., Rangan, C.P., Yung, M. (eds.) INDOCRYPT 2007. LNCS, vol. 4859, pp. 341–350. Springer, Heidelberg (2007)
6. Arnault, F., Berger, T.P., Minier, M.: Some Results on FCSR Automata With Applications to the Security of FCSR-Based Pseudorandom Generators. IEEE Transactions on Information Theory 54(2), 836–840 (2008)
7. Berbain, C., Billet, O., Canteaut, A., Courtois, N., Gilbert, H., Goubin, L., Gouget, A., Granboulan, L., Lauradoux, C., Minier, M., Pornin, T., Sibert, H.: Sosemanuk: a fast oriented software-oriented stream cipher. In: ECRYPT - Network of Excellence in Cryptology, Call for stream Cipher Primitives - Phase 2 (2005), http://www.ecrypt.eu.org/stream/
8. Berbain, C., Gilbert, H.: On the security of IV dependent stream ciphers. In: Biryukov, A. (ed.) FSE 2007. LNCS, vol. 4593, pp. 254–273. Springer, Heidelberg (2007)
9. Biham, E.: New types of cryptoanalytic attacks using related keys (extended abstract). In: Rueppel, R.A. (ed.) EUROCRYPT 1992. LNCS, vol. 658, pp. 398–409. Springer, Heidelberg (1993)
10. de Cannières, C.: eSTREAM Optimized Code HOWTO (2005), http://www.ecrypt.eu.org/stream/perf

11. Fischer, S., Meier, W., Stegemann, D.: Equivalent Representations of the F-FCSR Keystream Generator. In: ECRYPT Network of Excellence - SASC Workshop, pp. 87–94 (2008), http://www.ecrypt.eu.org/stvl/sasc2008/
12. Goresky, M., Klapper, A.: Arithmetic crosscorrelations of feedback with carry shift register sequences. IEEE Transactions on Information Theory 43(4), 1342–1345 (1997)
13. Goresky, M., Klapper, A.: Fibonacci and Galois representations of feedback-with-carry shift registers. IEEE Transactions on Information Theory 48(11), 2826–2836 (2002)
14. Goresky, M., Klapper, A.: Periodicity and distribution properties of combined fcsr sequences. In: Gong, G., Helleseth, T., Song, H.-Y., Yang, K. (eds.) SETA 2006. LNCS, vol. 4086, pp. 334–341. Springer, Heidelberg (2006)
15. Granboulan, L., Levieil, É., Piret, G.: Pseudorandom permutation families over abelian groups. In: Robshaw, M.J.B. (ed.) FSE 2006. LNCS, vol. 4047, pp. 57–77. Springer, Heidelberg (2006)
16. Hell, M., Johansson, T.: Breaking the F-FCSR-H stream cipher in real time. In: Pieprzyk, J. (ed.) ASIACRYPT 2008. LNCS, vol. 5350, pp. 557–569. Springer, Heidelberg (2008)
17. Hong, S., Kim, J., Lee, S., Preneel, B.: Related-key rectangle attacks on reduced versions of SHACAL-1 and AES-192. In: Gilbert, H., Handschuh, H. (eds.) FSE 2005. LNCS, vol. 3557, pp. 368–383. Springer, Heidelberg (2005)
18. Klapper, A., Goresky, M.: 2-adic shift registers. In: Anderson, R. (ed.) FSE 1993. LNCS, vol. 809, pp. 174–178. Springer, Heidelberg (1994)
19. Lewis, T.G., Payne, W.H.: Generalized feedback shift register pseudorandom number algorithm. J. ACM 20(3), 456–468 (1973)
20. Marsaglia, G.: Xorshift RNGs. Journal of Statistical Software 8(14), 1–6 (2003)
21. Matsumoto, M., Kurita, Y.: Twisted GFSR generators. ACM Trans. Model. Comput. Simul. 2(3), 179–194 (1992)
22. Matsumoto, M., Nishimura, T.: Mersenne twister: A 623-dimensionally equidistributed uniform pseudo-random number generator. ACM Trans. Model. Comput. Simul. 8(1), 3–30 (1998)
23. Niederreiter, H.: The multiple-recursive matrix method for pseudorandom number generation. Finite Fields Appl. 1(1), 3–30 (1995)
24. Panneton, F., L'Ecuyer, P.: On the xorshift random number generators. ACM Trans. Model. Comput. Simul. 15(4), 346–361 (2005)
25. Rivest, R.: The RC4 encryption algorithm. RSA Data Security (1992)
26. Röck, A.: Stream ciphers using a random update function: Study of the entropy of the inner state. In: Vaudenay, S. (ed.) AFRICACRYPT 2008. LNCS, vol. 5023, pp. 258–275. Springer, Heidelberg (2008)
27. Roggeman, Y.: Varying feedback shift registers. In: Quisquater, J.-J., Vandewalle, J. (eds.) EUROCRYPT 1989. LNCS, vol. 434, pp. 670–679. Springer, Heidelberg (1990)
28. Stankovski, P., Hell, M., Johansson, T.: An efficient state recovery attack on X-FCSR-256. In: Dunkelman, O. (ed.) FSE 2009. LNCS, vol. 5665, pp. 23–37. Springer, Heidelberg (2009)

A   Random Algorithms to Pick Good qs

Algorithm 1. Algorithm to pick randomly a FCSR with a good software design

    Input: k the word size. n the length of the FCSR to seek with $k|n$.
           $f \leq n/k$ the number of word-feedbacks to place.
    Output: A transition matrix T define by block with a cost of f shift and
             word-adder operations and such that its feedback polynomial is
             primitive of degree n.

  begin
    repeat

$$T \leftarrow (t_{i,j})_{0 \leq i,j < n/k} \text{ where } t_{i,j} = \begin{cases} I_k & \text{if } j \equiv i+1 \mod n/k \\ 0 & \text{otherwise} \end{cases};$$

$$From \leftarrow Random([0, n/k]^f);$$
$$To \leftarrow Random([0, n/k]^f);$$
$$Shift \leftarrow Random\left(([-k/2, k/2] \setminus \{0\})^f \right);$$

      for $l \leftarrow 0$ **to** $f - 1$ **do**

$$t_{To[l],From[l]} \leftarrow t_{To[l],From[l]} + \begin{cases} SL^{Shift[l]} & \text{if } Shift[l] > 0 \\ SR^{-Shift[l]} & \text{otherwise} \end{cases};$$

$$q \leftarrow \det(I - 2 \cdot T);$$
    until q *is primitive* ;
    return T;
  end

This algorithm picks random word-feedbacks positions and shift values, and computes the associated feedback polynomial.

B   The T Matrix

The following matrix T is the one used in X-FCSR-128 v2. It is a 32 bit word 16×16 matrix:

$$\begin{pmatrix}
0 & I & 0 & 0 & 0 & 0 & 0 & 0 & 0 & 0 & 0 & 0 & 0 & 0 & 0 & 0 \\
0 & 0 & I & SL^{10} & 0 & 0 & 0 & 0 & 0 & 0 & 0 & 0 & 0 & 0 & 0 & 0 \\
0 & 0 & 0 & I & 0 & SR^7 & 0 & 0 & 0 & 0 & 0 & 0 & 0 & 0 & 0 & 0 \\
0 & 0 & 0 & 0 & I & 0 & 0 & 0 & 0 & 0 & 0 & 0 & 0 & 0 & 0 & 0 \\
0 & 0 & 0 & 0 & 0 & I & 0 & 0 & 0 & 0 & 0 & 0 & I & 0 & 0 & 0 \\
0 & 0 & SL^7 & 0 & 0 & 0 & I & 0 & 0 & 0 & 0 & 0 & 0 & 0 & 0 & 0 \\
0 & SR^{10} & 0 & 0 & 0 & 0 & 0 & I & 0 & 0 & 0 & 0 & 0 & 0 & 0 & 0 \\
0 & 0 & 0 & 0 & 0 & 0 & 0 & 0 & I & 0 & 0 & 0 & 0 & SR^6 & 0 & 0 \\
0 & 0 & 0 & 0 & 0 & 0 & 0 & 0 & 0 & I & 0 & SL^3 & 0 & 0 & 0 & 0 \\
0 & 0 & 0 & 0 & 0 & 0 & 0 & 0 & 0 & 0 & I & 0 & 0 & 0 & SL^8 & 0 \\
SR^4 & 0 & 0 & 0 & 0 & 0 & 0 & 0 & 0 & 0 & 0 & I & 0 & 0 & 0 & 0 \\
0 & 0 & 0 & 0 & 0 & 0 & 0 & 0 & 0 & 0 & 0 & 0 & I & 0 & 0 & 0 \\
0 & 0 & 0 & 0 & 0 & 0 & 0 & 0 & 0 & 0 & 0 & 0 & 0 & I & 0 & 0 \\
0 & 0 & 0 & 0 & 0 & 0 & 0 & 0 & 0 & 0 & 0 & 0 & 0 & 0 & I & 0 \\
0 & 0 & 0 & 0 & 0 & 0 & 0 & 0 & 0 & 0 & 0 & 0 & 0 & 0 & 0 & I \\
I & 0 & 0 & 0 & 0 & 0 & 0 & 0 & 0 & 0 & 0 & 0 & 0 & 0 & 0 & 0
\end{pmatrix}$$

Fig. 2. The matrix used in X-FCSR-128 v2

This matrix has 9 feedbacks words. $|q|$ is equal in hexadecimal notation to

$0x1$ $596D$ $63EF$ $BD0C$ $36EF$ $147B$ $FB44$ $F791$ $685C$ $A2BB$ 4832
$E9B7$ $A021$ $291E$ $421C$ $C180$ $0C67$ $473D$ $5FF9$ $ED90$ $818A$ $2B1D$
$AB66$ $9AB9$ $7B9A$ $AA50$ $2A32$ $D3F4$ $7E30$ $96FE$ 1382 8781 $121D$

The diameter Di of the graph corresponding with the matrix T is $Di = 37$. We also have $\log_2(q) = 512.432238323$ and 2 is primitive $\bmod\ q$ leading to a maximal order and producing ℓ-sequences.

C   The S-Box S

We have designed our S-box using the requirements defined in [15] except that all the steps are performed here on $GF(2)^8$ into itself. The S-box is given in tab. 3 in hexadecimal notation. It has been chosen to have a good resistance against differential and linear cryptanalyses, an high algebraic degree, an high nonlinear order and a degree between inputs and outputs equal to three. The S-box was generated using the key schedule algorithm KSA of RC4 ([25]) algorithm initialized with a key of 26 bytes length equal to the string "To design our streamcipher". Then after 48574 iterations of this algorithm, we obtain the following S-box:

Table 3. the chosen S-box

52	c3	45	ce	9	cf	a8	f8	fd	ab	b8	6d	95	2	31	8
56	f4	cb	40	61	7	12	39	62	bb	ef	5d	3a	a9	fb	2c
78	ad	75	77	10	ca	55	66	9e	65	7b	9b	13	76	c7	1c
71	d	18	3f	50	6c	28	64	a3	b7	d0	be	e6	9c	b9	94
fc	bc	a1	cd	3b	48	4c	99	cc	3e	79	24	f2	c1	da	d8
de	f	e8	67	2e	16	53	c4	9d	57	c0	4f	f0	d6	4e	81
69	8a	ae	f9	8b	ee	43	3d	e4	23	97	68	b	32	e1	b2
ec	e9	59	1	c2	34	b5	1f	2a	29	d7	d5	b0	96	11	c6
7d	91	2d	72	8f	87	1d	e7	ba	19	25	15	5e	d9	98	70
4a	ed	51	a6	88	86	58	c5	5f	eb	49	0	ff	1b	2f	6a
82	1a	af	9f	8c	6b	a2	f1	e	5	7f	73	92	3c	f5	d2
54	14	ac	83	20	90	c9	22	fa	74	d3	27	37	38	a5	33
85	6	4	b3	e2	5b	e3	47	1e	8d	4b	b1	36	46	bd	35
dc	6e	d1	7c	a7	41	c	42	a0	aa	26	5a	4d	e5	5c	80
21	3	f3	63	ea	44	dd	89	8e	7e	b4	30	a	a4	60	f6
bf	fe	e0	f7	c8	d4	9a	db	84	7a	6f	2b	b6	17	93	df

The chosen S-box has the following properties:

- The best differential trail is $DP(S) = \text{Max}_{a,b \in (GF(2)^8)^2 \setminus \{0,0\}} \#\{x | S(x \oplus a) \oplus S(x) = b\} = 10$.
- The best linear trail is $LP(S) = \text{Max}_{a,b \in (GF(2)^8)^2 \setminus \{0,0\}} |\#\{x | a \cdot S(x) = b \cdot x\} - 128| = 32$.
- The algebraic degree is equal to 7.
- The non-linear order is equal to 6.
- The degree between inputs and outputs is equal to three. There is no equation of degree two.

On the Symmetric Negabent Boolean Functions

Sumanta Sarkar

Projet SECRET, INRIA-Rocquencourt
Domaine de Voluceau, B. P. 105,
78153 Le Chesnay Cedex France
Sumanta.Sarkar@inria.fr

Abstract. We study the negabent Boolean functions which are symmetric. The Boolean function which has equal absolute spectral values under the nega-Hadamard transform is called a negabent function. For a bent function, the absolute spectral values are the same under the Hadamard-Walsh transform. Unlike bent functions, negabent functions can exist on odd number of variables. Moreover, all the affine functions are negabent.

We prove that a symmetric Boolean function is negabent if and only if it is affine.

Keywords: Boolean function, symmetric Boolean function, negabent function, nega-Hadamard transform, bent function, Krawtchouk polynomial.

1 Introduction

In 1976, Rothaus [6] introduced the class of bent functions which have the maximum possible distance from the affine functions. These functions exist only on even number of variables and an n-variable bent function can have the degree at most $\frac{n}{2}$. If a function is bent, then all the spectral values under the Hadamard-Walsh transformation are equal in absolute term.

Negabent functions have been studied in [2,8,3,4]. These functions have equal absolute spectral values under the nega-Hadamard transform. In [2] some classes of Boolean functions which are both bent and negabent have been identified. In another paper [8], construction of negabent functions has been shown in the class of Maiorana-McFarland bent functions. It is interesting to note that all the affine functions (both odd and even variables) are negabent [2, Proposition 1].

Symmetric Boolean functions form a subclass of Boolean functions. A Boolean function is called symmetric if the outputs of the function are the same for all the inputs of the same weight. In [7], Savicky showed that a symmetric function is bent if and only if it is quadratic.

In this paper, we study the symmetric negabent Boolean functions. We prove that a symmetric function is negabent if and only if it is affine. This also tells that there is no symmetric Boolean function on even number of variables which is both bent and negabent.

B. Roy and N. Sendrier (Eds.): INDOCRYPT 2009, LNCS 5922, pp. 136–143, 2009.
© Springer-Verlag Berlin Heidelberg 2009

2   Preliminary

Let $\mathbb{F}_2^n$ be the vector space formed by the 2^n binary n-tuples. An n-variable Boolean function is a mapping $f : \mathbb{F}_2^n \mapsto \mathbb{F}_2$. Let $\mathcal{B}_n$ denote the set of all n-variable Boolean functions. The Hamming weight of a binary string S is the number of 1's in S and it is denoted by $wt(S)$. A function $f \in \mathcal{B}_n$ can be written as a function of $x_1, \ldots, x_n$ variables as follows

$$f(x_1, x_2, \ldots, x_n) = \bigoplus_{a=(a_1,\ldots,a_n)\in\mathbb{F}_2^n} \mu_a(\prod_{i=1}^{n} x_i^{a_i}), \text{ where } \mu_a \in \mathbb{F}_2.$$

This is called the algebraic normal form (ANF) of f. The algebraic degree, $\deg(f)$, of f is defined as $\max_{a\in\mathbb{F}_2^n}\{wt(a) : \mu_a \neq 0\}$.

Let $\lambda = (\lambda_1, \ldots, \lambda_n)$ and $x = (x_1, \ldots, x_n)$ be two elements in $\mathbb{F}_2^n$ and $\lambda \cdot x = \lambda_1 x_1 \oplus \ldots \oplus \lambda_n x_n$. Then the Hadamard-Walsh transform value of $f \in \mathcal{B}_n$ at λ is given by

$$\mathcal{H}_f(\lambda) = \frac{1}{2^{\frac{n}{2}}} \sum_{x\in\mathbb{F}_2^n} (-1)^{f(x)\oplus\lambda\cdot x}. \tag{1}$$

The function f is called bent if $|\mathcal{H}_f(\lambda)| = 1$ for all $\lambda \in \mathbb{F}_2^n$. For $a \in \mathbb{F}_2^n$, the autocorrelation spectrum value of f is computed as

$$\tau_a = \sum_{x\in\mathbb{F}_2^n} (-1)^{f(x)\oplus f(x\oplus y)}.$$

A Boolean function f is bent if and only for all $a \in \mathbb{F}_2^n$ the value τ_a is 0. The value τ_a is referred to as the periodic autocorrelation coefficient of f at $a \in \mathbb{F}_2^n$ [2].

The nega-Hadamard transform value of $f \in \mathcal{B}_n$ at $\lambda \in \mathbb{F}_2^n$ is given by

$$\mathcal{N}_f(\lambda) = \frac{1}{2^{\frac{n}{2}}} \sum_{x\in\mathbb{F}_2^n} (-1)^{f(x)\oplus\lambda\cdot x} i^{wt(x)}, \tag{2}$$

where $i = \sqrt{-1}$. A function $f \in \mathcal{B}_n$ is called negabent [2] if $|\mathcal{N}_f(\lambda)| = 1$ for all $\lambda \in \mathbb{F}_2^n$. We state the following result from [8, Lemma 1].

Lemma 1. [8] For any $\lambda \in \mathbb{F}_2^n$,

$$\sum_{x\in\mathbb{F}_2^n} (-1)^{\lambda\cdot x} i^{wt(x)} = 2^{\frac{n}{2}} \omega^n i^{-wt(\lambda)},$$

where $\omega = \frac{1}{\sqrt{2}} + \frac{i}{\sqrt{2}}$ is a primitive 8-th root of unity.

Note that $|\omega| = 1$ and $|i| = 1$. Then the following result directly follows from this lemma which is also stated in [2,8].

Proposition 1. All the affine functions are negabent.

Therefore, negabent functions exist on odd number of variables too.

The negaperiodic autocorrelation coefficient [2] of $f \in \mathcal{B}_n$ is defined as,

$$n_a = \sum_{x \in \mathbb{F}_2} (-1)^{f(x) \oplus f(x \oplus a)} (-1)^{wt(x \oplus a)} (-1)^{x \cdot a}.$$

In [2, Theorem 2], it was shown that a Boolean function is negabent if and only if all its negaperiodic autocorrelation values are 0 which is analogous to the result concerning the autocorrelation values of a bent function. Therefore, functions which are both bent and negabent are interesting and these functions exist in deed. For instance ([2, Example 2]), $x_1 x_2 \oplus x_2 x_3 \oplus x_3 x_4$ is both bent and negabent function on 4-variables.

A Boolean function $f \in \mathcal{B}_n$ is said to be symmetric if $f(x) = f(y)$ for all $x, y \in \mathbb{F}_2^n$ such that $wt(x) = wt(y)$. Therefore, f can be represented by the $(n+1)$-length binary string $[c_0, c_1, \ldots, c_n]$, called the value vector of f, where c_i is the output of f at an input of weight i. If one monomial of degree k is present in the ANF of a symmetric function, then all the other monomials of degree k are also present.

A Boolean function with degree at most 1 is called affine. For each n, there are exactly 4 affine n-variable symmetric Boolean functions. They are as follows.

(i) $f(x_1, \ldots, x_n) = 0$ for all $(x_1, \ldots, x_n) \in \mathbb{F}_2^n$.
(ii) $f(x_1, \ldots, x_n) = 1$ for all $(x_1, \ldots, x_n) \in \mathbb{F}_2^n$.
(iii) $f(x_1, \ldots, x_n) = x_1 \oplus x_2 \oplus \ldots \oplus x_n$.
(iv) $f(x_1, \ldots, x_n) = 1 \oplus x_1 \oplus x_2 \oplus \ldots \oplus x_n$.

If $[c_0, \ldots, c_n]$ is the value vector of the symmetric function $f(x_1, \ldots, x_n) = x_1 \oplus x_2 \oplus \ldots \oplus x_n$, then $c_i = \begin{cases} 0 \text{ if } i = 0 \mod 2 \\ 1 \text{ if } i = 1 \mod 2 \end{cases}$.

Savicky [7] showed that the Hadamard-Walsh coefficients of a symmetric Boolean function are directly related to the Krawtchouk polynomials as follows. Let f be an n-variable symmetric Boolean function with the value vector $[c_0, \ldots, c_n]$. From (1) we get,

$$\mathcal{H}_f(\lambda) = \frac{1}{2^{\frac{n}{2}}} \sum_{k=0}^{n} (-1)^{c_k} \sum_{wt(x)=k} (-1)^{\lambda \cdot x}. \tag{3}$$

We have,

$$\sum_{wt(x)=k} (-1)^{\lambda \cdot x} = \sum_{j=0}^{k} (-1)^j \binom{wt(\lambda)}{j} \binom{n - wt(\lambda)}{k - j} = P_k(wt(\lambda), n), \tag{4}$$

where $P_k(wt(\lambda), n)$ is the Krawtchouk polynomial [1]. Therefore,

$$\mathcal{H}_f(\lambda) = \frac{1}{2^{\frac{n}{2}}} \sum_{k=0}^{n} (-1)^{c_k} P_k(wt(\lambda), n).$$

Thus, $\mathcal{H}_f(\lambda') = \mathcal{H}_f(\lambda'')$ if $wt(\lambda') = wt(\lambda'')$, for $\lambda', \lambda'' \in \mathbb{F}_2^n$. Therefore, the values of $\mathcal{H}_f(\lambda)$ for different weights of λ's describe the whole spectrum. Note that the Krawtchouk polynomials have the following generating function

$$(1 - z)^j (1 + z)^{n-j} = \sum_{k=0}^{n} P_k(j, n) z^k. \tag{5}$$

Using the above results, Savicky proved that a symmetric function is bent if and only if it is of degree 2.

3   Symmetric Negabent Function

In this section, we study the symmetric negabent functions. Let f be an n-variable symmetric Boolean function whose value vector is $[c_0, \ldots, c_n]$. Then from (2) we get

$$\mathcal{N}_f(\lambda) = \frac{1}{2^{\frac{n}{2}}} \sum_{k=0}^{n} (-1)^{c_k} i^k \sum_{wt(x)=k} (-1)^{\lambda \cdot x}.$$

Then using (4), we have

$$\mathcal{N}_f(\lambda) = \frac{1}{2^{\frac{n}{2}}} \sum_{k=0}^{n} (-1)^{c_k} i^k P_k(wt(\lambda), n). \tag{6}$$

This also implies that $\mathcal{N}_f(\lambda') = \mathcal{N}_f(\lambda'')$ if $wt(\lambda') = wt(\lambda'')$, for $\lambda', \lambda'' \in \mathbb{F}_2^n$.

In the following lemma, we state the values of $P_k(j, n)$ for all $k = 0, 1, \ldots, n$ and for some values of j which we require later.

Lemma 2. *Let k be an integer in the range $\{0, 1, \ldots, n\}$.*

(i) Let n be even, then $P_k(\frac{n}{2}, n) = \begin{cases} 0 & \text{if } k \text{ odd} \\ (-1)^l \binom{\frac{n}{2}}{l} & \text{if } k = 2l \end{cases}$.

(ii) Let n be even, then

$$P_k(\frac{n}{2} - 1, n) = \begin{cases} 2(-1)^l \binom{\frac{n}{2}-1}{l} & \text{if } k = 2l + 1 \\ (-1)^l [\binom{\frac{n}{2}-1}{l} - \binom{\frac{n}{2}-1}{l-1}] & \text{if } k = 2l \end{cases}.$$

(iii) Let n be odd, then

$$P_k(\frac{n-1}{2}, n) = \begin{cases} (-1)^l \binom{\frac{n-1}{2}}{l} & \text{if } k = 2l + 1 \\ (-1)^l \binom{\frac{n-1}{2}}{l} & \text{if } k = 2l \end{cases}.$$

Proof. The proofs of (i), (ii) and (iii) follow from (5) by replacing $j = \frac{n}{2}, j = \frac{n}{2} - 1$ and $j = \frac{n-1}{2}$ respectively.

The following lemmas are useful in proving our main result.

Lemma 3. *Let n be even and f be an n-variable symmetric Boolean function with the value vector $[c_0, \ldots, c_n]$. If $|\mathcal{N}_f(\lambda)| = 1$ for a $\lambda \in \mathbb{F}_2^n$ such that $wt(\lambda) = \frac{n}{2}$, then $c_{2r+2} = c_{2r}$ holds for all integer $r = 0, \ldots, \frac{n}{2} - 1$.*

Proof. From (6) we have

$$\mathcal{N}_f(\lambda) = \frac{1}{2^{\frac{n}{2}}} \left[\sum_{l=0}^{\frac{n}{2}} (-1)^{c_{2l}} i^{2l} P_{2l}\left(\frac{n}{2}, n\right) + \sum_{l=0}^{\frac{n}{2}-1} (-1)^{c_{2l+1}} i^{2l+1} P_{2l+1}\left(\frac{n}{2}, n\right) \right].$$

Then using (i) of Lemma 2, we get

$$\mathcal{N}_f(\lambda) = \frac{1}{2^{\frac{n}{2}}} [\sum_{l=0}^{\frac{n}{2}} (-1)^{c_{2l}} (-1)^l (-1)^l \binom{\frac{n}{2}}{l} + 0]$$

$$= \frac{1}{2^{\frac{n}{2}}} \sum_{l=0}^{\frac{n}{2}} (-1)^{c_{2l}} \binom{\frac{n}{2}}{l}. \tag{7}$$

If we assume that $c_{2r+2} = c_{2r} \oplus 1$ holds for some $r \in \{0, \ldots, \frac{n}{2} - 1\}$, then (7) contains two nonzero integers of opposite sign. In that case,

$$|\mathcal{N}_f(\lambda)| < \frac{1}{2^{\frac{n}{2}}} \sum_{l=0}^{\frac{n}{2}} \binom{\frac{n}{2}}{l} = \frac{1}{2^{\frac{n}{2}}} \cdot 2^{\frac{n}{2}} = 1.$$

This contradicts that $|\mathcal{N}_f(\lambda)| = 1$ for $wt(\lambda) = \frac{n}{2}$. Therefore, $c_{2r+2} = c_{2r}$ holds for all integer $r = 0, \ldots, \frac{n}{2} - 1$.

Lemma 4. *Let n be even and f be an n-variable symmetric Boolean function with the value vector $[c_0, \ldots, c_n]$. Let $|\mathcal{N}_f(\beta)| = 1$ for a $\beta \in \mathbb{F}_2^n$ such that $wt(\beta) = \frac{n}{2}$. If $|\mathcal{N}_f(\lambda)| = 1$ for a $\lambda \in \mathbb{F}_2^n$ such that $wt(\lambda) = \frac{n}{2} - 1$, then $c_{2r+3} = c_{2r+1}$ holds for all integer $r = 0, \ldots, \frac{n}{2} - 2$.*

Proof. From (6) we have

$$\mathcal{N}_f(\lambda) = \frac{1}{2^{\frac{n}{2}}} [\sum_{l=0}^{\frac{n}{2}} (-1)^{c_{2l}} i^{2l} P_{2l}\left(\frac{n}{2} - 1, n\right) + \sum_{l=0}^{\frac{n}{2}-1} (-1)^{c_{2l+1}} i^{2l+1} P_{2l+1}\left(\frac{n}{2} - 1, n\right)].$$

Since $|\mathcal{N}_f(\beta)| = 1$, where $wt(\beta) = \frac{n}{2}$, then by Lemma 3, we have $c_{2r+2} = c_{2r}$ for all $r = 0, \ldots, \frac{n}{2} - 1$. Therefore,

$$\mathcal{N}_f(\lambda) = \frac{1}{2^{\frac{n}{2}}} [(-1)^{c_0} \sum_{l=0}^{\frac{n}{2}} i^{2l} P_{2l}\left(\frac{n}{2} - 1, n\right) + \sum_{l=0}^{\frac{n}{2}-1} (-1)^{c_{2l+1}} i^{2l+1} P_{2l+1}\left(\frac{n}{2} - 1, n\right)].$$

Then using (ii) of Lemma 2 we get

$$\mathcal{N}_f(\lambda) = \frac{1}{2^{\frac{n}{2}}} [(-1)^{c_0} \sum_{l=0}^{\frac{n}{2}} (-1)^l (-1)^l \left[\binom{\frac{n}{2}-1}{l} - \binom{\frac{n}{2}-1}{l-1} \right]$$

$$+ \sum_{l=0}^{\frac{n}{2}-1} (-1)^{c_{2l+1}} i (-1)^l 2 (-1)^l \binom{\frac{n}{2}-1}{l}]$$

$$= \frac{1}{2^{\frac{n}{2}}} [(-1)^{c_0} \sum_{l=0}^{\frac{n}{2}} \left[\binom{\frac{n}{2}-1}{l} - \binom{\frac{n}{2}-1}{l-1} \right] + 2i \sum_{l=0}^{\frac{n}{2}-1} (-1)^{c_{2l+1}} \binom{\frac{n}{2}-1}{l}]$$

$$= \frac{1}{2^{\frac{n}{2}}} [0 + 2i \sum_{l=0}^{\frac{n}{2}-1} (-1)^{c_{2l+1}} \binom{\frac{n}{2}-1}{l}]. \tag{8}$$

If we assume that $c_{2r+3} = c_{2r+1} \oplus 1$ holds for some $r \in \{0, \ldots, \frac{n}{2} - 2\}$, then in the sum $\sum_{l=0}^{\frac{n}{2}-1} (-1)^{c_{2l+1}} \binom{\frac{n}{2}-1}{l}$, there are two nonzero integers with opposite sign. Therefore,

$$|\mathcal{N}_f(\lambda)| < \frac{1}{2^{\frac{n}{2}}} \cdot 2 \sum_{l=0}^{\frac{n}{2}-1} \binom{\frac{n}{2}-1}{l} = \frac{1}{2^{\frac{n}{2}}} \cdot 2 \cdot 2^{\frac{n}{2}-1} = 1.$$

Thus we reach at a contradiction. Therefore, $c_{2r+3} = c_{2r+1}$ holds for all integer $r = 0, \ldots, \frac{n}{2} - 2$.

Lemma 5. *Let n be odd and f be an n-variable symmetric Boolean function with the value vector $[c_0, \ldots, c_n]$. If $|\mathcal{N}_f(\lambda)| = 1$ for a $\lambda \in \mathbb{F}_2^n$ such that $wt(\lambda) = \frac{n-1}{2}$, then $c_{2r+2} = c_{2r}$ holds for all integer $r = 0, \ldots, \frac{n-3}{2}$ and $c_{2r+3} = c_{2r+1}$ holds for all integer $r = 0, \ldots, \frac{n-3}{2}$.*

Proof. From (6) we have

$$\mathcal{N}_f(\lambda) = \frac{1}{2^{\frac{n}{2}}} [\sum_{l=0}^{\frac{n-1}{2}} (-1)^{c_{2l}} i^{2l} P_{2l}(\frac{n-1}{2}, n) + \sum_{l=0}^{\frac{n-1}{2}} (-1)^{c_{2l+1}} i^{2l+1} P_{2l+1}(\frac{n-1}{2}, n)].$$

Then using (iii) of Lemma 2, we get

$$\mathcal{N}_f(\lambda) = \frac{1}{2^{\frac{n}{2}}} [\sum_{l=0}^{\frac{n-1}{2}} (-1)^{c_{2l}} (-1)^l (-1)^l \binom{\frac{n-1}{2}}{l} + \sum_{l=0}^{\frac{n-1}{2}} (-1)^{c_{2l+1}} (-1)^l (-1)^l i \binom{\frac{n-1}{2}}{l}]$$

$$= \frac{1}{2^{\frac{n}{2}}} [\sum_{l=0}^{\frac{n-1}{2}} (-1)^{c_{2l}} \binom{\frac{n-1}{2}}{l} + i \sum_{l=0}^{\frac{n-1}{2}} (-1)^{c_{2l+1}} \binom{\frac{n-1}{2}}{l}].$$

Therefore,

$$|\mathcal{N}_f(\lambda)| = \frac{1}{2^{\frac{n}{2}}} \sqrt{(\sum_{l=0}^{\frac{n-1}{2}} (-1)^{c_{2l}} \binom{\frac{n-1}{2}}{l})^2 + (\sum_{l=0}^{\frac{n-1}{2}} (-1)^{c_{2l+1}} \binom{\frac{n-1}{2}}{l})^2}.$$

If we assume that $c_{2r+2} = c_{2r} \oplus 1$ holds for some $r \in \{0, \ldots, \frac{n-3}{2}\}$, then there will be two nonzero integers of opposite sign in the sum $\sum_{l=0}^{\frac{n-1}{2}} (-1)^{c_{2l}} \binom{\frac{n-1}{2}}{l}$. On the other hand, if we assume that $c_{2r+3} = c_{2r+1} \oplus 1$ holds for some $r \in \{0, \ldots, \frac{n-3}{2}\}$, then the sum $\sum_{l=0}^{\frac{n-1}{2}} (-1)^{c_{2l+1}} \binom{\frac{n-1}{2}}{l}$, contains two nonzero integers of opposite sign. Then in both of the cases,

$$|\mathcal{N}_f(\lambda)| < \frac{1}{2^{\frac{n}{2}}} \sqrt{(\sum_{l=0}^{\frac{n-1}{2}} \binom{\frac{n-1}{2}}{l})^2 + (\sum_{l=0}^{\frac{n-1}{2}} \binom{\frac{n-1}{2}}{l})^2}$$

$$= \frac{1}{2^{\frac{n}{2}}} \sqrt{2^{n-1} + 2^{n-1}} = 1$$

Thus we reach at a contradiction. Hence the result follows. Therefore, $c_{2r+2} = c_{2r}$ holds for all integer $r = 0, \ldots, \frac{n-3}{2}$ and $c_{2r+3} = c_{2r+1}$ holds for all integer $r = 0, \ldots, \frac{n-3}{2}$.

Now we prove our main result.

Theorem 1. *An n-variable symmetric Boolean function is negabent if and only if it is affine.*

Proof. From Proposition 1 we know that all the affine functions are negabent.

Next we prove that if an n-variable symmetric Boolean function f with the value vector $[c_0, c_1, \ldots, c_n]$ is negabent then it is affine.

First we consider that n is even. Then by Lemma 3 and Lemma 4 we have, $c_{2r+2} = c_{2r}$ for all $r = 0, \ldots, \frac{n}{2} - 1$ and also $c_{2r+3} = c_{2r+1}$ for all $r = 0, \ldots, \frac{n}{2} - 2$. Therefore, when $c_0 = c_1$, then $c_0 = c_2 = \ldots = c_n = c_1 = c_3 = \ldots = c_{n-1}$, in this case f is a constant function. On the other hand, when $c_0 = c_1 \oplus 1$, then $c_0 = c_2 = \ldots = c_n = c_1 \oplus 1 = c_3 \oplus 1 = \ldots = c_n \oplus 1$, in this case f is the linear function or its complement. Thus in both the cases we see that f is affine.

If we consider that n is odd, then by Lemma 5, we have $c_{2r+2} = c_{2r}$ for all $r = 0, \ldots, \frac{n-3}{2}$ and $c_{2r+3} = c_{2r+1}$ for all $r = 0, \ldots, \frac{n-3}{2}$. If $c_0 = c_1$, then $c_0 = c_2 = \ldots = c_{n-1} = c_1 = c_3 = \ldots = c_n$, in this case, f is a constant function. On the other hand, if $c_0 = c_1 \oplus 1$, then $c_0 = c_2 = \ldots = c_{n-1} = c_1 \oplus 1 = c_3 \oplus 1 = \ldots = c_n \oplus 1$. In this case, f is the linear function or its complement. Therefore, in both the cases, f is affine.

Hence the theorem.

Corollary 1. *For even n, there is no n-variable symmetric Boolean function which is both bent and negabent.*

4   Conclusions

Savicky [7] showed that the Hadamard-Walsh transform values of a symmetric Boolean function are related to the Krawtchouk polynomial and using this he proved that all the symmetric bent functions are quadratic. In this paper we have shown that the nega-Hadamard transform values of a symmetric Boolean function are also related to the Krawtchouk polynomial. Then we have used the properties of the Krawtchouk polynomial to prove that the symmetric negabent Boolean functions are all affine. This also tells that there is no symmetric Boolean function on even number of variables which is both bent and negabent. So to construct new classes of functions which are both bent and negabent we have to look beyond the class of symmetric Boolean functions. On the other hand, for odd number of variables, quadratic negabent functions have been characterized in [5,2]. It is interesting to construct higher degree negabent functions on odd number of variables for which we have to look at the Boolean functions which are not symmetric.

Acknowledgments. The author would like to thank the anonymous reviewers for their valuable suggestions on this paper.

References

1. MacWillams, F.J., Sloane, N.J.A.: The Theory of Error Correcting Codes. North Holland, The Netherlands (1977)
2. Parker, M.G., Pott, A.: On Boolean functions which are bent and negabent. In: Golomb, S.W., Gong, G., Helleseth, T., Song, H.-Y. (eds.) SSC 2007. LNCS, vol. 4893, pp. 9–23. Springer, Heidelberg (2007)
3. Parker, M.G.: Constabent properties of Golay-Davis-Jedwab sequences. In: Int. Symp. Information Theory, p. 302. IEEE, Sorrento (2000)
4. Riera, C., Parker, M.G.: One and two-variable interlace polynomials: A spectral interpretation. In: Ytrehus, Ø. (ed.) WCC 2005. LNCS, vol. 3969, pp. 397–411. Springer, Heidelberg (2006)
5. Riera, C., Parker, M.G.: Generalized bent criteria for Boolean functions. IEEE Trans. Inform. Theory 52(9), 4142–4159 (2006)
6. Rothaus, O.S.: On bent functions. J. Comb. Theory (A) 20, 300–305 (1976)
7. Savicky, P.: On the bent Boolean functions that are symmetric. Euro. J. Comb. 15, 407–410 (1994)
8. Schmidt, K.-U., Parker, M.G., Pott, A.: Negabent functions in the Maiorana-McFarland class. In: Golomb, S.W., Parker, M.G., Pott, A., Winterhof, A. (eds.) SETA 2008. LNCS, vol. 5203, pp. 390–402. Springer, Heidelberg (2008)

Improved Meet-in-the-Middle Attacks on AES

Hüseyin Demirci, İhsan Taşkın, Mustafa Çoban, and Adnan Baysal

TÜBİTAK UEKAE, 41470 Gebze, Kocaeli, Turkey
{huseyind,ihsan,mcoban,adnan}@uekae.tubitak.gov.tr

Abstract. We improve the existing distinguishers of AES. Our work is mainly built upon the works by Gilbert& Miner [17] and Demirci & Selçuk [14]. We find out that some part of the inner encryption function of AES can be expressed with relatively few constants under certain conditions. These new distinguishers are exploited to develop a meet-in-the-middle attack on 7 rounds of AES-128 and AES-192, and on 8 rounds of AES-256. The proposed attack is faster than the existing attacks [15,17] for key size of 128 at the expense of an increase in the complexities of memory and precomputation.

Keywords: AES, Rijndael, cryptanalysis, meet-in-the-middle attack.

1 Introduction

Rijndael has been announced as the Advanced Encryption Standard (AES) in 2001. After DES, it is one of the most widely used and analyzed ciphers in the world. AES is a 128-bit block cipher and accepts key sizes of 128, 192 and 256 bits. These versions of AES are called AES-128, AES-192 and AES-256 and the number of rounds for these versions are 10, 12 and 14 respectively. It has an SP-network structure. The interaction between the operations is chosen so that after two rounds full diffusion is satisfied. The AES S-box has been chosen considering differential and linear cryptanalysis.

There has been recent developments in the cryptanalysis of AES. In [8] there is a related key attack on 10 rounds of AES-192 and AES-256 with practical complexity. Biryukov et al. [9,10] have constructed related key attacks on the full AES-192 and AES-256. Moreover, chosen plaintext attacks work up to 7 rounds of AES-128 and 8 rounds of AES-192 and AES-256 [1,2,13,14,17,21,27]. Also timing cache attacks are an important threat againts AES [3].

In [17] it has been observed that one entry after 3 rounds of AES encryption can be expressed using 10 bytes if 15 entries of the plaintexts are fixed, only one entry takes every possible value. In [14] the expressions of [17] has been carried to a 4 round property. An entry after 4 rounds of encryption can be expressed with 26 bytes, which makes to attack on AES-128 unfeasible using this property. In this paper, we show that these expressions can be simplified for some instances. Hence we are able to carry the meet in the middle attacks on AES. To the best of our knowledge, this is the best attack on AES-128 with respect to online time complexity excluding related key attacks.

B. Roy and N. Sendrier (Eds.): INDOCRYPT 2009, LNCS 5922, pp. 144–156, 2009.
© Springer-Verlag Berlin Heidelberg 2009

This paper proceeds as follows: In Section 2 we briefly explain the AES block cipher and give a survey of the previous attacks. Section 3 is dedicated to previous work [17] and [14] which are related to our study. In Section 4, first we point out some errors in [14]. We show that under some conditions, the expression of the encryption function for one entry can be simplified in Section 4.1. Hence, we are able to reduce the number of constants used in this expression. Section 4.2 presents a meet-in-the middle attack on 7 rounds of AES by exploiting this reduced formula. In Section 4.3, we use Gilbert and Minier's collision property in a differential scenario to reduce the number of constants in the encryption function. Next, we extend the attack to 8 rounds of AES-256 in Section 4.4. In Section 4.5 we compare the results of this work with previous studies. We conclude the paper with a summary of the results in Section 5.

2   The AES Encryption Algorithm

In the encryption function of AES, 128-bit plaintext is considered as a 4×4 matrix in $GF(2^8)$, and the entries of the matrix are represented as 1-byte values. Each round function, except the final one, consists of 4 inner functions; the S-box substitution (SB), shift row (SR), mix column (MC), and add round key (ARK) operations, applied in that order. These functions make use of the finite field arithmetic and some matrix operations. The single S-box substitution is used for all entries of the table, and it is based on the inverse mapping in $GF(2^8)$, and an affine mapping, which is strong against differential and linear attacks [23]. In the SR operation, rows are shifted to the left by 0, 1, 2, and 3 bytes, from the first row to the last. MC operation provides efficient confusion on columns of the matrix, since it is an MDS matrix multiplication. The MDS matrix used in AES is

$$\begin{pmatrix} 02\ 03\ 01\ 01 \\ 01\ 02\ 03\ 01 \\ 01\ 01\ 02\ 03 \\ 03\ 01\ 01\ 02 \end{pmatrix}$$

In the ARK, the state is simply XORed with the 128-bit round key. This design of AES round function guarantees full diffusion after two round function calls. The AES encryption function consists of an initial key addition (*whitening*), necessary number of round functions, and the final round which is a round function without the MC operation. For the details of the encryption, decryption, and key scheduling algorithms, one can refer to [16].

There has been many attempts to analyze AES. First, the designers of AES break the 6 round version of AES-128 by the square attack using 2^{32} chosen plaintexts with about complexity of 2^{72} encryptions [13]. This attack has been improved and the workload has been reduced to 2^{44} in [15]. For AES-192 and AES-256, by the help of the key schedule, the attack of [22] can be successful for 7 rounds. In [17], Gilbert and Minier found an attack based on a collision property after three rounds of encryption. 7 rounds of AES-192 and AES-256 are broken using 2^{32} chosen plaintexts, and with the complexity of 2^{140} encryptions.

Moreover, the attack is faster than exhaustive search for AES-128. In [6,11,24] [26,25], the so called impossible differential attack is proposed for 7 rounds of AES, but it has higher complexity than the square attack. There are some new impossible differential attacks [1,2,21,27] on AES which reduces the time complexities of the previous attacks. Boomerang attack is applied by Biryukov [7] for the 5 and 6 rounds of the cipher. It breaks 5 rounds of AES-128 using 2^{46} adaptive chosen plaintexts in 2^{46} steps of analysis, whereas the 6-round attack needs 2^{78} chosen plaintexts, 2^{78} steps of analysis, and 2^{36} bytes of memory. A class of algebraic attacks on AES is examined in [12]. In this paper, the AES S-box is written as a system of implicit quadratic equations, resulting the conversion of the cryptanalysis to solving a huge system of quadratic equations. In [12], XSL method is suggested if the system of equations is overdefined and sparse which is the case for AES. Recently, related key attacks, which work up to 10 rounds of AES-192 and AES-256, have been applied to the cipher [4,5,8,18,19,20,28]. Finally, Biryukov et al. [9,10] have succeeded to attack the full AES-192 and AES-256.

2.1   Notation

Throughout the paper, we use $K^{(r)}$ and $C^{(r)}$ to denote the round key and the ciphertext of the rth round; $K_{ij}^{(r)}$ and $C_{ij}^{(r)}$ denote the byte values at row i, column j. The arithmetic operations among table entries are in $GF(2^8)$, where addition is the same as bit-wise XOR. By one round AES encryption, we mean an inner round without whitening or exclusion of the mixcolumn operation unless otherwise stated. By an active entry, we mean an entry that takes all byte values between 0 and 255 exactly once over a given set of plaintexts. By a passive entry we mean an entry that is fixed to a constant byte value. We use Δ to denote the difference with respect to XOR operation.

3   A 4-Round Distinguisher of AES

In [17], Gilbert and Minier showed an interesting distinguishing property for 4 rounds of AES: Consider the evolution of the plaintexts with 15 entries are passive but the first entry is active over 4 inner rounds, with no whitening. Let a_{ij} denote the ith row, jth column of the plaintext. After the first S-box transformation, define $t_{ij} = S(a_{ij})$. At the end of round 1, the state matrix is of the form:

$2t_{11} + c_1$	m_{12}	m_{13}	m_{14}
$t_{11} + c_2$	m_{22}	m_{23}	m_{24}
$t_{11} + c_3$	m_{32}	m_{33}	m_{34}
$3t_{11} + c_4$	m_{42}	m_{43}	m_{44}

where m_{ij} and c_i, $1 \leq i \leq 4$, $2 \leq j \leq 4$, are fixed values that depend on the passive entries and subkey values. At the end of the second round, the first main diagonal entry $C_{11}^{(2)}$ can be determined by the following equation:

$$C_{11}^{(2)} = 2S(2t_{11} + c_1) + 3S(m_{22}) + S(m_{33}) + S(m_{44}) + K_{11}^{(2)}$$
$$= 2S(2t_{11} + c_1) + c_5,$$

for some fixed value c_5. Applying round function, similar equations can be written for the other main diagonal entries. At the end of the second round, the main diagonal entries are of the form:

$$C_{11}^{(2)} = 2S(2t_{11} + c_1) + c_5$$
$$C_{22}^{(2)} = S(3t_{11} + c_4) + c_6$$
$$C_{33}^{(2)} = 2S(t_{11} + c_3) + c_7$$
$$C_{44}^{(2)} = S(t_{11} + c_2) + c_8$$

for some fixed values c_5, c_6, c_7, c_8. Since

$$C_{11}^{(3)} = 2S(C_{11}^{(2)}) + 3S(C_{22}^{(2)}) + S(C_{33}^{(2)}) + S(C_{44}^{(2)}) + K_{11}^{(3)},$$

we can summarize the above observations with the following proposition:

Proposition 1 ([17]). *Consider a set of 256 plaintexts where the entry a_{11} is active and all the other entries are passive. Encrypt this set with 3 rounds of AES. Then, the function which maps a_{11} to $C_{11}^{(3)}$ is entirely determined by 9 fixed 1-byte parameters.*

Remark 1. Proposition 1 can be generalized: Note that the argument preceding the proposition applies to any other third round ciphertext entry and hence the statement is true for any $C_{ij}^{(3)}$. Similarly, any other a_{ij} can be taken as the active byte instead of a_{11}.

Gilbert and Minier [17] observed that the constants c_1, c_2, c_3, and c_4 depend on the values (a_{21}, a_{31}, a_{41}) on the first column, whereas the other constants c_5, c_6, c_7, and c_8 are independent of these variables. They used this information to find collisions over 3 rounds of the cipher:

Proposition 2 ([17]). *Assume that c_1, c_2, c_3, and c_4 behave as random functions of the variables (a_{21}, a_{31}, a_{41}). If about 2^{16} random (a_{21}, a_{31}, a_{41}) values are taken and the other passive entries of the plaintext are fixed, then there is a non negligible probability that two different values of (a_{21}, a_{31}, a_{41}) produce identical functions $f, f' : a_{11} \to C_{11}^{(3)}$.*

This distinguishing property was used to build attacks on AES up to 7 rounds. Furthermore, Demirci and Selçuk developed the observations of Gilbert and Minier [17] and found a 4-round distinguisher of AES in [14]. Namely, the function which maps a_{11} to $C_{11}^{(4)}$ is entirely determined by 25 fixed 1-byte parameters under certain assumptions.

Proposition 3 ([14]). *Consider a set of 256 plaintexts where the entry a_{11} is active and all the other entries are passive. Encrypt this set with 4 rounds of AES. Then, the function which maps a_{11} to $C_{11}^{(4)}$ is entirely determined by 25 fixed 1-byte parameters.*

4   A New Attack on AES

In this section, we show how to improve the observations of Demirci and Selçuk
[14]. This improvement makes it possible to apply the attack on 7 rounds of all
versions of AES. We have two different approaches to advance the distinguishing
properties. The first method is based on reducing the number of parameters
which determine the function of the output of the 4-rounds of AES. The other
approach exploits the Gilbert and Minier's collision property and considers the
difference of two sets. Before stating these, we point out some corrections in
previous work [14].

In [14] it has been stated that 3 rounds of encryption can be expressed with
the following 9 constants:

$$C_{11}^{(3)} = 2S(2S(2t_{11} + c_1) + c_5) + 3S(2S(2t_{11} + c_4) + c_6)$$
$$+S(S(t_{11} + c_3) + c_7) + S(S(t_{11} + c_2) + c_8) + K_{11}^{(3)}. \qquad (1)$$

We observe that the equation (1) has 2 errors. These errors do not affect the
applicability of the attacks of [14]. However, in case (1) had been true, then we
would have

$$C_{11}^{(3)} = S(2S(2t_{11} + c_1) + c_5) \qquad (2)$$

when $c_1 = c_4, c_5 = c_6, c_2 = c_3$ and $c_7 = c_8$. Thus, it would show that the
function which maps the active entry a_{11} to $C_{11}^{(3)}$ is wholly determined by two
byte constants only with probability 2^{-32}.

The correct form of the equation (1) is

$$C_{11}^{(3)} = 2S(2S(2t_{11} + c_1) + c_5) + 3S(S(3t_{11} + c_4) + c_6)$$
$$+S(2S(t_{11} + c_3) + c_7) + S(S(t_{11} + c_2) + c_8) + K_{11}^{(3)}. \qquad (3)$$

Hence, such a direct simplification of the equation is impossible. Moreover, there
are also errors in $C_{22}^{(3)}$ and $C_{44}^{(3)}$. The right formulas for these are:

$$C_{22}^{(3)} = S(S(3t_{11} + c_4) + c_9) + 2S(3S(t_{11} + c_3) + c_{10})$$
$$+3S(S(t_{11} + c_2) + c_{11}) + S(3S(2t_{11} + c_1) + c_{12}) + K_{22}^{(3)} \qquad (4)$$
$$C_{44}^{(3)} = 3S(3S(t_{11} + c_2) + c_{17}) + S(S(2t_{11} + c_1) + c_{18})$$
$$+S(3S(3t_{11} + c_4) + c_{19}) + 2S(S(t_{11} + c_3) + c_{20}) + K_{44}^{(3)}. \qquad (5)$$

There is no fault in $C_{33}^{(3)}$ that is:

$$C_{33}^{(3)} = S(S(t_{11} + c_3) + c_{13}) + S(2S(t_{11} + c_2) + c_{14})$$
$$+2S(S(2t_{11} + c_1) + c_{15}) + 3S(2S(3t_{11} + c_4) + c_{16}) + K_{33}^{(3)}. \qquad (6)$$

Although there is no scenario that the parameters are annihilated directly, we
can still reduce the number of parameters under certain assumptions. In the
following sections, we will provide alternative methods for this reason.

4.1   A 4-Round Differential Distinguisher

In this part, we present how Proposition 3 is improved. First, we obtain the improved 4-round distinguisher of AES. We utilize an advantageous map

$$\Delta : (a_{11}, \tilde{a}_{11}) \rightarrow f(a_{11}) + f(\tilde{a}_{11}) = C_{11}^{(4)} + \tilde{C}_{11}^{(4)} = \Delta(C_{11}^{(4)})$$

to get an efficient attack. The next proposition gives this distinguishing property.

Proposition 4. *Consider a set of 256 plaintexts where the entry a_{11} is active and all the other entries are passive. Encrypt this set with 4 rounds of AES. Then, the function which maps a_{11} to $\Delta(C_{11}^{(4)})$ is entirely determined by 15 fixed 1-byte parameters with probability 2^{-72}.*

Proof. One can consider all constants $c_1, c_2, \cdots, c_{20}$ in (3),(4),(5) and (6) as random variables. Hence,

$$Pr(c_{12}=3c_5=3c_{15}=3c_{18}, 2c_{17}=3c_{14}=6c_8=6c_{11}, 3c_7=2c_{10}=6c_{13}=6c_{20})=2^{-72}(7)$$

If we take

$$S(2t_{11} + c_1) = x_1$$
$$S(t_{11} + c_2) = x_2$$
$$S(t_{11} + c_3) = x_3$$
$$S(3t_{11} + c_4) = x_4$$

and

$$d_1 = c_5, d_2 = c_6, d_3 = c_8, d_4 = c_9$$
$$d_5 = c_{16}, d_6 = c_{19}, d_7 = c_{20}$$

then

$$C_{11}^{(3)} = 2S(2x_1 + d_1) + S(x_2 + d_3) \tag{8}$$
$$+S(2x_3 + 2d_7) + 3S(x_4 + d_2) + K_{11}^{(3)}.$$
$$C_{22}^{(3)} = 3S(3x_1 + 3d_1) + 3S(x_2 + d_3)$$
$$+2S(3x_3 + 3d_7) + S(x_4 + d_4) + K_{22}^{(3)}, \tag{9}$$
$$C_{33}^{(3)} = 2S(x_1 + d_1) + S(2x_2 + 2d_3)$$
$$+S(x_3 + d_7) + 3S(2x_4 + d_5) + K_{33}^{(3)} \tag{10}$$
$$C_{44}^{(3)} = S(x_1 + d_1) + 3S(3x_2 + 3d_3)$$
$$+2S(x_3 + d_7) + S(3x_4 + d_6) + K_{44}^{(3)}. \tag{11}$$

with a probability 2^{-72}. Since

$$C_{11}^{(4)} = 2S(C_{11}^{(3)}) + 3S(C_{22}^{(3)}) + S(C_{33}^{(3)}) + S(C_{44}^{(3)}) + K_{11}^{(4)}, \tag{12}$$

the terms $K_{11}^{(4)}$ are canceled by taking a difference $\Delta(C_{11}^{(4)})$ from two different $C_{11}^{(4)}$ with respect to $+$. Thus, the fixed values

$$\left(c_1, c_2, c_3, c_4, d_1, \cdots, d_7, K_{11}^{(3)}, K_{22}^{(3)}, K_{33}^{(3)}, K_{44}^{(3)}\right) \qquad (13)$$

are sufficient to express the function $a_{11} \to \Delta(C_{11}^{(4)})$ with a probability 2^{-72}.   □

Note that chosen relations about parameters do not have any specific meaning. The number of equalities in (7) are chosen so that the complexity of resulting attack in Section 4.2 does not exceed exhaustive search.

4.2   The Attack

In this section, we describe a meet-in-the-middle attack on 7-round AES based on the distinguishing property observed in Section 4.1. In this attack, we first precompute $a_{11} \to \Delta(C_{11}^{(4)}) = f(i) + f(0)$ for all $1 \le i \le 32$ instead of $1 \le i \le 255$ according to Proposition 4 which not only reduces the precomputation time complexity in [14] but also gives sufficiently small probability explained in the sixth step. Then we choose and encrypt a suitable plaintext set. We search certain key bytes, do a partial decryption on the ciphertext set, and compare the values obtained by this decryption to the values in the precomputed set. When a match is found, the key value tried is most likely the right key value. The details of the attacks are as follows:

1. For each of the 2^{120} possible values of the parameters in (13), calculate the function $f : a_{11} \to C_{11}^{(4)}$, for each $0 \le a_{11} \le 32$ according to equations (8–11) and (12). Compute and store

   $$\Delta(C_{11}^{(4)}) = f(i) + f(0)$$

   for $1 \le i \le 32$.
2. Choose 2^{48} sets of 2^{32} plaintexts where the main diagonal entries take every possible value and the other entries are constant. Then at the end of round 1, there are 2^{72} different sets of 256 plaintexts having active first entry. Encrypt all chosen plaintexts with 7 rounds AES.
3. Let K_{final} denote the subkey blocks $(K_{11}^{(7)}, K_{24}^{(7)}, K_{33}^{(7)}, K_{42}^{(7)}, k^{(6)})$, where $k^{(6)}$ denotes $0E \cdot K_{11}^{(6)} + 0B \cdot K_{21}^{(6)} + 0D \cdot K_{31}^{(6)} + 09 \cdot K_{41}^{(6)}$. Search over all possible values of K_{final}. Using K_{final}, do a partial decryption of the ciphertext bytes $C_{11}^{(7)}, C_{24}^{(7)}, C_{33}^{(7)}$ and $C_{42}^{(7)}$ to obtain the entry $C_{11}^{(5)}$. Store all the values of $C_{11}^{(5)}$.
4. Let K_{init} denote the initial whitening subkey blocks $(K_{11}^{(0)}, K_{22}^{(0)}, K_{33}^{(0)}, K_{44}^{(0)})$. For each possible value of K_{init} and $K_{11}^{(1)}$ encrypt all chosen plaintexts with single round to guess the value of $C_{11}^{(1)}$. This step classifies 2^{72} sets of 256 plaintexts to satisfy that the first entry takes every value from 0 to 255 and all the other entries are fixed at the end of round 1.

5. For each of 2^{72} sets containing 256 plaintexts obtained in step 4, select the plaintexts of which the first entries of the first round output takes all the values from $i = 0$ to 32 and accordingly collect the 33 values of $C_{11}^{(5)}$ via using step 3. Next, calculate the values of $\Delta(C_{11}^{(5)})$.

6. Compare the sequence of the 32 $\Delta(C_{11}^{(5)})$ values obtained in Step 5 to the sequences obtained in precomputation. Now if the K_{init}, $K_{11}^{(1)}$ and K_{final} subkeys are guessed correctly, the function $C_{11}^{(1)} \rightarrow \Delta(C_{11}^{(5)})$ must match one of the functions obtained in the precomputation stage. Once a match is found, corresponding K_{init} and K_{final} are correct keys by an overwhelming probability, since the probability of having a match for a wrong key is approximately

$$2^{8 \times 15} 2^{-8 \times 32} = 2^{-136}.$$

7. Repeat the attack one more time with different target value, $C_{21}^{(5)}$, $C_{31}^{(5)}$, or $C_{41}^{(5)}$, instead of $C_{11}^{(5)}$, using the same plaintext set. This attack gives us another 5 key bytes from the final two rounds.

8. The remaining key bytes can be searched after recovering most of the key bytes.

Summary of the attack can be given as follows:

Step 1. (Precomputation Phase) Construct the table having 32 rows and 2^{120} columns. This table determines $f(i) + f(0)$ for any $f : a_{11} \rightarrow C_{11}^{(4)}$ where $1 \leq i \leq 32$.

Step 2. (Selection of Plaintexts and Encryption Phase) Choose 2^{72} sets of 256 plaintexts satisfying suitable conditions. Then, encrypt all chosen plaintexts with 7 rounds AES.

Step 3. (Decryption and Collection) Search K_{final} values and do partial decryption of the ciphertext bytes to store all the values of $C_{11}^{(5)}$.

Step 4. Search K_{init} and $K_{11}^{(1)}$ values. Then, for each possible value of these keys encrypt all chosen plaintexts with single round.

Step 5.-6. (Matching Phase) Calculate $\Delta(C_{11}^{(5)})$ for chosen plaintexts and compare the results with the precomputed table.

Step 7. (Discovery of More Key Bytes) Repeat the attack one more time with different target value.

Step 8. (Final Phase) For remaining key bytes, search exhaustively.

Since a set of 2^{32} plaintexts which are active in the diagonal entries gives 2^{24} plaintext sets which will be used in Step 2 in our attack, this attack requires 2^{80} chosen plaintexts. Therefore, we expect that the event

$$3c_5 = c_{12} = 3c_{15} = 3c_{18}, 6c_8 = 6c_{11} = 3c_{14} = 2c_{17}, 3c_7 = 2_{10} = 6c_{13} = 6c_{20}$$

occurs, the first entry $C_{11}^{(1)}$ takes every possible value and the rest remain constant. There is a precomputation step which calculates 2^{120} possible values for 32 plaintexts. Therefore the complexity of this step, which will be done only once, is 2^{125} evaluations of the function f. As the 7 round encryption of AES takes approximately four times evaluation of f, complexity of the precomputation reduces to 2^{123}.

In the key search phase, for every combination of K_{final}, we do partial decryption over 2^{80} ciphertexts which makes 2^{120} partial decryptions and for every combination of K_{init} and $K_{11}^{(1)}$, we do partial encryption over 2^{80} plaintexts which makes 2^{120} partial encryptions. As in [13] and [15], we assume that 2^8 partial decryptions take approximately the time of a single encryption. Also, we assume that 2^8 partial encryptions take approximately the time of a single encryption. Therefore the processing complexity of the attack is comparable to 2^{113} encryptions.

As we take the target entries used in Step 7 to be on the same column as $C_{11}^{(5)}$, such as $C_{21}^{(5)}$, equations (8–11) will remain identical in these computations, and the only change will be on a few coefficients in equation (12). Hence, there won't be a need for a separate precomputation; the necessary values for $C_{11}^{(1)} \rightarrow \Delta(C_{21}^{(5)})$ can be obtained with a slight overhead. However, we will need separate memory to store the obtained values. Thus, the memory requirement of the precomputation phase, the dominant factor of the memory complexity, is $2 \times 2^{125} = 2^{126}$ bytes, which is equivalent to 2^{122} AES blocks.

Note that the complexities above are for average expected values with approximately 50 % success rate. One can apply the attack using more sets of chosen plaintexts to increase the success probability.

4.3   A 4-Round Collision-Differential Distinguisher of AES

According to the work of Gilbert and Minier [17], it is possible to find a collision over 3 rounds of the cipher for a fixed entry (See Section 3.3 in [17]). That is if we take about 2^{16} sets which consist of 256 plaintexts, then one can find $c_1 = \tilde{c}_1, \cdots, c_8 = \tilde{c}_8$ with nonnegligible probability. Next proposition uses this fact to reduce the number of parameters expressing the encryption function.

Proposition 5. *Assume that a collision for $C_{11}^{(3)}$ holds. Then the probability to find a collision also for $C_{22}^{(3)}$ and $C_{33}^{(3)}$ is 2^{-64}.*

Proof. By the assumption, we have $c_1 = \tilde{c}_1, \cdots, c_8 = \tilde{c}_8$. Observe that

$$c_i = \tilde{c}_i \text{ for any } 9 \le i \le 16$$

occurs with probability 2^{-64}.

Corollary 1. *Suppose we have a collection of 2^{80} sets consisting of 32 plaintexts as follows:*

1. *The first entry a_{11} takes 32 different value.*
2. *The other entries of the first column (a_{21}, a_{31}, a_{41}) change over 2^{16} different combinations.*
3. *The remaining entries change over 2^{64} different values.*

Then, after 4 rounds of AES encryption, there exists some function which maps a_{11} to $\Delta(C_{11}^{(4)})$ is entirely determined by 13 fixed 1-byte parameters with non negligible probability.

Proof. We may find $c_1 = \tilde{c}_1, \cdots, c_8 = \tilde{c}_8$ with nonnegligible probability via Proposition 2 and the second assumption in corollary. By applying Proposition 5 and the third assumption in corollary,

$$\forall i, \ 1 \leq i \leq 3, \ C_{ii}^{(3)} + \tilde{C}_{ii}^{(3)} = 0$$

takes place with a significant probability. Therefore,

$$\Delta(C_{11}^{(4)}) = S(C_{44}^{(3)}) + S(\tilde{C}_{44}^{(3)}).$$

If we fix $c_1 = \tilde{c}_1 = d_1$, $c_2 = \tilde{c}_2 = d_2$, $c_3 = \tilde{c}_3 = d_3$, $c_4 = \tilde{c}_4 = d_4$, $c_{17} = d_5$, $\tilde{c}_{17} = d_6$, $c_{18} = d_7$, $\tilde{c}_{18} = d_8$, $c_{19} = d_9$, $\tilde{c}_{19} = d_{10}$, $c_{20} = d_{11}$, $\tilde{c}_{20} = d_{12}$, then

$$\left(d_1, d_2, \ldots, d_{12}, K_{44}^{(3)} \right) \tag{14}$$

are sufficient to express the function $a_{11} \rightarrow \Delta(C_{11}^{(4)})$ with a non negligible probability.   □

Note that we could use Corollary 1 to prepare an attack on AES. But, the complexity of such an attack exceeds the key length of AES-128.

4.4 Extension to 8 Rounds

We can successfully attack 8 rounds of AES using almost the same steps of the 7-round attack followed by an exhaustive search of the last round key. The only difference is the computation of the function $\Delta(C_{11}^{(4)})$ for each $0 \leq a_{11} \leq 64$ instead of $0 \leq a_{11} \leq 32$ in step 1. We use these 64 values in the comparison phase to increase the elimination power of the attack. In this case, the precomputation and memory complexities are doubled and the complexity of the key search phase rises by a factor of 2^{128} in spite of the fact that the data complexity does not alter. Therefore, the time complexity of the attack on 8-round AES-256 becomes 2^{241}. Our attack has more time complexity than [15] and [14]. However, our attack is more advantageous in terms of precomputation and memory than [14]. When compared to [15], there is a significant improvement in terms of the number of plaintexts needed.

4.5 Comparison of Attacks on AES

There are six previous attacks [1,2,15,17,21,27] on 7-round AES-128. The attack [17] by Gilbert and Minier uses 2^{32} plaintexts and 2^{96} memory but is slightly faster than exhaustive search. On the other hand, the attack of Ferguson et al. [15] uses almost the entire codebook with 2^{120} time and 2^{64} memory complexity. The remaining attacks [1,2,21,27] are in type of impossible differential attacks. Our attack has a precomputation phase having 2^{123} complexity, but the constructed table can be used for any AES key. The data complexity is between [17] and [21]. The online time complexity of the proposed attack is the best among the others. The comparison of the results are illustrated in Table 1.

Table 1. Summary of Attacks on AES Excluding the Related-Key Model

Block Cipher	Paper	Rounds	Type	Data (CP)	Complexity Memory	Time	Pre.
AES-128	[17]	7	Collision	2^{32}	2^{96}	$< 2^{128}$	2^{96}
	[1]	7	Impossible Differential	$2^{117.5}$		2^{121}	–
	[2,27]	7	Impossible Differential	$2^{115.5}$		2^{119}	–
	[15]	7	Square	$2^{128} - 2^{119}$	2^{64}	2^{120}	–
	[21]	7	Impossible Differential	$2^{112.2}$	$2^{89.2}$	$2^{117.2}$ MA	–
	This paper	7	MitM	2^{80}	2^{122}	2^{113}	2^{123}
AES-192	[17]	7	Collision	2^{32}	2^{84}	2^{140}	2^{84}
	[25]	7	Imp. Differential	2^{92}	2^{153}	2^{186}	–
	[22]	7	Square	2^{32}	2^{32}	2^{184}	–
	[15]	7	Square	$19 \cdot 2^{32}$	2^{32}	2^{155}	–
	[15]	7	Square	$2^{128} - 2^{119}$	2^{64}	2^{120}	–
	[27]	7	Impossible Differential	$2^{115.5}$		2^{119}	–
	[27]	7	Impossible Differential	2^{92}		2^{162}	–
	[21]	7	Impossible Differential	$2^{113.8}$	$2^{89.2}$	$2^{118.8}$ MA	–
	[21]	7	Impossible Differential	$2^{91.2}$	2^{61}	$2^{139.2}$	–
	[14]	7	MitM	2^{32}	2^{206}	2^{72}	2^{208}
	[14]	7	MitM-TM	2^{34+n}	2^{206-n}	2^{74+n}	2^{208-n}
	[15]	8	Square	$2^{128} - 2^{119}$	2^{64}	2^{188}	–
	This paper	7	MitM	2^{80}	2^{122}	2^{113}	2^{123}
AES-256	[22]	7	Square	2^{32}	2^{32}	2^{200}	–
	[17]	7	Collision	2^{32}	2^{84}	2^{140}	2^{84}
	[15]	7	Square	$21 \cdot 2^{32}$	2^{32}	2^{172}	–
	[15]	7	Square	$2^{128} - 2^{119}$	2^{64}	2^{120}	–
	[25]	7	Imp. Differential	$2^{92.5}$	2^{153}	$2^{250.5}$	–
	[27]	7	Impossible Differential	$2^{115.5}$		2^{119}	–
	[27]	8	Impossible Differential	$2^{116.5}$		$2^{247.5}$	–
	[21]	7	Impossible Differential	$2^{113.8}$	$2^{89.2}$	$2^{118.8}$ MA	–
	[21]	7	Impossible Differential	2^{92}	2^{61}	2^{163} MA	–
	[21]	8	Impossible Differential	$2^{111.1}$	$2^{112.1}$	$2^{227.8}$ MA	–
	[21]	8	Impossible Differential	$2^{89.1}$	2^{97}	$2^{229.7}$ MA	–
	[14]	7	MitM	2^{32}	2^{206}	2^{72}	2^{208}
	[14]	7	MitM-TM	2^{34+n}	2^{206-n}	2^{74+n}	2^{208-n}
	This paper	7	MitM	2^{80}	2^{122}	2^{113}	2^{123}
	[15]	8	Square	$2^{128} - 2^{119}$	2^{104}	2^{204}	–
	[14]	8	MitM	2^{32}	2^{206}	2^{200}	2^{208}
	[14]	8	MitM-TM	2^{34+n}	2^{206-n}	2^{202+n}	2^{208-n}
	This paper	8	MitM	2^{80}	2^{123}	2^{241}	2^{124}

MA-Memory Accesses, CP-Chosen plaintext.

Time complexity is measured in encryption units unless mentioned otherwise. The unit of memory complexity is AES block.

5   Conclusion

In this work we have found two different methods that one entry of the ciphertext after 4 rounds of AES encryption is expressed with only 15 or 13 fixed bytes respectively, rather than 25 bytes [14]. The first method utilizes the equality of the parameters to reduce the number of parameters. The second approach exploits the collision property [17] in a differential scenario. Using the first method, we have developed an attack on 7 rounds of AES-128, AES-192 and 8 rounds of AES-256. The proposed attack on AES-128 is advantageous from the existing attacks in terms of time complexity.

Acknowledgments

We would like to thank Ali Aydın Selçuk for his review and many valuable comments on the paper.

References

1. Bahrak, B., Aref, M.R.: A novel impossible differential cryptanalysis of AES. In: Proceedings of the Western European Workshop on Research in Cryptology, volume Bochum of Germany (2007)
2. Bahrak, B., Aref, M.R.: Impossible differential attack on seven-round AES-128. IET Information Security Journal 2, 28–32 (2008)
3. Bernstein, D.J.: Cache-timing attacks on AES (2005), http://cr.yp.to/antiforgery/cachetiming-20050414.pdf
4. Biham, E., Dunkelman, O., Keller, N.: Related-key and boomerang attacks. In: Cramer, R. (ed.) EUROCRYPT 2005. LNCS, vol. 3494, pp. 507–525. Springer, Heidelberg (2005)
5. Biham, E., Dunkelman, O., Keller, N.: Related-key impossible differential attacks on AES-192. In: Pointcheval, D. (ed.) CT-RSA 2006. LNCS, vol. 3860, pp. 21–31. Springer, Heidelberg (2006)
6. Biham, E., Keller, N.: Cryptanalysis of reduced variants of Rijndael. In: The Third AES Candidate Conference (2000)
7. Biryukov, A.: Boomerang attack on 5 and 6-round AES. In: The Fourth Conference on Advanced Encryption Standard (2004)
8. Biryukov, A., Dunkelman, O., Keller, N., Khovratovich, D., Shamir, A.: Key recovery attacks of practical complexity on aes variants with up to 10 rounds (2009), http://eprint.iacr.org/2009/374.pdf
9. Biryukov, A., Khovratovich, D.: Related-key cryptanalysis of the full AES-192 and AES-256 (2009), http://eprint.iacr.org/2009/317.pdf
10. Biryukov, A., Khovratovich, D., Nikolić, I.: Distinguisher and related-key attack on the full aes-256 (extended version). In: Halevi, S. (ed.) CRYPTO 2009. LNCS, vol. 5677, pp. 231–249. Springer, Heidelberg (2009)
11. Cheon, J.H., Kim, M.J., Kim, K., Lee, J., Kang, S.: Improved impossible differential cryptanalysis of Rijndael. In: Kim, K.-c. (ed.) ICISC 2001. LNCS, vol. 2288, pp. 39–49. Springer, Heidelberg (2002)
12. Courtois, N.T., Pieprzyk, J.: Cryptanalysis of block ciphers with overdefined systems of equations. In: Zheng, Y. (ed.) ASIACRYPT 2002. LNCS, vol. 2501, pp. 267–287. Springer, Heidelberg (2002)
13. Daemen, J., Knudsen, L., Rijmen, V.: The block cipher SQUARE. In: Biham, E. (ed.) FSE 1997. LNCS, vol. 1267, pp. 149–165. Springer, Heidelberg (1997)
14. Demirci, H., Selçuk, A.A.: A meet in the middle attack on 8-round AES. In: Nyberg, K. (ed.) FSE 2008. LNCS, vol. 5086, pp. 116–126. Springer, Heidelberg (2008)

15. Ferguson, N., Kelsey, J., Lucks, S., Schneier, B., Stay, M., Wagner, D., Whiting, D.: Improved cryptanalysis of Rijndael. In: Schneier, B. (ed.) FSE 2000. LNCS, vol. 1978, pp. 213–230. Springer, Heidelberg (2001)
16. Fips-197: Advanced Encrption Standart (November 2001), http://csrc.nist.gov/publications/fips/fips197/fips-197.pdf
17. Gilbert, H., Minier, M.: A collision attack on 7 rounds of Rijndael. In: The Third AES Candidate Conference (2000)
18. Hong, S., Kim, J., Lee, S., Preneel, B.: Related-key rectangle attacks on reduced versions of SHACAL-1 and AES-192. In: Gilbert, H., Handschuh, H. (eds.) FSE 2005. LNCS, vol. 3557, pp. 368–383. Springer, Heidelberg (2005)
19. Jakimoski, G., Desmedt, Y.: Related-key differential cryptanalysis of 192-bit key AES variants. In: Matsui, M., Zuccherato, R.J. (eds.) SAC 2003. LNCS, vol. 3006, pp. 208–221. Springer, Heidelberg (2004)
20. Kim, J., Hong, S., Preneel, B.: Related-key rectangle attacks on reduced AES-192 and AES 256. In: Biryukov, A. (ed.) FSE 2007. LNCS, vol. 4593, pp. 225–241. Springer, Heidelberg (2007)
21. Lu, J., Dunkelman, O., Keller, N., Kim, J.: New impossible differential attacks on AES. In: Chowdhury, D.R., Rijmen, V., Das, A. (eds.) INDOCRYPT 2008. LNCS, vol. 5365, pp. 279–293. Springer, Heidelberg (2008)
22. Lucks, S.: Attacking seven rounds of Rijndael under 192-bit and 256-bit keys. In: The Third AES Candidate Conference (2000)
23. Nyberg, K., Knudsen, L.R.: Provable security against a differential attack. Journal of Cryptology 8(1), 27–38 (1995)
24. Phan, R.C.W.: Classes of impossible differentials of advanced encryption standard. IEE Electronics Letters 38(11), 508–510 (2002)
25. Phan, R.C.W.: Impossible differential cryptanalysis of 7-round advanced encryption standard AES. Information Processing Letters 91, 33–38 (2004)
26. Phan, R.C.W., Siddiqi, M.U.: Generalized impossible differentials of advanced encryption standard. IEE Electronics Letters 37(14), 896–898 (2001)
27. Zhang, W., Wun, W., Feng, D.: New results on impossible differential cryptanalysis of reduced AES. In: Nam, K.-H., Rhee, G. (eds.) ICISC 2007. LNCS, vol. 4817, pp. 239–250. Springer, Heidelberg (2007)
28. Zhang, W., Wun, W., Zhang, L., Feng, D.: Improved related-key impossible differential attacks on reduced round AES-192. In: Biham, E., Youssef, A.M. (eds.) SAC 2006. LNCS, vol. 4356, pp. 15–27. Springer, Heidelberg (2007)

Related-Key Rectangle Attack of the Full HAS-160 Encryption Mode

Orr Dunkelman[1], Ewan Fleischmann[2], Michael Gorski[2], and Stefan Lucks[2]

[1] Ecole Normale Superieure, France
Orr.Dunkelman@ens.fr
[2] Bauhaus-University Weimar, Germany
{Ewan.Fleischmann,Michael.Gorski,Stefan.Lucks}@uni-weimar.de

Abstract. In this paper we investigate the security of the encryption mode of the HAS-160 hash function. HAS-160 is a Korean hash standard which is widely used in Korean industry. The structure of HAS-160 is similar to SHA-1 besides some modifications. In this paper, we present the first cryptographic attack that breaks the encryption mode of the full 80-round HAS-160. SHACAL-1 and the encryption mode of HAS-160 are both blockciphers with key size 512 bits and plain-/ciphertext size of 160 bits.

We apply a key recovery attack that needs about 2^{155} chosen plaintexts and $2^{377.5}$ 80-round HAS-160 encryptions. The attack does not aim for a collision, preimage or 2nd-preimage attack, but it shows that HAS-160 used as a block cipher can be differentiated from an ideal cipher faster than exhaustive search.

Keywords: differential cryptanalysis, related-key rectangle attack, HAS-160.

1 Introduction

HAS-160 is a hash function that is widely used by the Korean industry. It is a hash function standardized by the Korean government (TTAS.KO-12.0011/R1) [1]. Based on the MERKLE-DAMGÅRD structure [9, 17], it uses a compression function with input size of 512 bits and a chaining and output value of 160 bits. HAS-160 consists of a round function which is applied 80 times for each input message block. The overall design of the compression function is similar to the design of SHA-1 [18] and the MD family [19, 20], except some modifications in the rotation constants and in the message expansion.

Up to now there are only a few cryptographic results on HAS-160. Yun et al. [23] found a collision on 45-round HAS-160 with complexity 2^{12} by using the techniques introduced by Wang et al. [22]. Cho et al. [7] extended the previous result to break 53-round HAS-160 in time 2^{55}. At ICISC 2007 Mendel and Rijmen [15] improved the attack complexity of the attack in [7] to 2^{35} hash computations and they were able to present a colliding message pair for the 53-round version of HAS-160. They also showed how the attack can be extended to 59-round HAS-160 with a complexity of 2^{55}.

B. Roy and N. Sendrier (Eds.): INDOCRYPT 2009, LNCS 5922, pp. 157–168, 2009.

HAS-160 in encryption mode is resistant to many attacks that can be applied to SHACAL-1, since its rotation constants are different and in each round its key schedule (which is equal to the message expansion) does not offer any sliding properties. Nevertheless, it has a high degree of linearity which makes it vulnerable to related-key attacks.

In this paper we analyze the internal block cipher of HAS-160 and present the first cryptographic result on the full HAS-160 in encryption mode. Using a related-key rectangle attack with four related keys we can break the full 80-rounds, i.e., recovering some key bits faster than exhaustive search. Our attack uses about 2^{155} chosen plaintexts and runs in time of about $2^{377.5}$ 80-round HAS-160 encryptions, while an exhaustive key search requires about 2^{512} 80-round HAS-160 encryptions.

The paper is organized as follows: In Section 2 we give a brief description of the HAS-160 encryption mode. Section 3 discusses some crucial properties of HAS-160. In Section 4 we describe the related-key rectangle attack. Section 5 presents our related-key rectangle attack on the full HAS-160 encryption mode. Section 6 concludes the paper.

2   Description of the HAS-160 Encryption Mode

2.1   Notation

The following notations are used in this paper:

$\oplus$: bitwise XOR operation
$\wedge$: bitwise AND operation
$\vee$: bitwise OR operation
$X^{\lll k}$: bit-rotation of X by k positions to the left.
$\boxplus$: addition modulo 2^{32} operation
$\neg$: bitwise complement operation
e_i : a 32-bit word with zeros in all positions except for bit i, $(0 \leq i \leq 31)$
$e_{i_1,\ldots,i_l}$: $e_{i_1} \oplus \cdots \oplus e_{i_l}$

The bit positions of a 32-bit word are labeled as $31, 30, \ldots, 1, 0$, where bit 31 is the most significant bit and bit 0 is the least significant bit.

2.2   HAS-160

Now we show the structure of HAS-160 an how it is used as a block cipher. The inner block cipher operates on a 160-bit message block and a 512-bit master key. A 160-bit plaintext $P_0 = A_0||B_0||C_0||D_0||E_0$ is divided into five 32-bit words A_0, B_0, C_0, D_0, E_0. HAS-160 consists of 4 passes of 20 rounds each, i.e., the round function is applied 80 times in total. The corresponding ciphertext P_{80} is denoted by $A_{80}||B_{80}||C_{80}||D_{80}||E_{80}$. The round function at round i $(i = 1, \ldots, 80)$ can be described as follows:

$$A_i \leftarrow A_{i-1}^{\lll s_{1,i}} \boxplus f_i(B_{i-1}, C_{i-1}, D_{i-1}) \boxplus E_{i-1} \boxplus k_i + c_i,$$
$$B_i \leftarrow A_{i-1},$$
$$C_i \leftarrow B_{i-1}^{\lll s_{2,i}},$$
$$D_i \leftarrow C_{i-1},$$
$$E_i \leftarrow D_{i-1},$$

where c_i and k_i represents the i-th round constant and the i-th round key respectively, while $f_i(\cdot)$ represents a boolean function. The function $f_i(\cdot)$ and the constant c_i of round i can be found in Table 1.

Table 1. Boolean functions and constants

Pass	Round (i)	Boolean function (f_i)	Constant (c_i)
1	$1 - 20$	$(x \wedge y) \vee (\neg x \wedge z)$	0
2	$21 - 40$	$x \oplus y \oplus z$	$0x5a827999$
3	$41 - 60$	$(x \vee \neg z) \oplus y$	$0x6ed9eba1$
4	$61 - 80$	$x \oplus y \oplus z$	$0x8f1bbcdc$

The rotation constant $s_{1,i}$ used in round i are given in Table 2.

Table 2. The bit rotation s_1

Round $(i \bmod 20) + 1$	1	2	3	4	5	6	7	8	9	10	11	12	13	14	15	16	17	18	19	20
$s_{1,i}$	13	5	11	7	15	6	13	8	14	7	12	9	11	8	15	6	12	9	14	5

The rotation constant $s_{2,i}$ depends on the pass, i.e., it changes the value if the pass is changed but it is constant in each pass. The pass-dependent values of $s_{2,i}$ are:

- Pass 1: $s_{2,i} = 10$
- Pass 2: $s_{2,i} = 17$
- Pass 3: $s_{2,i} = 25$
- Pass 4: $s_{2,i} = 30$

The 80 round keys k_i, $i \in \{1, 2, \ldots, 80\}$ are derived from the master key K, which consists of sixteen 32-bit words $K = x_0, x_1, \ldots, x_{15}$. The round keys k_i are obtained from the key schedule described in Table 3.

Figure 1 shows the round function of HAS-160.

Table 3. The key schedule

Round ($i \bmod 20$) + 1	Pass 1	Pass 2	Pass 3	Pass 4
1	$x_8 \oplus x_9$ $\oplus x_{10} \oplus x_{11}$	$x_{11} \oplus x_{14}$ $\oplus x_1 \oplus x_4$	$x_4 \oplus x_{13}$ $\oplus x_6 \oplus x_{15}$	$x_{15} \oplus x_{10}$ $\oplus x_5 \oplus x_0$
2	x_0	x_3	x_{12}	x_4
3	x_1	x_6	x_5	x_2
4	x_2	x_9	x_{14}	x_{13}
5	x_3	x_{12}	x_7	x_8
6	$x_{12} \oplus x_{13}$ $\oplus x_{14} \oplus x_{15}$	$x_7 \oplus x_{10}$ $\oplus x_{13} \oplus x_0$	$x_8 \oplus x_1$ $\oplus x_{10} \oplus x_3$	$x_{11} \oplus x_6$ $\oplus x_1 \oplus x_{12}$
7	x_4	x_{15}	x_0	x_3
8	x_5	x_2	x_9	x_{14}
9	x_6	x_5	x_2	x_9
10	x_7	x_8	x_{11}	x_4
11	$x_0 \oplus x_1$ $\oplus x_2 \oplus x_3$	$x_3 \oplus x_6$ $\oplus x_9 \oplus x_{12}$	$x_{12} \oplus x_5$ $\oplus x_{14} \oplus x_7$	$x_7 \oplus x_2$ $\oplus x_{13} \oplus x_8$
12	x_8	x_{11}	x_4	x_{15}
13	x_9	x_{14}	x_{13}	x_{10}
14	x_{10}	x_{14}	x_6	x_5
15	x_{11}	x_4	x_{15}	x_0
16	$x_4 \oplus x_5$ $\oplus x_6 \oplus x_7$	$x_{15} \oplus x_2$ $\oplus x_5 \oplus x_8$	$x_0 \oplus x_9$ $\oplus x_2 \oplus x_{11}$	$x_3 \oplus x_{14}$ $\oplus x_9 \oplus x_4$
17	x_{12}	x_7	x_8	x_{11}
18	x_{13}	x_{10}	x_1	x_6
19	x_{14}	x_{13}	x_{10}	x_1
20	x_{15}	x_0	x_3	x_{12}

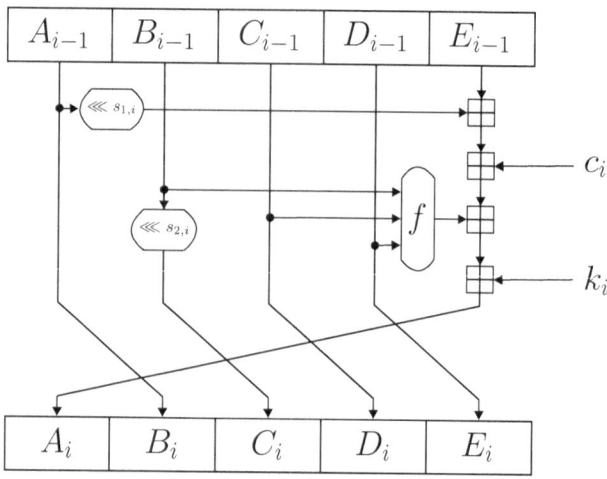

Fig. 1. The round function of HAS-160

3   Properties in HAS-160

Property 1. (from [10]) Let $Z = X \boxplus Y$ and $Z^* = X^* \boxplus Y^*$ with X, Y, X^*, Y^* being 32-bit words. Then, the following properties hold:

1. If $X \oplus X^* = e_j$ and $Y = Y^*$, then $Z \oplus Z^* = e_{j,j+1,\cdots,j+k-1}$ holds with probability 2^{-k} ($j < 31, k \geq 1$ and $j + k - 1 \leq 30$). In addition, in case $j = 31$, $Z \oplus Z^* = e_{31}$ holds with probability 1.
2. If $X \oplus X^* = e_j$ and $Y \oplus Y^* = e_j$, then $Z \oplus Z^* = e_{j+1,\cdots,j+k-1}$ holds with probability 2^{-k} ($j < 31, k \geq 1$ and $j + k - 1 \leq 30$). In addition, in case $j = 31$ $Z = Z^*$ holds with probability 1.

A more general description of these properties can be derived from the following theorem.

Theorem 1. *(from [14]) Given three 32-bit XOR differences $\Delta X, \Delta Y$ and ΔZ. If the probability $\Pr[(\Delta X, \Delta Y) \overset{\boxplus}{\to} \Delta Z] > 0$, then*

$$\Pr[(\Delta X, \Delta Y) \overset{\boxplus}{\to} \Delta Z] = 2^{-k},$$

where the integer k is given by $k = \#\{i | 0 \leq i \leq 30, \text{ not } ((\Delta X)_i = (\Delta Y)_i = (\Delta Z)_i)\}$.

Property 2. Consider the difference $\Delta P_i = (\Delta A_i, \Delta B_i, \Delta C_i, \Delta D_i, \Delta E_i)$ of a message pair in round i. Then we know some 32 differences in round $i + 1, i + 2, i + 3$ and $i + 4$. The known word differences are as follows:

$$(\Delta B_{i+1}, \Delta C_{i+1}, \Delta D_{i+1}, \Delta E_{i+1}) = (\Delta A_i, \Delta B_i \lll s_{2,i+1}, \Delta C_i, \Delta D_i),$$
$$(\Delta C_{i+2}, \Delta D_{i+2}, \Delta E_{i+2}) = (\Delta A_i \lll s_{2,i+2}, \Delta B_i \lll s_{2,i+1}, \Delta C_i),$$
$$(\Delta D_{i+3}, \Delta E_{i+3}) = (\Delta A_i \lll s_{2,i+2}, \Delta B_i \lll s_{2,i+1}),$$
$$(\Delta E_{i+4}) = (\Delta A_i \lll s_{2,i+2})$$

4   The Related-Key Rectangle Attack

The boomerang attack [21] is an extension to differential cryptanalysis [5] using adaptive chosen plaintexts and ciphertexts to attack block ciphers. The amplified boomerang attack [12] transforms the ordinary boomerang attack into a chosen plaintext attack. This attack can be improved by using all possible differentials instead of two. The resulting attack is called the rectangle attack [3]. The related-key rectangle attack was e.g. published in [13, 4, 11]. It is a combination of the related-key attack [2] and the rectangle attack. The attack can be described as follows.

A block cipher $E : \{0,1\}^n \times \{0,1\}^k \to \{0,1\}^n$ with $E_K(\cdot) := E(K, \cdot)$ is treated as a cascade of two sub-ciphers $E_{K^i}(P) = E1_{K^i}(E0_{K^i}(P))$, where P is then plaintext encrypted under the key K^i. It is assumed that there exists a related-key differential $\alpha \to \beta$ which holds with probability p for $E0$, i.e., $\Pr[E0_{K^a}(P^a) \oplus E0_{K^b}(P^b) = \beta | P^a \oplus P^b = \alpha] = p$, where K^a and $K^b = K^a \oplus \Delta K^*$

are two related keys and ΔK^* is a known key difference (the same holds for $\Pr[E0_{K^c}(P^c) \oplus E0_{K^d}(P^d) = \beta | P^c \oplus P^d = \alpha] = p$, where K^c and $K^d = K^c \oplus \Delta K^*$ are two related keys). Let $X^i = E0_{K^i}(P^i)$, $i \in \{a, b, c, d\}$ be an intermediate encryption value. We assume a related-key differential $\gamma \to \delta$ which holds with probability q for $E1$, i.e., $\Pr[E1_{K^a}(X^a) \oplus E1_{K^c}(X^c) = \delta | X^a \oplus X^c = \gamma] = q$, where the keys K^a and K^c are related as $K^a \oplus K^c = \Delta K'$ and $\Delta K'$ is a known key difference (the same holds for $\Pr[E1_{K^b}(X^b) \oplus E1_{K^d}(X^d) = \delta | X^b \oplus X^d = \gamma] = q$ where the keys K^b and K^d are related as $K^b \oplus K^d = \Delta K'$). In our attack we use four different keys but one can also apply the attack with more or less keys.

Let a plaintext quartet (P^a, P^b, P^c, P^d) with $P^a \oplus P^b = \alpha = P^c \oplus P^d$, where P^i is encrypted under the key K^i, $i \in \{a, b, c, d\}$. Out of N pairs of plaintexts with the related-key difference α about $N \cdot p$ pairs have an output difference β after $E0$. These pairs can be combined into about $\frac{(N \cdot p)^2}{2}$ quartets, such that each quartet satisfies $E0_{K^a}(P^a) \oplus E0_{K^b}(P^b) = \beta$ and $E0_{K^c}(P^c) \oplus E0_{K^d}(P^d) = \beta$. We assume that the intermediate values after $E0$ distribute uniformly over all possible values. Thus, $E0_{K^a}(P^a) \oplus E0_{K^c}(P^c) = \gamma$ holds with probability 2^{-n}. If this occurs, $E0_{K^b}(P^b) \oplus E0_{K^d}(P^d) = \gamma$ holds as well, since the following condition holds:

$$(E0_{K^a}(P^a) \oplus E0_{K^b}(P^b)) \oplus (E0_{K^c}(P^c) \oplus E0_{K^d}(P^d))$$
$$\oplus (E0_{K^a}(P^a) \oplus E0_{K^c}(P^c)) =$$
$$(X^a \oplus X^b) \oplus (X^c \oplus X^d) \oplus (X^a \oplus X^c) =$$
$$\beta \oplus \beta \oplus \gamma = \gamma$$

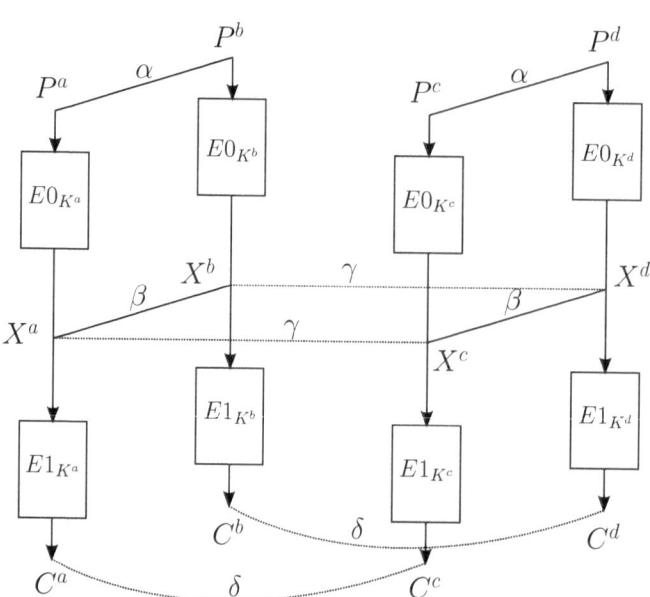

Fig. 2. The related-key rectangle distinguisher

The expected number of quartets satisfying both $E1_{K^a}(X^a) \oplus E1_{K^c}(X^c) = \delta$ and $E1_{K^b}(X^b) \oplus E1_{K^d}(X^d) = \delta$ is

$$\sum_{\beta,\gamma}(N \cdot p)^2 \cdot 2^{-n} \cdot q^2 = N^2 \cdot 2^{-n} \cdot (p \cdot q)^2.$$

For a random cipher, the expected number of correct quartets is about $N^2 \cdot 2^{-2n}$. Therefore, if $p \cdot q > 2^{-n/2}$ and N is sufficiently large, the related-key rectangle distinguisher can distinguish between E and a random cipher. Figure 2 visualizes the structure of the related-key rectangle distinguisher.

5 Related-Key Rectangle Attack on the Full HAS-160 Encryption Mode

In this section, we give a 71-round related-key rectangle distinguisher, which can be used to mount a related-key rectangle attack on the full 80-round HAS-160 encryption mode. We can use Property 2 to partially determine whether a candidate quartet is a right one or if it is not. A wrong quartet can be discarded during the stepwise computation, which reduces the complexity of the subsequent steps and also the overall complexity of the attack. Thus, our technique is in some way similar to the early abort technique presented by Lu et al. [14].

5.1 A 71-Round Related-Key Rectangle Distinguisher

Let K be a master key which can be written as $K = x_0, x_1, \ldots, x_{15}$, where x_i is a 32-bit word. We use four different – but related – master keys K^a, K^b, K^c and K^d to mount our related-key rectangle attack on the full HAS-160 encryption mode. The master key differences are as follows:

$$\Delta K^* = K^a \oplus K^b = K^c \oplus K^d = (e_{31}, 0, 0, 0, 0, 0, 0, 0, 0, 0, e_{31}, 0, 0, 0, 0, 0), \quad (1)$$
$$\Delta K' = K^a \oplus K^c = K^b \oplus K^d = (0, 0, 0, 0, 0, 0, 0, 0, 0, 0, 0, 0, e_{31}, 0, e_{31}, 0).$$

Since the key schedule of HAS-160 offers a high degree of linearity we can easily determine all the 80 round key differences derived from the master key differences ΔK^* and $\Delta K'$ respectively. We observe that if we choose $\Delta x_0 = \Delta x_{10}$ and the remaining word differences as zero, i.e., $\Delta x_i = 0$, $i = 1, 2, \ldots, 8, 9, 11, 12, \ldots, 15$, then a zero difference can be obtained starting from round 14 up to round 37. We use this observation for the related-key differential for E0. Moreover, we can observe that if $\Delta x_{12} = \Delta x_{14}$ holds and the remaining word differences in $\Delta K'$ are all zero, then a zero difference can be obtained from round 44 to round 65. This observation is used in our related-key differential for E1.

Considering Property 1 and Theorem 1 we have found a 39-round related-key differential from round 0 to 39 for E0 ($\alpha \rightarrow \beta$) using the master key difference ΔK^*. The related-key differential is:

$$(e_7, e_1, 0, e_{5,19,31}, e_{12,26,31}) \rightarrow (e_{4,31}, e_{31}, 0, 0, 0).$$

The related-key differential $E0$ is shown in Table 4.[1]

Table 4. The Related-Key Differential $E0$

i	ΔA_i	ΔB_i	ΔC_i	ΔD_i	ΔE_i	Δk_i	Prob.
0	e_7	e_1	0	$e_{5,19,31}$	$e_{12,26,31}$	$-$	2^{-7}
1	e_{26}	e_7	e_{11}	0	$e_{5,19,31}$	e_{31}	2^{-5}
2	e_{19}	e_{26}	e_{17}	e_{11}	0	e_{31}	2^{-6}
3	0	e_{19}	e_4	e_{17}	e_{11}	0	2^{-5}
4	e_{11}	0	e_{29}	e_4	e_{17}	0	2^{-3}
5	e_{23}	e_{11}	0	e_{29}	e_4	0	2^{-4}
6	e_{21}	e_{23}	e_{21}	0	e_{29}	0	2^{-4}
7	0	e_{21}	e_1	e_{21}	0	0	2^{-3}
8	0	0	e_{31}	e_1	e_{21}	0	2^{-3}
9	e_{21}	0	0	e_{31}	e_1	0	2^{-3}
10	0	e_{21}	0	0	e_{31}	0	2^{-2}
11	0	0	e_{31}	0	0	e_{31}	2^{-1}
12	0	0	0	e_{31}	0	0	2^{-1}
13	0	0	0	0	e_{31}	0	1
14	0	0	0	0	0	e_{31}	1
15	0	0	0	0	0	0	1
$\vdots$	$\vdots$	$\vdots$	$\vdots$	$\vdots$	$\vdots$	$\vdots$	$\vdots$
37	0	0	0	0	0	0	1
38	e_{31}	0	0	0	0	e_{31}	2^{-1}
39	$e_{4,31}$	e_{31}	0	0	0	0	

We exploit a 32-round related-key differential for $E1$ ($\gamma \rightarrow \delta$) that covers rounds 39 to 71 using the key difference $\Delta K'$. The related-key differential is:

$$(e_6, 0, 0, 0, e_{19}) \rightarrow (e_{5,6,7,14,17,18,19,28,29,30}, e_{5,8,9,19,21,29}, e_{5,26,27}, e_{19}, e_5)$$

The 160-bit difference δ can be written as a concatenation of five 32-bit word differences

$$\delta = (\delta_A, \delta_B, \delta_C, \delta_D, \delta_E) = (\Delta A_{71}, \Delta B_{71}, \Delta C_{71}, \Delta D_{71}, \Delta E_{71}). \qquad (2)$$

The related-key differential $E1$ is shown in Table 5. The probability for the differential $E0$ is 2^{-48} due to Table 4, while the probability for $E1$ is 2^{-24} from Table 5. Thus, the probability of our related-key rectangle distinguisher for round 1–71 is:

$$\left(2^{-48} \cdot 2^{-24}\right)^2 \cdot 2^{-160} = 2^{-304}$$

---

[1] Note that $\Pr[(\Delta c_i, \Delta k_i) \overset{\boxplus}{\rightarrow} \Delta k_i] = 1$ always holds due to Property 1. This is true since Δc_i is equal to zero for all i and Δk_i is either zero or e_{31}.

Table 5. The Related-Key Differential $E1$

i	ΔA_i	ΔB_i	ΔC_i	ΔD_i	ΔE_i	Δk_i	Prob.
39	e_6	0	0	0	e_{19}	$-$	2^{-1}
40	0	e_6	0	0	0	0	2^{-1}
41	0	0	e_{31}	0	0	0	1
42	0	0	0	e_{31}	0	e_{31}	2^{-1}
43	0	0	0	0	e_{31}	0	1
44	0	0	0	0	0	e_{31}	1
45	0	0	0	0	0	0	1
$\vdots$	$\vdots$	$\vdots$	$\vdots$	$\vdots$	$\vdots$	$\vdots$	$\vdots$
65	0	0	0	0	0	0	1
66	e_{31}	0	0	0	0	e_{31}	2^{-1}
67	e_7	e_{31}	0	0	0	0	2^{-1}
68	e_{21}	e_7	e_{29}	0	0	e_{31}	2^{-3}
69	$e_{7,28,29}$	e_{21}	e_5	e_{29}	0	0	2^{-6}
70	$e_{5,8,9,19,21,29}$	$e_{7,28,29}$	e_{19}	e_5	e_{29}	0	2^{-10}
71	$e_{5,6,7,14,17,18,19,28,29,30}$	$e_{5,8,9,19,21,29}$	$e_{5,26,27}$	e_{19}	e_5		

However, the correct difference δ occurs in two ciphertext pairs of a ciphertext quartet for a random cipher with probability $(2^{-160})^2 = 2^{-320}$.

5.2 The Attack on the Full HAS-160 Encryption Mode

Our attack uses four related keys K^a, K^b, K^c and K^d where each two of the four master keys are related as stated in (2). It is assumed that an attacker knows the two master key differences ΔK^* and $\Delta K'$, but not the maser keys themselves. In the first step we apply our 71-round related-key rectangle distinguisher to obtain a small amount of subkey candidates in rounds $72, 73, 74, 76, 77, 78, 80$. In the second step we find the remaining subkey candidates by an exhaustive search for the obtained subkey candidates and the remaining subkeys to recover the four 512-bit master keys K^a, K^b, K^c and K^d.
The attack works as follows:

1. Choose 2^{155} plaintexts $P_i^a = (A_i, B_i, C_i, D_i, E_i)$, $i = 1, 2, \ldots, 2^{155}$. Compute 2^{155} plaintexts P_i^b, i.e., $P_i^b = P_i^a \oplus \alpha$, where α is a fixed 160-bit word as stated above. Set $P_i^c = P_i^a$ and $P_i^d = P_i^b$. In a chosen plaintext attack scenario ask for the encryption of the plaintexts $P_i^a, P_i^b, P_i^c, P_i^d$ under K^a, K^b, K^c and K^d, respectively and obtain the ciphertexts C_i^a, C_i^b, C_i^c and C_i^d.
2. Guess seven 32-bit round keys $k_{80}^a, k_{79}^a, k_{78}^a, k_{77}^a, k_{76}^a, k_{75}^a, k_{74}^a$ and compute $k_{80}^l, k_{79}^l, k_{78}^l, k_{77}^l, k_{76}^l, k_{75}^l, k_{74}^l$, $l \in \{b, c, d\}$ using the known round key differences.
   2.1. Decrypt each of the ciphertexts $C_i^a, C_i^b, C_i^c, C_i^d$ under $k_{80}^l, k_{79}^l, k_{78}^l, k_{77}^l, k_{76}^l$, k_{75}^l, k_{74}^l, $l \in \{a, b, c, d\}$ respectively and obtain the intermediate encryption

values $C_{73,i}^a$, $C_{73,i}^b$, $C_{73,i}^c$ and $C_{73,i}^d$, respectively. From Property 2 we know the value of the 96-bit difference $\delta_{A \lll 30}$, $\delta_{B \lll 30}$ and δ_C, see (2).

2.2. Check whether the following conditions are fulfilled for any quartet $(C_{73,j}^a, C_{73,j}^b, C_{73,j}^c, C_{73,j}^d)$:

$$C_{73,j}^a \oplus C_{73,j}^c = \delta_{A \lll 30} = C_{73,j}^b \oplus C_{73,j}^d,$$
$$D_{73,j}^a \oplus D_{73,j}^c = \delta_{B \lll 30} = D_{73,j}^b \oplus D_{73,j}^d,$$
$$E_{73,j}^a \oplus E_{73,j}^c = \delta_C = E_{73,j}^b \oplus E_{73,j}^d.$$

Record $k_{80}^l, k_{79}^l, k_{78}^l, k_{77}^l, k_{76}^l, k_{75}^l, k_{74}^l$, $l \in \{a, b, c, d\}$ and discard all the quartets that do not satisfy the above conditions and discard the quartets that do not satisfy this condition.

3. Guess a 32-bit round key k_{73}^a and compute k_{73}^l, $l \in \{b, c, d\}$ using the known round key differences.

3.1. Decrypt each remaining quartet $(C_{73,j}^a, C_{73,j}^b, C_{73,j}^c, C_{73,j}^d)$ under k_{73}^l, $l \in \{a, b, c, d\}$, respectively and obtain the quartets $(C_{72,j}^a, C_{72,j}^b, C_{72,j}^c, C_{72,j}^d)$. From Property 2 we know the value of the 32-bit difference δ_D.

3.2. Check whether $E_{72,j}^a \oplus E_{72,j}^c = \delta_D = E_{72,j}^b \oplus E_{72,j}^d$ holds. Record $k_{80}^l, k_{79}^l, k_{78}^l, k_{77}^l, k_{76}^l, k_{75}^l, k_{74}^l, k_{73}^l$, $l \in \{a, b, c, d\}$ and discard all the quartets that do not satisfy the above condition.

4. Guess one 32-bit round keys k_{72}^a and compute k_{72}^l, $l \in \{b, c, d\}$ using the known round key differences.

4.1. Decrypt each remaining quartet $(C_{72,j}^a, C_{72,j}^b, C_{72,j}^c, C_{72,j}^d)$ under k_{72}^l, $l \in \{a, b, c, d\}$ respectively and obtain the quartets $(C_{71,j}^a, C_{71,j}^b, C_{71,j}^c, C_{71,j}^d)$. From Property 2 we know the value of the 32-bit difference δ_E.

4.2. Check whether $E_{71,j}^a \oplus E_{71,j}^c = \delta_E = E_{71,j}^b \oplus E_{71,j}^d$ holds. If there exist at least 21 quartets passing the above condition, record $k_{80}^l, k_{79}^l, k_{78}^l, k_{77}^l, k_{76}^l, k_{75}^l, k_{74}^l, k_{73}^l, k_{72}^l$, $l \in \{a, b, c, d\}$ and go to Step 5. Otherwise go to Step 4 with another guessed round key. If all the possible round keys for k_{72}^a are tested, then repeat Step 3 with another guessed round key k_{73}^a. If all the possible round keys for k_{73}^a are tested, then go to Step 2 with another guess for the round keys $k_{80}^a, k_{79}^a, k_{78}^a, k_{77}^a, k_{76}^a, k_{75}^a, k_{74}^a$.

5. For a suggested $(k_{80}^l, k_{79}^l, k_{78}^l, k_{77}^l, k_{76}^l, k_{75}^l, k_{74}^l, k_{73}^l, k_{72}^l)$, do an exhaustive key search for the remaining $512 - 9 \cdot 32 = 224$ key bits by trial encryption. If a 512-bit key is suggested, output it as the master key of the full HAS-160 encryption mode. Otherwise restart the algorithm.

5.3   Analysis of the Attack

There are 2^{155} pairs (P_i^a, P_i^b) and 2^{155} pairs (P_i^c, P_i^d) of plaintexts, thus we have $(2^{155})^2 = 2^{310}$ quartets. The data complexity of Step 1 is $2^2 \cdot 2^{155} = 2^{157}$ chosen plaintexts. The time complexity of Step 1 is about $2^2 \cdot 2^{155} = 2^{157}$ encryptions. Step 2.1 requires time about $2^{224} \cdot 2^2 \cdot 2^{155} \cdot (7/80) \approx 2^{377.5}$ eighty round encryptions. The number of remaining quartets after Step 2.2 is $2^{310} \cdot (2^{-96})^2 = 2^{118}$, since we have a 96-bit filtering condition on both pairs of a quartet. The time complexity of Step 3.1 is about $2^{256} \cdot 2^2 \cdot 2^{118} \cdot (1/80) \approx 2^{370}$ encryptions. After Step 3.2 about $2^{118} \cdot (2^{-32})^2 = 2^{54}$ quartets remain, since we have a 32-bit filtering condition on both pairs of a quartet. The time complexity of Step 4.1 is $2^{288} \cdot 2^2 \cdot 2^{54} \cdot (1/80) \approx 2^{337.5}$ encryptions. After Step 4.2 the number of remaining quartets is about $2^{54} \cdot (2^{-32})^2 = 2^{-10}$, since we have a 32-bit filtering condition on both pairs of a quartet. Thus, we do not expect wrong quartets after the distinguisher step remaining either for the correct or the false round keys. The expected number of quartets that remain for the correct round keys are about $2^{310} \cdot 2^{-304} = 2^6$.

Using the Poisson distribution we can compute the success rate of our attack. The probability that the number of remaining quartets for each false key bit combination is larger then 21 is $Y_i \sim Poisson(\mu = 2^{-10})$, $\Pr(Y_i \geq 22) \approx 0$, where i indicates a wrong key. Thus, for all the $2^{288} - 1$ wrong keys we expect that about $2^{188} \cdot 2^{189} = 2^{-1}$ quartets are counted. The probability that the number of quartets counted for the correct key bits is at least 21 is $Z \sim Poisson(\mu = 2^6)$, $\Pr(Z \geq 22) \approx 1$. The data complexity of our attack is $2^{155} \cdot 2^2 = 2^{157}$ chosen plaintexts, while the time complexity is about $2^{377.5}$ full HAS-160 encryptions. Our attack has a success rate of 1.

6   Conclusion

In this paper we present the first cryptanalytic result on the inner block cipher of the Korean hash algorithm standard HAS-160. Our related-key rectangle attack can break the full 80-round HAS-160 encryption mode. A more complex and non-linear key schedule would have defended our attack. Moreover, to strengthen the cipher against differential attacks, we propose to use the f-function more often in each round and so the f-function may influence more than one word in each round. Note that this analysis does not seem to say anything about the collision, preimage or 2nd-preimage resistance of HAS-160, but it shows some interesting properties that occur if HAS-160 is used as a block cipher. It shows that HAS-160 as a block cipher can be differentiated efficiently from a random cipher and the key bits can be found much faster than exhaustive search.

References

[1] Telecommunications Technology Association. Hash Function Standard Part 2: Hash Function Algorithm Standard (HAS-160). TTAS.KO-12.0011/R1 (December 2000)

[2] Biham, E.: New Types of Cryptanalytic Attacks Using Related Keys. J. Cryptology 7(4), 229–246 (1994)

[3] Biham, E., Dunkelman, O., Keller, N.: The Rectangle Attack - Rectangling the Serpent. In: Pfitzmann, B. (ed.) EUROCRYPT 2001. LNCS, vol. 2045, pp. 340–357. Springer, Heidelberg (2001)

[4] Biham, E., Dunkelman, O., Keller, N.: Related-Key Boomerang and Rectangle Attacks. In: Cramer (ed.) [8], pp. 507–525

[5] Biham, E., Shamir, A.: Differential Cryptanalysis of DES-like Cryptosystems. In: Menezes, A., Vanstone, S.A. (eds.) [16], pp. 2–21

[6] Brassard, G. (ed.): CRYPTO 1989. LNCS, vol. 435. Springer, Heidelberg (1990)

[7] Cho, H.-S., Park, S., Sung, S.H., Yun, A.: Collision Search Attack for 53-Step HAS-160. In: Rhee, M.S., Lee, B. (eds.) ICISC 2006. LNCS, vol. 4296, pp. 286–295. Springer, Heidelberg (2006)

[8] Cramer, R. (ed.): EUROCRYPT 2005. LNCS, vol. 3494. Springer, Heidelberg (2005)

[9] Damgård, I.: A Design Principle for Hash Functions. In: Brassard, G. (ed.) [6], pp. 416–427

[10] Hong, S., Kim, J., Kim, G., Sung, J., Lee, C., Lee, S.: Impossible Differential Attack on 30-Round SHACAL-2. In: Johansson, T., Maitra, S. (eds.) INDOCRYPT 2003. LNCS, vol. 2904, pp. 97–106. Springer, Heidelberg (2003)

[11] Hong, S., Kim, J., Lee, S., Preneel, B.: Related-Key Rectangle Attacks on Reduced Versions of SHACAL-1 and AES-192. In: Gilbert, H., Handschuh, H. (eds.) FSE 2005. LNCS, vol. 3557, pp. 368–383. Springer, Heidelberg (2005)

[12] Kelsey, J., Kohno, T., Schneier, B.: Amplified Boomerang Attacks Against Reduced-Round MARS and Serpent. In: Schneier, B. (ed.) FSE 2000. LNCS, vol. 1978, pp. 75–93. Springer, Heidelberg (2001)

[13] Kim, J., Kim, G., Hong, S., Lee, S., Hong, D.: The Related-Key Rectangle Attack - Application to SHACAL-1. In: Wang, H., Pieprzyk, J., Varadharajan, V. (eds.) ACISP 2004. LNCS, vol. 3108, pp. 123–136. Springer, Heidelberg (2004)

[14] Lu, J., Kim, J., Keller, N., Dunkelman, O.: Related-Key Rectangle Attack on 42-Round SHACAL-2. In: Katsikas, S.K., López, J., Backes, M., Gritzalis, S., Preneel, B. (eds.) ISC 2006. LNCS, vol. 4176, pp. 85–100. Springer, Heidelberg (2006)

[15] Mendel, F., Rijmen, V.: Colliding Message Pair for 53-Step HAS-160. In: Nam, K.-H., Rhee, G. (eds.) ICISC 2007. LNCS, vol. 4817, pp. 324–334. Springer, Heidelberg (2007)

[16] Menezes, A., Vanstone, S.A. (eds.): CRYPTO 1990. LNCS, vol. 537. Springer, Heidelberg (1991)

[17] Merkle, R.C.: One Way Hash Functions and DES. In: Brassard (ed.) [6], pp. 428–446

[18] National Institute of Standards and Technology. FIPS 180-1: Secure Hash Standard (April 1995), http://csrc.nist.gov

[19] Rivest, R.: The MD5 Message-Digest Algorithm. Request for Comments: 1321 (April 1992), http://tools.ietf.org/html/rfc1321

[20] Rivest, R.L.: The MD4 Message Digest Algorithm. In: Menezes, A., Vanstone, S.A. (eds.) [16], pp. 303–311

[21] Wagner, D.: The Boomerang Attack. In: Knudsen, L.R. (ed.) FSE 1999. LNCS, vol. 1636, pp. 156–170. Springer, Heidelberg (1999)

[22] Wang, X., Lai, X., Feng, D., Chen, H., Yu, X.: Cryptanalysis of the Hash Functions MD4 and RIPEMD. In: Cramer, R. (ed.) [8], pp. 1–18

[23] Yun, A., Sung, S.H., Park, S., Chang, D., Hong, S., Cho, H.-S.: Finding Collision on 45-Step HAS-160. In: Won, D.H., Kim, S. (eds.) ICISC 2005. LNCS, vol. 3935, pp. 146–155. Springer, Heidelberg (2006)

Second Preimage Attack on SHAMATA-512

Kota Ideguchi and Dai Watanabe

Systems Development Laboratory, Hitachi, LTD
{kota.ideguchi.yf,dai.watanabe.td}@hitachi.com

Abstract. We present a second preimage attack on SHAMATA-512, which is a hash function of 512-bit output and one of the first round candidates of the SHA-3 competition. The attack controls several message blocks to fix some variables of internal state and uses a meet-in-the-middle approach to find second preimages. The time complexity is about $2^{452.7}$ computations of the step function and the memory complexity is about $2^{451.4}$ blocks of 128 bits.

Keywords: hash function, second preimage attack, SHAMATA, SHA-3 candidate.

1 Introduction

Cryptographic hash functions are important cryptographic primitives and used in many applications including HMAC, PRNG and signature schemes. After the discovery of the attacks [1,2] on NIST's standard hash function SHA-1, cryptographic community has much interest in building secure and efficient hash functions. Indeed, NIST demands a new standard hash function, SHA-3 [3], which will be selected through a competition among the hash functions proposed by researchers from all over the world. The hash functions are expected to have preimage, second preimage and collision resistances. For the hash functions of n-bit output, it is expected that a preimage, a second preimage and a collision are not found faster than 2^n, 2^n and $2^{n/2}$ operations, respectively.

There are several types of hash functions proposed to SHA-3 competition. Among them, one of the most interesting designs is the sponge structure [4]. Several hash functions based on the sponge structure adapt stream-cipher design and thus these hash functions are more likely to have good performance of throughput speed. Besides, hash functions based on the sponge structure use a permutation as a update transformation of internal state. Due to invertibility of the permutation, a meet-in-the-middle technique [5] becomes a powerful tool to attack these hash functions. Indeed, several candidates of SHA-3 competition were attacked by this technique in the paper [6].

SHAMATA [7] is the hash function based on sponge structure and stream-cipher design which is proposed by Atalay et al. and one of the first round candidates of SHA-3 competition. There were some cryptanalyses on SHAMATA. An internal component of SHAMATA was analyzed as a block cipher in the papers [8,9]. However, this result does not give direct implication about security of

B. Roy and N. Sendrier (Eds.): INDOCRYPT 2009, LNCS 5922, pp. 169–181, 2009.

SHAMATA as a hash function. A collision attack was mounted on SHAMATA by Indesteege et al [10]. They found a collision of SHAMATA-256 with time complexity of about 2^{40} and proposed a theoretical collision attack on SHAMATA-512 with time complexity of about 2^{110}. To our knowledge, there is no published work on other security criteria, such as second preimage resistance and preimage resistance, of SHAMATA. Our main contribution is to give a security analysis about second preimage resistance of SHAMATA.

In this paper, we analyze SHAMATA and propose a second preimage attack on SHAMATA-512 requiring $2^{452.7}$ computations of the step function. This is less than 2^{512} computations required for generic attack. Our attack fixes some variables of internal state by controlling several message blocks and uses a meet-in-the-middle technique to obtain second preimages. Furthermore, we point out some properties of the hash function which enable our attack. Interestingly, the designers of the hash function adopted these properties with an aim to increase security.

The paper is organized as follows. In Section 2, the specification of SHAMATA is briefly explained. In Section 3, we observe some properties of SHAMATA that are used in our attack. In Section 4, a second preimage attack on SHAMATA-512 is presented, and then some discussion about designer's security claim is given in Section 5. Finally, we conclude this paper in Section 6.

2   The SHAMATA Hash Function

In this section, we briefly describe the specification of SHAMATA. We skip details that are not relevant to our attack. We refer to the original paper [7] for these.

The hash function SHAMATA is a hash function based on stream-cipher design. A message is padded to a multiple of 128 bits and the message blocks are processed by a step function sequentially. Let $pad(x) = M_0||M_1||\cdots||M_{l-1}$ be a l-block padded message. The hash function consists of three stages; Initialization, Update and Finalization stages. The hash value $y = H(x)$ is computed as follows:

Initialization Stage: $S_0 = Initialization(IV)$,

Update Stage: $S_{i+1} = StepFunction(S_i, M_i, i)$, $i = 0, 1, \ldots, l - 1$,

Finalization Stage: $y = Finalization(S_l, l)$,

where S_i is the internal state before the i-th step is applied[1]. We call the update process, described by $S_{i+1} = StepFunction(S_i, M_i, i)$, the i-th step. We will not explain details of the initialization and finalization stages because our attack does not need the details.

The internal state is of 2048-bit length and stored in sixteen 128-bit registers; four B registers $\{B[0], \ldots, B[3]\}$ and twelve K registers $\{K[0], \ldots, K[11]\}$. We

---

[1] The $StepFunction$ is called $UpdateRegister$ in the specification [7] of the hash function.

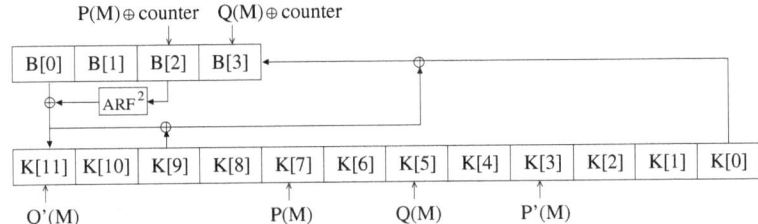

Fig. 1. The shift register of *StepFunction*

denote values of the registers $B[n]$ and $K[n]$ before the i-th step by $B[n]_i$ and $K[n]_i$, respectively. Hence, the internal state S_i before i-th step is $\{B[0]_i, \ldots, B[3]_i, K[0]_i, \ldots, K[11]_i\}$.

In a process of the step function, firstly register values are xored with linear transformations of a message block and then the shift register is clocked twice. The step function is depicted at Figure 1 and can be expressed as the following equations.

$$B[0]_{i+1} = B[2]_i \oplus P(M_i) \oplus (i+1),$$
$$B[1]_{i+1} = B[3]_i \oplus Q(M_i) \oplus (i+1),$$
$$B[2]_{i+1} = K[0]_i \oplus K[9]_i \oplus B[0]_i \oplus ARF^2(B[2]_i \oplus P(M_i) \oplus (i+1)),$$
$$B[3]_{i+1} = K[1]_i \oplus K[10]_i \oplus B[1]_i \oplus ARF^2(B[3]_i \oplus Q(M_i) \oplus (i+1)),$$
$$K[n]_{i+1} = K[n+2]_i, \quad n = 0, 2, 4, 6, 7, 8,$$
$$K[1]_{i+1} = K[3]_i \oplus P'(M_i),$$
$$K[3]_{i+1} = K[5]_i \oplus Q(M_i),$$
$$K[5]_{i+1} = K[7]_i \oplus P(M_i),$$
$$K[9]_{i+1} = K[11]_i \oplus Q'(M_i),$$
$$K[10]_{i+1} = B[0]_i \oplus ARF^2(B[2]_i \oplus P(M_i) \oplus (i+1)),$$
$$K[11]_{i+1} = B[1]_i \oplus ARF^2(B[3]_i \oplus Q(M_i) \oplus (i+1)),$$

where the functions P and Q are linear and invertible functions, P' and Q' are linear functions and ARF is the AES round function without AddRoundKey.

3   Observation: Another Description of the Shift Register

In this section, we give another description of the shift register in Figure 1.

We divide the registers into two sets, the registers with even number index and the registers with odd number index. The step function can be described by two shift registers interacting with each other only at the points of the feedbacks. This is depicted in Figure 2. One shift register is formed by the even registers and the other is formed by the odd registers. In the step function, firstly the register values are xored with the linear transformations of the message block and then two shift registers are clocked simultaneously and once.

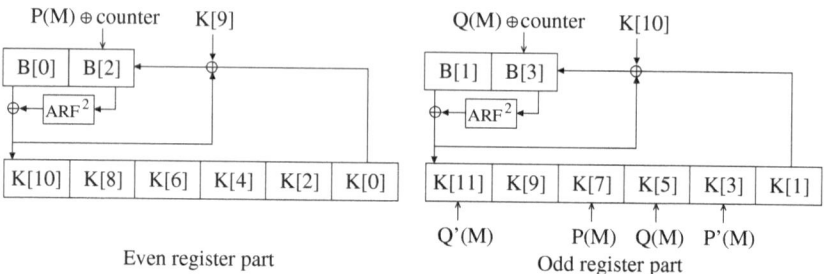

Fig. 2. Another description of *StepFunction*

We can see the following two properties from this description.

Property 1. For the even register part, a message block is xored only with $B[2]$ register. Especially, K registers with even number indices are not xored with message blocks.

Property 2. The linear transformation of the message block which is xored with $K[7]$ register is the same as that of the message block xored with $B[2]$ register.

As will be seen in Section 4.3 and 4.4, these properties are used in our attack.

4   Second Preimage Attack on SHAMATA-512

In this section, we describe a second preimage attack on SHAMATA-512. First, we describe notations and basic setting of the attack in Section 4.1. Then, we present a main procedure of the attack in Section 4.2 and sub-procedures which are used in the main procedure in Section 4.3 and 4.4. Finally, the computational complexity of the attack is shown in Section 4.5.

4.1   Notations and Setting of Second Preimage Attack

Let $x^{(0)}$ and $y^{(0)}$ be the target message and its hash value respectively.

$$y^{(0)} = H(x^{(0)}). \tag{1}$$

Let the padded message of $x^{(0)}$ consist of l 128-bit message blocks, $pad(x^{(0)}) = M_0^{(0)}||M_1^{(0)}||\cdots||M_{l-1}^{(0)}$. The internal state before the i-th step is denoted by $S_i^{(0)}$. The values of registers $B[n]$ and $K[n]$ before the i-th step are denoted by $B[n]_i^{(0)}$ and $K[n]_i^{(0)}$, respectively.

The goal of the attack is to find a message x which is not equal to $x^{(0)}$ and gives the same hash value as $x^{(0)}$ does, i.e.

$$y^{(0)} = H(x), \quad x \neq x^{(0)}. \tag{2}$$

Our attack aims to find a second preimage x such that the block length of $pad(x)$ is the same as that of $pad(x^{(0)})$, which is l. We denote the padded message of x by

$pad(x) = M_0||M_1|| \cdots ||M_{l-1}$. The internal state before the i-th step is denoted by S_i. The values of registers $B[n]$ and $K[n]$ before the i-th step is denoted by $B[n]_i$ and $K[n]_i$, respectively. The differences between the values related to $x^{(0)}$ and those related to x are defined as follows:

$$b[n]_i = B[n]_i \oplus B[n]_i^{(0)}, \quad k[n]_i = K[n]_i \oplus K[n]_i^{(0)}, \quad m_i = M_i \oplus M_i^{(0)},$$

$$\sigma_i = S_i \oplus S_i^{(0)} = \{b[0]_i, \ldots, b[3]_i, k[0]_i, \ldots, k[11]_i\}.$$

where $S_i \oplus S_i^{(0)}$ is defined as component-wise differences.

The finalization function depends on the internal state after processing the last message block and the total number of messages blocks. Hence, if the internal state difference σ_l after processing the last message block is zero, the difference of the hash value is also zero. Our attack aims to obtain the message which cause this internal collision, $\sigma_l = 0$.

4.2 Procedure of Second Preimage Attack

Our attack controls message blocks over several blocks and can be applied when the length of the padded message is greater than or equal to 27, that is $l \geq 27$. We assume that this condition holds.

Our attack uses a meet-in-the-middle approach. The attacker divides a message into two segments: the first λ message blocks $M_0|| \cdots ||M_{\lambda-1}$ and the last $(l - \lambda)$ message blocks $M_\lambda|| \cdots ||M_{l-1}$. The integer λ is arbitrarily determined by the attacker under the conditions, $\lambda \geq 13$ and $(l - \lambda) \geq 14$. Such a λ exists, because $l \geq 27$. It is explained in Section 4.3 and 4.4 why these conditions are needed.

A procedure of the attack is as follows.

Step 1. As candidates of the first segment $M_0|| \cdots ||M_{\lambda-1}$, we build 2^{448} messages of λ blocks such that when each of these message is used to update the initial internal state difference $\sigma_0 = 0$, an internal state after the $\lambda - 1$-th step, σ_λ, satisfies the following equations:

$$b[0]_\lambda = k[0]_\lambda = k[2]_\lambda = k[4]_\lambda = k[6]_\lambda = k[8]_\lambda = k[10]_\lambda = 0,$$
$$b[2]_\lambda = k[7]_\lambda, \quad k[5]_\lambda = 0. \tag{3}$$

The message candidates and the corresponding internal states σ_λ are stored in pairs on a storage. The set of 2^{448} pairs is denoted by V_1. A way to build message candidates of the first segment is described in section 4.3.

Step 2. As a candidate of the second (last) segment $M_\lambda|| \cdots ||M_{k-1}$, we build a message of $(l - \lambda)$ blocks such that when this message is used to reverse the final internal state difference $\sigma_l = 0$, an internal state difference before the λ-th step, σ_λ, satisfies the equations (3). A way to build message candidates of the second segment is described in section 4.4.

Step 3. We check the obtained internal state σ_λ is found in V_1 which is made in Step 1. If found, the message candidate of the first segment paired with this internal state in V_1 and the message candidate of the second segment which

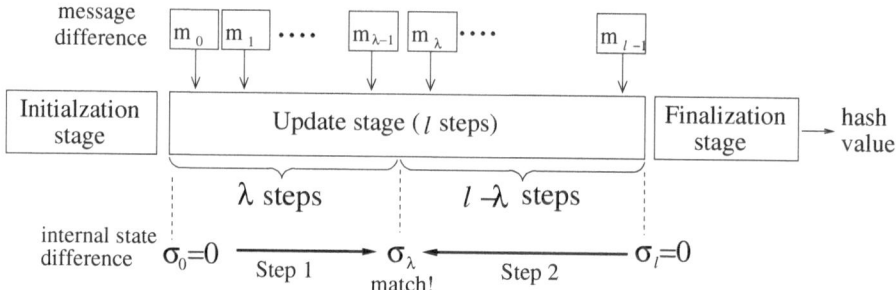

Fig. 3. Overview of attack

is now tested are concatenated to form a second preimage. If not found, go back to Step 2.

An overview of the attack is depicted in Figure 3.

Because the space of the internal state difference restricted by the equations (3) is 896-bit volume and the number of the internal state belonging to V_1 is 2^{448}, we need to build about $2^{896-448}$ message candidates of the second segment at Step 2 before a second preimage is obtained.

4.3   Building Message Candidates of the First Segment of Message

In this section, we show how to obtain message candidates of λ blocks $M_0|| \cdots ||M_{\lambda-1}$ that are used to update the initial internal state difference σ_0 to an internal state differences σ_λ satisfying equations (3).

Firstly, let us see the update of an internal state difference by the step function.

$$b[0]_{i+1} = b[2]_i \oplus P(m_i), \tag{4}$$

$$b[1]_{i+1} = b[3]_i \oplus Q(m_i), \tag{5}$$

$$b[2]_{i+1} = k[0]_i \oplus k[9]_i \oplus b[0]_i \oplus \Delta_{X_i^{(0)}}(b[2]_i \oplus P(m_i)), \tag{6}$$

$$b[3]_{i+1} = k[1]_i \oplus k[10]_i \oplus b[1]_i \oplus \Delta_{Y_i^{(0)}}(b[3]_i \oplus Q(m_i)), \tag{7}$$

$$k[n]_{i+1} = k[n+2]_i, \quad n = 0, 2, 4, 6, 8 \tag{8}$$

$$k[1]_{i+1} = k[3]_i \oplus P'(m_i), \tag{9}$$

$$k[3]_{i+1} = k[5]_i \oplus Q(m_i), \tag{10}$$

$$k[5]_{i+1} = k[7]_i \oplus P(m_i), \tag{11}$$

$$k[7]_{i+1} = k[9]_i, \tag{12}$$

$$k[9]_{i+1} = k[11]_i \oplus Q'(m_i), \tag{13}$$

$$k[10]_{i+1} = b[0]_i \oplus \Delta_{X_i^{(0)}}(b[2]_i \oplus P(m_i)), \tag{14}$$

$$k[11]_{i+1} = b[1]_i \oplus \Delta_{Y_i^{(0)}}(b[3]_i \oplus Q(m_i)), \tag{15}$$

where $\Delta_X(r)$, $X_i^{(0)}$, and $Y_i^{(0)}$ are defined as follows,

$$\Delta_X(r) = ARF^2(r) \oplus ARF^2(X \oplus r),$$

$$X_i^{(0)} = B[2]_i^{(0)} \oplus P(M_i^{(0)}) \oplus (i+1),$$
$$Y_i^{(0)} = B[3]_i^{(0)} \oplus Q(M_i^{(0)}) \oplus (i+1).$$

By controlling nine message block differences, we can fix nine variables of the internal state as the following theorem.

Theorem 1. *Consider any internal state difference before the j-th step σ_j. If nine message block differences $m_j, \ldots, m_{j+8}$ are set by the equations $P(m_i) = b[2]_i$ for $i = j, j+1, \ldots, j+8$, then an internal state difference after the $(j+8)$-th step σ_{j+9} satisfies the following equations:*

$$b[0]_{j+9} = k[0]_{j+9} = k[2]_{j+9} = k[4]_{j+9} = k[6]_{j+9} = k[8]_{j+9} = k[10]_{j+9} = 0,$$
$$b[2]_{j+9} = k[7]_{j+9}, \quad k[5]_{j+9} = 0. \tag{16}$$

Proof. We prove the theorem by using the equations (4)-(15) and $P(m_i) = b[2]_i$, for $i = j, \ldots, j+8$.
First, by using the equation (4) and $P(m_i) = b[2]_i$, for $i = j, \ldots, j+8$, the following equations hold:

$$b[0]_i = 0, \quad i = j+1, \ldots, j+9. \tag{17}$$

If $P(m_i) = b[2]_i$, the input difference of ARF^2 at the equation (6) becomes zero and then the output difference of ARF^2 also becomes zero. Therefore, by using the equations (14) and (17), the following equations hold:

$$k[10]_i = 0, \quad i = j+2, \ldots, j+9. \tag{18}$$

Then, by using the equations (8) and (18), the following equations hold.

$$k[8]_i = 0, \quad i = j+3, \ldots, j+9, \tag{19}$$
$$k[6]_i = 0, \quad i = j+4, \ldots, j+9, \tag{20}$$
$$k[4]_i = 0, \quad i = j+5, \ldots, j+9, \tag{21}$$
$$k[2]_i = 0, \quad i = j+6, \ldots, j+9, \tag{22}$$
$$k[0]_i = 0. \quad i = j+7, \ldots, j+9. \tag{23}$$

Next, by using the equations (6), (17), (23) and $P(m_i) = b[2]_i$ for $i = j+7, j+8$, $b[2]_{i+1}$ is equal to $k[9]_i$ for $i = j+7, j+8$. Then, together with the equation (12), the following equations hold.

$$k[7]_i = b[2]_i, \quad i = j+8, j+9. \tag{24}$$

Finally, we obtain the following equation by using the equations (11) and (24).

$$k[5]_{j+9} = k[7]_{j+8} \oplus P(m_{j+8}) = k[7]_{j+8} \oplus b[2]_{j+8} = 0. \tag{25}$$

$\square$

This message control is well understood in the description of the step function in Section 3. From Property 1, it is expected that the even registers can be easily controlled. Indeed, by setting $P(m_i) = b[2]_i$, the difference at $B[2]$ is cancelled before a clock of the shift register and an input of ARF function at the even register part has no difference. Repeating this cancellation between $b[2]_i$ and $P(m)_i$ during nine steps for $i = j, \ldots, j+8$, all differences after $(j+8)$-th step of even register values except that of $B[2]$ become zero and the value $b[2]_{j+9}$ is the same as the value $k[7]_{j+9}$. Furthermore, since the linear transformation of the message difference at $K[7]$ is the same as that at $B[2]$ (Property 2), the value $k[7]_{j+9}$ vanishes. This is what happens in the message control in Theorem 1.

Now, we present the procedure to obtain message candidates required in Step 1 in Section 4.2.

Step 1-1. We arbitrarily fix a message-block difference of $(\lambda - 13)$-block length, $m_0 || \cdots || m_{\lambda-14}$. Using this, we update the internal state difference $\sigma_0 = 0$ and obtain $\sigma_{\lambda-13}$.

Step 1-2. We randomly choose a message-block difference of four-block length, $m_{\lambda-13} || \cdots || m_{\lambda-10}$, and update the internal state difference $\sigma_{\lambda-13}$ to $\sigma_{\lambda-9}$.

Step 1-3. We determine a message-block difference of nine-block length, $m_{\lambda-9} || \cdots || m_{\lambda-1}$, by using Theorem 1 with $j = \lambda - 9$ and obtain the internal state difference σ_λ satisfying the equations (3). Then, a message candidate is obtained by xoring $M_0^{(0)} || \cdots || M_{\lambda-1}^{(0)}$ with $m_0 || \cdots || m_{\lambda-1}$.

In order to build 2^{448} message candidates of the first segment, we execute Step 1-1 once and repeat 2^{448} times the procedure from Step 1-2 to Step 1-3. Because message-block differences of four-block length, $m_{\lambda-14} || \cdots || m_{\lambda-10}$, is of 512-bit length, we can choose 2^{448} different message-block differences at Step 1-2. Therefore, we can build different 2^{448} message candidates. Of course, a way to generate random internal state differences $\sigma_{\lambda-9}$ is more flexible. We can use any 448-bit degrees of freedom from $m_0, \ldots, m_{\lambda-10}$.

The value λ should be greater or equal to 13 because Step 1-2 and 1-3 require 4 and 9 message blocks, respectively. When $\lambda = 13$, Step 1-1 is omitted.

Because an execution of Step 1-2 and Step 1-3 needs 4 and 9 evaluations of the step function respectively, building a message candidate and the corresponding internal state difference requires 13 evaluations of the step function. Thus, Step 1 in Section 4.2 requires 13×2^{448} evaluations of the step function.

4.4 Building Message Candidates for the Second Segment of Message

In this section, we show how to obtain message candidates of $(l - \lambda)$ blocks $M_\lambda || \cdots || M_{l-1}$ that is used to reversely update the internal state difference $\sigma_l = 0$ after processing the last message block to an internal state difference σ_λ before the λ-th step satisfying the equations (3).

Let us see the inverse transformation of the step function. Solving the equations (4)-(15) for $b[n]_i$'s and $k[n]_i$'s, the inverse function of the step function is described by the following equations,

$$b[0]_i = k[10]_{i+1} \oplus \Delta_{X_i^{(0)}}(b[0]_{i+1}), \qquad b[2]_i = b[0]_{i+1} \oplus P(m_i),$$

$$k[0]_i = b[2]_{i+1} \oplus k[10]_{i+1} \oplus k[7]_{i+1}, \quad k[n]_i = k[n-2]_{i+1}, \ n = 2, 4, 6, 8, 10$$

$$b[1]_i = k[11]_{i+1} \oplus \Delta_{Y_i^{(0)}}(b[1]_{i+1}), \qquad b[3]_i = b[1]_{i+1} \oplus Q(m_i),$$

$$k[1]_i = b[3]_{i+1} \oplus k[11]_{i+1} \oplus k[8]_{i+1},$$

$$k[5]_i = k[3]_{i+1} \oplus Q(m_i), \qquad\qquad\quad k[3]_i = k[1]_{i+1} \oplus P'(m_i), \qquad (26)$$

$$k[9]_i = k[7]_{i+1}, \qquad\qquad\qquad\qquad k[7]_i = k[5]_{i+1} \oplus P(m_i),$$

$$k[11]_i = k[9]_{i+1} \oplus Q'(m_i).$$

Theorem 2. *Consider any internal state difference after the $(j+8)$-th step σ_{j+9}. For simplicity of notation, we denote this internal state difference by*

$$b[n]_{j+9} = r_n, \ (n = 0, 1, 2, 3) \qquad k[n]_{j+9} = s_n, \ (n = 0, \ldots, 11)$$

If the nine message block differences $m_j, \ldots, m_{j+8}$ is set by the equations (28)-(36), then the internal state difference before j-th step σ_j, that is obtained by reversely updating σ_{j+9}, satisfies the equations (27).

$$b[0]_j = k[0]_j = k[2]_j = k[4]_j = k[6]_j = k[8]_j = k[10]_j = 0,$$

$$b[2]_j = k[7]_j, \quad k[5]_j = 0, \qquad\qquad\qquad\qquad\qquad\qquad\qquad (27)$$

$$Q(m_{j+8}) = \tilde{s}_{10} \oplus s_6 \oplus s_3 \oplus \Delta_{X_j^{(0)}}(\tilde{r}_0), \qquad\qquad\qquad\qquad\qquad (28)$$

$$Q(m_{j+7}) = \tilde{s}_8 \oplus s_4 \oplus s_1 \oplus P'(m_{j+8}), \qquad\qquad\qquad\qquad\qquad (29)$$

$$Q(m_{j+6}) = s_8 \oplus \tilde{s}_6 \oplus s_2 \oplus r_3 \oplus s_{11} \oplus P'(m_{j+7}), \qquad\qquad\qquad\quad (30)$$

$$Q(m_{j+5}) = s_6 \oplus \tilde{s}_4 \oplus s_0 \oplus r_1 \oplus s_9 \oplus P'(m_{j+6}) \oplus Q(m_{j+8}) \oplus Q'(m_{j+8)}, \quad (31)$$

$$Q(m_{j+4}) = r_2 \oplus s_{10} \oplus s_4 \oplus \tilde{s}_2 \oplus \tilde{s}_{11} \oplus P'(m_{j+5}) \oplus Q(m_{j+7}) \oplus Q'(m_{j+7}), \ (32)$$

$$Q(m_{j+3}) = r_0 \oplus s_8 \oplus s_2 \oplus \tilde{s}_0 \oplus \tilde{s}_9$$
$$\oplus P(m_{j+8}) \oplus P'(m_{j+4}) \oplus Q(m_{j+6}) \oplus Q'(m_{j+8}) \oplus Q'(m_{j+6}), \ (33)$$

$$Q(m_{j+2}) = \tilde{r}_2 \oplus \tilde{s}_{10} \oplus s_6 \oplus s_0 \oplus s_7 \oplus \Delta_{Y_{j+6}^{(0)}}(\tilde{s}_9 \oplus Q'(m_{j+8}))$$
$$\oplus P(m_{j+7}) \oplus P'(m_{j+3}) \oplus Q(m_{j+5}) \oplus Q'(m_{j+5}) \oplus Q'(m_{j+7}), \ (34)$$

$$Q(m_{j+1}) = r_2 \oplus \tilde{r}_0 \oplus s_{10} \oplus s_7 \oplus s_5 \oplus s_1 \oplus$$
$$\Delta_{Y_{j+5}^{(0)}}(s_7 \oplus \Delta_{Y_{j+6}^{(0)}}(\tilde{s}_9 \oplus Q'(m_{j+8})) \oplus Q'(m_{j+7}))$$
$$\oplus P(m_{j+8}) \oplus P(m_{j+6}) \oplus P'(m_{j+8}) \oplus P'(m_{j+2}) \oplus Q(m_{j+4})$$
$$\oplus Q(m_{j+7}) \oplus Q'(m_{j+4}) \oplus Q'(m_{j+6}), \qquad\qquad\qquad\qquad (35)$$

$$Q(m_j) = r_0 \oplus r_3 \oplus s_{11} \oplus s_5 \oplus s_3$$
$$\oplus \Delta_{Y_{j+4}^{(0)}}(s_5 \oplus \Delta_{Y_{j+5}^{(0)}}(s_7 \oplus \Delta_{Y_{j+6}^{(0)}}(\tilde{s}_9 \oplus Q'(m_{j+8}))$$
$$\oplus Q'(m_{j+7})) \oplus P(m_{j+8}) \oplus Q'(m_{j+6}))$$
$$\oplus P(m_{j+5}) \oplus P(m_{j+7}) \oplus P'(m_{j+1}) \oplus P'(m_{j+7})$$
$$\oplus Q(m_{j+8}) \oplus Q(m_{j+3}) \oplus Q(m_{j+6}) \oplus Q'(m_{j+3}) \oplus Q'(m_{j+5}), \ (36)$$

where $\tilde{s}_n$'s and $\tilde{r}_0$ are defined as follows:

$$\tilde{s}_{10} = s_{10} \oplus \Delta_{X_{j+8}^{(0)}}(r_0),$$

$$\tilde{s}_8 = s_8 \oplus \Delta_{X_{j+7}^{(0)}}(\tilde{s}_{10}),$$

$$\tilde{s}_6 = s_6 \oplus \Delta_{X_{j+6}^{(0)}}(\tilde{s}_8),$$

$$\tilde{s}_4 = s_4 \oplus \Delta_{X_{j+5}^{(0)}}(\tilde{s}_6),$$

$$\tilde{s}_2 = s_2 \oplus \Delta_{X_{j+4}^{(0)}}(\tilde{s}_4),$$

$$\tilde{s}_0 = s_0 \oplus \Delta_{X_{j+3}^{(0)}}(\tilde{s}_2),$$

$$\tilde{r}_2 = r_2 \oplus s_{10} \oplus s_7 \oplus \Delta_{X_{j+2}^{(0)}}(\tilde{s}_0),$$

$$\tilde{r}_0 = r_0 \oplus s_8 \oplus s_5 \oplus \Delta_{X_{j+1}^{(0)}}(\tilde{r}_2),$$

$$\tilde{s}_{11} = s_{11} \oplus \Delta_{Y_{j+8}^{(0)}}(r_1),$$

$$\tilde{s}_9 = s_9 \oplus \Delta_{Y_{j+7}^{(0)}}(\tilde{s}_{11}).$$

Before proving Theorem 2, we show that the equations (28)-(36) are solved for $m_j, \ldots, m_{j+8}$ in negligible computational cost. First, m_{j+8} is determined by the equation (28) because Q is invertible. Then, m_{j+7} is determined by the equation (29) because m_{j+8} is already determined. Like this, m_{j+6}, m_{j+5}, m_{j+4}, m_{j+3}, m_{j+2}, m_{j+1} and m_j are determined by the equations (30), (31), (32), (33), (34), (35) and (36), respectively and sequentially.

Now, we prove Theorem 2.

Proof (of Theorem 2). First, using the equations of the inverse transformation of the step function (26) nine times iteratively, we can express the internal state difference before the $\lambda + 1$-th step, σ_j, by σ_{j+9} and $m_j, \ldots, m_{j+8}$. Especially, $b[0]_j$, $k[10]_j$, $k[8]_j$, $k[6]_j$, $k[4]_j$, $k[2]_j$, $k[0]_j$, $b[2]_j$, $k[7]_j$ and $k[5]_j$ are expressed as the follows:

$$b[0]_j = \tilde{s}_{10} \oplus s_6 \oplus s_3 \oplus \Delta_{X_j^{(0)}}(\tilde{r}_0) \oplus Q(m_{j+8}), \tag{37}$$

$$k[10]_j = \tilde{s}_8 \oplus s_4 \oplus s_1 \oplus P'(m_{j+8}) \oplus Q(m_{j+7}), \tag{38}$$

$$k[8]_j = s_8 \oplus \tilde{s}_6 \oplus s_2 \oplus r_3 \oplus s_{11} \oplus P'(m_{j+7}) \oplus Q(m_{j+6}), \tag{39}$$

$$k[6]_j = s_6 \oplus \tilde{s}_4 \oplus s_0 \oplus r_1 \oplus s_9$$
$$\oplus P'(m_{j+6}) \oplus Q(m_{j+8}) \oplus Q'(m_{j+8}) \oplus Q(m_{j+5}), \tag{40}$$

$$k[4]_j = r_2 \oplus s_{10} \oplus s_4 \oplus \tilde{s}_2 \oplus \tilde{s}_{11}$$
$$\oplus P'(m_{j+5}) \oplus Q(m_{j+7}) \oplus Q'(m_{j+7}) \oplus Q(m_{j+4}), \tag{41}$$

$$k[2]_j = r_0 \oplus s_8 \oplus s_2 \oplus \tilde{s}_0 \oplus \tilde{s}_9 \oplus P(m_{j+8}) \oplus P'(m_{j+4})$$
$$\oplus Q(m_{j+6}) \oplus Q'(m_{j+8}) \oplus Q'(m_{j+6}) \oplus Q(m_{j+3}), \tag{42}$$

$$k[0]_j = \tilde{r}_2 \oplus \tilde{s}_{10} \oplus s_6 \oplus s_0 \oplus s_7 \oplus \Delta_{Y_{j+6}^{(0)}}(\tilde{s}_9 \oplus Q'(m_{j+8})) \oplus P(m_{j+7})$$
$$\oplus P'(m_{j+3}) \oplus Q(m_{j+5}) \oplus Q'(m_{j+5}) \oplus Q'(m_{j+7}) \oplus Q(m_{j+2}), \tag{43}$$

$$b[2]_j = \tilde{r}_0 \oplus P(m_j), \tag{44}$$

$$k[7]_j = r_2 \oplus s_{10} \oplus s_7 \oplus s_5 \oplus s_1$$
$$\oplus \Delta_{Y_{j+5}^{(0)}}(s_7 \oplus \Delta_{Y_{j+6}^{(0)}}(\tilde{s}_9 \oplus Q'(m_{j+8})) \oplus Q'(m_{j+7}))$$
$$\oplus P(m_{j+8}) \oplus P(m_j) \oplus P(m_{j+6}) \oplus P'(m_{j+8}) \oplus P'(m_{j+2})$$
$$\oplus Q(m_{j+4}) \oplus Q(m_{j+7}) \oplus Q'(m_{j+4}) \oplus Q'(m_{j+6}) \oplus Q(m_{j+1}), \tag{45}$$

$$k[5]_j = r_0 \oplus r_3 \oplus s_{11} \oplus s_5 \oplus s_3$$

$$\oplus \Delta_{Y_{j+4}^{(0)}} \left(s_5 \oplus \Delta_{Y_{j+5}^{(0)}} \left(s_7 \oplus \Delta_{Y_{j+6}^{(0)}} \left(\tilde{s}_9 \oplus Q'(m_{j+8}) \right) \right) \right.$$

$$\left. \oplus Q'(m_{j+7}) \right) \oplus P(m_{j+8}) \oplus Q'(m_{j+6}))$$

$$\oplus P(m_{j+5}) \oplus P(m_{j+7}) \oplus P'(m_{j+1}) \oplus P'(m_{j+7}) \oplus Q(m_{j+8})$$

$$\oplus Q(m_{j+3}) \oplus Q(m_{j+6}) \oplus Q'(m_{j+3}) \oplus Q'(m_{j+5}) \oplus Q(m_j). \qquad (46)$$

From the equations (28) and (37), the equation $b[0]_j = 0$ follows. Similarly, $k[10]_j = 0$ is derived from the equations (29) and (38), $k[8]_j = 0$ from the equations (30) and (39), $k[6]_j = 0$ from the equations (31) and (40), $k[4]_j = 0$ from the equations (32) and (41), $k[2]_j = 0$ from the equations (33) and (42), $k[0]_j = 0$ from the equations (34) and (43), $b[2]_j = k[7]_j$ from the equations (35), (44) and (45), and $k[5]_j = 0$ from the equations (36) and (46). $\qquad \square$

Now, we present a procedure to obtain message candidates of the second segment required in Step 2 in Section 4.2.

Step 2-1. We arbitrarily fix a message-block difference of $(l - \lambda - 13)$-block length, $m_{\lambda+13} || \cdots || m_{l-1}$. Using this difference, we reversely update the final internal state difference $\sigma_l = 0$ and obtain $\sigma_{\lambda+13}$.

Step 2-2. We randomly choose a message-block difference of four-block length, $m_{\lambda+9} || \cdots || m_{\lambda+12}$, and reversely update the internal state difference $\sigma_{\lambda+13}$ to $\sigma_{\lambda+9}$.

Step 2-3. We determine a message-block difference of nine-block length, $m_\lambda || \cdots || m_{\lambda+8}$, by using Theorem 2 with $j = \lambda$ and obtain the internal state difference σ_λ satisfying equations (3). Then, a message candidate is obtained by xoring $M_\lambda^{(0)} || \cdots || M_{l-1}^{(0)}$ with $m_\lambda || \cdots || m_{l-1}$.

In order to build 2^{448} message candidates of the second segment, we execute Step 2-1 once and repeat 2^{448} times the procedure from Step 2-2 to Step 2-3. Because message-block differences of four-block length, $m_{\lambda+9} || \cdots || m_{\lambda+12}$, is of 512-bit length, we can choose 2^{448} different message-block differences at Step 2-2. Therefore, we can build different 2^{448} message candidates. Of course, a way to generate random internal state differences $\sigma_{\lambda+9}$ is more flexible. We can use any 448-bit degrees of freedom from $m_{\lambda+9}, \ldots, m_{l-1}$ except for padding bits.

The value $l - \lambda$ should be greater or equal to 14 because Step 2-2 and 2-3 require 4 and 9 message blocks respectively and Step 2-1 requires at least 1 message block containing padding bits.

Because an execution of Step 2-2 and Step 2-3 needs 4 and 9 evaluations of the step function respectively, building a message candidate of the second segment and the corresponding internal state difference requires 13 evaluations of the step function. Thus, Step 2 in Section 4.2 requires 13×2^{448} evaluations of the step function.

4.5   Complexity of the Attack

Here, we show complexity of the attack.

For Step 1 of the attack, as will be explained in Section 4.3, we need 13 computations of the step function to build a message candidate of the first segment. Thus, 13×2^{448} step function evaluations are required for Step 1. As of memory complexity, we need to store four message blocks $M_{\lambda-13}||M_{\lambda-12}||M_{\lambda-11}||M_{\lambda-10}$ and seven variables of internal state σ_λ which are not fixed by the equations (3) per a pair of a message candidate and an internal state. Thus, we need 11×2^{448} 128-bit memory to store V_1.

For Step 2 and 3 of the attack, as will be explained in Section 4.4, we need 13 computations of the inverse of the step function to build a message candidate of the second segment. Thus, 13×2^{448} inverse step function evaluations are required for Step 2 and 3. Notice that the time complexity of an invocation of the inverse step function is the same as that of the step function.

Thus, total time complexity of the attack is $13 \times 2^{448} + 13 \times 2^{448} \approx 2^{452.7}$ evaluations of the step function and total memory requirement is $11 \times 2^{448} \approx 2^{451.4}$ 128-bit blocks.

5 Discussion about Designer's Security Claim

The designers of SHAMATA prove the following statement (Corollary 1 in Section 5.1 in the specification [7]):

> "It is impossible to find a collision on CV's by imposing differences only on eighth consecutive blocks."

We would like to point out that our attack does not contradict with this statement because the attack needs 27 message blocks at least.

In the proof of the above statement, the designers use two properties mentioned in Section 3. One property is that K registers with even indices are not xored with message blocks, and the other is that the linear transformation of the message blocks at register $B[2]$ is the same as that at register $K[7]$. These properties play an important role for the hash function to resist attacks based on internal collision using up to eight consecutive message blocks. On the contrary, when 27 or more message blocks are used, it is these properties to make our attack possible.

6 Conclusion

In this paper, we presented a second preimage attack on SHAMATA-512. The attack uses differential paths that hold with a probability one and a meet-in-the-middle approach to find second preimages. The time complexity is about $2^{452.7}$ computations of the step function and the memory complexity is about $2^{451.4}$ blocks of 128 bits. Our attack uses two properties of SHAMATA, which the designers seem to consider, make the function more resistant to cryptographic attacks. Our results reveal that the effect of the properties is opposite to their expectation.

Acknowledgements

The authors would like to thank Hirotaka Yoshida for reading the manuscript and Yasuko Fukuzawa, Toru Owada, Hisayoshi Sato, and Yasuo Hatano for continuous encouragement.

References

1. Wang, X., Yin, Y.L., Yu, H.: Finding Collisions in the Full SHA-1. In: Shoup, V. (ed.) CRYPTO 2005. LNCS, vol. 3621, pp. 17–36. Springer, Heidelberg (2005)
2. De Cannière, C., Rechberger, C.: Finding SHA-1 characteristics: General results and applications. In: Lai, X., Chen, K. (eds.) ASIACRYPT 2006. LNCS, vol. 4284, pp. 1–20. Springer, Heidelberg (2006)
3. National Institute of Standards and Technology, Announcing Request for Candidate Algorithm Nominations for a New Cryptographic Hash Algorithm (SHA-3) Family, Federal Register 27(212), 62212-62220 (November 2007)
4. Bertoni, G., Daemen, J., Peeters, M., Van Assche, G.: Sponge Functions. Ecrypt Hash Workshop (2007)
5. Diffie, W., Hellman, M.E.: Exhaustive Cryptanalysis of the NBS Data Encryption Standard. Computer 10, 74–84 (1977)
6. Khovratovich, D., Nikolić, I., Weinmann, R.-P.: Meet-in-the-Middle Attacks on SHA-3 Candidates. In: Dunkelman, O. (ed.) FSE 2009. LNCS, vol. 5665, pp. 260–276. Springer, Heidelberg (2009)
7. Atalay, A., Kara, O., Karakoc, F., Manap, C.: SHAMATA Hash Function Algorithm Specifications (2008)
8. Fleischmann, E., Gorski, M.: Some Observations on SHAMATA (2008),
   `http://www.uni-weimar.de/cms/fileadmin/medien/medsicherheit/Research/`
   `SHA3/Observations_for_SHAMATA.pdf`.
9. Atalay, A., Kara, O., Karakoc, F.: Improved Cryptanalysis of SHAMATA-BC (2008),
   `http://www.uekae.tubitak.gov.tr/uekae_content_files/crypto/`
   `improved_analysis_of_Shamata-BC.pdf`.
10. Indesteege, S., Mendel, F., Preneel, B., Schläffer, M.: Practical Collisions for SHAMATA. In: Jacobson Jr., M.J., Rijmen, V., Safavi-Naini, R. (eds.) SAC 2009. LNCS, vol. 5867, pp. 1–15. Springer, Heidelberg (2009)

Towards Secure and Practical MACs
for Body Sensor Networks

Zheng Gong[1], Pieter Hartel[1], Svetla Nikova[1,2], and Bo Zhu[3]

[1] Faculty of EWI, University of Twente, The Netherlands
{z.gong,pieter.hartel,s.nikova}@utwente.nl
[2] Dept. ESAT/SCD-COSIC, Katholieke Universiteit Leuven, Belguim
[3] Dept. Computer Science and Engineering, Shanghai Jiaotong University, China
zhubo03@gmail.com

Abstract. In this paper, some practical problems with the Message Authentication Codes (MACs), which are suggested in the current security architectures for wireless sensor network (WSN), are reconsidered. The analysis exploits the fact that the recommended MACs for WSN, e.g., TinySec (CBC-MAC), MiniSec (OCB-MAC), and SenSec (XCBC-MAC), are not exactly suitable for body sensor network (BSN). Particularly a dedicated attack is elaborated on the XCBC-MAC. Considering the hardware limitations of BSN, we propose a tunable lightweight MAC based on the PRESENT block cipher, which is named TuLP. A 128-bit variant TuLP-128 is proposed for a higher resistance against internal collisions. Compared to the existing schemes, our lightweight MACs are time and resource efficient on hardware-constrained devices.

1 Introduction

Traditional wireless sensor networks (WSNs) are used to collect public information in the environment, such as temperature, humidity, fire alarm, etc. Body sensor network (BSN, also called wireless medical sensor network) [33], which can be developed from WSN, is a key technology for long term monitoring of biological events or any abnormal condition of patients for realizing the Ambient Assisted Living (AAL) vision [1]. Since monitored health data from a person with BSN will be a part of personal Electronic Health Record (EHR), a higher level of assessment and protection is required for BSN communications. The existing EHR standards (ISO 27001, 27799, openEHR/ISO 18308, etc.) oblige BSN to be secured with strong cryptography. However, strong cryptography entails more resources. Since BSN nodes are either worn or implanted by a patient, the power consumption should be low to minimize radiation and maximize durability. Moreover, BSN sensors also have limited computational ability and memory, typically with a low-end CPU and RAM in KBytes level. These factors are important not only in the implantable but also in the external sensor settings because they determine how "hidden" and "pervasive" the sensors are.

Considering the highly constrained resources that a BSN node can have, a better trade-off has to be found such that the security is maximized, while minimizing the resource requirement. Unfortunately, because of the heterogeneity of BSN, the secure protocols for static networks might not applicable for BSN. Also the methods proposed

B. Roy and N. Sendrier (Eds.): INDOCRYPT 2009, LNCS 5922, pp. 182–198, 2009.

for *ad hoc* networks such as asymmetric cryptography techniques would be costly for BSN applications. Due to the constraints in power consumption and computational ability, it remains a great challenge to design secure and practical cryptographic primitives which are both time and resource efficient for BSN applications.

To ensure the authenticity and integrity of WSN communication, security protocols via different Message Authentication Codes (MACs, different from the term "Medium Access Control") are proposed. MAC is a symmetric-key primitive that inputs a key-message pair to produce a unique tag. The integrity and the authenticity of the message are protected by the tag and the key respectively. One widely used method is the Security Protocol for Sensor Networks (SPINS) [29], which consists of μTESLA (micro version of the Timed, Efficient, Streaming, Loss-tolerant Authentication) and SNEP (Secure Network Encryption Protocol) for broadcasting messages. Following SPINS, many lightweight security architectures have been proposed for WSN, e.g., TinySec [21], SenSec [24] and MiniSec [25]. All these architectures considered which MAC will be suitable in the WSN packet/message authentication. For instance, TinySec and MiniSec recommend the well-known CBC-MAC [19] and OCB-MAC [30] respectively, whilst SenSec uses a novel scheme called XCBC-MAC [24]. All the recommended MACs are based on the operation modes of block cipher, and suggest 32-bit length tag for WSN. In contrast, since dedicated hash functions (such as MD5 and SHA-1) are primarily designed to be collision resistant for preventing forgery of digitally signed documents, it was exploited that MACs based on hash functions (e.g., HMAC [16]) might be less competitive than block-cipher-based ones for highly constrained devices [10]. Nevertheless, it is recognized by the BSN research community that authentication in BSN protocols is usually for short messages in network processing [33]. This property implies that the candidates of MACs, which focus more on the one-wayness than on the collision-resistance, will be more practical for BSN applications.

Since typical BSN nodes have limited resources, an appropriate security level should be imposed to realize authenticity and confidentiality in applications. Intuitively, 32-bit security level for WSN is not suitable even for the one-wayness of the transmitted data in BSN. As a comparable case for sensitive data authenticity, the authentication of Electronic Funds Transfer in the US Federal Reserve System uses a 64-bit CBC-MAC, and additionally a secret value for IV is daily changed and synchronized by the member banks. In other applications, certain authorities even recommended to implement a MAC with a longer length of 128-bit. Although an appropriate security level for BSN applications will be ensured case by case, a 64-bit security bound is widely-accepted for resisting sensible threats in such hardware-limited devices. As power and RAM are normally the most constrained resources on a BSN node, the design of a MAC should consider applicable trade-offs towards time and resource efficient in practice.

The contributions of this work are three-fold. Firstly, we describe some practical problems of the MACs recommended in popular security architectures for WSN, such as TinySec (CBC-MAC), MiniSec (OCB-MAC) and SenSec (XCBC-MAC). In particular, we demonstrate an existential forgery attack on XCBC-MAC, which implies that the authenticity of SenSec is broken. Secondly, a performance comparison is presented on efficient MACs from different design principles, e.g., CBC-MAC, OCB-MAC, ALPHA-MAC [12]. Thirdly, taking into account the requirements for authenticity in BSN, we propose a tunable lightweight MAC based on the PRESENT block cipher [9], which is named TuLP. The structure of TuLP is inspired by the generic construction ALRED [12]. A 128-bit variant TuLP-128 is proposed for the higher resistance against internal collisions. Compared to the existing schemes, our lightweight MACs show a better performance on MICAz node with less memory costs, and also energy-efficient in the level of gate equivalents.

The remainder of this paper is organized as follows. Section 2 describes some definitions and notions which will be used throughout the paper. The problems with the MACs recommended in the proposed security architectures for WSN are described in Section 3. Section 4 gives a performance comparison of some efficient MACs for BSN authenticity. The designs of TuLP and TuLP-128 follow in Section 5 along with a detailed analysis of the security and the performance. Section 6 concludes the paper.

2 Preliminaries

Here we review some definitions and primitives which will be used in the following sections. Exclusive-or (xor) will be denoted by $\oplus$. A message $M = a\|b$ denotes the concatenation of two strings a and b. Let $\mathcal{M}$ and $\mathcal{K}$ be the message and key spaces respectively.

ALRED. The ALRED construction is a generic MAC design introduced by Daemen and Rijmen [12]. The ALRED construction consists of the following steps:

1. **Initialization**: Fill the state with an all-zero block and encrypt it with a full encryption E with an authentication key k.
2. **Chaining**: For each message, iteratively perform an *injection layout* to map the bits of the message to the same dimensions as a sequence of r round keys of E. Then apply a sequence of r times round function of E to the state by using the output of the injection layout as the round keys.
3. **Finalization**: Apply a full encryption E with the authentication key k to the final state. The tag is the first ℓ_m bits of the output.

By using AES as the underlying block cipher, Daemen and Rijmen also presented two paradigms called ALPHA-MAC [12] and Pelican [13] based on ALRED. Recently, many papers exploited that ALPHA-MAC and Pelican might be threatened under the internal collisions [18], the side-channel attack [5] and the impossible differential analysis [32]. We note that all those cryptanalyses are based on the internal structures of ALPHA-MAC and Pelican, which do not endanger the security of ALRED.

PRESENT. At CHES 2007, Bogdanov *et al.* proposed an ultra-lightweight block cipher which is named PRESENT [9]. PRESENT is an example of an SP-network and consists of 31 rounds. The block length is 64 bits and two key lengths of 80 and 128 bits are supported. The hardware requirements for PRESENT are competitive. Using the *Virtual Silicon* (VST) standard cell library based on *UMC L180 0.18µm 1P6M Logic Process* (UMCL18G212T3), PRESENT-80 and PRESENT-128 are estimated to require 1570 and 1886 gate equivalents, respectively [9]. Since Bogdanov *et al.* do not expect the

128-bit key version to be used until a rigorous analysis is given, the term PRESENT means 80-bit key version in hereafter.

Further details about the specification of PRESENT can be found in Bogdanov *et al.* [9], including basic results of the differential and linear cryptanalyses, which can be summarized as follows.

Theorem 1. *Any five-round differential characteristic of PRESENT has a minimum of 10 active S-boxes.*

Theorem 2. *Let ϵ_{4R} be the maximal bias of a linear approximation of four rounds of PRESENT. Then $\epsilon_{4R} \leq 2^{-7}$.*

Based on PRESENT, Bogdanov *et al.* [10] propose some low-energy block-cipher-based hash functions (e.g., single and double block length construction DM-PRESENT and H-PRESENT respectively) which are more practical than dedicated or AES-based hash functions on highly constrained devices, such as RFID tags.

Recently, many cryptanalysis results have been given on the PRESENT block cipher. Wang [31] presents a differential attack on 16-round PRESENT with the complexities of about 2^{64} chosen plaintexts, 2^{32} 6-bit counters, and 2^{64} memory accesses. Collard and Standaert [11] show a statistical saturation attack against 24-round PRESENT. The saturation attack [11] depends on a simplified key schedule algorithm such that the same subkey should be used in each round. Özen *et al.* [27] provide a related-key rectangle attack on 17-round PRESENT-128. Albrecht and Cid [2] present an algebraic differential attack on 19-round PRESENT-128. However the known attacks on PRESENT with 80-bit keys, without any simplification, so far are bounded with 16 rounds [31].

3   Problems with the MACs Recommended for WSN

For ensuring the security of the communication in WSN, many schemes have been proposed for the different layers of WSN. Basically, data link layer security is fundamental for other security properties in the higher layers, e.g., secure routing in network layer and non-repudiation in application layer. In practice, there exist three widely-cited schemes for the security of data link layer, which are TinySec [21], SenSec [24], and MiniSec [25]. For confidentiality, all the three schemes suggest using a lightweight block cipher for data encryption. But for authenticity, three totally different MAC functions are recommended, which are claimed to be suitable for WSN. In this section, we will give a comparative analysis of the three recommended MAC functions in the three schemes [21,24,25].

CBC-MAC. In TinySec [21], Karlof *et al.* suggest to use CBC-MAC [19] as the underlying MAC function. CBC-MAC uses a cipher block chaining construction for computing and verifying MACs. The first advantage of CBC-MAC is simplicity, as it relies on a block cipher which minimizes the number of cryptographic primitives that must be implemented on BSN nodes with a limited memory. For BSN applications, the disadvantage of CBC-MAC is that independent keys should be used for encryption and authentication. Furthermore, the one-key CBC-MAC construction [4] is not secure for

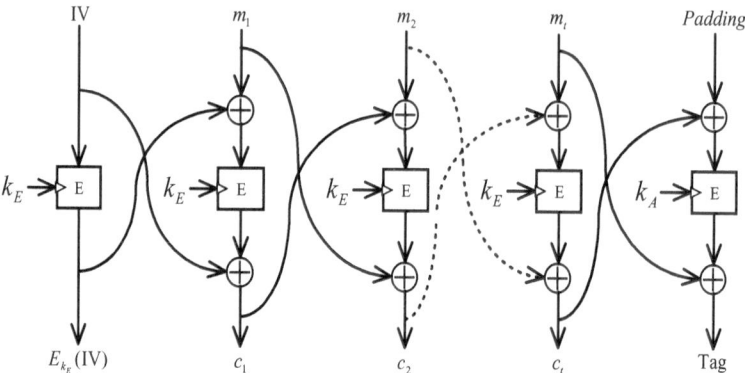

Fig. 1. The XCBC algorithm proposed in SenSec [24]

arbitrary length messages, which allows adversaries can forge a tag for certain messages. To preserve the provable security for arbitrary length messages, a variant of CBC-MAC uses three different keys for the authentication [7]. Although the three-key construction solves the arbitrary length message problem and avoids unnecessary message padding, it raises another typical risk with respect to the key management in BSN. Compared to the one-key construction, the extra keys will impose a heavy burden on key generation, distribution and storage. The risk of the key management indicates that a *provably secure* CBC-MAC might be less practical for BSN applications.

XCBC-MAC. The XCBC-MAC algorithm proposed by Li *et al.* [24] is part of the authenticated encryption mode for SenSec. Let k_A and k_E be the authentication key and the encryption key, respectively. Let message $M = m_1||m_2||...||m_t$. Figure 1 depicts the construction of XCBC-MAC. In general, the XCBC-MAC algorithm can be viewed as a variant of the two-key CBC mode. Unfortunately, we have found a practical existential forgery on XCBC-MAC by implementing a chosen-message attack. One can easily build two different messages with the same tag under the XCBC mode. The forgery can be described in the following steps:

1. First, adversary $\mathcal{A}$ obtains IV, $E_{k_E}(\text{IV})$ from the first block of any former ciphertext under k_E.
2. Next, $\mathcal{A}$ requests the encryptions on the two different blocks $E_{k_E}(\text{IV}) \oplus m_1$ and $E_{k_E}(\text{IV}) \oplus m_1'$ in the XCBC mode. The ciphers will be $E_{k_E}(m_1) \oplus \text{IV}$ and $E_{k_E}(m_1') \oplus \text{IV}$. $\mathcal{A}$ obtains $E_{k_E}(m_1)$ and $E_{k_E}(m_1')$ by xoring the ciphers with IV.
3. Finally, $\mathcal{A}$ arbitrarily selects a message M', and then outputs two different messages M_1, M_2, where $M_1 = E_{k_E}(\text{IV}) \oplus m_1||E_{k_E}(m_1)||0||M'$ and $M_2 = E_{k_E}(\text{IV}) \oplus m_1'||E_{k_E}(m_1')||0||M'$.

It is easy to see that two different prefixes $E_{k_E}(\text{IV}) \oplus m_1||E_{k_E}(m_1)||0$ and $E_{k_E}(\text{IV}) \oplus m_1'||E_{k_E}(m_1')||0$ will produce the same zero output to the next step. Thus the two different messages M_1 and M_2 will have the same tag. The attack is difficult to detect since IV is a publick-known value and the prefixes are computationally indistinguishable from a randomized query. Although the above attack can be avoided by using a one-time randomized IV, this assumption is impractical in WSN and BSN. If IV can frequently be updated, all nodes should immediately synchronize the value. Otherwise the receiver cannot correctly decrypt any packet from the sender. Since synchronization is costly in sensor networks, it is impractical for an IV to be distributed just for one-time usage. Due to the above analysis, the XCBC-MAC algorithm proposed in SenSec [24] is insecure under the chosen message attack and should be abandoned in any circumstance of WSN/BSN authentication.

OCB-MAC. In MiniSec [25], Luk *et al.* suggest using the OCB mode [30], which is an efficient authenticated encryption scheme, as the MAC function for message authenticity and integrity. Since its publication OCB has received some attention, but little cryptanalysis. We believe this has two reasons. First, the security proof of OCB [30] seems to imply that cryptanalysis is useless. The proof is quite complicated and analysis of the proof details is restricted to those people who are well-versed in formal proof techniques. Second, the OCB mode has been patented. There is a significant cost, both directly and indirectly, associated with using a patented algorithm. The last reason is the main reason for the lack of rigorous cryptanalysis. Spending time on OCB will only help the patent-holders to sell their licenses without any further compensation to the cryptanalyst. Moreover, Ferguson also presents a collision attack on OCB with arbitrary length messages [15]. To keep adequate authentication security of OCB, one has to limit the amount of data that the MAC algorithm processes. Since the offset values used in OCB require extra time/memory costs with respect to the message length, the area and the power consumption will be increased for the computation and storage. The above reasons are relevant to real-life applications on BSN, and cast doubts on the wisdom of using OCB.

4   A Comparison of Some Practical MACs for BSN

We have shown that the MAC functions proposed for WSN in the literature are not exactly suitable for BSN. Many different MAC Functions have been proposed in the past decades. Driven by the highly constrained resources of BSN node, the performance and security of those candidates should be rigorously examined before they are implemented. Basically, there are three approaches towards designing MAC functions. The first is to design a new primitive from scratch, such as UMAC [6]. The second is to define a new mode of operation for existing primitives. Such as variants of encryption modes of block ciphers: CBC-MAC [19] and OCB-MAC [30]; Or variants mode of hash functions: HMAC/NMAC [3,16]. The third approach, which can be viewed as a hybrid of the first and the second approach, is to design new MAC functions using components of existing primitives, such as ALPHA-MAC [12].

Based on the security and performance requirements of BSN, we will give a detailed comparison of some popular MAC candidates, which are claimed to be efficient from the three different approaches. To be fair, all MACs based on block cipher use AES-128 as the underlying block cipher, as well as input messages can be of arbitrary length. The timing of the keysetup and the message processing are estimated from the performance data given by the NESSIE consortium [26] (Pentium III/Linux Platform), such that the

Table 1. The comparison of some practical MAC functions

	CBC-MAC [19]	OCB-MAC [30]	ALPHA-MAC [12]	HMAC (SHA-1) [16]
Based on	cipher mode	cipher mode	AES components	hash mode
Keysetup	616	644	1032	1346
Finalization	1440	1444	416	3351
Message processing	26	30	10.6	15
Area in GE (estimate)	4764	6812	4424	8120 [14]

message processing time is measured in cycles/byte, while the keysetup and keysetup + finalization are measured in cycles. The area in *gate equivalents* (GE) can be calculated from two parts: the area of the underlying component or primitive, and the area for internal operations and storages. In order to compare the area requirements independently it is common to state the area in GE, where one GE is equal to the area which is required by two-input NAND gate with the lowest driving strength of the appropriate technology [28]. By following the same method [10,14], we also use the *Virtual Silicon* (VST) standard cell library based on *UMC L180 0.18µm 1P6M Logic Process* (UMCL18G212T3) to estimate each area in GE of the candidates. According to the related experiments [14], the area for AES-128 encryption is estimated to be 3400 GE, as well as 64-bit storing and exclusive-or require 512 GE and 170 GE, respectively.

For chips built with CMOS technology, the power consumption is the sum of two parts: the static and the dynamic costs. The static part is roughly proportional to the area, namely the larger size of the chip the larger energy costs, whilst the dynamic part is proportional to the operating frequency. For the devices with a lower operating frequency, the static power consumption is the most significant. For this reason, the area of gate equivalents is often used as a simplified benchmark for energy efficiency. The comparison in Table 1 shows that ALPHA-MAC has merits on both of the message processing speed and the area of GE, which indicates that one could also build a time and energy efficient MAC from the ALRED construction by using a lightweight block cipher.

5   Two New Lightweight MACs from ALRED

In this section, we will propose a tunable lightweight MAC based on PRESENT, which is named TuLP. To raise the security bound of resisting internal collisions, we will also give a wide-pipe version of TuLP, which is called TuLP-128. Both of our schemes use the experiences of ALPHA-MAC [12] and Pelican [13]. Next, the security of our schemes will be analyzed. Finally, the performance of our lightweight schemes will be given. Compared to the results in Table 2, our new MAC functions are time-efficient with less memory usage, and also energy-efficient in the number of gate equivalents.

5.1   TuLP and TuLP-128

By using the round function of PRESENT [9], first a new MAC function TuLP is built from a modification of the ALRED construction. TuLP is a lightweight MAC function with an 80-bit key length at maximum and 64-bit block length, which consists of the following steps:

1. **Padding.** Let k be an authentication key such that $|k| \leq 80$ bits. If $|k|$ is less than 80 bits, it should be iteratively padded with 1 and 0 as $10101\cdots$. First pad M with $\lambda(M, k)$ where $\lambda(M, k)$ returns the concatenation of bitwise lengths of M and k. Then pad the concatenated string to a multiple of 64 bits, e.g., appending a single bit 1 followed by necessary d bits 0. Finally Split the result $pad(M)$ into 64-bit blocks $m_1, m_2, \cdots, m_t, t = \frac{|pad(M)|}{64}$, such that

$$pad(M) = M||\lambda(M, k)||10^d.$$

2. **Initialization.** Apply one full-round PRESENT encryption E to the initial value IV with the (padded) authentication key k, then obtain $s_0 = E_k(\text{IV})$ as the initial state.

3. **Compression.** For each message block m_i where $i \in \{1, 2, \cdots, t\}$, xor m_i with the current state s_i as the 64 most significant bits of the key k_i for current r times PRESENT round function ρ. The rest 16 bits of the key k_i is derived from the 16 most significant bits of the authentication key k (denote by $\text{MSB}^{16}(k)$). By executing the same key schedule algorithm of PRESENT, apply r times ρ on the state s_{i-1}, such that

$$s_i = \rho^r_{m_i \oplus s_{i-1}||\text{MSB}^{16}(k)}(s_{i-1}).$$

4. **Finalization.** Apply one full-round PRESENT encryption to the state s_t under the key k, and then truncate the first ℓ_m bits of the final state s_{t+1} as the tag of the message M.

$$s_{t+1} = E_k(s_t), \ tag_M = \text{Trunc}^{\ell_m}(s_{t+1}).$$

Since the length of internal state is only 64 bits, TuLP is not strong enough to resist the birthday attack on internal states for an existential forgery. Although this "weakness" is not fatal in some BSN applications, we still provide a wide-pipe version, which is called TuLP-128, to increase the state and the maximum tag lengths to be 128 bits. The key length of TuLP-128 is up to 160 bits. We note that the design principle is inspired by MDC-2 [20] and the padding rule is identical to TuLP.

1. **Padding.** Let k be an authentication key such that $|k| \leq 160$ bits. By using the same padding rule of TuLP, split the result $pad(M) = M||\lambda(M, k)||10^d$ into 64-bit blocks $m_1, m_2, \cdots, m_t, t = \frac{|pad(M)|}{64}$.

2. **State Initialization.** Divide the (padded) authentication key k into two 80-bit key $k_l||k_r$. Then apply one full-round PRESENT encryption to two different 64-bit initial values IV_1 and IV_2 under k_l and k_r, respectively. Obtain the outputs as the *left* and *right* initial states $s_{l,0}$ and $s_{r,0}$, such that

$$s_{l,0} = E_{k_l}(\text{IV}_1), s_{r,0} = E_{k_r}(\text{IV}_2).$$

3. **Compression.** For each message block m_i where $i \in \{1, 2, \cdots, t\}$, first split the last left and right states $s_{l,i-1}$ and $s_{r,i-1}$ into four 32-bit blocks. Then exchange the least significant 32 bits of the left state (denoted by $\text{LSB}^{32}(.)$) with the most significant 32 bits of the right state. The exchanged input states are denoted by

$\hat{s}_{l,i-1}$ and $\hat{s}_{r,i-1}$. By following the same algorithm of the compression in TuLP, apply r PRESENT round functions on the exchanged input states $\hat{s}_{l,i-1}$ and $\hat{s}_{r,i-1}$ respectively.

$$\hat{s}_{l,i-1} = \text{MSB}^{32}(s_{l,i-1})||\text{MSB}^{32}(s_{r,i-1}), 3$$
$$\hat{s}_{r,i-1} = \text{LSB}^{32}(s_{l,i-1})||\text{LSB}^{32}(s_{r,i-1});$$
$$s_{l,i} = \rho^r_{m_i \oplus s_{l,i-1}||\text{MSB}^{16}(k_l)}(\hat{s}_{l,i-1}),$$
$$s_{r,i} = \rho^r_{m_i \oplus s_{r,i-1}||\text{MSB}^{16}(k_r)}(\hat{s}_{r,i-1}).$$

4. **Finalization.** Apply one full-round PRESENT encryption to the left and the right states under the divided keys k_l and k_r respectively. Then truncate the first ℓ_m bits of the concatenation of the final states as the tag of the message M.

$$\hat{s}_{l,t} = \text{MSB}^{32}(s_{l,t})||\text{MSB}^{32}(s_{r,t}),$$
$$\hat{s}_{r,t} = \text{LSB}^{32}(s_{l,t})||\text{LSB}^{32}(s_{r,t});$$
$$s_{l,t+1} = E_{k_l}(\hat{s}_{l,t}), \ s_{r,t+1} = E_{k_r}(\hat{s}_{r,t});$$
$$tag_M = \text{Trunc}^{\ell_m}(s_{l,t+1}||s_{r,t+1}).$$

Figure 2 and 3 depict the high-level algorithms of TuLP and TuLP-128, respectively. Referring to the security issues of ALPHA-MAC and Pelican [5,10,32], the advantages of our schemes are as follows.

- In ALPHA-MAC [12], all message blocks directly become the round keys after the message injections, so the attacker can execute side-channel attacks in the *known message scenario*. Biryukov et al. [5] present a side-channel attack on ALPHA-MAC, which relies on the fact that the round keys of ALPHA-MAC are public-known by the attacker. In TuLP, round keys are not computed from a deterministic function of input message blocks. Thus, a side-channel attack is unlikely to make a hypothesis on any intermediate states of the algorithm. The xor operation between the state and the input message block can resist the attacker to implement similar side-channel attacks [5] on TuLP and TuLP-128.
- Like in Pelican [13], the message injection layer is also removed in TuLP and TuLP-128 for simplicity. Because it can hardly improve the resistance against linear and differential attacks. In Pelican, the message block is xored with the last output state as the input for current round. But in our schemes, the message block is xored with the state as a part of the subkey for next round. We note that the iteration of $E_{k \oplus m}(k)$ is proven to be collision and preimage resistant in the black-box analysis of the PGV constructions [8].
- The bitwise lengths of message and key are appended to the end of the message. This message padding rule can avoid some trivial attacks on the internal collision and the extension. ALPHA-MAC and Pelican only pad message with a single 1 followed by the minimum number of 0 bits to suffice a block.
- Benefit from the ALRED construction, the security of our schemes can be reduced to the security of PRESENT if internal collisions are not involved. The proofs are provided in the security analysis of Section 5.2. Since the compressions in TuLP and TuLP-128 are different from the PRESENT encryption, encryption and authentication can use the same secret key.

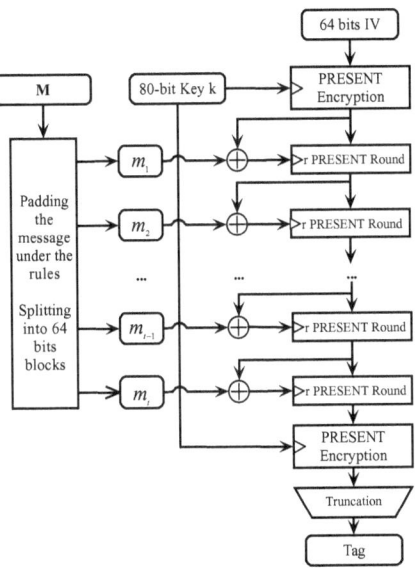

Fig. 2. The illustration of TuLP

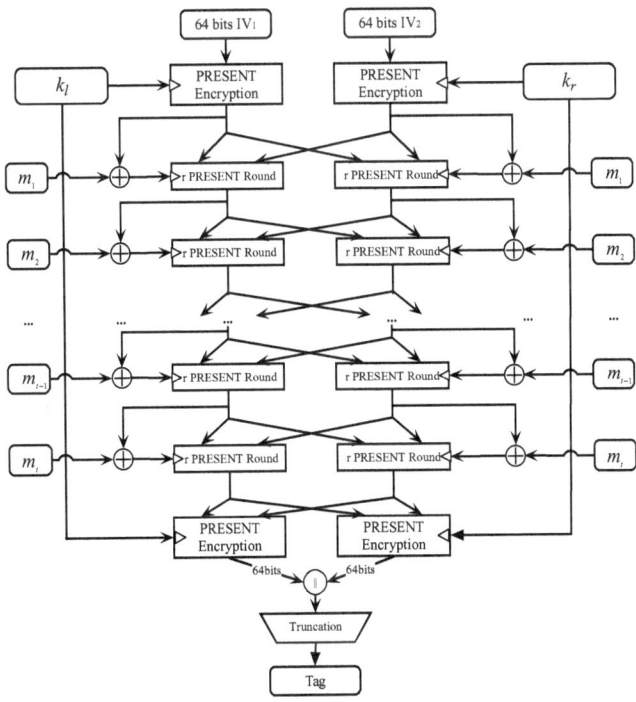

Fig. 3. The illustration of TuLP-128

- TuLP is designed for rapid message processing. The computational costs of the message processing are equivalent to $\frac{r}{31}$ of one PRESENT encryption. Whilst TuLP-128 provides a wider intermediate state and maximum 128-bit tag length for collision resistance, such that the costs of message processing only require $\frac{2 \cdot r}{31}$ of one PRESENT encryption.
- The choice of r rounds PRESENT in the compression is *tunable* by consideration of the practical balance of security and performance. Since key management in sensor network is expensive on computation and energy, the length of authentication key is *tunable* since the padding rules considered dynamic key length. To give practical instances for the analysis in the following section, we will consider $r=16$ in the compression of TuLP and TuLP-128, whilst $\mathrm{IV} = \mathrm{IV}_1 = 0123456789\mathrm{ABCDEF}$ and $\mathrm{IV}_2 = \mathrm{FEDCBA9876543210}$.

5.2 Security Analysis

In this section, we first prove that TuLP is as strong as the PRESENT block cipher with respect to key recovery and existential forgery attacks without internal collisions. Then we give a synthetic analysis of TuLP when internal collisions are considered. Finally, a similar security analysis is given on TuLP-128.

Since the ALRED construction has a similar internal structure with the CBC mode, which typically implies the security between the construction and the underlying cryptographic primitives. Derived from the provability results of the ALRED construction in [12], it is easy to derive a similar result on TuLP as follows.

Theorem 3. *Any key recovery attack on* TuLP *requiring t (adaptively) chosen messages, can be converted to a key recovery attack on the PRESENT block cipher requiring $t + 1$ adaptively chosen plaintexts.*

Proof. Let $\mathcal{A}$ be a successful attacker requiring t tag values corresponding to t (adaptively) chosen messages m_i yielding the key k, where $i \in \{1, 2, \cdots, t\}$. Then we derive a key recovery attack on the PRESENT block cipher as follows.

1. Request the first state $s_0 = E_k(\mathrm{IV})$.
2. For $i = 1$ to t, compute the intermediate state $s_i = \chi(s_0, m_i)$, where χ denotes the compression function of TuLP.
3. For $i = 1$ to t, request $tag_i = \mathrm{Trunc}(E_k(s_i))$.
4. Submit t tag values to $\mathcal{A}$ to recover the key k.

The above attack requires t chosen messages and one chosen message on $E_k(\mathrm{IV})$. So the theorem follows.   □

Similar to Theorem 3, the provability of TuLP can be extended to the existential forgery attack and the fixed point attack as follows. The proofs are omitted here due to the page limit.

Lemma 1. *Any existential forgery attack on* TuLP *without internal collisions requiring t (adaptively) chosen messages, can be converted to a ciphertext guessing attack on the PRESENT block cipher requiring $t + 1$ adaptively chosen plaintexts.*

Lemma 2. *Any existential forgery attack on* TuLP, *requiring t (adaptively) chosen messages for a fixed point* $\{(m, s)|E_{m \oplus s}(s) = s, m \in \mathcal{M}, s \in \mathcal{K}\}$, *can be converted to a fixed point attack* $\{(m', k)|E_{m'}(k) = k, m \in \mathcal{M}, k \in \mathcal{K}\}$ *on the PRESENT block cipher requiring t + 1 adaptively chosen plaintexts.*

Now we analyze the security with respect to internal collisions. The reason why we choose $r=16$ in the compression of TuLP (and TuLP-128) to resist the internal collisions from the linear and differential cryptanalysis are briefly described as follows.

Theorem 4. *Consider $r=16$ in the compression of* TuLP. *The minimum extinguishing differential in* TuLP *imposes a differential characteristic of about 2^{-64}. Whilst the maximum bias of the linear analysis with the probability of about 2^{-28} with 2^{56} known plaintext/ciphertext pairs.*

Proof. Based on the differential and the linear cryptanalyses that are given by Bogdanov *et al.* [9], any 5 rounds differential characteristic of PRESENT has a minimum of 10 active S-boxes. One round PRESENT has one S-box, all 31 rounds use the same. For differential cryptanalysis, we have:

1. One S-box provides maximum 2^{-2} possibility for differential characteristic, thus 16 rounds provide a lower bound $(2^{-2})^{r*10/5} = 2^{-64}$ for the probability of a characteristic. The probability is not greater than the birthday attack on the intermediate states (2^{-32} and 2^{-64} for TuLP and TuLP-128 respectively).
2. This differential cryptanalysis would require the memory complexity of about 2^{64} known plaintext/ciphertext pairs.

For linear cryptanalysis, we have:

1. Any 4 rounds provide the maximal bias of a linear approximation $\epsilon_{4R} \leq 2^{-7}$. Hence 16 rounds provide the maximum bias of a linear approximation $(2^{-7})^{r/4} = 2^{-28}$.
2. This linear cryptanalysis would require the memory complexity of about $1/(2^{-28})^2 = 2^{56}$ known plaintext/ciphertext pairs.

So the theorem follows.   □

Consider a typical BSN application consisting of 100 nodes, each node transfers an 8-byte message under the same authentication key per 15 seconds for monitoring. Although the above linear analysis has a non-negligible bias, the time and the memory complexities of obtaining 2^{56} plaintext/ciphertext pairs (about 2^{19} TB) would be impractical.

By using multi-collisions, Knudsen *et al.* [22] provide a collision attack and preimage attacks on the MDC-2 construction with the time complexities of about $(\log_2(n)/n) \cdot 2^n$ and 2^n where the block length is n. The preimage attacks make new trade-offs so that the most efficient attack requires time and memory of about 2^n. Whilst the meet-in-the-middle attack on MDC-2 [23] requires time and memory about $2^{3n/2}$ and 2^n. Based on the security analysis of the MDC-2 construction and TuLP, the security of TuLP-128 with the internal collisions is as follows.

Theorem 5. *Consider r=16 in the compression of TuLP-128. The internal collision and preimage attacks on TuLP-128 have the complexities of about $2^{61.3}$ and 2^{64}, respectively.*

Proof. The proof is based on the security that r=16 in the compression of TuLP-128. One S-box provides a maximum 2^{-2} possibility for differential characteristic, 16-round PRESENT provide a lower bound 2^{-64} for the probability of a characteristic. The minimum extinguishing differential in TuLP-128 imposes a differential characteristic of about 2^{-64} in the left state and the same in the right state. 16 rounds provide a maximum bias of a linear approximation 2^{-28}. But both the differential analysis and the linear cryptanalysis require a memory complexity no less than 2^{56} known plaintext/ciphertext pairs, which is impractical in BSN. Since PRESENT is an SP-network block cipher and the iteration of $E_{k \oplus m}(k)$ is proven to be collision and preimage resistant in the black-box analysis by Black *et al.* [8], and TuLP-128 has a MDC-2 like construction. Each round of the compression in TuLP-128 exchanges the right most 32 bits of the left state with the left-most 32 bits of the right state. Due to Knudsen *et al.*'s cryptanalysis of MDC-2 [22], the internal collision attack and the preimage attack on TuLP-128 would require the time complexity of about $(\log_2(64)/64) \cdot 2^{64} \approx 2^{61.3}$ and 2^{64}, respectively. Therefore, the complexity of an internal collision is about $2^{-61.3}$ via the multi-collision attack with a negligible memory requirement. Whilst the preimage attack requires time and memory of about 2^{64}. So the theorem follows.   □

Although TuLP-128 does not achieve the ideal upper bounds of collision and preimage resistances, the MDC-2 like structure in TuLP-128 still yields many practical advantages. For example, symmetric left and right pipes can minimize the area in hardware, or the memory usage in software implementation. And the simple permutation layer between left and right states saves redundant logical gates. Nevertheless, a $2^{61.3}$ level of time complexity on finding an internal collision is still beyond the computational bound in practice. Now we consider the security of TuLP-128 without internal collisions.

Theorem 6. *Any key recovery attack on TuLP-128 requiring t (adaptively) chosen messages, can be converted to a key recovery attack on PRESENT requiring $t + 2$ adaptively chosen plaintexts.*

Proof. Consider the situation that $k_l = k_r = k$. Let $\mathcal{A}$ be a successful attacker requiring t tag values corresponding to t (adaptively) chosen messages m_i yielding the key k, where $i \in \{1, 2, \cdots, t\}$. Let χ be the compression function of TuLP. $\text{MSB}^{32}(\cdot)$ and $\text{LSB}^{32}(\cdot)$ denote the truncation of the most and the least significant 32 bits, respectively. Then we derive a key recovery attack on the PRESENT block cipher as follows.

1. Request the initial left and right states $s_{l,0} = E_k(\text{IV}_1)$ and $s_{r,0} = E_k(\text{IV}_2)$.
2. For $i = 1$ to t, compute the left state $s_{l,i} = \chi(\text{MSB}^{32}(s_{l,i})||\text{MSB}^{32}(s_{r,i}), m_i)$ and the right state $s_{r,i} = \chi(\text{LSB}^{32}(s_{l,i})||\text{LSB}^{32}(s_{r,i}), m_i)$.
3. For $i = 1$ to t, request $tag_i = \text{Trunc}(E_k(s_{l,i})||E_k(s_{r,i}))$.
4. Submit t tag values to $\mathcal{A}$ to recover the key k.

The above attack needs t chosen messages except $E_k(IV_1)$ and $E_k(IV_2)$. So the theorem follows.   □

Similar to Theorem 6, it is easy to obtain the following lemmas on TuLP-128. The proofs are omitted here due to the page limit.

Lemma 3. *Any existential forgery attack on* TuLP-128 *without internal collisions of requiring* t *(adaptively) chosen messages, can be converted to a ciphertext guessing attack on PRESENT requiring* $t + 2$ *adaptively chosen plaintexts.*

Lemma 4. *Any existential forgery attack on* TuLP-128 *with a fixed point of requiring* t *(adaptively) chosen messages, can be converted to a fixed point attack on PRESENT requiring* $t + 2$ *adaptively chosen plaintexts.*

5.3   Performance

Before we study the performance of TuLP and TuLP-128, first we program an optimized implementation of PRESENT by using 1K bytes look-up table on MICAz nodes. From our performance tuning, we find that the bit permutation of PRESENT is costly in software implementation. Compared to the best known result of AES-128 software implementation on MICAz nodes [17], our optimized implementation of PRESENT still shows a competitive processing speed per block and promising lower memory costs. Since PRESENT has already been proven to be a better choice than AES in hardware implementation [10], our optimized implementation shows that PRESENT is also practical in software.

Table 2. The comparison of AES and PRESENT implementations

Encryption	Software (MICAz)			Hardware [10]		
	RAM (byte)	ROM (byte)	Processing speed	Logic process	Cycles per block	Area
AES-128 [10,17]	1915	12720	1.46ms / 16Bytes	0.35μm	1032	3400 GE
PRESENT-80	1040	1926	1.82ms / 8Bytes	0.18μm	32	1570 GE

As a point of comparison, we select DM-PRESENT [10], which is derived from the Davies-Meyer construction and the PRESENT with an 80-bit key, as the underlying hash function for HMAC [16]. We also choose one-key CBC-MAC based on PRESENT as a benchmark for comparability. The area in GE is estimated by using the *Virtual Silicon* (VST) standard cell library based on *UMC L180 0.18μm 1P6M Logic Process* (UMCL18G212T3). All experiments are based the MICAz nodes (*TinyOS version 2.10*), which are popular in both of WSN and BSN. The results in the entries of processing speed (in milliseconds) are averaged by iterating 100 times experiments with/without the optimization in the keysetup.

If we choose r=16 in the compression of TuLP, TuLP will be about 2 times faster than PRESENT encryption in message processing. Table 3 shows that TuLP approaches 1.6 and 1.8 times faster than HMAC with DM-PRESENT and one-key CBC-MAC based on PRESENT respectively, where message length from 8 bytes to 1024 bytes. The keysetup costs in our schemes, which require one (or two) PRESENT encryption(s) to generate an

Table 3. The comparison amongst some PRESENT-based MAC functions

	TuLP	TuLP-128	CBC-MAC (PRESENT)	HMAC (DM-PRESENT)
Key length (bit)	80	160	80	80
Intermediate state (bit)	64	128	64	64
RAM / ROM (byte)	1048 / 3302	1056 / 3718	1040 / 2970	1056 / 3484
Area in GE (estimate)	2252	2764	2252	2213 [10]
Processing Speed (ms)	TuLP	TuLP-128	CBC-MAC (PRESENT)	HMAC (DM-PRESENT)
8 bytes	4.46 / 6.63	8.91 / 13.24	6.51	10.90
16 bytes	5.59 / 7.75	11.17 / 15.49	8.70	13.08
32 bytes	7.87 / 10.03	15.72 / 20.05	13.05	17.43
64 bytes	12.39 / 14.56	24.76 / 29.09	21.77	23.97
128 bytes	21.43 / 23.59	42.84 / 47.17	39.20	37.04
256 bytes	39.50 / 41.67	79.00 / 83.33	74.06	65.35
512 bytes	75.65 / 77.81	151.53 / 155.66	143.78	122.01
1024 bytes	147.94 / 150.10	295.97 / 300.31	283.21	233.04

encrypted IV, mainly lack TuLP (or TuLP-128) in processing the messages shorter than 32 bytes. We note that the keysetup can be optimized by precomputing the encrypted IV before the authentications with the same keys, and the values can be reused in the latter authentication with the same keys. Same optimization can be implemented in TuLP-128 to boost the processing of short messages. We note that HMAC also can precompute the initialization values for optimization, but the values must be treated and protected (128 bits for a certain key in DM-PRESENT) in the same manner as secret keys [16]. While the optimization for our schemes only increases a smaller storage (one encrypted IV is 64-bit) without need to be insulated. Although the lengths of internal state and tag are doubled, the performance of TuLP-128 is still comparable to one-key CBC-MAC based on PRESENT. Obviously, TuLP-128 will be faster than HMAC with a double block length hash function based on PRESENT. Nevertheless, if a higher security bound is required, one can tweak the rounds in the compressions of TuLP and TuLP-128. For instance, increase 16 rounds to 20 will decrease about 4/16=25% performance in message processing. In return, a 20-round PRESENT will have a lower bound $(2^{-2})^{20*10/5} = 2^{-80}$ for a differential characteristic. And the maximal bias of a linear approximation $(2^{-7})^{20/4} = 2^{-35}$, which requires 2^{70} known plaintext/ciphertext.

6   Conclusion

By considering the restrictions of BSN, two lightweight MACs TuLP and TuLP-128 have been proposed. The security of our schemes is analyzed with respect to the crypt-analyses on ALRED and the results on PRESENT. The key length and the number of round functions in the compression are tunable in our lightweight schemes, which support practical trade-offs between security and performance in BSN applications. The statistics strongly support that TuLP and TuLP-128 are promising on devices with constrained resources. Since both PRESENT and ALRED are new proposals, we suggest that rigorous analysis should be imposed to avoid any potential weakness inside the cryptosystems based on them.

Acknowledgement. We would like to thank Vicent Rijmen and Xuejia Lai for their helpful advice. And also thank many anonymous reviewers for their valuable comments. The first author acknowledges the financial support of SenterNovem for the ALwEN project, grant PNE07007. The last author is supported by NSFC (No.60573032, 60773092, 60803146), National "863" Program of China (No. 2009AA01Z418) and National "973" Program of China (No.2007CB311201).

References

1. AAL: The Ambient Assisted Living Joint Programme. European Union (January 2008), http://www.aal-europe.eu/about-aal
2. Albrecht, M., Cid, C.: Algebraic Techniques in Differential Cryptanalysis. In: Dunkelman, O. (ed.) FSE 2009. LNCS, vol. 5665, pp. 193–208. Springer, Heidelberg (2009)
3. Bellare, M., Canetti, R., Krawczyk, H.: Keying hash functions for message authentication. In: Koblitz, N. (ed.) CRYPTO 1996. LNCS, vol. 1109, pp. 1–15. Springer, Heidelberg (1996)
4. Bellare, M., Kilian, J., Rogaway, P.: The security of the cipher block chaining message authentication code. Journal of Computer and System Sciences 61(3), 362–399 (2000)
5. Biryukov, A., Bogdanov, A., Khovratovich, D., Kasper, T.: Collision Attacks on AES-Based MAC: Alpha-MAC. In: Paillier, P., Verbauwhede, I. (eds.) CHES 2007. LNCS, vol. 4727, pp. 166–180. Springer, Heidelberg (2007)
6. Black, J., Halevi, S., Krawczyk, H., Krovetz, T., Rogaway, P.: UMAC: Fast and Secure Massage Authentication. In: Wiener, M. (ed.) CRYPTO 1999. LNCS, vol. 1666, pp. 216–233. Springer, Heidelberg (1999)
7. Black, J., Rogaway, P.: CBC MACs for Arbitrary-Length Messages: The Three-Key Constructions. Journal of Cryptology 18(2), 111–131 (2005)
8. Black, J., Rogaway, P., Shrimpton, T.: Black-Box Analysis of the Block-Cipher-Based Hash-Function Constructions from PGV. In: Yung, M. (ed.) CRYPTO 2002. LNCS, vol. 2442, pp. 320–335. Springer, Heidelberg (2002)
9. Bogdanov, A., Knudsen, L.R., Leander, G., Paar, C., Poschmann, A., Robshaw, M.J.B., Seurin, Y., Vikkelsoe, C.: PRESENT: An Ultra-Lightweight Block Cipher. In: Paillier, P., Verbauwhede, I. (eds.) CHES 2007. LNCS, vol. 4727, pp. 450–466. Springer, Heidelberg (2007)
10. Bogdanov, A., Leander, G., Paar, C., Poschmann, A., Robshaw, M.J.B., Seurin, Y.: Hash Functions and RFID Tags: Mind the Gap. In: Oswald, E., Rohatgi, P. (eds.) CHES 2008. LNCS, vol. 5154, pp. 283–299. Springer, Heidelberg (2008)
11. Collard, B., Standaert, F.-X.: A Statistical Saturation Attack against the Block Cipher PRESENT. In: Fischlin, M. (ed.) CT-RSA 2009. LNCS, vol. 5473, pp. 195–210. Springer, Heidelberg (2009)
12. Daemen, J., Rijmen, V.: A New MAC Construction ALRED and a Specific Instance ALPHA-MAC. In: Gilbert, H., Handschuh, H. (eds.) FSE 2005. LNCS, vol. 3557, pp. 1–17. Springer, Heidelberg (2005)
13. Daemen, J., Rijmen, V.: The Pelican MAC Function. Unpublished manuscript, http://eprint.iacr.org/2005/088
14. Feldhofer, M., Rechberger, C.: A Case Against Currently Used Hash Functions in RFID Protocols. In: Meersman, R., Tari, Z., Herrero, P. (eds.) OTM 2006 Workshops. LNCS, vol. 4277, pp. 372–381. Springer, Heidelberg (2006)

15. Ferguson, N.: Collision attacks on OCB. Preprint (Febuary 2002)
16. Federal Information Processing Standard 198, The Keyed-Hash Message Authentication Code (HMAC), NIST, U.S. Department of Commerce (March 2002)
17. Healy, M., Newe, T., Lewis, E.: Analysis of Hardware Encryption Versus Software Encryption on Wireless Sensor Network Motes. In: Mukhopadhyay, S.C., Gupta, G.S. (eds.) Smart Sensors and Sensing Technology. Springer, Heidelberg (2008)
18. Huang, J., Seberry, J., Susilo, W.: On the internal Structure of ALPHA-MAC. In: Nguyên, P.Q. (ed.) VIETCRYPT 2006. LNCS, vol. 4341, pp. 271–285. Springer, Heidelberg (2006)
19. ISO/IEC 9797-1, Information technology - Security Techniques - Message Authentication Codes (MACs) - Part 1: Mechanisms using a block cipher, ISO (1999)
20. ISO/IEC 10118-2:1994. Information technology - Security techniques - Hash-functions - Part 2: Hash-functions using an n-bit block cipher algorithm, Revised in (2000)
21. Karlof, C., Sastry, N., Wagner, D.: TinySec: A Link Layer Security Architecture for Wireless Sensor Networks. In: SenSys 2004, Baltimore, Maryland, USA, November 3-5 (2004)
22. Knudsen, L., Mendel, F., Rechberger, C., Thomsen, S.: Cryptanalysis of MDC-2. In: Ghilardi, S. (ed.) EUROCRYPT 2009. LNCS, vol. 5479, pp. 106–120. Springer, Heidelberg (2009)
23. Lai, X., Massey, J.: Hash Functions Based on Block Ciphers. In: Rueppel, R.A. (ed.) EUROCRYPT 1992. LNCS, vol. 658, pp. 474–494. Springer, Heidelberg (1993)
24. Li, T., Wu, H., Wang, X., Bao, F.: SenSec Design. I^{2}R Sensor Network Flagship Project (SNFP: security part): Technical Report-TR v1.0 (February 2005)
25. Luk, M., Mezzour, G., Perrig, A., Gligor, V.: MiniSec: A Secure Sensor Network Communication Architecture. In: IPSN 2007, Cambridge, Massachusetts, USA, April 25-27 (2007)
26. Performance of optimized implementations of the NESSIE primitives, v2.0, The NESSIE Consortium (2003),
    https://www.cosic.esat.kuleuven.be/nessie/deliverables/D21-v2.pdf
27. Özen, O., Varici, K., Tezcan, C., Kocair, Ç.: Lightweight Block Ciphers Revisited: Cryptanalysis of Reduced Round PRESENT and HIGHT. In: Boyd, C., Nieto, J.G. (eds.) ACISP 2009. LNCS, vol. 5594, pp. 90–107. Springer, Heidelberg (2009)
28. Paar, C., Poschmann, A., Robshaw, M.: New Designs in Lightweight Symmetric Encryption. In: Kitsos, P., Zhang, Y. (eds.) RFID Security: Techniques, Protocols and System-on-Chip Design, pp. 349–371. Springer, Heidelberg (2008)
29. Perrig, A., Szewczyk, R., Wen, V., Culler, D., Tygar, J.D.: SPINS: security protocols for sensor networks. In: Proceedings of the 7th annual international conference on Mobile computing and networking, Rome, Italy, pp. 189–199 (July 2001)
30. Rogaway, P., Bellare, M., Black, J.: OCB: A block-cipher mode of operation for efficient authenticated encryption. ACM Transactions on Information and System Security (TISSEC) 6(3), 365–403 (2003)
31. Wang, M.: Differential Cryptanalysis of Reduced-Round PRESENT. In: Vaudenay, S. (ed.) AFRICACRYPT 2008. LNCS, vol. 5023, pp. 40–49. Springer, Heidelberg (2008)
32. Wang, W., Wang, X., Xu, G.: Impossible Differential Cryptanalysis of PELICAN, MT-MAC-AES and PC-MAC-AES, http://eprint.iacr.org/2009/005
33. Yang, G.Z. (ed.): Body Sensor Network. Springer, London (2003)

Indifferentiability Characterization of Hash Functions and Optimal Bounds of Popular Domain Extensions

Rishiraj Bhattacharyya[1], Avradip Mandal[2], and Mridul Nandi[3]

[1] Applied Statistics Unit, Indian Statistical Institute, Kolkata, India
rishi_r@isical.ac.in
[2] Université du Luxembourg, Luxembourg
avradip.mandal@uni.lu
[3] NIST, USA
mridul.nandi@gmail.com

Abstract. Understanding the principle behind designing a good hash function is important. Nowadays it is getting more importance due to the current SHA3 competition which intends to make a new standard for cryptogrpahic hash functions. Indifferentiability, introduced by Maurer *et al* in TCC'04, is an appropriate notion for modeling (pseudo)random oracles based on ideal primitives. It also gives a strong security notion for hash-designs. Since then, we know several results providing indifferentiability upper bounds for many hash-designs. Here, we introduce a unified framework for indifferentiability security analysis by providing an indifferentiability upper bound for a wide class of hash designs GDE or *generalized domain extension*. In our framework, we present an unified simulator and avoid the problem of defining different simulators for different constructions. We show, the probability of some bad event (based on interaction of the attacker with the GDE and the underlying ideal primitve) is actually an upper bound for indifferentiable security. As immediate applications of our result, we provide simple and improved (in fact optimal) indifferentiability upper bounds for HAIFA and tree (with counter) mode of operations. In particular, we show that n-bit HAIFA and tree-hashing with counter have optimal indifferentiability bounds $\Theta(q\sigma/2^n)$ and $\Theta(q^2 \log \ell/2^n)$ respectively, where ℓ is the maximum number of blocks in a single query and σ is the total number of blocks in all q queries made by the distinguisher.

Keywords: Indifferentiability, Merkle-Damgård , HAIFA, Tree mode of operations with counter.

1 Introduction

Random Oracle method, introduced by Bellare and Rogaway [1], is a very popular platform for proving security of cryptographic protocol. In this model all the participating parties, including the adversary, is given access to a truly random function R. Unfortunately, it is impossible to realize a truly random function in practice. So while implementing the protocol the most natural choice is to instantiate R by an *ideal* hash function H. The formal proofs in Random Oracle model indicate that there is no structural flaw in the designed protocol. But how can we make sure, that replacing the random function R with a *good* hash function H will not make the protocol insecure? In

B. Roy and N. Sendrier (Eds.): INDOCRYPT 2009, LNCS 5922, pp. 199–218, 2009.

fact recent results [13,16] show that theoretically it is possible to construct some patho-
logical protocols that are secure in random oracle model but completely insecure in
standard model. Fortunately those separation results do not imply an immediate serious
threat to any widely used cryptosystem, proven to be secure in random oracle model.
So one can hope that any attack, which fails when a protocol is instantiated with R but
succeeds when the protocol is instantiated with H, will use some structural flaw of H
itself. So the above question boils down to the following. *How can we guarantee the
structural robustness of a hash function H?*

Indifferentiability of Hash Functions: Motivated by above question, Coron et al. studied *Indifferentiability* of some known iterated hash designs[5], based on Maurer's indifferentiability framework [15]. Informally speaking, to prove indifferentiability of an
iterated hash function C (based on some ideal primitive f), one has to design a simulator S. The job of S is to simulate the behavior of f while maintaining consistency
with R. Now if no distinguisher D can distinguish the output distribution of the pair
(C^f, f) from that of (R, S^R), the construction C is said to be indifferentiable from
an RO. In [5], the authors proved that the well known Merkle-Damgård Hash function is indifferentiable from a random oracle under some specific prefix free padding
rule. Subsequently, authors of [2,4,9,12] proved indifferentiability of different iterated
hash function constructions. Today indifferentiability is considered to be an essential
property of any cryptographic hash function.

Related Work: In [14], Maurer introduced a concept of random systems and showed
some techniques of proving *indistinguishability* of two random systems which can
be useful to prove indistinguishability or even indifferentiability. However, Maurer's
methodology can only be applied once one can prove the conditional probability distribution of the view (input/output) given non-ocurrance of bad event, remain identical in
the two worlds. So far there is no known generic technique for finding the bad event and
proving the distributions are actually identical. In [11], the authors introduced the concept of preimage awareness to prove the indifferentiability of MD with post-processor
(modeled as an independent random oracle). More precisely, it was shown that if H is
preimage-aware (a weaker notion than random oracle model) and R is a post-processor
modeled as a random oracle then $R(H(\cdot))$ is indifferentiable. In[10], a particular tree
mode of operation (4-ary tree) with specific counter scheme is shown to be indifferentiable secure.

Our Motivation: Although many known hash function constructions have been shown
to be indifferentiable from an RO, the proof of these results are usually complicated
(many times, due to numerous game hopings and hybrid arguments). Also, they require
different simulators for each individual hash design. There are no known sufficient conditions for hash functions to be indifferentiable from an RO. From a different perspective, the existing security bounds for different constructions are not always optimal. In
fact, to the best of our knowledge none of the known bounds was proven to be tight.
The results of [11,14] do not directly imply to improve the indifferentiability bounds for
general iterated hash functions based on a single random oracle. The methods of [10]
does not give us any optimal bound either. So a natural question to ask is: *Can we characterize the minimal conditions of a cryptographic hash function to be indifferentiable
from a Random Oracle and achieve optimal bound?*

Our Result: In this paper, we present a unified technique of proving indifferentiabile security for a major class of iterated hash functions, called Generalized Domain Extensions. We extend the technique of [14] to the indifferentiability framework. We identify a set of events (called BAD events) and show that any distinguisher, even with unbounded computational power, has to provoke the BAD events in order to distinguish the hash function C from a random function R. Moreover we prove that, to argue indifferentiability of a construction C^f, one has only to show that the probability that any distinguisher invokes those BAD events, while interacting with the pair (C^f, f), is negligible. **We avoid the cumbersome process of defining simulator for each construction separately by providing a unified simulator for a wide range of constructions. To prove indifferentiability one simply need to compute the probability of provoking the BAD event when interacting with (C^f, f).**

In the second part of this paper, we apply our technique to some popular domain extension algorithms to provide optimal indifferentiable bounds. In particular, we consider Merkle-Damgård with HAIFA and tree mode with specific counter scheme.Many of candidates of *SHA3* competition actually use these two modes of operations. So, our result can also be viewd as an **optimal** indifferentiability guarantee of these candidates. We briefly describe our results below:

1. **MD with counter** or HAIFA: Let C^f be MD with counter where the last block counter is zero (all other counters are non-zero). Many SHA3 candidates such as BLAKE, LANE, SHAvite-3 etc are in this category. In Theorem 3 and Theorem 5, we show that the (tight) indifferentiable bound for C is $\Theta(\sigma q/2^n)$ where q is the number of queries, n is the size of the hash output and σ is total number of blocks in all the queries. The so far best known bound for HAIFA mode is $\sigma^2/2^n$ [5].

2. **Tree-mode with counter**: Tree mode with counter (e.g. the mode used in MD6) is known to be indifferentiable secure with upper bound $q^2\ell^2/2^n$ [10]. In Theorem 4 and Theorem 6, we are provide an optimal indifferentiable bound $\Theta(q^2 \log \ell/2^n)$.

2 Notations and Preliminaries

Let us begin with recalling the notion of indifferentiability, introduced by Maurer in [15]. Loosely speaking, if an ideal primitive $\mathcal{G}$ is indifferentiable from a construction C based on another ideal primitive $\mathcal{F}$, then $\mathcal{G}$ can be safely replaced by $C^{\mathcal{F}}$ in any cryptographic construction. In other terms if a cryptographic construction is secure in $\mathcal{G}$ model then it is secure in $\mathcal{F}$ model.

Definition 1. Indifferentiability [15]
A Turing machine C with oracle access to an ideal primitive $\mathcal{F}$ is said to be $(t, q_C, q_{\mathcal{F}}, \varepsilon)$ indifferentiable from an ideal primitive $\mathcal{G}$ if there exists a simulator S with an oracle access to $\mathcal{G}$ and running time at most t, such that for any distinguisher D, $|\Pr[D^{C^{\mathcal{F}}, \mathcal{F}} = 1] - \Pr[D^{\mathcal{G}, S^{\mathcal{G}}} = 1]| < \varepsilon$. The distinguisher makes at most q_C queries to C or $\mathcal{G}$ and at most $q_{\mathcal{F}}$ queries to $\mathcal{F}$ or S. Similarly, $C^{\mathcal{F}}$ is said to be (computationally) indifferentiable from $\mathcal{G}$ if running time of D is bounded by some polynomial in the security parameter k and ε is a negligible function of k.

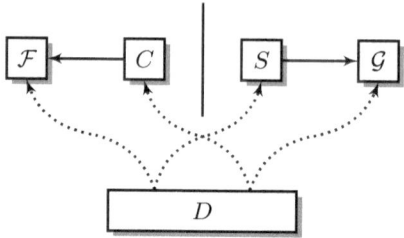

Fig. 1. The indifferentiability notion

We stress that in the above definition $\mathcal{G}$ and $\mathcal{F}$ can be two completely different primitives. As shown in Fig 1 the role of the simulator is to not only simulate the behavior of $\mathcal{F}$ but also remain consistent with the behavior of $\mathcal{G}$. Note that, the simulator does not know the queries made directly to $\mathcal{G}$, although it can query $\mathcal{G}$ whenever it needs.

For the rest of the paper C represents the domain extension algorithm of an iterated hash function. We consider $\mathcal{G}$ and $\mathcal{F}$ to be the same primitive; a random oracle. The only difference is $\mathcal{F}$ is a fixed length random oracle whereas $\mathcal{G}$ is a variable length random oracle. Intuitively a random function (oracle) is a function $f : X \rightarrow Y$ chosen uniformly at random from the set of all functions from X to Y.

Definition 2. $f : X \rightarrow Y$ *is said to be a* random oracle *if for each $x \in X$ the value of $f(x)$ is chosen uniformly at random from Y. More precisely, for $x \notin \{x_1, \ldots, x_q\}$ and $y, y_1, \cdots, y_q \in Y$ we have*

$$\Pr[f(x) = y \mid f(x_1) = y_1, f(x_2) = y_2, \cdots, f(x_q) = y_q] = \frac{1}{|Y|}$$

Most of the hash functions used in practice are iterated hash functions. The construction of an iterated hash function starts with a length compressing function $f : \{0,1\}^{m'} \rightarrow \{0,1\}^n$. Then we apply a domain extension technique, like the well known Merkle-Damgård , to realize a hash function $C^f : \{0,1\}^* \rightarrow \{0,1\}^n$. Intuitively, any practical domain extension technique applies the underlying compression function f in a sequence, where inputs of f are determined by previous outputs and the message $M \in \{0,1\}^*$ (for parallel constructions, inputs only depend on the message). Finally the output $C^f(M)$ is a function of all the previous intermediate outputs and the message M. The *Generalized Domain Extension* (GDE) are the domain extension techniques where u_ℓ is the input to final invocation of f and $C^f(M) = f(u_\ell)$. A domain extension algorithm from the class GDE is completely characterized by the following two functions:

1. **Length function**: $\ell : \{0,1\}^* \rightarrow \mathbb{N}$ is called *length function*, which actually measures the number of invocation of f. More precisely, given a message $M \in \{0,1\}^*$, $\ell = \ell(M)$ denotes the number of times f is applied while computing $C^f(M)$.

2. **Input function**: For each $j \in \mathbb{N}$, $U_j : \{0,1\}^* \times (\{0,1\}^n)^j \rightarrow \{0,1\}^{m'}$, called j^{th} *input function*. It computes the input of jth invocation of f. This is computed from the message M and all $(j-1)$ previous outputs of f. In other words,

$U_j(M, v_0, v_1, \cdots, v_{j-1})$ is the input of jth invocation of f while computing $C^f(M)$, where $v_1, \cdots, v_{j-1}$ denote the first $(j-1)$ outputs of f and v_0 is a constant depending on the construction. The input function usually depend on message block, instead of whole message and hence we may not need to wait to get the complete message to start invoking f.

The above functions are independent of the underlying function f. Note that the padding rule of a domain extension is implicitly defined by the input functions defined above. At first sight, it may seem that GDE does not capture the constructions with independent post processor. But we argue that, when the underlying primitive is modeled like a random oracle, then queries to the post processor can be viewed as queries to same oracle (as in the intermediate queries) but with different padding. Namely in case of NMAC like constructions, we can consider a GDE construction where the inputs to the intermediate queries are padded with 1 and the final query is padded with 0. Similarly, one can incorporate domain extensions which use more than one random oracle.

Definition 3. (GDE: **Generalized Domain Extension**)
Let $S = (\ell, \langle U_j \rangle_{j \geq 1})$ be tuple of deterministic functions as stated above. For any function $f : \{0,1\}^{m'} \to \{0,1\}^n$ and a message M, $\mathsf{GDE}_S^f(M)$ is defined to be v_ℓ, where $\ell = \ell(M)$ and for $1 \leq j \leq \ell$,

$$v_j = f\big(U_j(M, v_0, v_1, \cdots, v_{j-1})\big).$$

The $u_j = U_j(M, v_0, v_1, \cdots, v_{j-1})$ is called the jth intermediate input for the message M and the function f, $1 \leq j \leq \ell$. Similarly, $v_j = f(u_j)$ is called j^{th} intermediate output, $1 \leq j \leq \ell - 1$. The last intermediate input u_ℓ is also called final (intermediate) input. The tuple of functions S completely characterizes the domain extension and is called the **structure** *of the domain extension GDE_S.*

Note that we can safely assign $v_0 = IV$, the Initialization Vector, used in many domain extensions. In Fig 2 we describe the concept of GDE. Each G_i is an algorithm which computes the ith intermediate input u_i, using the input-function U_i defined above. The wires between G_i and G_{i+1} is thick. In fact it contains all the previous input, output and the state information. In this paper we describe sufficient conditions to make a Generalized Domain Extension technique indifferentiable from a Random Oracle (RO). In the next section we show a hybrid technique to characterize the conditions and prove its correctness.

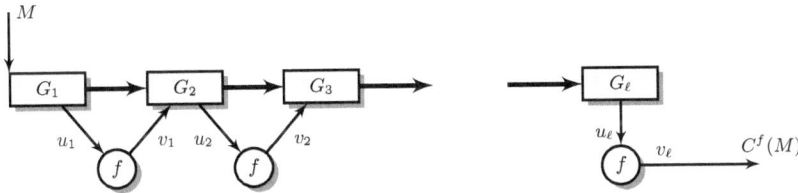

Fig. 2. The Generalized Domain Extension Circuit

3   Indifferentiability of GDE

In this section we discuss the sufficient condition for a domain extension algorithm C of the class GDE to be indifferentiable from a random oracle $\mathcal{R}$. Let C queries a fixed input length random oracle f. Recall that to prove the indifferentiability, for any distinguisher D running in time bounded by some polynomial of the security parameter κ, we need to define a simulator S such that

$$|\Pr[D^{C^f,f} = 1] - \Pr[D^{\mathcal{R},S^{\mathcal{R}}} = 1]| < \varepsilon(\kappa).$$

Here $\varepsilon(\kappa)$ is a negligible function and the probabilities are taken over random coin tosses of D and randomness of f and R. Let *right query* denote the queries to R/C^f and *left query* denote the queries to S^R/f. The simulator keeps a list L, initialized to empty. If u_i is the ith query to the simulator and the response of the simulator was v_i then the ith entry of L is the tuple (i, u_i, v_i).

Definition 4. *Let $C \in$ GDE. We say that $C^f(M)$ for a message M is computable from a list $L = \{(1, u_1, v_1), \cdots, (k, u_k, v_k)\}$ if there are $\ell = \ell(M)$ tuples $(i_1, u_{i_1}, v_{i_1}), \cdots, (i_\ell, u_{i_\ell}, v_{i_\ell}) \in L$ such that for all $t \in \{1, 2, \cdots, \ell\}$,*

$$u_{i_t} = U_t(M, v_0, v_{i_1}, \cdots, v_{i_{t-1}}).$$

Intuitively for any simulator to work, C must have the following property:

Message Reconstruction: There should an efficient algorithm $\mathcal{P}^1$ such that given a set $L = \{(1, u_1, v_1), \cdots, (k, u_k, v_k)\}$, input-output of k many f queries and an input $u \in \{0,1\}^{m'}$ (in the domain of f); $\mathcal{P}(L, u)$ outputs M if $C^f(M)$ is computable from $L \cup \{(k+1, u, v)\}$ for all $v \in \{0,1\}^n$ where $u_\ell = u$ (as in Definition 4). If no such M exists $\mathcal{P}$ outputs $\perp$. If there are more than one such M, we assume $\mathcal{P}$ outputs any one of them.[2]

We argue that this is a very general property and is satisfied by all known secure domain extensions. In fact, the Message reconstruction algorithm $\mathcal{P}$ defined above is similar to the extractor of Preimage Awareness (PrA) of [11]. This is very natural as the notion of PrA is much relaxed notion than that of PRO and every PRO is essentially PrA [11]. However existence of such an algorithm does not guarantee indifferentiability from a Random Oracle. For example, the traditional Merkle-Damgård construction is PrA but not PRO. In fact, The method of [11] is only applicable to prove indifferentiability when the final query is made to an independent post processor. On the other hand, Our contribution in this paper is to show a set of sufficient conditions along with the existence of extractor for a domain extension of the class GDE (where the final query can be made to that same function) to be a PRO.

Our simulator works as follows. Suppose the kth query to the simulator is u. Then

- If $(i, u, v) \in L$ for some $i < k$ and some $v \in \{0,1\}^n$, then $L = L \cup \{(k, u, v\}$ and return v.

---

[1] Note that the exact description of $\mathcal{P}$ depends on specific implementation.

[2] For example, $\mathcal{P}$ can choose a message randomly among all such messages. However, it will actually invoke BAD event.

- If $\mathcal{P}(L, u) = M$
  - $L = L \cup \{(k, u, R(M))\}$
  - return $R(M)$
- If $\mathcal{P}(L, u) = \perp$
  - Sample $h \in_R \{0,1\}^n$
  - $L = L \cup \{(k, u, h)\}$
  - return h

Without loss of generality, we can assume adversary maintains two lists L_{right} and L_{left} to keep the query-responses made to R/C^f and S^R/f respectively.

3.1   Security Games

To prove the indifferentiability of **GDE** we shall use hybrid technique. We start with the scenario when the distinguisher D is interacting with C^f, f.

A left query **S(u)**	A right query **C(M)**
1. return $COM\_RO(u)$.	1. $v_0 = \lambda$.
	2. $\ell = \ell(M)$.
COM_RO(u)	3. for $i = 1$ to ℓ
	$\quad$ (a) $u_i = U_i(M, v_0, v_1, \cdots, v_{i-1})$.
1. return $f(u)$.	$\quad$ (b) $v_i = COM\_RO(u_i)$.
	4. return v_ℓ.

Fig. 3. Procedures of Game 0

Game 0: In this game the distinguisher is given access to an oracle S for the left queries. Additionally, both C and S is given access to another oracle COM_RO which can make f queries. Note that C or S do not have direct access to f. S on an input (u), queries $COM\_RO(u)$. COM_RO on input u returns $f(u)$. Formally, Game 0 can be viewed as Fig 3. Since the view of the distinguisher remains unchanged in this game we have
$$Pr[D^{C^f, f} = 1] = Pr[G_0 = 1]$$
where G_0 is the event when the distinguisher outputs 1 in Game 0.

Game 1: Now we change the description of the subroutine COM_RO and gives it an access to random oracle R as well. In this game COM_RO takes a 3-tuple (u, M, tag) as input where $u \in \{0,1\}^{m'}, M \in \{0,1\}^m$ and $tag \in \{0,1\}$. COM_RO returns $f(u)$ when $tag = 0$ and returns $R(M)$ otherwise. We also change the procedure to handle left and right query. In this game, the algorithm S maintains a list L containing the query number, input, output of previous left queries. While processing a right query M, the algorithm queries COM_RO with $tag = 1$ when querying with u_ℓ and makes $tag = 0$ for all other queries. Informally speaking, for a right query M, the algorithm C behaves almost similarly as game 0, except it returns $R(M)$ as the response. Similarly when a left query is a trivially derived from L and some message M, the algorithm sets $tag = 1$ before querying COM_RO and sets $tag = 0$ otherwise. Formally $Game1$ can be viewed as Figure 4.

A left query $\mathbf{S}(u)$	A right query $\mathbf{C}(M)$

A left query $\mathbf{S}(u)$

1. If $(j, u, v) \in L$ for some v, j, return v.
2. If $\mathcal{P}(L, u) = M \neq \perp$
   (a) $v = COM\_RO(u, M, 1)$.
   (b) $index = index + 1$.
   (c) ADD $(index, u, v)$ to L
   (d) return v
3. else $\backslash\backslash \mathcal{P}(L, u) = \perp$
   (a) $v = COM\_RO(u, \lambda, 0)$.
   (b) $index = index + 1$.
   (c) ADD $(index, u, v)$ to L
   (d) return v

A right query $\mathbf{C}(M)$

1. $v_0 = IV$.
2. $\ell = \ell(M)$.
3. for $i = 1$ to $\ell - 1$
   (a) $u_i = U_i(M, v_0, v_1, \cdots, v_{i-1})$.
   (b) $v_i = COM\_RO(u_i, \lambda, 0)$.
4. $u_\ell = U_i(M, v_0, v_1, \cdots, v_{\ell-1})$.
5. $v_\ell = COM\_RO(u_\ell, M, 1)$.
6. return v_ℓ.

$\mathbf{COM\_RO}(u, M, tag)$

1. if $tag = 0$ return $f(u)$.
2. else return $R(M)$

Fig. 4. Procedures of Game 1. The variable $index$ represents the number of distinct queries made to S, so far; i. e. $index$ is the size of the list L. Initially index is set to 0. λ represent the empty string.

Definition 5. *Trivial Query*
A left query u is said to be a trivially derived query (in short, trivial query) if there exist a $M \in L_{right}$ and k tuples $(i_1, u_{i_1}, v_{i_1}), \cdots, (i_k, u_{i_k}, v_{i_k}) \in L_{left}$ such that

- $u_{i_t} = U_t(M, v_0, v_{i_1}, \cdots, v_{i_{t-1}})$ *for all $t \in \{1, 2, \cdots, k\}$*
- $u = U_{k+1}(M, v_0, v_{i_1}, \cdots, v_{i_k})$

Similarly a right query M is said to be a trivial query if M is computable from L_{left}. Any other queries are said to be nontrivial queries.

Definition 6. BAD *Events for Game 0 and Game 1*
Let D make q queries to a game (either Game 0 or Game 1). Let u_j be the jth query when it is a left query and M_j be the jth query when it is a right query. For i^{th} right query M_i, let u_i^f be the input to final COM_RO query and $u_{in,1}^i, u_{in,2}^i, \cdots$ be the inputs to the non-final intermediate COM_RO queries. The ith query is said to set the BAD *event if one of the following happens*

- *for nontrivial right query $(M_i, right)$*
  - **Collision in final input** *The final input is same as final input of a previous right query. $u_i^f = u_j^f; i \neq j$ and $M_i \neq M_j$.*
  - **Collision between final and non-final intermediate input**
    * *The final input is same as intermediate input of a previous right query, $u_i^f = u_{in,j}^k$ for some $k \leq i$ and $j < l(M_k)$.*
    * *One of the intermediate input is same as the final input of a previous right query. $u_{in,k}^i = u_j^f$ for some $j < i$ and $k \leq l(M_i)$*
  - **Collision between final input and nontrivial left query** *The final input is same as a non-trivial left query u_j; $u_i^f = u_j$ for some $j < i$ but u_j is not a trivial query for M_i.*
- *for left query $(u_i, left)$*

- **Collision between nontrivial left query and final input of a right query** $u_i = u_j^f$ *for some $j < i$ but u_i is not trivially derived.*

Let us concentrate on how each of the event defined above can help the distinguisher. When nontrivial collision between the final input of two right (say M_i and M_j) query happens, the output of two queries will surely be a collision in Game 0. But in case of Game 1, the collision probability will be negligible. When final intermediate input of right query M_i collides with non-final intermediate input of another right query M_j, it may not be obvious how D can exploit this event. But we note that in that case output distribution of these two queries may not be independent in Game 0. The well known length extension attack can also be seen as exploiting this event. Finally if the final input of some right query M_j collides with input of some nontrivial left query u_i, the outputs of these two queries are same in Game 0. But it is easy to check that, in Game 1, they will be same with negligible probability. We stress that unless the nontrivial left query is same as the final input, adversary cannot gain anything. In fact in both of the games the output distribution remains same, even if the nontrivial left query collides with some non-final intermediate input of some right query.

Theorem 1. *Let $C \in$ GDE be a domain extension algorithm. Let BAD event be as defined in Definition 6. Then for any distinguisher D,*

$$| \Pr[D^{C^f,f} = 1] - \Pr[D^{R,S^R} = 1]| \leq \Pr[\text{BAD}^{C^f,f}]$$

where $\text{BAD}^{C^f,f}$ *denotes the* BAD *event when D is interacting with (C^f, f).*

Proof. To prove the theorem we will show the following relations. Let G_1 denote the event that the distinguisher outputs 1 in Game 1,

1. $| \Pr[G_0 = 1] - \Pr[G_1 = 1]| \leq \Pr[\text{BAD}^0]$.
2. $\Pr[G_1 = 1] = \Pr[D^{R,S^R} = 1]$

As $Pr[D^{C^f,f} = 1] = Pr[G_0 = 1]$ and $\Pr[\text{BAD}^0] = \Pr[\text{BAD}^{C^f,f}]$, the theorem will follow immediately. First we shall prove that if BAD events do not happen, then the input output distributions of Game 0 and Game 1 are identical. It is easy to check that $\neg$BAD is a monotone event as once BAD event happens (flag is set) it remains so for future queries. Now if the BAD events do not happen, then the final input of a right query is always "fresh" in both the games. So the output distribution remains same. On the other hand, if an input to a nontrivial left query is not same as the final input of a previous right query, then in both the cases the outputs are same and the output distribution of the left query is consistent with the previous outputs. Similar to [14], we view each input, output and internal states as random variables. We call the set of input, output and internal states as the transcript of the game. Let T_i^j denote the transcript of Game j after i^{th} query, $j = 0, 1$. Let BAD_i^0 and BAD_i^1 be the random variable of BAD event in i^{th} query in Game 0 and Game 1 respectively. The following lemma shows that the probability of BAD event occuring first in i^{th} query is same in both Game 0 and Game 1. Moreover if BAD does not happen in first i queries then the transcript after i^{th} query is identiaclly distributed in both the games.

Lemma 1.   *1.* $\Pr[\text{BAD}_i^0 \wedge \neg(\cup_{k=1}^{i-1} \text{BAD}_k^0)] = \Pr[\text{BAD}_i^1 \wedge \neg(\cup_{k=1}^{i-1} \text{BAD}_k^1)]$
    2. $\Pr[T_i^0|\neg \cup_{k=1}^{i} \text{BAD}_k^1] = \Pr[T_i^1|\neg \cup_{k=1}^{i} \text{BAD}_k^1]$

For a detail proof of the above Lemma, we refer the reader to Appendix A. As a direct application of this Lemma, we get the following results.

Corollary 1. *Let* BAD^j *denote the event that,* D *invokes* BAD *in Game* j. *Then we have,*

    1. $\Pr[\text{BAD}^0] = \Pr[\text{BAD}^1]$
    2. $\Pr[D^{G_0} \wedge \neg\text{BAD}^0] = \Pr[D^{G_1} \wedge \neg\text{BAD}^1]$

Using Corollary 1 one can get the following lemma.

Lemma 2. *Let* G_1 *denote the event that the distinguisher outputs* 1 *in Game* 1.

$$|\Pr[G_0 = 1] - \Pr[G_1 = 1]| \leq \Pr[\text{BAD}^0]$$

For the proof of Lemma 2 we refer the reader to the full version of the paper. Now we shall prove that $\Pr[G_1 = 1] = \Pr[D^{R,S^R} = 1]$. We prove it by hybrid arguments.

Game 2: In this game we change the description of C. Here we remove the lines $1 - 4$ in the description of C in Game 1 and change the query in line 5 to $COM\_RO(\lambda, M, 1)$ where λ is an empty string. So C does not anymore query COM_RO with $tag = 0$.

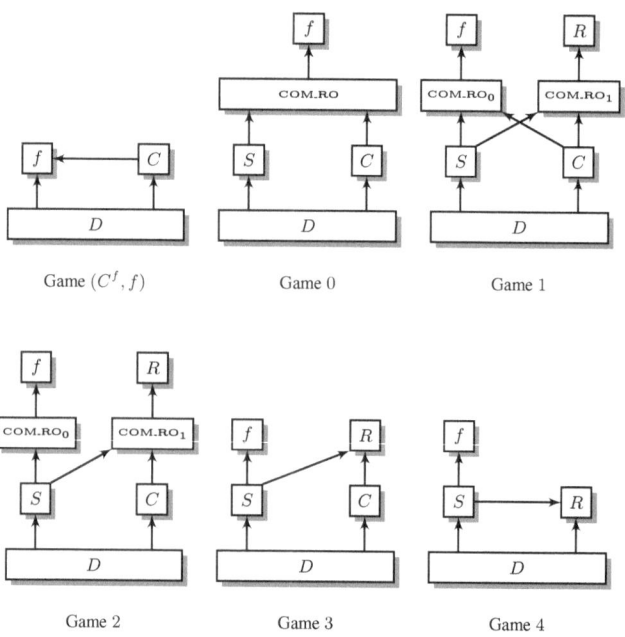

Fig. 5. Security Games

Note that output of C is still $R(M)$. So the changes does not affect the input output distribution of the game. Hence

$$\Pr[G_2 = 1] = \Pr[G_1 = 1]$$

where G_2 is the event D outputs 1 in Game 2.

Game 3: Now we give S and C a direct access to f and R. So we replace the query $COM\_RO(u, M, 0)$ by $f(u)$. Similarly we write $R(M)$ in place of COM_RO $(u, M, 1)$. As D did not have direct access to COM_RO and COM_RO did not modify any list, Game 3 is essentially same as Game 2. So

$$\Pr[G_3 = 1] = \Pr[G_2 = 1]$$

where G_3 is the event D outputs 1 in Game 3.

Game 4: In this game we remove the subroutine C. So the distinguisher D has direct access to R. Now as the simulator S had no access to internal variables of C, the input output distribution remains same after this change. So

$$\Pr[G_4 = 1] = \Pr[G_3 = 1]$$

where G_4 is the event D outputs 1 in Game 4.

The final observation we make is that S need not query f. Instead it can choose a uniform random value from $\{0,1\}^n$. Note that f is modeled as random function. So we changed a random variable of the game with another random variable of same distribution. Hence all the input, output, internal state distribution remains same. This makes S exactly the same simulator we defined.

$$\Pr[G_4 = 1] = \Pr[D^{R,S^R} = 1].$$

As the Game 0 is equivalent to the pair (C^f, f) we obtain our main result of the section (using triangle inequality):

$$|\Pr[D^{C^f,f} = 1] - \Pr[D^{R,S^R} = 1]| \leq \Pr[\text{BAD}^0] = \Pr[\text{BAD}^{C^f,f}] \qquad \square$$

4   Applications to Popular Mode of Operations

In this section we show the indifferentiability of different popular mode of operations from a Random Oracle. We note that, according to Theorem 1 to upper bound distinguisher's advantage one needs to calculate the probability of BAD event defined in previous section. Moreover we can only concentrate on the specific mode of operation rather than the output of the simulator.

4.1   Merkle-Damgård with Prefix Free Padding

It is well known that the usual Merkle-Damgård domain extension fails to satisfy indifferentiability property because of the length extension attacks. So we need to use some prefix free padding on the input message. Let g be the padding function. On input of message M and with oracle access to $f : \{0,1\}^{m'} \to \{0,1\}^n$, the MD domain extension computes the hash value using the following algorithm.

Merkle-Damgård $(MD^f(M))$

1. let $y_0 = 0^n$ (more generally, some fixed IV value can be used)
2. let $g(M) = (M_1, ..., M_l)$
3. for $i = 1$ to l
   - do $y_i = f(y_{i-1}, M_i)$
4. return y_l.

In [6], Coron et. al. proved indifferentiability of Merkle-Damgård Construction for prefix free padding. We reprove the result using Theorem 1 in a simpler way.

Theorem 2. *The prefix free Merkle-Damgård construction is $(t_S, q_C, q_F, \varepsilon)$ - indifferentiable from a random oracle, with $t_S = \ell \cdot \mathcal{O}(q^2)$ and $\varepsilon = \mathcal{O}(\frac{\sigma^2}{2^n})$, where ℓ is the maximum length of a query made by the distinguisher D, σ is the sum of the lengths of the queries made by the distinguisher and $q = q_C + q_F$.*

Note that for prefix free Merkle-Damgård constructions our simulator defined in Section 3 is similar to that of [12]. As shown in that paper, the simulator's running time is $\ell \cdot \mathcal{O}(q^2)$. For the proof of the above Theorem, the reader is referred to the full version of the paper. In this paper we concentrate on MD with a special padding rule, HAIFA.

4.2   Merkle-Damgård with HAIFA

Now we consider Merkle-Damgård mode of operation another variant of prefix free padding; HAIFA. In this padding we append a counter (indicating the block number) with each but last block of the message. The last block is padded with 0 (see Fig 6). It is easy to check that Merkle-Damgård with HAIFA belongs to **GDE**. In this case the reconstruction algorithm works as follows. Let t denote the length of the padding. On input of a f query u; check whether the last t bit of u is 0. If not return $\perp$. Otherwise parse u as $h_0 \| m_0$ where h_0 is of n bits. Find, whether h_0 is in the output column of a query in the list L. If no return $\perp$. If such a query exists select corresponding input u_i. Now last t bit of u_i will be $\ell - 1$, where ℓ is the number of blocks in possible message. We call such an u_i as $u_{\ell-1}$. Now for $j = \ell - 1$ to 2; parse u_j as $h_{j-1} \| m_j$. find whether h_{j-1} exist in the output column of L where the corresponding input has padding $j - 1$. If no return $\perp$. Else select the input and call it u_{j-1}. Repeat the above three steps until we find a u_j with padding 1. If we can find such u_is, then construct the message $M = m_1 \| m_2 \| \cdots m_\ell \| m_0$ and return M. Check that for i^{th} query the algorithm P runs in time $\mathcal{O}(i\ell)$ where ℓ is the maximum block length of a query. Hence the total running time of P and hence of the simulator is $\mathcal{O}(q^2\ell)$.

For finding the probability of BAD events, the HAIFA padding rule gives us the following advantage. While computing $C^f(M)$ for any message M, all the intermediate

Fig. 6. Merkle-Damgård with padding rule HAIFA

inputs are unique. In fact the final input is always different from any intermediate input. So if no f query with same counter padding has collision in the output, the output of the penultimate f queries do not have collision in output and no nontrivial left query input is same as the final input of some right query, BAD event does not happen. If BAD event does not happen in i^{th} query, the output of ith query is uniformly distributed over $Y = \{0,1\}^n$. Without loss of generality, we assume that D does not make any trivial query as trivial queries do not raise a BAD event. Moreover we can consider only a deterministic (albeit adaptive) distinguisher as the general case can easily be reduced to this case [17]. So input to the ith query is uniquely determined by previous $i-1$ outputs. We represent the output of the nontrivial queries as the view (V) of the distinguisher. Let $f : \{0,1\}^{m'} \to \{0,1\}^n$ be a fixed input length random oracle. If D makes q nontrivial queries and $\mathcal{V}$ is the set of all possible views then $|\mathcal{V}| = |Y|^q$. We write V as $\cap_{i=1}^q V_i$, where V_i is the output corresponding to i^{th} query. Now for any $V \in \mathcal{V}$, we define an event BAD'^V which occurs whenever there is a collision between intermediate inputs, final inputs and left query inputs. In fact, $\neg\text{BAD}'^V \cap V \subseteq \neg\text{BAD} \cap V$. We split, BAD'^V as $\cup_{i=1}^q \text{BAD}_i'^V$. $\text{BAD}_i'^V$ occurs whenever any intermediate input (final or non-final) of ith right query collides with any intermediate inputs of any other distinct right query or with input of any nontrivial left query. Although we are working with an adaptive attacker, future query inputs are fixed by V. Note that, if i^{th} query is left query $\text{BAD}_i'^V$ never occurs. Suppose ℓ_i is the number of blocks in i^{th} query.

Suppose the ith query made by the distinguisher is a right query. For $\neg\text{BAD}_i'^V$ to happen, any intermediate input (final or non-final) has to be different from previous intermediate/final inputs. Because of HAIFA padding, no final input will be same with any intermediate input. So if $\neg\text{BAD}_i'^V$ has to be true, every intermediate input of ith has to be different from the intermediate inputs with same counter of previous $i-1$ queries. Also any intermediate input can not be same as future left query inputs or future right query intermediate inputs fixed by the view. There only q many such candidates. So for any intermediate(final) input there are at most $i-1+q < 2q$ bad values. Hence,

$$\Pr[\neg\text{BAD}_i'^V \cap V_i \mid \cap_{j=1}^{i-1} (\neg\text{BAD}_j'^V \cap V_j)] \geq \left(\frac{|Y|-2q}{|Y|}\right)^{\ell_i-1} \cdot \frac{1}{|Y|}.$$

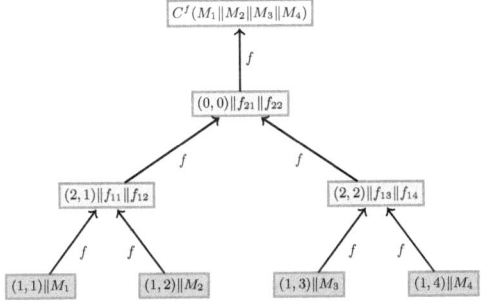

Fig. 7. Tree Mode of Operation with Sequential Padding where $\frac{m'}{n} = 2$

If the ith query is nontrivial left query,

$$\Pr[\neg\text{BAD}_i'^V \cap V_i | \cap_{j=1}^{i-1} (\neg\text{BAD}_j'^V \cap V_j)] = \frac{1}{|Y|}.$$

So one can calculate the probability of $\neg\text{BAD}$ as

$$
\begin{aligned}
\Pr[\neg\text{BAD}] &= \sum_{V \in \mathcal{V}} \Pr[\neg\text{BAD} \cap V] \geq \sum_{V \in \mathcal{V}} \Pr[\neg\text{BAD}'^V \cap V] \\
&= \sum_{V \in \mathcal{V}} \Pr[\cap_{i=1}^q (\neg\text{BAD}_i'^V \cap V_i)] \\
&= \sum_{V \in \mathcal{V}} \Pr[\neg\text{BAD}_1'^V \cap V_1] \prod_{i=2}^q \Pr[\neg\text{BAD}_i'^V \cap V_i | \cap_{j=1}^{i-1} (\neg\text{BAD}_j'^V \cap V_j)] \\
&\geq \sum_{V \in \mathcal{V}} \prod_{i=1}^q \left(\frac{|Y| - 2q}{|Y|} \right)^{\ell_i - 1} \cdot \frac{1}{|Y|} \\
&\geq \sum_{V \in \mathcal{V}} \left(1 - \mathcal{O}(\frac{\sigma q}{|Y|}) \right) \cdot \frac{1}{|Y|^q} = 1 - \mathcal{O}(\frac{\sigma q}{|Y|})
\end{aligned}
$$

Here $Y = \{0,1\}^n$ and $\sigma = \sum_{i=1}^q \ell_i$. So $\Pr[\text{BAD}] \leq \mathcal{O}(\frac{\sigma q}{2^n})$.

Theorem 3. *The Merkle-Damgård construction with HAIFA padding rule based on a FIL-RO is $(t_S, q_C, q_{\mathcal{F}}, \varepsilon)$ - indifferentiable from a random oracle, with $t_S = \ell \cdot \mathcal{O}(q^2)$ and $\varepsilon = \mathcal{O}(\frac{\sigma q}{2^n})$, where ℓ is the maximum length of a query made by the distinguisher D, σ is the sum of the lengths of the queries made by the distinguisher and $q = q_C + q_{\mathcal{F}}$.*

In [5], Coron et al. considered a specific prefix-free padding rule which is similar to HAIFA. There they proved indifferentiability bound as $\mathcal{O}(\frac{\sigma^2}{2^n})$. So Theorem 3 can be seen as improving that bound as well. In Section 5.1 we show that the bound we prove in Theorem 3 is tight.

4.3 Tree Mode of Operation with Counter

Tree mode of operation is another popular mode of operation. *MD6*, a SHA3 candidate uses this mode of operation. Let $f : \{0,1\}^{m'} \rightarrow \{0,1\}^n$. The input message is divided in blocks and can be viewed as the leaf nodes. The edges are the function f. Any internal node can be viewed as the concatenation of the outputs of f on its child nodes. The output of the hash function is the output of f applied on the root.

   Now with each node we associate a tag $\langle height, index \rangle$ where $height$ denotes the height of the node in the tree and $index$ represents the index of the node in the level it is in (see Figure 7). Each node is padded with the tag. This padding makes, like HAIFA, each input unique in the evaluation tree of $C^f(M)$ for any fixed message M. One can easily construct the computable algorithm $\mathcal{P}$ using the same method as in HAIFA. Due to space constraint we don't describe the it here. Let M_i and M_j be two distinct right queries (for simplicity, both of length ℓ) made by distinguisher. Let k be an index such that k^{th} block of M_i and M_j is different. Consider the path from node $(1, k)$ to the root.

It is easy to check that if no collision happens in this path, the final input of f query does not collide while computing $C^f(M_i)$ and $C^f(M_j)$. Length of this path is $\log \ell$ (height of the tree). On the other hand a nontrivial left query input can collide with at most one intermediate input of a right query. Hence, using a method similar to proof of Theorem 3, one can prove the following theorem

Theorem 4. *Let $\mathcal{F}$ be a FIL-RO and C be the tree mode of operation with the counter padding. $C^{\mathcal{F}}$ is $(t_S, q_C, q_{\mathcal{F}}, \varepsilon)$ - indifferentiable from a random oracle, with $t_S = \ell \cdot \mathcal{O}(q^2)$ and $\varepsilon = \mathcal{O}(\frac{q^2 \log \ell}{2^n})$, where ℓ is the maximum length of a query made by the distinguisher D and $q = q_C + q_{\mathcal{F}}$.*

We refer the reader to the full version of the paper for a proof of the above theorem.

5 Indistinguishability Attacks on Popular Mode of Operations

In this section we show a lower bound for the advantage of a distinguishing attacker against Merkle-Damgård constructions with HAIFA padding and Tree mode of operations with counter padding scheme. The bound we achieve actually reaches the corresponding upper bound shown before. Note, if all the queries are of length ℓ, then $q^2 \ell = q\sigma$.

5.1 Distinguishing Attacks on Merkle-Damgård Constructions

Consider q messages $M_1, \cdots, M_q$ such that,

$$\text{PAD}(M_1) = M_1^1 \| M^2 \| \cdots \| M^\ell$$
$$\text{PAD}(M_2) = M_2^1 \| M^2 \| \cdots \| M^\ell$$

$$\vdots$$

$$\text{PAD}(M_q) = M_q^1 \| M^2 \| \cdots \| M^\ell$$

Let COLL be the event denoting collision among $C^f(M_1), \cdots, C^f(M_q)$. We shall prove that, $\Pr[\text{COLL}] = \Omega(\frac{q^2 \ell}{2^n})$ Let COLL_{ij} be the event denoting the collision between $C^f(M_i)$ and $C^f(M_j)$. Hence,

$$\Pr[\text{COLL}] = \Pr[\bigcup_{1 \le i < j \le q} \text{COLL}_{ij}].$$

Using principle of inclusion-exclusion we get,

$$\Pr[\bigcup_{1 \le i < j \le q} \text{COLL}_{ij}] \ge \sum_{1 \le i < j \le q} \Pr[\text{COLL}_{ij}] - \sum_{1 \le i < j < k \le q} \left(\Pr[\text{COLL}_{ij} \cap \text{COLL}_{jk}] \right.$$
$$+ \Pr[\text{COLL}_{ij} \cap \text{COLL}_{ik}] + \Pr[\text{COLL}_{ik} \cap \text{COLL}_{jk}] \right)$$
$$- \sum_{1 \le i < j < k < r \le q} \left(\Pr[\text{COLL}_{ij} \cap \text{COLL}_{kr}] + \Pr[\text{COLL}_{ik} \cap \text{COLL}_{jr}] \right.$$
$$+ \Pr[\text{COLL}_{ir} \cap \text{COLL}_{jk}] \right) \tag{1}$$

In the full version of the paper, we prove the following Lemma.

Lemma 3. Let $Y = \{0,1\}^n$ and $1 \leq i < j < k < r \leq q$. If $\ell - 1 \leq 2^n$, then

1. $\Pr[\text{COLL}_{ij}] \geq \frac{\ell}{2|Y|}$
2. $\Pr[\text{COLL}_{ij} \cap \text{COLL}_{jk}] \leq \frac{2\ell^2}{|Y|^2}$
3. $\Pr[\text{COLL}_{ij} \cap \text{COLL}_{kr}] \leq \frac{\ell^2}{|Y|^2} + \frac{6\ell^3}{|Y|^3}$

Using Equation 1 and Lemma 3 one can prove,

$$\Pr[\text{COLL}] \geq \binom{q}{2}\frac{\ell}{2|Y|} - 3\binom{q}{3}\frac{2\ell^2}{|Y|^2} - 3\binom{q}{4}\left(\frac{\ell^2}{|Y|^2} + \frac{6\ell^3}{|Y|^3}\right) \approx \frac{\alpha}{4} - \frac{\alpha^2}{8} \geq \frac{\alpha}{8}$$

where $\alpha = \frac{q^2\ell}{2^n} < 1$. By Birthday Bound, for a random function R, the collision probability for q different messages is $\Theta(\frac{q^2}{2^n})$. Hence for a distinguisher D which queries messages $M_1, \cdots, M_q$, the advantage of the distinguisher is $\Omega(\frac{q^2\ell}{2^n})$. Also we can easily construct such q messages for any prefix free Merkle-Damgård scheme, specifically HAIFA.

Theorem 5. Let C be the Merkle-Damgård domain extension with a prefix free padding. There exist a distinguisher D, such that

$$|\Pr[D^{C^f,f} = 1] - \Pr[D^{S^R,R} = 1]| \geq \Omega(\frac{q^2\ell}{2^n})$$

where D makes q queries and length of each query is at most ℓ.

5.2 Distinguishing Attacks on Tree Mode

Similar to previous attack we choose q messages $M_1, \cdots, M_q$ such that after padding only first block of these messages are different. Formally

$$\text{PAD}(M_i) = M_i^1||M^2||\cdots||M^\ell.$$

Now for these massages the tree mode works like a Merkle-Damgård mode with messages $\overline{M}_1, \cdots, \overline{M}_q$ where

$$\text{PAD}(\overline{M}_i) = M_i^1||\overline{M}^2||\cdots||\overline{M}^h \quad \forall i = 1, 2, \cdots, q$$

$h = \lceil \log \ell \rceil$ is the height of the tree. Hence using the similar method to previous section we get the following Theorem.

Theorem 6. Let C be the Tree mode domain extension with the sequential counter padding. There exist a distinguisher D, such that

$$|\Pr[D^{C^f,f} = 1] - \Pr[D^{S^R,R} = 1]| \geq \Omega(\frac{q^2 \log \ell}{2^n})$$

where D makes q queries and length of each query is atmost ℓ.

6   Conclusion and Future Work

In this paper we proposed a unified method to prove indifferentiability of a wide class of iterated hash function, called **GDE**. Using our method we proved optimal indifferentiability bounds for Merkle-Damgård construction with counter (e.g. HAIFA) mode and for Tree Mode constructions with a similar sequential padding. This result shows tight indifferentiability bound (when the underlying compression functions are realized as random oracles) for many SHA3 candidates like BLAKE, LANE, SHAvite-3, MD6 etc. We strongly believe that tight indifferentiability bounds for MD constructions with independent post-processor [11] can also be proved using our method.

References

1. Bellare, M., Rogaway, P.: Random Oracles Are Practical: A Paradigm for Designing Efficient Protocols. In: 1st Conference on Computing and Communications Security, pp. 62–73. ACM, New York (1993)
2. Bellare, M., Ristenpart, T.: Multi-Property-Preserving Hash Domain Extension and the EMD Transform. In: Lai, X., Chen, K. (eds.) ASIACRYPT 2006. LNCS, vol. 4284, pp. 299–314. Springer, Heidelberg (2006)
3. Barke, R.: On the Security of Iterated MACs. Diploma Thesis 2003. ETH Zurich
4. Bertoni, G., Daemen, J., Peeters, M., Van Assche, G.: On the indifferentiability of the sponge construction. In: Smart, N.P. (ed.) EUROCRYPT 2008. LNCS, vol. 4965, pp. 181–197. Springer, Heidelberg (2008)
5. Coron, J.S., Dodis, Y., Malinaud, C., Puniya, P.: Merkle-Damgard Revisited: How to Construct a Hash Function. In: Shoup, V. (ed.) CRYPTO 2005. LNCS, vol. 3621, pp. 430–448. Springer, Heidelberg (2005)
6. Coron, J.S., Dodis, Y., Malinaud, C., Puniya, P.: Merkle-Damgard Revisited: How to Construct a Hash Function (full version of [5]),
   http://cs.nyu.edu/~dodis/ps/merkle.ps
7. Coron, J.S., Patarin, J., Seurin, Y.: The Random Oracle Model and the Ideal Cipher Model Are Equivalent. In: Wagner, D. (ed.) CRYPTO 2008. LNCS, vol. 5157, pp. 1–20. Springer, Heidelberg (2008)
8. Damgård, I.: A Design Principles for hash functions. In: Brassard, G. (ed.) CRYPTO 1989. LNCS, vol. 435, pp. 416–427. Springer, Heidelberg (1990)
9. Dodis, Y., Pietrzak, K., Puniya, P.: A new mode of operation for block ciphers and length-preserving MACs. In: Smart, N.P. (ed.) EUROCRYPT 2008. LNCS, vol. 4965, pp. 198–219. Springer, Heidelberg (2008)
10. Dodis, Y., Reyzin, L., Rivest, R., Shen, E.: Indifferentiability of Permutation-Based Compression Functions and Tree-Based Modes of Operation, with Applications to MD6. In: Dunkelman, O. (ed.) FSE 2009. LNCS, vol. 5665, pp. 104–123. Springer, Heidelberg (2009)
11. Dodis, Y., Ristenpart, T., Shrimpton, T.: Salvaging Merkle-Damgård for Practical Applications. In: Ghilardi, S. (ed.) EUROCRYPT 2009. LNCS, vol. 5479, pp. 371–388. Springer, Heidelberg (2009)
12. Chang, D., Lee, S., Nandi, M., Yung, M.: Indifferentiable security analysis of popular hash functions with prefix-free padding. In: Lai, X., Chen, K. (eds.) ASIACRYPT 2006. LNCS, vol. 4284, pp. 283–298. Springer, Heidelberg (2006)
13. Canetti, R., Goldreich, O., Halevi, S.: The random oracle methodology, revisited. In: STOC 1998. ACM, New York (1998)

14. Maurer, U.: Indistinguishability of Random Systems. In: Knudsen, L.R. (ed.) EUROCRYPT 2002. LNCS, vol. 2332, pp. 110–132. Springer, Heidelberg (2002)
15. Maurer, U., Renner, R., Holenstein, C.: Indifferentiability, Impossibility Results on Reductions, and Applications to the Random Oracle Methodology. In: Naor, M. (ed.) TCC 2004. LNCS, vol. 2951, pp. 21–39. Springer, Heidelberg (2004)
16. Nielsen, J.: Separating Random Oracle Proofs from Complexity Theoretic Proofs: The Non-committing Encryption Case. In: Yung, M. (ed.) CRYPTO 2002. LNCS, vol. 2442, pp. 191–214. Springer, Heidelberg (2002)
17. Nandi, M.: A Simple and Unified Method of Proving Indistinguishability. In: Barua, R., Lange, T. (eds.) INDOCRYPT 2006. LNCS, vol. 4329, pp. 317–334. Springer, Heidelberg (2006)
18. SHA 3 official website,
http://csrc.nist.gov/groups/ST/hash/sha-3/Round1/
submissions_rnd1.html

Appendix A   Proof of Lemma 1

Let $X_1^j, X_2^j, \cdots, X_q^j \in \mathcal{X}$ and $Y_1^j, Y_2^j, \cdots, Y_q^j \in \mathcal{Y}$ be input random variables and output random variables respectively of Game j; $j \in \{0,1\}$. Let $U_{1,i}^j, U_{2,i}^j, \cdots, U_{\ell_i,i}^j$ be the internal random variables (output of internal queries) of ith query in Game j. As previously We call the set of input,output and internal states, the transcript of the game. Let T_i^j denote the transcript of Game j after i^{th} query.

In this proof,w.l.g., we assume that Distinguisher does not repeat queries. Let q be the number queries the adversary make. We shall prove the Lemma 1 by induction on i.

CASE $i = 1$: We start from the observation that

$$\Pr_D[X_1^0] = \Pr_D[X_1^1].$$

If X_1 is a right query $(M_1, right)$

$$\Pr_{D,f}[(U_1^0, \cdots, U_{\ell_1,1}^0)|X_1^0] = \Pr_{D,f}[(U_1^1, \cdots, U_{\ell_1,1}^1)|X_1^1].$$

Hence

$$\Pr_{D,f}[X_1^0, U_{1,1}^0, U_{2,1}^0, \cdots, U_{\ell_1,1}^0] = \Pr_{D,f,R}[X_1^1, U_{1,1}^1, U_{2,1}^1, \cdots, U_{\ell_1,1}^1].$$

It is easy to check that for the first query BAD event can only be set by a right query. Also note that it happens when the final query is same with some non-final intermediate query. So

$$\Pr_{D,f}[BAD_1^0|X_1^0, U_{1,1}^0, U_{2,1}^0, \cdots, U_{\ell_1,1}^0] = \Pr_{D,R,f}[BAD_1^1|X_1^0, U_{1,1}^0, U_{2,1}^0, \cdots, U_{\ell_1,1}^0].$$

Hence

$$\Pr_{D,f}[BAD_1^0] = \Pr_{D,R,f}[BAD_1^1]$$

If $\neg BAD_1$ is true then $u_1^f \notin I_{M_1}$. As f and R are random oracles, we have

$$\Pr_f[f(u_1^f) = v] = \Pr_R[R(M_1) = v] \forall v \in \{0,1\}^n.$$

On the other hand if the first query is $(u, left)$ for any u, then $Y_1 = f(u)$ in both the games. So, $\forall v \in \{0,1\}^n$

$$\Pr_{D,f}[Y_1^0 = v | X_1^0, U_{1,1}^0, U_{2,1}^0, \cdots, U_{\ell_1,1}^0 \wedge \neg \text{BAD}_1^0]$$
$$= \Pr_{D,R,f}[Y_1^1 = v | X_1^1, U_{1,1}^1, U_{2,1}^1, \cdots, U_{\ell_1,1}^1 \wedge \neg \text{BAD}_1^1].$$

Hence,

$$\Pr_{D,f}[X_1^0, U_{1,1}^0, U_{2,1}^0, \cdots, U_{\ell_1,1}^0, Y_1^0 | \neg \text{BAD}_1^0]$$
$$= \Pr_{D,f,R}[X_1^1, U_{1,1}^1, U_{2,1}^1, \cdots, U_{\ell_1,1}^1, Y_1^0 | \neg \text{BAD}_1^1].$$

This Implies that the distribution of transcript after first query is identical in both the games if $\neg \text{BAD}_1$ is true. This finishes the proof of the case $i = 1$.

Suppose the lemma is true for all $i < t$.

CASE $i = t$: By Induction Hypothesis, we have,

$$\Pr_{D,f}[T_{t-1}^0 | \neg(\cup_{k=1}^{t-1} \text{BAD}_k^0)] = \Pr_{D,f,R}[T_{t-1}^1 | \neg(\cup_{k=1}^{t-1} \text{BAD}_k^1)].$$

As the input/output distribution of two games are same if $\neg(\cup_{k=1}^{t-1} \text{BAD}_k^1)$ is true, the distribution of tth query must be same for both the games.

$$\Pr_{D,f}[X_t^0 | T_{t-1}^0 \wedge \neg(\cup_{k=1}^{t-1} \text{BAD}_k^0)] = \Pr_{D,f,R}[X_t^1 | T_{t-1}^1 \wedge \neg(\cup_{k=1}^{t-1} \text{BAD}_k^1)]$$

When $X_t = (u_t, left)$ is a non trivial left query then $Y_t = f(u_t)$ in both the games. Now if $\neg(\cup_{i=1}^{t-1} \text{BAD}_i)$ is true then, from induction hypothesis, the transcript distribution after t queries is same for both the games. The probability that u_t^f collides with some final input of any previous query is same for both the games. So for the left query

$$\Pr[\text{BAD}_t^0 | \neg(\cup_{k=1}^{t-1} \text{BAD}_k^0)] = \Pr[\text{BAD}_t^0 | \neg(\cup_{k=1}^{t-1} \text{BAD}_k^1)]$$

When $X_t = (M_t, right)$ then we have,

$$\Pr_{D,f}[X_t^0 | T_{t-1}^0 \wedge \neg \text{BAD}^0] = \Pr_{D,f,R}[X_t^1 | T_{t-1}^1 \wedge \neg \text{BAD}^1]$$

Notice that if the distribution of tth query is same for both the games then the distribution of internal queries is also same for both the games. Hence

$$\Pr_{D,f}[X_t^0, U_{1,1}^0, \cdots, U_{\ell(M_t),(t)}^0 | T_{t-1}^0 \wedge \neg(\cup_{k=1}^{t-1} \text{BAD}_k^0)]$$
$$= \Pr_{D,f}[X_t^1, U_{1,1}^1, \cdots, U_{\ell(M_t),(t)}^1 | T_{t-1}^1 \wedge \neg(\cup_{k=1}^{t-1} \text{BAD}_k^1)].$$

Hence

$$\Pr_{D,f}[\text{BAD}_t^0 | \neg(\cup_{k=1}^{t-1} \text{BAD}_k^0)] = \Pr_{R,D,f}[\text{BAD}_t^1 | \neg(\cup_{k=1}^{t-1} \text{BAD}_k^1)]$$

For a non-trivial left query $(u_t, left)$, both the game queries $f(u_t)$. if $\neg(\cup_{k=1}^{t}\mathrm{BAD}_k^1)$ is true then $u_t \neq u_j^f$ for all $j < t$. On the other hand , for a right query $(M_t, right)$, if $\neg(\cup_{k=1}^{t}\mathrm{BAD}_k^1)$ is true then u_t^f has never been queried before. Then $\Pr_f[f(u_t^f) = v] = \Pr_R[R(M_t) = v]$ for all $v \in \{0,1\}^n$. So

$$\Pr_{D,f}[Y_t^0, X_t^0, U_{1,1}^0, \cdots, U_{\ell(M_t),(t)}^0 | T_{t-1}^0 \wedge \neg(\cup_{k=1}^{t}\mathrm{BAD}_k^0)]$$
$$= \Pr_{D,R,f}[Y_t^1, X_t^1, U_{1,1}^1, \cdots, U_{\ell(M_t),(t)}^1 | T_{t-1}^1 \wedge \neg(\cup_{k=1}^{t}\mathrm{BAD}_k^1)].$$

This implies

$$\Pr_{D,f}[T_t^0 | \neg(\cup_{k=1}^{i}\mathrm{BAD}_k^0)] = \Pr_{D,R,f}[T_t^1, \cdots, U_{\ell_i,i}^1) | \neg(\cup_{k=1}^{i}\mathrm{BAD}_k^1)] \qquad \square$$

A Distinguisher for the Compression Function of SIMD-512

Florian Mendel and Tomislav Nad

Institute for Applied Information Processing and Communications (IAIK)
Graz University of Technology, Inffeldgasse 16a, A-8010 Graz, Austria
Tomislav.Nad@iaik.tugraz.at

Abstract. SIMD is one of the round 2 candidates of the public SHA-3 competition hosted by NIST. It was designed by Leurent *et al.*. In this paper, we present a distinguisher attack on the compression function of SIMD-512. By linearizing the compression function we construct a linear code. Using techniques from coding theory to search for low Hamming weight codewords, we can find differential characteristics with low Hamming weight (and hence high probability). In the attack the differences are introduced only in the *IV*. Such a characteristic is the base for our distinguisher, which can distinguish the compression function of SIMD-512 from random with a complexity of $5 \cdot 2^{425.28}$ compression function calls. Furthermore, we can distinguish the output transformation of SIMD-512 from random with a complexity of about $22 \cdot 2^{425.28}$ compression function calls. So far this is the first cryptanalytic result for the SIMD hash function.

Keywords: SHA-3 candidate, SIMD, cryptanalysis, distinguisher.

1 Introduction

Recently, the NIST hash function competition [12] has started. In this public competition to find an alternative hash function to replace the SHA-1 and SHA-2 hash functions, many new designs have been proposed. In November 2008, round one has started and in total 51 out of 64 submissions have been accepted. Recently, the 14 round 2 candidates were announced. SIMD, designed by Leurent *et al.* [8], is one of them. It is an iterative hash function based on the Merkle-Damgård design principle [5,11]. It is a wide-pipe design [9] producing a hash value up to 512 bits, denoted by SIMD-n, where n is the output length. For the remainder of this paper wherever we mention SIMD we refer to SIMD-512. The design of the compression function is similar to the MD4 family. Furthermore, there exist several proofs [4,10] for the mode of operation used by SIMD. The designers additionally provide bounds for a large class of differential attacks. Most of the security is based on the message expansion. In this paper, we present a distinguisher attack on the compression function of SIMD-512 with a complexity of $5 \cdot 2^{425.28}$ compression function calls. Including the output transformation we can distinguish the output of SIMD-512 from random with a complexity of about

B. Roy and N. Sendrier (Eds.): INDOCRYPT 2009, LNCS 5922, pp. 219–232, 2009.

$22 \cdot 2^{425.28}$ compression function calls. The distinguisher is based on a differential characteristic with differences only in the IV. A characteristic with high success probability is found by using techniques from coding theory. By linearizing the compression function we define a linear code where each codeword represents a differential characteristic. Using an algorithm to find low Hamming weight codewords, we found characteristics which lead to the above attack complexity.

Even if we do not attack the whole hash function, we show unexpected non-random properties of the SIMD-512 compression function. However, our attack does not invalidate the security claims of the designers, since most of the security comes from the message expansion, but note that the non-randomness of the compression function of SIMD effects the applicability of the proofs for the mode of operation build upon it.

The structure of this paper is as follows. A short description of SIMD is given in Section 2. Section 3 gives an overview of the basic attack strategy. Section 4 shows in which way we linearized the compression function of SIMD. Followed by Section 5 containing the description of the techniques from coding theory to find good characteristics. Finally, the distinguisher for full SIMD is presented in Section 6.

2   Description of SIMD

SIMD is an iterative hash function that follows the Merkle-Damgård design. The main component of a Merkle-Damgård hash function is the compression function. In the case of SIMD-512 to compute the hash of a message M, it is first divided into k chunks of 1024 bits. By the use of a message expansion one block is expanded to 8192 bits. Then the compression function is used to compress the message chunks and the internal state. The padding rule to fill the last blocks is known as the Merkle-Damgård strengthening. The initial value of the internal state is called IV and is fixed in the specification of the hash function. The output of the hash function is given by computing a finalization function on the last internal state, which is a truncation for SIMD. The internal state of SIMD contains 32 32-bit words and is therefore twice as large as the output. SIMD consist of 4 rounds where each round consist of 8 steps. The feed-forward consists of four additional steps with the IV as message input. Since we apply a compression function attack independent from the message expansion, we omit the description of the message expansion. For a detailed description of the hash function we refer to [8].

2.1   SIMD Step Function

The core part of SIMD is the step function of the state update. Figure 1 illustrates the step function at step t. The state update consists of eight step functions in parallel. To make the step function dependent from each other, $(A_{p^t(i)}^{t-1} \lll r^t)$ is included in a modular addition, where $p^t(i)$ is a permutation, which is different for each step.

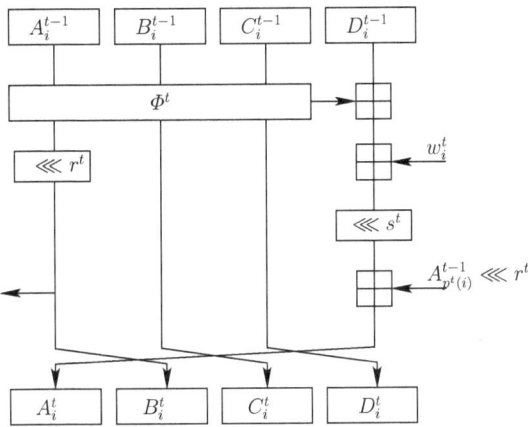

Fig. 1. Update function of SIMD at step t. $i = 0, \cdots, 7$

Equation (1) is the formal definition of the step function, where $\boxplus$ denotes the addition modulo 2^{32}.

$$A_i^t = (D_i^{t-1} \boxplus w_i^t \boxplus \Phi(A_i^{t-1}.B_i^{t-1}, C_i^{t-1})) \lll s^t \boxplus (A_{p^t(i)}^{t-1} \lll r^t)$$
$$B_i^t = A_i^{t-1} \lll r^t$$
$$C_i^t = B_i^{t-1} \tag{1}$$
$$D_i^t = C_i^{t-1}$$

The permutation p is separated in 4 different permutations:

$$p^0(x) = \begin{cases} x+1 \pmod 8, & \text{if } x = 0 \pmod 2 \\ x-1 \pmod 8, & \text{otherwise} \end{cases}$$

$$p^1(x) = \begin{cases} x+2 \pmod 8, & \text{if } x = 0 \pmod 4 \text{ or } x = 1 \pmod 4 \\ x-2 \pmod 8, & \text{otherwise} \end{cases}$$

$$p^2(x) = 7 - x \pmod 8$$

$$p^3(x) = x + 4 \pmod 8$$

The permutation used at step t is $p^{t \bmod 4}$. As mentioned before, the 32 steps of SIMD are divided into 4 rounds, each consisting of 8 steps. The boolean function Φ and the rotation constants (s and r) for a round are given in Table 1. In Table 2 the rotation constants for each round are given. The feed-forward consist of four steps using the same step function. Table 3 lists the used Boolean function and the rotation constants for the feed-forward.

Table 1. Φ and rotation constants for a round

step	Φ	r	s
0	IF	π_0	π_1
1	IF	π_1	π_2
2	IF	π_2	π_3
3	IF	π_3	π_0
4	MAJ	π_0	π_1
5	MAJ	π_1	π_2
6	MAJ	π_2	π_3
7	MAJ	π_3	π_0

Table 2. Rotation constants for each round

round	π_0	π_1	π_2	π_3
0	3	20	14	27
1	26	4	23	11
2	19	28	7	22
3	15	5	29	9

Table 3. Φ and rotation constants for the feed-forward of SIMD

step	Φ	r	s
0	IF	15	5
1	IF	5	29
2	IF	29	9
3	IF	9	15

3   The Basic Attack Strategy

In this section, we briefly describe the attack strategy to construct a distinguisher for the compression function. The attack can be summarized as follows:

1. Find a differential characteristic for the compression function of SIMD with differences in the IV, which holds with high probability.
2. Use message modification technique to increase the probability.

To find a good characteristic for the compression function, we use a linearized model of it. Finding a characteristic in a linear code is not difficult. Since the security of SIMD is heavily based on the message expansion, we concentrate on characteristics with differences only in the IV. The probability that the characteristic holds in the original compression function is related to the Hamming weight of the characteristic. In general, a differential characteristic with low Hamming weight has a higher probability than one with a high Hamming weight. Finding a characteristic with high probability (low Hamming weight) is related to finding a low weight word in linear codes. Therefore, we use the probabilistic algorithm from Canteaut and Chabaud [2] to find a good characteristic for the compression function of SIMD. It has been shown in the past, for instance the cryptanalysis of SHA-0 [3], SHA-1 [13] or EnRUPT [7] that this technique works well for finding differential characteristics with low Hamming weight. Furthermore, we can improve the probability of the characteristic using message modification, which was introduced by Wang *et al.* in [15].

4   Linearization of SIMD

Since we have only differences in the IV, we can omit the message expansion and assume that the message words have no differences. The step function (1) is the only part of SIMD which has to be linearized. The nonlinear parts of this function are the modular additions and the Boolean function Φ. In the attack, we replace all modular addition by XORs. The function Φ depends on the current step and is either the IF function or the MAJ function. To have a good approximation for those, we have to take a closer look on the differential behavior of them.

4.1   Differential Behavior of IF and MAJ

The differential behavior of IF and MAJ is already discussed in [6]. IF and MAJ have three inputs. Table 4 shows the differential propagation of the Boolean functions regarding XOR-differences.

Table 4. Differential propagation of IF and MAJ

Δx	Δy	Δz	ΔIF	ΔMAJ
0	0	0	0	0
0	0	1	$x \oplus 1$	$x \oplus y$
0	1	0	x	$x \oplus z$
0	1	1	1	$y \oplus z \oplus 1$
1	0	0	$y \oplus z$	$y \oplus z$
1	0	1	$x \oplus y \oplus z$	$x \oplus z \oplus 1$
1	1	0	$x \oplus y \oplus z \oplus 1$	$x \oplus y \oplus 1$
1	1	1	$y \oplus z \oplus 1$	1

Since we aim for a low weight characteristic, we replace the Boolean function Φ with the 0-function, *i.e.* we block each input difference in Φ, no matter if IF or MAJ is used. This has probability $1/2$ in most cases. One can see that there is exactly one input difference for IF and one for MAJ where the output difference is always one. We discard characteristics with such properties, except in the feed-forward. There we manually correct the characteristic, resulting in a slightly higher Hamming weight. Furthermore, we use the non-linearity of the IF function in the feed-forward to decrease the Hamming weight significantly (see Section 6.2).

Finally, the linearized step function looks as follows:

$$
\begin{aligned}
A_i^t &= (D_i^{t-1} \oplus w_i^t \oplus 0) \lll s^t \oplus (A_{p^t(i)}^{t-1} \lll r^t) \\
B_i^t &= A_i^{t-1} \lll r^t \\
C_i^t &= B_i^{t-1} \\
D_i^t &= C_i^{t-1}
\end{aligned}
\tag{2}
$$

Note that for the feed-forward w_i^t is equal to one word of the IV.

5   Finding Good Characteristics

As observed by Rijmen and Oswald [14], all differential characteristics for a linearized hash function can be seen as the codewords of a linear code. Our aim is to find good characteristics. Therefore, we have to include each part where differences could decrease the success probability. Let the vector

$$
\Delta cv^t := (\Delta A_i^t | \Delta B_i^t | \Delta C_i^t | \Delta D_i^t),
\tag{3}
$$

for $i = 0, \cdots, 7$ and $cv^t \in \{0,1\}^{1024}$ be the concatenated difference of all chaining values (in bit representation) at step t. Then the vector

$$
\Delta dc := (\Delta IV, \Delta cv^1, \cdots, \Delta cv^{36}),
$$

where $\Delta dc \in \{0,1\}^{37 \cdot 1024}$, represents the differences in the IV, chaining values after each step and the output of the SIMD compression function, including the feed-forward. Δdc is one codeword of the linear code and therefore a differential characteristic. To construct the generator matrix for the linear code, we proceed as follows:

1. Compute Δdc_j with the input difference $\Delta IV_j = e_j$, where $e_j \in \{0,1\}^{1024}$ is the j-th unit vector.
2. Repeat the computation for $j = 1, \ldots, 1024$.

The resulting systematic generator matrix of the linear code for the linearized SIMD compression function is defined in the following way:

$$
G_{1024 \times 37 \cdot 1024} := [I_{1024 \times 1024} | CV],
\tag{4}
$$

where CV is defined by

$$
\begin{pmatrix} \Delta dc_1 \\ \vdots \\ \Delta dc_{1024} \end{pmatrix}.
$$

5.1   Reducing the Code Length

Depending on the number of steps, the linear code can get large. If we take a closer look on the dependencies of each chaining value, one can see that only the A_i's are updated at each step and the other values only depend on them. Therefore, we can reduce the code size by only considering the A_i's at each step function. The definition of Δcv^t in Equation (3) changes to

$$\Delta cv^t := (\Delta A_i^t), \tag{5}$$

Following the same procedure above, the resulting generator matrix is much smaller, namely

$$G_{1024 \times 10240} := [I_{1024 \times 1024} | CV]. \tag{6}$$

Therefore, the performance of the search for low Hamming weight codewords is increased.

5.2   Low Weight Search

We implemented the probabilistic algorithm from Canteaut and Chabaud [2] to search for codewords with low Hamming weight and applied some optimizations to speed up the search. This iterative algorithm basically looks for small Hamming weight codewords in a smaller code. Such a codeword is considered as a good candidate for a low Hamming weight codeword for the whole code. Considering a systematic generator matrix like (6) the algorithm randomly selects σ columns of it and split the selection in two submatrices of equal size. By computing all linear combination of p rows (usually 2 or 3) for each submatrix and storing their weight, the algorithm searches for a collision of both weights which allow to search for codewords of $2p$. Then two randomly selected columns are interchanged, followed by one Gaussian elimination step. This procedure is repeated until a sufficiently small Hamming weight was found. Additionally, we check for each codeword if each difference at the input of the Boolean function can be blocked. If it is not possible we discard the codeword. We omit this check in the feed-forward (see Section 4.1).

In the case of the codes originating from the linearized SIMD compression function we found several low weight codewords in less than an hour on a PC.

5.3   Estimating the Probability for a Characteristic

To compute the probability of the found differential characteristic, we have to consider the differences entering the Boolean function Φ and the modular additions.

The Boolean function Φ. The probability for blocking a difference in one bit at the input of Φ is $1/2$ or 0 for some cases, but then the characteristic is discarded (see Section 4.1). Hence, the total probability is determined by the sum of all differences at the input. Note, that differences at the same bit positions are counted only once. The overall probability for step t is defined by 2^{-x}, where x is given by

$$\sum_{i=0}^{7} hw(\Delta A_i^{t-1} \vee \Delta B_i^{t-1} \vee \Delta C_i^{t-1})$$

and $hw(\cdot)$ is the bit-wise Hamming weight of a 32-bit word.

The modular additions. Consider the additions (7) from the step function (1).

$$(\Delta D_i^{t-1} \boxplus \Delta w_i^t) \lll s^t \boxplus (\Delta A_{p^t(i)}^{t-1} \lll r^t) \tag{7}$$

We could consider each modular addition separately and prevent a carry for each bit difference, but this would result in a rather conservative approximation. Therefore, we want to give a more detailed analysis. By allowing carries in the first addition, we can compensate them at the second addition. However, this is not that easy, because of the rotation after the first modular addition.

First we take a look at the following addition:

$$\Delta D_i^{t-1} \boxplus \Delta w_i^t.$$

If we have a difference at the same bit position, we can cancel them out with probability $1/2$. The overall probability to cancel out such differences for step t is 2^{-y}, where y is defined by

$$\sum_{i=0}^{7} hw(\Delta D_i^{t-1} \wedge \Delta w_i^t).$$

Note that $\Delta w_i^t \neq 0$ only for the feed-forward. If there is only a difference in one input of the modular addition (bit-wise), we allow carries. However, we do not want that the carry expansion is destroyed, due to the rotation to left by s^t bits, since we cannot compensate this in the second addition. To take care of this problem we have to consider two cases.

Let be l_j the bit position of the j-th difference in ΔD_i^{t-1} before the rotation, l_j' after the rotation and $d_{\mathrm{MSB}}(l_j)$ ($d_{\mathrm{MSB}}(l_j')$) the distance of l_j (l_j') to the most significant bit (MSB). The first case is $d_{\mathrm{MSB}}(l_j) < s^t$, i.e. the difference is rotated over the MSB. Therefore, we have to ensure that the carry expands at most to the MSB from the position of the difference *before* the rotation. The probability for that is

$$1 - 2^{-d_{\mathrm{MSB}}(l_j)}.$$

The second case considers $d_{\mathrm{MSB}}(l_j) \geq s^t$, i.e. the difference is not rotated over the MSB. In this case we have to ensure that the carry expands at most to the MSB from the position of the difference *after* the rotation. The probability for that is

$$1 - 2^{-d_{\mathrm{MSB}}(l_j')}.$$

This differentiation has to be done for each difference in ΔD_i^{t-1}. The overall probability is given by the product of all single probabilities.

In the last modular addition

$$(\Delta D_i^{t-1} \lll s^t) \boxplus (\Delta A_{p^t(i)}^{t-1} \lll r^t)$$

we first cancel out differences at the same bit positions of both variables with probability $1/2$ for each such difference. In the last step we compensate the carries from the first addition with the same probability. Finally, the overall success probability for the second modular addition is 2^{-z}, where z is defined as follows:

$$\sum_{i=0}^{7} hw(\Delta D_i^{t-1} \lll s^t \vee \Delta A_{p^t(i)}^{t-1} \lll r^t).$$

Note, that we ignore differences in the MSB for these calculations, which results in a small improvement.

Message modification. To improve the success probability of the differential characteristic we use message modification. We have the freedom to choosing the actual values of the IV and the message words. Regarding the message words, we assume that we can increase the success probability in the first 4 steps to 1. Since one message block in SIMD has 1024 bit and is expanded to 8192, we can at least choose the first 32 expanded message words w, but not completely arbitrary. The message modification for the first 4 steps results in a significant improvement of the overall success probability, since this probability is low in these steps. However, the message expansion needs to be studied in more detail to get a good view on the security of SIMD. It might be possible to improve the attack by using more sophisticated message modification techniques.

6   Distinguisher for Full SIMD

In this section, we present a distinguisher for the full (32 steps and feed-forward) compression function of SIMD. It is based on the differential multicollision distinguisher introduced by Biryukov et al. [1] and high probability differential characteristics for the compression function of SIMD. This characteristic was found by using the techniques described in the previous section. Before describing the differential characteristic in detail, we first have to discuss the setting we use to show non-randomness in the compression function of SIMD.

6.1   Differential q-Multicollision

The notion of differential q-multicollision was introduced by Biryukov et al. in the cryptanalysis of AES-256. They show that differential q-multicollision can be found for AES-256 with a complexity of $q \cdot 2^{67}$, while for an ideal cipher an adversary needs at least

$$O(q \cdot 2^{\frac{q-2}{q+2} \cdot n}) \tag{8}$$

time. Note that in [1] the attack is described for a block cipher. However, it can be easily adapted for a random function. Below we repeat the basic definition and lemma, we need for the distinguishing attack for the compression function of SIMD.

Definition 1. *A set of two differences and q pairs*

$$\{\Delta IV, \Delta M; (IV_1, M_1), (IV_2, M_2), \cdots, (IV_q, M_q)\}$$

is called a differential q-multicollision for $f_{IV}(\cdot)$ *if*

$$f_{IV_1}(M_1) \oplus f_{IV_1 \oplus \Delta IV}(M_1 \oplus \Delta M) = f_{IV_2}(M_2) \oplus f_{IV_2 \oplus \Delta IV}(M_2 \oplus \Delta M)$$
$$= \cdots = f_{IV_q}(M_q) \oplus f_{IV_q \oplus \Delta IV}(M_q \oplus \Delta M).$$

In the case of SIMD, f is the compression function and ΔM is equal 0.

Lemma 1. *To construct a differential q-multicollision for an ideal function with an n-bit output an adversary needs at least* $O(q \cdot 2^{\frac{q-2}{q+2} \cdot n})$ *queries on the average.*

The proof for Lemma 1 works similar as in [1] for an ideal cipher.

In this section, we show how to find a differential q-multicollision for the SIMD compression function with a complexity of about $q \cdot 2^{425.28}$ instead of the expected

$$q \cdot 2^{\frac{q-2}{q+2} \cdot 1024}.$$

This is described in detail in the subsequent sections.

6.2   The Differential Characteristic

We have found several characteristics with low Hamming weight. The best ones have a weight of 504 in all chaining variables. We can further reduce the weight by using the non-linearity of the IF function in the feed-forward. If we do not block all input differences in the Boolean function, we can cancel out additional differences, which results in a lower Hamming weight for the subsequent steps. Thus, the overall success probability of the characteristic is increased. In that way we can improve the characteristics to a weight of 486. By a detailed analysis (see Section 5.3) we determine the success probability of the characteristics with $\approx 2^{-507.34}$ without message modification. If we use additionally message modification as described in Section 5.3, we increase the probability to $\approx 2^{-425.28}$. Table 5 presents one of the differential characteristics with weight 486. Due to space restriction we do not show the complete characteristic but the differences in the IV, which is enough to reconstruct the whole differential path. In Appendix A the characteristic in the steps of the feed-forward, including the above modifications, is given.

Table 6 splits the probability estimation into rounds and steps (for readability the probabilities are given in $\log_2$).

The characteristic in Table 5 leads to a guaranteed difference in one bit at the output of Φ in the third step of the feed-forward. By correcting this manually, the success probability is slightly decreased, which is already included in the overall probability.

Table 5. Differences in the IV

i	A_i^0	B_i^0	C_i^0	D_i^0
0	00000000	00000000	00000000	00000000
1	00000000	00000000	00000000	00000000
2	00000000	00000000	00000000	00000000
3	00000000	104804a0	00000000	00000000
4	00000000	00000000	050e0010	00000000
5	00000000	00000000	00000000	00000000
6	00000000	00000000	00000000	68801201
7	04004400	00000000	00000000	00000000

Table 6. Probabilities in $\log_2$ for each round and step

round \ step	0	1	2	3	4	5	6	7
0	-23.85	-23.03	-19.09	-16.19	-15.12	-12.09	-9	-8.03
1	-7.09	-5	-4	-4	-3	-2	-2	-2
2	-1	-1	-1	-2	-3	-4	-4	-3
3	-4.19	-6	-9	-12	-16	-19.42	-19	-23.30
feed-forward	-31.05	-46.09	-69.46	-77.34				

6.3 The Complexity of the Attack

The differential characteristic described in the previous section can be used to construct a distinguisher for the compression function of SIMD. It is easy to see that by using the differential characteristic q times one can find a differential q-multicollision with a complexity of about $q \cdot 2^{507.34}$ compression function evaluations. Furthermore, by using message modification (see Section 5.3) in the first 4 steps the complexity of the attack can be significantly reduced, resulting in a complexity of about $q \cdot 2^{425.28}$. Note that the generic attack has a complexity of about

$$q \cdot 2^{\frac{q-2}{q+2} \cdot 1024}$$

compression function evaluations. Hence, one can distinguish the compression function of SIMD from a random function with a complexity of about $q \cdot 2^{507.34}$ and $q \cdot 2^{425.28}$ for $q = 6$ and $q = 5$, respectively.

In a similar way as we can distinguish the compression function of SIMD from random, we can also distinguish the output transformation (last iteration of SIMD) from random. While the complexity for constructing a differential q-multicollision for the output transformation using the differential characteristic described in the previous section is the same as before, the complexity of the generic attack has changed, since the output is only 512 instead of 1024 bits in the last iteration due to the truncation at the end. Hence, the complexity of the generic attack is

$$q \cdot 2^{\frac{q-2}{q+2} \cdot 512}.$$

Table 7. Summary of the attack complexities

message modification	compression function		output transformation	
	generic	our attack	generic	our attack
no	$6 \cdot 2^{\frac{4}{8} \cdot 1024}$	$6 \cdot 2^{507.34}$	$438 \cdot 2^{\frac{436}{440} \cdot 512}$	$438 \cdot 2^{507.34}$
yes	$5 \cdot 2^{\frac{3}{7} \cdot 1024}$	$5 \cdot 2^{425.28}$	$22 \cdot 2^{\frac{20}{24} \cdot 512}$	$22 \cdot 2^{425.28}$

However, by setting $q = 438$ and $q = 22$ for the case with message modification in the first 4 rounds, we can distinguish the output transformation of SIMD from random with a complexity of about $438 \cdot 2^{507.34}$ and $22 \cdot 2^{425.28}$, respectively. Table 7 provides a summary of the complexities for our distinguisher and the generic complexities.

7   Conclusions

In this paper, we presented a distinguishing attack on the compression function of SIMD-512. We used techniques from coding theory to search for differential characteristics with low Hamming weight. We have found several characteristics with weight 486. Our attack strategy for the distinguisher is similar to the multicollision distinguisher introduced by Biryukov et al. [1]. By using the characteristic with the highest success probability, we are able to construct a distinguisher, which complexity is below the generic bound in [1], even with a still conservative probability estimation. We are able to distinguish the compression function from random with a complexity of $5 \cdot 2^{425.28}$ compression function calls. Including the output transformation the complexities are still below the generic bound, i.e. we can distinguish the output transformation of SIMD from random with a complexity of about $22 \cdot 2^{425.28}$ compression function calls.

Even if we do not attack the whole hash function, we show unexpected properties for the SIMD-512 compression function. However, our attack does not invalidate the security claims of the designers, since most of the security comes from the message expansion, but note that the non-randomness of the compression function of SIMD effect the applicability of the proofs for the mode of operation build upon it.

This is the first external cryptanalysis of the SIMD hash function. However, the desigerns have tweaked the design to avoid this attack.

Acknowledgements

The authors wish to thank Gaëtan Leurent for validating our attack, Christian Rechberger, Vincent Rijmen and the anonymous referees for useful comments and discussions. The work in this paper has been supported in part by the European Commission under contract ICT-2007-216646 (ECRYPT II) and by the Austrian Science Fund (FWF), project P19863.

References

1. Alex Biryukov, D.K., Nikolić, I.: Distinguisher and Related-Key Attack on the Full AES-256. In: Halevi, S. (ed.) Crypto. LNCS, vol. 5677, pp. 231–249. Springer, Heidelberg (2009)
2. Canteaut, A., Chabaud, F.: A New Algorithm for Finding Minimum-Weight Words in a Linear Code: Application to McEliece's Cryptosystem and to Narrow-Sense BCH Codes of Length 511. IEEE Transactions on Information Theory 44(1), 367–378 (1998)
3. Chabaud, F., Joux, A.: Differential Collisions in SHA-0. In: Krawczyk, H. (ed.) CRYPTO 1998. LNCS, vol. 1462, pp. 56–71. Springer, Heidelberg (1998)
4. Chang, D., Nandi, M.: Improved Indifferentiability Security Analysis of chopMD Hash Function. In: Nyberg, K. (ed.) FSE 2008. LNCS, vol. 5086, pp. 429–443. Springer, Heidelberg (2008)
5. Damgård, I.B.: A Design Principle for Hash Functions. In: Brassard, G. (ed.) CRYPTO 1989. LNCS, vol. 435, pp. 416–427. Springer, Heidelberg (1990)
6. Daum, M.: Cryptanalysis of Hash Functions of the MD4-Family. Ph.D. thesis, Ruhr-Universität Bochum (May 2005), http://www.cits.rub.de/imperia/md/content/magnus/dissmd4.pdf
7. Indesteege, S., Preneel, B.: Practical Collisions for EnRUPT. In: Dunkelman, O. (ed.) FSE 2009. LNCS, vol. 5665, pp. 246–259. Springer, Heidelberg (2009)
8. Leurent, G., Bouillaguet, C., Fouque, P.A.: SIMD Is a Message Digest. Submission to NIST (2008), http://www.di.ens.fr/~leurent/files/SIMD.pdf
9. Lucks, S.: A Failure-Friendly Design Principle for Hash Functions. In: Roy, B. K. (ed.) ASIACRYPT 2005. LNCS, vol. 3788, pp. 474–494. Springer, Heidelberg (2005)
10. Maurer, U.M., Tessaro, S.: Domain Extension of Public Random Functions: Beyond the Birthday Barrier. In: Menezes, A. (ed.) CRYPTO 2007. LNCS, vol. 4622, pp. 187–204. Springer, Heidelberg (2007)
11. Merkle, R.C.: One Way Hash Functions and DES. In: Brassard, G. (ed.) CRYPTO 1989. LNCS, vol. 435, pp. 428–446. Springer, Heidelberg (1990)
12. National Institute of Standards and Technology: Announcing Request for Candidate Algorithm Nominations for a New Cryptographic Hash Algorithm (SHA-3) Family. Federal Register Notice, (November 2007), http://csrc.nist.gov
13. Pramstaller, N., Rechberger, C., Rijmen, V.: Exploiting Coding Theory for Collision Attacks on SHA-1. In: Smart, N.P. (ed.) Cryptography and Coding 2005. LNCS, vol. 3796, pp. 78–95. Springer, Heidelberg (2005)
14. Rijmen, V., Oswald, E.: Update on SHA-1. In: Menezes, A. (ed.) CT-RSA 2005. LNCS, vol. 3376, pp. 58–71. Springer, Heidelberg (2005)
15. Wang, X., Yu, H.: How to Break MD5 and Other Hash Functions. In: Cramer, R. (ed.) EUROCRYPT 2005. LNCS, vol. 3494, pp. 19–35. Springer, Heidelberg (2005)

A Differential Characteristic for the 4 Steps in the Feed-Forward

Table 8. Differences in the chaining values in the feed-forward

(t,i)	A_i^t	B_i^t	C_i^t	D_i^t
$(33,0)$	00000000	00000000	00000000	00000000
$(33,1)$	00000000	00000000	00000000	00000000
$(33,2)$	00000000	00000000	00000000	00000000
$(33,3)$	00000000	00000000	83801001	00000000
$(33,4)$	00000000	00000000	00000000	0000c008
$(33,5)$	00000000	00000000	00000000	00000000
$(33,6)$	84d0c901	00000000	00000000	00000000
$(33,7)$	80088000	8410c1c0	00000000	00000000
$(34,0)$	00000000	00000000	00000000	00000000
$(34,1)$	00000000	00000000	00000000	00000000
$(34,2)$	00000000	00000000	00000000	00000000
$(34,3)$	02090094	00000000	00000000	83801001
$(34,4)$	9a193831	00000000	00000000	00000000
$(34,5)$	01100010	00000000	00000000	00000000
$(34,6)$	00000000	9a192030	00000000	00000000
$(34,7)$	00000000	01100010	8410c1c0	00000000
$(35,0)$	00000000	00000000	00000000	00000000
$(35,1)$	00000000	00000000	00000000	00000000
$(35,2)$	00220002	00000000	00000000	00000000
$(35,3)$	21620401	80412012	00000000	00000000
$(35,4)$	8c010008	33432706	00000000	00000000
$(35,5)$	00000000	00220002	00000000	00000000
$(35,6)$	00000000	00000000	9a192030	00000000
$(35,7)$	20000000	00000000	01100010	8410c1c0
$(36,0)$	02001118	00000000	00000000	00000000
$(36,1)$	00000000	00000000	00000000	00000000
$(36,2)$	00000000	44000400	00000000	00000000
$(36,3)$	00000040	c4080242	80412012	00000000
$(36,4)$	00000000	02001118	33432706	00000000
$(36,5)$	00000000	00000000	00220002	00000000
$(36,6)$	4d00b040	00000000	00000000	9a192030
$(36,7)$	a4e04042	00000040	00000000	01100010

Sampling from Signed Quadratic Residues: RSA Group Is Pseudofree

Mahabir Prasad Jhanwar and Rana Barua

Indian Statistical Institute
Stat-Math Unit
203 B.T. Road, Kolkata
India
mahabir_r@isical.ac.in, rana@isical.ac.in

Abstract. Rivest (TCC 2004) explored the notion of a pseudo-free group from cryptographic perspective. He made the conjecture that the RSA group $\mathbb{Z}_N^*$ is a plausible pseudo-free group. Daniele Micciancio proved that (to appear in Journal of Cryptology), under strong RSA assumption, $\mathbb{Z}_N^*$ is pseudo-free. The proof uses the fact that N is the product of two safe primes, and **elements are sampled uniformly at random from the subgroup QR_N of quadratic residues**. He asked whether the proof can be carried over if elements are sampled uniformly at random from the whole of $\mathbb{Z}_N^*$. In this article, we show that one can sample uniformly at random from the subgroup QR_N^+ of signed quadratic residues to prove that $\mathbb{Z}_N^*$ is pseudo-free. Consequently, we believe one can show $\mathbb{Z}_N^*$ pseudo-free where elements are sampled from $QR_N \cup QR_N^+$, thus enlarging the set from which elements are sampled.

Keywords: RSA Group, Free Group, Quadratic Residues.

1 Introduction

Given a computational problem (Computational Assumption: this problem is "hard" to solve) over a finite group, often a cryptographic scheme is designed over this group in such a way that security (of the scheme) could be achieved without **extra assumptions**. The only way to formally prove such a fact is by showing that an attacker against the scheme can be used as a sub-part in an algorithm that can break the underlying computational assumption.

For example, the RSA public-key cryptosystem [23] is based on the multiplicative group $\mathbb{Z}_N^*$, where N is the product of two large primes. The security of RSA scheme depends upon the "RSA assumption" [23]. Informally this assumption is that it is hard to solve the equation $x^e \equiv a \pmod{N}$ given only $N, a \in \mathbb{N}_N^*$ and $e(\gcd(e, \phi(N) = 1))$. Similarly, the Cramer-Shoup cryptosystem and signature scheme [6], [7] depend upon the "Strong RSA Assumption", [10], [3], which similarly assumes the hardness of solving the equation $x^e \equiv a \pmod{N}$, though here the adversary is allowed to solve the equation for exponent $e > 1$ of **her choice**.

B. Roy and N. Sendrier (Eds.): INDOCRYPT 2009, LNCS 5922, pp. 233–247, 2009.

Within $\mathbb{Z}_N^*$, Rivest [22] takes this progression one step further. He examine the situation where the adversary may choose whatever equation (as long as the equation is "nontrivial"-unsatisfiable in the "corresponding" free group, with appropriate care for some details) and try to solve. The $\mathbb{Z}_N^*$ **is pseudo-free** assumption is that the adversary will succeed with at most negligible probability. The notion of pseudo-free group was introduced by Hohenberger [12]. Rivest [22], explored this notion and provided an alternative stronger definition. He defined pseudo-freeness of a "family of computational groups". The assumption of pseudo-freeness may be made for arbitrary finite group, such as an elliptic curve group or even a noncommutative group.

Rivest [22], studied the assumption that a group is pseudo-free or, more specifically, pseudo-free abelian, and showed how it implies some known standard assumptions on the group. Thus assuming that a finite group is pseudo-free appears to be quite a strong assumption and formulating and studying such a strong assumption may indicate a course taken against the traditional style of making only the minimal complexity theoretic assumptions necessary for a cryptographic scheme. Rivest [22], provides motivation and justifications for studying pseudo-free groups and some of them are as follows:

- $\mathbb{Z}_N^*$ is possibly a natural candidate for pseudo-free group.
- It may turn out that the pseudo-freeness is in fact not a "stronger" assumption. It may be implied by some standard assumptions and in fact in [14], Micciancio vindicated the belief by proving that $\mathbb{Z}_N^*$ is pseudo-free is implied by the strong RSA assumption [3].
- Using a stronger assumption may make proofs easier.
- Reasoning in a free group can be quite simple and intuitive, so assuming pseudo-freeness allows one to capture "natural" security proofs in a plausible framework. This was Hohenberger's [12] motivation. In [12], pseudo-freeness has been linked to the construction of specific cryptographic primitives, like directed transitive signature schemes, for which no solution is currently known. See [18] for a recent work in this area.

Free groups are widely used in computer science, and most modern cryptography relies on the hardness of computational problems over finite groups. As argued in [22], pseudo-free groups can be a very interesting notion from a cryptographic perspective. As pointed out by Micciancio [14], (non abelian) free groups are used in the so called Dolev-Yao model [8] for the symbolic analysis of public key cryptographic protocols. In the last few years, there have been several effort to bridge the gap between the symbolic model of [8] and the standard computational model used in cryptography (see for example [1],[2],[13],[15],[16],[17]). An intersting question is whether pseudo-free groups can be used to extend (in a computationally sound way) the Dolev-Yao model (in which encryption and decryption are viewed as black-box operations with no algebraic properties) with richer data structures and cryptographic functions (e.g., homomorphic encryption schemes) that make fundamental use of computational groups.

The main question left open by Rivest in [22] is: do pseudo-free group exists? Rivest [22], made the conjecture that the RSA group $\mathbb{Z}_N^*$ (where $N = P \cdot Q$ is the product of two large primes) is pseudo-free and nicknamed the their conjecture the *super strong RSA assumption*.

In [14], Micciancio very elegantly resolved this conjecture by providing an affirmative answer. Micciancio proved that $\mathbb{Z}_N^*$ is pseudofree under the strong RSA assumption, at least when $N = P \cdot Q$ is the product of two "safe primes" (i.e., P and Q are of the form $2p+1$ and $2q+1$ respectively such that p and q are primes). In other words $\mathbb{Z}_N^*$ is pseudo-free is implied by strong RSA assumption. Micciancio [14], further proved that the RSA group $\mathbb{Z}_N^*$ satisfies an even stronger version of the pseudo-freeness property than the one defined in [22]: he proved that no adversary can efficiently compute an unsatisfiable system of equations (as opposed to a single equation) together with a solution in the given computational group.

In order to successfully work out pseudo-freeness of $\mathbb{Z}_N^*$, [14] considered the computational group $\mathbb{Z}_N^*$ together with a different sampling procedure that chooses elements at random from the subgroup QR_N, the set of quadratic residues modulo N. One of the questions asked by Micciancio is that if one can prove pseudo-freeness of $\mathbb{Z}_N^*$ if elements are sampled uniformly at random from the whole group $\mathbb{Z}_N^*$.

Our Contribution: We prove that one can show $\mathbb{Z}_N^*$ to be pseudo-free when elements are sampled uniformly at random from a different subgroup of $\mathbb{Z}_N^*$. This subgroup is set of signed quadratic residues modulo N, denoted as QR_N^+. Consequently, we believe one can show $\mathbb{Z}_N^*$ pseudo-free where elements are sampled from $QR_N \cup QR_N^+$, thus enlarging the set from which elements are sampled. The group QR_N^+ has been suggested by Fischlin and Schnorr in [9] (in the different context of hard-core bits of generalized Rabin functions [21],[9]) and later Hoftheinz and Kiltz [11] demonstrated the usefulness of this group for cryptographic purpose.

2   Preliminaries

Statistical Distance
Let X and Y be two random variables tamking values in a finite set S. The *statistical distance* between X and Y is defined to be

$$\text{Dist}(X, Y) = \tfrac{1}{2} \cdot \sum_{s \in S} |\text{Prob}[X = s] - \text{Prob}[Y = s]|$$

Mathematical Group
We recall the definition of a mathematical group. A group $G = (S, \circ)$ consists of a set S of elements together with a binary operation $\circ$ on S satisfying the following properties. Closure property requires that for all $x, y \in S$, we have $x \circ y \in S$. There should be an identity element in S, denoted as 1, such that for all elements $x \in S$, we have $x \circ 1 = 1 \circ x = 1$. Associativity requires that for all elements $x, y, z \in S$, we have $x \circ (y \circ z) = (x \circ y) \circ z$ and finally for every element $x \in S$, there should be a element $y \in S$ (y is called inverse of x often denoted as x^{-1}) such that $x \circ y = y \circ x = 1$. G is called abelian if $\circ$ is commutative i.e., for all $x, y \in S$, we have $x \circ y = y \circ x$.

Computational Group

In cryptography, for a mathematical group G, often a "suitable" representation $\langle \cdot \rangle : G \to \{0,1\}^*$ of G is what one looks for. Such a representation $\langle \cdot \rangle : G \to \{0,1\}^*$ is called a computational group implementing the underlying mathematical group. Clearly many computational groups may implement the same mathematical group. Below we define, a family of computational groups implementing a family of finite mathematical groups.

Let $\mathcal{G} = \{G_N\}_{N \in \mathcal{N}}$ be a family of finite mathematical groups indexed by $N \in \mathcal{N} \in \{0,1\}^*$. A computational group family implementing $\mathcal{G}$ is defined by a collection of representations $\langle \cdot \rangle_N : G_N \to \{0,1\}^*$ (for $N \in \mathcal{N}$) such that the following operations can be carried out in polynomial time in the bit-size of N.

- Composition: given $N \in \mathcal{N}$, representations $\langle x \rangle_N$ and $\langle y \rangle_N$ of group elements $x, y \in G_N$, compute representation $\langle x \circ y \rangle_N$ of $x \circ y$.
- Identity: given N, compute a representation $\langle 1 \rangle_N$ of the identity element 1 of the group G_N.
- Inverses: given N and $\langle x \rangle_N$ (for some $x \in G_N$), compute $\langle x^{-1} \rangle_N$.
- Recognizing elements from a group: given $N \in \mathcal{N}$ and $x \in \{0,1\}^*$, determine if there exists a $y \in G_N$ such that $x = \langle y \rangle_N$.
- Sampling group elements: on input $N \in \mathcal{N}$, output the representation $\langle x \rangle_N$ of a randomly chosen group element $x \in G_N$ (with not necessarily uniform probability distribution).

2.1 Free Abelian Groups

Let G be a mathematical abelian group and $A = \{a_1, \ldots, a_k\} \subset G$. Consider the subgroup $\langle A \rangle$ of G generated by A,

$$\langle A \rangle = \{a_1^{t_1} \cdots a_k^{t_k} : t_i \in \mathbb{Z}\}$$

If $\langle A \rangle = G$, then we call A to be a generating set of G. Assume that $G = \langle A \rangle$. We call G a free group if

$$a_1^{t_1} \cdots a_k^{t_k} = 1 \text{ implies } t_i = 0 \text{ for all } i.$$

We then denote G by $\mathcal{F}(A)$. Thus for a free group G, for any two distinct tuples $(t_1, \ldots, t_k), (u_1, \ldots, u_k) \in \mathbb{Z}^k$ the corresponding group elements $a_1^{t_1} \cdots a_k^{t_k}$ and $a_1^{u_1} \cdots a_k^{u_k}$ are distinct. We call G to be a free group of rank k and clearly it is isomorphic to k copies of $\mathbb{Z}$. Thus free groups are necessarily infinite.

We remark that the fundamental property of a free group is that there **does-not exists a non-trivial relation among its generators** (inparticular $\nexists$ a nonzero tuple $(t_1, \ldots, t_k) \in \mathbb{Z}^k$ such that $\prod_{i=1}^{k} a_i^{t_i} = 1$).

So if for some finite group G, given any randomly chosen elements $g_1, \ldots, g_n \in G$, it is "computationally" hard to find a non-trivial relation (we will show later that it correspond to some non-trivial equation over the "corresponding" free group) among $g_1, \ldots, g_n$, then G captures the fundamental property of a free group and *informally* we call G a pseudo-free group.

2.2 Pseudo Free Abelian Groups

First we describe equations in free groups. Let X and A be two disjoint set of variable and constant symbols. A group equation over variables X and constants A, is $E : w_1 = w_2$, where w_1 and w_2 are words over alphabets $(X \cup X^{-1})^*$ and $(A \cup A^{-1})^*$ respectively. Note that $(A \cup A^{-1})^*$ is nothing but the free abelian group $\mathcal{F}(A)$ generated by A. Unless otherwise specified, we interpret E as an equation over the free group $\mathcal{F}(A)$. A solution to $E : w_1 = w_2$ (over the free group $\mathcal{F}(A)$) is a function $\sigma : X \to \mathcal{F}(A)$ such that $\sigma(w_1) = w_2$ (in $\mathcal{F}(A)$), where σ is extended to words over $X \cup X^{-1}$ homomorphically in the natural way. We say that an equation $E : w_1 = w_2$ is **satisfiable** over the free group $\mathcal{F}(A)$ if it admits a solution. We say it is **unsatisfiable** otherwise.

Let G be a computational group. A group equation over G is defined by an equation E over variables X and constants A, and a function $\alpha : A \to G$ (α will sample $|A|$ many element from the group G) and is denoted as E_α. A solution to equation $E_\alpha : w_1 = w_2$ is a function $\xi : X \to G$ such that $\xi(w_1) = \alpha(w_2)$.

Before we formally introduce pseudo-free groups, observe that for any finite group G, given any element $a \in G$, the following equation $E : x^{|G|+1} = a$ is unsatisfiable over the free group $\mathcal{F}(\{a\})$ but has solution $x = a$ over G. In order to properly define pseudo-free groups we need to consider families of groups $\{G_N\}$ (N is chosen at randomen) so that given a randomly chosen N, it should be hard to compute the corresponding group order $|G_N|$. Technically, we assume the set of indexes $\mathcal{N}$ is endowed with a sequence of probability distributions $(\mathcal{N}_k)_k$ such that $\mathcal{N}_k$ can be sampled in (expected) polynomial (in k) time. Typically, $\mathcal{N}_k$ is the uniform distribution over all strings in $\mathcal{N}$ of length k, but other distributions are possible. The set of indexes $\mathcal{N}$ together with the polynomial time sampling algorithm and associated probability distribution $\mathcal{N}_k$ is called a **probability ensemble**.

Definition 1. *[22],[14] Let $\mathcal{G} = \{G_N\}_{N \in \mathcal{N}}$ be a family of computational groups. $\mathcal{G}$ is called pseudo-free if for any probabilistic polynomial (in k, security parameter) time algorithm $\mathcal{A}$, the probability that on input a polynomial sized set A ($|A| = p(k)$), a randomly chosen group index $N \in \mathcal{N}_k$, and $\alpha : A \to G_N$ (it chooses independently at random $|A|$ many group elements according to the computational group sampling procedure), $\mathcal{A}$ outputs (E, ξ) such that E (equation over variables X and constans A) is unsatisfiable over $\mathcal{F}(A)$ and $\xi : X \to G_N$ is a solution to E_α over G_N is a negligible function in k.*

3 Signed Quadratic Residues

Let N be an odd integer. Elements of $\mathbb{Z}_N$ are represented as signed integers in the set $\{-\frac{N-1}{2}, \ldots, -1, 0, 1, \ldots, \frac{N-1}{2}\}$. For $x \in \mathbb{Z}_N$, we define $|x|$ as the absolute value of x

For a subgroup G of $\mathbb{Z}_N^*$, consider the following set:

$$G^+ := \{|x| : x \in G\}$$

Define an operation 'o' on G^+ as follows. For $g, h \in G^+$, $g \circ h = |g \cdot h \pmod{N}|$. One may check that $(G^+, \circ)$ becomes a group. One may note that elements in G^+ are not necessarily in G. For completeness we work out the closure property. The rest of the group properties can be checked easily.

Closure Property: Given $g, h \in G^+$, show $g \circ h \in G^+$

Case-1: $g, h \in G$. This trivially shows that $g \circ h$ belongs to G^+.

Case-2: Either of g or h is not in G. Without loss of generality say g is not in G and $h \in G$. As $g \in G^+$, clearly $-g \in G$. Thus $-g \cdot h \pmod{N} \in G$. Therefor $|-g \cdot h \pmod{N}| \in G^+$. But $|-g \cdot h \pmod{N}| = |g \cdot h \pmod{N}| = g \circ h$. Thus $g \circ h \in G^+$.

Case-3: Both g, h are not in G. Then $-g, -h \in G$. Thus $(-g) \cdot (-h) \pmod{N} \in G$. Therefor $|(-g) \cdot (-h) \pmod{N}| \in G^+$. But $|(-g) \cdot (-h) \pmod{N}| = |g \cdot h \pmod{N}| = g \circ h$. Thus $g \circ h \in G^+$.

For an integer x we define,

$$g^{\underline{x}} = g \circ \cdots \circ g = |g^x \pmod{N}|$$

More complicated expressions in the exponents are computed modulo the group order. For example,

$$g^{\underline{1/2}} = g^{\underline{2^{-1} \bmod \mathrm{ord}(G^+)}}$$

Define the following map $\phi : G \to G^+$ as follows: For $x \in G$, $\phi(x) = |x|$. One may check that, for $x, y \in G$

$$\phi(x \cdot y) = \phi(x) \circ \phi(y)$$

i.e. ϕ is a group homomorphism. The kernel of this homomorphism is trivial if -1 is not in G and else it is $\{-1, 1\}$ and for the former case, ϕ becomes an isomorphism.

3.1   Our Choice for N and G

We take $N = P \cdot Q$, the product of two prime numbers where P and Q are of the form $2p + 1$ and $2q + 1$ respectively with p, q themselves primes. Clearly $P, Q \equiv 3 \pmod{4}$ i.e. N is a Blum integer. We study the RSA group $\mathbb{Z}_N^*$. For the rest of this paper the elements of $\mathbb{Z}_N$ are represented as signed integers in the set $\{-\frac{N-1}{2}, \ldots, -1, 0, 1, \ldots, \frac{N-1}{2}\}$. For $x \in \mathbb{Z}_N$, we define $|x|$ as the absolute value of x. We will take G to be the group QR_N of quadratic residues modulo N. Thus

$$QR_N^+ = \{|x| : x \in QR_N\}$$

As N is a Blum integer, -1 is not a quadratic reside and thus ϕ becomes isomorphism. Now as QR_N is a cyclic group of order pq and ϕ is an isomorphism, QR_N^+ is also a cyclic group of order pq. Another fundamental property of the group QR_N^+, where it is different from QR_N, is, that membership in QR_N^+ is efficiently recognizable whereas computing square root still remains hard. It is due to the fact that as a set $QR_N^+ = J(N) \cap (0, \frac{N-1}{2}]$ where $J(N) = \{x \in \mathbb{Z}_N^* : \text{Jacobi symbol } (\frac{x}{N}) = 1\}$. One may note that recognizing membership of elements in $J(N)$ can be performed efficiently as in particular Jacobi symbols can be efficiently computed. Thus QR_N^+ is a "gap group" [19], in which the computational problem (i.e computing a square root) is as hard as factoring, whereas the corresponding decisional problem (i.e., deciding if an element is a signed square) is easy.

As we noted earlier in the general case, $x \in QR_N^+$ does not imply that x is a quadratic residue modulo N. For $-y \in QR_N$ implies $| - y| = y \in QR_N^+$. But as $y = (-1) \cdot (-y)$ and -1 is quadratic non-residue, y is quadratic non-residue. Thus for the rest of this article elements of QR_N^+ will be characterized as follows. For an element $x \in QR_N^+$, either $x \in QR_N$ or there exists a unique quadratic residue $y \in QR_N$ such that $-x \equiv y \pmod{N}$. This y is nothing but the element $N - x$.

4   Strong Signed QR-RSA (SQR-RSA) Assumption

We let, for $k \geq 1$, $\mathcal{N}_k$ be the set of all safe prime products of bit-size bounded by k with some standard probability distribution (used in cryptography) on $\mathcal{N}_k$. We first recall some computational assumptions that are conjectured to be asymptotically hard and are related to this work.

Strong RSA problem [3]: given a random integer $N \in \mathcal{N}_k$, and a randomly chosen group element $\gamma \in \mathbb{Z}_N^*$, output an integer $e > 1$ and a group element $\xi \in \mathbb{Z}_N^*$ such that $\xi^e \equiv \gamma \pmod{N}$.

Strong QR-RSA problem [7]: given a random integer $N \in \mathcal{N}_k$, and a randomly chosen quadratic residue $\gamma \in QR_N$, output an integer $e > 1$ and a group element $\xi \in \mathbb{Z}_N^*$ such that $\xi^e \equiv \gamma \pmod{N}$.

In [7], it has been observed that strong QR-RSA problem is as hard as strong RSA problem. For our work we propose a new variant of strong RSA problem. We call it strong signed QR-RSA problem.

Strong SQR-RSA problem: given a random integer $N \in \mathcal{N}_k$, and a randomly chosen $\gamma \in QR_N^+$, output an integer $e > 1$ and a group element $\xi \in \mathbb{Z}_N^*$ such that $\xi^e \equiv \gamma \pmod{N}$.

We will show below that this problem is as hard as Strong QR-RSA problem.

Theorem 1. *If the strong QR-RSA problem is asymptotically hard where the underlying modulus N is chosen randomly from the set $\mathcal{N}_k$ of all safe prime products of bit size bounded by k, then the strong SQR-RSA problem is also asymptotically hard for the same N.*

Assume the existence of a PPT algorithm $\mathcal{A}$ which, given a input (N, γ), where $\gamma \in QR_N^+$, outputs a element $\xi \in \mathbb{Z}_N^*$ and an integer $e > 1$ such that $\xi^e \equiv \gamma \pmod{N}$. We will use $\mathcal{A}$ as an oracle to solve strong QR-RSA problem. Let an input of the strong QR-RSA problem be given as (N, γ) where $\gamma \in QR_N$. Consider the following cases:

Case-1: Check if $0 < \gamma \leq \frac{N-1}{2}$. If yes, then $\gamma \in QR_N^+$. Pass (N, γ) to $\mathcal{A}$. Clearly the solution given by $\mathcal{A}$ will also be a solution to this strong QR-RSA instance.

Case-2: Let $-\frac{N-1}{2} \leq \gamma < 0$. Then $\gamma = -t$ where $0 < t \leq \frac{N-1}{2}$. As $\gamma \in QR_N$, $t = |\gamma| \in QR_N^+$. With (N, t) as an input to $\mathcal{A}$, it will output an element $\xi \in \mathbb{Z}_N^*$ and a positive integer $e > 1$ such that $\xi^e \equiv t \pmod{N}$. Here we claim that this e is necessarily odd. If e is even, t becomes a quadratic residue which is not possible as $-t = \gamma \in QR_N$. Thus we now output $\xi' = -\xi$ as a solution to (N, γ) as we can see,

$$(\xi')^e \equiv (-\xi)^e \equiv -1 \cdot \xi^e \equiv -t \equiv \gamma \pmod{N} \qquad \square$$

We also need the following lemma in the proof of our main theorem.

Lemma 1. *Let $N = p \cdot q$, product of two safe primes. QR_N and QR_N^+ denotes the subgroup of quadratic residues and signed quadratic residues respectively. For an element x, chosen randomly from QR_N^+, the probability that x also belongs to QR_N is $\frac{1}{2} + o(1)$, where $o(1)$ is negligible.*

Proof: In 1918, Polya[20] and Vinogradov[24], proved independently the following remarkable inequality,

$$\left| \sum_{a=N+1}^{N+M} \left(\frac{a}{p} \right) \right| \leq \sqrt{p} \cdot \log p$$

where p is prime and N, M are arbitrary $(0 \leq N < N + M < p)$. Putting $N = 0$, $M = \frac{p-1}{2}$ and $N = \frac{p-1}{2}$, $M = \frac{p-1}{2}$ respectively, we have the following inequalities,

$$\left| \sum_{a=1}^{\frac{p-1}{2}} \left(\frac{a}{p} \right) \right| \leq \sqrt{p} \cdot \log p \quad \text{and} \quad \left| \sum_{a=\frac{p+1}{2}}^{p-1} \left(\frac{a}{p} \right) \right| \leq \sqrt{p} \cdot \log p$$

The above inequality clearly shows that for an element x, chosen randomly in the range $1 \leq x \leq \frac{p-1}{2}$ (resp. $\frac{p-1}{2} < x \leq p-1$), the probability that x is a quadratic residue modulo p is $\frac{1}{2} + o(1)$ (resp. $\frac{1}{2} + o(1)$). Also note that for x chosen uniformly at random in an interval $[1, m]$, where m is a multiple of p (p is prime), $x \pmod{p}$ is uniformly distributed in $[0, p-1]$. So for $x \in_R \mathbb{Z}_N^* \cap [1, \frac{N-1}{2}]$, $x \pmod{p}$ and $x \pmod{q}$ are independent and approximately (elements not co-prime to N are ignored) uniformly distributed in $[1, p-1]$ and $[1, q-1]$ respectively.

So for x chosen uniformly at random in $\mathbb{Z}_N^* \cap [1, \frac{N-1}{2}]$, $\text{Prob}[x \in QR_N] = \text{Prob}[x \pmod{p}) \in QR_p$ and $x \pmod{q}) \in QR_q] = \text{Prob}[x \pmod{p}) \in QR_p] \cdot \text{Prob}[x \pmod{q}) \in QR_q]$.

Now $\text{Prob}[x \pmod{p}) \in QR_p] = \text{Prob}[x \pmod{p}) \in QR_p | 1 \leq x \pmod{p}) \leq \frac{p-1}{2}] \cdot \text{Prob}[1 \leq x \pmod{p}) \leq \frac{p-1}{2}] + \text{Prob}[x \pmod{p}) \in QR_p | \frac{p-1}{2} < x \pmod{p}) \leq p-1] \cdot \text{Prob}[\frac{p-1}{2} < x \pmod{p}) \leq p-1] = (\frac{1}{2} + o(1))(\frac{1}{2} + o(1)) + (\frac{1}{2} + o(1))(\frac{1}{2} + o(1)) = \frac{1}{2} + o(1)$. Similarly, $\text{Prob}[x \pmod{q}) \in QR_q] = \frac{1}{2} + o(1)$. Thus,

$\text{Prob}[x \in QR_N] = \text{Prob}[x \pmod p) \in QR_p] \cdot \text{Prob}[x \pmod q) \in QR_q] = (\frac{1}{2} + o(1)) \cdot (\frac{1}{2} + o(1)) = \frac{1}{4} + o(1).$

So QR_N constitutes approximately $\frac{1}{4}$th of $\mathbb{Z}_N^* \cap [1, \frac{N-1}{2}]$. The cardinality of $\mathbb{Z}_N^* \cap [1, \frac{N-1}{2}]$ and $J(N) \cap [1, \frac{N-1}{2}]$ are $\frac{\phi(N)}{2}$ and $\frac{\phi(N)}{4}$ respectively. As $QR_N \cap [1, \frac{N-1}{2}] \subset J(N) \cap [1, \frac{N-1}{2}]$, the proportion of $QR_N \cap [1, \frac{N-1}{2}]$ in $J(N) \cap [1, \frac{N-1}{2}]$ is approximately (i.e. modulo a negligible quantity) $\frac{1}{2}$. Hence for an element x, chosen randomly from $QR_N^+ = J(N) \cap [1, \frac{N-1}{2}]$, the probability that x also belongs to QR_N is $\frac{1}{2} + o(1)$.

$\square$

Remark: Vinogradov also proved a generalization of their result in which the prime p is replaced by a composite k. Sharper estimate of the above inequality for prime modulus was obtained by D.A. Burgess [4],[5].

5 $\mathbb{Z}_N^*$ Is Pseudo-free

The proof of our main Theorem below is along the lines of the proof of Theorem-2 in [14] with necessary modifications. We have essentially managed to sample elements uniformly at random from a **isomorphic copy** (QR_N^+) of QR_N in $\mathbb{Z}_N^*$ to prove $\mathbb{Z}_N^*$ is pseudo-free.

Theorem 2. *Assume the strong RSA problem is asymptotically hard with respect to a distribution ensemble $\mathcal{N}$ over the safe prime products. Then the computational group family of $\mathbb{Z}_N^*$ of invertible integers modulo $N \in \mathcal{N}$ (with the modular multiplication group operation, and uniform sampling procedure over the signed quadratic residue group QR_N^+) is pseudo-free with respect to the same distribution ensemble $\mathcal{N}$.*

Assume that $\mathbb{Z}_N^*$ is not pseudofree, i.e. there is a PPT algorithm $\mathcal{A}$ that on input a randomly chosen $N \in \mathcal{N}_k$ and random group elements $\alpha : A \to QR_N^+$ (for some polynomial sized set A), outputs an equation $E : w_1 = w_2$ (over constants in A and variables in X) which is unsatisfiable over $\mathcal{F}(A)$, together with a solution $\xi : X \to \mathbb{Z}_N^*$ to E_α over the group $\mathbb{Z}_N^*$.

We use $\mathcal{A}$ to solve the strong SQR-RSA problem for the same distribution of the modulus N. Thus, given a randomly chosen $N \in \mathcal{N}_k$ and $\gamma \in QR_N^+$, we compute an integer $e > 1$ and a group element $\xi \in \mathbb{Z}_N^*$ such that $\xi^e \equiv \gamma \pmod N$. By Theorem 1 this also implies an algorithm to solve the strong QR-RSA Problem and which in turn yield an algorithm [7] which will solve strong RSA problem. The reduction works as follows.

Let (N, γ) be an instance of the strong SQR-RSA problem. We begin by checking if γ is a generator of QR_N^+. Below we outline a sufficient condition for γ to be a generator of QR_N^+. For this we need the following result [14] which for elements γ in QR_N checks if γ is a generator for QR_N.

Lemma 2. *[14] Let $N = P \cdot Q$ be the products of two distinct safe primes, and $\gamma \in QR_N$ a quadratic residue. Then γ is a generator for QR_N iff $\gcd(\gamma - 1, N) = 1$.*

Lemma 3. *Let $N = P \cdot Q$ be the products of two distinct safe primes, and $\gamma \in QR_N^+$. If,*

$$gcd(\gamma - 1, N) = 1 \ and \ gcd(-\gamma - 1, N) = 1$$

then γ is a generator for QR_N^+.

Proof: We know for a Blum integer N, the map $\phi : QR_N \rightarrow QR_N^+$ ($\phi(x) = |x|$) is a group isomorphism. The inverse of ϕ ($\phi^{-1} : QR_N^+ \rightarrow QR_N$) is defined as follows:

$$\phi^{-1}(x) = \begin{array}{l} x \ if \ x \in QR_N \\ -x \ if \ x \notin QR_N \end{array}$$

We are given a Blum integer N and $\gamma \in QR_N^+$ such that $gcd(\gamma - 1, N) = 1$ and $gcd(-\gamma - 1, N) = 1$. We will show that γ is a generator of QR_N^+.

Case-1: Say $\gamma \in QR_N$. Then $\phi^{-1}(\gamma) = \gamma$. Now as $gcd(\gamma - 1, N) = 1$, by Lemma-2, γ is a generator of QR_N. Now as a generator is mapped into a generator under isomorphism and $\phi(\gamma) = |\gamma| = \gamma \in QR_N^+$, γ is a generator of QR_N^+.

Case-2: Say $\gamma \notin QR_N$. Then $\phi^{-1}(\gamma) = -\gamma \in QR_N$. Now as $gcd(-\gamma - 1, N) = 1$, by Lemma-2, $-\gamma$ is a generator of QR_N. Similarly as generators are mapped into generators under isomorphism and $\phi(-\gamma) = |-\gamma| = \gamma \in QR_N^+$, γ is a generator of QR_N^+. $\square$

So for given $\gamma \in QR_N^+$ we first compute $g = gcd(\gamma - 1, N)$ and $g' = gcd(-\gamma - 1, N)$. Since $N = P \cdot Q$, we have $g, g' \in \{1, P, Q, PQ\}$. We consider below all the cases.

- Case-1: Either of g or g' is in $\{P, Q\}$. W.l.o.g. say $g \in \{P, Q\}$. Then we can easily compute $\phi(N) = (P - 1) \cdot (Q - 1)$ and output $(\xi, e) = (\gamma, \phi(N) + 1)$ as a solution to the strong SQR-RSA problem input (N, γ).

- Case-2: As $\gamma \in QR_N^+$, therefore $0 < \gamma \leq \frac{N-1}{2}$. Thus $gcd(-\gamma - 1, N)$ will never be N. So if $g' \notin \{P, Q\}$ then g' must be equal to 1. Now if $g = N$, then $\gamma \equiv 1 \pmod{N}$ and we can immediately output a solution to the strong SQR-RSA problem input (N, γ), e.g. $(\xi, e) = (1, 2)$

- Case-3: g and g' are both equal to 1. Then by Lemma-3, γ is a generator for QR_N^+.

For rest of the proof we assume that γ is a generator of QR_N^+. Now we generate an input instance (N, α) for algorithm $\mathcal{A}$ where for a polynomial sized set A, α samples $|A|$ many elements from QR_N^+. Since $\mathcal{A}$ works only with non negligible probability, we need the input values $\alpha(a)$ to be distributed (almost) uniformly at random over QR_N^+. The following lemma shows that γ, being a generator of QR_N^+, can be used to sample QR_N^+ almost uniformly at random.

Lemma 4. *[14] For any cyclic group G and generator $\gamma \in G$, if $\nu \in \{0, \ldots, B - 1\}$ is chosen uniformly at random, then the statistical distance between γ^ν and the uniform distribution over G is at most $\frac{|G|}{2B}$.*

So for any polynomial sized set A, we sample $|A|$ many elements almost uniformly at random from QR_N^+ as follows. For $a \in A$, choose $\nu_a \in \{0, \ldots, N \cdot |A| \cdot K - 1\}$ uniformly at random for some super polynomial function $K(k) = k^{\omega(1)}$ and set $\alpha(a) = \gamma^{\nu_a}$ (note that $\gamma^{\nu_a} = |\gamma^{\nu_a} \pmod{N}|$). There are two things to check here.

1. $\alpha(a)$ is uniformly distributed over QR_N^+
2. Among all the assignments $\alpha : A \to QR_N^+$ to sample QR_N^+ almost uniformly at random, our choice of α where $\alpha(a) = \gamma^{\nu_a}$ is uniformly selected.

For the first property, By Lemma-4, the statistical distance between $\alpha(a)$ and the uniform distribution over QR_N^+ is at most $\frac{|QR_N^+|}{2N|A|K} \leq \frac{1}{2|A|K}$. For later, we know that algorithm $\mathcal{A}$ will be successful with non-negligible probability on input N and assignment $\alpha : A \to QR_N^+$ provided α is distributed uniformly at random. Since the value $\alpha(a)$ are independently chosen, the statistical distance between α and a uniformly chosen assignment is at most $\frac{1}{2K} = \frac{1}{k^{\omega(1)}}$ and thus $\mathcal{A}$ succeeds on input α ($\alpha(a) = \gamma^{\nu_a}$) with non-negligible probability $\delta(k) - \frac{1}{K(k)}$ where $\delta(k)$ is the non-negligible probability of $\mathcal{A}$'s success on input (N, α) when the assignment α is distributed uniformly at random.

In the rest of the proof, we assume $\mathcal{A}$ is successful, and we consider the conditional success probability of the reduction and show that it will turn out to be at least $\frac{3}{16} + o(1)$, where $o(1)$ is negligible.

We now first workout some more details about our assignment α. We know, for every $a \in A$, we set $\alpha(a) = \gamma^{\nu_a}$ for a randomly chosen $\nu_a \in \{0, \ldots, N \cdot |A| \cdot K - 1\}$. With each of this ν_a one can associate two unique numbers modulo $\frac{\phi(N)}{4} = pq$. They are respectively, the remainder w_a and the quotient z_a of ν_a when divided by pq. Thus $w_a \equiv \nu_a \pmod{pq}$ and $z_a = \frac{\nu_a - w_a}{pq}$. Eventhough they exists, given ν_a, it is hard to compute z_a and w_a due to the unavailability of $\phi(N)$. Thus we will use w_a and z_a only in the analysis of the reduction.

Notice that, given w_a, the conditional distribution of z_a is uniform over the set

$$S_a = \left\{ 0, \ldots, \left\lfloor \frac{N \cdot |A| \cdot K - 1 - w_a}{pq} \right\rfloor \right\}$$

The size of S_a is at least

$$|S_a| \geq 1 + \left\lfloor \frac{N \cdot |A| \cdot K - 1 - w_a}{pq} \right\rfloor \overset{[w_a \leq pq-1]}{\geq} \left\lfloor \frac{N \cdot |A| \cdot K}{pq} \right\rfloor \overset{[N > 4pq]}{\geq} 4|A|K \geq 4$$

Also, given w_a, the value of $\alpha(a) = \gamma^{\nu_a} = \gamma^{w_a}$ is uniquely determined, and z_a is uniformly distributed over the set S_a independently from α, E and ξ.

Assume that $\mathcal{A}$ is successful, i.e., $E : w_1 = w_2$ is not satisfiable over $\mathcal{F}(A)$, and $\xi : X \to \mathbb{Z}_N^*$ is a valid solution to E_α, i.e. $\xi(w_1) = \alpha(w_2)$. Like typical reduction, we use equation E and solution ξ to output a solution to strong SQR-RSA problem input (N, γ). This is done in two steps. First, we transform equation E and solution ξ (to E_α) into a new equation E' (unsatisfiable over the same $\mathcal{F}(A)$) containing only one variable and a solution ξ' to E_α'. Then E' and ξ' will be used to solve the given instance (N, γ) of strong SQR-RSA problem. The following lemma will show how to transform (E, ξ) into a univariate equation and solution (E', ξ').

Lemma 5. *[14] For any computational group family $\mathcal{G}$, there is a polynomial time algorithm that on input a group G from $\mathcal{G}$, and an equation E, over a set X of variables and set A of constants, and a variable assignment $\xi : X \to G$, outputs a univariate equation E', over the same set A of constants, and a value $\xi' \in G$, such that*

Prop-1: if E is unsatisfiable over the free group $\mathcal{F}(A)$, then E' is also unsatisfiable over $\mathcal{F}(A)$, and

Prop-2: for any assignment $\alpha : A \to G$, if ξ is a solution to E_α then ξ' is a solution to E'_α.

In particular for input equation $E : \prod_{x \in X} x^{e_x} = \prod_{a \in A} a^{d_a}$, where $e_x, d_a \in \mathbb{Z}$ and input assignment $\xi : X \to G$, the algorithm $\mathcal{A}$ outputs equation $E' : x^e = \prod_{a \in A} a^{d_a}$ and the value ξ' in G, $\xi' = \prod_{x \in X} \xi(x)^{\frac{e_x}{e}}$.

At this point, as an output of Lemma-5, we are having an univariate equation E' : $x^e = \prod_{a \in A} a^{d_a}$ which is unsatisfiable over $\mathcal{F}(A)$ and a solution $\xi' \in \mathbb{Z}_N^*$ to E'_α, i.e.,

$$(\xi')^e = \prod_{a \in A} \alpha(a)^{d_a} = \gamma^{\underline{d}} \tag{1}$$

where $d = \sum_{a \in A} \nu_a d_a$. Notice that E' is satisfiable over the free group $\mathcal{F}(A)$ iff $e \mid \gcd(d_a : a \in A)$. So necessarily here, $e \nmid \gcd(d_a : a \in A)$.

In the rest of the proof we distinguish various cases, depending on the all possible values of $\gcd(e, pq)$ and they are,

Case-1: $e = 0$ ($=> \gcd(e, pq) = pq$)
Case-2: $e \neq 0$ and $\gcd(e, pq) = pq$
Case-3: $e \neq 0$ and $\gcd(e, pq) \in \{p, q\}$
Case-4: $e \neq 0$ and $\gcd(e, pq) = 1$

Case-1: $e = 0$.
In this case we first calculate the probability that $d = \sum_a \nu_a d_a = 0$.

Lemma 6. *[14] Given α, $e = 0$ and $\{d_a : a \in A\}$ such that $e \nmid \gcd\{d_a : a \in A\}$, the conditional probability that $d = \sum_{a \in A} \nu_a d_a \neq 0$ is at least $\frac{3}{4}$.*

Assuming $d \neq 0$ (which, by Lemma-6, happens with probability at least $\frac{3}{4}$), we have $|d| + 1 > |d| \geq 1$. Now,

$$\gamma^{\underline{|d|}} = \gamma^{\pm d} \overset{[\text{Equation}-1]}{=} (\xi')^{\pm e} = (\xi')^{\pm 0} = 1$$

But $\gamma^{\pm d} = 1$
$=> |\gamma^{\pm d} \pmod N| = 1$
$=> \gamma^{\pm d} \pmod N = \pm 1$.

We want to rule out the case when $\gamma^{\pm d} \pmod{N} = -1$. γ is given in QR_N^+. By Lemma-1, the probability that γ is also in QR_N is $\frac{1}{2} + o(1)$. Now assume $\gamma \in QR_N$ (happens with probability $\frac{1}{2} + o(1)$), then $\gamma^{\pm d} \pmod{N} \neq -1$ as $-1 \notin QR_N$. Thus we have $\gamma^{\pm d} \pmod{N} = 1$. Now we can output $(\gamma, |d|+1)$ as a valid solution to strong SQR-RSA problem input (N, γ) as

$$\gamma^{|d|+1} = \gamma \cdot \gamma^{|d|} = \gamma \cdot \gamma^{\pm d} \stackrel{[\gamma^{\pm d} \pmod{N}=1]}{=} \gamma$$

Thus $(\gamma, |d|+1))$ is a valid solution provided $d \neq 0$ and $\gamma \in QR_N$. These two events are clearly independent. Thus
Prob $[(\gamma, |d|+1)$ is a valid solution]
$\geq$ Prob $[d \neq 0$ and $\gamma \in QR_N]$
$= $ Prob $[d \neq 0] \cdot$ Prob $[\gamma \in QR_N] \stackrel{[\text{Lemma--6,Lemma--1}]}{\geq} \frac{3}{4} \cdot (\frac{1}{2} + o(1)) = \frac{3}{8} + o(1)$

Case-2: $e \neq 0$ and $\gcd(e, pq) = pq$.
As $\gamma \in QR_N^+$, $\gamma^{\phi(N)/4} = \gamma^{pq} = 1$ and therefore as $pq \mid e$, $\gamma^{\underline{e}} = 1$. Now $\gamma^{\underline{e}} = |\gamma^e \pmod{N}|$. Thus $\gamma^{\underline{e}} = 1$ implies $|\gamma^e \pmod{N}| = 1$, i.e., $\gamma^e \pmod{N} = \pm 1$. We want to rule out the case when $\gamma^e \pmod{N} = -1$. Like earlier, assuming γ to be quadratic residue will help us rule out this case and $\gamma \in QR_N$ happens with probability $\frac{1}{2} + o(1)$. So we now assume that $\gamma \in QR_N$ and out put $(\gamma, |e|+1)$ as a valid solution to the strong SQR-RSA problem instance (N, γ) as

$$\gamma^{|e|+1} = \gamma \cdot \gamma^{\pm e} = \gamma \cdot 1 = \gamma$$

So Prob$[(\gamma, |e|+1)$ is a valid solution$] \geq$ Prob$[\gamma \in QR_N] = \frac{1}{2} + o(1)$. We remark that, although we cannot compute $\gcd(e, pq)$ (or even check if $\gcd(e, pq) = pq$) because pq is not know, we can guess that this is the case, and simply check if $(\gamma, |e|+1)$ is indeed a solution to the given strong SQR-RSA problem input. Similar remarks apply to the other cases below.

Case-3: $e \neq 0$ and $\gcd(e, pq) \in \{p, q\}$.
Here $o(\gamma^{\underline{e}}) = \frac{pq}{\gcd(e, pq)} \in \{p, q\}$. Thus $\gamma^{\underline{e}}$ is not a generator of QR_N^+. Assume that $\gamma^{\underline{e}}$ also belongs to QR_N and this happens with probability $\frac{1}{2} + o(1)$. Now as $\gamma^{\underline{e}}$ is not a generator of QR_N^+, it is also not a generator of QR_N. Then by Lemma-2 $\gcd(\gamma^{\underline{e}} - 1, N) \neq 1$. Again as γ is a generator of QR_N^+ and $\gcd(e, pq) \in \{p, q\}$ implies that $\gamma^{\underline{e}} \not\equiv 1 \pmod{N}$. Thus $\gcd(\gamma^{\underline{e}} - 1, N) \neq N$. Then $\gcd(\gamma^{\underline{e}} - 1, N) \in \{P, Q\}$. So we can compute $\phi(N)$, and output the solution $(\gamma, \phi(N) + 1)$ to the strong SQR-RSA problem input (N, γ). So the probability of success in outputting a valid solution in this case is depends on the probability that given $\gamma \in QR_N^+$ is also in QR_N and this probability is $\frac{1}{2} + o(1)$.

Case-4: $e \neq 0$ and $\gcd(e, pq) = 1$
In this case first we see that $e \nmid d$ with probability at least $\frac{3}{8}$.

Lemma 7. [14] Given $\alpha, \gcd(e, pq) = 1$, and $\{d_a : a \in A\}$ such that $e \nmid \gcd\{d_a : a \in A\}$, the conditional probability that e does not divide $d = \sum_{a \in A} \nu_a d_a$ is at least $\frac{3}{8}$

Let $e' = \frac{e}{t}$ and $d' = \frac{d}{t}$ where $t = \gcd(e, d)$. Assuming $e \nmid d$ (which, by Lemma-7, happens with probability at least $\frac{3}{8}$), we have $t \neq e$, and consequently $e' = \frac{e}{t} > 1$.

Also note that from $\gcd(e, pq) = 1$ and $t \mid e$, we get $\gcd(t, o(QR_N^+)) = \gcd(t, pq) = 1$. Now we have as output (equation-1) from the algorithm $\mathcal{A}$,

$(\xi')^e = \gamma^{\underline{d}}$
i.e. $(\xi')^e \equiv \pm\gamma^d \pmod{N}$
i.e. $((\xi')^e)^2 \equiv (\pm\gamma^d)^2 \equiv \gamma^{2d} \pmod{N}$
i.e. $(\xi')^{2e't} \equiv \gamma^{2d't} \pmod{N}$.

Now clearly $(\xi')^{2e'}, \gamma^{2d'} \in QR_N$, and as $\gcd(t, o(QR_N) = o(QR_N^+)) = 1$ we have $(\xi')^{2e'} \equiv (\xi')^{2et^{-1} \pmod{o(QR_N)}} \equiv \gamma^{2dt^{-1} \pmod{o(QR_N)}} \equiv \gamma^{2d} \pmod{N}$. At this point, we have (γ, ξ', e', d') such that $(\xi')^{2e'} \equiv \gamma^{2d'} \pmod{N}$, $e' > 1$ and $\gcd(e', d') = 1$. $(\xi')^{2e'} \equiv \gamma^{2d'} \pmod{N}$ tells that $N \mid ((\xi')^{e'} - \gamma^{d'})((\xi')^{e'} + \gamma^{d'})$. If $(\xi')^{e'} \neq \pm\gamma^{d'}$, then computing $\gcd(N, (\xi')^{e'} - \gamma^{d'})$ and $\gcd(N, (\xi')^{e'} + \gamma^{d'})$ will surely yields $\{P, Q\}$ and we can immediately output a solution $(\gamma, \phi(N) + 1)$ to the strong SQR-RSA problem input (N, γ). Now we consider the case when $(\xi')^{e'} = \pm\gamma^{d'}$. If $(\xi')^{e'} = \gamma^{d'}$, use the Euclidean algorithm to compute two integers e'' and d'' such that $e'e'' + d'd'' = \gcd(e', d') = 1$. Now we output $((\xi')^{d''}\gamma^{e''}, e')$ as a valid solution to the strong SQR-RSA problem input (N, γ) as $e' > 1$ (as a consequence of Lemma-7) and $((\xi')^{d''}\gamma^{e''})^{e'} = (\xi')^{e'd''}\gamma^{e'e''} = \gamma^{d'd'' + e'e''} = \gamma$. Finally we consider the case when $(\xi')^{e'} = -\gamma^{d'}$. In this case we assume that γ belongs to QR_N and this happens with probability $\frac{1}{2} + o(1)$. As $\gamma \in QR_N$, implies $\gamma^{d'}$ is also in QR_N. Also as N is a Blum integer, $-1 \notin QR_N$ and thus $-\gamma^{d'} \notin QR_N$. As $(\xi')^{e'} = -\gamma^{d'}$, therefor e' is necessarily odd (e' even implies $(\xi')^{e'} = -\gamma^{d'} \in QR_N$). Thus $\gamma^{d'} = -(\xi')^{e'} = (-1)^{e'} \cdot (\xi')^{e'} = (-\xi')^{e'}$. So by replacing ξ' with $-\xi'$, this last case $(\xi')^{e'} = -\gamma^{d'}$ reduces to the previous one $(\xi')^{e'} = \gamma^{d'}$.

So in Case-4 ($e \neq 0$ and $\gcd(e, pq) = 1$), the probability that we will successfully output a valid solution depends on the two independent events and they are $e \nmid d$ and $\gamma \in QR_N$ and the probability that both these events occur is atleast $\frac{3}{8} \cdot (\frac{1}{2} + o(1)) = \frac{3}{16} + o(1)$.

Acknowledgments

We would like to thank one of the reviewers whose careful reading and suggestions helped us in improving the technical quality of the paper. The first author likes to acknowledge the National Board for Higher Mathematics (NBHM), India for supporting his research fellowship.

References

1. Abadi, M., Rogaway, P.: Reconciling two views of cryptography (the computational soundness of formal encryption). Journal of Cryptology 15(2), 103–127 (2002)
2. Backes, M., Pfitzmann, B., Waidner, M.: A composable cryptographic library with nested operations. In: ACM Conference on Computer and Communications Security, pp. 220–230 (2003)

3. Barić, N., Pfitzmann, B.: Collision-free accumulators and fail-stop signature schemes without trees. In: Fumy, W. (ed.) EUROCRYPT 1997. LNCS, vol. 1233, pp. 480–494. Springer, Heidelberg (1997)
4. Burgess, D.A.: The distribution of quadratic residues and non-residues. Mathematika 4, 106–112 (1957)
5. Burgess, D.A.: On character sums and primitive roots. Proc. London Math. Soc. 12(3), 179–192 (1962)
6. Cramer, R., Shoup, V.: A practical public key cryptosystem provably secure against adaptive chosen ciphertext attack. In: Krawczyk, H. (ed.) CRYPTO 1998. LNCS, vol. 1462, pp. 13–25. Springer, Heidelberg (1998)
7. Cramer, R., Shoup, V.: Signature schemes based on the strong rsa assumption. In: ACM Conference on Computer and Communications Security, pp. 46–51 (1999)
8. Dolev, D., Yao, A.C.-C.: On the security of public key protocols. IEEE Transactions on Information Theory 29(2), 198–207 (1983)
9. Fischlin, R., Schnorr, C.-P.: Stronger security proofs for rsa and rabin bits. J. Cryptology 13(2), 221–244 (2000)
10. Fujisaki, E., Okamoto, T.: Statistical zero knowledge protocols to prove modular polynomial relations. In: Kaliski Jr., B.S. (ed.) CRYPTO 1997. LNCS, vol. 1294, pp. 16–30. Springer, Heidelberg (1997)
11. Hofheinz, D., Kiltz, E.: The group of signed quadratic residues and applications. In: Halevi, S. (ed.) CRYPTO 2009. LNCS, vol. 5677, pp. 231–249. Springer, Heidelberg (2009)
12. Hohenberger, S.: The cryptographic impact of groups with infeasible inversion. In: Master's thesis, EECS Dept., MIT (June 2003)
13. Impagliazzo, R., Kapron, B.M.: Logics for reasoning about cryptographic constructions. In: FOCS, pp. 372–383 (2003)
14. Micciancio, D.: The rsa group is pseudo-free. Journal of Cryptology. A preliminary version appeared in Eurocrypt (2005) (to appear), http://cseweb.ucsd.edu/~daniele/
15. Micciancio, D., Panjwani, S.: Adaptive security of symbolic encryption. In: Kilian, J. (ed.) TCC 2005. LNCS, vol. 3378, pp. 169–187. Springer, Heidelberg (2005)
16. Micciancio, D., Warinschi, B.: Soundness of formal encryption in the presence of active adversaries. In: Naor, M. (ed.) TCC 2004. LNCS, vol. 2951, pp. 133–151. Springer, Heidelberg (2004)
17. Mitchell, J.C., Ramanathan, A., Scedrov, A., Teague, V.: A probabilistic polynomial-time process calculus for the analysis of cryptographic protocols. Theor. Comput. Sci. 353(1-3), 118–164 (2006)
18. Neven, G.: A simple transitive signature scheme for directed trees. Theor. Comput. Sci. 396(1-3), 277–282 (2008)
19. Okamoto, T., Pointcheval, D.: The gap-problems: A new class of problems for the security of cryptographic schemes. In: Kim, K.-c. (ed.) PKC 2001. LNCS, vol. 1992, pp. 104–118. Springer, Heidelberg (2001)
20. Pólya, G.: Über die verteilung der quadratischen reste und nichtreste. Göttinger Nachrichte, pp. 21–29 (1918)
21. Rabin. Digital signatures and public key functions as intractable as factorization. Technical Report MIT/LCS/TR-212 (January 1979)
22. Rivest, R.L.: On the notion of pseudo-free groups. In: Naor, M. (ed.) TCC 2004. LNCS, vol. 2951, pp. 505–521. Springer, Heidelberg (2004)
23. Rivest, R.L., Shamir, A., Adleman, L.M.: A method for obtaining digital signatures and public-key cryptosystems. Communications of the ACM 21(2), 120–126 (1978)
24. Vinogradov, I.M.: Sur la distribution des résidus et des non-résidus des puissances. J. Phys.-Math. Soc. Perm. (1), 94–96 (1918)

Software Implementation of Pairing-Based Cryptography on Sensor Networks Using the MSP430 Microcontroller

Conrado Porto Lopes Gouvêa and Julio López

Instituto de Computação, Universidade Estadual de Campinas
conrado.gouvea@students.ic.unicamp.br, jlopez@ic.unicamp.br

Abstract. The software implementation of cryptographic schemes for wireless sensor networks poses a challenge due to the limited capabilites of the platform. Nevertheless, its feasibility has been shown in recent papers. In this work we describe a software implementation of pairing-based cryptography and elliptic curve cryptography for the MSP430 microcontroller, which is used in some wireless sensors including the Tmote Sky and TelosB. We have implemented the pairing computation for the MNT and BN curves over prime fields along with the ECDSA scheme. The main result of this work is a platform-specific optimization for the multiplication and reduction routines that leads to a 28% speedup in the field multiplication compared to the best known timings published. This optimization consequently improves the speed of both pairing computation and point multiplication.

Keywords: pairing based cryptography, wireless sensor networks, software implementation.

1 Introduction

Wireless sensor networks (WSN) have been the subject of a lot of research recently due to their vast number of applications. One of the challenges they bring is how to secure their communication against eavesdropping or malicious manipulation. These can be addressed through many cryptographic schemes; but since these nodes are highly constrained environments, these schemes must be implemented with great efficiency.

The advantages of asymmetric over symmetric cryptography for WSNs is well established in the literature. For that reason, we chose to implement two types of asymmetric cryptosystems: pairing-based and elliptic curve cryptography. The security levels being considered are the 64/70-bit, being the most feasible and where most of the work so far has focused; and the 128-bit, which can be expensive but may be necessary in the coming years and has not been well explored for WSNs. The main contributions of this work are a platform-specific optimization to improve the speed of both types of cryptosystems and timings for computations in those two different security levels.

B. Roy and N. Sendrier (Eds.): INDOCRYPT 2009, LNCS 5922, pp. 248–262, 2009.

The remainder of this work is organized as follows. In Section 2 we give an introduction to the MSP430 microcontroller, describing its features and limitations. Subsequently, in Section 3, the fundamental operations of multiplication and reduction are described along with our proposed optimization. The implementation and results of pairing-based cryptography is described in Section 4. In Section 5, the implementation and results of elliptic curve cryptography is detailed. Finally, this paper in concluded in Section 6.

2   The MSP430 Microcontroller

The MSP430 from Texas Instruments is a family of 16-bit microcontrollers mostly known for its low power consumption and it is used in wireless sensors such as the Tmote Sky from Moteiv and the TelosB from Crossbow. It features 12 general purpose registers and a 27 instructions set including one bit only shifts and byte swapping. Memory (bytes and words) can be addressed through four addressing modes: *register direct*, *register indexed* (with an offset word), *register indirect* and *register indirect with post-increment*. Destination operands can be addressed only with register direct and indexed modes.

Each instruction can be represented by up to three words (one for the instruction and two offset words). With only a few exceptions, it is relatively simple to calculate the number of cycles spent in each instruction: one for each word in the instruction, plus one for each memory read and two for each memory write. Short immediate constants $(-1, 0, 1, 2, 4$ and $8)$ can be encoded without using offset words with a clever usage of two special registers (for example, zeroing a register the "naive way" – moving 0 to it – takes only one cycle).

Still, there is a critical issue with the instruction set: it lacks both multiply and divide. This is partially addressed with a hardware multiplier present in some of the MSP430 models. It is a memory mapped peripheral that supports four operations: *multiply, signed multiply, multiply and accumulate* and *signed multiply and accumulate*. In order to use them, it is necessary to write the first operand into one of four specific addresses (MPY, MPYS, MAC, MACS; respectively) according to the operation to be issued. Then, the second operand can be written into another specific address (OP2) and the double precision result will be available with a two cycle delay in two addresses (RESLO, RESHI). The *multiply and accumulate* operations also set the carry flag of the addition into another address (SUMEXT).

An important consequence of the hardware multiplier is that it implies an unusual overhead since the operands must be written to and read from memory. Also, there is no instruction for division, therefore it must be carried out in software which is rather expensive.

When timing the algorithms, we have measured the number of cycles taken by the procedures. Timings in seconds or milliseconds are calculated assuming a 8,000,000 Hz clock; the exact maximum clock varies in each device from the MSP430 family. For that reason, it is recommended to compare running times by their number of cycles. We have used the MSPGCC compiler version 3.2.3 with the -O2 optimization flag unless noted otherwise.

3   Multiplication and Reduction

Field multiplication over $\mathbb{F}_p$ sums about 75% of the running time of point multiplication and pairing computation. Consequently, it is crucial to implement it using assembly language since this leads to a speedup greater than two-fold, according to our experiments. Multiplication in $\mathbb{F}_p$ consists of two operations: the plain multiplication of the operands into a double precision number and its subsequent reduction modulo a prime.

3.1   Multiplication

The standard algorithm for multiplication is the Comba method [1], which is a column-wise variant of the row-wise standard schoolbook version that reduces memory accesses. Recently, it has been suggested a variant of the Comba method, the Hybrid method [2], that mixes the row-wise and column-wise techniques. It can be seen as the plain Comba method, with the difference that each "digit" is now stored in multiple machine integers, and the digit-digit multiplication is carried out with the row-wise schoolbook technique. Both methods are illustrated in Figure 1.

The advantage of the Hybrid method is that, in a digit-digit multiplication, all of the integers of the first digit can be stored in registers, reducing memory reads. Consequently, this method is appropriate for platforms with a relatively large number of registers. In [3], the authors present an even more optimized version of the Hybrid method, using *carry-catcher* registers in order to simplify its carry handling. They have also studied its application on many platforms, including the MSP430, where they were able to obtain a 15.4% speed improvement compared to the Comba method.

It appears that the Hybrid method is always superior to the plain Comba method when there are sufficient registers available, but this fails to take into account the characteristics of the platform. Analyzing the running time of the Comba method, it can be concluded that the majority of the time is spent at one repeated step: multiply and accumulate. For each column of the result, it is necessary to compute many products and accumulate them in order to obtain the result of that column and the carries of the next two columns. The importance of the multiply and accumulate step (which we will refer to as "MulAcc") was noted before in [2,4]. However, what has been overlooked so far is the fact that the MulAcc is exactly what is provided by the MAC (Multiply and Accumulate) operation of the MSP430 hardware multiplier.

The MulAcc step is illustrated in Figure 2. It consists of the reading of two integers, one from each operand, followed by their multiplication into a double precision integer, and finally the addition of those two integers to a triple precision accumulator (the third only accumulates the carries of those additions).

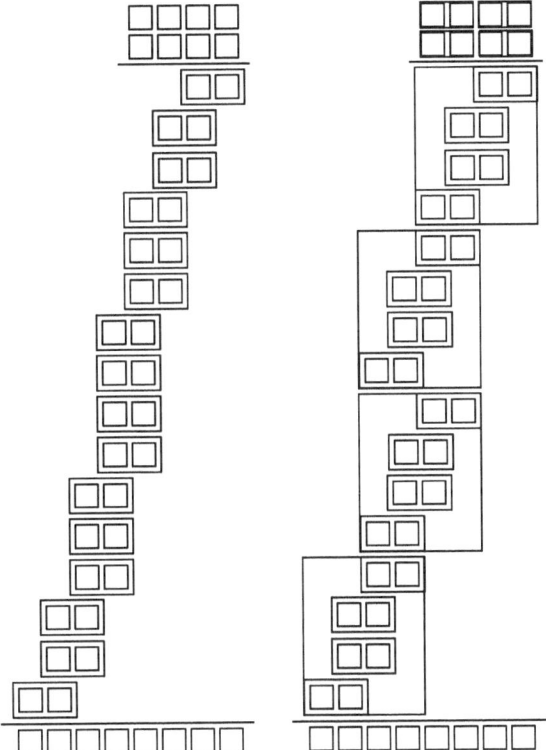

Fig. 1. Comparison of multiplication methods: Comba to the left, Hybrid to the right

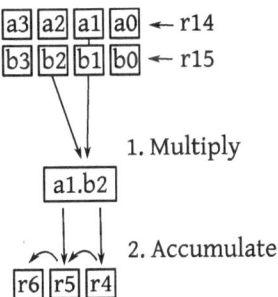

Fig. 2. The MulAcc step, using as example the step for words a1 and b2. The registers r14 and r15 hold the pointers to the two 4-word operands

The pseudo-assembly code for the MulAcc step without using MAC is listed in Algorithm 1 and using MAC in Algorithm 2. Compared to Algorithm 1, Algorithm 2 has two less instructions, one less memory read and one less address in extension words, saving four cycles in total. This leads to a great speedup since the MulAcc step is repeated n^2 times with n being the size of the operands in machine integers.

Algorithm 1. Plain MulAcc step

Input: x, the offset address of an integer in the first operand (pointed by r14); y, the offset address of an integer in the second operand (pointed by r15)

Ouput: The multiplication of the integers and their accumulation into r4, r5, r6

```
mov x(r14),&__MPY ;move first operand, specify unsigned multiplication
mov y(r15),&__OP2 ;move second operand
add &__RESLO,r4 ;add low part of the result
addc &__RESHI,r5 ;add high part of the result
adc r6 ;add the carry
```

Algorithm 2. MulAcc step using MAC

Input: x, the offset address of an integer in the first operand (pointed by r14); y, the offset address of an integer in the second operand (pointed by r15)

Ouput: Multiplication and accumulation into RESLO, RESHI, r6

```
mov x(r14),&__MAC; move first operand; specify multiply and accumulate
mov y(r15),&__OP2 ;move second operand
add &__SUMEXT,r6 ;add the carry
```

The main advantage of using plain Comba with MAC compared to the Hybrid method is that the latter uses all of the 12 available registers, while the former leaves 8 free registers. These can be used as a simple cache for the operands. Additionally, one register can be used to save the address of the SUMEXT in order to add using the *register indirect mode* instead of *register indexed*, saving one more cycle in each MulAcc step (this requires a reordering of the instructions since otherwise the SUMEXT is fetched before the two cycle delay of the hardware multiplier). Table 1 compares the instruction counts of our implementation and those from [3]. It can be readily seen that the greatest savings come from the smaller number of add instructions, since the hardware multiplier does most of the additions by itself. Also, one cycle can be saved in each step due to the linear nature of the access of the first operand, which can be read with the *register indirect with post-increment* addressing mode (mov @reg+,&label).

The multiplication timings are detailed in Table 2, where is clear that the Comba multiplier using the MAC optimization is indeed effective, and 9.2% faster than the Hybrid multiplier given in [3]. We have found that using Karatsuba multiplication with a 128-bit Comba multiplier is a little faster than using 256-bit Comba, and it also requires less code space.

Table 1. Comparison of instruction counts of 160-bit multiplication

Instruction	CPI	Comba MAC		Hybrid in [5]	
		Instructions	Cycles	Instructions	Cycles
add @reg,reg	2	99	198		
Other additions				309	709
mov x(reg),&label	6	20	120	45	270
mov reg,x(reg)	4			20	80
mov reg,reg	1			27	27
mov reg,&label	4	89	356	100	400
mov x(reg),reg	3	13	39	45	135
mov @reg+,&label	5	100	500		
mov @reg,&label	5	29	145		
mov @reg,x(reg)	5	20	100		
other			128		167
Totals			1586		1746

Table 2. Timings for multiplication and squaring

Algorithm	Cycles	Time (ms)
160-bit multiplication		
Hybrid in [3]	1,746	0.22
Comba MAC	1,586	0.20
160-bit squaring		
Comba MAC	1,371	0.19
256-bit multiplication		
Hybrid (Karatsuba, 128-bit Comba)	4,025	0.50
Comba MAC (Karatsuba, 128-bit Comba)	3,597	0.45
Comba MAC (256-bit Comba)	3,689	0.46
256-bit squaring		
Comba MAC (Karatsuba, 128-bit Comba)	2,960	0.37

3.2   Reduction

Traditional modular reduction can be an expensive operation because it needs costly divisions. Since the MSP430 has no divide instruction at all, they would need to be computed in software, which would be even more prohibitive. We have selected two algorithms in the literature that do not require divisions: Montgomery reduction [6] and Barrett reduction [7].

Montgomery reduction requires the operands to be transformed into a special Montgomery form. This is often not a problem since we can use the Montgomery

Table 3. Timings for reduction

Algorithm	Cycles	Time (ms)
Modulo 160-bit prime		
Montgomery in [5] (estimated)	2,988	0.37
Montgomery MAC	1,785	0.22
SECG (prime: $2^{160} - 2^{31} - 1$)	342	0.04
Modulo 256-bit prime		
Montgomery	4,761	0.60
Montgomery MAC	3,989	0.50
Barrett	4,773	0.60
NIST (prime: $2^{256} - 2^{224} + 2^{192} + 2^{96} - 1$)	709	0.09

form as the "official" representation of all numbers in the cryptographic protocol being used and they would only need to be converted back, for example, to be printed on the screen for human reading. Montgomery reduction also requires a precomputed constant that is dependent of the machine integer size.

The Montgomery reduction algorithm has almost the same structure as the Comba multiplication, with the first operand being the lower part of the double precision number to be reduced and the second operand being the prime modulus. Therefore, one can employ the same MAC optimization to speed up the reduction.

Barrett reduction is slightly more complex and it involves half precision Comba multiplications. Each of these multiplications can also use the MAC optimization. It also requires a precomputed constant which is dependent of the prime modulus.

There also are specific algorithms for reduction when the prime modulus has a special form. For primes of the form $2^k - c$ such as the 160-bit primes from the SECG standard [8] the algorithm is described in [9]. For "NIST primes" [10], the algorithm is described in [11].

The reduction timings are presented in Table 3. The reduction timing from [5] was estimated by subtracting the reported multiplication timing in [3] from the field multiplication timing in [5]. While an exact comparison may be hard to

Table 4. Timings for field multiplication (using Montgomery reduction)

Algorithm	Cycles	Time (ms)
160-bit		
Hybrid in [5]	4,734	0.59
MAC	3,389	0.42
256-bit		
Hybrid	8,855	1.11
MAC	7,604	0.95

make due to this inexact estimate, we notice again that the MAC optimization is very effective. The Barrett reduction was slower than Montgomery reduction, but since we have focused on optimizing Montgomery, we believe its speed can be further improved. As expected, reduction modulo a special form prime is much faster.

Finally, the running times of algorithms for field multiplication – multiplication followed by reduction – are given in Table 4. Compared to [5], field multiplication using MAC is about 28% faster.

4   Identity Based Cryptography Using Pairings

It has been shown recently that identity-based cryptography using bilinear pairings is very appropriate in the wireless sensor network scenario [12]. There are many identity-based cryptographic schemes, but the most useful in this context probably is the non-interactive key agreement scheme [13,14,15] that allows two parties to compute a mutual key without interaction in order to bootstrap a secure channel using symmetric encryption, and will be described next.

Let $e : G_1 \times G_2 \to G_T$ be a bilinear pairing with G_1 and G_2 being additive groups and G_T a multiplicative group, all of them with a prime order r. Let $H_1 : \{0,1\}^* \to G_1$ and $H_2 : \{0,1\}^* \to G_2$ be two hash functions. The master key generation is done by the key generation center by choosing a random $s \in \{1, ..., r - 1\}$. The private key distribution is done before the deployment of the sensors by assigning a sensor A the identity ID_A and private keys $S_{1A} = sH_1(ID_A)$ and $S_{2A} = sH_2(ID_A)$.

Now, suppose sensors A and B wish to compute a shared key. If G_1 and G_2 were the same group and the pairing was symmetric, then the two hash functions would be the same and the two private keys of each node would be equal. Therefore, A could compute $e(S_{1A}, H_1(ID_B))$ and B could compute $e(H_1(ID_A), S_{1B})$. Due to the bilinearity and symmetry, we have

$$
\begin{aligned}
e(S_{1A}, H_1(ID_B)) &= e(sH_1(ID_A), H_1(ID_B)) \\
&= e(H_1(ID_A), sH_1(ID_B)) \\
&= e(H_1(ID_A), S_{1B}) \\
&= e(S_{1B}, H_1(ID_A)) \, .
\end{aligned}
$$

Then both parties can generate the same value, which can be used to derive a shared key. In our case, though, the pairing is asymmetric since the elliptic curves used are ordinary. Therefore, we need two private keys for each sensor, the hash functions are different, and the last step in the equation is not valid. Still, we have two useful equations which can be easily verified: $e(S_{1A}, H_2(ID_B)) = e(H_1(ID_A), S_{2B})$ and $e(H_1(ID_B), S_{2A}) = e(S_{1B}, H_2(ID_A))$. In [14], it is suggested that each party should multiply their sides of those two equations in order to compute the shared key, but this requires two pairing computations. In [5] it is suggested that the sensors could agree on which equation they should use with a little amount of communication. Instead, there is a simpler fix that maintains the non-interactive aspect of the protocol. It can be defined that the sensor with the smaller ID in lexicographical order should use its first private key in the first pairing parameter and the other its second private key in the second pairing parameter, therefore choosing one of the equations without any interaction.

4.1 MNT Curve over a 160-Bit Field

For 160-bit fields, we have implemented two security levels. To allow comparisons, the first one is the same described in [5] which uses a MNT curve of embedding degree 4. These parameters where chosen in order to provide minimum acceptable security; the 640-bit extension field used gives approximately 64 bits of security [16]. The authors chose the Tate pairing instead of the faster Ate pairing since hashing a identity to a point in G_2 is simpler in the Tate pairing. The Miller loop is implemented using the sliding window technique with $w = 3$. The second level of security chosen follows a similar implementation but using a MNT curve with embedding degree 6. This results in a 960-bit extension field that provides approximately 70 bits of security [17].

The respective finite field operation and pairing computation timings are detailed in Table 5, which shows that the MAC optimization leads to a 20.2% speedup in the 64-bit level. It is important to remark that in [5] the authors chose to compile their code with optimization turned off; the reason given is that the difference in speed obtained by using different compilers is very significant when using optimization and that would make any comparisons harder.

Table 5. Timings for field operations and pairing computations on MNT curves

Algorithm	Optimization	Cycles	Time (ms)
Field operations			
Multiplication		3,389	0.42
Squaring		3,172	0.40
Inversion		187,575	23.45
MNT curve, $k = 4$			
Tate [5]	Off	37,739,040	4,717
Our Tate (MAC)	Off	30,125,088	3,766
Our Tate (MAC)	On	26,553,690	3,319
MNT curve, $k = 6$			
Our Tate (MAC)	Off	51,199,102	6,400
Our Tate (MAC)	On	40,869,215	5,109

Still, we feel that providing the timings for the optimized versions would lead to more interesting comparisons.

4.2   BN Curve over a 256-Bit Field

For the 128 bits security level, the Barreto-Naehrig family of curves [18] was chosen. They have an embedding degree of 12 and provide a sextic twist that allows the doubling and adding of Miller's algorithm to be performed on the curve over $\mathbb{F}_{p^2}$ instead of the costly $\mathbb{F}_{p^{12}}$. The curve chosen is the one generated by the x value of $-0x4080000000000001$ suggested in [19]. Regarding the BN formulas, one can find in the literature different values for $p(x)$: the original paper [18] uses $p(x) = 36x^4 + 36x^3 + 24x^2 + 6x + 1$ but some other papers [19,20] use $p(x) = 36x^4 - 36x^3 + 24x^2 - 6x + 1$, which gives the same value when using x with inverted sign. We use the original version.

The pairings chosen were the Optimal Ate [21], R-ate [22] and Xate [19]; all of them optimal pairings as defined in [21]. They provide optimal speed by truncating the Miller loop by a quarter. We follow the approach detailed in [20] but using the final exponentiation optimization from [23]. Since the Miller loop runs through the bits of $6x + 2$ (or x in Xate), which has low Hamming weight, the sliding window technique is not appropriate and was not used.

We present the timings for the finite field operations and pairing computations in Table 6. The pairing computation is much more expensive than in the MNT curve, and probably unacceptable for the wireless sensor scenario. As noted in [24], it is important to keep in mind that the pairing computation scales more-or-less like RSA rather than like elliptic curve cryptography. It is also worth noticing that the three kind of pairings give almost the same speed, with the Xate pairing being a little faster. We describe the Xate pairing for BN curves in Algorithm 3.

The ROM and RAM requirements of the pairing computation program are listed in Table 7. To put them in perspective, we note that popular sensors have such as Tmote Sky and TelosB have 48KB of ROM and 10K of RAM. The code size is still large; though it is only possible to determine its feasibility by analyzing specific applications. The amount of RAM allocated is probably tolerable, since most of it is allocated from the stack and freed after the computation.

5   Elliptic Curve Cryptography

While identity based schemes built with pairings seem ideal for the wireless sensor scenario, they still are expensive, mainly in the higher 128-bit level of security. For that reason, we have also implemented the cheaper elliptic curve cryptography in order to allow comparison with pairing-based cryptography. To illustrate a concrete use, the ECDSA (Elliptic Curve Digital Signature Algorithm) [10]

Algorithm 3. Xate pairing for BN curves

Input: $x \in \mathbb{Z}$ (the BN parameter), $Q \in E'(\mathbb{F}_{p^2})$, $P \in E(\mathbb{F}_p)$
Ouput: $\zeta(Q, P) \in \mathbb{F}_{p^{12}}$
1: $v, xQ \Leftarrow f_{|x|,Q}(P)$ {$f_{r,Q}$ if the Miller function, it also computes rQ}
2: **if** $x > 0$ **then**
3:    $v \Leftarrow 1/v$
4:    $xQ = -xQ$
5: **end if**
6: $v \Leftarrow v^{1+p+p^3+p^{10}}$
7: $v, A \Leftarrow g_{xQ,pxQ}(P)$ {$g_{P,Q}$ is the line function from the Miller function, it also computes $P + Q$ }
8: $v, B \Leftarrow g_{p^3 xQ, p^{10} xQ}(P)$
9: $v, C \Leftarrow g_{A,B}(P)$
10: **return** $v^{(p^{12}-1)/r}$

Table 6. Timings for field operations and pairing computations on the BN curve

Algorithm	Cycles	Time (ms)
Field operations		
Multiplication	7,569	0.95
Squaring	6,952	0.87
Inversion	380,254	47.53
Pairings		
Optimal Ate	117,597,798	14,700
R-ate	117,514,219	14,689
Xate	116,130,546	14,516

Table 7. ROM and maximum allocated RAM size for pairing programs

Version	ROM (KB)	RAM (KB)
BN 256 bits, Karatsuba w/ Comba 128	32.3	4.7
BN 256 bits, Comba 256	36.2	4.7
MNT 160 bits, Comba 160	28.9	2.3
MNT 160 bits, Comba 160 in [5]	34.9	3.4

was chosen for its popularity and wide standardization. However, it is important to notice that elliptic curve cryptography still requires the expensive public key authentication which is outside the scope of this work.

The ECDSA is composed by key generation, signature generation and verification. The key and signature generation require a fixed point multiplication that is their most expensive operation. In our implementation, we have used the Comb algorithm with window size 4 [11] which requires the precomputation of 15 elliptic curve points. For the signature verification, we have used the interleaving algorithm with NAF [11] of width 5 and 4 for the fixed and random points, respectively.

At the 80-bit level of security, the secg160r1 [8] curve was chosen which allows fast reduction [9] due to its special form modulus. This curve has -3 as its b parameter to enable a known optimization in the point doubling. At the 128-bit level of security, the P-256 curve [10] was chosen which also provides fast reduction [11] due to its special form modulus ("NIST prime"). This curve also has -3 as its b parameter.

We present the timings for the finite field operations and point multiplication in Table 8 and the ECDSA timings in Table 9. The timings results of our implementation are faster than [25], but they do acknowledge that their work leaves room for much optimization. Also notice that the 5NAF is not adequate since it is just a little faster than 4NAF but requires double storage space. The Montgomery ladder method [26], while secure against side-channel attacks (timing and power analysis), is 40–50% slower than 4NAF.

The ROM and RAM requirements for the ECDSA program are listed in Table 10. The ROM sizes are about 5% smaller than the pairing-based cryptography, and seem to be acceptable, specially in the 80-bit level of security. The RAM requirements are also realistic since most of it is freed after the computation.

Table 8. Timings for field operations and point multiplication for the given curves

Algorithm	secg160r1		P-256	
	Cycles	Time (ms)	Cycles	Time (ms)
Field operations				
Multiplication	1,952	0.24	4,327	0.54
Squaring	1,734	0.22	3,679	0.46
Inversion	187,575	19.27	292,170	36.52
Random point multiplication				
4NAF	4,417,661	0.552	13,372,271	1.672
5NAF	4,433,104	0.554	13,188,903	1.649
Montgomery ladder	6.319,383	0.790	20,476,234	2.560
Unknown from [25]		0.800		
Fixed point multiplication				
Comb, $w = 4$	1,831,063	0.229	5,688,793	0.711
Comb, $w = 4$ in [27]		0.720		
Sliding window, $w = 4$ in [25]		0.720		
Simultaneous point mult.				
Interleaved	5,204,544	0.651	15,784,176	1.973

Table 9. Timings for ECDSA

Algorithm	secg160r1		P-256	
	Cycles	Time (s)	Cycles	Time (s)
Key Generation	1,849,903	0.231	5,682,433	0.710
Sign	2,166,906	0.270	5,969,593	0.746
Verify	5,488,568	0.686	16,139,555	2.017

Table 10. ROM and maximum allocated RAM size for elliptic curve programs

Version	ROM (KB)	RAM (KB)
256 bits, Karatsuba w/ Comba 128	25.7	3.5
256 bits, Comba 256	29.5	3.5
160 bits, Comba 160	23.5	2.5
160 bits, Comba 160 in [27]	31.3	2.9

6   Conclusion

Implementing efficient cryptographic schemes on wireless sensor networks is a difficult task, but feasible. It is important to analyze every feature offered by the platform in order to get the best results, as can be seen with the simple but effective optimization using the MAC operation from the hardware multiplier of the MSP430. Still, there is plenty of work to be done. As our implementation has shown, there is a steep price to be paid in the 128-bit level of security pairing computation (14.5 seconds). Some relevant future work that we would suggest is to provide a fast implementation of identity based cryptography in other security levels and implement in software the recently proposed method to speed up finite field arithmetic for BN curves [28].

References

1. Comba, P.: Exponentiation cryptosystems on the IBM PC. IBM Systems Journal 29(4), 526–538 (1990)
2. Gura, N., Patel, A., Wander, A., Eberle, H., Shantz, S.: Comparing elliptic curve cryptography and RSA on 8-bit CPUs. In: Joye, M., Quisquater, J.-J. (eds.) CHES 2004. LNCS, vol. 3156, pp. 925–943. Springer, Heidelberg (2004)
3. Scott, M., Szczechowiak, P.: Optimizing multiprecision multiplication for public key cryptography. Cryptology ePrint Archive, Report 2007/299 (2007), http://eprint.iacr.org/
4. Großschädl, J.: Instruction Set Extension for Long Integer Modulo Arithmetic on RISC-Based Smart Cards. In: Symposium on Computer Architecture and High Performance Computing, pp. 13–19 (2002)

5. Szczechowiak, P., Kargl, A., Scott, M., Collier, M.: On the application of pairing based cryptography to wireless sensor networks. In: Proceedings of the second ACM conference on Wireless network security, pp. 1–12. ACM, New York (2009)
6. Montgomery, P.: Modular multiplication without trial division. Mathematics of computation 44(170), 519–521 (1985)
7. Barrett, P.: Implementing the rivest shamir and adleman public key encryption algorithm on a standard digital signal processor. In: Odlyzko, A.M. (ed.) CRYPTO 1986. LNCS, vol. 263, pp. 311–323. Springer, Heidelberg (1987)
8. Certicom Research: SEC 2: Recommended Elliptic Curve Domain Parameters (2006), http://www.secg.org/
9. Menezes, A., Van Oorschot, P., Vanstone, S.: Handbook of Applied Cryptography. CRC Press, Boca Raton (1997)
10. National Institute of Standards and Technology: FIPS 186-3: Digital Signature Standard (DSS) (2009), http://www.itl.nist.gov
11. Hankerson, D., Vanstone, S., Menezes, A.: Guide to Elliptic Curve Cryptography. Springer, Heidelberg (2004)
12. Oliveira, L., Aranha, D., Morais, E., Daguano, F., Lopez, J., Dahab, R.: TinyTate: computing the tate pairing in resource-constrained sensor nodes. In: Sixth IEEE International Symposium on Network Computing and Applications, NCA 2007, pp. 318–323 (2007)
13. Sakai, R., Ohgishi, K., Kasahara, M.: Cryptosystems based on pairing. In: The 2000 Symposium on Cryptography and Information Security, Okinawa, Japan (2000)
14. Dupont, R., Enge, A.: Provably secure non-interactive key distribution based on pairings. Discrete Applied Mathematics 154(2), 270–276 (2006)
15. Oliveira, L., Scott, M., Lopez, J., Dahab, R.: TinyPBC: Pairings for authenticated identity-based non-interactive key distribution in sensor networks. In: 5th International Conference on Networked Sensing Systems, INSS, pp. 173–180 (2008)
16. Lenstra, A.K.: Key Lengths. In: Handbook of Information Security. John Wiley & Sons, Chichester (2004)
17. Lenstra, A., Verheul, E.: Selecting Cryptographic Key Sizes. Journal of Cryptology 14(4), 255–293 (2001)
18. Barreto, P., Naehrig, M.: Pairing-Friendly Elliptic Curves of Prime Order. In: Preneel, B., Tavares, S. (eds.) SAC 2005. LNCS, vol. 3897, pp. 319–331. Springer, Heidelberg (2006)
19. Nogami, Y., Akane, M., Sakemi, Y., Kato, H., Morikawa, Y.: Integer Variable χ-Based Ate Pairing. In: Galbraith, S.D., Paterson, K.G. (eds.) Pairing 2008. LNCS, vol. 5209, pp. 178–191. Springer, Heidelberg (2008)
20. Devegili, A., Scott, M., Dahab, R.: Implementing Cryptographic Pairings over Barreto-Naehrig Curves. In: Takagi, T., Okamoto, T., Okamoto, E., Okamoto, T. (eds.) Pairing 2007. LNCS, vol. 4575, pp. 197–207. Springer, Heidelberg (2007)
21. Vercauteren, F.: Optimal pairings. Cryptology ePrint Archive, Report 2008/096 (2008), http://eprint.iacr.org/
22. Lee, E., Lee, H.S., Park, C.M.: Efficient and generalized pairing computation on abelian varieties. Cryptology ePrint Archive, Report 2008/040 (2008), http://eprint.iacr.org/
23. Scott, M., Benger, N., Charlemagne, M., Perez, L.J.D., Kachisa, E.J.: On the final exponentiation for calculating pairings on ordinary elliptic curves. Cryptology ePrint Archive, Report 2008/490 (2008), http://eprint.iacr.org/
24. Galbraith, S., Paterson, K., Smart, N.: Pairings for cryptographers. Discrete Applied Mathematics 156(16), 3113–3121 (2008)

25. Wang, H., Li, Q.: Efficient Implementation of Public Key Cryptosystems on Mote Sensors (Short Paper). In: Ning, P., Qing, S., Li, N. (eds.) ICICS 2006. LNCS, vol. 4307, pp. 519–528. Springer, Heidelberg (2006)
26. Montgomery, P.: Speeding the Pollard and elliptic curve methods of factorization. Mathematics of Computation 48(177), 243–264 (1987)
27. Szczechowiak, P., Oliveira, L., Scott, M., Collier, M., Dahab, R.: NanoECC: Testing the Limits of Elliptic Curve Cryptography in Sensor Networks. In: Verdone, R. (ed.) EWSN 2008. LNCS, vol. 4913, pp. 305–320. Springer, Heidelberg (2008)
28. Fan, J., Vercauteren, F., Verbauwhede, I.: Faster Fp-arithmetic for Cryptographic Pairings on Barreto-Naehrig Curves. In: Clavier, C., Gaj, K. (eds.) CHES 2009. LNCS, vol. 5747, pp. 240–253. Springer, Heidelberg (2009)

A New Hard-Core Predicate of Paillier's Trapdoor Function[*]

Dong Su and Kewei Lv

State Key Laboratory of Information Security
Graduate University of Chinese Academy of Sciences
P.O. Box 4588, Beijing 100049, P.R. China
sudong.tom@gmail.com, kwlu@gucas.ac.cn

Abstract. At EuroCrypt '01, Catalano *et al.* [1] proved that for Paillier's trapdoor function if computing residuosity class is hard, then given a random $w \in \mathbb{Z}_{N^2}^*$ the least significant bit of its class is a hard-core predicate. In this paper, we reconsider the bit security of Paillier's trapdoor function and show that under the same assumption, the most significant bit of the class of w is also a hard-core predicate. In our proof, we use the "guessing and trimming" technique [2] to find a polynomial number of possible values of the class and devise a result checking method to test the validity of them.

Keywords: Paillier's trapdoor function, Hard-core Predicate, Most significant bit.

1 Introduction

Modern cryptography is based on the existence of one-way (trapdoor) functions. A function is said to be *one-way* if it is easy to compute but hard to invert. A concept tightly connected to one-way functions is the notion of *hard-core predicates*, introduced by Blum and Micali [3]. A polynomial-time algorithm predicate $B : \{0, 1\}^* \to \{0, 1\}$ is called a hard-core predicate of a function f, if all efficient algorithm, given $f(x)$, can guess $B(x)$ with success probability only negligibly better than half. Another way of saying this is that if x is chosen at random then $B(x)$ looks random (to a polynomial time observer) even when given $f(x)$. Blum and Micali [3] showed that for a finite field $\mathbb{F}_p$ and $\mathbb{F}_p^*$'s generator g, the most significant bit (MSB) of the discrete logarithm function $\mathrm{DL}(y) = x$ is a hard-core predicate, where $x \in \mathbb{Z}_{p-1}$, $y = g^x \mod p$. This was done by reducing the problem of inverting exponentiation function $\mathrm{EXP}(x) = g^x \mod p$ (which is believed to be one-way) to the problem of guessing the most significant bit of x with any non-negligible advantage. Soon after, Alexi *et al.* [4] presented that the least significant bit (LSB) in an RSA/Rabin encrypted message is a hard-core predicate. In 1989, Goldreich and Levin [5] proved that every one-way function has a hard-core predicate. Although such general result has already been proved, for some specific one-way functions, we still need to find their hard-core predicates.

[*] This work is partially supported by National Natural Science Foundation of China (No.60970154) and NGR Project "973" of China (No.2007CB311202).

B. Roy and N. Sendrier (Eds.): INDOCRYPT 2009, LNCS 5922, pp. 263–271, 2009.
© Springer-Verlag Berlin Heidelberg 2009

The concept of *the simultaneously security of bits* is a generalization of hard-core predicates. Intuitively, a sequence of bits associated to a one-way function f is said to be simultaneously secure if no efficient algorithm can gain any information about the given sequence of bits in x, given $f(x)$. The simultaneous security of a one-way function is beneficial to the construction of more efficient pseudorandom generators as well as to the improvement of other cryptographic applications. Long and Wigderson [6] and Peralta [7] showed that $\log \log p$ bits of the discrete logarithm function modulo a prime number p are simultaneous secure. Alexi *et al.* [4] showed that the RSA/Rabin function hides $\log \log N$ bits simultaneously, where N is an RSA modulus. For one way function $f_{N,g}(x) = g^x \mod N$, where N is an RSA modulus, Goldreich and Rosen [2] presented the simultaneous hardness of upper half bits of $f_{N,g}(\cdot)$. Although this result is the same as the result proven by Håstad, Schrift and Shamir [8], Goldreich and Rosen's proof is much simple and elegant.

MOTIVATION AND PREVIOUS WORK. At Eurocrypt '99, Paillier [9] proposed a new homomorphic trapdoor permutation over $\mathbb{Z}^*_{N^2}$, where N is an RSA modulus, and use it to construct a probabilistic public key encryption scheme. To encrypt a message $c \in \mathbb{Z}_N$, one can choose a random integer $y \in \mathbb{Z}^*_N$ and compute $w = g^c y^N \mod N^2$, where $g \in \mathbb{Z}^*_{N^2}$ whose order is a nonzero multiple of N. c is called the *class* of w relative to g, denoted $Class_{N,g}(w)$. It is shown in [9] that, knowing the factorization of N, computing $Class_{N,g}(w) = c$ is easy. Paillier defined *Computational Composite Residuosity Class Problem*, denoted Class[N], as the problem of computing the class c given w and g, and thought it is hard to be solved.

In 2001, Catalano, Gennaro and Howgrave-Grahm [1] analyzed the bit security of this scheme and showed that the LSB of the class is a hard-core predicate of Paillier's trapdoor function under the assumption that computing residuosity class is hard. They also proved that Paillier's trapdoor function hides $n - b$ (up to $O(n)$) bits under the assumption that computing the class c of a random w remains hard even when we are told that $c < 2^b$. This assumption is also called *B-hard assumption*. Their proof technique, called "zeroing and shifting", can be briefly described below. Suppose an adversary has a LSB oracle which given input $w = g^c y^N \mod N^2$, where $c \in \mathbb{Z}_N$, predict the LSB of c. Once he knows the LSB of c from the oracle, he zeros it and shifts c by one bit to the right. He iterates the above procedure to compute all bits of c. If the LSB oracle is always correct in prediction, the above procedure goes well. But if the oracle is erroneous, randomization is needed to amplify the statistical advantage of the oracle on predicting the LSB. The way to learn the information of one bit of plaintext from ciphertext $w = g^c y^N \mod N^2$ is to consider $w' = w \cdot g^r s^N = g^{(c+r)}(ys)^N \mod N^2$, where r is randomly selected from $\mathbb{Z}_N$ and s is randomly selected from $\mathbb{Z}^*_N$, then to query the LSB oracle on several randomized w', and to count the oracle answers on 1 or 0 to determine the bit. A natural question arises: dose the MSB of the class is also a hard-core predicate for Paillier's trapdoor function under the assumption that computing residuosity class is hard? The above proof technique is infeasible for studying the MSB of c, since we can not prevent the disturbance of carries from lower bits and the wrap around problem when computing $c + r \mod N$. We need to find another way.

In [2], Goldreich and Rosen devised a proof technique to solve the following problem: given a noisy MSB oracle and $g^x \mod N$, find a polynomial time algorithm to recover x, where N is an n bits RSA modulus and $x \in_R \{0,1\}^n$. The basic idea is that: for $i = n, \ldots, 1$, guess all of the possible values of $x_n \cdots x_i$ and group them into a sorted list L_i, then use the information from the MSB oracle to trim some invalid list elements off in order to keep the size of L_i bounded by a polynomial. On the last stage, a polynomial size list L_1 which contains x can be obtained. The way of trimming invalid candidates off by using the MSB oracle is called "trimming rule". And we refer to this proof technique as "guessing and trimming".

OUR CONTRIBUTION. In this paper, we find a new hard-core predicate of Paillier's trapdoor function. We prove that, assuming computing residuosity class is hard, given a random $w \in \mathbb{Z}_{N^2}^*$, the MSB of $c = Class_{N,g}(w)$ is a hard-core predicate. In our proof, we apply "guessing and trimming" technique to find a polynomial number of possible class values and we devise a method to test the validity of them.

1.1   Notations

Let $a \in_R A$ denote selecting an element a from the set A randomly and uniformly. For an integer x, let $lsb(x)$ denote the least significant bit of x and let $msb(x)$ denote the most significant bit of x. Let N_n be the set of all n bits integers $N = P \cdot Q$, where P and Q are two large primes of equal length. Let P_n be the set of pairs $\langle N, g \rangle$, where $N \in_R N_n$, and g is an element of $\mathbb{Z}_{N^2}^*$ whose multiplicative order is a nonzero multiple of N. We use log to denote the logarithm function with base 2. We use $\epsilon(n)$ to represent some non-negligible function with $\epsilon(n) > \frac{1}{p(n)}$ for some polynomial $p(n)$. We use ϵ instead of $\epsilon(n)$ for simplicity. For $x \in \{0,1\}^n$, we denote by $x_n \ldots x_2 x_1$ the bit expansion of x, by x_i the ith bit of x, and by $x_{i,j}$ the substring of x including the bits from position j to position i, where $1 \le j \le i \le n$. Let $x \circ y$ denote the concatenation of two binary strings x and y.

1.2   Organization

The paper is orgainzed as follows. In section 2, we give a brief description of Paillier's scheme and the definition hard-core predicate. In section 3, we show that the most significant bit of the class is a hard-core bit of Paillier's trapdoor function.

2   Preliminaries

2.1   Paillier's Scheme

In [9], Paillier proposed a new probabilistic encryption scheme based on computations in the group $\mathbb{Z}_{N^2}^*$, where N is an RSA modulus. This scheme is homomorphic, semantic secure against chosen plaintext attack and efficient in decryption. Specifically, for $\langle N, g \rangle \in P_n$, consider the following map:

$$\mathcal{E}_{N,g} : \mathbb{Z}_N \times \mathbb{Z}_N^* \to \mathbb{Z}_{N^2}^*   \qquad \mathcal{E}_{N,g}(c, y) = g^c y^N \mod N^2.$$

Paillier showed that $\mathcal{E}_{N,g}$ is a trapdoor permutation. The trapdoor information is the factorization of N. By the bijective property of $\mathcal{E}_{N,g}$, given $\langle N, g \rangle \in P_n$, for an element $w \in \mathbb{Z}_{N^2}^*$, there exists an unique pair $(c, y) \in \mathbb{Z}_N \times \mathbb{Z}_N^*$ such that $w = g^c y^N \mod N^2$. Here c is said to be the *class* of w relative to g, we denote it with $Class_{N,g}(w)$. And y is called *Paillier N-th root*. We define the *Computational Composite Residuosity Class Problem* as the problem of computing c given w, and assume it is hard to solve.

Definition 1. *We say that computing the function $Class_{N,g}(\cdot)$ is hard if, for every probabilistic polynomial time algorithm $\mathcal{A}$, there exists a negligible function $\mathrm{negl}(\cdot)$ such that*

$$\Pr \begin{bmatrix} \langle N, g \rangle \in_R P_n; c \in_R \mathbb{Z}_N; \\ y \in_R \mathbb{Z}_N^*; w = g^c y^N \mod N^2; \\ \mathcal{A}(N, g, w) = c \end{bmatrix} \leq \mathrm{negl}(n).$$

If the factorization of $N = PQ$ is known, one can solve this problem. Indeed, let $\lambda = \lambda(N) = \mathrm{lcm}(P-1, Q-1)$, then $Class_{N,g}(w) = \frac{L(w^\lambda \mod N^2)}{L(g^\lambda \mod N^2)} \mod N$, where L is defined as $L(u) = (u-1)/N$. On the other hand, if the factorization of N is not known, no polynomial strategy to solve the problem has been discovered. This leads to the following assumption.

Assumption 1. *If N is a modulus of unknown factorization, there exists no probabilistic polynomial time algorithm for the Computational Composite Residuosity Class Problem.*

2.2 Hard-Core Predicate

Definition 2. *(from [10]) A polynomial-time-computable predicate $b : \{0,1\}^* \to \{0,1\}$ is called a hard-core predicate of a function $f : \{0,1\}^* \to \{0,1\}^*$ if for every probabilistic polynomial-time algorithm A', every positive polynomial $p(\cdot)$, and all sufficiently large n's,*

$$\Pr[\mathcal{A}'(f(U_n)) = B(U_n)] < \frac{1}{2} + \frac{1}{p(n)},$$

where U_n is a random variable uniformly distributed over $\{0,1\}^n$.

3 The Most Significant Bit of *Class* Is Hard

In this section, we present the hardness of the most significant bit of Paillier's trapdoor function's class.

Theorem 1. *Let $\langle N, g \rangle \in P_n$. If the function $Class_{N,g}(\cdot)$ is hard, then the predicate $msb(\cdot)$ is hard for it.*

Proof. Suppose that predicate $msb(\cdot)$ is not hard, we assume that there exist an MSB oracle for predicting $msb(\cdot)$, then this oracle can be used to construct a probabilistic polynomial time algorithm to compute the hard function $Class_{N,g}(\cdot)$. That is, given $w \in \mathbb{Z}_{N^2}^*$ such that $w = \mathcal{E}_{N,g}(c, y) = g^c y^N \mod N^2$, and an oracle $\mathcal{O}_{N,g}(w) = msb(c)$, we show how to compute $c = Class_{N,g}(w)$ in probabilistic polynomial time.

Our proof can be divided into two cases, depending on whether the MSB oracle is erroneous or not.

The perfect oracle case: Suppose that oracle $\mathcal{O}_{N,g}$ is perfect, that is, $\Pr_w[\mathcal{O}_{N,g}(w) = msb(Class_{N,g}(w))] = 1$, we can use it to find $Class_{N,g}(w)$, given $w \in \mathbb{Z}^*_{N^2}$. We use two strategies:

Left shifting: By $w = w^2 \mod N^2$, we can shift class c by one bit to the left.

Zeroing: By computing $w = w \cdot g^{-2^{(n-1)}} \mod N^2$, we can zero the n-st bit of class c, if this bit is 1.

Fig.1 is the detailed description of this algorithm.

FindingClass-usingPerfectOracle $(\mathcal{O}_{N,g},N,g,w)$

1. $c = ()$;
2. **for**$(i = 1$ to $n)$
3. $b = \mathcal{O}_{N,g}(w)$;
4.   **append**(c,b);   (append bit b to the end of string c)
5.   **if**(b==1) **then**
6. $w = wg^{-2^{(n-1)}} \mod N^2$;   (bit zeroing)
7. $w = w^2 \mod N^2$;   (bit left shifting)
8. **end for**
9. **return** c;

Fig. 1. Finding Class using a Perfect Oracle

The imperfect oracle case: In this case, the MSB oracle might give some erroneous answers, that is, $\Pr_w[\mathcal{O}_{N,g}(w) = msb(x)] \geq \frac{1}{2} + \epsilon(n)$, where $\epsilon(n) > \frac{1}{p(n)}$ for some polynomial $p(n)$. A straightforward way to learn the MSB of class c, as illustrated in [1], is to use randomization to amplify the statistical advantage of the oracle in guessing the bit. This is done by considering $w' = w \cdot g^r s^N$, where $r \in_R \mathbb{Z}_N$ and $s \in_R \mathbb{Z}^*_N$, querying $\mathcal{O}_{N,g}(w')$ on several randomized w', and counting 1-answers and 0-answers to decide c's MSB. However, it is infeasible since there exist the disturbance of carries from lower bits and the wrap around problem, when we perform $c + r \mod N$. So, we need to find another way.

A proof technique developed by Goldreich and Rosen [2] can be applied here. One of the features in this technique is to use "guessing and trimming" strategy rather than use the "zeroing and shifting" strategy as illustrated in the perfect oracle case. The formal description of our class finding algorithm using an imperfect oracle is presented in Fig. 2.

First, we guess the m most significant bits of class c to create the environment to invoke the Trimming-Rule algorithm [2] (see Fig. 3), where $m = 1 - \log \epsilon$. Note that $2^m = 2/\epsilon$ is a polynomial number of choices. And we denote by d the correct assignment of the m leading bits of c. Second, we iterate from the $(n - m)$th bit down

FindingClass-usingImperfectOracle($\mathcal{O}_{N,g}$, N, g, w)

1. **for** every possible assignment d of the m MSBs of $Class_{N,g}(w)$, where $m = 1 - \log \epsilon$;
2.   let list $L_{n-m} = \{0, 1\}$;   (list forming and trimming)
3.   **for**($l = n - m - 1$ to 1)
4.   let $L_l = \{2u, 2u + 1 : u \in L_{l+1}\}$;
5.   sort L_l from the largest element v^l_{max} to the smallest element v^l_{min};
6.   **while**($v^l_{max} - v^l_{min} > 2^m$)
7.   Trimming-Rule(N, g, L_l, v^l_{max}, v^l_{min}, $n - m$);
8.   **end while**
9.   **end for**
10. $y_1 \in_R \mathbb{Z}_N^*$;   (results checking)
11.   **for**($v \in L_1$)
12.   valid=true; $v' = d \circ v$;   (concatenate v to the end of d)
13.   compute $w_1 = (w/g^{v'})^{2^{(n-m)}} \cdot y_1^N \mod N^2$;
14.   **for**($i = 1$ to m)
15. $x = $ **Randomized-Query**($\mathcal{O}_{N,g}$, N, g, w_1);
16.   **If**($x == 1$)
17.   valid=false;
18.   **break**;
19.   **else**
20. $w_1 = w_1^2$;
21.   **end for**
22.   **if**(valid==true)
23.   **return** v';
24.   **end for**
25.   **return** Error;
26. **end for**

Fig. 2. Finding Class Using Imperfect Oracle

to the 1st bit, that is, letting index l go down from $n - m$ to 1, and creating *sorted* lists $L_l = \{c|c - e \cdot 2^l \in \{0, \ldots, 2^l - 1\}\}$. In other words, list L_l contains all of the possible bits of class c from position $n - m$ to position l. Initially, $L_{n-m} = \{0, 1\}$. The transformation from the $(l+1)$st list to the lth list is done by letting L_l contain all the values v such that $v = 2u$ or $v = 2u + 1$, where $u \in L_{l+1}$. This makes the size of L_l twice the size of L_{l+1}. But the size of L_l should be small. So we use the Trimming-Rule algorithm [2] (see Fig. 3) to keep the size of L_l bounded by a polynomial. Roughly speaking, this rule use the partial information from the MSB oracle to eliminate those invalid elements from list L_l. Since L_l is sorted, it must contains two extreme elements: the largest candidate v^l_{max} and the smallest candidate v^l_{min}. At least one of them is not the correct value of $c_{n-m,l}$. If $v^l_{max} - v^l_{min} \leq 2^m$, the size of L_l is less than 2^m. So, if $v^l_{max} - v^l_{min} > 2^m$, we repeatedly use the Trimming-Rule algorithm to discard one of them until the difference is less than 2^m. (See line 3-9 in Fig. 2.) In the Trimming-Rule algorithm (See Fig. 3), a special position of c' determines validity of v^l_{max} and v^l_{min}, where

$$g^{c'} = (g^c \cdot g^{-v_{min} \cdot 2^l})^e \mod N \quad \text{and} \quad e = \lceil 2^{2m} / (v^l_{max} - v^l_{min}) \rceil.$$

Trimming-Rule $(\mathcal{O}_{N,g}, N, g, L_l, v_{\max}^l, v_{\min}^l, n)$

1. Compute $Y' = g^{c'} = (Yg^{v_{\min}^l 2^l})^e$, where $Y = g^c y^N, y \in_R \mathbb{Z}_N^*$ and $e = \lceil 2^{2m}/(v_{\max}^l - v_{\min}^l) \rceil$;
2. $cp = l + 2m + 1$;   (Set crucial point)
3. $Y'' = (Y')^{2^{n-cp}}$;   (Shift c''s crucial position to nth bit)
4. Randomly pick $t(n) = n^4/\epsilon^2$ elements $r_1, \ldots, r_{t(n)} \in \{0,1\}^{n-1}$;
5. Set $b = 0$;
6. **for**$(k = 1$ to $t(n))$
7. $b_k = \mathcal{O}_{N,g}(Y'' g^{r_k})$;
8. $b = b + b_k$;
9. **end for**
10. $M = b/t(n)$;
11. **If**$(M \le 1/2)$ **then**
12.   discard $v_{\max}^l$ from the list L_l;
13. **else**
14.   discard $v_{\min}^l$ from the list L_l;

Fig. 3. Trimming Rule

Randomized-Query $(\mathcal{O}_{N,g}, N, g, w)$

1. $\tau = \frac{2n}{\epsilon^2}$;
2. $countZero = 0, countOne = 0$;
3. **for**$(i = 1$ to $\tau)$
4. $r \in_R \mathbb{Z}_N, s \in_R \mathbb{Z}_N^*$;
5. $\hat{w} = w \cdot g^r s^N = g^{c+r}(ys)^N \mod N^2$;
6. $b = \mathcal{O}_{N,g}(\hat{w})$;
7.   **if**$(b == msb(r))$ **then**
8. $countZero = CountZero + 1$;
9.   **else**
10. $countOne = CountOne + 1$;
11. **end for**
12. **If**$(countZero > countOne)$
13.   **return** 0;
14. **else**
15.   **return** 1;

Fig. 4. Randomized-Query

This special position of c', also called *crucial position* (shortly denoted cp), is defined to be $cp = l + 2m + 1$. It is shown in [2] that:

1. If $c_{n-m,l} = v_{\min}$, the cp-bit of x' is 0, and the m bits to its right are also 0;
2. If $c_{n-m,l} = v_{\max}$, the cp-bit of x' is 1, and the m bits to its right are 0.

Therefore, we can shift c' by $n - cp$ bits to the left to place the cp of c' on n location. Then, we can call the imperfect MSB oracle to learn the cp bit of c'. We use randomization to amplify the statistical advantage of the oracle. For further detail, please refer to [2].

On the last iteration, we can have a polynomial size list L_1 which contains a value equal to $c_{n-m} \cdots c_1$.

HOW TO CHECK THE RESULTS?   Once we obtain the class candidates list $L_1 = \{v_1, \ldots, v_t\}$, where $t \leq 2^m$, we must check each element v in L_1 to see whether $v' = d \circ v = Class_{N,g}(w)$. But since $w = g^c y^N \mod N^2$ and we do not have any knowledge of y, we can not check any value in L_1 by simply encrypting it. We use the Randomized-Query algorithm [1] (see Fig. 4) to resolve this difficulty. Catalano *et al.* [1] used this procedure to amplify the statistical advantage of an imperfect LSB oracle.

Specifically, for any $v \in L_1$, we randomly select $y_1 \in \mathbb{Z}_{N^2}^*$, then we compute $v' = d \circ v$ and

$$w_1 = (w/g^{v'})g^{2^{n-m}} y_1^N = g^{(c-v') \cdot 2^{n-m}} (y \cdot y_1)^N \mod N^2.$$

By doing these, all those remaining non-zero m bits of $c - v' \mod N$ have been shifted to the left end, since the trimming rule assures that $|c - v'| \leq 2^m$. Next, we invoke Randomized-Query algorithm m times to see whether $Class_{N,g}(w_1)$ is zero or not. If it is not zero, we discard this candidate and try another one. This is because that $Class_{N,g}(w_1)$ is non-zero if and only if the algorithm returns one non-zero answers during m calls, regardless of the wrap around and carrying problems brought by computing $(c - v')2^{n-m} \mod N$.

Now we give the probability and time analysis of the whole class finding algorithm with an imperfect MSB oracle (see Fig. 2). According to [2], the error probability of the Trimming-Rule algorithm is exponentially small, specifically, less than 2^{-n}. And its overhead is $O(n^4/\epsilon^2)$. In the class class finding algorithm, the while loop (lines 6-8) calls the trimming rule algorithm at most $2^m = 2^{1-\log \epsilon} = 2/\epsilon$ times. The results checking part (lines 10-25) takes time at most $m2^m$. Since at the beginning of the algorithm we must guess the m most significant bits of c, the whole algorithm takes time $O(\frac{n^5}{\epsilon^4})$. Since the error probability of the trimming rule algorithm is exponentially small and this algorithm is called polynomial times, we can get correct c with a very high probability.

In sum, we construct a polynomial time algorithm to compute class c with the help of a MSB oracle, whether it is perfect or not, which contradicts Assumption 1. Now we complete the proof.   □

4 Conclusion

In this paper, we present the bit security analysis of Paillier's trapdoor function and show that, for $w \in \mathbb{Z}_{N^2}^*$, the most significant bit of w's class is a hard-core bit. There are several open questions in this area. Are all n bits of the class of w are simultaneously hard-core bits under the assumption that computing residuosity class is hard? This will be an improvement of the simultaneous security result proven by Catalano [1] under the B-hard assumption. Another intriguing direction is to study the bit security of the Paillier N-th root under the RSA assumption or factoring assumption.

References

1. Catalano, D., Gennaro, R., Howgrave-Graham, N.: Paillier's trapdoor function hides up to $O(n)$ bits. Journal of Cryptology 15(4), 251–269 (2002)
2. Goldreich, O., Rosen, V.: On the security of modular exponentiation with application to the construction of pseudorandom generators. Journal of Cryptology 16(2), 71–93 (2003)
3. Blum, M., Micali, S.: How to generate cryptographically strong sequences of pseudo-random bits. Journal on Computing 13(4), 850–864 (1984)
4. Alexi, W., Chor, B., Goldreich, O., Schnorr, C.: Rsa and rabin functions: Certain parts are as hard as the whole. SIAM J. Computing 17(2), 194–209 (1988)
5. Goldreich, O., Levin, L.: A hard-core predicate for all one-way functions. In: Proc. 21st ACM Symposium on Theory of Computing, pp. 25–32 (1989)
6. Long, D.L., Wigderson, A.: The discrete log hides $O(\log n)$ bits. SIAM J. Computing 17(2), 363–372 (1988)
7. Peralta, R.: Simultaneous security of bits in the discrete log. In: Pichler, F. (ed.) EURO-CRYPT 1985. LNCS, vol. 219, pp. 66–72. Springer, Heidelberg (1986)
8. Håstad, J., Schrift, A.W., Shamir, A.: The discrete logarithm modulo a composite hides $O(n)$ bits. Journal of Computer and System Sciences 47, 376–404 (1993)
9. Paillier, P.: Public-key cryptosystems based on composite degree residuosity class. In: Stern, J. (ed.) EUROCRYPT 1999. LNCS, vol. 1592, pp. 223–238. Springer, Heidelberg (1999)
10. Goldreich, O.: Fundation of Cryptography–Basic Tools. Cambridge University Press, Cambridge (2001)

Private Interrogation of Devices via Identification Codes[*]

Julien Bringer[1], Hervé Chabanne[1,2], Gérard Cohen[2], and Bruno Kindarji[1,2]

[1] Sagem Sécurité
[2] Télécom ParisTech

Abstract. Consider a device that wants to communicate with another device (for instance a contactless one). We focus on how to withstand privacy threats in such a situation, and we here describe how to query the device and then identify it, with a new identification protocol solution. The interrogation step uses the concept of identification codes introduced by Ahlswede and Dueck. We show that this probabilistic coding scheme indeed protects the device against an eavesdropper who wants to track it. In particular, when using a special class of identification codes due to Moulin and Koetter that are based on Reed-Solomon codes, we directly depend on the hardness of a cryptographic assumption known as the Polynomial Reconstruction problem. We analyse the security and privacy properties of our proposal in the privacy model for contactless devices introduced by Vaudenay at ASIACRYPT 2007. We finally explain how to apply our scheme with very low-cost devices.

Keywords: Identification, Privacy, Polynomial Reconstruction Problem.

1 Introduction

In the field of contactless communication, a verifier (often called a sensor or reader of devices) is used to identify the objects by verifying the validity of the attached contactless devices. This is the case for Radio Frequency IDentification (RFID) systems, where devices are attached to physical objects. The verification is realized through an authentication protocol between a device and the verifier. Once authenticated, the verifier manages the object and allows the owner of the object to access some service. Applications examples include in stock management application for real-time item identification and inventory tracking, e-passport applications, etc. Devices can also be part of a sensor network that gives information on the related infrastructure around a geographical zone.

In this context, a verifier has often to manage many devices at the same time in the same area. Main issues are then efficiency, security and cost, and, of course, the problem very specific to the field of contactless communication: privacy. Many schemes to handle the latter problem have been proposed so far

---

[*] This work was partially funded by the ANR T2TIT project.

B. Roy and N. Sendrier (Eds.): INDOCRYPT 2009, LNCS 5922, pp. 272–289, 2009.

(e.g. [17, 20, 30, 28, 22, 19, 11, 7, 27, 24, 26, 21, 3]; see [8] for a more exhaustive list), but finding an efficient solution enabling privacy of devices is still an active field of research.

Contactless devices are generally assumed to respond automatically to any verifier scan. We follow, in this work, an idea [23] that suggests that the verifier directly addresses the device with which it wants to communicate. To this aim, the verifier broadcasts the device identifier and then the corresponding device responds accordingly. However, the emission of the device identifier enables an eavesdropper to track it. We here look for a solution which does not require many computations and many communications efforts, while preventing an eavesdropper to be able to track a particular device. Changing the paradigm from the situation where a device initiates the protocol to a situation where the device identifies first the interrogation request enables to envisage new solutions.

We show that Identification Codes [1] perfectly fit to our needs. They were introduced by Ahlswede and Dueck to enable the identification of an element out of $\{1, \ldots, n\}$ by only conveying $\log \log n$ bits. While transmission codes enable to correct messages under some noise tolerance property – i.e. to answer the question *What is the received message?*, an identification code detects if a particular message m has been transmitted – i.e. answers the question *Is it the message m?*. We show that such a probabilistic coding scheme increases a lot the job of the eavesdropper as the same identifying bit string is not used twice except with a small probability. In particular, for the class of identification codes of [18], a reduction to the cryptographic assumption of [15] is possible.

Our introduction of Identification Codes for authenticating devices can be viewed in the more general context of challenge-response protocols. Each device has an identifier m and the prover broadcasts a challenge associated to m. Here our scheme does not rely neither on hash functions nor on a random generator on the device side. Moreover, our work shows that our solution is very efficient in terms of channel usage.

We first describe a general scheme based on these identification codes and show that our scheme satisfies good security and privacy properties by analysing it in the privacy model defined in [28]. We then explain how the scheme is suited to very low-cost devices.

Note that the problematic of this article is not limited to interrogation of low-cost devices; in fact, we focus on interrogation protocols and any independent component that communicates over a noisy broadcasting channel is a potential target (as e.g. in [4]).

2   Identification Codes

We wish to communicate mainly with contactless devices, which means that all the communications are to pass through radio waves. As a direct consequence, a message that is sent over the channel is publicly available to any eavesdropper. In a realistic model where a verifier sequentially communicates with wireless devices, it is the verifier that will initiate the communication. To that purpose, the verifier first beckons the device with which it wants to communicate. The most efficient way for doing so is to use an identification code.

2.1   General Definition

Let $\mathcal{X}, \mathcal{Y}$ be two alphabets, and W^η a channel from $\mathcal{X}^\eta$ to $\mathcal{Y}^\eta$. W^η is defined as the probability to receive a message $y^\eta \in \mathcal{Y}^\eta$ given a transmitted message $x^\eta \in \mathcal{X}^\eta$. By extension, for a given subset $E \subset \mathcal{Y}^\eta$, $W^\eta(E|x^\eta)$ is the probability to receive a message belonging to E when x^η has been transmitted.

Definition 1 (Identification Code, [1]). *A $(\eta, N, \lambda_1, \lambda_2)$-identification code from $\mathcal{X}$ to $\mathcal{Y}$ is given by a family $\{(Q(\cdot|i), \mathcal{D}_i)\}_i$ with $i \in \{1, \ldots, N\}$ where:*

- *$Q(\cdot|i)$ is a probability distribution over $\mathcal{X}^\eta$, that encodes i,*
- *$D_i \subset \mathcal{Y}^\eta$ is the **decoding set**,*
- *λ_1 and λ_2 are the first-kind and second-kind error rates, with*

$$\lambda_1 \geq \sum_{x^\eta \in \mathcal{X}^\eta} Q(x^\eta|i) W^\eta(\overline{D_i}|x^\eta)$$

and

$$\lambda_2 \geq \sum_{x^\eta \in \mathcal{X}^\eta} Q(x^\eta|j) W^\eta(D_i|x^\eta)$$

(where $W^\eta(D_i|x^\eta)$ is the probability to be in the decoding set D_i given a transmitted message x^η and $W^\eta(\overline{D_i}|x^\eta)$ the probability to be outside the decoding set)

for all $i, j \in \{1, \ldots, N\}$ such that $i \neq j$.

Given $Q(\cdot|i)$, the **encoding set** of i is defined as the set of messages x^η for which $Q(x^\eta|i) > 0$.

   Informally, an identification code is given by a set of (probabilistic) coding functions, along with (deterministic) decoding sets. The error rate λ_1 gives the probability of a false-negative, and λ_2, of a false-positive identification. We stress that the use of an identification code in our case is more interesting than using a transmission code for the following reasons:

- The efficiency in terms of information rate: the rate of such a code is defined as $R = \frac{1}{\eta} \log \log N$ and can (see [1, Theorem 1]) be made arbitrary close to the (Shannon) capacity of the channel. This means that it is possible to identify $N = 2^{2^{R\eta}}$ devices with a message of length η, with constant error rates (λ_1, λ_2). A regular **transmission** code permits only to identify $2^{R\eta}$ devices.
- The transmission of an element of D_i to identify the device i permits its identification without completely giving away the identity i. Indeed, an eavesdropper only gets the message sent $x^\eta \in Y^\eta$, not the associated index i. The use of an identification code is thus a good way to enhance privacy in the beckoning of wireless devices. This notion is formalized in Section 3.

The proof of the result stated in [1, Theorem 1] is based on a generic construction, exhibited hereafter. Let $A_1, \ldots, A_N \subset X^\eta$ be N subsets such that each A_i has cardinal n and each intersection $A_i \cap A_j$ for $i \neq j$ contains at most λn elements. The encoding distribution $Q(\cdot|i)$ is defined as the uniform distribution over A_i; in the noiseless case (the channel W^η is the identity function) the decoding sets are also the A_i's. Note that in that case the false-negative rate λ_1 is equal to 0 and the false-positive rate λ_2 is λ.

This theoretical construction gives way to multiple practical identification codes based on constant-weight codes, such as [16, 29, 6]. We focus on [18] which provides a simple though efficient identification code well suited to our application.

2.2 Moulin and Koetter Identification Codes Family

We here recall a simple construction of identification codes proposed by Moulin and Koetter [18].

The identification code detailed in [18] is based on an Error-Correcting Code C of length n, size $N = |C|$ and minimum distance d over some alphabet. For a word $c_i = (c_i^{(1)}, \ldots c_i^{(n)}) \in C$, the corresponding set A_i is the collection of all $(u, c_i^{(u)})$, for $u \in \{1, \ldots, n\}$. Note that we indeed have sets A_i of constant size n; moreover, the intersection of two different sets $A_i \cap A_j$ contains at most $n - d$ elements, which induces $\lambda_2 = \frac{n-d}{n} = 1 - \frac{d}{n}$.

A Reed-Solomon code over a finite field $A = \mathbb{F}_q$, of length $n < q - 1$, and dimension k, is the set of the evaluations of all polynomials $P \in \mathbb{F}_q[X]$ of degree less than $k-1$, over a subset $F \subset \mathbb{F}_q$ of size n ($F = \{\alpha_1, \ldots, \alpha_n\}$). In other words, for each k-tuple $(x_0, \ldots, x_{k-1}) \in \mathbb{F}_q^k$, the corresponding Reed-Solomon word is the n-tuple $(y_1, \ldots, y_n)$ where $y_i = \sum_{j=0}^{k-1} x_j \alpha_i^j$. In the sequel, we identify a source word $(x_0, \ldots, x_{k-1}) \in \mathbb{F}_q^k$ with the corresponding polynomial $P = \sum_{j=0}^{k-1} x_j X^j \in \mathbb{F}_q[X]$.

Definition 2 (Moulin-Koetter RS-Identification Codes). *Let $\mathbb{F}_q$ be a finite field of size q, $k \leq n \leq q - 1$ and an evaluation domain $F = \{\alpha_1, \ldots, \alpha_n\} \in \mathbb{F}_q$. Set $A_P = \{(j, P(\alpha_j)) | j \in \{1, \ldots, n\}\}$ for P any polynomial on $\mathbb{F}_q$ of degree at most $k - 1$.*

The Moulin-Koetter RS-Identification Codes is defined by the family of encoding and decoding sets $\{(A_P, A_P)\}_{P \in \mathbb{F}_q[X], \deg P < k}$.

This leads to a $(\log_2 n + \log_2 q, q^k, 0, \frac{k-1}{n})$-identification code from $\{0, 1\}$ to $\{0, 1\}$.

Using a Reed-Solomon code of dimension k, this gives $\lambda_2 = \frac{k-1}{n}$ since $d = n-k+1$ (Reed-Solomon codes are Maximum Distance Separable).

2.3 Application to Our Setting

Back to our original problem of devices interrogation, here comes a brief description of a set-up that enables the use of identification codes to initiate a protocol between a verifier and a device. A more formal description is given in Section 4.

A set of $M < q^k$ devices is constructed, and each of them is associated with a different random polynomial $p_l \in \mathbb{F}_q[X]$ of degree less than $k - 1$. The memory of these devices is then filled with a set of $p_l(\alpha_j)$, for $\alpha_j \in F$, with F a public subset of $\mathbb{F}_q$, *i.e.* the devices contain the evaluation of p_l over a subset of $\mathbb{F}_q$. The verifier is given the polynomial p_l.

When the verifier wants to initiate communication with the device number l associated with the identifier p_l, it selects a random $\alpha_j \in F$ and sends $(j, p_l(\alpha_j))$ over the wireless channel. A device that receives this message checks whether the value stored in its memory at the corresponding address is equal to $p_l(\alpha_j)$, *i.e.* computes an equality test of two bit strings. If the test is successful, it replies and goes through the authentication protocol described in Section 4. Otherwise, it remains silent.

Consequently, only a legitimate verifier can interrogate a specific device. Next sections emphasize the security properties reached thanks to this principle.

3   Vaudenay's Model for Privacy

We briefly recall in this section the model for privacy, correctness and soundness described in [28]. Our main concern is interrogation of devices, but it can be easily seen as an authentication protocol, so we use almost the same model.

Following [28], we consider that provers are equipped with ContactLess Device (CLD) to identify themselves. CLDs are transponders identified by a unique Serial Number (SN). During the identification phase, a random virtual serial number (vSN) is used to address them.

An identification protocol is defined as algorithms: First to setup the system made of a verifier and several CLDs, secondly to run a protocol between CLDs and verifiers. Note that we need an authority who publishes a mathematical structure.

Setup Algorithms

- SETUPAUTHORITY$(1^k) \mapsto (KA_s, KA_p)$ generates the system parameters defined by an authority (KA_s stands for the private parameters and KA_p for the parameters publicly available).
- SETUPVERIFIER$_{KA_p}$ initializes a verifier. It may generate a private/public set of parameters (KV_s, KV_p), associated to the verifier.
- SETUPCLD$^b_{KA_p, KV_p}$(SN) generates the parameters of the CLD identified by SN. This algorithm outputs a couple (s, I) where s denotes the secret (if any) parameters of the CLD, I its identity within the system. It enables to initialize the internal state of the CLD, which may be updated afterwards during an execution of the protocol. If $b = 1$, it also stores the pair (I,SN) in a database which may be made available to the verifier. If $b = 0$ it is a illegitimate device.

Communication Protocol $\mathcal{P}$. Along with these setup algorithms, the identification protocol between a CLD and a verifier consists of messages sent by the two parties. Protocol instances are hereafter denoted by π.

Oracles. To formalize possible actions of an adversary, different oracles are defined to represent ways for him to interact with verifiers or CLDs, or to eavesdrop communications. The use of different oracles leads to different privacy levels.

Given a public set of parameters KV_p, the adversary has access to:

- CREATECLD^b(SN): creates a CLD with serial number SN initialized via SETUPCLD^b. At this point, it is a free CLD, i.e. not yet in the system.
- DRAWCLD($distr$)$\mapsto$((vSN_1, b_1),...,(vSN_n, b_n)): this oracle moves a random subset of n CLDs according to a given distribution from the set of free CLDs into the set of drawn CLDs in the system. Virtual serial numbers vSN_i can be used to refer to these CLDs. If b_i is one, this indicates whether a CLD is legitimate. This oracle creates and keeps a table of correspondences $\mathcal{T}$ where $\mathcal{T}(\text{vSN})$=SN. Adversary has no knowledge of this table $\mathcal{T}$.
- FREE(vSN): moves the drawn CLD vSN to the set of free CLDs, i.e. vSN cannot be used any more to query the CLD.
- LAUNCH $\mapsto \pi$: makes the verifier launch a new protocol instance π.
- SENDVERIFIER(m, π) $\mapsto m'$: sends the message m for the protocol instance π to the verifier who may respond m'.
- SENDCLD(m', π) $\mapsto m$: sends the message m' to the CLD who may respond m.
- RESULT(π) $\mapsto x$: when π is a complete instance of $\mathcal{P}$, it returns 1 if the verifier succeeds in identifying a CLD from π and 0 otherwise.
- CORRUPT(vSN)$\mapsto S$: returns the internal state S of the CLD vSN.

Types of Adversary

- **Strong** adversary is allowed to use all of the above oracles.
- **Destructive** adversary cannot use a corrupted CLD another time.
- **Forward** adversary cannot use any oracle after one CORRUPT query, i.e. destroys the system when he corrupts one CLD.
- **Weak** adversary is not allowed to use the CORRUPT oracle.
- **Narrow** adversary is not allowed to use the RESULT oracle.

This defines 8 kinds of adversaries because a narrow adversary may also have restrictions on the use of the CORRUPT oracle. For instance, an adversary can be narrow and forward, he is then denoted by narrow-forward.

Remark 1. The notion of **destructive** adversary is an intermediate notion between **strong** and **forward** adversaries. As explained in [19], **destructive** notion is different from **forward** notion only when the system enables the introduction of some correlated secrets between CLDs. This is not our case in the sequel, so we will no further distinguish these two notions.

Three security notions are defined in this model: correctness, resistance against impersonation and privacy.

Definition 3. *A scheme is* **correct** *if the identification of a legitimate CLD fails only with negligible probability.*

Resistance against Impersonation Attacks. The definition of resistance against impersonation attacks (Definition 4) deals with active adversaries. Active adversaries may impersonate verifiers and CLDs, and eavesdrop and modify communications. This property of resistance against impersonation attacks has also repercussions regarding privacy properties (cf. Lemma 1).

Definition 4. *A scheme is* **resistant against Impersonation Attacks** *if any polynomially bounded* **strong** *adversary is not identified by a verifier except with a negligible probability. Adversaries are authorized to use different devices at the same time while they communicate with the verifier. Nevertheless, the resulting protocol transcript must neither be equal to an outputted one between a legitimate CLD and the verifier nor lead to the identification of a corrupted CLD.*

Remark 2. Obviously this means that a scheme is not resistant against impersonation attacks if an adversary is able to modify on the fly outputs from a prover without affecting the identification result.

In addition to this definition, in order to mitigate replay attacks, a legitimate verifier should not output twice the same values in two complete protocol instances, except with a negligible probability.

Note that following Remark 1, the CORRUPT oracle will be useless for impersonation attacks against our scheme (as secret are not correlated between devices).

Similarly, and as in [22], we introduce the **resistance against impersonation of verifier** where an adversary should not be able to be identified as a legitimate verifier by a non-corrupted CLD except by replaying an eavesdropped transcript. This is related to the notion of verifier authentication. Note that we introduce a slight restriction in Section 5.3 as our scheme aims only at ensuring validity of the verifier against a pre-fixed CLD.

Privacy. Privacy is defined as an advantage of an adversary over the system. To formalize this, [28] proposes to challenge the adversary once with the legitimate oracles and a second time with simulated oracles. In this setting, the adversary is free to define a game and an algorithm $\mathcal{A}$ to solve his game. If the two challenges results are distinguishable, i.e. if the system cannot be simulated, then there is a privacy leakage. A game with three phases is imposed. In the first phase, $\mathcal{A}$ has access to the whole system using oracles. In a second phase, the hidden table $\mathcal{T}$ of correspondences is transmitted to $\mathcal{A}$ (note that this table is never learned by the simulator). In a third phase, $\mathcal{A}$, who is no longer allowed to use the oracles, outputs its result. A scheme is defined as **private** if for any game, all adversaries are trivial (the formal definition is given in Appendix A, Definition 7).

The following lemma established by Vaudenay in [28] emphasizes the link between impersonation resistance and privacy:

Lemma 1. *A scheme secure against impersonation attacks and narrow-weak (resp. narrow-forward) private is weak (resp. forward) private.*

The proof relies on the fact that an adversary is not able to simulate any CLD if the scheme is sound. This implies that the RESULT oracle is easily simulated.

Remark 3. Our model aims at dealing with identification of multiple devices. It is therefore reasonable to amend the privacy model by stating that the SEND-CLD(m', π) oracle cannot communicate with a single CLD, but broadcasts the message m' to all the CLDs in the vicinity. Moreover, as it was shown in D'Arco *et al.* [5], no privacy is possible if the adversary can deactivate a CLD, which is possible if we allow the adversary to manipulate the CLDs one by one.

[28] proves also that narrow-strong privacy implies the use of public key cryptography and that strong privacy is impossible in this model. In the sequel we stick to symmetric cryptography, and that is why we do not analyse the narrow-strong privacy any further. Furthermore, as explained in the previous remark, we exclude from our model of threats the situation where the adversary communicates with one isolated device.

4 Our Protocol for Interrogation

Our aim is for a CLD to recognize itself into a verifier request, but authentication of the CLD toward the verifier is handled as well. That is how we set-up the system:

- SETUPAUTHORITY(1^ℓ) generates a set of parameters KA_p defining two integers η, N, two alphabets $\mathcal{X}$, $\mathcal{Y}$, and two error rates λ_1, λ_2. No private parameter is defined.
- SETUPVERIFIER$_{KA_p}$ constructs an $(\eta, N, \lambda_1, \lambda_2)$-identification code from $\mathcal{X}$ to $\mathcal{Y}$ following Definition 1, $\mathcal{IC} = \{(Q(\cdot|i), \mathcal{D}_i)\}_{i \in \{1,...,N\}}$, and sets $KV_p = \mathcal{IC}$. $\mathcal{IC}$ is based on the Moulin-Koetter construction [18] (cf. Definition 2).
- SETUPCLD$_{KV_p}$(SN) first returns randomly chosen $(i, j) \in \{1, ..., N\}$, $i \neq j$ as the parameters of the CLD identified by SN. It then initializes the CLD with the storage of a description of the decoding set D_i of the identifier i and the description of $Q(\cdot|j)$, the encoding probability mass function for index j. It also stores (i, j, SN) in the verifier database.

A verifier and a set of devices are set-up as above and the following steps are then processed to interrogate and authenticate a specific CLD.

- The verifier, who wants to interrogate the CLD of identifier SN, recovers its identifier i in the database and encodes it via $Q(\cdot|i)$ into a message $x \in \mathcal{X}^\eta$. The verifier broadcasts the message (ACK, x), where ACK is an acknowledgement number which will help the verifier to sort the received answers when it emits simultaneously several such messages.
- Any listening CLD that receives the message (ACK, y) uses its own decoding set $D_{i_{CLD}}$ to determine whether y encodes i_{CLD}.
- If a CLD identifies y as an encoding of its identifier i_{CLD}, then it sends the message (ACK, x') to the verifier, where ACK is the incoming acknowledgement number and x' is an encoding of j_{CLD} obtained via $Q(\cdot|j_{CLD})$.

- Upon receiving this message, the verifier then checks whether the received message y' is a member of the decoding set D_j of the aimed CLD. If so, then the CLD is declared as authenticated.

Note that here x' has to be chosen in relation with the value of y so that impersonation of a CLD is not easy.

Remark 4. As a practical assumption, our interrogation protocol works as a broadcast channel and we assume that a legitimate verifier is interrogating several CLDs during the same period. Although it might look restrictive, recall that our goal is to address applications where a verifier has to manage efficiently a cloud of CLDs. More formally, we assume that a cloud of M CLDs is present in the broadcast area of the verifier and that the verifier interrogates them uniformly in a random order. In particular, an adversary is not able to *a priori* distinguish the devices without trying to exploit the content of messages exchanged.

4.1   Specifications Using Reed-Solomon Based Identification Codes

We now consider only the Moulin-Koetter setting, in particular for the security analysis in the next sections. The description is given below (see also Fig. 1).

In this setting, a set of CLDs is constructed where each of them – say CLD_l – is associated with two different random polynomial identifiers p_l, $p'_l \in \mathbb{F}_q[X]$ of degree at most $k-1$. Here p_l and p'_l are good descriptions of the associated encoding functions and the decoding sets; they are both stored on the CLD side and on the verifier database.

When the verifier wants to initiate communication with CLD_l (with identifiers p_l, p'_l), it selects a random $\alpha_j \in F \subset \mathbb{F}_q[X]$ and broadcasts $(ACK, j, p_l(\alpha_j))$ over the wireless channel. A CLD with identifiers p, p' that receives this message checks whether the polynomial p stored in its memory evaluated in α_j is equal to $p_l(\alpha_j)$. If the test is successful, it responds with the value $(ACK, p'(\alpha_j))$. Otherwise, it remains silent. The verifier authenticates the CLD if the received value $p'(\alpha_j)$ is equal to $p'_l(\alpha_j)$.

Remark 5. For privacy purposes, we do not want replay attacks to be possible at all. In order to avoid them, we add to each devices a flag bit that tells if the α_j

CLD	parameters	Verifier
identifiers p, p'	$\mathbb{F}_q, (\alpha_1, \ldots, \alpha_n)$	(l, p_l, p'_l)

$$\xleftarrow{\quad (ACK, j, a = p_l(\alpha_j)) \quad} \quad \text{Pick } j$$

If $p(\alpha_j) = a$ $\xrightarrow{\quad (ACK, b = p'(\alpha_j)) \quad}$ Check whether $p'_l(\alpha_j) = b$

Fig. 1. CLD identification via Moulin-Koetter identification codes

was already used or not; this bit is flipped on at the reception of $(j, p(\alpha_j))$; after that, a device no longer accepts such a message. This can be seen as coupons enabling a limited number of interrogations by a legitimate verifier.

When communicating with an isolated device, it may enable an adversary to track the device via a replay attack by listening whether the device responses. In our situation, this does not lead to a privacy threat as the adversary is only able to interrogate a cloud of devices which is continuously evolving.

5   Security Analysis

Remark first that the scheme is correct: In the Moulin-Koetter construction (cf. Section 2.2) the false-negative error rate (λ_1) is zero, thus the correct CLD will always answer and be authenticated.

5.1   Assumptions

Part of our results are directly linked to solving the problem of polynomial reconstruction (PR) [15, 14, 13, 12]:

Definition 5 ([15]). *Given n, k, t such that $n \geq t \geq 1$, $n \geq k$ and $z, y \in \mathbb{F}_q^n$, with $z_i \neq z_j$ for $i \neq j$, output all (p, I) where $p \in \mathbb{F}_q[X]$, $\deg(P) < k$, $I \subset \{1, \ldots, n\}$, $|I| \geq t$, and $\forall i \in I, p(z_i) = y_i$. Such an instance of this problem is noted $PR_{n,k,t}^z$.*

The Guruswami-Sudan algorithm [10] for the **list decoding** of Reed-Solomon codes gives a way to solve the polynomial reconstruction problem when $t \geq \sqrt{kn}$. However, no efficient solution to this problem exists when $t < \sqrt{kn}$ and it is reputed hard. If $t < k$, PR is unconditionally secure (in the information-theoretical meaning).

Based on the assumed intractability of PR, [15] derives the Decisional PR (DPR) problem which consists, given an instance y of $PR_{n,k,t}^z$ for which there exists a solution (p, I), in determining whether a given $i \in \{1, \ldots, n\}$ is in I. Thanks to the DPR assumption (hardness of the DPR problem), it is shown [15] that PR instances are pseudo-random and that they do not leak any partial information on the polynomial values.

Remark 6. In the sequel we assume that the PR and DPR problems remain hard (with respect to the security parameter ℓ) even in our setting – where the noise is generated by the other queries and responses. M will be chosen so that the DPR assumption holds when the noise is assumed to be random. To justify this choice, we can refer to [9] which explains the link between Reed-Solomon list decoding and the previous works on polynomial reconstruction in the mixture model. An algorithm to reconstruct polynomials from mixed values is designed in [2]. When considering mixed evaluations of M polynomials of degree at most $k - 1$, it enables to reconstruct one of these polynomials when at least $M(k-1)$ related values are available in the mixture. In the sequel, we set M greater than $\sqrt{\frac{n}{k}}$ so that $M(k - 1)$ is approximately greater than $\sqrt{nk}$, i.e. that we obtain the same bound as for the solvability of PR instances. This algorithm is the basis – although a bit simpler – of the list decoding algorithm [10] and this fact suggests that when we get less than $M(k-1)$ values for each polynomial with M large, the problem of reconstructing one polynomial remains hard even without a perfectly random noise.

5.2   Effect of Passive Eavesdropping

When listening on the channel to the queries made by a legitimate verifier and the replies produced by legitimate CLDs, an eavesdropper sees messages of this kind: $(ACK_i, j_i, p_{l_{j_i}}(\alpha_{j_i}))$, $(ACK_i, p'_{l'_{j_i}}(\alpha_{j_i}))$ (for l'_j such that $p_{l'_j}(\alpha_j) = p_{l_j}(\alpha_j)$), for some number of i's (say $i \in \{1, \dots, T\}$). Note that we may also have collisions on the α_j used (i.e. $j_i = j_{i'}$ may occur for some $i \neq i'$). This means that the adversary obtains a set S of several PR instances of length less or equal to n (the length of the overall code, see Section 2.2). Targeting a specific CLD, of identifier p and p', then there are at least two corresponding PR instances, $PR^{z_1}_{n_1,k,t_1}$ and $PR^{z_2}_{n_2,k,t_2}$ where p is one solution of the first one and p' a solution of the latter, among the set S of all those PR instances. One difficulty for the adversary is to sort the different messages and to deal with the collisions to extract such instances. If we assume that there is no collision (then necessarily $T \leq n$) and that the verifier queries uniformly the M CLDs (cf. Remark 4), then it implies that the adversary can recover these instances, but with $t_i \approx \frac{n_i}{M}$. So if M is greater than $\sqrt{\frac{n}{k}}$ then the PR instances are hard.

Moreover, when the number of received messages is large, the t_i's above may be greater than $\sqrt{kn}$ but the adversary has to deal with the collisions and to try all the different instances until the recovery of a solvable instance. Another strategy is to see the problem as one longer PR instance. This is related to the **list recovery problem** which is analysed in [25]. This is hard as well given some restriction on the number of eavesdropped messages. In the sequel, we assume that the list recovery problem in the mixture model is hard when $t < \sqrt{nk \times l}$ with l the maximum number of collisions per z_i.

Proposition 1. *Assume that the number M of devices simultaneously queried by the verifier is such that $\sqrt{q} \geq M \geq e\sqrt{\frac{n}{k}}$ (with $e = exp(1)$). Then a passive adversary, who eavesdrops at most T requests with $T < M^2 k$, cannot reconstruct the polynomial identifiers, except with a negligible probability.*

Proof. Assume that the adversary has eavesdropped T different requests with $T/M \geq \sqrt{kn}$, then there may exist solvable PR instances. Now he has to find these solvable instances among all possible instances. Following Remark 4 on uniformity of the queries made by a verifier, we assume that the number of different requests to each device is exactly $t = T/M$. (Due to the false-positive error rate of the underlying identification code, one request will address several additional devices and imply as many replies. In fact, as the polynomials are chosen independently and uniformly, the number of devices addressed by one query is strictly greater than 1 only if there is a collision during the evaluation of several polynomials. The assumption $M \le \sqrt{q}$ enables us to neglect this point, but the result is easily generalizable to the case $M > \sqrt{q}$.)

Let $M \ge \gamma\sqrt{\frac{n}{k}}$ where γ will be determined later. Note that if $T/M < k$ then it is unconditionally secure and if $T < \gamma n$ then $T/M < \sqrt{nk}$ so that the PR instances are hard. Assume that $T \ge \gamma n$, thus the number of collisions per α_j is expected to be about T/n (note that $T/M \le n$ as each device is linked to at most n different requests). To make computation more tractable, we assume below that the number of collisions per α_j is exactly T/n.

The adversary has to reconstruct one polynomial corresponding to some part of the eavesdropped values.

The first strategy for the adversary is to find a solvable PR instance in the classical meaning, i.e. without any collision. The number of possible PR instances is then expected to be $B = \left(\frac{T}{n}\right)^n$ whereas the number of solvable instances is $A = M \times \binom{T/M}{\lceil\sqrt{kn}\rceil}\left(\frac{T}{n}\right)^{n-\lceil\sqrt{kn}\rceil}$. If the ratio $\rho = \frac{A}{B}$ of the number of solvable instances over the number of all possible instances is negligible then the adversary would not find a solvable instance in polynomial time. In fact ρ is equal to

$$M\binom{T/M}{\lceil\sqrt{kn}\rceil}\left(\frac{T}{n}\right)^{-\lceil\sqrt{nk}\rceil}.$$

To approximate ρ, note $R = \frac{k}{n}$ the rate of the Reed-Solomon code as eavesdropped by the adversary. We also introduce $\theta > 1$ such as $\frac{T}{M} = \theta\sqrt{kn}$. The notations give $M = \frac{\gamma}{\sqrt{R}}$ and $\frac{T}{n} = \theta\gamma$. A good approximation of $\binom{T/M}{\lceil\sqrt{kn}\rceil}$ is, for $\theta > 2$, $2^{\frac{T}{M}h_2\left(\frac{M\sqrt{kn}}{T}\right)} = 2^{n\sqrt{R}\theta h_2\left(\frac{1}{\theta}\right)}$ where h_2 is the binary entropy function. This shows that ρ can be fairly approximated by

$$\rho \approx \frac{\gamma}{\sqrt{R}}2^{n\sqrt{R}\left(\theta h_2\left(\frac{1}{\theta}\right)-\log_2(\theta\gamma)\right)}.$$

Taking a closer look at the exponent, we see that $\theta h_2(\frac{1}{\theta}) - \log_2(\theta\gamma) = (\theta - 1)\log_2(\frac{\theta}{\theta-1}) - \log_2(\gamma)$ is negative only if $\gamma > \left(1 + \frac{1}{\theta-1}\right)^{\theta-1}$. As $\forall x \in \mathbb{R}^\star, \log(1 + \frac{1}{x}) < \frac{1}{x}$, we deduce that if $\gamma \ge e$, then $\theta h_2(\frac{1}{\theta}) - \log_2(\theta\gamma) < 0$. Thus, $\rho \le M2^{-n\sqrt{R}\log_2(\frac{\gamma}{e})}$ is negligible.

This gives a negligible probability for the adversary to find a solvable instance. This conclusion can be generalized to non-constant number of collisions as soon as the j picked by the verifier is chosen uniformly and independently among the different requests.

The general strategy is to apply the list recovery technique [25] derived from the list decoding algorithm [10]. This becomes tractable as soon as T/M is greater than $\sqrt{nk} \times l$ with l the maximum number of collisions per α_j (roughly, this corresponds to solving a PR instance of length nl). Here $l = T/n$ and the condition $T/M \ge \sqrt{nkl} = \sqrt{Tk}$ is equivalent to the condition $T \ge M^2k$. Due to our hypothesis on the number of eavesdropped messages, the algorithm cannot be applied. Finally if there exists an adversary able to reconstruct a polynomial with any other strategy, then we can exploit it to simplify the list recovery problem within the mixture model. This would contradict its difficulty when $T/M < \sqrt{nk \times l}$.   □

Note that in practice, the cloud of devices is dynamic, some devices may exit or enter the cloud around a verifier, so that the difficulty for the attacker can only increase.

Following this proposition and via the DPR problem, then a passive adversary cannot distinguish the answers as soon as the same interrogation request does not appear twice. The proofs of the following results are in Appendix B.

Proposition 2. *Assume $\sqrt{q} \geq M \geq e\sqrt{\frac{n}{k}}$ and $T < M^2 k$. A passive adversary cannot determine whether two requests correspond to the same CLD except if there is a collision, that happens only with probability $1/\sqrt{n}$.*

5.3   Security against Impersonation

In our protocol, a CLD replies to the verifier only if it believes that the verifier is legitimate. It is thus close to mutual authentication – although here the authentication of the verifier is only probabilistic with respect to the false-positive error rate of an identification code. It is a weaker result than general verifier authentication: a verifier cannot be impersonated in order to interrogate a pre-fixed CLD.

Proposition 3. *Assume $\sqrt{q} \geq M \geq e\sqrt{\frac{n}{k}}$ and $T < M^2 k$. In our scheme, given a non-corrupted CLD, an adversary cannot impersonate a verifier to interrogate this specific CLD, without replaying an eavesdropped transcript, except with probability $\frac{1}{q}$.*

Of course, if no specific CLD is fixed, then impersonation of an interrogation towards a member of a large set of CLDs is easier. With M CLDs, the probability to reach one of them correctly is $\frac{M}{q}$.

Given this difficulty of impersonating a verifier against a chosen CLD and the uselessness of eavesdropping (cf. Proposition 1), we deduce the resistance of CLDs against impersonation attacks.

Proposition 4. *Assume $\sqrt{q} \geq M \geq e\sqrt{\frac{n}{k}}$ and $T < M^2 k$. Our scheme is secure against impersonation of a CLD, i.e. an adversary will fail with probability $1 - \frac{1}{q}$.*

Replay attacks on the verifier side are not important from a security point of view as replaying a query does not give additional information to the adversary. However, they are prevented in the scheme to maintain privacy (with replay attacks, an adversary could track a device).

5.4   Privacy

Proposition 5. *If $\sqrt{q} \geq M \geq e\sqrt{\frac{n}{k}}$ and $T < M^2 k$, then our scheme is weak private.*

See the proofs in Appendix B.

Moreover, even if not forward private, as the identifiers are independently chosen among devices, the corruption of one device directly affects only this device. Although, this level of privacy could seem low, it is exactly what we intended to achieve and it is important to notice that contrary to the protocols described in [28], devices do not need the use of any internal random number generator to implement the protocol.

6   Advantages for Very Low-Cost Devices

For low-cost devices, instead of storing the two polynomial identifiers p, p', we store directly the values $p(\alpha_1), \ldots, p(\alpha_n)$ and $p'(\alpha_1), \ldots, p'(\alpha_n)$ within the device. So doing, no computation is needed on the device side. Depending on the amount of memory available per device, we can also limit the number of such values by restricting ourselves to a basis of evaluation of size $L < n$, e.g. $(\alpha_1, \ldots, \alpha_L)$.

An additional advantage is that the scheme can be adapted simply to work over a noisy channel by storing encoded versions – through some error-correcting code – of these values $p(\alpha_1), \ldots, p(\alpha_L)$ and $p'(\alpha_1), \ldots, p'(\alpha_L)$ and the corresponding index $1, \ldots, L$. The devices will only have to compute the distance between the received message and the stored one.

7   Practical Parameters

For real-life low-cost CLDs, we can imagine a non-volatile memory of about $2^{18} = 256k$ bits. We aim at a field size $q = 2^{64}$, which permits to store $2^{12} = 4096$ fields elements in the memory, *i.e.* 2048 evaluations of the two polynomials p_l, p'_l (which implies that the length $n \leq q - 1$ of the corresponding code is $n = 2^{11}$).

With these parameters, we suggest the use of polynomials of dimension $k = 2^8$. Using such a dimension permits to define $q^k = 2^{64 \times 256}$ possible polynomials; the number M of devices needed in the cloud around a verifier has then to be greater than $e \times \sqrt{\frac{n}{k}}$, i.e. at least 8. With $M = 256$, this leads to the restriction $T < 2^{24}$, which is automatically satisfied here as $T \leq Mn = 2^{19}$.

These parameters enable 2048 interrogations of the same device without compromising the device identity - both in terms of impersonation and of weak privacy.

Remark 7. We can suppress the identification-code structure, and replace it with a random one (*i.e.* replace $p(\alpha_i), p'(\alpha_i)$ by random $\beta_i, \beta'_i \in \{0, 1\}^{\log_2 q}$). However, instead of storing $k \cdot \log_2 q$ bits per device at the verifier's side, we need to store for each device the $n \cdot \log_2 q$ bits that are stored in it. With these parameters, this implies a storage space 8 times larger.

8 Conclusion

Finally, it is possible to further extend the scheme toward reaching forward privacy (equivalent to destructive privacy in this context of non-correlated identifiers): we store $L < k$ values for each identifier p, p' of degree at most $k - 1$ and erase the values $p(\alpha_j)$ and $p'(\alpha_j)$ after replying to the associated query. Because we erase the values after, a corruption will not give direct access to these values and because $L < k$, it is unconditionally impossible for an adversary to recover the missing values by polynomial interpolation. Hence, the destructive privacy is fulfilled. In this case, the false-positive rate should be quite small to avoid quick waste of the coupons of the devices.

Acknowledgements. The authors thank the referees for their helpful comments.

References

1. Ahlswede, R., Dueck, G.: Identification via channels. IEEE Transactions on Information Theory 35(1), 15–29 (1989)
2. Ar, S., Lipton, R.J., Rubinfeld, R., Sudan, M.: Reconstructing algebraic functions from mixed data. SIAM J. Comput. 28(2), 487–510 (1998)
3. Bringer, J., Chabanne, H., Icart, T.: Improved Privacy of the Tree-Based Hash Protocols Using Physically Unclonable Function. In: Ostrovsky, R., De Prisco, R., Visconti, I. (eds.) SCN 2008. LNCS, vol. 5229, pp. 77–91. Springer, Heidelberg (2008)
4. Bringer, J., Chabanne, H., Icart, T.: Efficient Zero-Knowledge Identification Schemes which respect Privacy. In: ACM Symposium on Information, Computer and Communication Security – ASIACCS 2009, Sydney, Australia (March 2009)
5. Arco, P.D., Scafuro, A., Visconti, I.: Semi-destructive privacy in RFID systems. In: Workshop on RFID Security (2009)
6. Eswaran, K.: Identification via channels and constant-weight codes, http://www.eecs.berkeley.edu/ ananth/229BSpr05/Reports/ KrishEswaran.pdf
7. Fung, B., Al-Hussaeni, K., Cao, M.: Preserving RFID Data Privacy. In: IEEE International Conference on RFID – RFID 2009, Orlando, Florida, USA (April 2009)
8. Information Security Group. RFID security & privacy lounge, http://www.avoine.net/rfid/
9. Guruswami, V., Sudan, M.: Reflections on improved decoding of reed-solomon andalgebraic-geometric codes (2002)
10. Guruswami, V., Sudan, M.: Improved decoding of reed-solomon and algebraic-geometry codes. IEEE Transactions on Information Theory 45(6), 1757–1767 (1999)
11. Juels, A., Weis, S.A.: Defining strong privacy for RFID. In: PERCOMW, pp. 342–347. IEEE Computer Society, Los Alamitos (2007)
12. Kiayias, A., Yung, M.: Polynomial reconstruction based cryptography. In: Vaudenay, S., Youssef, A.M. (eds.) SAC 2001. LNCS, vol. 2259, pp. 129–133. Springer, Heidelberg (2001)

13. Kiayias, A., Yung, M.: Cryptographic hardness based on the decoding of reed-solomon codes. In: Widmayer, P., Triguero, F., Morales, R., Hennessy, M., Eidenbenz, S., Conejo, R. (eds.) ICALP 2002. LNCS, vol. 2380, pp. 232–243. Springer, Heidelberg (2002)

14. Kiayias, A., Yung, M.: Cryptographic hardness based on the decoding of reed-solomon codes with applications. In: Electronic Colloquium on Computational Complexity (ECCC), vol. 017 (2002)

15. Kiayias, A., Yung, M.: Cryptographic hardness based on the decoding of reed-solomon codes. IEEE Transactions on Information Theory 54(6), 2752–2769 (2008)

16. Kurosawa, K., Yoshida, T.: Strongly universal hashing and identification codes via channels. IEEE Transactions on Information Theory 45(6), 2091–2095 (1999)

17. Molnar, D., Wagner, D.: Privacy and security in library RFID: issues, practices, and architectures. In: CCS, pp. 210–219. ACM, New York (2004)

18. Moulin, P., Koetter, R.: A framework for the design of good watermark identification codes. In: Delp III, E.J., Wong, P.W. (eds.) SPIE, vol. 6072, p. 60721H. SPIE, San Jose (2006)

19. Ng, C.Y., Susilo, W., Mu, Y., Safavi-Naini, R.: RFID privacy models revisited. In: Jajodia, S., López, J. (eds.) ESORICS 2008. LNCS, vol. 5283, pp. 251–266. Springer, Heidelberg (2008)

20. Ohkubo, M., Suzuki, K., Kinoshita, S.: RFID privacy issues and technical challenges 48(9), 66–71 (2005)

21. Ouafi, K., Phan, R.C.-W.: Traceable Privacy of Recent Provably-Secure RFID Protocols. In: Bellovin, S.M., Gennaro, R., Keromytis, A.D., Yung, M. (eds.) ACNS 2008. LNCS, vol. 5037, pp. 479–489. Springer, Heidelberg (2008)

22. Paise, R.-I., Vaudenay, S.: Mutual authentication in RFID: security and privacy. In: Abe, M., Gligor, V.D. (eds.) ASIACCS, pp. 292–299. ACM, New York (2008)

23. PEARS. Privacy Ensuring Affordable RFID System. European Project

24. Rieback, M.R.: Security and Privacy of Radio Frequency Identification. PhD thesis, Vrije Universiteit, Amsterdam, The Netherlands (2008)

25. Rudra, A.: List Decoding and Property Testing of Error Correcting Codes. PhD thesis, University of Washington (2007)

26. Sadeghi, A.-R., Visconti, I., Wachsmann, C.: User Privacy in Transport Systems Based on RFID E-Tickets. In: Workshop on Privacy in Location-Based Applications – PILBA 2008, Malaga, Spain (October 2008)

27. Spiekermann, S., Evdokimov, S.: Privacy Enhancing Technologies for RFID - A Critical Investigation of State of the Art Research. In: IEEE Privacy and Security (2009)

28. Vaudenay, S.: On privacy models for RFID. In: Kurosawa, K. (ed.) ASIACRYPT 2007. LNCS, vol. 4833, pp. 68–87. Springer, Heidelberg (2007)

29. Verdu, S., Wei, V.K.: Explicit construction of optimal constant-weight codes for identification via channels. IEEE Transactions on Information Theory 39(1), 30–36 (1993)

30. Weis, S.A., Sarma, S.E., Rivest, R.L., Engels, D.W.: Security and privacy aspects of low-cost radio frequency identification systems. In: Hutter, D., Müller, G., Stephan, W., Ullmann, M. (eds.) Security in Pervasive Computing. LNCS, vol. 2802, pp. 201–212. Springer, Heidelberg (2004)

A   Formal Definition of Privacy

The definition given in [28] follows.

Definition 6. *A* **blinded** *adversary uses simulated oracles instead of the oracles* LAUNCH, SENDVERIFIER, SENDCLD *and* RESULT. *Simulations are made using an algorithm called a* **blinder** *denoted* $\mathcal{B}$.

To simulate oracles, a blinder has access neither to the provers secrets nor to the secret parameters KV_s. We denote $\mathcal{A}^{\mathcal{O}}$ the algorithm $\mathcal{A}$ when executed using legitimate oracles and $\mathcal{A}^{\mathcal{B}}$ the algorithm $\mathcal{A}$ when executed using the blinder.

Definition 7. *An adversary is* **trivial** *if there exists a blinder* $\mathcal{B}$ *such that the difference*

$$\left| \Pr\left[\mathcal{A}^{\mathcal{O}} \text{ wins}\right] - \Pr\left[\mathcal{A}^{\mathcal{B}} \text{ wins}\right] \right|$$

is negligible.

Hence, to prove privacy, it suffices to prove that an adversary cannot distinguish between the outputs of the blinder $\mathcal{B}$ and outputs made by legitimate oracles. As stated in [28], this definition of privacy is more general than anonymity and untraceability. To the different kinds of adversaries enumerated above correspond accordingly as many notions of privacy.

Note that CORRUPT queries are considered to always leak information on the CLDs' identity. For instance, an adversary can systematically open CLDs in order to track them. In this model, such an adversary is considered as a trivial one because a blinded adversary will succeed in the same way, as the CORRUPT oracle is not simulated. Strong privacy is defined only to ensure that CLDs cannot be tracked using their outputs even if their secrets are known.

B   Security Proofs

B.1   Security against Impersonation

Proposition 3. *Assume* $\sqrt{q} \geq M \geq e\sqrt{\frac{n}{k}}$ *and* $T < M^2 k$. *In our scheme, given a non-corrupted CLD, an adversary cannot impersonate a verifier to interrogate this specific CLD, without replaying an eavesdropped transcript, except with probability* $\frac{1}{q}$.

Proof. To interrogate a CLD, the only useful information for an adversary are the requests made by the verifier. Proposition 1 implies that this does not give an efficient solution to the adversary for obtaining information on one identifier.

Hence, the remaining solution to interrogate a CLD is to try at random to initiate a communication without prior knowledge of its identifier. The question is what is the probability to succeed out of a random couple (j, a)? If a specific CLD with identifier p is targeted, this probability is equal to $\Pr\left[p(\alpha_j) = a\right] = \frac{1}{q}$.
□

Proposition 4. *Assume $\sqrt{q} \geq M \geq e\sqrt{\frac{n}{k}}$ and $T < M^2 k$. Our scheme is secure against impersonation of a CLD, i.e. an adversary will fail with probability $1 - \frac{1}{q}$.*

Proof. As stated in the previous proposition, impersonation of a verifier is not possible except with probability $\frac{1}{q}$ and an adversary would need to succeed at least k times to reconstruct the p' polynomial of a CLD. Moreover, eavesdropping the devices responses does not give a solution to reconstruct an identifier or to obtain information on an identifier, as stated in Proposition 1. Furthermore corruption is not useful here as identifiers are not correlated between CLDs (following Definition 4, the adversary is not allowed to impersonate a corrupted CLD). The best choice for an adversary is thus to try at random.   □

B.2   Privacy

Proposition 5. *Assume $\sqrt{q} \geq M \geq e\sqrt{\frac{n}{k}}$ and $T < M^2 k$, then our scheme is weak private.*

Proof. We first prove the narrow-weak privacy; then, Lemma 1 together with Proposition 4 enables us to conclude. It is clear that all oracles are easy to simulate except SENDCLD and SENDVERIFIER (RESULT is not simulated in the narrow case). Concerning the latter, SENDVERIFIER is used to generate an interrogation request; it is simulated simply by sending a random value. As PR instances are not distinguishable from random sequences (cf. [15]), an adversary cannot distinguish the requests from non-simulated ones.

Concerning SENDCLD, the simulator needs to simulate the output of a CLD. For this, it can answer only on average to one request over M with a random value. As the adversary cannot impersonate a verifier, he cannot determine if a CLD is answering when beckoned or not. He cannot either distinguish the answered values from PR instances as above.   □

RFID Distance Bounding Multistate Enhancement

Gildas Avoine[1], Christian Floerkemeier[2], and Benjamin Martin[1]

[1] Université catholique de Louvain
Information Security Group
B-1348 Louvain-la-Neuve, Belgium
[2] Massachusetts Institute of Technology
Auto-ID Labs
Cambridge, MA 02139, USA

Abstract. Distance bounding protocols aim at avoiding relay attacks during an authentication process. Such protocols are especially important in RFID, where mounting a relay attack between a low-capability prover and a remote verifier is a realistic threat. Several distance bounding protocols suitable for RFID have been recently suggested, all of which aim to reduce the adversary's success probability and the number of rounds executed within the protocol. Peinado et al. introduced an efficient distance bounding protocol that uses the concept of void challenges. We present in this paper a generic technique called *MUltiState Enhancement* that is based on a more efficient use of void challenges. MUSE significantly improves the performances of the already-published distance bounding protocols and extends the void challenges to *p*-symbols.

Keywords: RFID, Authentication, Mafia fraud, Distance bounding.

1 Introduction

Radio Frequency IDentification (RFID) is a well-known technology that is used to identify or authenticate objects or subjects wirelessly. RFID systems consist of transponders called *tags*, and transceivers called *readers*. The proliferation of RFID technology during the last decades results from the decreasing cost and size of the tags and the increased volume in which they are deployed. Most of RFID systems deployed today are *passive*, meaning that the RFID tags do not carry a battery and harvest the power of the carrier wave generated by the RFID reader.

The capabilities of the tags are restricted and application-dependent. For example, a 10-cent tag only transmits a short unique identifier upon reception of a reader's request, while a 2-euro tag such as those used in electronic passports has an embedded microprocessor. The latter is able to perform cryptographic operations within a reasonable time period. Those in current electronic passports are typically able to compute RSA-1024 signatures. RFID tags are often also used in applications such as mass transportation, building access control, and event ticketing. In such applications, the computation capabilities of the tag rely on

B. Roy and N. Sendrier (Eds.): INDOCRYPT 2009, LNCS 5922, pp. 290–307, 2009.

wired logic only. Computations are thus restricted but, nevertheless, the tags allow for on-the-fly encryption of a few thousand bits. Strong security can thus also be achieved with tags that offer mid-range computational resources.

While identification is the primary purpose of RFID, authentication via an RFID tag is an important application. The common RFID-friendly authentication protocols implemented in practice are usually based on the ISO/IEC 9798 standard. Although these protocols are secure in a classical cryptographic model, they are susceptible to *Mafia fraud* [4]. This attack, presented by Desmedt, Goutier, and Bengio at Crypto 1987, actually defeats any authentication protocol because the adversary passes the authentication by relaying the messages between the legitimate verifier (in our case the reader) and the legitimate prover (in our case the tag). Mafia fraud is a major security issue for RFID systems, precisely because the tags answer to any query from a reader without the consent or awareness of their tag owner.

As illustrated by Avoine and Tchamkerten in [1], Mafia fraud may have a real impact in our daily lives. To illustrate the problem, the authors considered an RFID-based theater ticketing system. To buy a ticket, the customer needs to stay in the field of the ticket machine during the transaction. The presence of the customer in the vicinity of the machine is an implicit agreement of the transaction. Now, let's assume there is a line of customers waiting for a ticket. Bob and Charlie are the adversaries: Bob is at the end of the queue, close to the victim Alice, and Charlie is in front of the ticketing machine. When the machine initiates the transaction with Charlie, the latter transmits the received signal to Bob who transmits it in turn to Alice. Alice's card automatically replies to Bob and the signal is sent from Bob to the machine through Charlie. The transaction is thus transparently relayed between Alice and the machine.

Mafia fraud is not caught by the classical cryptographic models because it comprises a relay of the low-layer signal without any attempt to tamper with the carried information. Thwarting relay attacks can thus not only rely on cryptographic measures, but requires the evaluation of the distance between the prover and the verifier. This must be done without significantly increasing the required capabilities of the RFID tags, which eliminates computationally or resource intensive approaches, such as the use of global positioning systems. To decide whether the prover is in the neighborhood of the verifier, a common approach consists for the latter to measure the round trip time (RTT) of a message transmitted from the verifier to the prover, and then back from the prover to the verifier. Assuming that the signal propagation speed is known, the prover can define $\Delta t_{\max}$ that is the maximum expected RTT including propagation and processing delays. An RTT less than $\Delta t_{\max}$ demonstrates that the prover necessarily stays in the verifier's neighborhood.

The work presented in this paper is based on the 3-state approach introduced by Munilla, Ortiz, and Peinado [8,9]. Our contribution is three-fold. We show that, based on the assumptions provided in [8,9], the 3-state approach can be significantly improved, i.e., the number of rounds in the protocol can be reduced while maintaining the same security level. We then generalize the 3-state approach and introduce the generic concept of *multistate* that improves all existing distance bounding protocols. We demonstrate the effectiveness of our solution by applying it to some well-known protocols.

In Section 2, we introduce some background related to distance bounding, especially the protocols designed by Hancke and Kuhn [5] on one hand, and by Munilla and Peinado [9] on the other hand. In Section 3 our 3-state enhancement is presented, followed in Section 4 by its generalization to the p-state case. We show in Section 5 that the case $p = 4$ provides a fair trade-off between security and practicability, and analyze it when it is applied to the most common distance bounding protocols.

2   Primer on Distance Bounding

In this section, some background about RTT-based distance bounding protocols are provided. We present Hancke and Kuhn's protocol (HK) [5], then Munilla and Peinado's protocol (MP) [8,9] is detailed. The latter improves HK using the concept of *void challenges*.

As stated in [4], the measurement of the RTT should not be noised by arbitrary processing delays, including delays due to cryptographic operations. It is suggested in [4] that (a) $\Delta t_{\max}$ is computed from the speed of light, (b) each message used for the RTT measurement contains only one bit, and (c) there are no other computation processed during the measurement of the round trip time. These assumptions still apply today and are the foundations of all the published distance bounding protocols for RFID [1,2,3,5,6,7,10,11,12,13]. The protocol originally suggested by Munilla, Ortiz, and Peinado [8,9] is an exception in that it considers messages carrying three states: 0, 1, or *void*.

2.1   Hancke and Kuhn's Protocol

The HK protocol [5], depicted in Figure 1, is a key-reference protocol in terms of distance bounding devoted to RFID systems. HK is a simple and fast protocol, but it suffers from a high adversary success probability.

Initialization. The prover (P) and the verifier (V) share a secret x and agree on (a) a security parameter n, (b) a public pseudo random function H whose output size is $2n$, and (c) a given timing bound $\Delta t_{\max}$.

Protocol. HK consists of two phases: a slow one followed by a fast one. During the slow phase V generates a random nonce N_V and sends it to P. Reciprocally, P generates N_P and sends it to V. V and P then both compute $H^{2n} := H(x, N_P, N_V)$. In what follows, H_i $(1 \le i \le 2n)$ denotes the ith bit of H^{2n}, and $H_i \ldots H_j$ $(1 \le i < j \le 2n)$ denotes the concatenation of the bits from H_i to H_j. Then V and P split H^{2n} into two registers of length n: $R^0 := H_1 \ldots H_n$ and $R^1 := H_{n+1} \ldots H_{2n}$. The fast phase then consists of n rounds. In each of the rounds, V picks a random bit c_i (the challenge) and sends it to P. The latter immediately answers $r_i := R_i^{c_i}$ that is the ith bit of the register R^{c_i}.

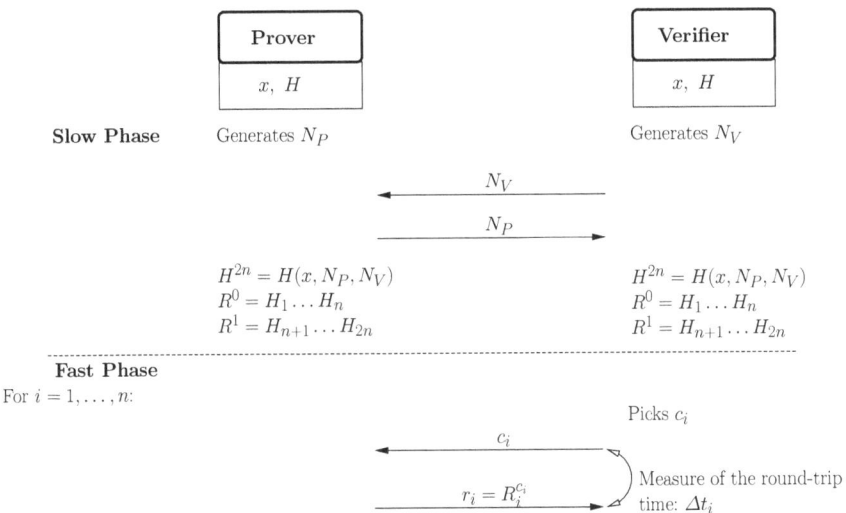

Fig. 1. Hancke and Kuhn's protocol

Verification. At the end of the fast phase, the verifier checks that the answers received from the prover are correct and that: $\forall\, i, 1 \leq i \leq n,\ \Delta t_i \leq \Delta t_{\max}$..

Computation of the adversary success probability. The best known attack is based on querying the tag with n 1-bit challenges between the slow and fast phases in order to obtain a full register. Without loss of generality, we can assume that the adversary obtains R^0 sending only 1-bit challenges equal to zero. Afterwards, when she tries to trick the reader, two cases occurs: (a) if $c_i = 0$ she definitely knows the right answer, (b) if $c_i = 1$, she has no clue about the right answer but she can try to guess it with probability $\frac{1}{2}$. Thereby, the adversary success probability, as explained in [5], is:

$$P_{\text{HK}} = \left(\frac{3}{4}\right)^n.\tag{1}$$

2.2   Munilla and Peinado's Protocol

In order to decrease the adversary success probability of HK, Munilla and Peinado [8,9] introduce the concept of void challenges. The basic idea is that challenges can be 0, 1, or *void*, where *void* means that no challenge is sent. Prover and verifier agree on which challenges should be *void*. Upon reception of 0 or 1 while a *void* challenge was expected, the prover detects the attack and gives up the protocol. Figure 2 describes MP.

Initialization. The prover (P) and the verifier (V) share a secret x and agree on (a) a security parameter n, (b) a public pseudo random function H whose output size is $4n$, and (c) a given timing bound $\Delta t_{\max}$.

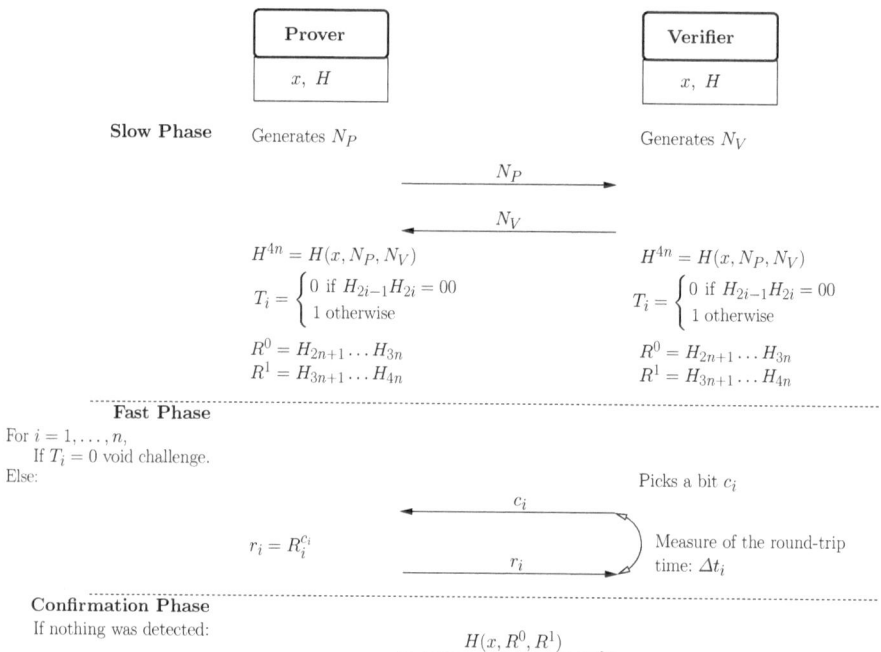

Fig. 2. Munilla and Peinado's protocol

Protocol. As with HK, V and P exchange nonces N_V and N_P. From these values, they compute $H^{4n} = H(x, N_P, N_V)$. $2n$ bits are used to generate a n-bit register T as follows: if $H_{2i-1}H_{2i} = 00$, 01, or 10 then $T_i = 1$, otherwise $T_i = 0$. Each T_i decides whether c_i is a void challenge ($T_i = 0$) or not ($T_i = 1$). In the latter case, c_i will be either 0 or 1, and will be called a *full* challenge. The $2n$ remaining bits are used to generate the two registers $R^0 = H_{2n+1} \ldots H_{3n}$ and $R^1 = H_{3n+1} \ldots H_{4n}$ as done by HK. Upon termination of the fast phase, if the prover did not detect any attack, he sends $H(x, R^0, R^1)$ to the verifier.

Verification. The verifier checks that the received $H(x, R^0, R^1)$ is correct, i.e, the prover did not detect an attack. Then the verifier checks the Δt_is and all the values r_is as it is done in HK.

Computation of the adversary success probability. In what follows, p_f denotes the probability that $T_i = 1$ ($1 \leq i \leq n$), i.e., a full challenge is expected in the ith round of the protocol. The adversary success probability clearly depends on p_f. It is shown in [9] that the optimal adversary success probability is obtained when $p_f = \frac{3}{5}$. However, obtaining such a probability is not trivial because T is obtained from the output of the random function H. Consequently, Munilla and Peinado suggest to take $p_f = \frac{3}{4}$, which is close to $\frac{3}{5}$ and easier to generate from H.

To compute the success probability of an adversary, one must know that an adversary may consider two strategies. The first strategy relies on the adversary querying the prover before the fast phase starts. In the second one, the adversary does not query the prover at all. In HK, it was clear that the best adversary's strategy was to query the prover in advance. In MP, the problem is more difficult because the prover aborts the protocol when he receives a challenge while expecting a void one.

In the case where the adversary does not ask in advance, the adversary succeeds if no void challenge appears and if he guesses the challenge. The probability is equal to $p_{\text{ask}} = \left(p_f \cdot \frac{3}{4}\right)^n$.

On the other side, without asking the tag in advance, $p_{noask} = \sum_{i=0}^{i=n} p(i) \cdot \left(\frac{1}{2}\right)^i$,

where $p(i)$ is the probability that exactly i full challenge appears. This latter is equal to $p(i) = \binom{n}{i} \cdot p_f^i \cdot (1 - p_f)^{(n-i)}$. At last $p_{noask} = \left(1 - \frac{p_f}{2}\right)^n$. When $p_f = \frac{3}{4}$ the adversary chooses the no-asking strategy and his success probability is:

$$P_{\text{MP}} = \left(\frac{5}{8}\right)^n. \tag{2}$$

3   MUSE-3 HK

MP is designed such that the prover always sends a void answer upon reception of a void challenge. We prove below that this approach does not exploit the full potential of the 3-state message approach. We also introduce an improvement which decreases the adversary success probability while the number of exchanged messages remains unchanged. This new protocol, called MUSE-3 HK, is an improvement over the 3-state message approach of HK. Throughout this paper, given a protocol $\mathcal{P}$, we denote by MUSE-p $\mathcal{P}$, the enhancement of $\mathcal{P}$ with p-state messages, where MUSE stands for MUltiState Enhancement.

In MUSE-3 HK, the initialization and verification steps do not differ from HK. We restrict our description of the core step which differs from the HK approach.

Protocol. Our enhancement is just like in MP [9] based on the introduction of 3-state messages rather than binary messages. However, in our approach the three states are not used in the same way. 0,1 and the void state are no longer treated differently and we simply refer to them as a 3-*symbol*. We denote these 3-symbols by $\{0, 1, 2\}$. Throughout this paper, given a protocol MUSE-p $\mathcal{P}$, we refer to a p-*symbol* as one of the p different p-states. We denote, by $\{0, \ldots, p-1\}$, the set of these p-symbols.

As with HK and MP, V and P exchange nonces N_V and N_P. From these values, they compute a bit string $H(x, N_P, N_V)$. We will discuss the length of $H(x, N_P, N_V)$ in a following section. With this bit string $H(x, N_P, N_V)$, they generate $3n$ 3-symbols $\{S_1, \ldots, S_{3n}\}$. These 3-symbols are used to fill up three registers R^0, R^1 and R^2. In fact, each one of the three registers R^j contains n 3-symbols $\{S_{j+1}, \ldots, S_{j+n}\}$.

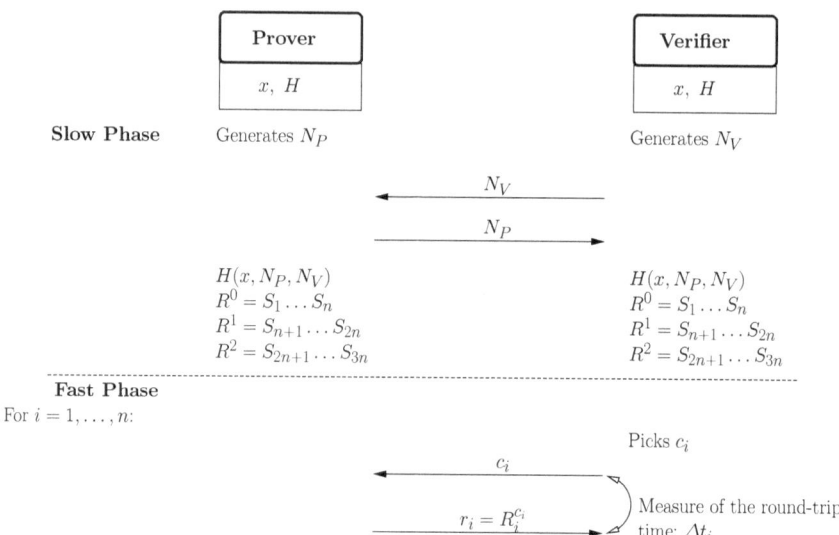

Fig. 3. Hancke and Kuhn's protocol with MUSE-3

After the fast phase begins, the verifier picks at random c_i from $\{0, 1, 2\}$ and sends it to the prover. The prover immediately answers $r_i = R_i^{c_i}$. Figure 3 illustrates this protocol.

Computation of the adversary success probability. In MUSE-3 HK, the prover is not able to abort the protocol because he has no means to detect an attack. Consequently, the success probability of the adversary is always higher when she queries the prover before the fast phase. In such a case, the adversary obtains one of the three registers, say R^0 without loss of generality. During the fast phase, when the adversary is challenged in a given round by the verifier with the challenge 0, she can definitely provide the right response; otherwise she answers randomly. Thereby, her success probability is $\frac{1}{3} \cdot 1 + \frac{2}{3} \cdot \frac{1}{3} = \frac{5}{9}$, for each round, and the overall probability is so:

$$P_{\text{MUSE-3 HK}} = \left(\frac{5}{9}\right)^n. \qquad (3)$$

From equations (2) and (3), we deduce that MUSE-3 HK performs better than MP: it provides a smaller adversary success probability with neither increasing the number of exchanges, nor adding new assumptions compared to [9]. This behavior can be explained by the fact that in MP the adversary earns some information with the use of void challenges. This leak of information is no longer an issue with MUSE-3, because the three different 3-states are used in an identical way. One may nevertheless stress that MUSE-3 HK needs more memory than MP since 3 registers are required in MUSE-3 HK while 2 registers are enough in MP. In the next section, we generalize the three-state enhancement to the p-state enhancement and analyze both success probability and memory consumption.

4 MUSE-p HK

4.1 Hancke and Kuhn's Protocol with MUSE-p

In this section, we consider MUSE-p HK, where $p \geq 2$. The new protocol, which generalizes MUSE-3 HK, is similar to it except that it uses:

- p-symbols from $\{0, 1, 2, ..., p-1\}$,
- p registers containing n p-symbols,
- challenges and answers are p-symbols.

There is a perfect match between MUSE-2 HK and HK, when $p = 2$, .

4.2 Computation of the Adversary Success Probability

In the case of HK, two different attacks strategies exist: to either query or not query the tag in advance. If the adversary chooses to not ask in advance, at each round she tries a response at random, so her success probability is $\left(\frac{1}{p}\right)^n$. Therefore, the best strategy for the adversary to perform a Mafia fraud when HK is used consists in querying the prover with some arbitrary bits before the fast phase starts. In MUSE-p HK, the same strategy is used, i.e., the adversary queries the prover with some random p-symbols obtaining thus one register of size n of a total of p registers. Without loss of generality, we assume that the adversary obtains R^0. When the adversary is challenged with 0, she is definitely able to provide the right answer, otherwise she correctly answers with probability $1/p$. We deduce the overall success probability of the adversary (depicted in Figure 4) as being:

$$P_{\text{MUSE-}p\ \text{HK}} = \left(\frac{2p-1}{p^2}\right)^n. \tag{4}$$

4.3 Generation of the Registers

We assume that the prover – in our framework, an RFID tag – is not able to directly generate and store p-symbols. Consequently, he must generate the symbols using a hash function that outputs bits only. The same problem occurs for the storage: the memory needed to store one p-symbol is $\lceil \log_2(p) \rceil$ bits. In other words, real p-symbols exist in practice only during their transit on the channel.

In order to generate the p-symbols, an arbitrary set $\mathcal{A} \subseteq \mathbb{F}_{2^{\lceil \log_2(p) \rceil}}$ is defined, such that the cardinality of $\mathcal{A}$ is equal to p i.e., $\mathcal{A}$ consists of p combinations of $\lceil \log_2(p) \rceil$ bits. Then the prover uses the following deterministic technique: firstly, he defines a bijection between the set $\{0, \ldots, p-1\}$ of p-symbols and $\mathcal{A}$. Secondly, he generates a stream of bits and regroups them by blocks of $\lceil \log_2(p) \rceil$ bits. A block belonging to $\mathcal{A}$ supplies one p-symbol; otherwise it is dropped.

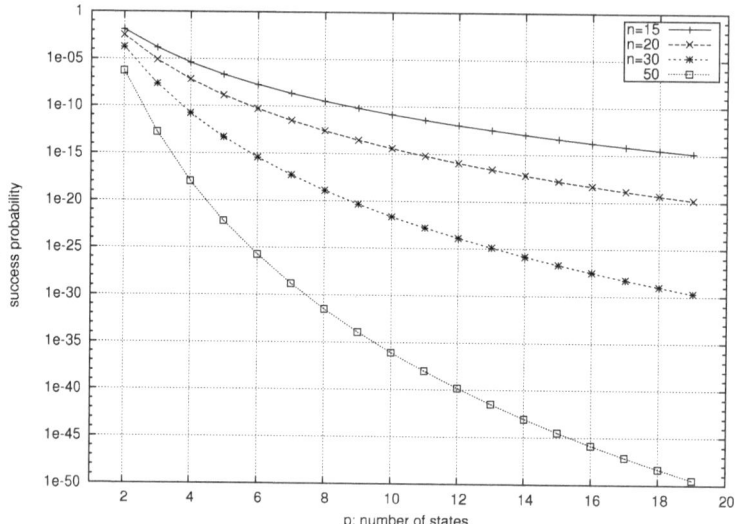

Fig. 4. Success probability for the Mafia fraud depending on the number of states

Let q be the probability of picking a given element of $\mathcal{A}$. Clearly, $\mathcal{A}$ is included in the set of all possible combinations of $\lceil \log_2(p) \rceil$ bits. Given that there is $2^{\lceil \log_2(p) \rceil}$ such combinations, we conclude that q is equal to $\frac{p}{2^{\lceil \log_2(p) \rceil}}$.

We now define A_i the event of picking an element of $\mathcal{A}$ at the ith draw. If this event happens, it means that the $(i-1)$th first draws failed (no element of $\mathcal{A}$ has been picked), and the ith succeeded (an element of $\mathcal{A}$ has been picked). As the draws are independent, we had shown that $P(A_i) = (1-q)^{i-1}q$. According to these observations, we deduce that $P(A_i)$ follows a geometric distribution. So the expectation of $P(A_i)$ (i.e., the average number of bit blocks of length $\lceil \log_2(p) \rceil$ needed to pick an element of $\mathcal{A}$) is $\frac{1}{q}$.

Thanks to the previous results we know that we need $\frac{1}{q} \cdot \lceil \log_2(p) \rceil$ bits to create a p-symbol. In order to filling up a register, n p-symbols have to be picked. At last the average number of bits to be generated in order to obtain a full register of n p-symbols is not $n \cdot \lceil \log_2(p) \rceil$ but:

$$n \cdot \lceil \log_2(p) \rceil \cdot \frac{2^{\lceil \log_2(p) \rceil}}{p}.$$

4.4 Memory Consumption

From a theoretical point of view, using MUSE allows to decrease the adversary success probability towards zero by increasing the value p. However the increase of p is bounded by the memory. So, if n is the number of rounds, HK needs to store $2n$ bits, MP $4n$ bits, and MUSE-p HK $np\lceil \log_2(p) \rceil$ bits. Figure 5 depicts the memory consumption given n and p. We see that memory grows quickly with the number of states. Large values of p are thus not realistic in practice. Moreover, in

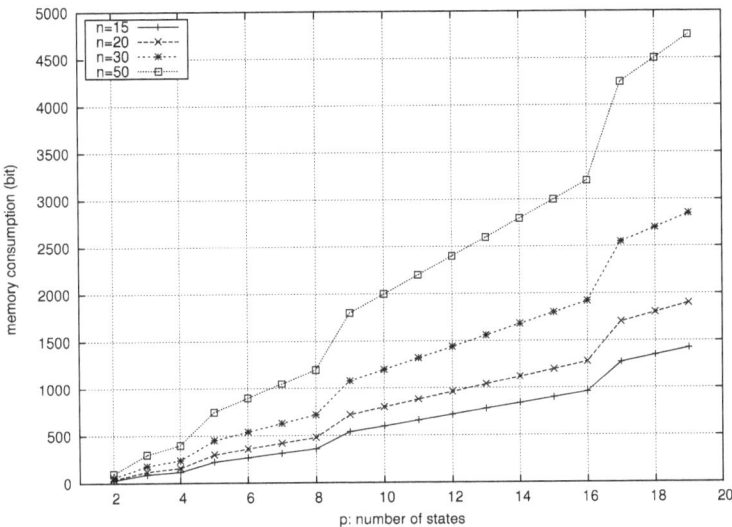

Fig. 5. Number of bits depending on the number of states

order to optimize the memory consumption, and the generation of the registers, and so ease the implementation, p has to be a power of two. Consequently, in Section 5 we provide an analysis of the performance of MUSE when $p = 4$. This is a good candidate because it is a small power of two which allows us to have a good trade-off between memory consumption, number of rounds and adversary success probability. Such a choice for p avoids the problem of generating symbols for the registers, because all of the 2-bits combinations represent a 4-symbol.

5   MUSE-4 Applied to Some Protocols

In this section, we apply MUSE-4 to some well-known distance bounding protocols and compare their performances with their original form.

5.1   Hancke and Kuhn

We begin by analyzing the performance of MUSE-4 HK with respect to memory and adversary's success probability. We then compare the results with the performances of the original HK, MUSE-3 HK, and MP.

Since MUSE-4 HK is a special case of MUSE-p HK analyzed in Section 4, the evaluation of the performances is trivial. From Section 4.4, we know that MUSE-4 HK requires the tag to store $4n$ bits where n is the number of rounds and from formula (4), we get:

$$P_{\text{MUSE-4 HK}} = \left(\frac{7}{16}\right)^n. \tag{5}$$

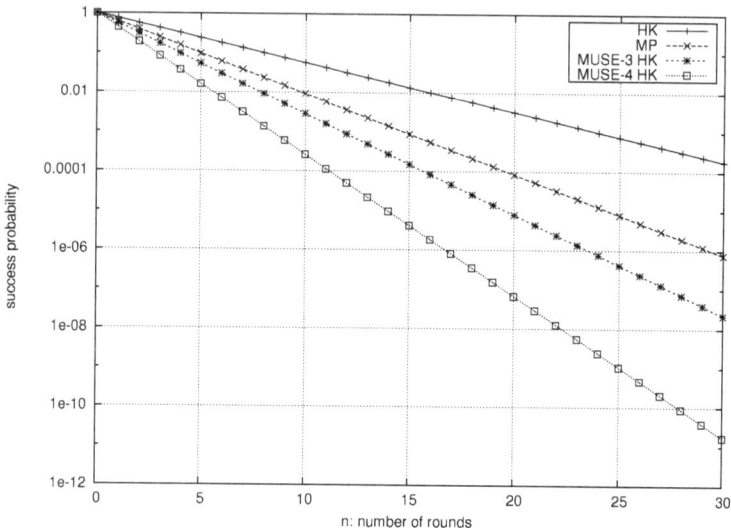

Fig. 6. Adversary's success probability

Table 1. Memory consumption, number of rounds, and adversary success probability

	HK		MP		MUSE-3 HK		MUSE-4 HK	
Probability	Memory	Rounds	Memory	Rounds	Memory	Rounds	Memory	Rounds
10^{-2}	32	16	36	9	42	7	40	5
10^{-4}	64	32	76	19	90	15	88	11
10^{-6}	94	47	116	29	138	23	128	16
10^{-8}	128	64	156	39	186	31	176	22
10^{-10}	160	80	192	48	234	39	216	27

The adversary success probabilities of HK, MP, MUSE-3 HK and MUSE-4 HK are respectively given in equations (1), (2),(3), and (5). Figure 6 shows that MUSE-4 HK clearly decreases the number of rounds of the protocol compared to HK, MUSE-3 HK, and MP, for any fixed adversary's success probability.

Figure 7 depicts the memory consumption according to the number of rounds. It shows that MUSE consumes more memory than the original versions of the protocols, but the loss is partly compensated by the reduced number of rounds. In particular, one may notice that MUSE-4 uses the memory optimally compared to MUSE-3 because 3 is not a power of 2. Table 1 summarizes our analysis for different values of adversary's success probability. It points out that MUSE-4 HK performs better than all the other candidates. For example, HK needs 32 fast phase rounds to get an adversary's success probability as low as 10^{-4}, while MUSE-4 HK needs only 11 rounds to reach the same security level.

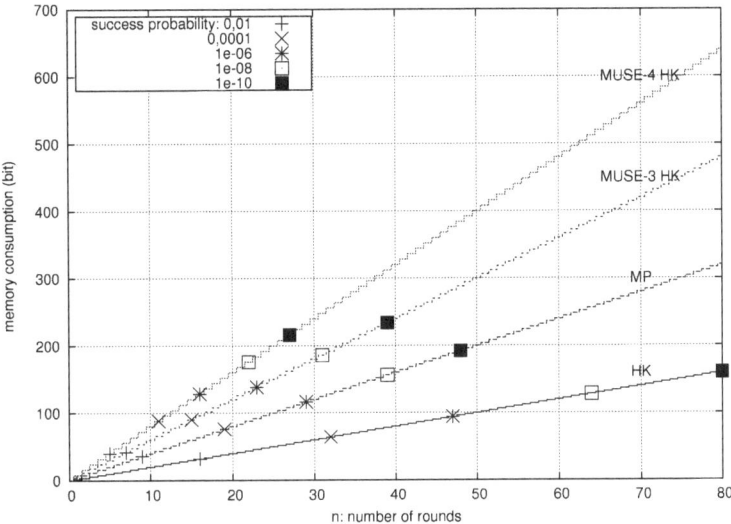

Fig. 7. Memory consumption and success probability according to the number of rounds

5.2 Kim and Avoine

Kim and Avoine's protocol (KA) [6] basically relies on *predefined* challenges. Predefined challenges allow the prover to detect that an attack occurs. However, contrarily to MP, the prover does not abort the protocol upon detection of an attack, but sends random responses to the adversary. The concept of the predefined challenges works as follows: the prover and the verifier agree on some predefined 1-bit challenges; if the adversary sends in advance a challenge to the prover that is different from the expected predefined challenge, then the prover detects the attack. The complete description of KA is provided below.

Initialization. The prover (P) and the verifier (V) share a secret x and agree on (a) a security parameter n, (b) a public pseudo random function H whose output size is $4n$, and (c) a given timing bound $\Delta t_{\max}$ and summarized in Figure 8.

Protocol. As previously, V and P exchange nonces N_P and N_V. From these values they compute $H^{4n} = H(x, N_P, N_V)$, and split it in four registers: $R^0 := H_1 \ldots H_n$ and $R^1 := H_{n+1} \ldots H_{2n}$ are the potential responses; the register $D := H_{3n+1} \ldots H_{4n}$ constitutes the potential predefined challenges; finally, the register $T := H_{2n+1} \ldots H_{3n}$ allows the verifier (resp. prover) to decide whether a predefined challenge should be sent (resp. received): in round i, if $T_i = 1$ then a random challenge is sent; if $T_i = 0$ then the predefined challenge D_i is sent instead of a random one.

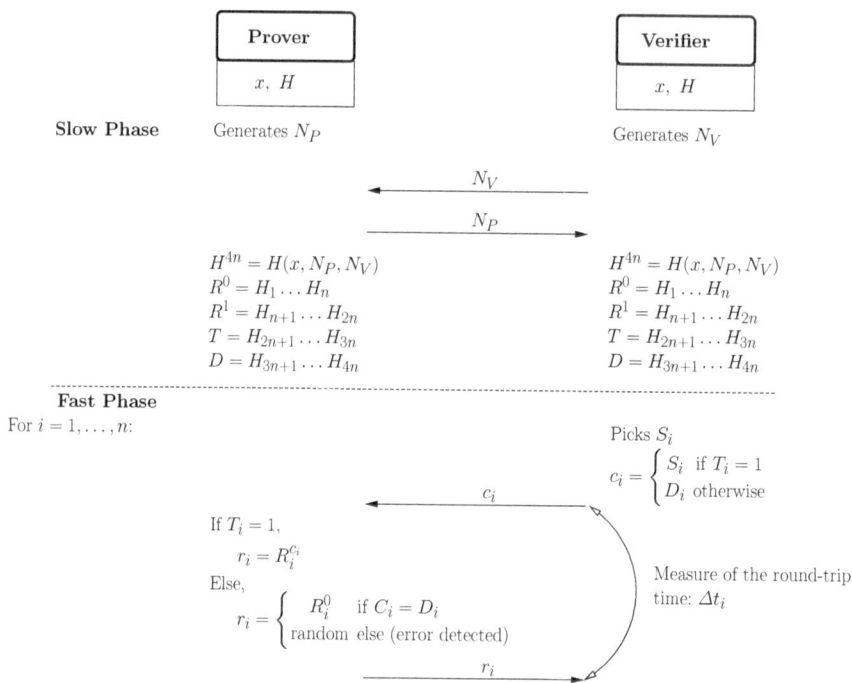

Fig. 8. Kim and Avoine's protocol

Verification. At the end of the fast phase, the verifier checks that the answers received from the prover are correct and that: $\forall\, i, i \in \{1, \ldots, n\}$, $\Delta t_i \leq \Delta t_{\max}$.

MUSE-4 KA. Applying MUSE to KA does not significantly modify the protocol. Except that R^0, R^1, two additional registers R^2, R^3, and D contain 4-symbols instead of bits, the basic principle of KA remains unchanged. In order to create these registers, $11n$ random bits must be generated instead of $4n$ for KA: $R^j = H_{2jn+1} \ldots H_{2n(j+1)}$ for $j \in \{0, 1, 2, 3\}$, $T = H_{8n+1} \ldots H_{9n}$, and $D = H_{9n+1} \ldots H_{11n}$. During the fast phase, the only difference between KA and MUSE-4 KA is that in the latter case the verifier (resp. prover) sends 4-symbol challenges (resp. responses) instead of binary challenges (resp. responses).

Comparison. In what follows, p_r is the probability that $T_i = 1$, i.e., a random challenge is expected in the ith rounds of the protocol. In the original paper [6], an adversary can choose to ask or not to ask the tag in advance. If she does not ask in advance, her success probability is $\left(\frac{1}{2}\right)^n$ for the original protocol, and it is $\left(\frac{1}{4}\right)^n$ with MUSE-4. If the adversary queries the tag in advance, the cumulated probability of not being detected by the reader in the ith round is

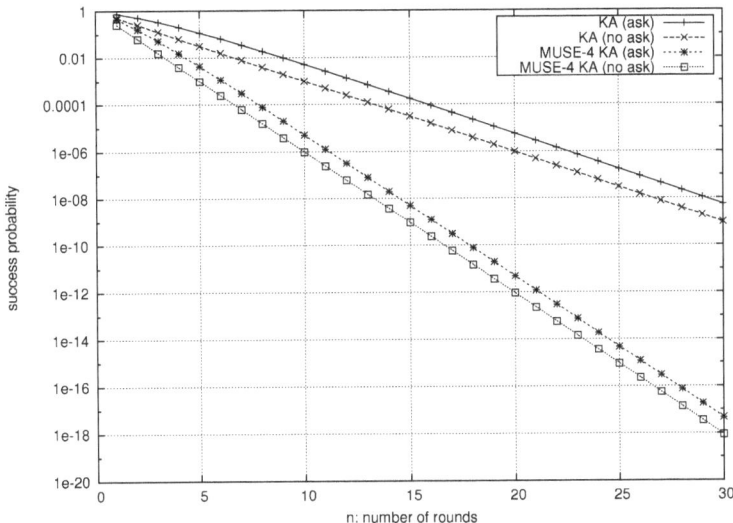

Fig. 9. Adversary's success probability when $p_r = 1/2$

Table 2. Memory consumption, number of rounds, and adversary success probability, when $p_r = 1/2$

	KA		MUSE-4 KA	
Probability	Memory	Rounds	Memory	Rounds
10^{-2}	48	12	66	6
10^{-4}	76	19	99	9
10^{-6}	88	22	121	11
10^{-8}	116	29	154	14
10^{-10}	140	35	187	17

$\frac{1}{2} + \frac{1}{4} \cdot \left(\frac{1}{2} + \frac{1}{2} \cdot p_r\right)^{i-1}$. With MUSE-4, and following the same computations as done in [6], we find that the cumulated probability of not being detected by the reader in the ith round is:

$$\frac{1}{4} + \frac{3}{16} \cdot \left(\frac{1}{4} + \frac{3}{4} \cdot p_r\right)^{i-1}.$$

Figure 9 shows how the adversary's success probability evolves, depending on the number of rounds, when $p_r = 1/2$.

As previously explained with HK, MUSE-4 KA requires the tag to store more bits than KA per round (11 bits instead of 4 per round). However, this drawback is partly compensated by the fact that MUSE-4 KA reduces the number of rounds, and so the total required memory. Table 2 points out that MUSE-4 divides by 2 the number of rounds when used with KA, while keeping the same security level.

5.3   Brands and Chaum

Brands and Chaum's protocol (BC) [2] is the earliest distance bounding protocol. BC is the protocol that provides the lowest adversary success probability for a given number of rounds that is $\left(\frac{1}{2}\right)^n$. This nice property is explained by the fact that BC requires a final signature after the fast phase of the protocol, as described below and summarized in Figure 10.

Initialization. The prover and the verifier share a secret x and agree on (a) a security parameter n, (b) a commit scheme, and (c) a given timing bound $\Delta t_{\max}$.

Protocol. Both of the prover and the verifier generate n bits, c_i for the verifier and m_i for the prover. Then the prover commits on n bits m_i using a secure commitment scheme. Afterwards, the fast phase begins. The verifier sends c_i to prover. The latter immediately answers $r_i = c_i \oplus m_i$. Once the n rounds are completed, an additional phase, called the *authentication phase* is executed: the prover opens the commitment, concatenates the $2n$ bits c_i and r_i into m, and signs it with his secret x.

Verification. After the commitment opening the verifier checks that the r_is are those he expected. Then he computes m in the same way than the prover did, and verifies that the signature is valid and that no adversary have changed the challenges or the responses. He finally checks that: $\forall\, i, 1 \leq i \leq n, \Delta t_i \leq \Delta t_{\max}$.

MUSE-4 BC. When using MUSE-4 BC, prover and verifier must each generate n 4-symbols, that is $2n$ bits: instead of picking some bits, they pick at random the m_i for the prover, and the c_i for the verifier in $\{0, 1, 2, 3\}$. The commit is done as usual, but the m_i are no longer encoded on one bit but on two bits.

For the fast phase, r_i is still equal to $c_i + m_i$, except that the is done modulo 4 instead of modulo 2.

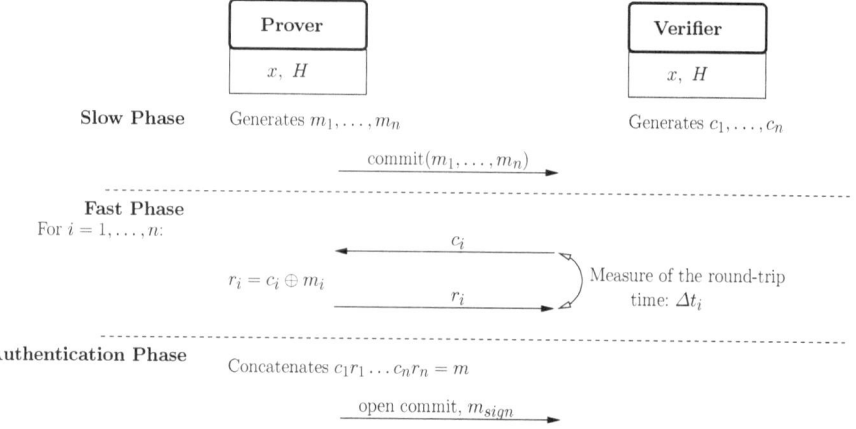

Fig. 10. Brands and Chaum's protocol

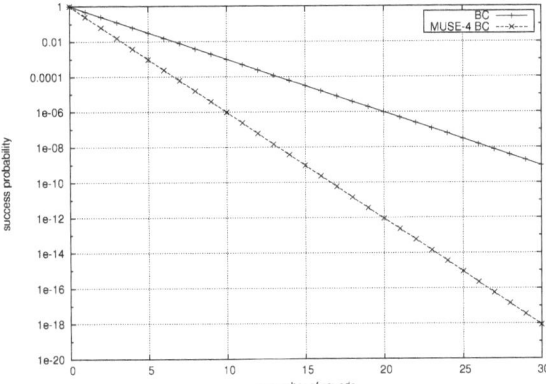

Fig. 11. Adversary success probability depending on the number of rounds for BC

For the authentication phase, the length of m is $4n$ bits: we have to map $\mathbb{F}_4$ on $\mathbb{F}_2 \times \mathbb{F}_2$. Afterwards the prover can send the signed bit-string.

Comparison. The use of MUSE-4 highly decreases the adversary success probability. For the original protocol [2], it is:

$$P_{\mathrm{BC}} = \left(\frac{1}{2}\right)^n. \tag{6}$$

This probability is explained by the fact that the adversary fails as soon as she sends a wrong challenge to the prover, due to the final signature. With MUSE-4, the adversary succeeds with probability $\frac{1}{4}$ at each round instead of $\frac{1}{2}$. We so obtain:

$$P_{\mathrm{MUSE\text{-}4\ BC}} = \left(\frac{1}{4}\right)^n. \tag{7}$$

Formulas (6) and (7), represented in Figure 11, point out the advantage of MUSE-4 BC over the original BC. Table 3 shows how the number of rounds and the memory consumption evolve for a given level of security. We can see that in the case of BC, MUSE-4 BC consumes the same memory than the original protocol, while it is twice faster.

6   On the Implementability of MUSE

Most RFID protocols in the HF and UHF frequency bands use amplitude modulation between two different states for signalling between reader and tag. For the reader-to-tag channel, the signal is typically modulated between one level that represents the carrier-wave amplitude and an attenuated level. Pulse duration coding where the duration for which the signal is attenuated is varied is used to encode two different logical symbols. For the tag-to-reader signaling, the tags

Table 3. Memory consumption, number of rounds and adversary success probability

	BC		MUSE-4 BC	
Probability	Memory	Rounds	Memory	Rounds
0.0156	12	6	12	3
0.0000153	32	16	32	8
$3.81 \cdot 10^{-6}$	36	18	36	9
$1.49 \cdot 10^{-8}$	52	26	52	13
$2.33 \cdot 10^{-10}$	64	32	64	16

either load modulate the reader signal (at LF and HF) or backscatter some of incident electromagnetic wave (UHF). Coding schemes used include Manchester, Miller, and FM0 encoding.

To accommodate MUSE-3, we need to encode three different symbol states on the reader-to-tag and tag-to-reader channel. This can be accomplished by using the existing coding schemes that define logical 0 and logical 1 and interpreting the absence of a modulated signal in the predefined timeslot for either the challenge or the response as the third symbol. This assumes that there is all other tags in the range of the reader will remain silent. Encoding MUSE-p with $p \geq 4$ using the same overall symbol periods require either more than two modulation levels, additional phase modulation or the use of higher bandwidth signals. All of which come at the expense of the signal-to-noise ratio required for reliable decoding of the signals and required complexity of the decoder.

The turn-around-times between reader and tag signaling are typically of the order of a few milliseconds in HF protocols and microseconds in UHF systems. The turn-around-times are needed to allow for the decoding of reader commands in the tag microchip and to reduce noise in the reader receiver circuitry resulting from the modulation of the reader signal. Detecting additional propagation delays resulting from relay attacks over short distances such as a few meters (corresponding to delays of the order of a tens of nanoseconds) will thus be difficult due to the large turn-around-times. In a sophisticated relay attack, the adversary can also reduce the processing delays resulting from the decoding of the original reader commands significantly by operating the tag emulator at a higher clock speed. This is possible because the emulated tag can be battery-powered and is thus not constrained by the limited power budget of an ordinary passive tag.

7   Conclusion

We introduced in this paper the concept of p-symbol that extends the void challenges suggested by Munilla, Ortiz, and Peinado, and we provided a generic p-symbol-based technique that behaves better than the original Munilla et al.'s protocol. Our solution, called MUSE, is generic in the sense that it can be used to improve any distance bounding protocols. We provided a formal analysis of MUSE in the general case, and illustrated it when $p = 3$ and $p = 4$.

We definitely believe that distance bounding protocols require further analysis since they form the only countermeasure known today against relay attacks. We are already surrounded by several billion RFID tags and so potential victims of relay attacks, especially when our tags serve as access keys or credit cards. Contactless smartcard manufacturers, and more generally RFID manufacturers, recently understood the strength of relay attacks and the threat for their business.

References

1. Avoine, G., Tchamkerten, A.: An efficient distance bounding RFID authentication protocol: balancing false-acceptance rate and memory requirement. In: Samarati, P., Yung, M., Martinelli, F., Ardagna, C.A. (eds.) ISC 2009. LNCS, vol. 5735, pp. 250–261. Springer, Heidelberg (2009)
2. Brands, S., Chaum, D.: Distance-bounding protocols. In: Helleseth, T. (ed.) EUROCRYPT 1993. LNCS, vol. 765, pp. 344–359. Springer, Heidelberg (1994)
3. Bussard, L., Bagga, W.: Distance-bounding proof of knowledge to avoid real-time attacks. In: SEC, pp. 223–238 (2005)
4. Desmedt, Y., Goutier, C., Bengio, S.: Special uses and abuses of the fiat-shamir passport protocol. In: Pomerance, C. (ed.) CRYPTO 1987. LNCS, vol. 293, pp. 21–39. Springer, Heidelberg (1988)
5. Hancke, G., Kuhn, M.: An RFID distance bounding protocol. In: Conference on Security and Privacy for Emerging Areas in Communication Networks – SecureComm 2005, Athens, Greece. IEEE, Los Alamitos (2005)
6. Kim, C.H., Avoine, G.: RFID distance bounding protocol with mixed challenges to prevent relay attacks. In: Cryptology ePrint Archive, Report 2009/310 (2009)
7. Kim, C.H., Avoine, G., Koeune, F., Standaert, F.-X., Pereira, O.: The Swiss-Knife RFID Distance Bounding Protocol. In: Lee, P.J., Cheon, J.H. (eds.) ICISC 2009. LNCS, vol. 5461, pp. 98–115. Springer, Heidelberg (2009)
8. Munilla, J., Ortiz, A., Peinado, A.: Distance Bounding Protocols with Void-Challenges for RFID. In: Workshop on RFID Security – RFIDSec 2006, Graz, Austria (July 2006) (Ecrypt)
9. Munilla, J., Peinado, A.: Distance Bounding Protocols for RFID Enhanced by using Void-Challenges and Analysis in Noisy Channels. Wireless Communications and Mobile Computing 8(9), 1227–1232 (2008)
10. Nikov, V., Vauclair, M.: Yet Another Secure Distance-Bounding Protocol. Cryptology ePrint Archive, Report 2008/319 (2008), http://eprint.iacr.org/
11. Reid, J., Neito, J.G., Tang, T., Senadji, B.: Detecting relay attacks with timing based protocols. In: Bao, F., Miller, S. (eds.) Proceedings of the 2nd ACM Symposium on Information, Computer and Communications Security – ASIACCS 2007, Singapore, Republic of Singapore, pp. 204–213. ACM, New York (2007)
12. Singelée, D., Preneel, B.: Distance bounding in noisy environments. In: Stajano, F., Meadows, C., Capkun, S., Moore, T. (eds.) ESAS 2007. LNCS, vol. 4572, pp. 101–115. Springer, Heidelberg (2007)
13. Tu, Y.-J., Piramuthu, S.: RFID Distance Bounding Protocols. In: First International EURASIP Workshop on RFID Technology, Vienna, Austria (September 2007)

Two Attacks against the F_f RFID Protocol[*]

Olivier Billet[1] and Kaoutar Elkhiyaoui[2]

[1] Orange Labs, Issy-les-Moulineaux, France
[2] Institut Eurécom, Valbonne, France
billet@eurecom.fr, kaoutar.elkhiyaoui@eurecom.fr

Abstract. This paper investigates a new family of RFID protocols called F_f that grew out of a proposal made at ESORICS 2007. This family has the property of having highly efficient implementations and simultaneously providing some security arguments which shares some features with the HB protocol family. In this work, we exhibit links between the F_f protocol and the LPN problem, and demonstrate two attacks against the F_f family of protocols which run with a time complexity of about 2^{52} and 2^{38} respectively against the instance proposed by the designers that has a 512-bit secret key. Our two attacks have the nice property that they only require interactions with the tag alone and does not involve the reader.

1 Introduction

Radio Frequency IDentifiers (RFID) are tiny electronic tags attached to items that allow them to be identified in an automatic way, without requiring physical access or line of sight. The main incentive to their introduction has been the ease and simplification of the supply chain management, but RFID tags already found a great variety of applications: postal tracking, tickets in transportation networks, airline luggage tracking, counterfeits fighting... The economics behind the above mentioned use-cases requires that RFID tags can be built at a very low cost, which translates into very strong design constraints for security. In particular, the memory available is very limited and the overall number of gates must be lower than a few thousand for most of the applications.

These constraints explain why the first RFID tags basically only hold a unique identifier. This however, posed a security threat as the RFID tags entered more and more into the life of end users, attached to the items they carry around. To solve these security issues, several proposals have been made, with different trade-offs between security and efficiency. As an example, forward-privacy was reached at the expense of embedding hash functions [15], whereas several authors tried to reduce the resources needed by common cryptographic primitives as much as possible: a lightweight block cipher, PRESENT, was proposed in [4], a clever tweak of Rabin's mapping, SQUASH, was introduced in [17]. One line of

---

[*] This work has been supported in part by the French Government through the ANR project RFID-AP.

B. Roy and N. Sendrier (Eds.): INDOCRYPT 2009, LNCS 5922, pp. 308–320, 2009.
© Springer-Verlag Berlin Heidelberg 2009

cryptographic designs that looked very promising is built around the problem of learning parity with noise (LPN) and was initiated by the introduction of the HB protocol [10]. But reaching high security requirements proved to be hard as shown by the cryptanalysis of the members of this family. The HB protocol is secure against passive attackers, but fails against a simple active attack. The HB⁺ protocol introduced in [11] corrected this but succumbed a more subtle active attack [7]. Almost every other proposals were flawed in some way [8], and the most robust proposal to date might be [9].

Although the simplicity of protocols from the HB family and the fact that they build on the LPN hard problem make them very attractive, they have the main drawback of requiring quite long secret keys to be able to reach a given level of security. Some alternatives to the HB family have recently appeared. One of these was introduced by Chichoń, Klonowski, and Kutyłowski in [6] where the secret consists in the knowledge of linear subspaces, but this proposal has been recently broken [12]. Another recent proposal that shares some features with HB-like protocols is the F_f protocol recently proposed in [2] which aims for an implementation that fits about 2kGE for which best known attacks require a time complexity of more than 2^{130}.

In this work, we study the security of the F_f protocol, and exhibit two key-recovery attacks on it. For the parameters chosen by the authors (512-bit secret keys) our best attack runs in time 2^{38}. Moreover, our two attacks only require to query the tag and do not need to interact with the reader. In order to explain our attacks, we first expose the LPN problem and give the best known algorithms to solve it. We then briefly describe the F_f protocol which shares some features with the HB protocol together with its main underlying building block, the f function, very similar in spirit to a universal hash function family. After this preliminary descriptions, we explain the connexions between the F_f protocol and the LPN problem. We then proceed to a study of the f function that unveils some of its properties that we use in our attacks. The first of our attacks indeed directly relies on the particularities of the function f to lower the complexity of the LPN problem underlying the F_f protocol. Our second attack relies on the existence of collisions in the random number generator used in F_f to mount a low complexity key-recovery.

2   Learning Parity with Noise

We now describe the problem of learning parity with noise (hereafter the LPN problem). To this end, let us denote the scalar product of two vectors x and y of $GF(2)^n$ by $x \cdot y$. The problem of recovering a binary vector $s \in GF(2)^n$ given the parity of $a \cdot s$ for randomly chosen vectors a of $GF(2)^n$ is easy: given any set $\{(a_i, a_i \cdot s)\}$ where the a_i span $GF(2)^n$, the value of s can be found by Gaussian elimination. In the case of LPN, the problem consists in learning the parity in the presence of noise: given enough values $(a, a \cdot s \oplus \nu)$ where a is randomly chosen and $\Pr[\nu = 1] = \epsilon$, recover the value s. The LPN problem is much more difficult and the best currently known algorithms have a time complexity of $2^{\Theta(n/\log(n))}$.

Let us denote by $x \xleftarrow{\Delta} X$ the random choice of an element x from X according to the probability distribution Δ. We also denote by $\$$ the uniform distribution, by Ber_ϵ the Bernouilli distribution of parameter $\epsilon \in]0, \frac{1}{2}[$, that is $\Pr[\nu = 1] = \epsilon$ and $\Pr[\nu = 0] = 1 - \epsilon$ for $\nu \xleftarrow{\mathrm{Ber}_\epsilon} \mathrm{GF}(2)$. The LPN problem can be stated more formally as follows:

Definition 1 (LPN Problem). *Let s be a vector randomly chosen from $\mathrm{GF}(2)^n$, $\epsilon \in]0, 1/2[$ be some noise parameter, and $\mathcal{O}_{s,\epsilon}$ be an oracle that outputs independent values according to the following distribution:*

$$\left\{ a \xleftarrow{\$} \mathrm{GF}(2)^n ; \nu \xleftarrow{\mathrm{Ber}_\epsilon} \mathrm{GF}(2) : (a, a \cdot s \oplus \nu) \right\}$$

An algorithm A such that

$$\Pr\left[s \xleftarrow{\$} \mathrm{GF}(2)^n : A^{\mathcal{O}_{s,\epsilon}}(1^n) = s \right] \geq \delta ,$$

running in time at most T using at most M memory and making at most q queries to oracle $\mathcal{O}_{s,\epsilon}$ is said to (q, T, M, δ)-solve the $\mathrm{LPN}_{n,\epsilon}$ problem.

The LPN problem can be reformulated as the problem of decoding a random linear code, which is well-known to be NP-complete [1]. Combined to the extreme simplicity of implementation of scalar products over $\mathrm{GF}(2)^n$, this hardness makes it a problem of choice for the design of cryptographic primitives. It has served, among other cryptographic uses, as main building block of various RFID protocols designs [10,11,9,5].

As stated above, the best known algorithms have a complexity of $2^{\Theta(n/\log(n))}$. The first algorithm to reach this complexity has been proposed by Blum, Kalai, and Wasserman in [3] and uses ideas similar to that put into use in the generalized birthday paradox [20]. By introducing the Walsh-transform during the last step of the BKW algorithm, Levieil and Fouque were able in [13] to give a sensible improvement of the complexity. Typical values of the complexity of the LF algorithm and stated in terms of memory sorting are given in Table 1. Finally, both algorithms given above require $2^{\Theta(n/\log(n))}$ queries. As noted in [14], it is possible to lower this number of queries to $\Theta(n)$ by first generating very low-weight linear combinations of the original set of queries; the loss of independence does not seem to have a great impact in practice [13].

Table 1. Complexity of the algorithm LF1 from [13] to solve an LPN problem over vectors of n bits and with an error probability of ϵ. The table should be read in the following way: it takes 2^{130} bytes of memory to solve LPN problem with $n = 512$ and a noise parameter of $\epsilon = .49$.

$\epsilon \backslash n$	128	192	256	512	640
0.0001	13	17	21	36	44
0.2500	34	41	55	89	109
0.4375	44	53	66	105	130
0.4900	55	67	88	130	162

3   The F_f Family of Protocols

At ESORICS 2007, a new RFID protocol was proposed [16] that relies on a lightweight function called DPM in order to perform identification. DPM is a function of degree two in the secret key and is very weak as it only involves very few of the set of possible monomials of degree two. Even more problematic is the fact that an attacker is able to access the output of the DPM function for various inputs, leading to very simple algebraic attacks [19,18].

In order to deal with these issues, a new family [2] of lightweight functions F_f was designed, and the RFID protocol was reworked. The rationale behind the design of this protocol is to minimize the workload on the tag. To this end, it uses a lightweight function with an output of very small size instead of the usual cryptographically strong hash functions. This, however, implies colliding outputs for a large number of the secret keys; the resulting ambiguity is resolved, as usual, by using a large number of interactions. The most interesting feature of this new protocol lies in the way it prevents an attacker from having direct access to F_f's output: instead of providing the reader (and thus, the attacker) with a lightweight function of a known random R and the secret key K, it manages to keep some level of uncertainty. This calls for a parallel with the HB family of protocols [10,11,9,5] where at each pass, a very simple function is used—a scalar product between R and K, but some uncertainty is ensured by adding noise.

Before describing the protocol that relies on it, let us first describe the F_f function family. The F_f function is built around a small fan-in function $f : \mathrm{GF}(2^{mt}) \times \mathrm{GF}(2^{mt}) \to \mathrm{GF}(2^t)$. The function f operates on the t-bit blocks of its mt-bit inputs. As described in Figure 1, F_f in turn operates on mt-bit blocks of lmt-bit

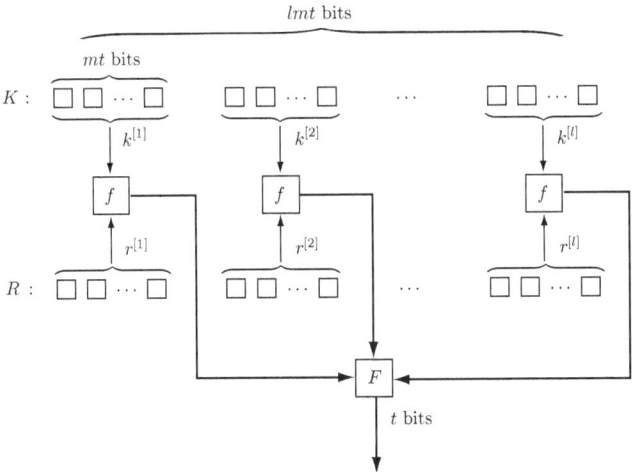

Fig. 1. The F_f function

inputs. Denoting by $x^{[i]}$ the i-th mt-bit block of any lmt-bit value X, we can define F_f as:

$$F_f(K, R) = \bigoplus_{i=1}^{l} f(k^{[i]}, r^{[i]}) \ .$$

We now turn to the description of the protocol itself. Each tag T_{ID} in the system is initialized with a pair of secret keys $(K_{\text{ID}}, K'_{\text{ID}})$ and the back-end system stores the corresponding tuples $(\text{ID}, K_{\text{ID}}, K'_{\text{ID}})$ in its database. An execution of the protocol proceeds as follows:

- the reader sends a nonce $N \in \text{GF}(2^{lmt})$ to the tag T_{ID};
- the tag T_{ID} replies with a seed ρ, and the following q values:

$$v_1 = F_f(K_{\text{ID}}, R_1^{a_1}) \oplus F_f(K'_{\text{ID}}, N_1) \ ,$$
$$v_2 = F_f(K_{\text{ID}}, R_2^{a_2}) \oplus F_f(K'_{\text{ID}}, N_2) \ ,$$
$$\vdots$$
$$v_q = F_f(K_{\text{ID}}, R_q^{a_q}) \oplus F_f(K'_{\text{ID}}, N_q) \ .$$

The seed ρ is used to generate q sets $\{R_i^1, \ldots, R_i^d\}$ consisting of d random values computed by the tag using a simple LFSR. To generate the i-th value sent to the reader, the tag T_{ID} first secretly selects a number a_i in $\{1, \ldots, d\}$ and then computes

$$F_f(K_{\text{ID}}, R_i^{a_i}) \oplus F_f(K'_{\text{ID}}, N_i)$$

using the corresponding $R_i^{a_i}$, one out of the d random values from the i-th set. The rational behind generating the q sets of d randoms is to avoid sending them over the air and thus, to prevent an active attacker from tampering with them. (In a similar way, the tag uses the same LFSR to derive the values $N_1, \ldots, N_q$ from the nonce N.)

On the reader side, the answer of the tag is processed as follows. From the seed ρ, the reader first derives the q sets of d random values $\{R_i^1, \ldots, R_i^d\}$. Then, for each of the q received values v_i, the reader discards from its database every identity j such that:

$$\forall a \in \{1, \ldots, d\} \qquad F_f(K_j, R_i^a) \oplus F_f(K'_j, N_i) \neq v_i \ .$$

Obviously, a valid tag is never discarded as v_i is obtained at least when $a = a_i$. Additionally, if the f function is well balanced, the parameters d and t can be chosen in such a way that by increasing q, the probability of accepting invalid tag is negligible, see [2] for further details.

Since it is well known how to design identification protocols with cryptographically strong hash functions, the main advantage of the F_f protocol is to allow for highly compact implementations. As cryptographic hash functions and lightweight block ciphers currently respectively require around 7 kGE and 5 kGE, the F_f protocol targets implementations of size about 2 kGE. The practical set of parameters given in [2] is

lmt	l	m	t	d	q
256	64	1	4	8	60

and the function $f : \mathrm{GF}(2^4) \times \mathrm{GF}(2^4) \to \mathrm{GF}(2^4)$, $(r, k) \mapsto z$ is such that

$$
\begin{aligned}
z_1 &= r_1 k_1 \oplus r_2 k_2 \oplus r_3 k_3 \oplus r_4 k_4 \oplus r_1 r_2 k_1 k_2 \oplus r_2 r_3 k_2 k_3 \oplus r_3 r_4 k_3 k_4 \ , \\
z_2 &= r_4 k_1 \oplus r_1 k_2 \oplus r_2 k_3 \oplus r_3 k_4 \oplus r_1 r_3 k_1 k_3 \oplus r_2 r_4 k_2 k_4 \oplus r_1 r_4 k_1 k_4 \ , \\
z_3 &= r_3 k_1 \oplus r_4 k_2 \oplus r_1 k_3 \oplus r_2 k_4 \oplus r_1 r_2 k_1 k_4 \oplus r_2 r_3 k_2 k_4 \oplus r_3 r_4 k_1 k_3 \ , \\
z_4 &= r_2 k_1 \oplus r_3 k_2 \oplus r_4 k_3 \oplus r_1 k_4 \oplus r_1 r_3 k_3 k_4 \oplus r_2 r_4 k_2 k_3 \oplus r_1 r_4 k_1 k_2 \ ,
\end{aligned}
\tag{1}
$$

where (r_1, r_2, r_3, r_4), (k_1, k_2, k_3, k_4), and (z_1, z_2, z_3, z_4) respectively stand for a representation of r, k, and z in $\mathrm{GF}(2)^4$. Let us also note the projection π_i from $\mathrm{GF}(2^4)$ to $\mathrm{GF}(2)$ that, according to this representation, sends any element of $\mathrm{GF}(2^4)$ to its i-th output bit: $\pi_i(z) = z_i$.

Our two attacks given below work for other values of t, but in order to ease the exposition, we focus on the choice of $t = 4$ made by the authors of F_f.

4 Preliminary Remarks for the Attacks

4.1 On the LPN Problem Underlying F_f

If we discard the anti-replay nonce, the problem of recovering the key K in the F_f protocol can be seen as an LPN problem. Indeed, each of the q values v_i sent by the tag to the reader yields an equation involving some R among d possible values $R_i^1, \ldots, R_i^d$. Therefore, the attacker can always collect the equations $F_f(R_i^1, K) = v_i, \ldots, F_f(R_i^d, K) = v_i$ for $i = 1, \ldots, q$ and for several executions of the protocol. Each equation (which is defined over $\mathrm{GF}(2^t)$) can be projected over $\mathrm{GF}(2)$. Then, for each i and each execution, at least one of the d values R_i^j yields t correct boolean equations, whereas the other ones are uniformly wrong or false when F_f is well balanced, as requested by the design. Therefore, the probability that a boolean equation from the set collected by the attacker is true is $\frac{1}{d} + \frac{d-1}{d} \frac{1}{2}$. Now the equations contain terms of degree 2 in the key bits: for the parameters chosen by the authors ($t = 4$ and 256-bit keys), there are $6 \cdot 64$ monomials of degree exactly two, and $4 \cdot 64$ linear terms. Moreover, the choice of $d = 8$ yields a huge noise of $\epsilon = .4375$. Therefore, as stated in Table 1, a direct tentative to solve the LPN problem underlying F_f by linearization of the 640 monomials would have a complexity of 2^{130}.

4.2 Structure of the f Function

The f function at the core of the F_f protocol is strongly constrained, and consequently exhibits a quite specific structure. Indeed, for the protocol to be both complete and sound (i.e. reject invalid keys with overwhelming probability), the

f function must be well balanced on its inputs. We now study the effect of the following function τ on the output values of f:

$$\tau : \mathrm{GF}(2^4) \to \mathrm{GF}(2) , \quad x \mapsto \pi_1(x) \oplus \pi_2(x) \oplus \pi_3(x) \oplus \pi_4(x) .$$

According to the definition (1) of f, we derive the following facts:

$$\begin{aligned}
\forall r \in \{\text{0x0}, \text{0xf}\} , & \quad \tau\big(f(k,r)\big) = 0 \\
\forall r \in \{\text{0x1}, \text{0x2}, \text{0x4}, \text{0x8}\} , & \quad \tau\big(f(k,r)\big) = k_1 \oplus k_2 \oplus k_3 \oplus k_4 \\
\forall r \in \{\text{0x5}, \text{0xc}\} , & \quad \tau\big(f(k,r)\big) = k_1 k_3 \oplus k_3 k_4 \\
\forall r \in \{\text{0x6}, \text{0xa}\} , & \quad \tau\big(f(k,r)\big) = k_2 k_3 \oplus k_2 k_4 \\
\forall r \in \{\text{0x3}, \text{0x9}\} , & \quad \tau\big(f(k,r)\big) = k_1 k_2 \oplus k_1 k_4
\end{aligned}$$

and

$$\begin{aligned}
\tau\big(f(k, \text{0xe})\big) &= (k_1 \oplus k_2 \oplus k_3 \oplus k_4) \oplus (k_1 k_3 \oplus k_3 k_4) \\
\tau\big(f(k, \text{0xb})\big) &= (k_1 \oplus k_2 \oplus k_3 \oplus k_4) \oplus (k_2 k_3 \oplus k_2 k_4) \\
\tau\big(f(k, \text{0xd})\big) &= (k_1 \oplus k_2 \oplus k_3 \oplus k_4) \oplus (k_1 k_2 \oplus k_1 k_4) \\
\tau\big(f(k, \text{0x7})\big) &= (k_1 \oplus k_2 \oplus k_3 \oplus k_4) \oplus (k_1 k_3 \oplus k_3 k_4) \oplus (k_2 k_3 \oplus k_2 k_4) \oplus (k_1 k_2 \oplus k_1 k_4)
\end{aligned}$$

where, in order to save space, an element (z_1, z_2, z_3, z_4) of $\mathrm{GF}(2)^4$ is denoted by the corresponding nibble '$\text{0x}z_1 z_2 z_3 z_4$'. Therefore, $\tau\big(f(k,r))\big)$ is always a linear combination of the four bits c_1, c_2, c_3, and c_4 defined as

$$\begin{aligned}
c_1 &= k_1 \oplus k_2 \oplus k_3 \oplus k_4 , \\
c_2 &= k_1 k_3 \oplus k_3 k_4 , \\
c_3 &= k_2 k_3 \oplus k_2 k_4 , \\
c_4 &= k_1 k_2 \oplus k_1 k_4 .
\end{aligned}$$

Our two attacks against the F_f protocol both lead to a step where we have to solve for the values of $c_1, \ldots, c_4$ instead of the values of $k_1, \ldots, k_4$. Although the underlying mapping that sends k to c is not one-to-one, we will show that k can be derived from the knowledge of c and a few interactions with the system, this for a very low computational complexity.

Direct implications for the F_f protocol. It is interesting to note that the structural property of f uncovered by τ reveals a whole set of weak keys. Indeed, it is easy to check that: $\forall r, \forall k, \tau(f(r,k)) = \tau(f(k,r))$. As an example, if K is such that for all i, $k^{[i]} \in \{\text{0x0}, \text{0xf}\}$ then $\forall r, \tau(f(r,k)) = 0$, a property that can be easily distinguished. Also, if $k^{[i]} \in \{\text{0x1}, \text{0x2}, \text{0x4}, \text{0x8}, \text{0x0}, \text{0xf}\}$ for all i, $\tau(f(r,k))$ is a linear combination of r, for any r; again, this can be distinguished. There are 2^{64} keys of the first type and $6^{64} \simeq 2^{165}$ keys of the second type.

Also, the symmetry of f with respect to r and k shows that there is a very large class of randoms N such that $F_f(K', N) = 0$. This fact can be used by an attacker to get information about $F_f(K, R)$ directly instead of through $F_f(K, R) \oplus F_f(K', N)$.

5   LPN Solving Attack

In the description of our first attack, we make use of the following property that was exhibited at the end of Section 4.2: while the tag answers with a value $F_f(K_{\text{ID}}, R_i^{a_i}) \oplus F_f(K'_{\text{ID}}, N_i)$ to the reader, the attacker—when simulating a reader—is able to choose "nonces" N (such as $N = 0$ for instance) so that $F_f(K'_{\text{ID}}, N) = 0$ for any K'_{ID}. In the following, we therefore assume without loss of generality that the tag directly answers with $F_f(K_{\text{ID}}, R_i^{a_i})$, and thus, that the attacker's goal is to recover the part K_{ID} of the tag's secret key. (We also note that once K_{ID} has been recovered, it is immediate to additionally recover K'_{ID} as the answers of the tag become deterministic in the bits of K'_{ID} and the solving complexity of a simple linearisation is negligible compared to the complexity of the rest of the attack.)

5.1   The LPN Problem through τ

As we have seen in Section 4.1, it is possible to put the F_f protocol into the framework of the LPN problem. However, the protocol parameters have been chosen to escape a straightforward attack. In order to lower the complexity, we take advantage of the properties of f exhibited in Section 4.2. This requires to consider the LPN problem associated with $\tau \circ f$ instead of with f.

Let us recall that during an execution of the protocol, the tag sends q values v_i defined over $\text{GF}(2^4)$ as $v_i = F_f(K_{\text{ID}}, R_i^{a_i})$. An attacker who collects equations of the type $\tau(v_i) = \tau\big(F_f(K_{\text{ID}}, R^a)\big)$ for every possible $a \in \{1, \ldots, d\}$ will get noisy equations on the bits of K_{ID}. What is exactly the corresponding noise ϵ? The probability that the above boolean equation is true is 1 in the case where $a = a_i$ and $\frac{1}{2}$ otherwise, so that $1 - \epsilon = \frac{1}{8} + \frac{7}{8}\frac{1}{2}$, that is $\epsilon = 0.4375$.

5.2   Lowering the Complexity of the LPN Problem

In order to lower the complexity of the above LPN attack, we seek to lower the number of unknowns involved, as this is the parameter having the strongest impact on the complexity. We can achieve a 25% reduction of the number of unknowns using the following fact stated in Section 4.2:

$$\Pr_r\big[\tau(f(k,r)) = 0\big] = \tfrac{2}{16} , \qquad \Pr_r\big[\tau(f(k,r)) = c_1\big] = \tfrac{4}{16}$$
$$\Pr_r\big[\tau(f(k,r)) = c_2\big] = \tfrac{2}{16} , \qquad \Pr_r\big[\tau(f(k,r)) = c_3\big] = \tfrac{2}{16} ,$$
$$\Pr_r\big[\tau(f(k,r)) = c_1 \oplus c_2\big] = \tfrac{1}{16} , \qquad \Pr_r\big[\tau(f(k,r)) = c_1 \oplus c_3\big] = \tfrac{1}{16} .$$

Indeed, the above values show that the probability over the randoms r that a 4-bit block contribution $f(k,r)$ to $F_f(K,R)$ only involves c_1, c_2, and c_3 instead of all four unknowns $c_1, \ldots, c_4$ is equal to $\mu = \frac{12}{16} \simeq 2^{-0.415}$. In order to lower the number of unknowns involved in the LPN problem from $4 \cdot 64$ bits to $3 \cdot 64$ bits, the attacker seeks a seed ρ such that at least one value among the qd randoms $R_1^1, \ldots, R_1^d, R_2^1, \ldots, R_q^d$ has all its 4-bit blocks of the requested form. This happens with probability $1 - (1 - \mu^{64})^{qd} \simeq qd\mu^{64}$. Thus, about $2^{17.6}$ interactions with the tag will give one boolean equation to solve the underlying LPN problem with noise $\epsilon = 0.4375$ on 192 unknowns. As explained in Section 2, it is enough to collect $4 \cdot 192$ equations to produce the number of samples by considering all linear combinations of weight four, yielding a total number of interactions with the tag lower than 2^{28}. As shown in Table 1, the cost for solving the LPN problem becomes about 2^{53}—to be compared to the complexity of 2^{130} of the original LPN problem.

Once the values of $c_1, \ldots, c_3$ are known, the attacker derives a new set of equations by interacting with the tag, this time removing the constraints on the initial random seed ρ chosen by the tag. This provides the attacker with a set of equations in the four values $c_1, \ldots, c_4$ for each 4-bit block in which the attacker substitutes the value of $c_1, \ldots, c_3$ just recovered: this yields another LPN problem with 64 unknowns the complexity of which is negligible compared to the complexity of the previous LPN problem. After this step, the attacker knows $c_1, \ldots, c_4$ for every 4-bit block of the key K.

5.3   Recovering the Key K

At this point, the attacker gained knowledge of $c_1, \ldots, c_4$ for each of the 64 blocks of 4 bits, and thus is able to predict the value $\tau(f(R, K))$ for any R. However, there still remains to get the value of the bits of K to be able to predict $F_f(R, K)$ and as explained in Section 4.2, the mapping from (k_1, k_2, k_3, k_4) to (c_1, c_2, c_3, c_4) is not one-to-one.

One possibility for the attacker to overcome this issue is to use her knowledge of $c_1, \ldots, c_4$ for each 4 bits block that allows her to predict with absolute certainty the value $\tau(F_f(R, K))$ *for any* R. Therefore, the attacker enters a few additional interactions with the tag (once again using nonces N_0 such that $F_f(N_0, K') = 0$). For each of the q values $v_i = F_f(R_i^a, K)$ returned by the tag during an interaction, the attacker computes the d values $b_j = \tau(F_f(R_i^j, K))$ for $j = 1, \ldots, d$. If exactly one of $\{b_1, \ldots, b_8\}$, say b_{j_0}, is equal to $\tau(v_i)$, then we know that necessarily $a = j_0$. This yields an exact equation over $GF(2^4)$, namely $F_f(R^{j_0}, K) = v_i$, involving all the bits of K. As this event happens only when the $d - 1$ values b_j where $j \neq a$ are equal to $v_i \oplus 1$, it occurs with probability $\frac{1}{2}^{d-1}$. In order to collect N exact equations on the key bits, the attacker needs $N\frac{1}{q}2^{d-1}$ interactions with tag, which is lower than 2^{10} for the parameters chosen by the authors of F_f (these parameters yields $N = 640$ different monomials in the key bits). The resulting system can then be solved with a complexity of $N^3 \simeq 2^{26}$.

6   A Resynchronization Attack

Contrary to the previous attack which recovers K, our second attack aims to recover K': even without the knowledge of K, the attacker is able to replay any valid execution of the protocol (this includes traces obtained when the attacker takes the role of the reader) by removing the contribution involving K' and an incorrect nonce from the trace and incorporating the correct value involving K' and the nonce challenged by the reader.

The starting point of our second attack to recover K' is the internal generator that produces the random numbers $R_1^1, \ldots, R_1^d, \ldots, R_q^1, \ldots, R_q^d$ of an execution of the protocol. As the goal of F_f is to fit under the 3kGE limit, this number generator was chosen with a 64-bit internal state. As this generator does not directly manipulate the key bits, the designers claimed that the uniformity of its output is the only constraint, and that the generator does not need to be cryptographically secure [2]:

> "We do not care about the secrecy or predictability of the internal state of PRNG, but only require (pseudo-)random properties for the Rs for statistical purposes as discussed in the next sections. Therefore, we can safely use a cheap LFSR to derive R with good enough randomness."

The authors therefore chose to implement it as an LFSR, but our attack only relies on its reduced entropy; it remains valid with any other pseudo-random generator with a 64-bit internal state.

6.1   Deriving Noisy Information on K'

The main idea of the attack to recover information about K' is to find collisions on the random seed ρ used to generate the randoms $R_1^1, \ldots, R_d^1, \ldots, R_d^q$. Indeed, the set of d randoms $\{R_i^1, \ldots, R_i^d\}$ used at the i-th round of one execution of the protocol will be identical for any two traces for which the random seeds ρ collide. As the generator producing the R_i^j has an internal state of 64 bits, it requires 2^{32} interactions with a tag to find such a collision on the seeds ρ.

Therefore, the attacker first chooses two nonces N_1 and N_2 and challenges the tag with each of these nonces 2^{32} times so that the seeds ρ will collide for an execution of the protocol involving the nonce N_1 and another execution involving the nonce N_2 about once. This way, the attacker is able to collect values $v_i^{(1)} = F_f(K, R_i^{a_{i,1}}) \oplus F_f(K', N_1)$ and $v_i^{(2)} = F_f(K, R_i^{a_{i,2}}) \oplus F_f(K', N_2)$ for $i = 1, \ldots, q$. In order to get information on K' alone, the attacker hopes that $F_f(K, R_i^{a_{i,1}}) = F_f(K, R_i^{a_{i,2}})$ so that:

$$v_i^{(1)} \oplus v_i^{(2)} = F_f(K', N_1) \oplus F_f(K', N_2) \ .$$

When the seeds ρ collide however, this equation only holds when $a_{i,1} = a_{i,2}$ or when $a_{i,1} \neq a_{i,2}$ but $F_f(K, R_i^{a_{i,1}}) = F_f(K, R_i^{a_{i,2}})$ over $\mathrm{GF}(2^t)$. There are d^2 possible couples $(R_i^{a_{i,1}}, R_i^{a_{i,2}})$ and the first case happens with probability $\frac{d}{d^2}$ while the second one happens with probability $\frac{1}{2^t}(1 - \frac{d}{d^2})$ since F_f is well balanced and the R_i are randomly chosen.

6.2   Decreasing the Noise and Solving for K'

A major issue with the approach described above is that the equations on K' collected by the attacker are very noisy—projected over $\mathrm{GF}(2)$ they are true with probability $\frac{1}{8} + \frac{7}{8}\frac{1}{2} = \frac{1}{2} + \frac{1}{16}$ for the parameters chosen by the authors. As explained earlier, the number of monomials in the bits of K' that occur in $F_f(K', N)$ is 640, and Table 1 shows that trying to solve the corresponding LPN problem requires a complexity of 2^{130}.

One possibility to overcome this issue is to decrease the noise affecting the collected equation. In contrast with what happened for our first attack, it is possible to get several noisy samples of *the same equation*. Therefore, by finding several collisions on ρ, the value $v_i^{(1)} \oplus v_i^{(2)}$ obtained by the attacker is more likely to be equal to $F_f(K', N_1) \oplus F_f(K', N_2)$ than to any other value. With enough collisions, the attacker is thus able to recover the value $F_f(K', N_1) \oplus F_f(K', N_2)$ by voting for the value that appears the most often. As the analysis of such a strategy is a little bit involved over $\mathrm{GF}(2^t)$, we instead project each collected equation over $\mathrm{GF}(2)^t$ and consider each of the t boolean equations independently: this yields a very lose upper-bound for the complexity of our attack.

Let us determine the probability that the majority vote for N versions of a boolean equation is correct. Recall that each boolean equation collected by the attacker is true with probability $\frac{1}{2} + \epsilon$ where $\epsilon = \frac{1}{16}$. Therefore, let us assume that the constant member is a random variable b distributed according to the probabilities $\Pr[b = 0] = \frac{1}{2} + \epsilon$ and $\Pr[b = 1] = \frac{1}{2} - \epsilon$. If we denote by b_i the constant member for the i-th version of the boolean equation, the mean value of the random variable $B = \bigoplus_{i=1}^{N} b_i$ is $(\frac{1}{2} - \epsilon)N$ and so the majority vote is wrong when $B > \frac{N}{2}$. The Chernoff bound shows that:

$$\Pr\left[B > \tfrac{N}{2}\right] < e^{-N\epsilon^2(1+2\epsilon)^{-1}} \ .$$

To make the probability of getting a wrong equation become η, the attacker has to perform a majority vote on $N = -2\epsilon^2 \ln(\eta)$ samples. To solve the linearized system of 640 monomials, we need to get 640 correct equations, which happens with probability $(1 - \eta)^{640}$. As there are $q = 60$ rounds in one execution of the protocol, the attacker needs $\tilde{N} = 2^{32} N \frac{1}{q} (1 - \eta)^{-640}$ interactions with the tag to get a linearized system in the 640 monomials which is correct with probability greater than $\frac{1}{2}$. For the parameters chosen by the authors, setting $N = 4096$ leads to an error probability $\eta = 0.00018$, and thus to a total number of interactions with the tag of $\tilde{N} = 2^{38.4}$. The complexity to solve the linearized system is less than 2^{28} and thus negligible compared to the above complexity.

7   Conclusion

In this paper we studied the connections between the F_f RFID protocol and the LPN problem. We showed several properties of the f function underlying the F_f protocol and described two key-recovery attacks that build on these properties. In our attacks, the adversary only requires interactions with the tag and does not need to interact with the reader.

References

1. Berlekamp, E., McEliece, R., van Tilborg, H.: On the inherent intractability of certain coding problems. IEEE Transactions on Information Theory 24(3), 384–386 (1978)
2. Blaß, E.-O., Kurmus, A., Molva, R., Noubir, G., Shikfa, A.: The F_f-family of protocols for RFID-privacy and authentication. In: Conference on RFID Security, Leuven, Belgium (July 2009)
3. Blum, A., Kalai, A., Wasserman, H.: Noise-tolerant learning, the parity problem, and the statistical query model. J. ACM 50(4), 506–519 (2003)
4. Bogdanov, A., Knudsen, L.R., Leander, G., Paar, C., Poschmann, A., Robshaw, M.J.B., Seurin, Y., Vikkelsoe, C.: PRESENT: An Ultra-Lightweight Block Cipher. In: Paillier, P., Verbauwhede, I. (eds.) CHES 2007. LNCS, vol. 4727, pp. 450–466. Springer, Heidelberg (2007)
5. Bringer, J., Chabanne, H., Dottax, E.: HB^{++}: a Lightweight Authentication Protocol Secure against Some Attacks. In: Security, Privacy and Trust in Pervasive and Ubiquitous Computing—SecPerU 2006, pp. 28–33. IEEE Computer Society, Los Alamitos (2006)
6. Cichon, J., Klonowski, M., Kutylowski, M.: Privacy Protection for RFID with Hidden Subset Identifiers. In: Indulska, J., Patterson, D.J., Rodden, T., Ott, M. (eds.) PERVASIVE 2008. LNCS, vol. 5013, pp. 298–314. Springer, Heidelberg (2008)
7. Gilbert, H., Robshaw, M., Sibert, H.: Active attack against HB^{+}: a provably secure lightweight authentication protocol. Electronics Letters 41(21), 1169–1170 (2005)
8. Gilbert, H., Robshaw, M.J.B., Seurin, Y.: Good Variants of HB^{+} Are Hard to Find. In: Tsudik, G. (ed.) FC 2008. LNCS, vol. 5143, pp. 156–170. Springer, Heidelberg (2008)
9. Gilbert, H., Robshaw, M.J.B., Seurin, Y.: $HB^{\#}$: Increasing the Security and Efficiency of HB^{+}. In: Smart, N.P. (ed.) EUROCRYPT 2008. LNCS, vol. 4965, pp. 361–378. Springer, Heidelberg (2008)
10. Hopper, N.J., Blum, M.: Secure human identification protocols. In: Boyd, C. (ed.) ASIACRYPT 2001. LNCS, vol. 2248, pp. 52–66. Springer, Heidelberg (2001)
11. Juels, A., Weis, S.A.: Authenticating Pervasive Devices with Human Protocols. In: Shoup, V. (ed.) CRYPTO 2005. LNCS, vol. 3621, pp. 293–308. Springer, Heidelberg (2005)
12. Krause, M., Stegemann, D.: More on the Security of Linear RFID Authentication Protocols. In: Jacobson Jr., M.J., Rijmen, V., Safavi-Naini, R. (eds.) SAC 2009. LNCS, vol. 5867, pp. 182–196. Springer, Heidelberg (2009)
13. Levieil, É., Fouque, P.-A.: An Improved LPN Algorithm. In: De Prisco, R., Yung, M. (eds.) SCN 2006. LNCS, vol. 4116, pp. 348–359. Springer, Heidelberg (2006)
14. Lyubashevsky, V.: The parity problem in the presence of noise, decoding random linear codes, and the subset sum problem. In: Chekuri, C., Jansen, K., Rolim, J.D.P., Trevisan, L. (eds.) APPROX 2005 and RANDOM 2005. LNCS, vol. 3624, pp. 378–389. Springer, Heidelberg (2005)
15. Ohkubo, M., Suzuki, K., Kinoshita, S.: Efficient hash-chain based RFID privacy protection scheme. In: Ubiquitous Computing – Privacy Workshop (2004)
16. Di Pietro, R., Molva, R.: Information Confinement, Privacy, and Security in RFID Systems. In: Biskup, J., López, J. (eds.) ESORICS 2007. LNCS, vol. 4734, pp. 187–202. Springer, Heidelberg (2007)

17. Shamir, A.: SQUASH–A New MAC with Provable Security Properties for Highly Constrained Devices Such as RFID Tags. In: Nyberg, K. (ed.) FSE 2008. LNCS, vol. 5086, pp. 144–157. Springer, Heidelberg (2008)
18. Soos, M.: Analysing the Molva and Di Pietro Private RFID Authentication Scheme. In: Conference on RFID Security, Budapest, Hungary (July 2008)
19. van Deursen, T., Mauw, S., Radomirović, S.: Untraceability of RFID Protocols. In: Onieva, J.A., Sauveron, D., Chaumette, S., Gollmann, D., Markantonakis, K. (eds.) WISTP 2008. LNCS, vol. 5019, pp. 1–15. Springer, Heidelberg (2008)
20. Wagner, D.: A generalized birthday problem. In: Yung, M. (ed.) CRYPTO 2002. LNCS, vol. 2442, pp. 288–303. Springer, Heidelberg (2002)

Efficient Constructions of Signcryption Schemes and Signcryption Composability

Takahiro Matsuda*, Kanta Matsuura, and Jacob C.N. Schuldt

The University of Tokyo, Japan
{tmatsuda,kanta,schuldt}@iis.u-tokyo.ac.jp

Abstract. In this paper, we investigate simple but efficient constructions of signcryption schemes. Firstly, we show how symmetric primitives can be used to efficiently achieve outsider multi-user security, leading to a signcryption scheme with the currently lowest ciphertext and
computational overhead. For the mixed security notions outsider confi-
dentiality/insider unforgeability and insider confidentiality/outsider unforgeability, this approach yields lower ciphertext overhead and a higher
level of security, respectively, compared to the current schemes. Secondly,
we show a simple optimization to the well known "sign-then-encrypt"
and "encrypt-then-sign" approaches to the construction of signcryption
schemes by using tag-based encryption. Instantiations with our proposed
tag-based schemes yield multi-user insider secure signcryption schemes
in the random oracle model which is at least as efficient as any other
existing scheme both in terms of ciphertext overhead and computational
cost. Furthermore, we show that very efficient standard model signcryption schemes can be constructed using this technique as well. Lastly,
we show how signatures and encryption can be combined in a non-black-
box manner to achieve higher efficiency than schemes based on the above
approach. We refer to signature and encryption schemes which can be
combined in this way as *signcryption composable*, and we show that a
number of the most efficient standard model encryption and signature
schemes satisfy this, leading to the most efficient standard model signcryption schemes. Since all of our constructions are fairly simple and
efficient, they provide a benchmark which can be used to evaluate future
signcryption schemes.

Keywords: signcryption, multi-user security, generic construction.

1 Introduction

The notion signcryption was introduced by Zheng [47] as a primitive providing
the combined functionality of signatures and encryption i.e. unforgeability, message confidentiality, and possibly non-repudiation. The main motivation given
in [47] for introducing signcryption as a new primitive was to achieve higher
efficiency than simply combining signature and encryption. While the scheme

---

* Takahiro Matsuda is supported by a JSPS fellowship.

B. Roy and N. Sendrier (Eds.): INDOCRYPT 2009, LNCS 5922, pp. 321–342, 2009.

proposed in [47] was not formally proved secure, this was done in subsequent works [5,6]. Furthermore, An *et al.* [3] formally analyzed the security of the simple composition of signature and public key encryption (PKE).

Since the introduction of the primitive, many signcryption schemes have been proposed, e.g. [47,3,24,29,30,18,8,28,20,42,43,44]. However, these schemes provide different security levels depending on the used security model. The simplest security model for a signcryption scheme considers a two-user system consisting only of a single sender and a single receiver. While two-user security models have been considered in some of the earlier papers (e.g. [3,18]), they are of limited interest since most practical systems will include many users, and for signcryption schemes, two-user security does not imply multi-user security[1]. Another aspect of the security model is whether the adversary is considered to be an *insider*, possibly playing the part of either the sender or receiver, or an *outsider* trying to attack an uncompromised sender and receiver pair. Note that many schemes are proved secure using a "mix" of these security notions. e.g. insider confidentiality and outsider unforgeability [5,6], or outsider confidentiality and insider unforgeability [24,20]. The efforts to construct schemes providing security in the strongest sense, i.e. insider security for both confidentiality and unforgeability, have met some challenges. For example, the scheme proposed in [31] was shown to be insecure in [38,46], "fixed" in [46], only to be broken again in [39]. Finally, Libert *et al.* [29] updated the original scheme [31] while Li *et al.* [28] independently proposed a scheme based on [46], which both seem to be resistant to the attacks in [38,46,39]. In a similar way, the scheme proposed in [32] was shown to be insecure in [40], updated in [33], only to be shown insecure in [41]. Lastly, Libert *et al.* [30] updated the original scheme to be resistant to the attack in [40]. This illustrates that care must be taken when designing fully insider secure signcryption schemes.

Except the composition results by An *et al.* [3] and the relation between key agreement and signcryption key encapsulation mechanisms (signcryption KEMs) studied by Gorantla *et al.* [20], most constructions of signcryption schemes make very little use of existing primitives and the established security properties of these. Furthermore, the proposed signcryption schemes are rarely compared to the often simpler constructions of signcryption using existing primitives and the efficiency achieved by these. As the proposed constructions get increasingly complex, as in the case of the recently proposed standard model schemes [42,43,44], this leaves open the question whether the direct constructions provide any advantages compared to the signcryption schemes relying on other primitives, when these are instantiated properly.

Our Contribution. We focus on simple but efficient constructions of signcryption using existing primitives or simple extension of these. Firstly, we show how the

---

[1] E.g. see [6] for a discussion of this. Furthermore, note that An *et al.* [3] showed how a simple composition of signatures and encryption achieving two-user security can be transformed into a scheme achieving multi-user security, but this transformation is not applicable in general.

properties of symmetric key encryption (SKE) and message authentication codes (MAC) can be used to provide outsider security. As a tool, we use a tag-based non-interactive key exchange (TNIKE) scheme, which is a simple extension of an ordinary non-interactive key exchange (NIKE) scheme [19,15] and is easy to instantiate in the random oracle model. The resulting scheme has a lower computational cost and ciphertext overhead than any of the existing signcryption schemes. If insider unforgeability is required (and only outsider confidentiality), this approach still yield the lowest ciphertext overhead (roughly 25% shorter than the scheme by Zheng [47]), but is not as computationally efficient as [47]. If insider confidentiality is required (and only outsider unforgeability), this approach yields a scheme with exactly the same ciphertext overhead and slightly more expensive computational cost than the currently most efficient scheme by Gorantla *et al.* [20] instantiated with HMQV [27]. However, our approach is secure in a stronger security model.

We furthermore propose a simple optimization of the "sign-then-encrypt" and "encrypt-then-sign" constructions of signcryption, using tag-based encryption (TBE) [34,25][2]. While both constructions are shown to be insider secure, the latter requires a special one-to-one property of the signature scheme which, in practice, limits instantiations to the random oracle model. However, the advantage of this approach is that it achieves strong unforgeability which is not achieved by the former approach. To instantiate these schemes, we show how the most efficient standard and random oracle model PKE schemes can be turned into TBE schemes with practically no additional cost. This leads to an insider secure random oracle model scheme that is at least as efficient as any other existing scheme both in terms of ciphertext overhead and computational cost, as well as efficient standard model schemes.

Lastly, we show how a signature scheme and an encryption scheme which satisfy a few special requirements can be combined in a non-black-box way to achieve higher efficiency than a simple composition. The basic idea of this approach is simple and essentially lets the signature and encryption use "shared randomness". We call schemes that can be combined in this way *signcryption-composable*, and we show that some of the most efficient standard model encryption and signature schemes satisfy this. The resulting signcryption schemes are the most efficient insider secure standard model schemes.

We emphasize that the advantage of the above compositions lies not only in the achieved efficiency by the obtained signcryption schemes, but also in their simplicity, which allows us to prove security using already established security results for the underlying primitives. We believe that the constructions obtained via our compositions can be used as a benchmark to evaluate future signcryption schemes.

While in this paper we concentrate on schemes providing the basic security properties of signcryption, i.e. confidentiality and unforgeability, we conjecture that schemes providing additional properties, such as non-repudiation and anonymity, can be constructed using similar techniques.

---

[2] TBE has previously been introduced under the name *encryption with labels* [37].

2   Building Blocks

In our constructions of signcryption schemes we will make use of a number of different primitives including tag-based encryption (TBE), tag-based key encapsulation mechanism (TBKEM), signatures, symmetric key encryption (SKE), data encapsulation mechanism (DEM), message authentication codes (MAC), and tag-based non-interactive key establishment (TNIKE).

A TBE scheme is a public key encryption scheme in which the encryption and decryption algorithm take a tag as an additional input, and has been used in several other papers (e.g [37,34,25]). We will use TBE schemes which provide full CCA security [25] and a weaker selective tag variant, which we will denote IND-tag-CCA and IND-stag-CCA, respectively. A TBKEM[3] is the key encapsulation analogue of a TBE scheme for which we will also consider the security notions IND-tag-CCA and IND-stag-CCA.

For signatures, we use the standard security definitions of weak and strong unforgeability [3], denoted wUF-CMA and sUF-CMA, for SKE we use the security notions IND-CPA, IND-CCA and INT-CTXT as defined in [7], and for MAC we use the security notions wUF-CMA and sUF-CMA [7]. We define a DEM to be a special case of a SKE in which the encryption algorithm is deterministic.

A non-interactive key exchange (NIKE), introduced in [19] and formally defined in [15], is given by a setup algorithm Setup which returns a set of public parameters par, a key generation algorithm KG which on input par returns a public/private key pair (pk, sk), a shared key generation algorithm Share which on input par, a public key of one entity pk_1 and a private key of another entity sk_2, returns a shared key K. It is required for all $par \leftarrow \text{Setup}(1^k)$ and all (pk_1, sk_1) and (pk_2, sk_2) output from KG(par) that Share(par, pk_1, sk_2) = Share(par, pk_2, sk_1). A TNIKE is a tag-based extension of a NIKE in which the shared key generation algorithm takes as additional input a tag. We require a (T)NIKE to be secure against *active attacks* [15].

Due to space limitations, the formal definitions of these primitives are not included, and we refer the reader to the full version of the paper [35] for these.

3   Signcryption

A signcryption scheme is given by the following algorithms: a setup algorithm Setup which on input 1^k returns a set of public parameters par; a sender key generation algorithm KG$_S$ which on input par returns a public/private sender key pair (pk_S, sk_S); a receiver key generation algorithm KG$_R$ which on input par returns a public/private receiver key pair (pk_R, sk_R); a signcryption algorithm SC which on input par, sk_S, pk_R, and a message m, returns a ciphertext c; an unsigncryption algorithm USC which on input par, pk_S, sk_R, and c, returns either m or an error symbol $\perp$.

---

[3] Note that this primitive is *different* from the *Tag-KEM* introduced in [2], although they are closely related. It is easy to see that every IND-CCA Tag-KEM can be used as an IND-tag-CCA TBKEM.

It is required for all $par \leftarrow \mathtt{Setup}(1^k)$, all $(pk_S, sk_S) \leftarrow \mathtt{KG}_S(par)$, all (pk_R, sk_R) $\leftarrow \mathtt{KG}_R(par)$, and all messages m that $m = \mathtt{USC}(par, pk_S, sk_R, \mathtt{SC}(par, sk_S, pk_R, m))$.

3.1   Security

As mentioned in the introduction, a multi-user security definition is required for signcryption schemes. However, a number of slightly different models have been introduced in the literature (e.g. see [3,6,31,20]). In the following definitions, the differences of these will be highlighted. We firstly consider security models with insider security, and then discuss the weaker outsider counterparts.

Confidentiality. The strongest notion of confidentiality was introduced in [31] and is based on a security model in which the adversary can freely choose all user keys, except the challenge receiver key. We refer to this model as the *dynamic multi-user* model, and in this model we consider the notion *indistinguishability against insider chosen ciphertext attacks* (dM-IND-iCCA). More specifically, for a signcryption scheme $SC = (\mathtt{Setup}, \mathtt{KG}_S, \mathtt{KG}_R, \mathtt{SC}, \mathtt{USC})$ and a security parameter 1^k, dM-IND-iCCA security is defined via the experiment $\mathtt{Exp}_{SC,\mathcal{A}}^{\mathtt{dM-IND-iCCA}}(k)$ shown in Fig. 1 (upper left). In the experiment, the adversary $\mathcal{A} = (\mathcal{A}_1, \mathcal{A}_2)$ has access to an unsigncryption oracle $\mathcal{O} = \{\mathtt{Unsigncrypt}\}$ which is defined as follows:

- $\mathtt{Unsigncrypt}$: Given a public sender key pk_S and ciphertext c, the oracle returns $m/\bot \leftarrow \mathtt{USC}(par, pk_S, sk_R^*, c)$ where sk_R^* is the private receiver key generated in the beginning of the experiment. A query of the form (pk_S^*, c^*), where pk_S^* is the challenge sender key specified by $\mathcal{A}$ and c^* is the challenge ciphertext, is not allowed.

A security model defining a slightly weaker security notion was used in [3,5]. In this security model, which we will refer to as the *fixed challenge key multi-user* model, the adversary cannot choose the challenge sender key. More specifically, in this model we define indistinguishability against insider chosen ciphertext attacks (fM-IND-iCCA) for a signcryption scheme SC and security parameter 1^k via the experiment $\mathtt{Exp}_{SC,\mathcal{A}}^{\mathtt{fM-IND-iCCA}}(k)$ shown in Fig. 1 (upper right). In the experiment, $\mathcal{A} = (\mathcal{A}_1, \mathcal{A}_2)$ has access to an unsigncryption oracle as defined above.

Definition 1. *A signcryption scheme SC is said to be* X-IND-iCCA *secure, if* $|\Pr[\mathtt{Exp}_{SC,\mathcal{A}}^{\mathtt{X-IND-iCCA}}(k) = 1] - 1/2|$ *is negligible in k for any probabilistic polynomial-time algorithm $\mathcal{A}$, where* X $\in \{$dM, fM$\}$.

Unforgeability. Like the confidentiality definition above, we consider unforgeability in both the dynamic and the fixed challenge key multi-user models. For a signcryption scheme SC and security parameter 1^k, we define (weak) unforgeability against insider chosen message attacks in the dynamic multi-user model (dM-wUF-iCMA) via experiment $\mathtt{Exp}_{SC,\mathcal{A}}^{\mathtt{dM-wUF-iCMA}}(k)$ shown in Fig. 1 (lower left). In the experiment, the adversary $\mathcal{A}$ has access to a signcryption oracle $\mathcal{O} = \{\mathtt{Signcrypt}\}$ defined as follows:

$\mathrm{Exp}_{SC,\mathcal{A}}^{\texttt{dM-IND-iCCA}}(k):$
    $par \leftarrow \mathsf{Setup}(1^k)$
    $(pk_R^*, sk_R^*) \leftarrow \mathsf{KG}_R(par)$
    $(pk_S^*, sk_S^*, m_0, m_1, st) \leftarrow \mathcal{A}_1^{\mathcal{O}}(par, pk_R^*)$
    $b \leftarrow \{0,1\};\quad c^* \leftarrow \mathsf{SC}(par, sk_S^*, pk_R^*, m_b)$
    $b' \leftarrow \mathcal{A}_2^{\mathcal{O}}(st, c^*)$
    If $b = b'$ return 1
    Else return 0

$\mathrm{Exp}_{SC,\mathcal{A}}^{\texttt{dM-wUF-iCMA}}(k):$
    $L \leftarrow \emptyset;\quad par \leftarrow \mathsf{Setup}(1^k)$
    $(pk_S^*, sk_S^*) \leftarrow \mathsf{KG}_S(par)$
    $(pk_R^*, sk_R^*, c^*) \leftarrow \mathcal{A}^{\mathcal{O}}(par, pk_S^*)$
    $m^* \leftarrow \mathsf{USC}(par, pk_S^*, sk_R^*, c^*)$
    If $m^* \neq \perp \wedge (m^*, pk_R^*) \notin L$ return 1
    Else return 0

$\mathrm{Exp}_{SC,\mathcal{A}}^{\texttt{fM-IND-iCCA}}(k):$
    $par \leftarrow \mathsf{Setup}(1^k)$
    $(pk_S^*, sk_S^*) \leftarrow \mathsf{KG}_S(par)$
    $(pk_R^*, sk_R^*) \leftarrow \mathsf{KG}_R(par)$
    $(m_0, m_1, st) \leftarrow \mathcal{A}_1^{\mathcal{O}}(par, pk_S^*, sk_S^*, pk_R^*,)$
    $b \leftarrow \{0,1\};\quad c^* \leftarrow \mathsf{SC}(par, sk_S^*, pk_R^*, m_b)$
    $b' \leftarrow \mathcal{A}_2^{\mathcal{O}}(st, c^*)$
    If $b = b'$ return 1
    Else return 0

$\mathrm{Exp}_{SC,\mathcal{A}}^{\texttt{fM-wUF-iCMA}}(k):$
    $L \leftarrow \emptyset;\quad par \leftarrow \mathsf{Setup}(1^k)$
    $(pk_S^*, sk_S^*) \leftarrow \mathsf{KG}_S(par);$
    $(pk_R^*, sk_R^*) \leftarrow \mathsf{KG}_R(par)$
    $c^* \leftarrow \mathcal{A}^{\mathcal{O}}(par, pk_S^*, pk_R^*, sk_R^*)$
    $m^* \leftarrow \mathsf{USC}(par, pk_S^*, sk_R^*, c^*)$
    If $m^* \neq \perp \wedge (m^*, pk_R^*) \notin L$ return 1
    Else return 0

Fig. 1. Experiments for confidentiality and unforgeability

- Signcrypt: Given a public receiver key pk_R and a message m, the oracle returns $c \leftarrow \mathsf{SC}(par, sk_S^*, pk_R, m)$, where sk_S^* is the secret sender key generated in the beginning of the experiment. Furthermore, (pk_R, m) is added to the list L.

Likewise, we define (weak) unforgeability against insider chosen message attacks in the fixed challenge key multi-user model (fM-wUF-iCMA) via experiment $\mathrm{Exp}_{SC,\mathcal{A}}^{\texttt{fM-UF-iCMA}}(k)$ shown in Fig. 1 (lower right), where $\mathcal{A}$ has access to a signcryption oracle as defined above.

Definition 2. *A signcryption scheme SC is said to be* X-wUF-iCMA *secure, if* $\Pr[\mathrm{Exp}_{SC,\mathcal{A}}^{\texttt{X-wUF-iCMA}}(k) = 1]$ *is negligible in* k *for any probabilistic polynomial-time algorithm* $\mathcal{A}$*, where* $\mathtt{X} \in \{\mathtt{dM}, \mathtt{fM}\}$*.*

Strong insider unforgeability (dM-sUF-iCMA and fM-sUF-iCMA security) is defined in a similar way to the above, with the only change that the list L now contains (pk_R, m, c) for signcryptions queries made by $\mathcal{A}$, and it is required that $(pk_R^*, m^*, c^*) \notin L$ for the forgery output by $\mathcal{A}$.

Note that Libert et al. [32,30] uses a different unforgeability definition which is concerned about signature extracted from a ciphertext. However, this does not imply the unforgeability mentioned here. (In fact, the scheme proposed in [30] is insecure according to the above definition.)

Outsider Security. While insider security is inherent in the dynamic multi-user model, we can consider a weaker version of the fixed challenge key multi-user model in which the adversary knows neither the private sender key nor the private receiver key for the challenge key pairs. This is modeled by limiting the input given to the adversary $\mathcal{A}$ to (par, pk_S^*, pk_R^*) in the experiments $\mathrm{Exp}_{SC,\mathcal{A}}^{\texttt{fM-IND-iCCA}}(k)$

and $\mathrm{Exp}_{SC,\mathcal{A}}^{\mathrm{fM-wUF-iCMA}}(k)$ defined above. However, with this limited input, $\mathcal{A}$ can no longer compute signcryptions using the challenge private sender key sk_S^* in $\mathrm{Exp}_{SC,\mathcal{A}}^{\mathrm{fM-IND-iCCA}}(k)$, and can no longer compute unsigncryptions using the challenge private receiver key sk_R^* in $\mathrm{Exp}_{SC,\mathcal{A}}^{\mathrm{fM-wUF-iCMA}}(k)$. Hence, in both experiments, $\mathcal{A}$ is given access to oracles $\mathcal{O} = \{\mathtt{Signcrypt}, \mathtt{Unsigncrypt}\}$ defined as in the above.

We denote these modified experiments $\mathrm{Exp}_{SC,\mathcal{A}}^{\mathrm{fM-IND-oCCA}}(k)$ and $\mathrm{Exp}_{SC,\mathcal{A}}^{\mathrm{fM-wUF-oCMA}}(k)$, and define the outsider security notions fM-IND-oCCA and fM-wUF-oCMA in a similar way to the corresponding insider security notions. We furthermore consider the strong variant of the unforgeability notion fM-wUF-oCMA which will be denoted fM-sUF-oCMA, and is defined in a similar way to the corresponding insider notion fM-sUF-iCMA.

Key Registration. In the above experiments, the adversary can freely choose the public keys submitted to signcryption and unsigncryption oracles. However, in systems based on a traditional PKI, users are required to obtain a certificate by registering their public key at a certificate authority before the public key can be used in interaction with other users. This allows additional security measures such as requiring that a user prove knowledge of the secret key corresponding to the public key he is registering. To model security in this scenario, we give the adversary access to a *key registration oracle* in addition to normal queries. The key registration oracle maintains a list L_{PK} of registered key pairs and interacts with $\mathcal{A}$ as follows:

Register-key: Given a key pair (pk, sk), the oracle checks if (pk, sk) is a valid key pair. If not, the oracle returns 0. Otherwise, it adds (pk, sk) to L_{PK}, and returns 1.

When $\mathcal{A}$ submits a signcryption query (pk_R, m) or an unsigncryption query (pk_S, c), it is then required that $(pk_R, *) \in L_{PK}$ and $(pk_S, *) \in L_{PK}$, respectively. We write, for example, dM-sUF-iCMA(KR) to mean dM-sUF-iCMA security with key registration in order to distinguish it from ordinary dM-sUF-iCMA.

Key registration has been used in connection with the dynamic multi-user model in [44]. Furthermore, Gorantla *et al.* [20] defines a multi-user security model in which the adversary cannot choose any of the keys used in the system, but is only given a list of public user keys and access to a corruption oracle. This model implicitly implies key registration and we refer to this as the *static multi-user* model (see [20] for the details of the security definitions in this model). Furthermore, we use the prefix sM- to denote this model. We note that dynamic and fixed challenge key multi-user security with key registration trivially implies the static multi-user security.

Comparison of Security Notions. The hierarchy of the above mentioned security notions is shown in Fig. 2. The proofs of the implications shown in the figure are straightforward and are not given here. We furthermore conjecture that a separation exists between all of the security notions shown in the figure.

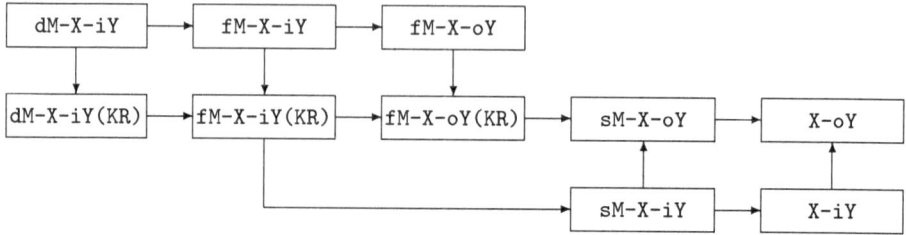

Fig. 2. Implications between security notions. In the figure, "A → B" means that security wrt. security notion A implies security wrt. security notion B. $(\mathtt{X}, \mathtt{Y})$ is $(\mathtt{IND}, \mathtt{CCA})$ for confidentiality, and is either $(\mathtt{wUF}, \mathtt{CMA})$ or $(\mathtt{sUF}, \mathtt{CMA})$ for unforgeability. The security notions without any prefix $\{\mathtt{dM\text{-}}, \mathtt{fM\text{-}}, \mathtt{sM\text{-}}\}$ indicate the two-user security notion.

$\mathbf{Setup}_{sc}(1^k):$	$\mathsf{SC}(par, sk_S, pk_R, m):$
$\quad par_n \leftarrow \mathbf{Setup}_n(1^k)$	$\quad \mathsf{tag} \leftarrow pk_S$
$\quad par_{te} \leftarrow \mathbf{Setup}_{te}(1^k)$	$\quad c_E \leftarrow \mathsf{TEnc}(par_{te}, pk_{R2}, \mathsf{tag}, m)$
$\quad$ Output $par \leftarrow (par_n, par_{te}).$	$\quad K \leftarrow \mathsf{Share}(par_n, pk_{R1}, sk_S)$
$\mathsf{KG}_S(par):$	$\quad \sigma \leftarrow \mathsf{Mac}(K, (pk_{R2} \| c_E))$
$\quad$ Output $(pk_S, sk_S) \leftarrow \mathsf{KG}_n(par_n).$	$\quad$ Output $c \leftarrow (c_E, \sigma).$
$\mathsf{KG}_R(par):$	$\mathsf{USC}(par, pk_S, sk_R, c):$
$\quad (pk_{R1}, sk_{R1}) \leftarrow \mathsf{KG}_n(par_n)$	$\quad$ Parse c as (c_E, σ). $\mathsf{tag} \leftarrow pk_S$
$\quad (pk_{R2}, sk_{R2}) \leftarrow \mathsf{KG}_{te}(par_{te})$	$\quad K \leftarrow \mathsf{Share}(par_n, pk_S, sk_{R1})$
$\quad pk_R \leftarrow (pk_{R1}, pk_{R2})$	$\quad$ If $\mathsf{MVer}(K, (pk_{R2} \| c_E), \sigma) = \bot$
$\quad sk_R \leftarrow (sk_{R1}, sk_{R2})$	$\qquad$ then output $\bot$ and stop.
$\quad$ Output $(pk_R, sk_R).$	$\quad$ Output $\mathsf{TDec}(par_{te}, sk_{R2}, \mathsf{tag}, c_E).$

Fig. 3. Simple composition using symmetric key primitives: TEtK&M

4   Simple Composition Using Symmetric Key Primitives

In this section we show that if only outsider security is required for either confidentiality or unforgeability (or for both), then symmetric key primitives can be used to construct efficient signcryption schemes. However, in order to make use of symmetric key primitives, sender and receiver must share a symmetric key. To achieve this, we employ a (T)NIKE which has the advantage of not requiring the sender and receiver to exchange messages to compute a shared key. As we will see, the combination of symmetric key primitives and (T)NIKE schemes secure against active attacks provides the strongest notion of outsider security. These constructions are only interesting if efficient instantiations of (T)NIKE schemes secure against active attacks can be constructed. However, in Section 7 we show that this is indeed possible. Due to space limitations, all proofs of the theorems in this section are given in the full version [35].

*Tag-based-Encrypt then Key-exchange and MAC (*TEtK&M*).* Firstly, we consider a construction in which outsider unforgeability is achieved by the combined use of a NIKE and a MAC scheme, and which we call *"Tag-based-Encrypt then*

$$
\begin{aligned}
&\text{Setup}_{sc}(1^k): \\
&\quad par_{tn} \leftarrow \text{Setup}_{tn}(1^k) \\
&\quad par_{sig} \leftarrow \text{Setup}_{sig}(1^k) \\
&\quad \text{Output } par \leftarrow (par_{tn}, par_{sig}). \\
&\text{KG}_S(par): \\
&\quad (pk_{S1}, sk_{S1}) \leftarrow \text{KG}_{tn}(par_{tn}) \\
&\quad (pk_{S2}, sk_{S2}) \leftarrow \text{KG}_{sig}(par_{sig}) \\
&\quad pk_S \leftarrow (pk_{S1}, pk_{S2}) \\
&\quad sk_S \leftarrow (sk_{S1}, sk_{S2}) \\
&\quad \text{Output } (pk_S, sk_S). \\
&\text{KG}_R(par): \\
&\quad \text{Output } (pk_R, sk_R) \leftarrow \text{KG}_{tn}(par_{tn}).
\end{aligned}
$$

$$
\begin{aligned}
&\text{SC}(par, sk_S, pk_R, m): \\
&\quad \text{tag} \leftarrow pk_{S2} \\
&\quad K \leftarrow \text{TShare}(par_{tn}, pk_R, sk_{S1}, \text{tag}) \\
&\quad c_E \leftarrow \text{SEnc}(K, m) \\
&\quad \sigma \leftarrow \text{Sign}(par_{sig}, sk_{S2}, (pk_R \| c_E)) \\
&\quad \text{Output } c \leftarrow (c_E, \sigma). \\
&\text{USC}(par, pk_S, sk_R, c): \\
&\quad \text{Parse } c \text{ as } (c_E, \sigma), \quad \text{tag} \leftarrow pk_{S2} \\
&\quad \text{If } \text{SVer}(par_{sig}, pk_{S2}, (pk_R \| c_E), \sigma) = \bot \\
&\quad\quad \text{then output } \bot \text{ and stop.} \\
&\quad K \leftarrow \text{TShare}(par_{tn}, pk_{S1}, sk_R, \text{tag}) \\
&\quad \text{Output } \text{SDec}(K, c_E).
\end{aligned}
$$

Fig. 4. Simple composition using symmetric key primitives: TK&SEtS

$$
\begin{aligned}
&\text{Setup}_{sc}(1^k): \\
&\quad \text{Output } par \leftarrow \text{Setup}_n(1^k). \\
\hline
&\text{KG}_S(par): \\
&\quad \text{Output } (pk_S, sk_S) \leftarrow \text{KG}_n(par). \\
\hline
&\text{KG}_R(par): \\
&\quad \text{Output } (pk_R, sk_R) \leftarrow \text{KG}_n(par).
\end{aligned}
$$

$$
\begin{aligned}
&\text{SC}(par, sk_S, pk_R, m): \\
&\quad K \leftarrow \text{Share}(par, pk_R, sk_S) \\
&\quad \text{Output } c \leftarrow \text{SEnc}(K, m). \\
\hline
&\text{USC}(par, pk_S, sk_R, c): \\
&\quad K \leftarrow \text{Share}(par, pk_S, sk_R) \\
&\quad \text{Output } \text{SDec}(K, c).
\end{aligned}
$$

Fig. 5. Simple composition using symmetric key primitives: K&SE

Key-exchange and MAC" (TEtK&M). More specifically, let $N = (\text{Setup}_n, \text{KG}_n, \text{Share})$ be a NIKE scheme, let $TE = (\text{Setup}_{te}, \text{KG}_{te}, \text{TEnc}, \text{TDec})$ be a TBE scheme, and let $M = (\text{Mac}, \text{MVer})$ be a MAC scheme. Then TEtK&M is defined as shown in Fig. 3. The security of the scheme is provided by the following theorems. Note that the MAC scheme M is required to be *one-to-one*[4] to guarantee confidentiality.

Theorem 3. *Assume TE is* IND-tag-CCA *(resp.* IND-stag-CCA*) secure and M is one-to-one. Then* TEtK&M *is* dM-IND-iCCA *(resp.* fM-IND-iCCA*) secure.*

Theorem 4. *Assume N is secure against active attacks and M is* sUF-CMA *(resp.* wUF-CMA*) secure. Then* TEtK&M *is* fM-sUF-oCMA *(resp.* fM-wUF-oCMA*) secure.*

*Tag-based-Key-exchange and Symmetric-key-Encrypt then Sign (*TK&SEtS*).* Using a similar approach to the above, we consider a signcryption scheme in which outsider confidentiality is achieved by the combined use of a TNIKE scheme and a SKE scheme, and which we call *"Tag-based-Key-exchange and Symmetric-key-Encrypt then Sign"* (TK&SEtS). For this scheme, the tag-based property of TNIKE is required to ensure that a ciphertext is only valid under a single public sender key. Specifically, let $TN = (\text{Setup}_{tn}, \text{KG}_{tn}, \text{TShare})$ be a TNIKE

---

[4] A MAC is said to be one-to-one if given a key K and a message m, there is only one MAC tag σ such that $\text{MVer}(K, m, \sigma) = \top$.

scheme, let $S = (\mathsf{Setup}_{sig}, \mathsf{KG}_{sig}, \mathsf{Sign}, \mathsf{SVer})$ be a signature scheme, and let $SE = (\mathsf{SEnc}, \mathsf{SDec})$ be a SKE scheme. Then TK&SEtS is defined as shown in Fig. 4. The security of this scheme is provided by the following theorems. Note that the SKE scheme SE is only required to be IND-CPA secure to guarantee confidentiality.

Theorem 5. *Assume S is* sUF-CMA *secure, TN is secure against active attacks, and SE is* IND-CPA *secure. Then* TK&SEtS *is* fM-IND-oCCA *secure.*

Theorem 6. *Assume S is* sUF-CMA *(resp.* wUF-CMA*) secure. Then* TK&SEtS *is* dM-sUF-iCMA *(resp.* dM-wUF-iCMA*) secure.*

*Key-exchange then Symmetric-key-Encrypt (*K&SE*).* Finally, we consider a signcryption scheme providing outsider unforgeability and outsider confidentiality. This scheme, which we call *"Key-exchange and Symmetric-key-Encrypt"* (K&SE), consists only of a NIKE scheme and a SKE scheme satisfying the security of *authenticated encryption* [7]. Interestingly, in this scheme a ciphertext consists only of the output of the underlying SKE scheme. Specifically, let $N = (\mathsf{Setup}_n, \mathsf{KG}_n, \mathsf{Share})$ be a NIKE scheme, and let $SE = (\mathsf{SEnc}, \mathsf{SDec})$ be a SKE scheme. Then K&SE is defined as shown in Fig. 5. The following state that K&SE satisfies both outsider confidentiality and outsider unforgeability.

Theorem 7. *Assume N is secure against active attacks and SE is* IND-CCA *secure. Then* K&SE *is* fM-IND-oCCA *secure.*

Theorem 8. *Assume N is secure against active attacks and SE is* INT-CTXT *secure. Then* K&SE *is* fM-sUF-oCMA *secure.*

5   Simple Composition Using Tag-Based Encryption

An *et al.* [3] analyzed the security of the simple composition of signature and encryption, and showed that both sign-then-encrypt and encrypt-then-sign are secure, but only for a weaker notion of confidentiality termed *generalized IND-CCA* security. If ordinary IND-CCA security is required, the latter becomes insecure, even if the used signature scheme is strongly unforgeable and the encryption scheme is IND-CCA secure. Furthermore, simple composition does not yield multi-user security. In [3], this is overcome by including the public sender key in the plaintext, and the public receiver key in the input to the signing algorithm. While this achieves multi-user security, it also introduces additional ciphertext overhead.

Here we show that by using a TBE scheme, multi-user security can be achieved without introducing additional ciphertext overhead. This is of course only useful if it is possible to construct TBE schemes which do not have a higher ciphertext overhead than ordinary PKE schemes. In Section 7 we show that this is indeed possible for the currently most efficient encryption schemes in both the standard and the random oracle model. Due to space limitations, the proofs of the theorems in this section are given in the full version [35].

$\text{Setup}_{sc}(1^k):$
  $par_{te} \leftarrow \text{Setup}_{te}(1^k)$
  $par_{sig} \leftarrow \text{Setup}_{sig}(1^k)$
  Output $par \leftarrow (par_{te}, par_{sig}).$

$\text{KG}_S(par):$
  Output $(pk_S, sk_S) \leftarrow \text{KG}_{sig}(par_{sig}).$
$\text{KG}_R(par):$
  Output $(pk_R, sk_R) \leftarrow \text{KG}_{te}(par_{te}).$

Sign-then-Tag-based-Encrypt StTE

$\text{SC}(par, sk_S, pk_R, m):$
  $\sigma \leftarrow \text{Sign}(par_{sig}, sk_S, (pk_R||m))$
  $\text{tag} \leftarrow pk_S$
  $c \leftarrow \text{TEnc}(par_{te}, pk_R, \text{tag}, (m||\sigma))$
  Output $c.$

$\text{USC}(par, pk_S, sk_R, c):$
  $\text{tag} \leftarrow pk_S$
  $(m||\sigma)/\bot \leftarrow \text{TDec}(par_{te}, sk_R, \text{tag}, c)$
    (if output is $\bot$, then output $\bot$ and stop.)
  If $\text{SVer}(par_{sig}, pk_S, (pk_R||m), \sigma) = \top$
    then output m, otherwise output $\bot$.

Tag-based-Encrypt-then-Sign TEtS

$\text{SC}(par, sk_S, pk_R, m):$
  $\text{tag} \leftarrow pk_S$
  $c_E \leftarrow \text{TEnc}(par_{te}, pk_R, \text{tag}, m)$
  $\sigma \leftarrow \text{Sign}(par_{sig}, sk_S, (pk_R||c_E))$
  Output $c \leftarrow (c_E, \sigma).$

$\text{USC}(par, pk_S, sk_R, c):$
  Parse c as $(c_E, \sigma),$ $\text{tag} \leftarrow pk_S$
  If $\text{SVer}(par_{sig}, pk_S, (pk_R||c_E), \sigma) = \bot$
    then output $\bot$ and stop.
  Output $\text{TDec}(par_{te}, sk_R, \text{tag}, c_E).$

Fig. 6. Simple composition of signature and TBE. Note that StTE and TEtS use the same setup and key generation algorithms.

Let $TE = (\text{Setup}_{te}, \text{KG}_{te}, \text{TEnc}, \text{TDec})$ be a TBE scheme and let $S = (\text{Setup}_{sig}, \text{KG}_{sig}, \text{Sign}, \text{SVer})$ be a signature scheme. Then the *"Sign-then-Tag-based-Encrypt"* (StTE) and *"Tag-based-Encrypt-then-Sign"* (TEtS) schemes are defined as shown in Fig. 6. We achieve the following security results for StTE.

Theorem 9. *Assume TE is* IND-tag-CCA *(resp.* IND-stag-CCA*) secure. Then* StTE *is* dM-IND-iCCA *(resp.* fM-IND-iCCA*) secure.*

Theorem 10. *Assume S is* wUF-CMA *secure. Then* StTE *is* dM-wUF-iCMA *secure.*

Note that the receiver trivially obtains a publicly verifiable signature of the sender on the sent message m when unsigncrypting a valid ciphertext. Hence, the receiver can convince any third party that the message m was indeed sent by the sender (this provides a similar type of non-repudiation to [32], which introduces the notion of *detachable signatures*).

Like the encrypt-then-sign approach, TEtS will generally not achieve IND-CCA security, even if the used TBE scheme is IND-CCA secure. However, if the signature scheme is *one-to-one*[5] the following results can be obtained.

Theorem 11. *Assume TE is* IND-tag-CCA *(resp.* IND-stag-CCA*) secure and S is one-to-one. Then* TEtS *is* dM-IND-iCCA *(resp.* fM-IND-iCCA*) secure.*

Furthermore, unlike StTE, if a strongly unforgeable signature scheme is used, TEtS will also be strongly unforgeable (note that the one-to-one property is not required in the following theorem).

---

[5] A signature scheme is said to be one-to-one if given public parameters par, a public key pk, and a message m, there exists only *one* signature σ such that $\text{SVer}(par, pk, m, \sigma) = \top$.

Theorem 12. *Assume* S *is* sUF-CMA *(resp.* wUF-CMA*) secure. Then* TEtS *is* dM-sUF-iCMA *(resp.* dM-wUF-iCMA*) secure.*

Currently, only random oracle model signature schemes, like BLS [10], have the one-to-one property. However, BLS is one of the most efficient schemes in terms of signature size and signing cost, and as we will see in Section 9, constructing TEtS using BLS and a tag-based variant of DHIES [1] (see also Section 7) will yield an insider secure signcryption scheme in the random oracle model, which is at least as efficient as the currently most efficient insider secure schemes by Libert *et al.* [29] and by Li *et al.* [28] which are also inspired by BLS and the DHIES scheme.

6   Signcryption Composability

While the simple composition of signature and TBE yields signcryption schemes which are at least as efficient as any other insider secure signcryption scheme (see Section 9), a part of the original motivation for considering signcryption as a separate primitive, is to achieve higher efficiency than such black-box compositions. In this section we show how to achieve insider secure signcryption schemes in the standard model which is more efficient than a black-box composition of the most efficient standard model signature and encryption schemes.

The idea behind our approach is fairly simple. Since both signature and encryption in the standard model are probabilistic, the sender could potentially reuse the same "randomness" for both signing and encryption. By doing so, both ciphertext and computational overhead can potentially be reduced. Naturally, a signature and an encryption schemes need to "match" to enable this, and to be able to prove security of the resulting signcryption scheme, we require the individual schemes to have a few special properties. We say that a pair of schemes satisfying these requirements are *signcryption composable* (SC-composable), and we will formally define the requirements below. Since we adopt the KEM/DEM approach, our SC-definition will be concerned with a signature scheme and a TBKEM scheme. We furthermore assume that both the TBKEM and the signature scheme are *patitionable*[6] i.e. for a TBKEM, it is required that the encapsulation algorithm can be divided into two deterministic algorithms TE_1 and TE_2 such that an encapsulation of a key can be computed by picking random $r \leftarrow \mathcal{R}$ (the randomness space $\mathcal{R}$ is specified by *par*), computing $c_1 \leftarrow \mathsf{TE}_1(par, r)$ and $(c_2, K) \leftarrow \mathsf{TE}_2(par, pk, \mathsf{tag}, r)$, and returning the encapsulation $c \leftarrow (c_1, c_2)$ and the encapsulated key K, and given c_1 and a tag, there is at most one c_2 and one K such that $\mathtt{TDecap}(par, sk, \mathsf{tag}, (c_1, c_2)) = K$. Partitionability of a signature scheme is defined in a similar way, and we let S_1 and S_2 denote the message independent part (taking only *par* and r as input) and the message dependent part of the signing algorithm, respectively.

Definition 13. *We say that a partitionable TBKEM $TK = (\mathtt{Setup}_{tk}, \mathsf{KG}_{tk},$ TEncap, TDecap) and a partitionalble signature scheme $S = (\mathtt{Setup}_{sig}, \mathsf{KG}_{sig},$*

---

[6] Partitionability of a signature scheme has previously been defined in [11].

Sign, SVer) *are* signcryption composable *(SC-composable) if they satisfy the following:*

- **Property 1.** *(Compatible Setup) There exists an algorithm* Setup'_{tk} *that, given public parameters* $par_{sig} \leftarrow \mathsf{Setup}_{sig}(1^k)$ *as input, generates* par_{tk} *distributed identically to the output of* $\mathsf{Setup}_{tk}(1^k)$. *Furthermore, there exists an algorithm* Setup'_{sig} *that, given* $par_{tk} \leftarrow \mathsf{Setup}_{tk}(1^k)$ *as input, generates* par_{sig} *distributed identically to the output of* $\mathsf{Setup}_{sig}(1^k)$.
- **Property 2.** *(Shared Randomness) Let* $\mathcal{R}_{tk}$ *and* $\mathcal{R}_{sig}$ *be the randomness spaces specified by* par_{tk} *and* par_{sig} *used by* TEncap *of* TK *and* Sign *of* S, *respectively. It is required that*
  - $\mathcal{R}_{sig} = \mathcal{R}_{tk} \times \mathcal{R}_{sig}^+$ *i.e. the randomness space for* TK *is shared by both* TK *and* S *(in the following we will use* $\mathcal{R}$ *to denote the common randomness space). We allow* $\mathcal{R}_{sig}^+$ *to be empty.*
  - *For all choices of* $(r, s) \in \mathcal{R} \times \mathcal{R}_{sig}^+$ *and all* $\sigma_1 \leftarrow \mathsf{S}_1(par_{sig}, (r, s))$, *it is required that* σ_1 *can be written as* $\sigma_1 = (c_1, \sigma_1')$ *such that* $c_1 = \mathsf{TE}_1(par_{tk}, r)$. *We allow* σ_1' *to be an empty string.*
- **Property 3.** *(Signature/Ciphertext Simulatability) There exist algorithms* S_1', S_2' *and* TE_2' *with the following properties:*
  - TE_2': *Given* par_{tk}, *a public/private key pair* $(pk_{tk}, sk_{tk}) \leftarrow \mathsf{KG}_{tk}(par_{tk})$, *a tag* tag, *and* $c_1 = \mathsf{TE}_1(par_{tk}, r)$ *for some* $r \in \mathcal{R}$, *this algorithm outputs* c_2 *and* K *such that* $(c_2, K) = \mathsf{TE}_2(par_{tk}, pk_{tk}, tag, r)$.
  - S_1': *Given* par_{sig}, $c_1 = \mathsf{TE}_1(par_{tk}, r)$ *for some* $r \in \mathcal{R}$, *and* $s \in \mathcal{R}_{sig}^+$, *this algorithm outputs* σ_1' *such that* $(c_1, \sigma_1') = \mathsf{S}_1(par_{sig}, (r, s))$. *If* $\mathcal{R}_{sig}^+$ *is empty, we do not consider this algorithm.*
  - S_2': *Given* par_{sig}, $(pk_{sig}, sk_{sig}) \leftarrow \mathsf{KG}_{sig}(par_{sig})$, *a message* m, $c_1 = \mathsf{TE}_1(par_{tk}, r)$ *for some* $r \in \mathcal{R}$, *and* $s \in \mathcal{R}_{sig}^+$, *this algorithm outputs* σ_2 *such that* $\sigma_2 = \mathsf{S}_2(par_{sig}, sk_{sig}, m, (r, s))$.

Although the requirements might seem somewhat restrictive, as shown in Section 8, tag-based variants of many of the existing standard model KEMs are in fact SC-composable with a number of standard model signature schemes.

6.1   Signcryption from SC-Composable Schemes

Let $TK = (\mathsf{Setup}_{tk}, \mathsf{KG}_{tk}, \mathsf{TEncap}, \mathsf{TDecap})$ be a partitionable TBKEM scheme in which $\mathsf{TEncap} = (\mathsf{TE}_1, \mathsf{TE}_2)$, let $S = (\mathsf{Setup}_{sig}, \mathsf{KG}_{sig}, \mathsf{Sign}, \mathsf{SVer})$ be a partitionable signature scheme in which $\mathsf{Sign} = (\mathsf{S}_1, \mathsf{S}_2)$, and let $D = (\mathsf{DEnc}, \mathsf{DDec})$ be a DEM. Furthermore, let TK and S be SC-composable with shared randomness space $\mathcal{R}$. We assume that the encapsulated-key space of TK and the key space of D is the same (if this is not the case, we can use an appropriate key derivation function).

Then, we construct a signcryption scheme SC as shown in Fig. 7. We note that our scheme allows c_2 in TK and σ_1' in S to be empty strings. The security of SC is guaranteed by the following theorems. To prove unforgeability, we require *key registration*, as introduced in Section 3.1.

$$
\begin{array}{l|l}
\textsf{Setup}_{sc}(1^k): & \textsf{KG}_S(par): \\
\quad par_{tk} \leftarrow \textsf{Setup}_{tk}(1^k) & \quad \text{Output } (pk_S, sk_S) \leftarrow \textsf{KG}_{sig}(par_{sig}). \\
\quad par_{sig} \leftarrow \textsf{Setup}'_{sig}(par_{tk}) & \textsf{KG}_R(par): \\
\quad \text{Output } par \leftarrow (par_{tk}, par_{sig}) & \quad \text{Output } (pk_R, sk_R) \leftarrow \textsf{KG}_{tk}(par_{tk}). \\
\textsf{SC}(par, sk_S, pk_R, m): & \textsf{USC}(par, pk_S, sk_R, c): \\
\quad (r, s) \leftarrow \mathcal{R} \times \mathcal{R}^+_{sig}, \quad \textsf{tag} \leftarrow pk_S & \quad \text{Parse } c \text{ as } (c_1, c_2, c_3). \quad \textsf{tag} \leftarrow pk_S \\
\quad (c_1, \sigma'_1) \leftarrow \textsf{S}_1(par_{sig}, (r, s)) & \quad K \leftarrow \textsf{TDecap}(par_{tk}, sk_R, \textsf{tag}, (c_1, c_2)) \\
\quad \sigma_2 \leftarrow \textsf{S}_2(par_{sig}, sk_S, (pk_R\|m), (r, s)) & \quad (m\|\sigma'_1\|\sigma_2) \leftarrow \textsf{DDec}(K, c_3) \\
\quad (c_2, K) \leftarrow \textsf{TE}_2(par_{tk}, pk_R, \textsf{tag}, r) & \quad \sigma \leftarrow (c_1, \sigma'_1, \sigma_2) \\
\quad c_3 \leftarrow \textsf{DEnc}(K, (m\|\sigma'_1\|\sigma_2)) & \quad \text{If } \textsf{SVer}(par_{sig}, pk_S, (pk_R\|m), \sigma) = \top \\
\quad \text{Output } c \leftarrow (c_1, c_2, c_3). & \quad \text{then output } m, \text{ otherwise output } \bot.
\end{array}
$$

Fig. 7. Proposed composition SC from SC-composable TBKEM and signature schemes

Theorem 14. *Assume* TK *is* IND-tag-CCA *(resp.* IND-stag-CCA*) secure,* D *is* IND-CCA *secure, and* TK *and* S *are SC-composable. Then* SC *is* dM-IND-iCCA *(resp.* fM-IND-iCCA*) secure.*

Theorem 15. *Assume* S *is* sUF-CMA *(resp.* wUF-CMA*) secure and* TK *and* S *are SC-composable. Then* SC *is* dM-sUF-iCMA(KR) *(resp.* dM-wUF-iCMA(KR)*) secure.*

The proofs of the above theorems are given in the full version [35]. Note that, unlike the simple compositions in the previous section, SC achieves strong unforgeability without imposing any restrictions which forces instantiations to be in the random oracle model. Note also that, like StTE, in the unsigncryption process the receiver obtains $\sigma = (c_1, \sigma'_1, \sigma_2)$ which is a publicly verifiable signature of the sender on the sent message m, and hence, the scheme can provide non-repudiation.

7   How to Obtain Tag-Based Primitives

The constructions in Sections 4, 5 and 6 depend on the existence of efficient (T)NIKE schemes, TBE schemes and TBKEM schemes. In this section we will show how existing schemes can be extended to tag-based schemes by exploiting their internal structure. Although this approach is not generic, it is simple, applicable to many of the existing schemes and, importantly, achieves tag-based schemes at practically no additional cost.

7.1   (T)NIKE Schemes in the Random Oracle Model

Consider the *Hashed Diffie-Hellman* (HDH) scheme which is defined as follows: The setup algorithm Setup picks a group $\mathbb{G}$ with prime order p, a generator $g \in \mathbb{G}$, and a hash function $H : \{0,1\}^* \to \{0,1\}^k$. The key generation algorithm KG picks $x \leftarrow \mathbb{Z}_p$ and sets $(pk, sk) \leftarrow (g^x, x)$. Suppose one party's key pair is $(pk_1, sk_1) = (g^x, x)$ and the other's is $(pk_2, sk_2) = (g^y, y)$, and suppose g^x is lexicographically smaller than g^y. Then the shared key algorithm Share outputs $K \leftarrow H(g^x, g^y, g^{xy})$.

It is relatively easy to show that this scheme is secure against active attacks in the random oracle model assuming the gap Diffie-Hellman (GDH) assumption holds in $\mathbb{G}$, using a proof similar to [15]. Furthermore, if the shared key is computed as $K \leftarrow H(g^x, g^y, g^{xy}, \mathsf{tag})$ where tag is a tag given as input to Share, the resulting scheme will be a TNIKE scheme which we will denote tHDH. In a similar manner to the HDH scheme, the security of tHDH can be shown assuming the GDH assumption holds in $\mathbb{G}$, using a proof similar to [15].

Lastly, note that a TNIKE scheme secure under the computational Diffie-Hellman (CDH) assumption can be obtained by making a similar modification to the Twin Diffie-Hellman protocol by [15], but at the cost of an increase in computational cost compared to tHDH.

7.2   TBE and TBKEM Schemes

It is possible to generically transform any IND-CCA secure PKE scheme into an IND-tag-CCA secure TBE scheme, simply by encrypting the tag together with the message [25]. Since a TBE is trivially a TBKEM, this approach also leads to a generic construction of TBKEMs. However, a drawback of this approach is that it leads to ciphertext expansion and possibly inefficient TBKEMs, and since our main concern is efficiency, we take a different approach in the following.

TBE Schemes in the Random Oracle Model. To construct an efficient TBE scheme, we consider the IND-CCA secure PKE schemes in the random oracle model which have hybrid structure i.e. they can be rewritten in the KEM/DEM style, and a random oracle is used as a key derivation function for a key of the DEM part. Typical examples of such schemes are the *DHIES* scheme [1] and the *Twin ElGamal* scheme [15]. We can turn such PKE schemes into IND-tag-CCA secure TBE schemes simply by inputting a tag into the key derivation function.

Here, as an example, we show in Fig. 8 a tag-based variant of the DHIES scheme which we denote tDHIES. We note that similar modification to the twin ElGamal scheme [15] will result in a corresponding secure tag-based variant (which we denote tTwin).

Since the standard KEM/DEM composition theorem [16] trivially applies to the composition of an IND-tag-CCA secure TBKEM and an IND-CCA secure DEM, it is sufficient to see that the TBKEM part of the tDHIES is actually IND-tag-CCA secure. It is known that the KEM part of the original DHIES is IND-CCA secure in the random oracle model based on the GDH assumption [17,21]. Since the proof of the IND-tag-CCA security of the TBKEM part of tDHIES is essentially the same as the IND-CCA security proof for the ECIES-KEM in [17], we omit the proof here.

TBKEM Schemes in the Standard Model. Here, we consider existing IND-CCA secure KEM schemes in the standard model that use a collision resistant hash function (CRHF) or a target CRHF (TCRHF) in the construction of an encapsulation. Specifically, we consider the very efficient and recently proposed schemes [13,26,23,22] which all use a (T)CRHF as a building block (to make

$\mathsf{Setup}_{te}(1^k)$:
   Pick a group $\mathbb{G}$ (order p) and $g \leftarrow \mathbb{G}$.
   Pick a DEM $D = (\mathsf{DEnc}, \mathsf{DDEM})$
     with key space $\{0,1\}^k$
   Pick $H : \{0,1\}^* \to \{0,1\}^k$.
   Output $par \leftarrow (p, g, \mathbb{G}, D, H)$.
$\mathsf{KG}_{te}(par)$:
   $x \leftarrow \mathbb{Z}_p$, $X \leftarrow g^x$
   Output $(pk, sk) \leftarrow (X, x)$.

$\mathsf{TEnc}(par, pk, \mathsf{tag}, m)$:
   $r \leftarrow \mathbb{Z}_p$, $\quad c_1 \leftarrow g^r$, $\quad K \leftarrow H(\mathsf{tag}\|c_1\|X^r)$
   $c_2 \leftarrow \mathsf{DEnc}(K, m)$
   $c \leftarrow (c_1, c_2)$
   Output (c, K).

$\mathsf{TDec}(par, sk, \mathsf{tag}, c)$:
   Parse c as (c_1, c_2). $\quad K \leftarrow H(\mathsf{tag}\|c_1\|c_1^x)$
   Output $m \leftarrow \mathsf{DDec}(K, c_2)$.

Fig. 8. A TBE scheme based on the DHIES scheme (tDHIES)

$\mathsf{Setup}_{tk}(1^k)$:
   Pick bilinear groups $(\mathbb{G}, \hat{\mathbb{G}}, \mathbb{G}_T)$ (order p)
     with $e : \mathbb{G} \times \hat{\mathbb{G}} \to \mathbb{G}_T$ and $\psi : \hat{\mathbb{G}} \to \mathbb{G}$
   Pick $\hat{g} \leftarrow \hat{\mathbb{G}}$, and set $g \leftarrow \psi(\hat{g})$.
   Pick a CRHF $\mathsf{CR} : \{0,1\}^* \to \{0,1\}^n$.
   Output $par \leftarrow (p, \mathbb{G}, \mathbb{G}_T, e, \psi, g, \hat{g}, \mathsf{CR})$.
$\mathsf{KG}_{tk}(par)$:
   $u', u_1, \ldots, u_n \leftarrow \mathbb{Z}_p$
   $U' \leftarrow g^{u'}$, $U_i \leftarrow g^{u_i}$ for $1 \le i \le n$
   $\alpha \leftarrow \mathbb{Z}_p$, $\quad \hat{h} \leftarrow \hat{g}^\alpha$, $\quad \mathsf{z} \leftarrow e(g, \hat{g})^\alpha$
   $pk \leftarrow (\mathsf{z}, U', U_1, \ldots, U_n)$
   $sk \leftarrow (\hat{h}, u', u_1, \ldots, u_n)$
   Output (pk, sk).

$\mathsf{TEncap}(par, pk, \mathsf{tag})$:
   $r \leftarrow \mathbb{Z}_p$, $\quad c_1 \leftarrow g^r$, $\quad t \leftarrow \mathsf{CR}(\mathsf{tag}\|c_1)$
   Let t be an n-bit string $t_1\|t_2\|\ldots\|t_n$
   $c_2 \leftarrow (U' \prod_{i=1}^n U_i^{t_i})^r$
   $c \leftarrow (c_1, c_2)$, $\quad K \leftarrow \mathsf{z}^r$
   Output (c, K).
$\mathsf{TDecap}(par, sk, \mathsf{tag}, c)$:
   Parse c as (c_1, c_2).
   $t \leftarrow \mathsf{CR}(\mathsf{tag}\|c_1)$
   Let t be an n-bit string $t_1\|t_2\|\ldots\|t_n$
   If $c_2 = c_1^{u' + \sum_{i=1}^n u_i t_i}$
     Output $K \leftarrow e(c_1, \hat{h})$
   Otherwise output $\bot$.

Fig. 9. TBKEM scheme based on the Boyen-Mei-Waters PKE (tBMW1)

[23] IND-CCA secure, we have to apply the technique from [4]). In these schemes, if we simply add a tag as an additional input to the hash function, we can achieve secure TBKEM schemes. As an example, we show in Fig. 9 a partitionable TBKEM scheme obtained from the practical PKE proposed by Boyen, Mei, and Waters [13] which we denote tBMW1 (note that the original scheme is a PKE scheme but here, we turn it into a TBKEM scheme).

Since the security proof is essentially the proof of the original BMW PKE scheme (whose proof is almost identical to that of the Waters IBE [45] which is adaptive identity chosen plaintext secure), the details are omitted here.

Several other KEMs share a similar structure to the Boyen *et al.* KEM [12] (e.g. [26,23,22,21]), and can be modified in a similar way to achieve TBKEMs. However, whether IND-tag-CCA or IND-stag-CCA security is achieved is dependent on how the original KEM is proved secure. In particular, the TBKEMs obtained from [26,23,22,21] will only achieve IND-stag-CCA security.

8 Concrete SC-Composable Schemes

We will now introduce a number of signature/TBKEM pairs which are SC-composable, using the TBKEMs introduced in the previous section. Consider the

TBKEM tBMW1 shown in Fig. 9. The scheme is partitionable with the algorithms $\mathsf{TE}_1(par, r) = g^r$ and $\mathsf{TE}_2(par, pk_R, \mathsf{tag}, r) = (c_2, K)$ where $c_2 \leftarrow (U' \prod_{i=1}^n U_i^{t_i})^r$, $K \leftarrow \mathsf{Z}^r$ and $t \leftarrow \mathsf{CR}(\mathsf{tag} \| g^r)$. An example of a suitable signature scheme to combine with this TBKEM is the scheme by Waters [45] (Waters). Here, we assume that Waters is implemented with the same bilinear groups as tBMW1 in Fig. 9. Signatures are of the form $\sigma = (g^r, g^\alpha \cdot \psi(\hat{V}' \prod_{i=1}^n \hat{V}_i^{m_i})^r) \in (\mathbb{G})^2$ where $g^\alpha \in \mathbb{G}$ and $(\hat{V}', \hat{V}_1, \ldots, \hat{V}_n) \in (\hat{\mathbb{G}})^{n+1}$ are elements of the private and public signer key, sk_S and pk_S, respectively, and m_i is the i-th bit of the message m (see [45] for a full description of the scheme). Furthermore, the scheme is partitionable with $\mathsf{S}_1(par, r) = g^r$ and $\mathsf{S}_2(par, sk_S, m, r) = g^\alpha \cdot \psi(\hat{V}' \prod_{i=1}^n \hat{V}_i^{m_i})^r$, where $r \in \mathbb{Z}_p$.

It is relatively easy to check that the two schemes satisfy the requirements about compatible setup (property 1) and shared randomness (property 2) of Definition 13 with shared randomness space $\mathbb{Z}_p$. Furthermore the algorithms TE'_2 and S'_2 for the scheme are defined as $\mathsf{TE}'_2(sk, \mathsf{tag}, g^r) = ((g^r)^{u' + \sum_{i=1}^n u_i t_i}, e(g^r, \hat{g}^\alpha))$ and $\mathsf{S}'_2(sk, m, g^r) = g^\alpha \cdot (g^r)^{u' + \sum_{i=1}^n u_i m_i}$, and satisfy the requirement about ciphertext/signature simulatability (property 3). Taking into account that tBMW1 is IND-tag-CCA secure and that Waters is wUF-CMA secure, Theorem 14 and 15 yields that the signcryption scheme SC shown in Fig. 7 is dM-IND-iCCA and dM-wUF-iCMA(KR) secure when instantiated with these schemes.

However, there are many other SC-composable pairs. For example, if a strongly unforgeable signcryption scheme is desired, Waters signatures can be replaced by the sUF-CMA secure variant proposed by Boneh et al. [11] (BSW). Alternatively, the signatures by Camenisch et al. [14] (CL) can be used to achieve a scheme with compact public sender keys (this scheme can furthermore be made sUF-CMA secure using the techniques from [11]). Likewise, the TBKEM can be replaced by any of the TBKEMs mentioned in the previous section to achieve signcryption schemes with various properties. Note that any combination of the mentioned signature schemes and TBKEMs will be SC-composable (see the full version [35] for details).

9   Comparison

In Fig. 10, we list the achieved security notions, underlying security assumptions and computational and ciphertext overhead for previously proposed signcryption schemes as well as the constructions discussed in this paper. All schemes are instantiated to obtain minimal ciphertext and computational overhead. Specifically, we assume that an IND-CCA secure DEM has no ciphertext overhead (i.e. is length preserving) and IND-CPA and IND-CCA secure SKE have ciphertext overheads which are of the size $|IV|$ and $|IV| + |\mathsf{MAC}|$ [7], respectively. In the original schemes of LYWDC [28] and LQ [29], the public sender key is included as part of the plaintext. However, this is only needed when considering anonymity, and we leave out the sender key from the plaintext in these schemes. Dent [18] and GBN [20] require a "signcryption DEM" which is a DEM that satisfies both IND-CCA and INT-CTXT security. To achieve this we assume that the Encrypt-then-MAC approach is used as discussed in [18].

Scheme	RO	Confidentiality	Unforgeability	Comp. Cost sc	Comp. Cost usc	Overhead Elements	Bits
Dent [18]	Yes	IND-oCCA / CDH	sUF-oCMA / CDH	[2,0;0]	[1,0;0]	$\|\mathbb{G}_e\| + \|\mathsf{MAC}\|$	240
BD [8]	Yes	IND-oCCA / GDH	sUF-iCMA / CDH	[3,0;0]	[0,2;0]	$\|\mathbb{G}_e\| + 2\|\mathbb{Z}_p\|$	480
GBN [20] + HMQV [27]	Yes	sM-IND-iCCA / CDH	sM-sUF-oCMA / CDH	[2,0;0]	[0,1;0]	$\|\mathbb{G}_e\| + \|\mathsf{MAC}\|$	240
Zheng [47,5,6]	Yes	fM-IND-oCCA / GDH	dM-sUF-iCMA / GDL	[1,0;0]	[1,1;0]	$2\|\mathbb{Z}_p\|$	320
LQ [29]	Yes	dM-IND-iCCA / co-CDH	dM-sUF-iCMA / co-CDH	[3,0;0]	[1,0;2]	$2\|\mathbb{G}_p\|$	342
LYWDC [28]	Yes	dM-IND-iCCA / co-CDH	dM-sUF-iCMA / co-CDH	[3,0;0]	[1,0;2]	$2\|\mathbb{G}_p\|$	342
Tan1 [42] + BB [9]	No	dM-IND-iCCA / DDH	sUF-iCMA / q-SDH	[3,1;0]	[0,2;1]	$2\|\mathbb{G}_e\| + \|\mathbb{G}_p\| + \|\mathbb{Z}_p\| + \|\mathsf{MAC}\|$	731
Tan2 [43] + BB [9]	No	dM-IND-iCCA / DDH	sUF-iCMA / q-SDH	[4,1;0]	[1,2;1]	$3\|\mathbb{G}_e\| + \|\mathbb{G}_p\| + \|\mathbb{Z}_p\|$	811
Tan3 [44]	No	dM-IND-iCCA / DBDH	dM-sUF-iCMA (KR) / q-SDH	[3,2;0]	[2,1;4]	$3\|\mathbb{G}_p\| + 2\|\mathbb{Z}_p\|$	833
K&SE(HDH)	Yes	fM-IND-oCCA / GDH	fM-sUF-oCMA / GDH	[1,0;0]	[1,0;0]	$\|IV\| + \|\mathsf{MAC}\|$	160
TK&SEtS(tHDH,BLS)	Yes	fM-IND-oCCA / GDH, co-CDH	dM-sUF-iCMA / co-CDH	[2,0;0]	[1,0;2]	$\|IV\| + \|\mathbb{G}_p\|$	251
TEtK&M(HDH,tDHIES)	Yes	dM-IND-iCCA / GDH	fM-sUF-oCMA / GDH	[3,0;0]	[2,0;0]	$\|\mathbb{G}_e\| + \|\mathsf{MAC}\|$	240
TEtS(tDHIES,BLS)	Yes	dM-IND-iCCA / GDH	dM-sUF-iCMA / co-CDH	[3,0;0]	[1,0;2]	$\|\mathbb{G}_e\| + \|\mathbb{G}_p\|$	331
TEtS(tTwin,BLS)	Yes	dM-IND-iCCA / CDH	dM-sUF-iCMA / co-CDH	[4,0;0]	[2,0;2]	$\|\mathbb{G}_e\| + \|\mathbb{G}_p\|$	331
StTE(tBMW1,Waters)	No	dM-IND-iCCA / DBDH	dM-wUF-iCMA / co-CDH	[5,0;0]	[1,0;3]	$4\|\mathbb{G}_p\|$	684
StTE(tBMW1,BB)	No	dM-IND-iCCA / DBDH	dM-wUF-iCMA / q-SDH	[4,0;0]	[1,1;2]	$3\|\mathbb{G}_p\| + \|\mathbb{Z}_p\|$	673
SC(tBMW2,CL)	No	fM-IND-iCCA / DBDH	dM-wUF-iCMA (KR) / LRSW	[4,1;0]	[1,0;6]	$4\|\mathbb{G}_p\|$	684
SC(tBMW2,CL')	No	fM-IND-iCCA / DBDH	dM-sUF-iCMA (KR) / LRSW	[4,2;0]	[1,1;6]	$4\|\mathbb{G}_p\| + \|\mathbb{Z}_p\|$	844
SC(tHaKu,Waters)	No	fM-IND-iCCA / CDH	dM-wUF-iCMA (KR) / co-CDH	[4+k,0;0]	[2+k,0;2]	$4\|\mathbb{G}_p\|$	684
SC(tHaKu,BSW)	No	fM-IND-iCCA / CDH	dM-sUF-iCMA (KR) / co-CDH	[4+k,1;0]	[2+k,1;2]	$4\|\mathbb{G}_p\| + \|\mathbb{Z}_p\|$	844
SC(tBMW1,Waters)	No	dM-IND-iCCA / DBDH	dM-wUF-iCMA (KR) / co-CDH	[4,0;0]	[1,0;3]	$3\|\mathbb{G}_p\|$	513
SC(tBMW1,BSW)	No	dM-IND-iCCA / DBDH	dM-sUF-iCMA (KR) / co-CDH	[4,1;0]	[1,1;3]	$3\|\mathbb{G}_p\| + \|\mathbb{Z}_p\|$	673

Fig. 10. Comparison of existing and proposed signcryption schemes. Column "Comp. Cost" lists the computational overhead for signcryption (sc) and unsigncryption (usc), where $[a, b; c]$ denotes a exponentiations, b multi-exponentiations and c pairing computations (multiplications, computation costs of hash functions and symmetric key primitives are ignored). In the overhead column, $\|\mathbb{G}_e\|$, $\|\mathbb{G}_p\|$, $\|\mathbb{Z}_p\|$, $\|IV\|$, and $\|\mathsf{MAC}\|$ denote the size of a group element on an ordinary elliptic curve, that of an elliptic curve equipped with an asymmetric pairing, the size of an exponent, the size of an initialization vector for SKE, and the size of a MAC tag, respectively. When instantiated to achieve 80 bits of security, we set $\|\mathbb{G}_e\| = \|\mathbb{Z}_p\| = \|H\| = 160$ bits, $\|\mathbb{G}_p\| = 171$ bits, $\|\mathbb{G}_{sp}\| = 237$ bits, $\|IV\| = 80$ bits, and $\|\mathsf{MAC}\| = 80$ bits. tBMW2 and tHaKu denote the TBKEMs obtained from [12] and [22] as explained in Section 7.2.

The scheme K&SE(HDH) has the lowest ciphertext and computational overhead of all signcryption schemes, while providing outsider multi-user security. This improves upon the Dent scheme [18] which is furthermore only shown to be secure in the two-user setting. If unforgeability against insiders is required, the scheme TK&SEtS(tHDH,BLS) provides the lowest ciphertext overhead, but the Zheng scheme [47,5,6] has lower computational cost. On the other hand, if confidentiality against insiders is required (but only outsider unforgeability), the schemes TEtK&M (HDH,tDHIES) and GBN [20] provides the same ciphertext overhead but GBN provides slightly lower computational overhead. However, GBN is only shown to be secure in the weaker static multi-user model which implies key registration, and in this aspect we consider TEtK&M(HDH,tDHIES) as an improvement upon GBN.

Considering schemes which provides full insider security, TEtS(tDHIES,BLS) improves upon LYWDC [28] and LQ [29] by providing slightly lower ciphertext overhead while having practically the same computational cost (an IND-CCA secure DEM vs. a one-time pad). The ciphertext overhead is in fact lower than BD [8] and only 11 bits larger than Zheng although these schemes provides a lower level of security.

The schemes based on SC-composable TBKEMs and signatures improves upon the previous standard model schemes by providing both lower ciphertext and computational overhead. The lowest overhead is achieved by SC(tBMW1,Waters) (and SC(tBMW2,Waters)). However, if strong unforgeability is desired, the slightly less efficient SC(tBMW1,BSW) is required. The only drawback of the schemes based on SC-composability is that key registration is required to guarantee unforgeability (note that previous standard model schemes requires key registration as well). If key registration is not feasible, the most efficient scheme would be StTE(tBMW1,Waters) or StTE(tBMW1,BB) where BB denotes the short signature scheme by Boneh et al. [9]. Lastly note that the schemes based on tBMW2 TBKEM and the signature scheme by Camenisch et al. [14] (CL) (or CL [14] modified with the technique from [11], denoted by CL') have the advantage of compact public sender and receiver keys.

References

1. Abdalla, M., Bellare, M., Rogaway, P.: The oracle Diffie-Hellman assumptions and an analysis of DHIES. In: Naccache, D. (ed.) CT-RSA 2001. LNCS, vol. 2020, pp. 143–158. Springer, Heidelberg (2001)
2. Abe, M., Gennaro, R., Kurosawa, K., Shoup, V.: Tag-KEM/DEM: A new framework for hybrid encryption and a new analysis of Kurosawa-Desmedt KEM. In: Cramer, R. (ed.) EUROCRYPT 2005. LNCS, vol. 3494, pp. 128–146. Springer, Heidelberg (2005)
3. An, J.H., Dodis, Y., Rabin, T.: On the security of joint signature and encryption. In: Knudsen, L.R. (ed.) EUROCRYPT 2002. LNCS, vol. 2332, pp. 83–107. Springer, Heidelberg (2002)
4. Baek, J., Galindo, D., Susilo, W., Zhou, J.: Constructing strong KEM from weak KEM (or how to revive the KEM/DEM framework). In: Ostrovsky, R., De Prisco, R., Visconti, I. (eds.) SCN 2008. LNCS, vol. 5229, pp. 358–374. Springer, Heidelberg (2008)

5. Baek, J., Steinfeld, R., Zheng, Y.: Formal proofs for the security of signcryption. In: Naccache, D., Paillier, P. (eds.) PKC 2002. LNCS, vol. 2274, pp. 80–98. Springer, Heidelberg (2002)

6. Baek, J., Steinfeld, R., Zheng, Y.: Formal proofs for the security of signcryption. J. Cryptology 20(2), 203–235 (2007)

7. Bellare, M., Namprempre, C.: Authenticated encryption: Relations among notions and analysis of the generic composition paradigm. In: Okamoto, T. (ed.) ASIACRYPT 2000. LNCS, vol. 1976, pp. 531–545. Springer, Heidelberg (2000)

8. Bjørstad, T.E., Dent, A.W.: Building better signcryption schemes with tag-KEMs. In: Yung, M., Dodis, Y., Kiayias, A., Malkin, T.G. (eds.) PKC 2006. LNCS, vol. 3958, pp. 491–507. Springer, Heidelberg (2006)

9. Boneh, D., Boyen, X.: Short signatures without random oracles. In: Cachin, C., Camenisch, J.L. (eds.) EUROCRYPT 2004. LNCS, vol. 3027, pp. 56–73. Springer, Heidelberg (2004)

10. Boneh, D., Lynn, B., Shacham, H.: Short signatures from the Weil pairing. J. Cryptology 17(4), 297–319 (2004)

11. Boneh, D., Shen, E., Waters, B.: Strongly unforgeable signatures based on computational Diffie-Hellman. In: Yung, M., Dodis, Y., Kiayias, A., Malkin, T.G. (eds.) PKC 2006. LNCS, vol. 3958, pp. 229–240. Springer, Heidelberg (2006)

12. Boyen, X., Mei, Q., Waters, B.: Direct chosen ciphertext security from identity-based techniques. In: Cryptology ePrint Archive, Report 2005/288 (2005)

13. Boyen, X., Mei, Q., Waters, B.: Direct chosen ciphertext security from identity-based techniques. In: ACM CCS 2005, pp. 320–329. ACM, New York (2005)

14. Camenisch, J., Lysyanskaya, A.: Signature schemes and anonymous credentials from bilinear maps. In: Franklin, M. (ed.) CRYPTO 2004. LNCS, vol. 3152, pp. 56–72. Springer, Heidelberg (2004)

15. Cash, D., Kiltz, E., Shoup, V.: The twin Diffie-Hellman problem and applications. In: Smart, N.P. (ed.) EUROCRYPT 2008. LNCS, vol. 4965, pp. 127–145. Springer, Heidelberg (2008)

16. Cramer, R., Shoup, V.: Design and analysis of practical public-key encryption schemes secure against chosen ciphertext attack. SIAM J. Computing 33(1), 167–226 (2003)

17. Dent, A.W.: ECIES-KEM vs. PSEC-KEM, Technical Report NES/DOC/RHU/WP5/028/2 (2002)

18. Dent, A.W.: Hybrid signcryption schemes with outsider security. In: Zhou, J., López, J., Deng, R.H., Bao, F. (eds.) ISC 2005. LNCS, vol. 3650, pp. 203–217. Springer, Heidelberg (2005)

19. Diffie, W., Hellman, M.E.: New directions in cryptography. IEEE Transactions on Information Theory IT-22(6), 644–654 (1976)

20. Gorantla, M.C., Boyd, C., Nieto, J.M.G.: On the connection between signcryption and one-pass key establishment. In: Galbraith, S.D. (ed.) Cryptography and Coding 2007. LNCS, vol. 4887, pp. 277–301. Springer, Heidelberg (2007)

21. Hanaoka, G., Imai, H., Ogawa, K., Watanabe, H.: Chosen ciphertext secure public key encryption with a simple structure. In: Matsuura, K., Fujisaki, E. (eds.) IWSEC 2008. LNCS, vol. 5312, pp. 20–33. Springer, Heidelberg (2008)

22. Hanaoka, G., Kurosawa, K.: Efficient chosen ciphertext secure public key encryption under the computational Diffie-Hellman assumption. In: Pieprzyk, J. (ed.) ASIACRYPT 2008. LNCS, vol. 5350, pp. 308–325. Springer, Heidelberg (2008)

23. Hofheinz, D., Kiltz, E.: Secure hybrid encryption from weakened key encapsulation. In: Menezes, A. (ed.) CRYPTO 2007. LNCS, vol. 4622, pp. 553–571. Springer, Heidelberg (2007)

24. Jeong, I.R., Jeong, H.Y., Rhee, H.S., Lee, D.H., Lim, J.I.: Provably secure encrypt-then-sign composition in hybrid signcryption. In: Lee, P.J., Lim, C.H. (eds.) ICISC 2002. LNCS, vol. 2587, pp. 16–34. Springer, Heidelberg (2003)

25. Kiltz, E.: Chosen-ciphertext security from tag-based encryption. In: Halevi, S., Rabin, T. (eds.) TCC 2006. LNCS, vol. 3876, pp. 581–600. Springer, Heidelberg (2006)

26. Kiltz, E.: Chosen-ciphertext secure key-encapsulation based on gap hashed Diffie-Hellman. In: Okamoto, T., Wang, X. (eds.) PKC 2007. LNCS, vol. 4450, pp. 282–297. Springer, Heidelberg (2007)

27. Krawczyk, H.: HMQV: A high-performance secure Diffie-Hellman protocol. In: Shoup, V. (ed.) CRYPTO 2005. LNCS, vol. 3621, pp. 546–566. Springer, Heidelberg (2005)

28. Li, C.K., Yang, G., Wong, D.S., Deng, X., Chow, S.S.M.: An efficient signcryption scheme with key privacy. In: López, J., Samarati, P., Ferrer, J.L. (eds.) EuroPKI 2007. LNCS, vol. 4582, pp. 78–93. Springer, Heidelberg (2007)

29. Libert, B., Quisquater, J.-J.: Efficient signcryption with key privacy from gap Diffie-Hellman groups. Updated version of[31], http://www.dice.ucl.ac.be/~libert/

30. Libert, B., Quisquater, J.-J.: Improved signcryption from q-Diffie-Hellman problems. Updated version of[32], http://www.dice.ucl.ac.be/~libert/

31. Libert, B., Quisquater, J.-J.: Efficient signcryption with key privacy from gap Diffie-Hellman groups. In: Bao, F., Deng, R., Zhou, J. (eds.) PKC 2004. LNCS, vol. 2947, pp. 187–200. Springer, Heidelberg (2004)

32. Libert, B., Quisquater, J.-J.: Improved signcryption from q-Diffie-Hellman problems. In: Blundo, C., Cimato, S. (eds.) SCN 2004. LNCS, vol. 3352, pp. 220–234. Springer, Heidelberg (2005)

33. Ma, C.: Efficient short signcryption scheme with public verifiability. In: Lipmaa, H., Yung, M., Lin, D. (eds.) INSCRYPT 2006. LNCS, vol. 4318, pp. 118–129. Springer, Heidelberg (2006)

34. MacKenzie, P.D., Reiter, M.K., Yang, K.: Alternatives to non-malleability: Definitions, constructions, and applications (extended abstract). In: Naor, M. (ed.) TCC 2004. LNCS, vol. 2951, pp. 171–190. Springer, Heidelberg (2004)

35. Matsuda, T., Matsuura, K., Schuldt, J.C.N.: Efficient constructions of signcryption schemes and signcryption composability, http://eprint.iacr.org

36. Shoup, V.: Sequences of games: a tool for taming complexity in security proofs. Cryptology ePrint Archive, Report 2004/332 (2004)

37. Shoup, V., Gennaro, R.: Securing threshold cryptosystems against chosen ciphertext attack. In: Nyberg, K. (ed.) EUROCRYPT 1998. LNCS, vol. 1403, pp. 1–16. Springer, Heidelberg (1998)

38. Tan, C.H.: On the security of signcryption scheme with key privacy. IEICE Transactions 88-A(4), 1093–1095 (2005)

39. Tan, C.H.: Analysis of improved signcryption scheme with key privacy. Inf. Process. Lett. 99(4), 135–138 (2006)

40. Tan, C.H.: Security analysis of signcryption scheme from q-Diffie-Hellman problems. IEICE Transactions 89-A(1), 206–208 (2006)

41. Tan, C.H.: Forgery of provable secure short signcryption scheme. IEICE Transactions 90-A(9), 1879–1880 (2007)

42. Tan, C.H.: Insider-secure hybrid signcryption scheme without random oracles. In: ARES 2007, pp. 1148–1154. IEEE Computer Society, Los Alamitos (2007)
43. Tan, C.H.: Insider-secure signcryption KEM/tag-KEM schemes without random oracles. In: ARES 2008, pp. 1275–1281. IEEE Computer Society, Los Alamitos (2008)
44. Tan, C.H.: Signcryption scheme in multi-user setting without random oracles. In: Matsuura, K., Fujisaki, E. (eds.) IWSEC 2008. LNCS, vol. 5312, pp. 64–82. Springer, Heidelberg (2008)
45. Waters, B.: Efficient identity-based encryption without random oracles. In: Cramer, R. (ed.) EUROCRYPT 2005. LNCS, vol. 3494, pp. 114–127. Springer, Heidelberg (2005)
46. Yang, G., Wong, D.S., Deng, X.: Analysis and improvement of a signcryption scheme with key privacy. In: Zhou, J., López, J., Deng, R.H., Bao, F. (eds.) ISC 2005. LNCS, vol. 3650, pp. 218–232. Springer, Heidelberg (2005)
47. Zheng, Y.: Digital signcryption or how to achieve cost(signature & encryption) << cost(signature) + cost(encryption). In: Kaliski Jr., B.S. (ed.) CRYPTO 1997. LNCS, vol. 1294, pp. 165–179. Springer, Heidelberg (1997)

On Generic Constructions of Designated Confirmer Signatures ⋆

(The "Encryption of a Signature" Paradigm Revisited)

Laila El Aimani

b-it (Bonn-Aachen International Center for Information Technology), Dahlmannstr.
2, 53113 Bonn, Germany
elaimani@bit.uni-bonn.de

Abstract. Designated Confirmer signatures were introduced to limit the verification property inherent to digital signatures. In fact, the verification in these signatures is replaced by a confirmation/denial protocol between the *designated confirmer* and some verifier. An intuitive way to obtain such signatures consists in first generating a digital signature on the message to be signed, then encrypting the result using a suitable encryption scheme. This approach, referred to as the "encryption of a signature" paradigm, requires the constituents (encryption and signature schemes) to meet the highest security notions in order to achieve secure constructions.

In this paper, we revisit this method and establish the necessary and sufficient assumptions on the building blocks in order to attain secure confirmer signatures. Our study concludes that the paradigm, used in its basic form, cannot allow a class of encryption schemes, which is vital for the efficiency of the confirmation/denial protocols. Next, we consider a slight variation of the paradigm, proposed in the context of undeniable signatures; we recast it in the confirmer signature framework along with changes that yield more flexibility, and we demonstrate its efficiency by explicitly describing its confirmation/denial protocols when instantiated with building blocks from a large class of signature/encryption schemes. Interestingly, the class of signatures we consider is very popular and has been for instance used to build efficient designated verifier signatures.

Keywords: Designated Confirmer signatures, Generic construction, Reduction/meta-reduction, Zero Knowledge.

1 Introduction

Digital signatures capture most of the properties met by signatures in the paper world, for instance, universal verification. However, in some applications, this property is not desired or at least needs to be controlled. Undeniable signatures were introduced in [12] for this purpose; they proved critical in situations where

---

⋆ This is an extended abstract. The full paper [15] is available at the Cryptology ePrint Archive, http://eprint.iacr.org.

B. Roy and N. Sendrier (Eds.): INDOCRYPT 2009, LNCS 5922, pp. 343–362, 2009.
© Springer-Verlag Berlin Heidelberg 2009

privacy or anonymity is a big concern, such as licensing software [12], electronic cash and electronic voting, and auctions. In these signatures, the verification can be only attained by means of a cooperation with the signer, called the confirmation/denial protocols. Unfortunately, this very virtue (verification with only the signer's help) became its major shortcoming for many practical applications. The flaw was later repaired in [10] by introducing the concept of *designated confirmer signatures*. In fact, this concept involves three entities, namely the signer who produces the signature, the designated confirmer who confirms or denies an alleged signature and finally the recipient of the signature. Designated confirmer signatures, or confirmer signatures for brevity, can have the additional feature of being converted, by the confirmer, to ordinary digital signatures.

1.1 Related Work

Since the introduction of confirmer signatures, researchers sought ways of producing them from digital signatures and other cryptographic primitives such as encryption and/or commitment schemes. We briefly review in this paragraph, in chronological order, the most important such attempts:

Okamoto (1994) [28]. The result proposes a construction of confirmer signatures from digital signatures, public key encryption, bit-commitment schemes and pseudo-random functions. The construction was used to prove equivalence between confirmer signatures and public key encryption with respect to existence. Thus, efficiency was not taken into account in the framework.

Michels and Stadler (1998) [25]. This approach builds efficient confirmer signatures from signatures obtained from the Fiat-Shamir paradigm and from commitment schemes. Thus, the resulting confirmer signatures can be only proven secure in the random oracle model (ROM), inheriting this property from the use of the Fiat-Shamir paradigm, which constitutes their major shortcoming. Actually, it is well known, according to [32], that most discrete-logarithm-based signatures obtained from the Fiat-Shamir technique are very unlikely to preserve the same level of security in the standard model.

Camenisch and Michels (2000) [8]. The authors present the "encryption of a signature" idea along with a security analysis of the resulting confirmer signatures. In fact, they require existentially unforgeable signatures and indistinguishable encryption in the strongest attack model (EUF-CMA signatures and IND-CCA secure encryption) to achieve unforgeable, invisible, and transcript-simulatable confirmer signatures. The major weakness of the construction lies in the resort, in the confirmation/denial protocols, to general concurrent zero knowledge (ZK) proofs of NP statements.

Goldwasser and Waisbard (2004) [23]. This result manages to circumvent partially the weakness of the above construction. In fact, from a large class of digital signatures, the authors propose a transformation to confirmer signatures by encrypting the former items under an IND-CCA secure encryption during the confirmation protocol. They consequently achieve an efficient confirmation, but at the expense of the transcript-simulatability, the invisibility and the length of the resulting signatures. For instance, the signature contains at least twice the number of the confirmation protocol's rounds of encryptions. Moreover, the denial protocol of the construction has still recourse to general concurrent ZK proofs of NP statements.

Gentry et al. (2005) [21]. This work gives the possibility of building confirmer signatures from digital signatures, encryption (IND-CCA) and commitment schemes. Although the resulting construction does not use random oracles, it still does not get rid completely of general ZK proofs since the confirmer has to prove in concurrent ZK the knowledge of the decryption of an IND-CCA encryption and of a string used for commitment.

Wang et al. (2007) [38]. In this work, the authors present two constructions. The first one fixes some flaws noticed in [21], however, it still requires concurrent ZK proofs of NP statements. The second construction does not require any encryption, but at the expense of the underlying security assumption. In fact, it has its invisibility resting on the decisional Diffie-Hellman assumption, which rules out using the scheme in bilinear groups and thus benefiting from the attractive features they present such as achieving short group elements. Moreover, the construction suffers also the recourse to the ROM. Finally, these constructions as well as the construction in [21] are not anonymous, as we will point later in this document.

Wikström (2007) [40]. The author in his work proposes a new model for convertible confirmer signatures along with a generic construction analyzed in this new model. The construction is similar to the one given in [8] with the exception of considering cryptosystems with labels. Although the construction requires a weaker security notion on the cryptosystem than IND-CCA, namely Δ-IND-CCA, it still resorts to general proofs of NP statements.

El Aimani (2008) [14]. This construction is a slight variation of the "encryption of a signature" paradigm which uses cryptosystems from the KEM/DEM paradigm and requires them to be only IND-CPA secure. The author claims that this impacts positively the efficiency of the confirmation/denial protocols by allowing homomorphic schemes in the design. However, such a claim lacks justification since the only illustrations provided in the paper (or in its full version [16]) are generic constructions from a class of pairing-based signatures, which are used with a specific cryptosystem (El Gamal encryption or the linear Diffie-Hellman KEM/DEM). Furthermore, one of the constructions uses a cryptosystem which operates on messages from $\mathbb{Z}_p^\times$ (for some prime p), thus, the resulting signatures will be quite long because of the size contrast between ring cryptography and elliptic-curve cryptography. This seems to violate the main expectation from appealing to elliptic curve cryptography, namely achieve short signatures.

Summing up the state-of-the art in confirmer signatures, we deduce that the most mountainous obstacle that faces the potentially anonymous generic constructions without ROM, namely those derived from variants of the "encryption of a signature" paradigm, lies in the resort to general zero knowledge (ZK) proofs of NP statements, e.g., proving in ZK the knowledge of the decryption of an IND-CCA encryption. In this paper, we revisit this paradigm. We basically address two questions: does the paradigm, used in its basic form [8], allow building blocks with weaker security assumptions, for instance IND-CPA cryptosystems and thus achieves efficient signatures as claimed in [14]? The second question concerns the alleged efficiency of the construction in [14]; how important is the contribution of the IND-CPA requirement to the efficiency of the confirmation/denial protocols?

1.2   Our Contributions

The results in this paper are twofold. First, we consider the plain "encryption of a signature" paradigm as described in [8]. We actually prove that EUF-CMA secure signatures are a sufficient and necessary requirement to obtain EUF-CMA secure convertible confirmer signatures. Next, we show that indistinguishable cryptosystems under a *plaintext checking attack* (IND-PCA) are already enough to obtain invisible signatures under a chosen message attack (INV-CMA). This contrasts the wide belief that the cryptosystems should be IND-CCA secure. We also show that this assumption on the cryptosystem (IND-PCA secure) is necessary to obtain invisible signatures. This rules out automatically from the design homomorphic cryptosystems, a class of cryptosystems which proved later to be vital for the efficiency of the confirmation/denial protocols.

   Next, we consider the proposal in [14] which builds a universally convertible undeniable signature scheme from secure digital signatures and IND-CPA secure cryptosystems obtained from the KEM/DEM paradigm. We propose a recast of the construction in the confirmer signature framework and we demonstrate its efficiency by explicitly describing the confirmation/denial protocols when instantiated from a large class of signature/encryption schemes. Interestingly, the class of signatures we consider has been already defined as an ingredient of an efficient construction of designated verifier signatures [36]. We conclude that our recast of [14] betters the previous constructions of confirmer signatures in terms of both efficiency and security. In fact, it gets rid of general ZK proofs of NP statements in the confirmation and/or the denial protocol, oppositely to the constructions in [28,8,23,21,38]. Moreover, the resulting signatures are not proven secure in the random oracle as in [25,38], and they enjoy a strong invisibility which captures both the traditional invisibility, defined in [8], and anonymity which was later defined in [19]. We prove for instance that the latter property is not met by the constructions in [21,38].

2   Convertible Designated Confirmer Signatures (CDCS)

Since their introduction, many definitions and security models for CDCS have emerged. We consider the default model adopted in most confirmer signature proposals [8,23,21,38,14]. This model was primally described in [8], where the sign_then_encrypt technique was first formally introduced.

   We refer to the full paper [15] for reminders of the necessary cryptographic primitives that will come into use, that are, digital signatures, public key encryption schemes, KEM/DEM mechanisms, and finally Σ protocols.

2.1   Syntax

A CDCS scheme consists of the following procedures:

Key generation. Generates probabilistically key pairs $(\mathsf{sk}_S, \mathsf{pk}_S)$ and $(\mathsf{sk}_C, \mathsf{pk}_C)$ for the signer and for the confirmer respectively, consisting of the private and the public key.

ConfirmSign. On input sk_S, pk_C and a message m, outputs a confirmer signature μ, then interacts with the signature recipient to convince him of the validity of the just generated signature.

Confirmation/Denial protocols. These are interactive protocols between the confirmer and a verifier. Their common input consists of pk_S, pk_C, the alleged signature μ, and the message m in question. The confirmer uses his private key sk_C to convince the verifier of the validity (invalidity) of the signature μ on m. At the end, the verifier either accepts or rejects the proof.

Selective conversion. This is an algorithm run by the confirmer using sk_C, in addition to pk_C and pk_S. The result is either $\perp$ or a string which can be universally verified as a valid digital signature. Some models, e.g. [40], require that the confirmer issues a protocol of the correctness of the conversion in case of a valid signature[1]. It is easy to see that such a proof of correctness is reduced, in case of constructions from the "encryption of a signature" paradigm, to a proof that a given ciphertext decrypts to a given message. This is theoretically possible since the last assertion is an NP statement which accepts a ZK proof system.

Selective verification. This is an algorithm for verifying converted signatures. It inputs the converted signature, the message and pk_S and outputs 0 or 1.

2.2   Security Model

The above algorithms must be complete. Moreover the confirmSign, confirmation and denial protocols must be complete, sound and non transferable (simulatable) (see [8])[2]. In the sequel, we describe further properties that a CDCS scheme should meet.

Security for the signer (unforgeability). It is defined through the following game: the adversary $\mathcal{A}$ is given the public parameters of the CDCS scheme, namely pk_S and pk_C, in addition to sk_C. $\mathcal{A}$ is further allowed to query the signer on polynomially many messages, say q_s. At the end, $\mathcal{A}$ outputs a pair consisting of a message m, that has not been queried yet, and a string μ. $\mathcal{A}$ wins the game if μ is a valid confirmer signature on m. We say that a CDCS scheme is (t, ϵ, q_s)-EUF-CMA secure if there is no adversary, operating in time t, that wins the above game with probability greater than ϵ.

---

[1] It is not the responsibility of the confirmer to provide proofs for ill-formed signatures.
[2] In [40], the author points a flaw in the definition of non transferability of [8] and proposes how to fix it (by having the simulator rewound). In all the constructions that will follow, the property of non transferability will be met as a direct consequence of using zero knowledge proofs.

Security for the confirmer (invisibility). Invisibility against a chosen message attack (INV1-CMA) is defined through the following game between an attacker $\mathcal{A}$ and his challenger $\mathcal{R}$: after $\mathcal{A}$ gets the public parameters of the scheme from $\mathcal{R}$, he starts **Phase 1** where he queries the signing, confirmation/denial, selective conversion oracles in an adaptive way. Once $\mathcal{A}$ decides that **Phase 1** is over, he outputs two messages m_0 and m_1 that have not been queried before to the signing oracle and requests a challenge signature $\mu^\star$. $\mathcal{R}$ picks uniformly at random a bit $b \in \{0, 1\}$. Then $\mu^\star$ is generated using the signing oracle on the message m_b. Next, $\mathcal{A}$ starts adaptively querying the previous oracles (**Phase 2**), with the exception of not querying m_0 and m_1 to the signing oracle and $(m_i, \mu^\star)$, $i = 0, 1$, to the confirmation/denial and selective conversion oracles. At the end, $\mathcal{A}$ outputs a bit b'. He wins the game if $b = b'$. We define $\mathcal{A}$'s advantage as $\mathsf{adv}(\mathcal{A}) = |\Pr[b = b'] - \frac{1}{2}|$. We say that a CDCS scheme is $(t, \epsilon, q_s, q_v, q_{sc})$-INV1-CMA secure if no adversary operating in time t, issuing q_s queries to the signing oracle, q_v queries to the confirmation/denial oracles and q_{sc} queries to the selective conversion oracle wins the above game with advantage greater that ϵ.

Anonymity of signatures. In some applications, it is required that the confirmer signatures are anonymous, i.e., do not leak the identity (public key) of the signer. We refer to [19] for the formal definition of anonymity of confirmer signatures under a chosen message attack (ANO-CMA).

A stronger notion of invisibility. To capture both anonymity and invisibility, Galbraith and Mao introduced in [19] a notion, which we denote INV2-CMA, that requires the confirmer signatures to be indistinguishable from random elements in the signature space. This new notion is proven to imply both INV1-CMA and ANO-CMA (Theorem 1 and Theorem 4 respectively of [19]).

3   The Plain "Encryption of a Signature" Paradigm

The paradigm devises a CDCS scheme by producing a digital signature on the message to be signed, then encrypting the result using a suitable cryptosystem. More precisely, let Σ be a digital signature scheme given by Σ.keygen which generates a key pair (private key $= \Sigma$.sk, public key$= \Sigma$.pk), Σ.sign and Σ.verify. Let furthermore Γ denote a cryptosystem described by Γ.keygen that generates the key pair (private key $= \Gamma$.sk, public key$= \Gamma$.pk), Γ.encrypt and Γ.decrypt. A confirmer signature on a message m is issued by first producing a digital signature $\sigma = \Sigma$.sign$_{\Sigma.\mathsf{sk}}(m)$ on m, then encrypting it using Γ.pk. The result is $\mu = \Gamma$.encrypt$_{\Gamma.\mathsf{pk}}(\sigma)$. It is obvious that Σ.sk forms the (DCSC) signer's private key, whereas Σ.pk is his public key. To confirm (deny) a confirmer signature μ, the confirmer uses Γ.sk to prove the knowledge of the decryption of μ which does (not) satisfy the equation defined by the algorithm Σ.verify. Such a proof of knowledge is possible as the considered statements are in NP (co-NP), and therefore accept zero knowledge proof systems (see [22]).

This technique was formally analyzed in [8]: it was shown that the construction is EUF-CMA secure if the underlying (digital) signature scheme is also EUF-CMA secure. Moreover, it is INV1-CMA secure if the underlying cryptosystem is IND-CCA secure. Finally, completeness, soundness and non-transferability of the involved protocols follow from using ZK proofs of knowledge.

In the sequel, we prove that the condition on the underlying signature scheme (EUF-CMA secure) is also necessary to achieve EUF-CMA secure confirmer signatures. Furthermore, we prove that IND-PCA secure cryptosystems are already enough, though mandatory, to achieve INV1-CMA signatures.

Theorem 1. *The above generic construction is (t, ϵ, q_s)-EUF-CMA secure if and only if the underlying digital signature scheme is (t, ϵ, q_s)-EUF-CMA secure.*

Proof. The If direction has been already proved in [8]. We prove now the other direction. Let $(m^\star, \sigma^\star)$ be an existential forgery against the digital signature scheme. One can derive a forgery against the confirmer signature by simply encrypting the signature $\sigma^\star$ using the public key of the confirmer. Simulation of the attacker's environment is easy; the reduction $\mathcal{R}$ (EUF-CMA attacker against the confirmer signature) will forward the appropriate parameters (those concerning the underlying digital signature) to the EUF-CMA attacker against the underlying signature scheme, denoted $\mathcal{A}$. For a signature query on a message m, $\mathcal{R}$ will first request his challenger for a confirmer signature μ that he decrypts using the universal trapdoor ($\mathcal{R}$ has access to such a trapdoor according to the EUF-CMA security game described in 2.2) in σ. Finally, $\mathcal{R}$ outputs σ to $\mathcal{A}$. □

Invisibility. In this paragraph, we prove that IND-PCA secure cryptosystems are mandatory and enough to achieve INV1-CMA secure undeniable signatures. To prove this assertion, we proceed as follows. We first show that the INV1-CMA security of the resulting signatures cannot rest on the NM-CPA security of the underlying cryptosystem. We do this by means of an efficient *meta-reduction* using such a reduction (the algorithm reducing NM-CPA breaking the underlying cryptosystem to INV1-CMA breaking the construction) to break the NM-CPA security of the cryptosystem. Thus, under the assumption that the cryptosystem is NM-CPA secure, the meta reduction forbids the existence of such a reduction. In case the cryptosystem is not NM-CPA secure, such a reduction will be useless. This result will rule out automatically all the other notions that are weaker than NM-CPA, namely, OW-CPA and IND-CPA. Next, we use a similar technique to exclude the OW-CCA notion. The next security notion to be considered is IND-PCA. Luckily, this notion turns out to be sufficient to obtain INV1-CMA secure signatures.

Note that meta-reductions have been successfully used in a number of important cryptographic results, e.g., the result in [5] which proves the impossibility of reducing factoring to the RSA problem, or the results in [32,30] which show that some well known signatures, which are proven secure in the random oracle, cannot conserve the same security in the standard model. All those impossibility results are partial as they apply only for certain reductions. Our result is in a first stage also partial since it requires the reduction $\mathcal{R}$, trying to attack a certain property of a cryptosystem given by the public key $\Gamma.\mathsf{pk}$, to provide the adversary against the confirmer signature with the confirmer public key $\Gamma.\mathsf{pk}$. We will denote such reductions by *key-preserving* reductions, inheriting the name from a wide and popular class of reductions which supply the adversary with the same public key as its challenge. Such reductions were for instance used in [31] to prove a separation between factoring and IND-CCA-breaking some factoring-based cryptosystems in the standard model. Our restriction to such a class of reductions is not unnatural since, to our best knowledge, all the reductions stemming the security of the generic constructions of confirmer signatures from the security of their underlying components, feed the adversary with the public keys of these components (signature scheme, encryption scheme, commitment scheme). Next, we use simular techniques to [31] to extend our impossibility results to arbitrary reductions.

Lemma 1. *Assume there exists a key-preserving reduction $\mathcal{R}$ that converts an INV1-CMA adversary $\mathcal{A}$ against the above construction to an NM-CPA adversary against the underlying cryptosystem. Then, there exists a meta-reduction $\mathcal{M}$ that NM-CPA breaks the cryptosystem in question.*

Let us first interpret this result. The lemma claims that under the assumption of the underlying cryptosystem being NM-CPA secure, there exists no key-preserving reduction $\mathcal{R}$ that reduces NM-CPA breaking the cryptosystem in question to INV1-CMA breaking the construction, or if there exists such an algorithm, the underlying cryptosystem is not NM-CPA secure, thus rendering such a reduction useless.

Proof. Let $\mathcal{R}$ be a key-preserving reduction that reduces NM-CPA breaking the cryptosystem underlying the construction to INV1-CMA breaking the construction itself. We will construct an algorithm $\mathcal{M}$ that uses $\mathcal{R}$ to NM-CPA break the same cryptosystem by simulating an execution of the INV1-CMA adversary $\mathcal{A}$ against the construction.

Let Γ be the cryptosystem $\mathcal{M}$ is trying to attack. $\mathcal{M}$ launches $\mathcal{R}$ over Γ with the same public key, say $\Gamma.\mathsf{pk}$. $\mathcal{M}$, acting as the INV1-CMA adversary $\mathcal{A}$ against the construction, queries $\mathcal{R}$ on $m_0, m_1 \xleftarrow{R} \{0,1\}^\star$ for confirmer signatures. Then he queries the resulting strings μ_0, μ_1 (corresponding to the confirmer signatures on m_0 and m_1 respectively) for a selective conversion. Let σ_0 and σ_1 be the output (digital) signatures on m_0 and m_1 respectively. At that point, $\mathcal{M}$ inputs $\mathcal{D} = \{\sigma_0, \sigma_1\}$ to his own challenger as a distribution probability from which the plaintexts will be drawn. He gets in response a challenge encryption $\mu^\star$, of either σ_0 or σ_1 under $\Gamma.\mathsf{pk}$, and is asked to produce a ciphertext μ' whose corresponding plaintext is meaningfully related to the decryption of $\mu^\star$. To do this, $\mathcal{M}$ chooses uniformly at random a bit $b \xleftarrow{R} \{0,1\}$. Then, he queries the presumed confirmer signature $\mu^\star$ on m_b for a selective conversion. If the result is different from $\perp$, i.e., $\mu^\star$ is the encryption of σ_b, then $\mathcal{M}$ will output $\Gamma.\mathsf{encrypt}_{\Gamma.\mathsf{pk}}(\overline{\sigma}_b)$ ($\overline{\sigma}_b$ refers to the bit-complement of the element σ_b) and the relation R: $R(m, m') = (m' = \overline{m})$. Otherwise, he will output $\Gamma.\mathsf{encrypt}_{\Gamma.\mathsf{pk}}(\overline{\sigma}_{1-b})$ and the same relation R. Finally $\mathcal{M}$ aborts the game (stops simulating an INV1-CMA attacker against the generic construction). $\qquad\square$

Lemma 2. *Assume there exists a key-preserving reduction $\mathcal{R}$ that converts an INV1-CMA adversary $\mathcal{A}$ against the above construction to a OW-CCA adversary against the underlying cryptosystem. Then, there exists a meta-reduction $\mathcal{M}$ that OW-CCA breaks the cryptosystem in question.*

Proof. The proof is similar to the one above. Let $\mathcal{R}$ be the key-preserving reduction that reduces OW-CCA breaking the cryptosystem underlying the construction to INV1-CMA breaking the construction itself. We will construct an algorithm $\mathcal{M}$ that uses $\mathcal{R}$ to OW-CCA break the same cryptosystem by simulating an execution of the INV1-CMA adversary $\mathcal{A}$ against the construction.

Let Γ be the cryptosystem $\mathcal{M}$ is trying to attack. $\mathcal{M}$ gets his challenge c and is equipped with a decryption oracle that he can query on all ciphertexts of his choice except of course on the challenge. $\mathcal{M}$ launches $\mathcal{R}$ over Γ with the same public key Γ.pk and the same challenge c. Obviously all decryption queries made by $\mathcal{R}$, which are by definition different from the challenge ciphertext c, can be forwarded to $\mathcal{M}$'s own challenger. At some point, $\mathcal{M}$, acting as an INV1-CMA attacker against the construction, will output two messages m_0, m_1 and gets as response a challenge signature $\mu^\star$ which he is required to tell to which message it corresponds. With overwhelming probability, $\mu^\star \neq c$, in fact, the challenge c is not the encryption of a certain σ such that σ is a valid (digital) signature on the message m_0 or the message m_1. Therefore, $\mathcal{M}$ queries his own challenger for the decryption of $\mu^\star$ (he can issue such a query since it is different from the challenge ciphertext). He checks whether the result, say σ, is a valid (digital) signature on m_0 or m_1. Then, he will simply output the result of this verification. Finally, when $\mathcal{R}$ outputs his answer, decryption of the ciphertext c, $\mathcal{M}$ will simply forward this result to his challenger. $\qquad\square$

Theorem 2. *The cryptosystem underlying the above construction must be at least IND-PCA secure, in case the considered reduction is key-preserving, in order to achieve INV1-CMA secure signatures.*

Proof. We proceed in this proof with elimination. Lemma 1 rules out the notion NM-CPA and thus the notions IND-CPA and OW-CPA. Moreover, Lemma 2 rules out OW-CCA and thus OW-PCA (and also OW-CPA). Thus, the next notion to be considered is IND-PCA. $\qquad\square$

Remark 1. The above theorem is only valid when the considered notions are those obtained from pairing a security goal GOAL $\in \{OW, IND, NM\}$ and an attack model ATK $\in \{CPA, PCA, CCA\}$. Presence of other notions will require an additional study, however, Lemmas 1 and 2 will be always of use when there exists a relation between these new notions and the notions OW-CCA and NM-CPA.

To extend the result to arbitrary reductions, we use the same techniques as in [31]. Namely, we first define the notion of *non malleability of a cryptosystem key generator* through the following two games:
In **Game 0**, we consider an algorithm $\mathcal{R}$ trying to break a cryptosystem Γ, w.r.t. a public key Γ.pk, in the sense of NM-CPA or OW-CCA using an adversary

$\mathcal{A}$ which solves a problem A, perfectly reducible to OW-CPA breaking the cryptosystem Γ. In this game, $\mathcal{R}$ launches $\mathcal{A}$ over his own challenge key Γ.pk and some other parameters chosen freely by $\mathcal{R}$. We will denote by $\mathsf{adv}_0(\mathcal{R}^{\mathcal{A}})$ the success probability of $\mathcal{R}$ in such a game, where the probability is taken over the random tapes of both $\mathcal{R}$ and $\mathcal{A}$. We further define $\mathsf{succ}_{\Gamma}^{\mathsf{Game0}}(\mathcal{A}) = \max_{\mathcal{R}} \mathsf{adv}_0(\mathcal{R}^{\mathcal{A}})$ to be the success in **Game 0** of the best reduction $\mathcal{R}$ making the best possible use of the adversary $\mathcal{A}$. In **Game 1**, we consider the same entities as in **Game 0**, with the exception of providing $\mathcal{R}$ with, in addition to $\mathcal{A}$, a OW-CPA oracle (i.e. a decryption oracle corresponding to Γ) that he can query w.r.t. any public key Γ.pk$' \neq \Gamma$.pk, where Γ.pk is the challenge public key of $\mathcal{R}$. Similarly, we define $\mathsf{adv}_1(\mathcal{R}^{\mathcal{A}})$ to be the success of $\mathcal{R}$ in such a game, and $\mathsf{succ}_{\Gamma}^{\mathsf{Game1}}(\mathcal{A}) = \max_{\mathcal{R}} \mathsf{adv}_0(\mathcal{R}^{\mathcal{A}})$ the success in **Game 1** of the reduction $\mathcal{R}$ making the best possible use of the adversary $\mathcal{A}$ and of the OW-CPA oracle.

Definition 1. *A cryptosystem Γ has a non malleable key generator if $\Delta = \max_{\mathcal{A}} |\mathsf{succ}_{\Gamma}^{\mathsf{Game1}}(\mathcal{A}) - \mathsf{succ}_{\Gamma}^{\mathsf{Game0}}(\mathcal{A})|$ is negligeable in the security parameter.*

This definition informally means that a cryptosystem has a non malleable key generator if NM-CPA or OW-CCA breaking it w.r.t. a key pk is no easier when given access to a decryption oracle w.r.t. any public key pk$' \neq$ pk.

Theorem 3. *If the cryptosystem underlying the above construction has a non malleable key generator, then it must be at least IND-PCA secure in order to achieve INV1-CMA secure confirmer signatures.*

The proof is provided in [15].

One can give an informal explanation to the result above as follows. It is well known that constructions obtained from the sign_then_encrypt paradigm are not *strongly unforgeable*. I.e., a polynomial adversary is able to produce, given a valid confirmer signature on a certain message, another valid confirmer signature on the same message without the help of the signer. Indeed, given a valid confirmer signature on a message, an attacker can request its corresponding digital signature from the selective conversion oracle, then he encrypts it under the cryptosystem public key and obtains a new confirmer signature on the same message. Therefore, any reduction $\mathcal{R}$ from the invisibility of the construction to the security of the underlying cryptosystem will need more than a list of records maintaining the queried messages along with the corresponding confirmer and digital signatures. Thus the insufficiency of notions like IND-CPA. In [8], the authors stipulate that the given reduction would need a decryption oracle (of the cryptosystem) in order to handle the queries made by the INV1-CMA attacker $\mathcal{A}$, which makes the invisibility of the construction rest on the IND-CCA security of the cryptosystem. In our work, we remark that the queries made by $\mathcal{A}$ are not completely uncontrolled by $\mathcal{R}$. In fact, they are encryptions of some data already released by $\mathcal{R}$, provided the digital signature scheme is strongly unforgeable, and thus known to him. Therefore, a plaintext checking oracle suffices to handle those queries.

Theorem 4. *The above construction is $(t, \epsilon, q_s, q_v, q_{sc})$-INV1-CMA secure if it uses a (t, ϵ', q_s)-SEUF-CMA secure digital signature and a $(t + q_s q_{sc}(q_{sc} + q_v), \epsilon \cdot (1 - \epsilon')^{(q_{sc} + q_v)}, q_{sc}(q_{sc} + q_v))$-IND-PCA secure cryptosystem.*

The proof is provided in [15].

Unfortunately, requiring the encryption scheme to be at least IND-PCA secure seems to impact negatively the efficiency of the construction as it excludes homomorphic schemes from use (a homomorphic cryptosystem cannot be IND-PCA secure). In fact, such schemes can be (as we will show later in this document) efficient decryption verifiable, i.e., they accept efficient ZK proofs of knowledge of the decryption of a given ciphertext. In the next section, we discuss an attempt to circumvent this problem.

Remark 2. There exists a simpler way to exclude homomorphic encryption from the design which consists in proceeding as follows:

First rule out the notions OW-CPA, IND-CPA and OW-PCA by remarking that ElGamal's encryption meets all those notions (under the CDH, DDH and GDH assumption resp.) but still cannot be used as an ingredient in the construction. In fact, ElGamal offers the possibility of, given a ciphertext, creating another ciphertext for the same message (multiply the first component by g^r, for some r, and the second one by y^r, where ($\mathsf{sk} = x, \mathsf{pk} = y = g^x$) is the key pair of the scheme). Now, let (μ, m_0, m_1) be a challenge to an INV1-CMA adversary $\mathcal{A}$. By construction, μ is an ElGamal encryption of some σ, which is a digital signature on either m_0 or m_1. By the argument above, $\mathcal{A}$ can create another confirmer signature μ', that is another encryption of σ, and that he can query to the selective conversion oracle and then answer his own challenge.

Next, conclude that the cryptosystem in constructions derived from the "encryption of signature" paradigm must be at least OW-CCA or NM-CPA or IND-PCA secure in order to lead to secure constructions. Finally, conclude by the fact that a homomorphic scheme cannot be NM-CPA nor OW-CCA nor IND-PCA secure[3].

However, in order to determine the exact security needed to achieve secure constructions from the mentioned paradigm, there seems no known simpler way to exist than the study provided in this section.

---

[3] Let $\mathbb{E}$ be a cryptosystem such that $\forall m, m' \in \mathcal{M}: \mathbb{E}.\mathsf{encrypt}(m \star m') = \mathbb{E}.\mathsf{encrypt}(m) \circ \mathbb{E}.\mathsf{encrypt}(m')$, where $\mathcal{M}$ is the message space, $\mathsf{encrypt}$ is the encryption algorithm and finally $\star$ and $\circ$ are some group laws defined by $\mathbb{E}$ on the message and ciphertext spaces resp. Let c be the NM-CPA challenge. An adversary can simply choose a random message $m' \xleftarrow{R} \mathcal{M}$, encrypt it in c' and finally output $c \circ c'$ and the relation $R = \star$. Now, let c be a OW-CCA challenge, an adversary can choose again a random message $m' \xleftarrow{R} \mathcal{M}$, encrypt it in c' and then query $c \star c'$ to the decryption oracle. Let $m"$ be the result, the adversary can simply output $m" \star m'^{-1}$ as the decryption of c (we assume that computing inverses in $\mathcal{M}$ is efficient). Similarly, a homomorphic scheme cannot be IND-PCA secure.

4   Efficient KEM/DEM-Based Constructions

One attempt to circumvent the problem of *strong forgeability* of constructions obtained from the plain "encryption of a signature" paradigm can be achieved by binding the digital signature to its encryption. In this way, from a digital signature σ and a message m, an adversary cannot create a new confirmer signature on m by just reencrypting σ. In fact, σ forms a digital signature on m and some data, say c, which uniquely defines the confirmer signature on m. Moreover, this data c has to be public in order to issue the confirmSign/confirmation/denial protocols. Such an idea has been implemented in [14] in the undeniable signature framework, using the KEM/DEM paradigm; in fact, given a message m, one first fixes the session key k and its encapsulation c, then generates a digital signature σ on the "augmented" message $m\|c$, finally encrypts σ using k and outputs the result as an undeniable signature on m.

In this section, we propose a recast of this construction in the CDCS framework. We also allow more flexibility without compromising the overall security by encrypting only one part of the signature and leaving out the other part, provided it does not reveal information about the key or the message. Moreover, we demonstrate the efficiency of the resulting construction by describing its confirmSign/confirmation/denial protocols when the underlying components belong to a wide class of encryption and digital signature schemes. Interestingly, the class of digital signatures we consider has been already used in a recent proposal [36] as an ingredient for a generic construction of designated-verifier signatures. Finally, we conclude with a comparison with the existing generic constructions.

4.1   The Construction

Let Σ be a digital signature scheme given by Σ.keygen which generates a key pair $(\Sigma.\text{sk}, \Sigma.\text{pk})$, Σ.sign and Σ.verify. Let furthermore $\mathcal{K}$ be a KEM given by $\mathcal{K}$.keygen which generates a key pair $(\mathcal{K}.\text{pk}, \mathcal{K}.\text{sk})$, $\mathcal{K}$.encap and $\mathcal{K}$.decap. Finally, we consider a DEM $\mathcal{D}$ given by $\mathcal{D}$.encrypt and $\mathcal{D}$.decrypt.

Without loss of generality, we consider that a digital signature σ generated using Σ on a message m, can be written on the form $\sigma = (s, r)$ where r reveals no information about m nor about $(\Sigma.\text{sk}, \Sigma.\text{pk})$. I.e., there exists an algorithm that inputs a message m and a key pair $(\Sigma.\text{sk}, \Sigma.\text{pk})$ and outputs a string indistinguishable from r, where the probability is taken over the message and the key pair spaces considered by Σ. Note that every signature scheme produces signatures of the given form, since a signature can be always written as the concatenation of itself and of the empty string (the message-key-independent part). We assume that s belongs to the message space of $\mathcal{D}$.

Let $\|$ denote the concatenation of two strings after appending to the first one the special character $\diamond$. Let $m \in \{0,1\}^\star$ a message not containing $\{\diamond\}$, we propose the following recast of the construction in [16]:

Key generation. Call Σ.keygen and $\mathcal{K}$.keygen to generate Σ.sk, Σ.pk, $\mathcal{K}$.pk and $\mathcal{K}$.sk respectively. Set the signer key pair to $(\Sigma.\text{sk}, \Sigma.\text{pk})$ and the confirmer key pair to $(\mathcal{K}.\text{sk}, \mathcal{K}.\text{pk})$.

ConfirmSign. Fix a key k together with its encapsulation e. Then compute a (digital) signature $\sigma = \Sigma.\text{sign}_{\Sigma.\text{sk}}(m\|e) = (s, r)$ on $m\|e$. Finally, output $\mu = (e, \mathcal{D}.\text{encrypt}_k(s), r)$ and prove the knowledge of s, decryption of $(e, \mathcal{D}.\text{encrypt}_k(s))$, which satisfies together with r $\Sigma.\text{verify}$. This proof is possible because the signer knows k and (s, r), and the last assertion defines an NP language which accepts a ZK proof system.

Confirmation/Denial protocol. To confirm (deny) a signature $\mu = (\mu_1, \mu_2, \mu_3)$, issued on a certain message m, the confirmer first computes $k = \mathcal{K}.\text{decap}_{\mathcal{K}.\text{sk}}(\mu_1)$ then calls $\Sigma.\text{verify}$ on $(\mathcal{D}.\text{decrypt}_k(\mu_2), \mu_3)$ and $m\|\mu_1$ using $\Sigma.\text{pk}$. According to the result, the signer issues a ZK proof of knowledge of the decryption of (μ_1, μ_2) that, together with μ_3, passes (does not pass) the verification algorithm $\Sigma.\text{verify}$. Again this proof is possible because the given assertion is an NP (co-NP) statement and thus accept a ZK proof system.

Selective conversion. To convert a given signature $\mu = (\mu_1, \mu_2, \mu_3)$ issued on a certain message m, the confirmer first checks its validity. In case it is valid, the confirmer computes $k = \mathcal{K}.\text{decap}_{\mathcal{K}.\text{sk}}(\mu_1)$ and outputs $(\mathcal{D}.\text{decrypt}_k(\mu_2), \mu_3)$ and proves that k is the decapsulation of μ_1, otherwise he outputs $\perp$.

Theorem 5. *The above construction is (t, ϵ, q_s)-EUF-CMA secure if the underlying digital signature scheme is (t, ϵ, q_s)-EUF-CMA secure.*

Theorem 6. *The proposed construction is $(t, \epsilon, q_s, q_v, q_{sc})$-INV2-CMA secure if it uses a (t, ϵ', q_s)-EUF-CMA secure digital signature, an INV-OT secure DEM and a $(t + q_s(q_v + q_{sc}), \epsilon \cdot (1 - \epsilon')^{q_v + q_{sc}})$-IND-CPA secure KEM.*

The proofs are similar to those provided in [16]. Note that the strong unforgeability of the underlying signature scheme is not needed here to achieve invisibility. In fact, if the adversary can come up with another digital signature σ' on a given $m\|c$, there is just one way to create the corresponding confirmer signature, namely, encrypt it using $k = \mathcal{K}.\text{decap}(c)$. Therefore, the reduction is able to handle a query requesting the confirmation/denial or selective conversion of such a signature by just maintaining a list of the queried messages, the issued confirmer signatures and their corresponding digital signatures.

4.2 Efficient Instantiations Using Certain Signatures and Cryptosystems

In this paragraph, we define the classes of signatures/cryptosystems that yield efficient instantiations of the construction defined earlier in this section. The class of digital signatures we consider is very similar to the one defined by [36] in the context of designated verifier signatures, whereas the class of cryptosystems spotlights the importance of homomorphic encryption in the framework.

Definition 2. *(The class $\mathbb{S}$ of signatures)* $\mathbb{S}$ *is the set of all digital signatures for which there exists a pair of algorithms, Convert and Retrieve, where Convert inputs a public key pk, a message m, and a valid signature σ on m (w.r.t. pk) and outputs the pair (s, r) such that:*

1. *there exists an algorithm that inputs a public key from the key space and a message from the message space, and outputs a string statistically indistinguishable from r.*
2. *there exists an algorithm* Compute *that on the input* pk, *the message m and r, computes a description of a* one-way *function $f : (\mathbb{G}, *) \to (\mathbb{H}, \circ_s)$ where:*
   - *$(\mathbb{G}, *)$ is a group and $\mathbb{H}$ is a set equipped with the binary operation $\circ_s$,*
   - *$\forall S, S' \in \mathbb{G}: f(S * S') = f(S) \circ_s f(S')$.*
   and an $I \in \mathbb{H}$, such that $f(s) = I$.

and Retrieve *is an algorithm that inputs* pk, *m and the correctly converted pair (s, r) and retrieves the signature σ on m.*

The class $\mathbb{S}$ differs from the class $\mathbb{C}$, introduced in [36], in the condition required for the one way function f. In fact, in our description of $\mathbb{S}$, the function f should satisfy a homomorphic property, whereas in the class $\mathbb{C}$, f should only possess an efficient Σ *protocol* for proving knowledge of a preimage of a value in its range. We show in Theorem 7 that signatures in $\mathbb{S}$ accept also efficient Σ *protocols* for proving knowledge of preimages, and thus belong to the class $\mathbb{C}$. Conversely, one can claim that signatures in $\mathbb{C}$ are also in $\mathbb{S}$, at least from a practical point of view, since it is not known how to achieve efficient Σ protocols for proving knowledge of preimages of f without having the latter item satisfy some homomorphic properties. It is worth noting that similar to the classes $\mathbb{S}$ and $\mathbb{C}$ is the class of signatures introduced in [23], where the condition of having an efficient Σ protocol for proving knowledge of preimages is weakened to having only a *witness hiding* proof of knowledge. Again, although this is a weaker assumption on f, all illustrations of signatures in this wider class happen to be also in $\mathbb{C}$ and $\mathbb{S}$. Our resort to specify the homomorphic property on f will be justified later when describing the confirmation/denial protocols of the resulting construction. In fact, these protocols are parallel composition of Σ protocols and therefore need a careful study as it is known that zero knowledge is not close under concurrent composition. Finally, the class $\mathbb{S}$ encompasses most proposals that were suggested so far, RSA-FDH [1], Schnorr [35], GHR [20], Modified ElGamal [33], Cramer-Shoup [13], Camenisch-Lysyanskaya-02 [6] and most pairing-based signatures such as [4,7,2,41,39].

1. The prover chooses $s' \xleftarrow{R} \mathbb{G}$, computes and sends $t_1 = I \circ_s f(s')$ to the verifier.
2. The verifier chooses $c \xleftarrow{R} \{0, 1\}$ and sends it to the prover.
3. If $c = 0$, the prover sends s'.
   Otherwise, he sends $s * s'$.
4. If $c = 0$, the verifier checks that t_1 is computed as in Step 1.
   Otherwise, he (verifier) accepts if $f(s * s') = t_1$.

Fig. 1. Proof system for membership to the language $\{s : f(s) = I\}$ Common input: I and Private input : s

Theorem 7. *The protocol depicted in Figure 1 is an efficient Σ protocol for proving knowledge of preimages of the function f described in Definition 2.*

The proof is given in [15].

Definition 3. *(The class $\mathbb{E}$ of cryptosystems)* $\mathbb{E}$ *is the set of encryption schemes Γ, obtained from the KEM/DEM paradigm, such that:*

1. *The message space is a group $\mathcal{M} = (\mathbb{G}, *)$ and the ciphertext space $\mathcal{C}$ is a set equipped with a binary operation $\circ_e$.*
2. *Let $m \in \mathcal{M}$ be a message and c its encryption with respect to a key* pk. *On the common input m and c, there exists an efficient ZK proof of m being the decryption of c with respect to* pk. *The private input of the prover is either the private key* sk, *corresponding to* pk, *or the randomness used to encrypt m in c (the randomness which is input to the KEM encapsulation algorithm).*
3. *$\forall m, m' \in \mathcal{M}, \forall$pk$: \Gamma.\mathsf{encrypt}_{\mathsf{pk}}(m * m') = \Gamma.\mathsf{encrypt}_{\mathsf{pk}}(m) \circ_e \Gamma.\mathsf{encrypt}_{\mathsf{pk}}(m')$. Moreover, given the randomness used to encrypt m in $\Gamma.\mathsf{encrypt}_{\mathsf{pk}}(m)$ and m' in $\Gamma.\mathsf{encrypt}_{\mathsf{pk}}(m')$, one can deduce (using only the public parameters) the randomness used to encrypt $m * m'$ in $\Gamma.\mathsf{encrypt}_{\mathsf{pk}}(m) \circ_e \Gamma.\mathsf{encrypt}_{\mathsf{pk}}(m')$.*

Examples of cryptosystems in the above class are ElGamal's encryption [17], or the cryptosystem defined in [3] which uses the linear Diffie-Hellman KEM. In fact, both cryptosystems are homomorphic and possess an efficient protocol for proving that a ciphertext decrypts to a given plaintext: the proof of equality of two discrete logarithms [11]. Paillier's [29] cryptosystem cannot be viewed as an instance of this class as it is not based on the KEM/DEM paradigm, however in [15], we provide a modified variant which belongs to the class $\mathbb{E}$ and thus is suitable for use in the construction.

Note that with this considered class of cryptosystems, the correctness of the selective conversion becomes easy since one can efficiently prove that a given ciphertext decrypts to a given message. In the sequel, we will see that, with this class it is also easy to prove knowledge of the decryption of a given ciphertext.

Theorem 8. *Let Γ be a OW-CPA secure cryptosystem from the class $\mathbb{E}$. Let furthermore c be an encryption of some message under some public key* pk. *The*

---

1. The prover chooses $s' \xleftarrow{R} \mathbb{G}$, computes and sends $t_2 = \Gamma.\mathsf{encrypt}(s') \circ_e (c, s_k)$ to the verifier
2. The verifier chooses $c \xleftarrow{R} \{0, 1\}$ and sends it to the signer.
3. If $c = 0$, the prover sends s' and the randomness used to encrypt it in $\Gamma.\mathsf{encrypt}(s')$.
   Otherwise, he sends $s' * s$ and proves that t_2 is an encryption of $s' * s$.
4. If $c = 0$, the verifier checks that t_2 is computed as in Step 1.
   Otherwise, he checks the proof of decryption of t_2:
   It it fails, he rejects the proof.

Fig. 2. Proof system for membership to the language $\{(e, s_k): \exists m : m = \Gamma.\mathsf{decrypt}(e, s_k)\}$ Common input: $(e, s_k, \Gamma.\mathsf{pk})$ and Private input: $\Gamma.\mathsf{sk}$ or randomness encrypting m in (e, s_k)

protocol depicted in Figure 2 is an efficient Σ protocol for proving knowledge of the decryption of c.

The proof is similar to the one of Theorem 7. □

The confirmation/denial protocols. We combine an EUF-CMA secure signature scheme $\Sigma \in \mathbb{S}$ and a cryptosystem $\Gamma \in \mathbb{E}$, where the underlying KEM $\mathcal{K}$ and DEM $\mathcal{D}$ are IND-CPA and INV-OT secure respectively, in the way described in Section 4. Namely, we first compute an encapsulation e together with its corresponding key k. Then compute a signature σ on the message to be signed concatenated with e. Finally convert σ to (s, r) using the Convert algorithm described in Definition 2 and encrypt s using k. The resulting confirmer signature is $(e, \mathcal{D}.\text{encrypt}_k(s), r)$. We describe in Figure 3 the confirmation/denial protocols corresponding to the resulting construction. Note that the confirmation protocol can be also run by the signer who wishes to confirm the validity of a just generated signature.

Remark 3. The prover in Figure 3 is either the confirmer of the signature (e, s_k, r) who can run the above protocols with the knowledge of his private key, or the signer who wishes to confirm the validity of a just generated signature (during the confirmSign protocol). In fact, with the knowledge of the randomness used to encrypt s in (e, s_k), where (s, r) is the converted pair obtained from $\sigma = \Sigma.\text{sign}(m\|e)$, the signer can issue the above confirmation protocol thanks to the properties satisfied by Γ.

Theorem 9. *The confirmation protocol (run either by the signer on a just generated signature or by the confirmer on any signature) described in Figure 3 is a Σ protocol if the underlying cryptosystem is OW-CPA secure.*

Theorem 10. *The denial protocol described in Figure 3 is a Σ protocol if the underlying cryptosystem is IND-CPA secure.*

The proofs of both theorems are given in [15].

---

1. The prover and verifier, given the public input, compute I as defined in Definition 2.
2. The prover chooses $s' \xleftarrow{R} \mathbb{G}$, computes and sends $t_1 = f(s') \circ_s I$ and $t_2 = \Gamma.\text{encrypt}(s') \circ_e (e, s_k)$ to the verifier
3. The verifier chooses $c \xleftarrow{R} \{0, 1\}$ and sends it to the prover.
4. If $c = 0$, the prover sends s' and the randomness used to encrypt s' in $\Gamma.\text{encrypt}(s')$.
   Otherwise, he sends $s' * s$ and proves that t_2 is an encryption of $s' * s$.
5. If $c = 0$, the verifier checks that t_1 and t_2 are computed as in Step 1.
   Otherwise, he checks the proof of decryption of t_2:
      It it fails, he rejects the proof.
      Otherwise:
         If the prover is confirming the signature, the verifier accepts if $f(s' * s) = t_1$.
         If the prover is denying the given signature, the verifier accepts the proof if $f(s' * s) \neq t_1$.

Fig. 3. Proof system for membership (non membership) to the language $\{(e, s_k, r): \exists s : s = \Gamma.\text{decrypt}(e, s_k) \wedge \Sigma.\text{verify}(\text{Retrieve}(s, r), m\|e) = (\neq)1\}$ Common input: $(e, s_k, r, \Sigma.\text{pk}, \Gamma.\text{pk})$ and Private input: $\Gamma.\text{sk}$ or randomness encrypting s in (e, s_k)

4.3 Comparisons and Possible Extentions

sign_then_encrypt variants. The construction presented in this section improves the plain paradigm [8] as it weakens the assumption on the underlying cryptosystem from being IND-CCA secure to only being IND-CPA secure. This impacts positively the efficiency of the construction from many sides. In fact, the resulting signature is shorter and its generation cost is smaller, since IND-CPA cryptosystems are simpler and allow faster encryption and shorter ciphertexts than IND-CCA ones. An illustration is given by ElGamal's encryption and its IND-CCA variant, namely Cramer-Shoup's encryption where the ciphertexts are at least twice longer than ElGamal's ciphertexts. Also, there is a multiplicative factor of at least two in favor of ElGamal's encryption/decryption cost. Moreover, the confirmation/denial protocols are rendered more efficient by the allowance of homomorphic cryptosystems as shown in 4.2. Such cryptosystems were not possible to use before, since a homomorphic scheme can never attain the IND-CCA security. Besides, even when the IND-CCA cryptosystem is decryption verifiable, e.g., Cramer-Shoup or the IND-CCA variant of Paillier's encryption [9], the involved protocols are much more expensive than the ones corresponding to their IND-CPA variant: in case of ElGamal, this protocol amounts to a proof of equality of two discrete logarithms, and in case of our modified variant of Paillier (described in [15]), this protocol comes to a proof of knowledge of an N-th root. The construction achieves also better performances than the proposal of [23], where the confirmer signature comprises k commitments and $2k$ IND-CCA encryptions, where k is the number of rounds used in the confirmation protocol. Moreover, the denial protocol presented in [23] suffers the resort to proofs of general NP statements (where the considered encryption is IND-CCA). Finally, the resulting signatures are not invisible.

Commitment-based constructions. Our construction does not use ROM, unlike the constructions in [25,38]. Moreover, it enjoys the strongest notion of invisibility (INV2-CMA) which captures both invisibility as defined in [8], and anonymity as defined in [19]. As mentioned in subsection 2.2, anonymity can be an important requirement for confirmer signatures in some settings. Unfortunately, many of the efficient generic constructions are not anonymous. In fact, constructions like [25,21,38] have a confirmer signature containing a commitment on the message to be signed and a valid digital signature on this commitment. Therefore, such constructions leak always a part of the signing key, namely the public key of the underlying digital signature. More precisely, an anonymity attacker $\mathcal{A}$, will get two public keys and a confirmer signature on a given message and has to tell the key under which the confirmer signature was created. To answer such a challenge, $\mathcal{A}$ will simply check the validity of the digital signature on the commitment (both are part of the confirmer signature) with regard to one public key (the confirmer signature public key includes the public key of the underlying digital signature). The result of such a verification is sufficient for $\mathcal{A}$ to conclude in case the two confirmer public keys do not share the same public key for the digital signature scheme.

The upshot is, our recast of the construction [14] achieves both maximal security (strong invisibility) without random oracles, and efficiency in terms of the signature length, generation, confirmation/denial and conversion cost. Furthermore, the construction readily extends to *directed signatures* [24] or *undeniable confirmer signatures* [26] by simply having the confirmer share his private key with the signer. Furthermore, one can extend the analysis provided in this paper to the other constructions instantiating the "encryption of a signature" paradigm, e.g., [23,40]. In fact, both constructions are not strongly unforgeable, thus the necessity of CCA or Δ-CCA security. To circumvent this problem, one can use similarly a cryptosystem derived from the hybrid encryption paradigm, and produce a signature on the message concatenated with the encapsulation. Hence, the resulting constructions will thrive on CPA or Δ-CPA security while conserving the same security, and thus will achieve better performances as we described above (short signature, small cost and many practical instantiations).

Acknowledgments

I thank the anonymous reviewers of IndoCrypt 2009 for their useful remarks. Thanks go also to an anonymous reviewer from ACNS 2009 for useful suggestions that substantially improved the quality of the present paper. Finally, I thank Joachim von zur Gathen for precious discussions throughout the realization of this project. This work is funded by the B-IT Foundation and the Land Nordrhein-Westfalen.

References

1. Bellare, M., Rogaway, P.: The Exact Security of Digital Signatures: How to Sign with RSA and Rabin. In: Maurer, U.M. (ed.) EUROCRYPT 1996. LNCS, vol. 1070, pp. 399–416. Springer, Heidelberg (1996)
2. Boneh, D., Boyen, X.: Short Signatures Without Random Oracles. In: Cachin, C., Camenisch, J.L. (eds.) EUROCRYPT 2004. LNCS, vol. 3027, pp. 56–73. Springer, Heidelberg (2004)
3. Boneh, D., Boyen, X., Shacham, H.: Short Group Signatures. In: Franklin, M.K. (ed.) [8], pp. 41–55
4. Boneh, D., Lynn, B., Shacham, H.: Short Signatures from the Weil Pairing. J. Cryptology 17(4), 297–319 (2004)
5. Boneh, D., Venkatesan, R.: Breaking RSA May Not Be Equivalent to Factoring. In: Nyberg, K. (ed.) [27], pp. 59–71
6. Camenisch, J., Lysyanskaya, A.: Dynamic Accumulators and Application to Efficient Revocation of Anonymous Credentials. In: Yung, M. (ed.) CRYPTO 2002. LNCS, vol. 2442, pp. 61–76. Springer, Heidelberg (2002)
7. Camenisch, J., Lysyanskaya, A.: Signature Schemes and Anonymous Credentials from Bilinear Maps. In: Franklin, M.K. (ed.) [18], pp. 56–72
8. Camenisch, J., Michels, M.: Confirmer Signature Schemes Secure against Adaptive Adversaries. In: Preneel, B. (ed.) EUROCRYPT 2000. LNCS, vol. 1807, pp. 243–258. Springer, Heidelberg (2000)

9. Camenisch, J., Shoup, V.: Practical Verifiable Encryption and Decryption of Discrete Logarithms. In: Boneh, D. (ed.) CRYPTO 2003. LNCS, vol. 2729, pp. 126–144. Springer, Heidelberg (2003)

10. Chaum, D.: Designated Confirmer Signatures. In: De Santis, A. (ed.) EURO-CRYPT 1994. LNCS, vol. 950, pp. 86–91. Springer, Heidelberg (1995)

11. Chaum, D., Pedersen, T.P.: Wallet Databases with Observers. In: Brickell, E.F. (ed.) CRYPTO 1992. LNCS, vol. 740, pp. 89–105. Springer, Heidelberg (1993)

12. Chaum, D., van Antwerpen, H.: Undeniable Signatures. In: Brassard, G. (ed.) CRYPTO 1989. LNCS, vol. 435, pp. 212–216. Springer, Heidelberg (1990)

13. Cramer, R., Shoup, V.: Signature schemes based on the strong RSA assumption. ACM Trans. Inf. Syst. Secur. 3(3), 161–185 (2000)

14. El Aimani, L.: Toward a Generic Construction of Universally Convertible Undeniable Signatures from Pairing-Based Signatures. In: Chowdhury, D.R., Rijmen, V., Das, A. (eds.) INDOCRYPT 2008. LNCS, vol. 5365, pp. 145–157. Springer, Heidelberg (2008)

15. El Aimani, L.: On Generic Constructions of Designated Confirmer Signatures (The Encryption of a Signature Paradigm Revisited), Cryptology ePrint Archive, Report 2009/403 (2009), http://eprint.iacr.org/

16. El Aimani, L.: Toward a Generic Construction of Convertible Undeniable Signatures from Pairing-Based Signatures, Cryptology ePrint Archive, Report 2009/362 (2009), http://eprint.iacr.org/

17. El Gamal, T.: A Public Key Cryptosystem and a Signature Scheme based on Discrete Logarithms. IEEE Trans. Inf. Theory 31, 469–472 (1985)

18. Franklin, M.K. (ed.): CRYPTO 2004. LNCS, vol. 3152. Springer, Heidelberg (2004)

19. Galbraith, S.D., Mao, W.: Invisibility and Anonymity of Undeniable and Confirmer Signatures.. In: Joye, M. (ed.) CT-RSA 2003. LNCS, vol. 2612, pp. 80–97. Springer, Heidelberg (2003)

20. Gennaro, R., Halevi, S., Rabin, T.: Secure Hash-and-Sign Signatures Without the Random Oracle. In: Stern, J. (ed.) [37], pp. 397–416

21. Gentry, C., Molnar, D., Ramzan, Z.: Efficient Designated Confirmer Signatures Without Random Oracles or General Zero-Knowledge Proofs. In: Roy, B. (ed.) [34], pp. 662–681

22. Goldreich, O.: Foundations of cryptography. Basic Tools. Cambridge University Press, Cambridge (2001)

23. Goldwasser, S., Waisbard, E.: Transformation of Digital Signature Schemes into Designated Confirmer Signature Schemes. In: Naor, M. (ed.) TCC 2004. LNCS, vol. 2951, pp. 77–100. Springer, Heidelberg (2004)

24. Lim, C.H., Lee, P.J.: Modified Maurer-Yacobi's scheme and its applications. In: Zheng, Y., Seberry, J. (eds.) AUSCRYPT 1992. LNCS, vol. 718, pp. 308–323. Springer, Heidelberg (1993)

25. Michels, M., Stadler, M.: Generic Constructions for Secure and Efficient Confirmer Signature Schemes. In: Nyberg, K. (ed.) [27], pp. 406–421

26. Nguyen, K.Q., Mu, Y., Varadharajan, V.: Undeniable Confirmer Signature. In: Zheng, Y., Mambo, M. (eds.) ISW 1999. LNCS, vol. 1729, pp. 235–246. Springer, Heidelberg (1999)

27. Nyberg, K. (ed.): EUROCRYPT 1998. LNCS, vol. 1403. Springer, Heidelberg (1998)

28. Okamoto, T.: Designated Confirmer Signatures and Public-Key Encryption are Equivalent. In: Desmedt, Y.G. (ed.) CRYPTO 1994. LNCS, vol. 839, pp. 61–74. Springer, Heidelberg (1994)

29. Paillier, P.: Public-Key Cryptosystems Based on Composite Degree Residuosity Classes. In: Stern, J. (ed.) [37], pp. 223–238
30. Paillier, P.: Impossibility Proofs for RSA Signatures in the Standard Model. In: Abe, M. (ed.) CT-RSA 2007. LNCS, vol. 4377, pp. 31–48. Springer, Heidelberg (2007)
31. Paillier, P., Villar, J.: Trading One-Wayness Against Chosen-Ciphertext Security in Factoring-Based Encryption. In: Lai, X., Chen, K. (eds.) ASIACRYPT 2006. LNCS, vol. 4284, pp. 252–266. Springer, Heidelberg (2006)
32. Paillier, P., Vergnaud, D.: Discrete-Log Based Signatures May Not Be Equivalent to Discrete-Log. In: Roy, B. (ed.) [34], pp. 1–20
33. Pointcheval, D., Stern, J.: Security Arguments for Digital Signatures and Blind Signatures. J. Cryptology 13(3), 361–396 (2000)
34. Roy, B. (ed.): ASIACRYPT 2005. LNCS, vol. 3788. Springer, Heidelberg (2005)
35. Schnorr, C.P.: Efficient signature generation by smart cards. J. Cryptology 4(3), 161–174 (1991)
36. Shahandashti, S.F., Safavi-Naini, R.: Construction of Universal Designated-Verifier Signatures and Identity-Based Signatures from Standard Signatures. In: Cramer, R. (ed.) PKC 2008. LNCS, vol. 4939, pp. 121–140. Springer, Heidelberg (2008)
37. Stern, J. (ed.): EUROCRYPT 1999. LNCS, vol. 1592. Springer, Heidelberg (1999)
38. Wang, G., Baek, J., Wong, D.S., Bao, F.: On the Generic and Efficient Constructions of Secure Designated Confirmer Signatures. In: Okamoto, T., Wang, X. (eds.) PKC 2007. LNCS, vol. 4450, pp. 43–60. Springer, Heidelberg (2007)
39. Waters, B.: Efficient Identity-Based Encryption Without Random Oracles. In: Cramer, R. (ed.) EUROCRYPT 2005. LNCS, vol. 3494, pp. 114–127. Springer, Heidelberg (2005)
40. Wikström, D.: Designated Confirmer Signatures Revisited. In: Vadhan, S.P. (ed.) TCC 2007. LNCS, vol. 4392, pp. 342–361. Springer, Heidelberg (2007)
41. Zhang, F., Safavi-Naini, R., Susilo, W.: An Efficient Signature Scheme from Bilinear Pairings and Its Applications. In: Bao, F., Deng, R., Zhou, J. (eds.) PKC 2004. LNCS, vol. 2947, pp. 277–290. Springer, Heidelberg (2004)

Verifiably Encrypted Signatures from RSA without NIZKs

Markus Rückert[*]

Cryptography and Computeralgebra
Department of Computer Science
TU Darmstadt
`rueckert@cdc.informatik.tu-darmstadt.de`

Abstract. Verifiably encrypted signature (VES) schemes allow a signer to encrypt a signature under the public key of a trusted party, the adjudicator, while maintaining public signature verifiability *without* interactive proofs. A popular application for this concept is fair online contract signing.

This paper answers the question of whether it is possible to implement a VES without pairings and zero-knowledge proofs. Our construction is based on RSA signatures and a Merkle hash tree. Hence, the scheme is stateful but relies on relatively mild assumptions in the random oracle model. Thus, we provide an alternative that does not rely on pairing-based assumptions.

The advantage of our approach over previous schemes is that widespread efficient hard- and software implementations of hash functions and RSA signatures can be easily reused for VES, i.e., we can avoid costly redevelopment. Furthermore, in contrast to using non-interactive zero-knowledge proofs, we only need a constant, small number of modular exponentiations.

Keywords: Online contract signing, Merkle hash trees, RSA.

1 Introduction

Verifiably encrypted signature (VES) schemes were introduced by Boneh, Gentry, Lynn, and Shacham [7]. They are built upon regular, i.e., non-encrypted, signature schemes and preserve their public verifiability, while hiding the signature itself from the public. There are three parties involved: the signer, the receiver, and a passive adjudicator. The signer computes a signature σ on a document m and outputs a masked signature ϖ. The general public can verify that ϖ contains a signature on m, but is unable to extract a valid regular signature. This also holds for the designated receiver. A popular application of this concept is *online contract signing* — an optimistic fair exchange protocol [3,1]. We assume two signers, who do not unconditionally trust each other, want to sign a contract. However, neither of them wants to sign first because each fears that

---

[*] This work was supported by CASED (`www.cased.de`).

B. Roy and N. Sendrier (Eds.): INDOCRYPT 2009, LNCS 5922, pp. 363–377, 2009.

the other party might back out at the last possible moment with a partly signed contract. Such a one-sided commitment to a contract may be used for blackmail or simply for negotiating a better deal elsewhere. In order to avoid this situation, both parties agree on the following protocol: 1. Exchange verifiably encrypted signatures; 2. Verify the encrypted signatures; 3. Exchange regular signatures.

In the case of a dispute, either party can appeal to the adjudicator, who is able to disclose both regular signatures. In contrast to other fair exchange protocols, VES schemes perform the initial signature exchange step more efficiently, in a single move.

Security of verifiably encrypted signatures comprises unforgeability and opacity [7], as well as extractability and abuse-freeness [18]. In [15], Huang et al. state that such protocols should be "ambiguous", which is not guaranteed by VES.

Along with the first security model, Boneh et al. proposed the BGLS construction that is provably secure in the random oracle model. Later on, Zhang et al. described a more efficient solution (ZSNS) [22] that seems to be provably secure in the random oracle model but lacks a formal proof of opacity. Lu et al. presented the first verifiably encrypted signature scheme (LOSSW) [16] that is secure in the standard model. The LOSSW scheme is based on the Waters signature scheme [21], which has a fairly large public key. In [18], Rückert and Schröder (RS) show a construction in the standard model with short keys. Lu et al. also sketch a generic construction using non-interactive zero-knowledge proofs (NIZKs). Since such constructions are typically very inefficient with respect to computational cost (esp. the number of modular exponentiations) and signature size, our work strictly focuses on direct and practical instantiations.

There is a second line of work on "verifiable encryption" in a more general scenario as described in, e.g., [11] or [2]. However, their objectives differ from the one in [7] as Boneh et al.'s work demands that transmitting and verifying an encrypted signature can be done in a single move. In particular, the verification process does not involve interactive zero-knowledge proofs as required in both [11] and [2]. Therefore, we focus on the line of research coming from Boneh et al.'s model.

To the best of our knowledge, all previous schemes use bilinear maps that yield very elegant constructions at the cost of new cryptographic assumptions, i.e., the bilinear Diffie-Hellman assumptions discussed in [6,13,19]. All these papers suggest that correctly applying and fully understanding these assumptions involves some pitfalls and it is safe to assume that this also applies to hardware and software implementations of the respective schemes. Furthermore, compared to hash functions and RSA signatures, the field of pairing based cryptography is young, which makes the newly developed complexity assumptions questionable.

Our contribution. Until now, it has been an open question whether efficient VES schemes in the sense of Boneh et al. can be realized without bilinear maps by using well-understood assumptions instead. We positively answer this question with our construction using full-domain hash RSA signatures [5] and a Merkle-style hash tree [17], which makes our scheme stateful. We also suggest a change

Table 1. Comparison of the different verifiably encrypted signature schemes. The column "R.O." states whether security is proven in the random oracle model. Let $\mathsf{ham}(m)$ be the hamming weight of a message m, mul a multiplication, and ex an exponentiation in the respective group or ring. Let pair be the cost for a pairing evaluation and hash be the cost for a hash function evaluation. The sizes are measured in group elements (G), ring elements (R), and hash values (H). S is the random seed to a pseudo random number generator. The parameter ℓ is a tree constant, e.g., $\ell = 20$ for 2^{20} verifiably encrypted signatures.

VES	R.O.	Keys (sk/pk)	Signature	Create	VesVf
BGLS	YES	G / G	2 G	$2\,\mathsf{ex}+\mathsf{mul}$	$3\,\mathsf{pair}$
ZSNS	YES	2 G / 2 G	G	ex	$2\,\mathsf{pair}$
LOSSW	NO	G / > 160 G (*)	3 G	$4\,\mathsf{ex} + (\mathsf{ham(m)} + 3)\,\mathsf{mul}$	$3\,\mathsf{pair}$
RS	NO	2 G / 4 G	3 G	$4\,\mathsf{ex} + 1\,\mathsf{mul}$	$2\,\mathsf{pair}$
Section 3	YES	R + S / 3 R + H	3 R + ℓ H	$2\,\mathsf{ex} + \mathsf{mul} + \mathcal{O}(\ell)\,\mathsf{hash}$	$2\,\mathsf{ex} + (\ell + 1)\,\mathsf{hash}$

(*) Depends on the size of the message space.

to the signer's key generation algorithm that involves an initial registration with the adjudicator, which be believe to be a sensible and practical extension.

When instantiated correctly, our construction is efficient and can even be implemented on smartcards, having RSA and hash co-processors. Compared to the previous constructions, our approach yields competitive performance for creation and verification of verifiably encrypted signatures. The key generation process in our construction, however, is costly and should be done on a more powerful device. This recommendation does not contradict the common requirement that private signing keys are not allowed to leave the signing device, such as a a smartcard, as the involved tree can be computed independently of the secret, security-sensitive RSA key.

Table 1 shows that only ZSNS has a faster Create method when omitting the constant (independent of the security parameter) number of hash evaluations in our scheme. NIZK constructions for RSA are not considered here because they involve many inefficient modular exponentiations and the number of ring elements in the signature grows with the security parameter. Moreover, using the secret key that often might increase the chance of a successful side-channel attack. Performance of the verification functions is hardly comparable but previous works suggest that pairing evaluations are costly. We, however, only need a constant number of typically very fast hash evaluations here.

As for the storage requirements, we state that they are slightly elevated in our scheme because of the authentication tree. The secret key can be compressed into a single random seed (for the secret leaves of the tree) and a secret RSA exponent. The public key comprises the public RSA key, an RSA signature, and one additional hash value. Note that a certain part of the user's key has to be trusted and will therefore be generated by the adjudicator. However, this does not limit the security of the signature scheme but merely allows the adjudicator to work correctly in case of a dispute.

As for the signature size, our scheme requires an overhead due to the Merkle authentication path. The overhead, however, is constant and does not grow with the security parameter. For instance, the tree depth ℓ can be set as small as 12, even if we assume that the signer works 365 days a year and signs 11 documents per day, where the key is also valid for one year. By increasing ℓ, the signature capability (2^ℓ) quickly becomes virtually unlimited. In the Merkle signature context, one typically sets $\ell = 20$, which allows for over a million signatures at manageable computational cost. In our case, we can manage even larger ℓ.

Finally, we state that it remains unclear whether it is possible to avoid both pairings and the random oracle methodology, which is encouraged by the famous work of Canetti, Goldreich, and Halevi [12].

Organization. We start by introducing our notation and some basic definitions in Section 2 before presenting our instantiation of verifiably encrypted signatures and proving its security in Section 3.

2   Preliminaries

In this section, we recall the specifications of digital signature schemes and of verifiably encrypted signature schemes along with their respective security model as well as Merkle authentication trees. Throughout the paper, n always denotes the security parameter.

2.1   Digital Signatures

The well-known definition of digital signatures along with its security model [14] and a specification of full-domain hash RSA signatures [5] can be found in Appendix A.1.

2.2   Verifiably Encrypted Signature Schemes

Verifiably encrypted signatures are specified in [7], which we slightly modify at the clearly marked spots below. A verifiably encrypted signature scheme VES = (AdjKg, Kg, Sign, Vf, Create, VesVf, Adj) consists of the following seven efficient algorithms.

Adjudicator Key Generation. $\mathsf{AdjKg}(1^n)$ outputs a key pair (ask, apk), where ask is the private key and apk the corresponding public key.

Key Generation, Signature Verification. Signature verification Vf is defined as with a digital signature scheme DSig (cf. Appendix A.1). The key generation algorithm of the signer is $\mathsf{Kg}(1^n, \mathsf{apk})$, which yields the secret key sk$'$ and the public key pk$'$. In [7], it is $\mathsf{Kg}(1^n)$. In addition, we need the signer to register with the adjudicator once, sending pk and receiving and additional key pair (sk$''$, pk$''$). The output is sk $=$ (sk$'$, sk$''$) and pk $=$ (pk$'$, pk$''$).

VES Creation. $\mathsf{Create}(\mathsf{sk}, \mathsf{apk}, m)$ takes as input a secret key sk, the adjudicator's public key apk, and a message $m \in \mathcal{M}$. It returns a verifiably encrypted signature ϖ for m.

VES Verification. The algorithm $\mathsf{VesVf}(\mathsf{apk}, \mathsf{pk}, \varpi, m)$ takes as input the adjudicator's public key apk, a public key pk, a verifiably encrypted signature ϖ, and a message m. It returns a bit.

Adjudication. The algorithm $\mathsf{Adj}(\mathsf{ask}, \mathsf{apk}, \mathsf{pk}, \varpi, m)$ accepts as input the key pair $(\mathsf{ask}, \mathsf{apk})$ of the adjudicator, the public key of the signer pk, a verifiably encrypted signature ϖ, and a message m. It extracts an ordinary signature σ on m and returns σ.

A verifiably encrypted signature scheme is *complete* if for all adjudication key pairs $(\mathsf{ask}, \mathsf{apk}) \leftarrow \mathsf{AdjKg}(1^n)$ and for all signature key pairs $(\mathsf{sk}, \mathsf{pk}) \leftarrow \mathsf{Kg}(1^n, \mathsf{apk})$ the following holds:

$$\mathsf{VesVf}(\mathsf{apk}, \mathsf{pk}, \mathsf{Create}(\mathsf{sk}, \mathsf{apk}, m), m) = 1 \quad \text{and}$$
$$\mathsf{Vf}(\mathsf{pk}, \mathsf{Adj}(\mathsf{ask}, \mathsf{apk}, \mathsf{pk}, \mathsf{Create}(\mathsf{sk}, \mathsf{apk}, m)), m) = 1 \quad \text{for all } m \in \mathcal{M}.$$

Security of verifiably encrypted signatures is defined via *unforgeability* and *opacity* as described in [7], as well as *extractability* and *abuse-freeness* as defined in [18]. Unforgeability requires that it is hard to forge a verifiably encrypted signature and opacity implies that it is difficult to extract an ordinary signature from a verifiably encrypted signature without the secret adjudication key. Extractability requires that the adjudicator can always extract valid regular signatures from valid verifiably encrypted signatures, even if the signer's key is not chosen honestly. The weaker definition, weak-extractability, assumes that the signer key is chosen correctly. As described in [18], weak-extractability can be improved to extractability by common key registration techniques. In Section 3, however, we follow the above modified model and let the adjudicator choose a non-critical part of the user's key that does not limit the security of the signature scheme.

The first two intuitions are formalized in experiments, where the adversary is given the public keys of the signer and of the adjudicator. Moreover, the adversary has access to two oracles: oracle Create returns a verifiably encrypted signature for a given message; oracle Adj extracts a regular signature from a valid verifiably encrypted signature.

A verifiably encrypted signature scheme VES is *secure* if the following holds:

Unforgeability. For any efficient algorithm $\mathcal{A}$, the probability that the following experiment evaluates to 1 is negligible.

> **Experiment** $\mathsf{Exp}^{\text{ves-forge}}_{\mathcal{A},\mathsf{VES}}(n)$
> $(\mathsf{ask}, \mathsf{apk}) \leftarrow \mathsf{AdjKg}(1^n)$
> $(\mathsf{sk}, \mathsf{pk}) \leftarrow \mathsf{Kg}(1^n, \mathsf{apk})$
> $(m^*, \varpi^*) \leftarrow \mathcal{A}^{\mathsf{Create}(\mathsf{sk},\mathsf{apk},\cdot),\mathsf{Adj}(\mathsf{ask},\mathsf{apk},\mathsf{pk},\cdot,\cdot)}(\mathsf{pk}, \mathsf{apk})$
> Return 1 iff $\mathsf{VesVf}(\mathsf{apk}, \mathsf{pk}, \varpi^*, m^*) = 1$ and
> $\mathcal{A}$ has never queried Create or Adj on m^*.

Opacity. For any efficient algorithm $\mathcal{A}$, the probability that the following experiment evaluates to 1 is negligible.

Experiment $\mathsf{Exp}_{\mathcal{A},\mathsf{VES}}^{\mathsf{ves\text{-}opac}}(n)$
  $(\mathsf{ask},\mathsf{apk}) \leftarrow \mathsf{AdjKg}(1^n)$
  $(\mathsf{sk},\mathsf{pk}) \leftarrow \mathsf{Kg}(1^n,\mathsf{apk})$
  $(m^*,\sigma^*) \leftarrow \mathcal{A}^{\mathsf{Create}(\mathsf{sk},\mathsf{apk},\cdot),\mathsf{Adj}(\mathsf{ask},\mathsf{apk},\mathsf{pk},\cdot,\cdot)}(\mathsf{pk},\mathsf{apk})$
  Return 1 iff $\mathsf{Vf}(\mathsf{pk},\sigma^*,m^*) = 1$ and
    $\mathcal{A}$ has never queried $\mathsf{Adj}(\mathsf{ask},\mathsf{apk},\mathsf{pk},\cdot,\cdot)$ on m^*.

A scheme is called $(t,q_{\mathsf{Create}},q_{\mathsf{Adj}},\epsilon)$-unforgeable (-opaque), if no adversary $\mathcal{A}$, running in time at most t, making at most q_{Create} verifiably encrypted signature oracle queries, and at most q_{Adj} adjudication oracle queries, can succeed with probability at least ϵ in the $\mathsf{Exp}_{\mathcal{A},\mathsf{VES}}^{\mathsf{ves\text{-}forge}}$ ($\mathsf{Exp}_{\mathcal{A},\mathsf{VES}}^{\mathsf{ves\text{-}opac}}$) experiment.

The scheme is *extractable* if for all adjudication keys $(\mathsf{ask},\mathsf{apk}) \leftarrow \mathsf{AdjKg}(1^n)$, for all signing key pairs $(\mathsf{sk},\mathsf{pk})$, and for all verifiably encrypted signatures ϖ on some message m the following holds: $\mathsf{VesVf}(\mathsf{apk},\mathsf{pk},\varpi,m) = 1 \implies \mathsf{Vf}(\mathsf{pk}, \mathsf{Adj}(\mathsf{ask},\mathsf{apk},\mathsf{pk},\varpi,m), m) = 1$. In [18], the authors introduce *abuse-freeness* as an additional property. It guarantees that even if signer and adjudicator collude, they cannot forge verifiably encrypted signatures on behalf of a third party. Due to a theorem in [18], we do not have to deal with abuse-freeness explicitly if a VES scheme is unforgeable, extractable, and key-independent. Key-independence is a property of the Create algorithm and states that it can be separated into a signing algorithm and an encryption algorithm, where the encryption algorithm is independent of the secret signature key. This is the case in Section 3.

2.3   Merkle Authentication Trees

A discussion of Merkle trees [17] and their efficient implementation can be found in Appendix A.2.

3   Our Construction

We present an efficient verifiably encrypted signature scheme based on RSA signatures in the random oracle model. Whereas previous constructions exploit the special properties of pairings in order to verifiably encrypt regular signatures, we use a Merkle hash tree to verifiably link encrypted signatures with regular ones. The core idea is that the signer masks the signature using a secret value x, encrypts x under the public key of the adjudicator, and attaches the encryption to the verifiably encrypted signature. Then, the signer uses authentication paths in a special Merkle tree to prove that x has been honestly encrypted. Observe that we make a sensible extension to the model of Boneh et al. and let the adjudicator generate a part of the user's key. This is a practical assumption because in real-world contract signing applications, the users simply register with the escrow beforehand. In the unlikely scenario, where there is more than one adjudicator, the signer has to create one public key per adjudicator.

Let $c = 2^\ell$ for an $\ell \in \mathbb{N}$ be the maximum number of messages to be signed under a single key and let $\mathsf{G} : \{0,1\}^* \to \{0,1\}^{k(n)}$, $k(n) = \omega(\log(n))$, and

$H : \{0,1\}^* \rightarrow \mathbb{Z}_{N_S}$ be collision resistant, one-way hash functions. The proposed verifiably encrypted signature scheme VERSA is a tuple (AdjKg, Kg, Sign, Vf, Create, VesVf, Adj), which is defined as follows.

Adjudicator Key Generation. $\mathsf{AdjKg}(1^n)$ uses $\mathsf{RSA.Kg}(1^n)$ to compute (N_E, e, d) and a second set (authsk,authpk) of RSA keys for key authenticity. It outputs $(N_E, e, \mathsf{authpk})$ as the public key and $(N_E, d, \mathsf{authsk})$ as the secret key.

Key Generation. $\mathsf{Kg}(1^n, (N_E, e, \mathsf{authpk}))$ uses $\mathsf{RSA.Kg}(1^n)$ to compute (N_S, v, s), such that $N_S > N_E$. Upon registration with the adjudicator, the authority randomly chooses c secret values $x_1, \ldots, x_c \leftarrow \mathbb{Z}_{N_E}$, such that they are invertible in $\mathbb{Z}_{N_S}$, and builds a binary tree T. The leaves of T are

$$\mathsf{G}(x_1^e \mod N_E || x_1^v \mod N_S), \ldots, \mathsf{G}(x_c^e \mod N_E || x_c^v \mod N_S) \,.$$

T can be represented by a single random seed to a pseudo random number generator that was used to generate the values $x_1, \ldots, x_c$.

Each inner node η has two children, $\mathsf{left}(\eta)$ and $\mathsf{right}(\eta)$. The value of η is formed recursively: $\eta \leftarrow \mathsf{G}(\mathsf{left}(\eta)||\mathsf{right}(\eta))$. Let ρ be the root of T. The adjudicator computes a signature: $\sigma_\rho \leftarrow \mathsf{RSA.Sign}(\mathsf{authsk}, \rho)$ and sends it to the user. The user's output is the private key (N_S, s, T) and the public key $(N_S, v, \rho, \sigma_\rho)$. The algorithm sets up a state comprising a signature counter $\imath \leftarrow 0$ and a small cache of $O(\ell)$ tree nodes in order to speed up the path computation (cf. Appendix A.2).

Signing, Signature Verification. As in RSA.

VES Creation. $\mathsf{Create}((N_S, s, T), (N_E, e, \mathsf{authpk}), m)$ increments the signature counter $\imath$ and computes

$$\sigma \leftarrow \mathsf{RSA.Sign}((N_S, s), m) \,,$$
$$\alpha \leftarrow \sigma \, x_\imath \mod N_S \,,$$
$$\beta \leftarrow x_\imath^e \mod N_E \,,$$
$$\text{and } \gamma \leftarrow x_\imath^v \mod N_S \,.$$

Then, it generates the authentication path π for $x_\imath$ in T, which is used to prove the relation between β and γ via the collision-resistance of G. The output is $\varpi = (\alpha, \beta, \gamma, \pi)$.

VES Verification. $\mathsf{VesVf}((N_E, e, \mathsf{authpk}), (N_S, v, \rho, \sigma_\rho), (\alpha, \beta, \gamma, \pi), m)$ is 1 iff

1. $0 \le \alpha < N_S$,
2. $\alpha^v \equiv \mathsf{H}(m)\,\gamma \pmod{N_S}$,
3. π correctly authenticates the leaf $\mathsf{G}(\beta||\gamma)$ for the given root ρ.
4. $\mathsf{RSA.Vf}(\mathsf{authpk}, \sigma_\rho, \rho) = 1$.

Adjudication. $\mathsf{Adj}((N_E, d, \mathsf{authsk}), (N_E, e, \mathsf{authpk}), (N_S, v, \rho, \sigma_\rho), (\alpha, \beta, \gamma, \pi), m)$ checks that the presented verifiably encrypted signature is valid. If so, it computes $x' \leftarrow \beta^d \mod N_E$, $\sigma \leftarrow \alpha/x' \mod N_S$, and returns σ.

See Appendix B for the proof of completeness. In the following paragraphs, we show that VERSA satisfies extractability, unforgeability, and opacity according to the model of Boneh et al. and its modifications in [18]. Due to the fact that Create works in two key-independent steps — sign with RSA.Sign and verifiably encrypt with additional secret values — our scheme is abuse-free according to [18, Theorem 5.4].

Extractability. We show that our scheme is extractable. For

$$\text{all adjudication keys:} \quad (N_E, e, d, \mathsf{authsk}, \mathsf{authpk}) \leftarrow \mathsf{AdjKg}(1^n),$$
$$\text{all signing keys:} \quad (N_S, v, \rho, s, T, \sigma_\rho),$$
$$\text{and all encrypted signatures:} \quad \varpi = (\alpha, \beta, \gamma, \pi) \text{ on some message } m,$$

$\mathsf{VesVf}((N_E, e, \mathsf{authpk}), (N_S, v, \rho, \sigma_\rho), \varpi, m) = 1$ guarantees the correctness of β and γ by conditions 3 and 4, i.e., they were computed from the same secret value x as long as G is collision resistant and RSA is unforgeable. In consequence, the adjudicator can always unmask α with the decryption of β. The resulting regular signature σ is always valid because of conditions 1 and 2 in VesVf.

For the following proofs, let $T_{\mathsf{AdjKg}}(n)$ and $T_{\mathsf{Kg}}(n)$ be the cost functions for adjudication and signature key generation and let $T_{\mathsf{Create}}(n), T_{\mathsf{VesVf}}(n)$, and $T_{\mathsf{Adj}}(n)$ be the cost functions for creation, verification, and adjudication of verifiably encrypted signatures.

Unforgeability. We show that our scheme is unforgeable, provided that the underlying signature scheme is unforgeable.

Theorem 1 (Unforgeability). VERSA *is* $(t, q_{\mathsf{Create}}, q_{\mathsf{Adj}}, \epsilon)$*-unforgeable if the* RSA *signature scheme is* $(t', q_{\mathsf{Create}}, \epsilon - \delta)$*-unforgeable with* $t' = T_{\mathsf{AdjKg}}(n) + T_{\mathsf{Kg}}(n) + q_{\mathsf{Create}} T_{\mathsf{Create}}(n) + q_{\mathsf{Adj}} T_{\mathsf{Adj}}(n)$ *and there is no polynomial-time adversary that can find collisions under* G *with probability* $\geq \delta$.

Proof. Towards contradiction, let's assume that there exists a successful polynomial time adversary $\mathcal{A}$ against the unforgeability of VERSA, running in time t and with success probability ϵ. Furthermore, assume that $\mathcal{A}$ makes q_{Create} verifiably encrypted signature queries and q_{Adj} adjudication queries. Via a black box simulation of $\mathcal{A}$, we construct an efficient and equally successful adversary $\mathcal{B}$ against the underlying signature scheme in the $\mathsf{Exp}_{\mathcal{A},\mathsf{RSA}}^{\mathsf{eu\text{-}cma}}$ experiment.

Setup. $\mathcal{B}$ gets as input the public verification key (N_S, v) and has access to a signing oracle $\mathsf{RSA.Sign}((N_S, s), \cdot)$. It generates its own adjudication key $(N_E, e, d, \mathsf{authsk}, \mathsf{authpk})$ and executes Kg in order to generate the secret values $(x_1, \ldots, x_c)$ as well as ρ and σ_ρ, accordingly. $\mathcal{B}$ simulates $\mathcal{A}$ with the input $(N_S, v, \rho, \sigma_\rho), (N_E, e, \mathsf{authpk})$.

VES Queries. Whenever $\mathcal{A}$ queries the verifiably encrypted signature oracle Create on some message m, algorithm $\mathcal{B}$ invokes its signing oracle $\sigma \leftarrow \mathsf{RSA.Sign}((N_S, s), \cdot)$ on m, masks the signature as described in Create, and outputs $(\alpha, \beta, \gamma, \pi)$.

Adjudication Queries. If $\mathcal{A}$ invokes the adjudication oracle Adj on a message m and on a verifiable encrypted signature $(\alpha, \beta, \gamma, \pi)$, $\mathcal{B}$ verifies it. If it is invalid, $\mathcal{B}$ returns fail. Otherwise, it extracts the signature by computing $x' \leftarrow \beta^d \mod N_E$, $\sigma \leftarrow \alpha/x' \mod N_S$, and returns σ.

Output. Finally, $\mathcal{A}$ halts, outputting a forged verifiably encrypted signature (m^*, ϖ^*), such that $\mathsf{VesVf}((N_E, e, \mathsf{authpk}), (N_S, v, \rho, \sigma_\rho), \varpi^*, m^*) = 1$ with $\varpi^* = (\alpha^*, \beta^*, \gamma^*, \pi^*)$. $\mathcal{B}$ extracts $\sigma^* \leftarrow \mathsf{Adj}((N_E, d, \mathsf{authsk}), (N_E, e, \mathsf{authpk}), (N_S, v, \rho, \sigma_\rho), \varpi^*, m^*)$ and stops, outputting (m^*, σ^*).

Analysis. Since $\mathcal{B}$ acts honestly on all queries and all keys are generated honestly, the environment of $\mathcal{A}$ is perfectly simulated. According to the security model, $\mathcal{A}$ is only successful if it returns a verifiably encrypted signature for a message which has never been signed before. In addition, extractability ensures that every verifiably encrypted signature yields a regular signature via adjudication. This step only fails if $\mathcal{A}$ can find collisions under G. Thus, $\mathcal{B}$'s success probability is at least $\epsilon - \delta$. As for the detailed complexity analysis, note that $\mathcal{B}$ queries the signature oracle whenever $\mathcal{A}$ queries the verifiably encrypted signature oracle. When $\mathcal{A}$ queries the adjudication oracle, $\mathcal{B}$ decrypts the query if it is valid. The overall overhead, including key generation, encryption, and adjudication, is at most $T_{\mathsf{AdjKg}}(n) + T_{\mathsf{Kg}}(n) + q_{\mathsf{Create}} T_{\mathsf{Create}}(n) + q_{\mathsf{Adj}} T_{\mathsf{Adj}}(n)$, which completes the proof. $\qquad\square$

Opacity. We prove that breaking opacity of VERSA implies being able to invert the RSA trapdoor. In order to emphasize the interesting case in the proof of opacity, where the adversary extracts a regular signature from an encrypted one, we omit the straightforward proof for the type of adversary that simply forges the underlying signature scheme. Inverting the RSA trapdoor with non-negligible probability, is assumed to be infeasible for all polynomially bounded algorithms, i.e., the problem is (t, ϵ)-hard for every non-negligible ϵ and any $t = \mathsf{poly}(n)$.

Theorem 2 (Opacity). *The* VERSA *scheme is* $(t, q_{\mathsf{Create}}, q_{\mathsf{Adj}}, \epsilon)$-*opaque if the* RSA *signature scheme is* $(t', q_{\mathsf{Create}}, \epsilon - \delta)$-*unforgeable, inverting the RSA trapdoor is* $(t', q_{\mathsf{Create}}, \epsilon')$-*hard with* $t' = t + T_{\mathsf{Kg}}(n) + T_{\mathsf{AdjKg}}(n) + q_{\mathsf{Create}} T_{\mathsf{Create}}(n) + q_{\mathsf{Adj}} T_{\mathsf{Adj}}(n)$ *and* $\epsilon' = \epsilon/q_{\mathsf{Create}}$, *and there is no polynomial-time adversary that can find collisions under* G *with probability* $\geq \delta$.

Proof. Assume there is a successful polynomial time adversary $\mathcal{A}$ against opacity of VERSA, running in time t and with success probability ϵ, which makes q_{Create} verifiably encrypted signature queries and q_{Adj} adjudication queries. Using $\mathcal{A}$, we construct an efficient algorithm $\mathcal{B}$ that is able to invert an RSA challenge $y \in \mathbb{Z}_{N_S}^*$. Thus, the goal of $\mathcal{B}$ is to find a value $x \in \mathbb{Z}_{N_S}$ with $x^v \equiv y \pmod{N_S}$ — see [4] for a formal definition.

Setup. $\mathcal{B}$ gets as input the public RSA key (N_S, v) and a challenge y. The algorithm executes AdjKg and Kg in order to generate $(N_E, e, d, \mathsf{authsk}, \mathsf{authpk})$ and $(x_1, \ldots, x_{j-1}, \square, x_{j+1}, \ldots, x_c)$, where $j \leftarrow \{1, \ldots, q_{\mathsf{Create}}\}$, $q_{\mathsf{Create}} \leq c$, is chosen uniformly at random. Then, it chooses $z \leftarrow \mathbb{Z}_{N_S}$ uniformly at random. Root ρ and signature σ_ρ of T is generated from

$$\left(\mathsf{G}(x_1^e\|x_1^v), \ldots, \mathsf{G}(x_{j-1}^e\|x_{j-1}^v), \mathsf{G}(y\|z^v/y), \mathsf{G}(x_{j+1}^e\|x_{j+1}^v), \ldots, \mathsf{G}(x_c^e\|x_c^v)\right),$$

where $\mathsf{G}(a\|b)$ is shorthand for $\mathsf{G}(a \bmod N_E \| b \bmod N_S)$. Algorithm $\mathcal{B}$ runs $\mathcal{A}$ on input $(N_S, v, \rho, \sigma_\rho), (N_E, e, \mathsf{authpk})$ in a black box simulation. $\mathcal{B}$ initializes a signature counter $\imath \leftarrow 0$. Furthermore, $\mathcal{B}$ maintains a list L_H of triples (m, r, σ) in order to simulate a consistent random oracle and the signature oracle.

Random Oracle Queries. On input m, algorithm $\mathcal{B}$ searches an entry $(m, r, \square)$ in L_H. If it does not exist, $\mathcal{B}$ randomly chooses an $\sigma \leftarrow \mathbb{Z}_{N_S}^*$ and adds $(m, r \leftarrow \sigma^v \bmod N_S, s)$ to L_H. The oracle returns r.

VES Queries. When $\mathcal{A}$ queries the oracle on a message m, algorithm $\mathcal{B}$ increments $\jmath$.

- Case $\imath = \jmath$: $\mathcal{B}$ adds $(m, y, 0)$ to L_H and sets

$$\alpha \leftarrow z \quad \bmod N_S,$$
$$\beta \leftarrow y \quad \bmod N_E,$$
$$\gamma \leftarrow z^v/y \quad \bmod N_S.$$

- Case $\imath \neq \jmath$: $\mathcal{B}$ executes $\mathsf{H}(m)$, yielding a triple $(m, r, \sigma) \in L_\mathsf{H}$, and sets

$$\alpha \leftarrow \sigma x_\imath \quad \bmod N_S,$$
$$\beta \leftarrow x_\imath^e \quad \bmod N_E,$$
$$\gamma \leftarrow x_\imath^v \quad \bmod N_S.$$

In both cases, the outputs is $(\alpha, \beta, \gamma, \pi)$, where π authenticates the $\imath$-th leaf.

Adjudication Queries. Whenever $\mathcal{A}$ invokes the adjudication oracle Adj on a message m and on a verifiable encrypted signature $\varpi = (\alpha, \beta, \gamma, \pi)$, algorithm $\mathcal{B}$ verifies its validity. If it is invalid, $\mathcal{B}$ answers with fail. If $\mathsf{H}(m) = y$, $\mathcal{B}$ stops and returns fail. Otherwise, it searches the list L_H for an entry (m, r, σ) and outputs σ. If it does not exists, $\mathcal{B}$ extracts the signature σ^* from ϖ. It stops and outputs the forgery (m, σ^*).

Output. When $\mathcal{A}$ halts, outputting a forged signature (m^*, σ^*). If m^* was never queried to Create, algorithm $\mathcal{B}$ outputs the forgery (m^*, σ^*). If m^* is in L_H, algorithm $\mathcal{B}$ returns σ^* as the v-th root of y modulo N_S.

Analysis. First, we have to show that $\mathcal{A}$'s queries are correctly answered by $\mathcal{B}$. The keys are chosen honestly except for the $\jmath$-th leaf of T. However, this deviation is not efficiently recognizable as the distribution of the arguments under G stays uniform. The random oracle and adjudication queries are perfectly simulated because $\mathcal{B}$ returns random hash values and valid signatures.

As for verifiably encrypted signature queries, we deal with the two cases separately. For $\imath \neq \jmath$, we use a standard random oracle technique for RSA signature simulation. The returned encrypted signatures are always valid. In case

$i = j$, algorithm $\mathcal{A}$ is given a tuple $(\alpha, \beta, \gamma, \pi)$ that is valid for m because $\alpha^v \equiv z^v \equiv z^v \, y/y \equiv \mathsf{H}(m)\,\gamma \pmod{N_S}$. Therefore, $\mathcal{A}$'s environment is simulated as expected. The computational overhead $T_{\mathsf{Kg}}(n) + T_{\mathsf{AdjKg}}(n) + q_{\mathsf{Create}}\, T_{\mathsf{Create}}(n) + q_{\mathsf{Adj}}\, T_{\mathsf{Adj}}(n)$ of the reduction is induced by the fact that $\mathcal{B}$ initially executes parts of Kg and AdjKg and that the simulation of Create and Adj can be performed at least as efficient as in the original scheme. As for Adj, the list-based simulation is even more efficient. Note that for brevity, our overhead analysis does not take the simulation of the random oracle into account. The success probability of $\mathcal{B}$ depends on the type of adversary $\mathcal{A}$. It may be an adversary that never queried m^* to Create. In this case, however, we have a direct forgery against the RSA signature scheme. The same holds in case that $\mathcal{A}$ queries Adj with a fresh message m because VERSA is extractable but with probability δ. In the interesting case, i.e., $\mathcal{A}$ queried m^* to Create, the success probability of $\mathcal{B}$ depends on the correct guess of the index j. If the guess is correct, $\mathcal{A}$ outputs (m^*, σ^*) with $\sigma^{*v} \equiv \mathsf{H}(m^*) \equiv y \pmod{N_S}$.

In consequence, if $\mathcal{A}$ is successful with noticeable probability ϵ then $\mathcal{B}$ is successful with probability $\epsilon/q_{\mathsf{Create}}$, which is still noticeable. $\qquad\square$

4 Conclusions

With our construction, we have shown that verifiably encrypted signatures can be constructed without pairings by using simple and efficient primitives instead. The main benefit of our result is that existing widespread hard- and software implementations of hash functions and RSA signatures can be easily reused in the VES setting. From a theoretical point of view, we introduced a new construction principle at the expense of making the scheme stateful. The remaining open question is whether the scheme can be made stateless and whether we can avoid the random oracle methodology.

Acknowledgments

The author would like to thank Dominique Schröder and Michael Schneider for many insightful discussions on the subject. Furthermore, the author thanks the anonymous reviewers of Indocrypt 2009 for their valuable comments.

References

1. Asokan, N., Shoup, V., Waidner, M.: Optimistic fair exchange of digital signatures. IEEE Journal on Selected Areas in Communications 18(4), 593–610 (2000)
2. Ateniese, G.: Verifiable encryption of digital signatures and applications. ACM Trans. Inf. Syst. Secur. 7(1), 1–20 (2004)
3. Bao, F., Deng, R.H., Mao, W.: Efficient and practical fair exchange protocols with off-line ttp. In: IEEE Symposium on Security and Privacy, pp. 77–85. IEEE Computer Society, Los Alamitos (1998)

4. Bellare, M., Namprempre, C., Pointcheval, D., Semanko, M.: The one-more-rsa-inversion problems and the security of chaum's blind signature scheme. J. Cryptology 16(3), 185–215 (2003)
5. Bellare, M., Rogaway, P.: The exact security of digital signatures - how to sign with RSA and rabin. In: Maurer, U.M. (ed.) EUROCRYPT 1996. LNCS, vol. 1070, pp. 399–416. Springer, Heidelberg (1996)
6. Boneh, D.: The decision diffie-hellman problem. In: Buhler, J.P. (ed.) ANTS 1998. LNCS, vol. 1423, pp. 48–63. Springer, Heidelberg (1998)
7. Boneh, D., Gentry, C., Lynn, B., Shacham, H.: Aggregate and verifiably encrypted signatures from bilinear maps. In: Biham, E. (ed.) EUROCRYPT 2003. LNCS, vol. 2656, pp. 416–432. Springer, Heidelberg (2003)
8. Buchmann, J., Dahmen, E., Klintsevich, E., Okeya, K., Vuillaume, C.: Merkle signatures with virtually unlimited signature capacity. In: Katz, J., Yung, M. (eds.) ACNS 2007. LNCS, vol. 4521, pp. 31–45. Springer, Heidelberg (2007)
9. Buchmann, J., Dahmen, E., Schneider, M.: Merkle tree traversal revisited. In: Buchmann, J., Ding, J. (eds.) PQCrypto 2008. LNCS, vol. 5299, pp. 63–78. Springer, Heidelberg (2008)
10. Buchmann, J., García, L.C.C., Dahmen, E., Döring, M., Klintsevich, E.: Cmss - an improved merkle signature scheme. In: Barua, R., Lange, T. (eds.) INDOCRYPT 2006. LNCS, vol. 4329, pp. 349–363. Springer, Heidelberg (2006)
11. Camenisch, J., Shoup, V.: Practical verifiable encryption and decryption of discrete logarithms. In: Boneh, D. (ed.) CRYPTO 2003. LNCS, vol. 2729, pp. 126–144. Springer, Heidelberg (2003)
12. Canetti, R., Goldreich, O., Halevi, S.: The random oracle methodology, revisited. J. ACM 51(4), 557–594 (2004)
13. Galbraith, S.D., Paterson, K.G., Smart, N.P.: Pairings for cryptographers. Cryptology ePrint Archive, Report 2006/165 (2006), http://eprint.iacr.org/
14. Goldwasser, S., Micali, S., Rivest, R.L.: A digital signature scheme secure against adaptive chosen-message attacks. SIAM J. Comput. 17(2), 281–308 (1988)
15. Huang, Q., Yang, G., Wong, D.S., Susilo, W.: Ambiguous optimistic fair exchange. In: Pieprzyk, J. (ed.) ASIACRYPT 2008. LNCS, vol. 5350, pp. 74–89. Springer, Heidelberg (2008)
16. Lu, S., Ostrovsky, R., Sahai, A., Shacham, H., Waters, B.: Sequential aggregate signatures and multisignatures without random oracles. In: Vaudenay, S. (ed.) EUROCRYPT 2006. LNCS, vol. 4004, pp. 465–485. Springer, Heidelberg (2006)
17. Merkle, R.C.: A certified digital signature. In: Brassard, G. (ed.) CRYPTO 1989. LNCS, vol. 435, pp. 218–238. Springer, Heidelberg (1990)
18. Rückert, M., Schröder, D.: Security of verifiably encrypted signatures and a construction without random oracles. In: Shacham, H., Waters, B. (eds.) Pairing 2009. LNCS, vol. 5671, pp. 17–34. Springer, Heidelberg (2009)
19. Smart, N.P., Vercauteren, F.: On computable isomorphisms in efficient asymmetric pairing-based systems. Discrete Applied Mathematics 155(4), 538–547 (2007)
20. Szydlo, M.: Merkle tree traversal in log space and time. In: Cachin, C., Camenisch, J.L. (eds.) EUROCRYPT 2004. LNCS, vol. 3027, pp. 541–554. Springer, Heidelberg (2004)
21. Waters, B.: Efficient identity-based encryption without random oracles. In: Cramer, R. (ed.) EUROCRYPT 2005. LNCS, vol. 3494, pp. 114–127. Springer, Heidelberg (2005)
22. Zhang, F., Safavi-Naini, R., Susilo, W.: Efficient verifiably encrypted signature and partially blind signature from bilinear pairings. In: Johansson, T., Maitra, S. (eds.) INDOCRYPT 2003. LNCS, vol. 2904, pp. 191–204. Springer, Heidelberg (2003)

A   Preliminaries

A.1   Digital Signatures

A signature scheme consists of a triple of efficient algorithms $\mathsf{DSig} = (\mathsf{Kg}, \mathsf{Sign}, \mathsf{Vf})$, where

Key Generation. $\mathsf{Kg}(1^n)$ outputs a private signing key sk and a public verification key pk.

Signing. $\mathsf{Sign}(\mathsf{sk}, m)$ outputs a signature σ on a message m from the message space $\mathcal{M}$ under sk.

Verification. The algorithm $\mathsf{Vf}(\mathsf{pk}, \sigma, m)$ outputs 1 if σ is a valid signature on m under pk, otherwise 0.

Signature schemes are complete if for any $(\mathsf{sk}, \mathsf{pk}) \leftarrow \mathsf{Kg}(1^n)$, any message $m \in \mathcal{M}$, and any $\sigma \leftarrow \mathsf{Sign}(\mathsf{sk}, m)$, we have $\mathsf{Vf}(\mathsf{pk}, \sigma, m) = 1$. Security of signature schemes is proven against existential forgery under chosen message attacks [14]. In this model, an adversary adaptively invokes a signing oracle and is successful if he outputs a valid signature on a *new* message.

A signature scheme $\mathsf{DSig} = (\mathsf{Kg}, \mathsf{Sign}, \mathsf{Vf})$ is called *existentially unforgeable under chosen message attacks* (EU-CMA) if for any efficient algorithm $\mathcal{A}$, the probability that the experiment $\mathsf{Exp}^{\mathsf{eu\text{-}cma}}_{\mathcal{A}, \mathsf{DSig}}$ evaluates to 1 is negligible.

Experiment $\mathsf{Exp}^{\mathsf{eu\text{-}cma}}_{\mathcal{A}, \mathsf{DSig}}(n)$
    $(\mathsf{sk}, \mathsf{pk}) \leftarrow \mathsf{Kg}(1^n)$
    $(m^*, \sigma^*) \leftarrow \mathcal{A}^{\mathsf{Sign}(\mathsf{sk}, \cdot)}(\mathsf{pk})$
    Let (m_i, σ_i) be the answer of $\mathsf{Sign}(\mathsf{sk}, \cdot)$ on input m_i, for $i = 1, \ldots, k$.
    Return 1 iff $\mathsf{Vf}(\mathsf{pk}, \sigma^*, m^*) = 1$ and $m^* \notin \{m_1, \ldots, m_k\}$.

A signature scheme DSig is $(t, q_{\mathsf{Sig}}, \epsilon)$-*unforgeable* if no adversary running in time at most t, invoking the signing oracle at most q_{Sig} times, outputs a valid forgery (m^*, σ^*) with probability at least ϵ.

Recall the definition of secure RSA signatures. Let $\mathsf{H} : \{0,1\}^* \rightarrow \mathbb{Z}_N^*$ be a collision resistant hash function for a given modulus N. The full-domain hash RSA signature scheme RSA [5] is a 3-tuple $(\mathsf{Kg}, \mathsf{Sign}, \mathsf{Vf})$, which is defined as follows.

Key Generation. $\mathsf{Kg}(1^n)$ receives the security parameter n and generates two primes p, q of bit length $n/2$. Let $N = pq$ be the public modulus. It chooses v relatively prime to $(p-1)(q-1)$, $s \leftarrow v^{-1} \pmod{(p-1)(q-1)}$, and returns the secret key (N, s) and the public key (N, v).

Signing. $\mathsf{Sign}((N, s), m)$ receives the modulus N, the private key s and a message $m \in \{0,1\}^*$. It computes $\sigma \leftarrow \mathsf{H}(m)^s \bmod N$ and returns σ.

Verification. $\mathsf{Vf}((N, v), \sigma, m)$ receives the public key (N, v), a signature σ and a message m. It returns 1 iff $0 \leq \sigma < N$ and $\sigma^v \equiv \mathsf{H}(m) \pmod{N}$.

It is well-known that RSA is complete and unforgeable in the random oracle model, when following the "hash-then-sign" paradigm [5].

A.2 Merkle Authentication Trees

In [17], Merkle describes a tree-based construction for digital signature schemes based on the collision-resistance of hash functions. Recall collision-resistance as a property of a hash function $G : D \to R$, which states that it is computationally infeasible to find distinct $x_1, x_2 \in D$, such that $G(x_1) = G(x_2)$.

At its core, Merkle's scheme relies on authenticating a large amount of data, the 2^ℓ leaves of a binary tree of depth ℓ, with a single public hash value, the root ρ of the binary tree, by providing authentication paths. The authentication path comprises all inner nodes, along with the relative position w.r.t. to their parent nodes, that are necessary to compute the value ρ. The path can be written as $\pi = [(I_1, E_1), \dots, (I_\ell, E_\ell)]$, where $I_i \in \{\mathsf{left}, \mathsf{right}\}$ and $E_i \in R$ for $i = 1 \dots, \ell$. For an example, see Figure 1.

The verification of the authentication path for a leaf X can be done by checking whether $\eta_\ell = \rho$, where

$$\eta_0 \leftarrow X,$$

$$\eta_i \leftarrow \begin{cases} G(E_i \| \eta_{i-1}) & \text{if } I_i = \mathsf{left} \\ G(\eta_{i-1} \| E_i) & \text{if } I_i = \mathsf{right} \end{cases} \quad \text{for } i = 1, \dots, \ell.$$

While authentication path creation and verification can be implemented using $O(\ell)$ hash evaluations by using a small cache of $O(\ell)$ hash values [17,20,9], the initial tree generation is rather costly. Setting $\ell = 20$, however, has proven to be a reasonable trade-off between signature capability and efficiency in the Merkle signature scheme [10] but there generalized constructions that allow for 2^{40} or even 2^{80} signatures without having to compute 2^{40} respectively 2^{80} hash values during the set-up phase [8].

In order to keep it more accessible, we do not apply these generalizations to our construction and state that leaf computation in our case is far less expensive than leaf computation in a Merkle signature scheme. Therefore, one can expect that the upper bound for the number of verifiably encrypted signatures can be

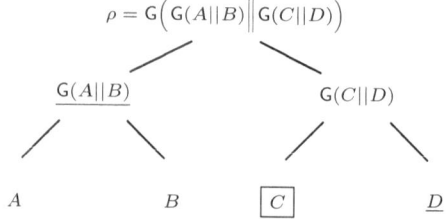

The authentication path for the leaf C: in order to compute ρ, it is necessary to publish D and $G(A\|B)$ along with their relative positions. The resulting path is $\pi = [(\mathsf{right}, D), (\mathsf{left}, G(A\|B))]$. Note that instead of publishing the relative position (left or right), it is sufficient to publish the zero-based index (2) of C.

Fig. 1. Merkle authentication tree

raised to 2^{30}. On a 2.4 GHz Opteron CPU, the overhead for tree generation with height $\ell = 30$ is about 30 minutes without further optimization or parallelization. Taking into account that hardly anyone will ever issue that many signatures in a lifetime, the computational overhead of our tree construction can be significantly reduced to 1 *minute* ($\ell = 25$), 1.5 *seconds* ($\ell = 20$), and 50 *milliseconds* ($\ell = 15$). Observe that, like the Merkle signature scheme, our construction scales well with the individual requirements of different application scenarios.

B   Completeness of Our Construction

For

$$
\begin{array}{ll}
\text{all adjudication keys} & (N_E, e, d, \mathsf{authsk}, \mathsf{authpk}) \leftarrow \mathsf{AdjKg}(1^n)\,, \\
\text{all signing keys} & (N_S, v, \rho, s, T, \sigma_\rho) \leftarrow \mathsf{Kg}(1^n, (N_E, e, \mathsf{authpk}))\,, \\
\text{all messages} & m \in \{0, 1\}^*\,, \\
\text{and encrypted signatures} & \varpi \leftarrow \mathsf{Create}((N_S, s, T), (N_E, e, \mathsf{authpk}), m)\,,
\end{array}
$$

we have

$$
\begin{aligned}
\varpi &= (\alpha, \beta, \gamma, \pi)\,, \\
\alpha &\equiv \mathsf{H}(m)^s\, x \pmod{N_S}\,, \\
\beta &\equiv x^e \pmod{N_E}\,, \\
\gamma &\equiv x^v \pmod{N_S}\,, \\
\pi &= [(I_1, E_1), \dots, (I_\ell, E_\ell)]\,.
\end{aligned}
$$

As for VesVf, condition 2 is satisfied because $\alpha^v \equiv \sigma^v\, x_i^v \equiv \mathsf{H}(m)\,\gamma \pmod{N_S}$ and condition 1 holds trivially. Conditions 3 and 4 are satisfied by construction of ρ and σ_ρ. Thus, $\mathsf{VesVf}((N_E, e, \mathsf{authpk}), (N_S, v, \rho, \sigma_\rho), (\alpha, \beta, \gamma, \pi), m) = 1$. As for Vf and Adj, we state state that Adj computes

$$
\begin{aligned}
x' &\leftarrow \beta^d \bmod N_E,\ x' \equiv x^{e\,d} \equiv x \pmod{N_E},\ x' \in \mathbb{Z}_{N_S}^*\,, \\
\sigma' &\leftarrow \alpha/x' \bmod N_S,\ \sigma' \equiv \mathsf{H}(m)^s\, x/x' \equiv \mathsf{H}(m)^s \pmod{N_S}
\end{aligned}
$$

and that, therefore, $\mathsf{Vf}((N_S, v), \sigma', m) = 1$. Thus, VERSA is complete.

Identity Based Aggregate Signcryption Schemes

S. Sharmila Deva Selvi[1], S. Sree Vivek[1,*], J. Shriram[2], S. Kalaivani[2],
and C. Pandu Rangan[1,*]

[1] Department of Computer Science and Engineering,
Indian Institute of Technology Madras
{sharmila,svivek,prangan}@iitm.ac.in
[2] National Institute of Technology Trichy, India
{shriram139,kalaivani.siva}@gmail.com

Abstract. An identity-based signature scheme allows any pair of users
to communicate securely and to verify each others signatures without exchanging public key certificates. For achieving both confidentiality and
authenticity simultaneously, signcryption schemes are used. An aggregate
signature scheme is a digital signature scheme that supports aggregation
of individual signatures. Given n signatures on n distinct messages signed
by n distinct users, it is possible to aggregate all these signatures into
a single signature. This signature will convince the verifier that all the
n signers have signed the corresponding n messages. In this paper, we
introduce the concept of aggregate signcryption which achieves confidentiality, authentication and aggregation efficiently. This helps in improving
the communication and the computation efficiency. Also, we extend the
scheme to achieve public verifiability with very efficient aggregate verification, that uses fixed number of pairings.

Keywords: Identity Based Cryptography, Aggregate Signcryption,
Provable Security, Bilinear Pairings, Random Oracle Model.

1 Introduction

The two most important functionalities offered by cryptography are authentication and confidentiality. In 1997 Zheng introduced the concept of signcryption which provides both confidentiality and authentication [22]. Signcryption is
more efficient than performing sign and encrypt independently on a single message using the most efficient signing and encryption algorithms. The first formal
security model and security proof was given by Baek et al. in 2002 [1]. Identity
based signcryption with formal security proof was introduced by Malone-Lee
in his paper [11]. But Malone-Lee's scheme was not secure and its weakness
was pointed out in [10]. Signcryption also provides several additional properties
such as cipher-text unlinkability, non repudiation and public verifiability. Many
efficient signcryption schemes have been proposed till date [4] [5] [8].

* Work supported by Project No. CSE/05-06/076/DITX/CPAN on Protocols for Secure Communication and Computation sponsored by Department of Information
Technology, Government of India.

B. Roy and N. Sendrier (Eds.): INDOCRYPT 2009, LNCS 5922, pp. 378–397, 2009.
© Springer-Verlag Berlin Heidelberg 2009

There are two major constraints to design an efficient signcryption scheme, namely computation and communication efficiency. With the advent of super computers, computational efficiency is not of a serious issue, but with increased technology, speed and density, the bandwidth is more a limiting condition. Thus communication efficiency is very important in the present scenario. The amount of data sent must be kept as close to the theoretical minimum for getting efficiency. For example in banking scenarios one may have to verify many signatures quickly and simultaneously. In order to reduce the verification cost and overhead of transmission, we use aggregate signatures.

In aggregate signatures multiple signatures from various users are combined into a single compact signature. Aggregation can be used to reduce the certificate chains in PKI settings. In the scheme in [9], multiple signatures from different signers on different documents can be aggregated to a single compact aggregate signature. The aggregate signatures has many real world applications ranging from traffic control to documents signed by directors of a company for official purpose. Another additional advantage of aggregate signature is that an adversary cannot remove a single signature from a set of signatures. There are two types of aggregation. In the first one the signatures can be aggregated in any order. On the other hand in sequential aggregation a signer adds his signature to the previous aggregate signature sent by the previous signer. Though sequential aggregation is comparatively weaker to the general signcryption, it has more practical applications in business scenario. Many aggregate signature schemes have been proposed till date [13] [20][9][2] [6][20]. Certain aggregate and batch verification schemes have been broken which is shown in [16].

In certain scenarios one may need to hide the message which he is sending so that only the receiver will be able to get back the message. In such cases signcryption comes into picture. We introduce the first identity based aggregate signcryption along with formal security model and formal security proof in this paper. Consider the scenario of online opinion poll. One may want his opinion to be secret. But the verifier has to ensure that all the concerned persons have polled their votes, in an efficient way. Only the verifier will be able to decrypt the messages and get the opinions. Consider another case where the directors of a company have to vote on some controversial issue. Each of them want their vote to be hidden from others since it may disrupt the friendly atmosphere prevailing in the company. In all these circumstances aggregate signcryption can be used to increase efficiency, provide secrecy and decrease the communication overhead. It has application in military communication also.

The idea of Identity Based Cryptography is to derive the public key of a user from an arbitrary string that uniquely identifies the user. It reduces the overhead of storing the public keys and the certificates of all the users. A central trusted authority called the Private Key Generator(PKG) is required to generate the private keys for the corresponding public keys. Identity based cryptography was introduced by Shamir in 1984 in [19]. Since then several ID based schemes have been proposed for both encryption and signatures. In 2001, Boneh and Franklin proposed the first practical identity-based encryption scheme based on Bilinear pairings [3].

Motivation: We give the various scenarios where this primitive will be useful.

1. Consider an online polling event which is a very common technology. The voters want to make sure that their vote is hidden and only the vote count register will be able to view the vote. The count register would also want to make sure that this is a valid vote by a valid user of the system. This calls for signcryption primitive which provides both confidentiality for the sender and authentication to the receiver. The count register will be a secure device but the computation power of the device might be limited. Providing high security and high computation power has a huge cost demand. But security of such devices cannot be relaxed and hence by relaxing the computation power, one can save a lot of cost involved. So with limited computation power, a count register will find it very difficult to verify the authenticity of each and every vote separately (since it may have millions of users voting). But by aggregate signcryption, the count register will easily be able to verify the authenticity of all the votes using a single verification step. Since a part of all the signcryptions are aggregated, the bandwidth is also saved. Thus aggregate signcryption can play a very important role in this scenario.

2. Consider a traffic management system. Assume in a particular area there are n traffic cameras. These traffic cameras collect the information about traffic in a particular zone. All these information has to be sent to the main server which requires instant updates about the traffic to monitor the traffic signals accordingly. These information are sensitive information and should not be sent in the open. The server also has to know that these information are authentic since an adversary in the middle should not be able to manipulate the data. This calls for the signcryption primitive. The server however powerful it is needs to execute instructions within matter of milli seconds and it should not waste any time in checking for authenticity of the data. By using aggregate signcryption technique, the server can easily verify all the data from the cameras instantly leading to no delay. This enables quick functioning of the server.

3. Aggregate signcryption can be used in routing scenarios. If many routers in the same locality wants to send some message to a particular computer in some other network and the routers also wants confidentiality since they do not want their message to be viewed by other routers in their own network (for e.g.. online bidding), then the routers can signcrypt their corresponding messages, then aggregate their signatures which saves them communication overhead and provides both authentication and confidentiality. Even anonymity is needed in certain scenarios which can be provided by signcryption.

4. Banking scenarios need both security and really fast computations. Signcryption is a necessity for online transactions. A common server can aggregate all the signcryptions before sending it to the bank which can unsigncrypt it and run the authenticate tests much faster than trying to test each signature separately for its validity. The banks can save a lot of time by using aggregation.

5. This primitive may also be used in Digital rights management (DRM). The interaction between the client/user and the rights providing authority usually takes place through a dealer. A dealer is an intermediate party who forwards the users request to the rights provider along with the appropriate funds. In this manner the rights providing authority (RPA)'s job is reduced and there is no direct interaction between the user and service provider. The users send their request signcrypted to the dealer. The dealer checks the authenticity of the users and forwards it to the rights provider. The rights provider having checked the reception of funds and authentication provides the license rights back to the user. Now consider the situation where each dealer deals with about 50 clients and the RPA is connected to about 50 dealers. If we use only signcryption, then the total number of verifications done by the RPA will be about 2500. But by using aggregation technique both at the dealer end and RPA end, we can reduce it to single verification step thus saving a lot of time and computation.

6. Aggregate signcryption can be used in many other similar scenarios such as military operations, online orders, medical reports communication and in many other major fields.

Related works: There is an established primitive called multi-signcryption where many singers encrypt and sign the same message m, such that the signature can be aggregated and also only one ciphertext is output by all n signers. This primitive is used in cases where many users needs to authenticate a single message like a certificate. There are few multi-signcryption schemes in the PKI based settings like [18] [14] [12]. So far, to the best of our knowledge there is only one multi-signcryption scheme in identity based settings by Jianhong et al. reported in [21]. But this scheme is proved insecure by Sharmila et al. [17]. Sharmila et al. in [17] proposed a fix to this identity based multi-signcryption which is secure. But the scheme in [17] requires interaction among the signers to generate a multi-signcryption. This interaction is undesirable in certain scenarios. If the signers are half way across the globe, this interaction could cause a lot of communication overhead. As of now, there has been no multi-signcryption scheme in identity based settings without any interaction among the signers.

Our Contribution: In this paper, we propose an aggregate signcryption scheme IBAS-1, which is a modification of Sakai et al.'s signature scheme [15]. We extend IBAS-1 to achieve public verifiability and sequential aggregation. Public verifiability is an important property in sequential aggregation. For a user to aggregate his signcryption to the aggregate signcryption from previous senders, the current user should be able to test the validity of the previous aggregate signcryption and then aggregate his signcryption to the verified aggregate signcryption. This is achieved in the second scheme IBAS-2 proposed in this paper. Finally, in IBAS-3, we present a new scheme which reduces the cost involved in unsigncryption, irrespective of the number of senders. IBAS-3 requires constant number of pairings for aggregate verification. Also, it is to be noted that unsigncryption is done by a single user and hence reducing the number of pairing operation during verification greatly improves the efficiency of the system. Also none of our schemes involve any kind of interaction among the signers which is an added advantage. To the best of our knowledge there is no scheme in aggregate signatures which achieves constant verification cost without any interaction among the signers. We formally prove all the aggregate signcryption schemes presented in this paper are unforgeable and is CCA-2 secure in the random oracle model. The existing secure aggregate signature schemes requires interaction between the signers before generating the aggregate signature, in order to perform efficient aggregate verification, which incorporates additional overhead to the system. We avoid such interaction between the signers in our aggregate signcryption scheme which is a major advantage.

2   Preliminaries

2.1   Bilinear Pairing

Let $\mathbb{G}$ be an additive cyclic group generated by P, with prime order q, and $\mathbb{G}_T$ be a multiplicative cyclic group of the same order q. Let $\hat{e}$ be a pairing defined as $\hat{e} : \mathbb{G} \times \mathbb{G} \to \mathbb{G}_T$. It satisfies the following properties.
For any P, Q, $R \epsilon \mathbb{G}$ and a, $b \epsilon \mathbb{Z}_q^*$.

- **Bilinearity :** $\hat{e}(aP, bQ) = \hat{e}(P, Q)^{ab}$.
- **Non Degenerate :** $\hat{e}(P, P) \neq 1$.
- **Easily Computable :** $\hat{e}(P, Q)$ must be easily and efficiently computable.

2.2   Computational Assumptions

In this section, we review the computational assumptions related to bilinear maps that are relevant to the protocols we discuss.

Bilinear Diffie-Hellman Problem (BDHP)
Given $(P, aP, bP, cP) \epsilon \mathbb{G}^4$ for unknown $a, b, c \epsilon \mathbb{Z}_q^*$, the BDH problem in $\mathbb{G}$ is to compute $\hat{e}(P, P)^{abc}$. The advantage of any probabilistic polynomial time algorithm A in solving the BDH problem in $\mathbb{G}$ is defined as

$$Adv_A^{BDH} = Pr[A(P, aP, bP, cP) = \hat{e}(P, P)^{abc} | a, b, c \epsilon \mathbb{Z}_q^*]$$

The BDH Assumption is that, for any probabilistic polynomial time algorithm A, the advantage Adv_A^{BDH} is negligibly small.

Decisional Bilinear Diffie-Hellman Problem (DBDHP)
Given $(P, aP, bP, cP, \alpha) \epsilon \mathbb{G}^4 \times \mathbb{G}_T$ for unknown $a, b, c \epsilon \mathbb{Z}_q^*$, the $DBDH$ problem in $\mathbb{G}$ is to decide if $\alpha \overset{?}{=} \hat{e}(P, P)^{abc}$. The advantage of any probabilistic polynomial time algorithm $\mathcal{A}$ in solving the DBDH problem in $\mathbb{G}$ is defined as

$$Adv_{\mathcal{A}}^{DBDH} = |Pr[\mathcal{A}(P, aP, bP, cP, \hat{e}(P, P)^{abc}) = 1] - Pr[\mathcal{A}(P, aP, bP, cP, \alpha) = 1]|$$

The DBDH Assumption is that, for any probabilistic polynomial time algorithm $\mathcal{A}$, the advantage $Adv_{\mathcal{A}}^{DBDH}$ is negligibly small.

Computation Diffie-Hellman Problem (CDHP)
Given $(P, aP, bP) \in \mathbb{G}^3$ for unknown $a, b \in \mathbb{Z}_q^*$, the $CDHP$ problem in $\mathbb{G}$ is to compute abP. The advantage of any probabilistic polynomial time algorithm $\mathcal{A}$ in solving the CDH problem in $\mathbb{G}$ is defined as

$$Adv_{\mathcal{A}}^{CDH} = Pr[\mathcal{A}(P, aP, bP) = abP | a, b \epsilon \mathbb{Z}_q^*]$$

The CDH Assumption is that, for any probabilistic polynomial time algorithm $\mathcal{A}$, the advantage $Adv_{\mathcal{A}}^{CDH}$ is negligibly small.

Modified Bilinear Diffie-Hellman Problem (MBDHP)
Given $(P, aP, bP) \in \mathbb{G}^3$ for unknown $a, b \in \mathbb{Z}_q^*$, the $MBDHP$ problem in $\mathbb{G}$ is to compute $\hat{e}(P, P)^{a^2 b}$. The advantage of any probabilistic polynomial time algorithm A in solving the MBDHP in $\mathbb{G}$ is defined as

$$Adv_{\mathcal{A}}^{MBDHP} = Pr[\mathcal{A}(P, aP, bP) = \hat{e}(P, P)^{a^2 b} | a, b \epsilon \mathbb{Z}_q^*]$$

The MBDH Assumption is that, for any probabilistic polynomial time algorithm $\mathcal{A}$, the advantage $Adv_{\mathcal{A}}^{MBDH}$ is negligibly small.

3   Identity Based Aggregate Signcryption(IBAS)

In this section, we define the general model for identity-based aggregate signcryption scheme. We then provide the security model for IBAS scheme.

3.1   Model for Identity Based Aggregate Signcryption(IBAS)

An IBAS consists of the following six algorithms,

- **IBAS.Setup :** The Private Key Generator(PKG) uses this algorithm to generate the system parameters $Params$ and master private key Msk, by providing the security parameter κ as input. The PKG makes $Params$ public and keeps Msk secret.
- **IBAS.KeyGen :** On providing the identity ID_i of user $\mathcal{U}_i$, master private key Msk and system parameters $Params$ as input by PKG, this algorithm outputs private key D_i corresponding to the user U_i. The PKG sends D_i to user $\mathcal{U}_i$ through a secure channel.
- **IBAS.Signcrypt :** For generating the signcryption of a message m_i from user $\mathcal{U}_i$ to $\mathcal{U}_B$, the user $\mathcal{U}_i$ with identity ID_i provides the message m_i, sender identity ID_i, private key D_i of ID_i, the receiver identity ID_B of user U_B and the system parameters $params$ as input to this algorithm. The $IBAS.Signcrypt$ algorithm outputs the valid signcryption σ_i for the message m_i from user $\mathcal{U}_i$ to $\mathcal{U}_B$

– **IBAS.Aggregate** : By taking different signcryptions σ_i ($for\ i = 1$ to n) (from the corresponding user U_i with identity ID_i to the user U_B with identity ID_B) as input , this algorithm outputs the aggregate signcryption σ_{Agg}. This algorithm is executed by any user $\mathcal{U}_i$, $i \in 1, 2, \ldots, n$ or by any other member who is not in the senders list.

– **IBAS.Unsigncrypt** : On input of a signcryption σ_i (from sender U_i to receiver U_B) with sender identity ID_i, receiver identity ID_B and private key D_B of the receiver $\mathcal{U}_B$, this algorithm outputs the message m_i if σ_i is a valid signcryption of message m_i from user $\mathcal{U}_i$ to $\mathcal{U}_B$.

– **IBAS.AggregateUnsigncrypt** : This algorithm takes, the aggregate signcryption σ_{Agg} from set of users with identity $\{ID_i\}_{(i=1,\ldots n)}$ to ID_B, the receiver identity ID_B and the private key D_B of the receiver U_B as input from the user U_B. Then $IBAS.AggregateUnsigncrypt$ outputs m_i (for $i = 1$ to n) if σ_{Agg} is a valid ciphertext on message m_i from user ID_i to ID_B ($for\ i = 1$ to n).

4   Security Model for Identity Based Aggregate Signcryption Scheme

4.1   Unforgeability

An IBAS scheme is existentially unforgeable under adaptive chosen identity and adaptive chosen message attack (EUF-IBAS-CMA) if no probabilistic polynomial time adversary $\mathcal{A}$ has a non-negligible advantage in the following game.

– **Setup Phase:** The challenger $\mathcal{B}$ runs the *Setup* algorithm, sets the system public parameters $Params$ and master private key Msk. $\mathcal{B}$ gives $Params$ to $\mathcal{A}$ and keeps the master private key Msk secret.

– **Training Phase :** $\mathcal{A}$ is allowed to access all the oracles with the queries of $\mathcal{A}$'s choice. The only restriction for $\mathcal{A}$ during training is, $\mathcal{A}$ should not query the private key corresponding to any target identities. If $\mathcal{A}$ asks such a query $\mathcal{B}$ aborts. $\mathcal{A}$ is given access to the following oracles.

   • **KeyGen Oracle :** When $\mathcal{A}$ makes a query with ID_i, $\mathcal{B}$ outputs the private key D_i corresponding to ID_i to $\mathcal{A}$.

   • **Signcrypt Oracle:** When $\mathcal{A}$ makes a query with the message m_i, the sender identity ID_i, the receiver identity ID_B as input. $\mathcal{B}$ outputs the signcryption σ_i on m_i from ID_i to ID_B.

   • **Unsigncrypt Oracle:** $\mathcal{A}$ submits the signcryption σ_i (from ID_i to ID_B) and receiver identity ID_B as input. $\mathcal{B}$ outputs corresponding message m_i if σ_i is a valid signcryption of m_i from ID_i to ID_B.

   • **AggregateUnsigncrypt Oracle :** $\mathcal{A}$ submits the aggregate signcryption σ_{Agg} which is the aggregate signcryption from users ID_i,(for i=1 to n) to the receiver ID_B . The challenger returns all the corresponding messages, m_i (for i = 1 to n) if σ_{Agg} is a valid aggregate signcryption on (m_i, ID_i) with ID_B as receiver.

Note that Aggregate oracle is not provided because it does not involve the private keys of any users.

- **Forgery :** The adversary $\mathcal{A}$ after having access to all the above oracles, outputs the aggregate signcryption σ_{Agg}^* on message m_i (i=1 to n) from users ID_i (for i=1 to n), to the receiver ID_B. $\mathcal{A}$ wins the game if σ_{Agg}^* is a valid forgery if $\mathcal{A}$ has not queried the private key of atleast one of the identities in the list of senders and $\mathcal{A}$ has not queried the signcrypt oracle for the corresponding message, user pair (m, ID_i), which is a part of the forgery (*i.e.*, σ_{Agg}^*).

4.2   Confidentiality

An IBAS scheme is semantically secure against adaptive chosen identity and adaptive chosen ciphertext attack (IND-IBAS-CCA2) if no probabilistic polynomial time adversary $\mathcal{A}$ has a non-negligible advantage in the following game.

- **Setup Phase :** The challenger $\mathcal{B}$ runs the *Setup* algorithm and sets the public parameters $Params$ and the master private key Msk. $\mathcal{B}$ gives $Params$ to $\mathcal{A}$ and keeps Msk secret.
- **Phase 1 :** $\mathcal{A}$ can have access to all the oracles as in the *Unforgeability* game.
- **Challenge :** After having sufficient training from the various oracles, $\mathcal{A}$ submits $(\{m_{0i}, m_{1i}\}, ID_i)_{i=1}^n, ID_B$ to $\mathcal{B}$. $\mathcal{B}$ checks if ID_B is one of target identity. If not, $\mathcal{B}$ aborts. Else the challenger chooses a random $b_i \in \{0, 1\}$, for $i = 1$ to n and signcrypts m_{b_i} using the sender private key D_i and receiver public key Q_B. $\mathcal{B}$ returns the aggregate signcryption σ_{Agg}^* to $\mathcal{A}$.
- **Phase 2 :** $\mathcal{A}$ makes similar kind of queries as in *Phase* 1. But it cannot make aggregate unsigncryption query on the challenge aggregate signcryption σ_{Agg}^*.
- **Output :** $\mathcal{A}$ outputs a bit b_i' for $i = 1$ to n. $\mathcal{A}$ wins the game if $b_i' = b_i$ for ($i = 1$ to n).
  The advantage of $\mathcal{A}$ is given by $ADV_{\mathcal{A}} = [\Pi_{i=1}^n Pr[b_i = b_i'] - \frac{1}{2^n}]$.

5   Identity Based Aggregate Signcryption Scheme (IBAS-1)

5.1   IBAS-1 Scheme

We present the IBAS-1 in this section. As mentioned in the general model of IBAS, the proposed IBAS-1 has six algorithms,

- **IBAS-1.Setup :** Let κ be the security parameter of the system. Let $\mathbb{G}_1$ be a additive group and $\mathbb{G}_2$ be a multiplicative group, both of same prime order q. Let $\hat{e}$ be a bilinear map defined by $\hat{e} : \mathbb{G}_1 \times \mathbb{G}_1 \to \mathbb{G}_2$. There are three hash functions defined as $H_1 : \{0, 1\}^* \to \mathbb{G}_1$, $H_2 : \{0, 1\}^* \times \mathbb{G}_2 \times \mathbb{G}_1 \times \{0, 1\}^* \to \mathbb{G}_1$ and $H_3 : \mathbb{G}_2 \times \{0, 1\}^* \to \{0, 1\}^{\bar{n}}$, where $\bar{n}$ is $|ID| + |m|$. Let the master private key Msk be $s \in_R \mathbb{Z}_q^*$. Let $P \in_R \mathbb{G}_1$ be a generator of the group $\mathbb{G}_1$ and the master public key $P_{pub} = sP$. Therefore, the public parameters $Params = \langle P, P_{pub}, \mathbb{G}_1, \mathbb{G}_2, \hat{e}, H_1, H_2, H_3 \rangle$ and the master private key is s.

– **IBAS-1.KeyGen** : On getting a request for private key corresponding to ID_i, PKG generates $Q_i = H_1(ID_i)$ and the private key $D_i = sQ_i$. PKG then delivers D_i to the user with identity ID_i over a secure channel.

– **IBAS-1.Signcrypt** : The signcryption of message m_i from ID_i to ID_B is performed by the user $\mathcal{U}_i$ as follows.
  - Selects a random r_i from $\mathbb{Z}_q^*$.
  - Computes $U_i = r_i P$.
  - Computes $\alpha_i = \hat{e}(r_i P_{pub}, Q_B)$ and $\hat{H}_i = H_2(m_i, \alpha_i, U_i, ID_B)$.
  - Computes $V_i = r_i \hat{H}_i + D_i$.
  - Computes $c_i = H_3(\alpha_i, ID_B) \oplus (ID_i \| m_i)$.

  The signcryption of m_i from ID_i to ID_B is $\sigma_i = \langle c_i, U_i, V_i \rangle$.

– **IBAS-1.AggregateSigncrypt** : The aggregation is done by any of the sender or by any third party. On receiving n individual signcryptions $\sigma_i = \langle c_i, U_i, V_i \rangle$, where $i = 1$ to n, the aggregation is done as follows,
  - Compute $V_{agg} = \Sigma_{i=1}^n V_i$
  - Output $\sigma_{Agg} = \langle \{c_i, U_i, ID_i\}_{i=1}^n, V_{agg} \rangle$.

– **IBAS-1.Unsigncrypt** : The receiver ID_B executes this algorithm with $\sigma_i = \langle c_i, U_i, V_i \rangle$, the sender identity ID_i and the private key D_B as input. The unsigncryption is done as follows,
  - $\alpha_i = \hat{e}(U_i, D_B)$.
  - $ID_i \| m_i = H_3(\alpha_i, ID_B) \oplus c_i$.
  - $\hat{H}_i = H_2(m_i, \alpha_i, U_i, ID_B)$.
  - Verifies $\hat{e}(V_i, P) \overset{?}{=} \hat{e}(\hat{H}_i, U_i)\hat{e}(Q_i, P_{pub})$. If this check passes, output the message (m_i, ID_i), else output *"Invalid"*

– **IBAS-1.AggregateUnsigncrypt** : The receiver ID_B for unsigncrypting $\sigma_{Agg} = \langle \{c_i, U_i, ID_i\}_{i=1}^n, V_{agg} \rangle$, uses his private key D_B and performs the following:

  For all $i = 1$ to n, do the following
  - $\alpha_i = \hat{e}(U_i, D_B)$
  - $ID_i \| m_i = H_3(\alpha_i, ID_B) \oplus c_i$
  - $\hat{H}_i = H_2(m_i, \alpha_i, U_i, ID_B)$
  - Verifies $\hat{e}(V_{agg}, P) \overset{?}{=} \prod_{i=1}^n \hat{e}(\hat{H}_i, U_i)\hat{e}(\Sigma_{i=1}^n Q_i, P_{pub})$. If this check passes output (m_i, ID_i)(for i=1 to n), else output *"Invalid"*

Correctness :

$$
\begin{aligned}
\hat{e}(V_{agg}, P) &= \hat{e}(\Sigma_{i=1}^n (r_i \hat{H}_i + D_i), P) \\
&= \hat{e}(\Sigma_{i=1}^n r_i \hat{H}_i, P)\hat{e}(\Sigma_{i=1}^n D_i, P) \\
&= \hat{e}(\Sigma_{i=1}^n \hat{H}_i, \Sigma_{i=1}^n r_i P)\hat{e}(\Sigma_{i=1}^n Q_i, P_{pub}) \\
&= \prod_{i=1}^n \hat{e}(\hat{H}_i, U_i)\hat{e}(\Sigma_{i=1}^n Q_i, P_{pub})
\end{aligned}
$$

5.2   Security Proof of IBAS-1

In this section, we give the formal security proof for IBAS-1.

Unforgeability

Theorem 1. *Our identity based aggregate signcryption scheme IBAS-1 is secure against any EUF-IBAS-CMA adversary $\mathcal{A}$ under adaptive chosen identity and adaptive chosen message attack in the random oracle model if MBDHP is hard in $\mathbb{G}_1$.*

Proof. The unforgeability proof is based on the Modified bilinear Diffie-Hellman Problem (MBDHP). MBDHP is the problem of computing $\hat{e}(P,P)^{a^2b}$ from the given instance (P, aP, bP) where a, b are chosen at random from $\mathbb{Z}_q^*$ and P is the generator of $\mathbb{G}_1$. We show how an algorithm $\mathcal{B}$ can solve $MBDHP$ by interacting with an adversary $\mathcal{A}$ that can break the existential unforgeability of IBAS-1 scheme.

Setup Phase : $\mathcal{B}$ sets the master public key $P_{pub} = aP$ and gives the system public parameters to $\mathcal{A}$.

Training Phase : During the training phase $\mathcal{A}$ can make polynomially bounded number of queries to the various oracles provided by $\mathcal{B}$. To maintain the consistency of the oracle responses, $\mathcal{B}$ maintains four lists namely LH_1list, LH_2list, LH_3list and $Slist$. The oracles and their responses are explained below,

H_1 **Oracle** : When $\mathcal{A}$ makes a request with ID_i, $\mathcal{B}$ does the following,

- $\mathcal{B}$ tosses a coin $coin_i$ and $Pr[coin_i = 0] = \mu$
- If $coin_i = 0$, $\mathcal{B}$ generates a random value $x_i \in \mathbb{Z}_q^*$ and responds with $Q_i = x_i bP$,
- Otherwise, $\mathcal{B}$ generates a random value $x_i \in \mathbb{Z}_q^*$ and outputs $Q_i = x_i P$ to $\mathcal{A}$. Also, $\mathcal{B}$ stores $ID_i, Q_i, x_i, coin_i$ in the LH_1List.

H_2 **Oracle** : When $\mathcal{A}$ makes a request with $(m_i, \alpha_i, U_i, ID_B)$, $\mathcal{B}$ outputs the corresponding value $\hat{H}_i$ if a tuple of the form $\langle m_i, \alpha_i, U_i, ID_B, \hat{H}_i, r_i' \rangle$, is already available in LH_2List. Else, $\mathcal{B}$ obtains Q_B from LH_1List and then chooses a random $r_i' \in \mathbb{Z}_q^*$ and outputs $\hat{H}_i = rQ_B + r_i'P$ to $\mathcal{A}$(Here r in randomly chosen from $\mathbb{Z}_q^*$ and is common for all H_2 oracle queries). $\mathcal{B}$ stores the tuple $\langle m_i, \alpha_i, U_i, ID_B, \hat{H}_i, r_i' \rangle$ in LH_2List.

H_3 **Oracle** : When $\mathcal{A}$ request with (α_i, ID_B), $\mathcal{B}$ outputs the corresponding h if an entry $\langle \alpha_i, ID_B, h \rangle$ is available in LH_3List, else chooses a random $h \in \{0,1\}^n$, outputs h to $\mathcal{A}$ and adds (α_i, ID_B, h) in the LH_3List.

Extract Oracle : When $\mathcal{A}$ makes an extract query with ID_i as input, $\mathcal{B}$ goes through the LH_1List to retrieve $coin_i$ corresponding to ID_i.

- If $coin_i = 0$, it is one of the target identities, so $\mathcal{B}$ aborts.
- If $coin_i = 1$, $\mathcal{B}$ responds with $Q_i = x_i P_{pub}$ where x_i is from LH_1 list.

Signcrypt Oracle : When $\mathcal{A}$ makes a signcryption query for the signcryption m_i with ID_i as sender and ID_B as receiver, $\mathcal{B}$ responds as follows:

- Checks the LH_1list corresponding to ID_i. If $coin_i = 1$, then $\mathcal{B}$ computes (c_i, U_i, V_i) as per the normal signcryption algorithm.

– If $coin_i = 0$, $\mathcal{B}$ performs the following,
  • Computes $\hat{H}_i = a_1 P - a_2 Q_i$, where a_1, a_2 are chosen at random from $\mathbb{Z}_q^*$ and Q_i is obtained from LH_1List.
  • Computes $U_i = a_2^{-1} P_{pub}$, $\alpha_i = \hat{e}(U_i, D_B)$, $V_i = a_1 a_2^{-1} P_{pub}$.
  • Finally, $\mathcal{B}$ computes $c_i = H_3(\alpha_i, ID_B) \oplus (ID_i \| m_i)$, where $H_3(\alpha_i, ID_B)$ is obtained by querying the H_3 $Oracle$.

We show that $\sigma_i = \langle c_i, U_i, V_i \rangle$ is a valid signcryption, since it passes the verification test

$$
\begin{aligned}
\hat{e}(\hat{H}_i, U_i)\hat{e}(Q_i, P_{pub}) &= \hat{e}(a_1 P - a_2 Q_i, a_2^{-1} P_{pub})\hat{e}(Q_i, P_{pub}) \\
&= \hat{e}(a_1 P, a_2^{-1} P_{pub})\hat{e}(-a_2 Q_i, a_2^{-1} P_{pub})\hat{e}(Q_i, P_{pub}) \\
&= \hat{e}(a_1 a_2^{-1} P_{pub}, P)\hat{e}(Q_i, P_{pub})^{-1}\hat{e}(Q_i, P_{pub}) \\
&= \hat{e}(a_1 a_2^{-1} P_{pub}, P) \\
&= \hat{e}(V_i, P)
\end{aligned}
$$

$\mathcal{B}$ outputs $\sigma_i = \langle c_i, U_i, V_i \rangle$ and stores $\langle m_i, \alpha_i, U_i, V_i, ID_B \rangle$ in the list, $Slist$.

Unsigncrypt Oracle : Note that unsigncryption during the unforgeability game is done in a different order from the actual protocol, because $\mathcal{C}$ does not know the private key of the identities with $coin_i = 0$ in list LH_1list. When $\mathcal{A}$ makes a unsigncryption query with $\sigma_i = \langle c_i, U_i, V_i \rangle$, ID_i as sender and ID_B as receiver, $\mathcal{B}$ responds as follows:

– Checks LH_1list for ID_B. If $coin_B = 1$, then $\mathcal{B}$ unsigncrypts σ_i as per the algorithm(as $\mathcal{B}$ knows the private of ID_B) and outputs m_i, ID_i if σ_i is a valid signcryption of m_i from ID_i to ID_B, Else output "$Invalid$" .
– If $coin_B = 0$, then ID_B is one of target identities. The $\mathcal{B}$ performs the following,
  1. Searches the LH_3List for the tuples corresponding to ID_B. If no matching tuple is present in LH_3list, then return "$Invalid$"
  2. For each entry $\langle \alpha_i, ID_B, h1_i \rangle$ corresponding to ID_B in LH_3list, compute $c_j \oplus h1_j$ and parse it as $ID_j \| m_j$ and check whether $ID_j = ID_i$. If no tuple with $ID_i = ID_j$ is found, output "$Invalid$".
  3. For each m_j, where $ID_j \| m_j = c_j \oplus h1_j$ in the previous step obtained from the LH_3list, find the matching tuples of the form $\langle m_i, \alpha_i, U_i, ID_B, \hat{H}_i, r_i' \rangle$ in LH_2list. If no matching tuple is present for any m_i in LH_2list, output "$Invalid$".
  4. For the matching tuple of the form $\langle m_i, \alpha_i, U_i, ID_B, \hat{H}_i, r_i' \rangle$ found in the previous step, check whether the following relationship holds.
  $$\alpha_i \overset{?}{=} \hat{e}(\tfrac{V_i - D_i}{r}, P_{pub})\hat{e}(\tfrac{r_i' P_{pub}}{r}, U_i)^{-1}$$
  We will prove that this check will be true for the correct tuple.
  $\alpha_i = \hat{e}(U_i, D_B)$,

$$
\begin{aligned}
\hat{e}(\tfrac{V_i - D_i}{r}, P_{pub})\hat{e}(\tfrac{r_i' P_{pub}}{r}, U_i)^{-1} & \\
&= \hat{e}(x_i Q_B, P_{pub})\hat{e}(\tfrac{r_i' x_i P}{r}, P_{pub})\hat{e}(\tfrac{r_i' x_i P}{r}, P_{pub})^{-1} \\
&= \hat{e}(s Q_B, x_i P) \\
&= \hat{e}(D_B, U_i)
\end{aligned}
$$

Then $\mathcal{B}$ checks whether $\hat{e}(V_i, P) \overset{?}{=} \hat{e}(\hat{H}_i, U_i)\hat{e}(Q_i, P_{pub})$. If both the above checks are true the tuple is accepted. Otherwise, the tuple is rejected.

5. If all tuples are rejected, then output "*Invalid*" else from the accepted tuple output m_i.

Note : There will exactly one tuple for which the tests will pass. Hence, only one m_i will be output from the above test.

Aggregate Unsigncrypt Oracle : When $\mathcal{A}$ makes aggregate unsigncrypt query with the signcryption $\sigma_{Agg} = \langle \{c_i, U_i, ID_i\}_{i=1}^n, V_{Agg} \rangle$ and ID_B as receiver, $\mathcal{B}$ responds as follows:

- Checks $LH_1 list$ for ID_B. If $coin_B = 1$, $\mathcal{B}$ knows the private key D_B and hence follows the aggregate unsigncrypt algorithm of IBAS-1.
- If $coin_i = 0$, $\mathcal{B}$ does not know the private key, so $\mathcal{B}$ cannot use the aggregate unsigncrypt algorithm of IBAS-1. Instead $\mathcal{B}$ does the following.
- $\mathcal{B}$ gets as input $\sigma_{Agg} = \langle \{c_i, U_i, ID_i\}_{i=1}^n, V_{Agg} \rangle$. $\mathcal{B}$ also knows the private key of all senders $\{ID_i\}_{i=1,\dots,n}$
- First, $\mathcal{B}$ collects the tuples of the form $\langle \alpha_i, ID_B, h1_i \rangle$ from $LH_3 List$.
- Computes $c_i \oplus h1_i$ and parse it as $m_i \| ID_i$, Check whether the ID_i belongs to sender list of σ_{Agg}.
- $\mathcal{B}$ collects all such m_i, ID_i pair corresponding to σ_{Agg}. If at least n such pairs are not present, then output "*Invalid*"
- $\mathcal{B}$ searches the $LH_2 List$ to find tuples of the form $\langle m_i, \alpha_i, U_i, ID_B, \hat{H}_i, r_i' \rangle$ corresponding to (m_i, U_i), $1 \le i \le n$ and performs the following operations.
  - Computes $\beta = \prod_{i=1}^n \alpha_i$.
  - Computes $X = V_{Agg} - \Sigma_{i=1}^n D_i = \Sigma r_i \hat{H}_i$
    $= \Sigma_{i=1}^n \{r_i(rQ_B + r_i'P)\}$
  - Computes $\beta' = (\hat{e}(X, P_{pub}) \prod_{i=1}^n \hat{e}(U_i, P_{pub})^{-r_i'})^{1/r}$
    $= \prod_{i=1}^n \hat{e}(r_i Q_B, P_{pub})$
    $= \prod_{i=1}^n \hat{e}(r_i D_B, P)$
    $= \prod_{i=1}^n \alpha_i$
  - Checks whether $\hat{e}(V_{agg}, P) \overset{?}{=} \prod_{i=1}^n \hat{e}(\hat{H}_i, U_i)\hat{e}(\Sigma_{i=1}^n Q_i, P_{pub})$ and $\beta' \overset{?}{=} \beta$.
  - If both the check passes, then $\mathcal{B}$ output m_i, ID_i, for all $i = 1, \dots, n$.
  - Else, output "*Invalid*"

Forgery : $\mathcal{A}$ chooses n sender identities $\{ID_i\}_{(i=1,\dots,n)}$ and a receiver identity ID_B and outputs the aggregate signcryption $\sigma_{Agg}^* = \langle \{c_i, U_i, ID_i\}_{i=1}^n, V_{agg}^* \rangle$ to $\mathcal{B}$. $\mathcal{A}$ wins the game if at least one of the identities is one of a target identities $(coin_i = 0)$ and $\mathcal{A}$ has not asked for a signcryption query of the corresponding m_i, ID_i pair (it is not a trivial forgery).

$\mathcal{B}$ has V_{agg}^* and $\mathcal{B}$ knows the private key of all the senders other than set of users who are the target identities. Let us assume these set of users form the first k identities of the list. Therefore $\mathcal{B}$ can compute,

$$V_{agg}^* - \Sigma_{i=k+1}^n D_i = \Sigma_{i=1}^n r_i \hat{H}_i + \Sigma_{i=1}^k D_i. \ \mathcal{B} \text{ has,}$$

$$\hat{e}(V_{Agg}^{*} - \Sigma_{i=k+1}^{n} D_i, P_{pub}) =$$
$$= \hat{e}(\Sigma_{i=1}^{n} r_i \hat{H}_i + \Sigma_{i=1}^{k} D_i, p_{pub})$$
$$= \hat{e}(\Sigma_{i=1}^{n} r_i r Q_B + r_i r_i' P, P_{pub}) \hat{e}(\Sigma_{i=1}^{k} D_i, P_{pub})$$
$$= \hat{e}(\Sigma_{i=1}^{n} r_i r Q_B, P_{pub}) \hat{e}(\Sigma_{i=1}^{n} r_i r_i' P, P_{pub}) \hat{e}(\Sigma_{i=1}^{k} D_i, P_{pub})$$
$$= \hat{e}(r D_B, \Sigma_{i=1}^{n} U_i) \Pi_{i=1}^{n} \hat{e}(U_i, r_i' P_{pub}) \hat{e}(\Sigma_{i=1}^{k} D_i, P_{pub})$$

$\mathcal{B}$ knows the values of r(stored in LH_2list), $\{r_i', U_i\}_{i=1\ to\ n}$, where U_i is available in the forged aggregate signcryption and r_i' stored in LH_2list, D_B (private key of ID_B is known to $\mathcal{B}$, ID_B is the identity of the receiver of σ_{Agg}^{*}) and P_{pub} (master public key).

Therefore, $\mathcal{B}$ can compute the inverse of the first two components in above equation. By multiplying
$\hat{e}(r D_B, \Sigma_{i=1}^{n} U_i)^{-1} \Pi_{i=1}^{n} \hat{e}(U_i, r_i' P_{pub})^{-1}$ with $\hat{e}(V_{agg}^{*} - \Sigma_{i=k+1}^{n} D_i, P_{pub})$, $\mathcal{B}$ gets
$\hat{e}(\Sigma_{i=1}^{k} D_i, P_{pub})$. However, since each $D_i = x_i abP$ and $P_{pub} = aP$, $\hat{e}(\Sigma_{i=1}^{k} D_i,$
$P_{pub}) = \hat{e}(P, P)^{a^2 b . \Sigma_{i=1}^{k} x_i}$. By raising this component to $\frac{1}{\Sigma_{i=1}^{k} x_i}$ (All x_i's are
obtained from the list LH_1list), $\mathcal{B}$ gets $\hat{e}(P, P)^{a^2 b}$ which is the solution to the instance of the hard problem.   □

Confidentiality

Theorem 2. *The identity-based aggregate signcryption scheme IBAS-1 is secure against IND-IBAS-CCA2 adversary $\mathcal{A}$ under adaptive chosen message and adaptive chosen identity attack in the random oracle model if BDHP is hard in $\mathbb{G}_1$.*

Proof. On getting a BDHP instance P, aP, bP, cP as challenge, the challenger $\mathcal{B}$ uses $\mathcal{A}$ who is capable of breaking the confidentiality of IBAS-1 to solve the Bilinear Diffie Hellman Problem(BDHP).

- **Setup Phase:** The challenger $\mathcal{B}$ sets the public parameters as follows. Sets two groups $\mathbb{G}_1$ and $\mathbb{G}_2$. $\mathcal{B}$ sets $P_{pub} = aP$ and gives system public parameters *params* to $\mathcal{A}$.
- **Phase 1:** $\mathcal{A}$ can ask all kinds of queries to the oracles. All the oracle are similar to the oracles in the $Unforgeabilty$ game of IBAS-1.
  - For H_1 oracle, when $\mathcal{A}$ queries for ID_i, $\mathcal{B}$ tosses a coin such that $Pr[coin_i = 0] = \mu$.
  - If $coin_i = 0$, $\mathcal{B}$ sets $Q_{ID} = x_i bP$ for some random $x_i \in Z_q^{*}$ returns Q_{ID} to $\mathcal{A}$.
  - Else $\mathcal{B}$ sets $Q_{ID} = x_i P$ and returns Q_{ID} to $\mathcal{A}$ and adds the tuple $\langle ID_i, Q_i, x_i, coin_i \rangle$ to the H_1list.
- **Challenge:**   After   getting   sufficient   training, $\mathcal{A}$ submits $(m_{0i}, m_{1i}, ID_i)_{i=1,...,n}$, receiver identity ID_B to $\mathcal{B}$. $\mathcal{B}$ checks the LH_1list for ID_B. If $coin_i = 1$, then $\mathcal{B}$ aborts. If not, $\mathcal{B}$ does the following.

- $\mathcal{B}$ chooses a random $k \epsilon$ [1,n].
- For each i $\mathcal{B}$ checks whether $i = k$. If not, $\mathcal{B}$ chooses a random $b \in \{0,1\}$ and signcrypts m_{b_i} as per the signcrypt algorithm using the senders private key and receivers public key.
- If $i = k$ then, $\mathcal{B}$
  - * Sets $U_i = cP$.
  - * Choose $x_i \in \mathbb{Z}_q^*$ and sets $\hat{H}_i = x_i P$.
  - * Compute $V_i = x_i cP + D_i$.
  - * Updates $LH_2 list$ and $LH_3 list$.
  - * Chooses a random c_i and sets the signcryption of message m_b as (c_i, U_i, V_i).
- $\mathcal{B}$ aggregates all the signatures σ_i, for $i = 1$ to n and gives the challenge aggregate signcryption $\sigma_{Agg}^* = \langle \{c_i, U_i, ID_i\}_{i=1}^n, V_{Agg}^* \rangle$ to $\mathcal{A}$.
- **Phase 2 :** This phase is similar to phase 1, But in phase 2, $\mathcal{A}$ cannot ask for aggregate unsigncryption on the challenge aggregate signcryption $\sigma_{Agg}^* = \langle \{c_i, U_i, ID_i\}_{i=1}^n, V_{Agg}^* \rangle$.
- **Output :** After $\mathcal{A}$ has made sufficient number of queries $\mathcal{A}$ outputs the guess b_i' for each $i = 1$ to $k - 1$. For the kth output, if the adversary aborts then the adversary has found out that it is not a valid signcryption of either of the messages. (We assume that the adversary is capable of doing this). If so, $\mathcal{B}$ gets $\langle h1_i, \alpha_i, ID_B \rangle$ from $LH_2 list$ (such a tuple exists because $\mathcal{A}$ must have queried the H_2 oracle with such a query to unsigncrypt the challenge ciphertext successfully and find out the error. The probability that $\mathcal{A}$ guesses the hash value is negligible) and outputs $\alpha_i^{\frac{1}{x_i}}$ as the solution to BDH problem where x_i is corresponding to ID_B in the $LH_1 list$.

$$\alpha_i^{\frac{1}{x_i}} = \hat{e}(U_i, D_B)^{\frac{1}{x_i}}$$
$$= \hat{e}(cP, x_i abP)^{\frac{1}{x_i}}$$
$$= \hat{e}(P, P)^{abc}$$

Note : Assume there are n such α_i's in the $LH_2 list$. One of them must be the solution to the BDH problem, without that hash value, $\mathcal{A}$ would not be able to unsigncrypt the challenge ciphertext. $\square$

6   Identity Based Aggregate Signcryption with Public Verifiability (IBAS-2)

6.1   IBAS-2 Scheme

The IBAS-2 scheme is a variant of IBAS-1, with the additional features such as public verification and sequential aggregation. Public verifiability is an important property in signcryption in certain scenarios. Achieving public verifiability without revealing any information about the message encrypted is a difficult task. IBAS-2 achieves it in sequential aggregation technique. Sequential aggregation is a weaker model compared to normal aggregation but has its practical applications like business scenarios and routing scenarios. IBAS-2 consists of the following algorithms.

- **IBAS-2.Setup** : Let κ be the security parameter of the system. Let $\mathbb{G}_1$ and $\mathbb{G}_2$ be two GDH groups of same prime order q. Let $\hat{e}$ be a bilinear map defined by $\hat{e} : \mathbb{G}_1 \times \mathbb{G}_1 \rightarrow \mathbb{G}_2$. The Hash Functions used in IBAS-2 are $H_1 : \{0,1\}^* \rightarrow \mathbb{G}_1$, $H_2 : \{0,1\}^* \times \mathbb{G}_2 \times \mathbb{G}_1 \times \{0,1\}^* \rightarrow \mathbb{G}_1$, $H_3 : \mathbb{G}_2 \times \{0,1\}^* \rightarrow \{0,1\}^n$ where $\bar{n}$ is $|ID| + |m|$, $H_4 : \{0,1\}^* \times \mathbb{G}_1 \rightarrow \mathbb{Z}_q^*$. Let the master private keys be s_1, $s_2 \epsilon_R \mathbb{Z}_q^*$ and let P be a generator of $\mathbb{G}_1$. Let the master public keys be $P_{pub1} = s_1 P$ and $P_{pub2} = s_2 P$. The public parameters $params$ pf the system are $\langle P, P_{pub1}, P_{pub2}, \mathbb{G}_1, \mathbb{G}_2, \hat{e}, H_1, H_2, H_3, H_4 \rangle$ and the master private keys are s_1 and s_2.

- **IBAS-2.KeyGen** : When user $\mathcal{U}_i$ submits his identity ID_i to the PKG, the PKG runs this algorithm to generate $D_{i1} = s_1 Q_i$ and $D_{i2} = s_2 Q_i$, where $Q_i = H_1(ID_i)$. PKG sends $D_i = \langle D_{i1}, D_{i2} \rangle$ to the user U_i over a secure channel.

- **IBAS-2.AggregateSigncrypt** : Let the sequence of users who will participate in the sequential aggregation be $\{\mathcal{U}_1, \mathcal{U}_2, \ldots, \mathcal{U}_n\}$, i.e user $\mathcal{U}_{i-1}$ does the aggregation of signcryption obtained from previous user $\mathcal{U}_{i-2}\}$ with his own signcryption and generates σ_{Agg}^{i-1}. Then $\mathcal{U}_{i-1}$ passes σ_{Agg}^{i-1} to user $\mathcal{U}_i$ for further aggregation or generation of σ_{Agg}^i by $\mathcal{U}_i$. For a user $\mathcal{U}_i$ to signcrypt a message m_i to receiver $\mathcal{U}_B$, the user $\mathcal{U}_i$ provides the message m_i, the sender identity ID_B, the private key D_i of sender ID_i, the receiver identity ID_B and the previous aggregate signcryption $\sigma_{Agg}^{(i-1)} = \langle \{c_j, U_j, ID_j\}_{j=1,\ldots,(i-1)}, V_{Agg}^{i-1}, W_{i-1} \rangle$ generated by user $\mathcal{U}_i$ as input and runs this algorithm.

  - First verifies whether $\sigma_{Agg}^{(i-1)}$ is valid by using $IBAS - 2.PublicVerify$ algorithm. If it is valid then proceeds.
  - Selects a random r_i from $\mathbb{Z}_q^*$.
  - Sets $U_i = r_i P$.
  - Computes $\alpha_i = \hat{e}(r_i P_{pub}, Q_B)$
  - Computes $\hat{H}_i = H_2(m_i, \alpha_i, U_i, ID_B)$ and $h_i = H_4(c_i \parallel c_{i-1} \parallel \cdots c_1, \Sigma_{j=1}^i U_j)$
  - Computes $V_i = r_i \hat{H}_i + D_{i1}$
  - Computes $V_{Agg}^i = V_{Agg}^{(i-1)} + V_i$
  - Computes $W_i = \frac{1}{r_i + h_i} D_{i2}$ and $c_i = H_3(\alpha_i, ID_B) \oplus (ID_i \parallel m_i)$
  - Outputs the aggregate signcryption $\sigma_{Agg}^{(i)} = \langle \{c_j, U_j, ID_j\}_{j=1,\ldots,i}, V_{agg}^{(i)}, W_i \rangle$

- **IBAS-2.PublicVerify** : The ith user on getting an aggregate signcryption $\sigma_{Agg}^{(i-1)} = \langle \{c_j, U_j, ID_j\}_{j=1}^{(i-1)}, V_{agg}^{(i-1)}, W_i \rangle$ from $i-1$ users and the list indicating the order in which the users have signed, uses this algorithm to check the validity of the aggregate signcryption. The verifier checks the following equality:

$$\hat{e}(W, (U_{i-1} + h_{i-1} P) \stackrel{?}{=} \hat{e}(Q_{i-1}, P_{pub2}), \text{ where } h_{i-1} = H_4(c_{i-1} \parallel c_{i-2} \parallel \cdots c_1, \Sigma_{j=1}^{i-1} U_j)$$

Since $\{U_i\}_{i=1,\ldots,i-1}$, W are available in $\sigma_{Agg}^{(i-1)}$ and P, P_{pub2} are public parameters, the above test can be performed by any user.

If the above check passes, this algorithm outputs "$Valid$", Else outputs "$Invalid$"

Correctness of the Verification :

$$\hat{e}(W, (U_{i-1} + h_{i-1}P) = \hat{e}(\frac{1}{r_{i-1}+h_{i-1}}D_{i2}, (r_{i-1} + h_{i-1})P)$$
$$= \hat{e}(D_{i2}, P)$$
$$= \hat{e}(Q_i, P_{pub2})$$

- **IBAS-2.AggregateUnsigncrypt :** The receiver $\mathcal{U}_B$ for unsigncrypting the aggregate signcryption $\sigma_{Agg}^{(n)} = \langle\{c_i, U_i, ID_i\}_{i=1,...,n}), V_{agg}^{(n)}, W_n\rangle$ performs the following.
  For each $i = (1, \ldots, n)$ calculates
    - Computes $\alpha_i = \hat{e}(U_i, D_{B1})$
    - Computes $ID_i \parallel m_i = H_3(\alpha_i, ID_B) \oplus c_i$
    - Checks $\hat{e}(V_{Agg}^{(n)}, P) \overset{?}{=} \prod_{i=1}^{n} \hat{e}(\hat{H}_i, U_i)\hat{e}(\Sigma_{i=1}^n Q_i, P_{pub})$, where $\hat{H}_i = H_2(m_i, \alpha_i, U_i, ID_B)$ and $h_i = H_4(c_i \parallel c_{i-1} \parallel \cdots c_1, \Sigma_{j=1}^i U_j)$.
    - Outputs all $\langle m_i, ID_i\rangle$ pairs for $i=1$ to n.

  Correctness of the Verification :

$$\hat{e}(V_{Agg}^{(n)}, P) = \hat{e}(\Sigma_{i=1}^n (r_i \hat{H}_i + D_i), P)$$
$$= \hat{e}(\Sigma_{i=1}^n r_i \hat{H}_i, P)\hat{e}(\Sigma_{i=1}^n D_i, P)$$
$$= \hat{e}(\Sigma_{i=1}^n \hat{H}_i, \Sigma_{i=1}^n r_i P)\hat{e}(\Sigma_{i=1}^n Q_i, P_{pub})$$
$$= \prod_{i=1}^n \hat{e}(\hat{H}_i, U_i)\hat{e}(\Sigma_{i=1}^n Q_i, P_{pub})$$

6.2 Security Proof

The security proof for this scheme is very much similar to IBAS-1 scheme. We are using the similar construct as the IBAS-1 in IBAS-2 with additional features, public verifiability.

7 Identity Based Aggregate Signcryption with Constant Verification Cost (IBAS-3)

7.1 IBAS-3 Scheme

IBAS-3 achieves constant number of pairing operation for aggregate verification irrespective of the number of senders. Hence this scheme is computationally efficient. This scheme consists of the following eight algorithms.

- **IBAS-3.Setup :** Let κ be the security parameter and let $\mathbb{G}_1$ and $\mathbb{G}_2$ be two GDH groups of the same prime order q. Let $\hat{e}$ be a bilinear map defined by $\hat{e} : \mathbb{G}_1 \times \mathbb{G}_1 \rightarrow \mathbb{G}_2$. The hash functions in IBAS-3 are defined as $H_1 : \{0,1\}^* \rightarrow \mathbb{G}_1$, $H_2 : \{0,1\}^* \times \mathbb{G}_2 \times \mathbb{G}_1 \times \{0,1\}^* \rightarrow \mathbb{Z}_q^*$, $H_3 : \mathbb{G}_2 \times \{0,1\}^* \rightarrow \{0,1\}^{\bar{n}}$ where $\bar{n} = | ID | + | m |$, and $H_4 : \{0,1\}^* \times \mathbb{G}_2 \times \mathbb{G}_1 \times \{0,1\}^* \times \mathbb{Z}_q^* \rightarrow \mathbb{Z}_q^*$. Let P be a random generator of $\mathbb{G}_1$ and the master private keys are $s_1, s_2 \in_R \mathbb{Z}_q^*$. The master public keys are $P_{pub1} = s_1 P$ and $P_{pub2} = s_2 P$. The system public parameters $params$ of the IBAS-3 system are $\langle P, P_{pub1}, P_{pub2}, \mathbb{G}_1, \mathbb{G}_2, \hat{e}, H_1, H_2, H_3, H_4\rangle$.

- **IBAS-3.KeyGen** : When user $\mathcal{U}_i$ with identity ID_i submits his identity to the PKG, the PKG runs this algorithm to generate $D_i = s_1 Q_i$, where $Q_i = H_1(ID_i)$. PKG sends D_i to the user U_i over a secure channel.
- **IBAS-3.Signcrypt** : When the user $\mathcal{U}_i$ with identity ID_i provides the message m_i, the receiver identity ID_B and his private key as input to this algorithm, signcryption of the message m_i is performed as follows.
  - Selects a random r_i from $\mathbb{Z}_{q^*}$.
  - Sets $U_i = r_i P$.
  - Computes $\alpha_i = \hat{e}(r_i P_{pub_1}, Q_B)$
  - Compute $c_i = H_3(\alpha_i, ID_B) \oplus (ID_i \parallel m_i)$
  - Computes $h1_i = H_2(m_i, \alpha_i, U_i, ID_B)$ and $h2_i = H_4(m_i, \alpha_i, U_i, ID_B, h1_i)$
  - Computes $V_i = r_i h1_i P_{pub_2} + h2_i D_i$
  - The signcryption $\sigma_i = \langle c_i, U_i, V_i \rangle$
- **IBAS-3.AggregateSigncrypt** : On providing n distinct signcryption $\sigma_i = \langle c_i, U_i, V_i \rangle$, for $i=1$ to n, the aggregate signcryption is formed as follows:

$$V_{Agg} = \Sigma_{i=1}^n V_i$$

Now $\langle \{c_i, U_i, ID_i\}_{i=1}^n, V_{Agg} \rangle$ is send as the aggregate signcryption to the receiver. It is to be noted that his algorithm can be run by one of the senders or any third party.
- **IBAS-3.Unsigncrypt** : The user ID_B to unsigncrypt $\sigma = \langle c_i, U_i, V_i \rangle$, (for $i = 1$ to n) uses his private key and does the following:
  - Computes $\alpha_i = \hat{e}(U_i, D_B)$.
  - Retrieves $ID_i \parallel m_i = H_3(\alpha_i, ID_B) \oplus c_i$.
  - Computes $h1_i = H_2(m_i, \alpha_i, U_i, ID_B)$ and $h2_i = H_4(m_i, \alpha_i, U_i, ID_B, h1_i)$.
  - Verifies $\hat{e}(V_i, P) \stackrel{?}{=} \hat{e}(P_{pub_2}, h1_i U i)\hat{e}(h2_i Q_i, P_{pub_1})$.
  - If the above test holds, the algorithm outputs (m_i, ID_i). Else, Outputs "*Invalid*"
- **IBAS-3.AggregateUnsigncrypt** : The user with identity ID_B, to unsigncrypt $\sigma_{Agg} = \langle \{c_i, U_i, ID_i\}_{i=1}^n, V_{Agg} \rangle$, uses his private key and does the following:

  Unsigncryption is carried out if σ_{Agg} passes public verification. For each i the user U_B calculates the following:
  - Computes $\alpha_i = \hat{e}(U_i, D_B)$.
  - Retrieves $ID_i \parallel m_i = H_3(\alpha_i, ID_B) \oplus c_i$.
  - Computes $h1_i = H_2(m_i, \alpha_i, U_i, ID_B)$ and $h2_i = H_4(m_i, \alpha_i, U_i, ID_B, h1_i)$.
  - Verifies $\hat{e}(V_{Agg}, P) \stackrel{?}{=} \hat{e}(P_{pub_2}, \Sigma_{i=1}^n h1_i U i)\hat{e}(\Sigma_{i=1}^n h2_i Q_i, P_{pub_1})$.
  - If the verification passes returns (m_i, ID_i) (for $i = 1$ to n). Else, Outputs "*Invalid*"
- **IBAS-3. Correctness** : The correctness of our scheme is proved as follows.
$\hat{e}(V_{Agg}, P) = \hat{e}(\Sigma_{i=1}^n r_i h1_i P_{pub_2}, P)\hat{e}(\Sigma_{i=1}^n h2_i D_i, P)$
$=\hat{e}(P_{pub_2}, \Sigma_{i=1}^n r_i h1_i P)\hat{e}(\Sigma_{i=1}^n h2_i Q_i, P_{pub_1})$
$=\hat{e}(P_{pub_2}, \Sigma_{i=1}^n h1_i U i)\hat{e}(\Sigma_{i=1}^n h2_i Q_i, P_{pub_1})$.

7.2   Security Proof of IBAS-3

Due to page restrictions we omit the proof here and provide it in the full version of this paper.

8   Efficiency

We have compared the efficiency of our scheme with the existing identity based signature scheme. From the table it is clear that our schemes are highly effective in computation. Also, the communication cost is highly reduced since the signature size is reduced by half. It cannot be completely reduced to constant value since one part of signature is needed for decryption. So only part of the signature can be aggregated.

Pt Mul - Scalar Point Multiplication.
Exp - Exponentiation in $\mathbb{G}_2$.
Pairing - Bilinear Pairing Operation.

In all the proposed schemes, we have aggregated only part of the signature. This provides sufficient amount of efficiency over sending each signcryption separately. Also, verification of number of signatures can be done in a single step rather than verifying each signature separately. This greatly reduces cost involved in verification. For example in banking systems, the verification of various transactions can be done in a single step rather than doing each verification separately. Secondly, instead of sending $2n$ components of signatures we send only n components. For large values of n this provides reduced cost with less bandwidth requirement in transmission. Though the number of components is still linear with respect to number of signers, it does save good amount of computation cost by reducing it into half.

The major advantage of our scheme is that the senders does not want to have any interactions as in Cheng et al.'s scheme [6] and Gentry et al.'s scheme [9], where all the senders agree upon a common random value R before performing the individual signatures which requires prior communication with all senders. In any aggregation scheme, different users must communicate the signcryption to the user who carries out the aggregation. This is the basic minimal cost inherent to the scheme.

Table 1. Efficiency comparison of Aggregate Signature Schemes

Schemes	Signing		Aggregate verify		
	Pt Mul	Pairing	Pt Mul	Exp	Pairing
Gentry et al.[9]	3		n		3
Bhaskar et al. [2]		1		n	n+1
X.Cheng et al. [6]	3		n		2
H.Yoon et al. [7]	3		n		n+1
Jing Xu et al. [20]	2				n+2
Our scheme IBAS-1	2				n+2
Our scheme IBAS-3	2		n		3

Any other communication done between the users/aggregator may be referred to as communication overhead. In our schemes, there is *NO* communication overhead. This also means that individual users may generate the signcryption in an off line fashion, except in the sequential aggregation scheme IBAS-2.

9 Conclusion and Open Problems

We have proposed the concept of aggregate signcryption by combining the functionalities of aggregate signature and signcryption. We have given three schemes each having its own advantage. We have formally proved the security of all the proposed schemes using adaptive identity in the random oracle model. These schemes have various practical applications. We leave as an open problem to device an efficient identity based aggregate signcryption scheme in the standard model. It will be interesting to investigate whether it is possible to reduce the number of pairing operations. It will be interesting to see a public verifiable aggregate signcryption with efficient aggregation and verification technique.

References

1. Baek, J., Steinfeld, R., Zheng, Y.: Formal proofs for the security of signcryption. In: Naccache, D., Paillier, P. (eds.) PKC 2002. LNCS, vol. 2274, pp. 80–98. Springer, Heidelberg (2002)
2. Bhaskar, R., Herranz, J., Laguillaumie, F.: Aggregate designated verifier signatures and application to secure routing. IJSN 2(3/4), 192–201 (2007)
3. Boneh, D., Franklin, M.K.: Identity-based encryption from the weil pairing. In: Kilian, J. (ed.) CRYPTO 2001. LNCS, vol. 2139, pp. 213–229. Springer, Heidelberg (2001)
4. Boyen, X.: Multipurpose identity-based signcryption (a swiss army knife for identity-based cryptography). In: Boneh, D. (ed.) CRYPTO 2003. LNCS, vol. 2729, pp. 383–399. Springer, Heidelberg (2003)
5. Chen, L., Malone-Lee, J.: Improved identity-based signcryption. In: Vaudenay, S. (ed.) PKC 2005. LNCS, vol. 3386, pp. 362–379. Springer, Heidelberg (2005)
6. Cheng, X., Liu, J., Wang, X.: Identity-based aggregate and verifiably encrypted signatures from bilinear pairing. In: ICCSA, vol. (4), pp. 1046–1054 (2005)
7. Cheon, J.H., Kim, Y., Yoon, H.J.: A new id-based signature with batch verification. Cryptology ePrint Archive, Report 2004/131 (2004)
8. Chow, S.S.M., Yiu, S.-M., Hui, L.C.K., Chow, K.P.: Efficient forward and provably secure id-based signcryption scheme with public verifiability and public ciphertext authenticity. In: Lim, J.-I., Lee, D.-H. (eds.) ICISC 2003. LNCS, vol. 2971, pp. 352–369. Springer, Heidelberg (2004)
9. Gentry, C., Ramzan, Z.: Identity-based aggregate signatures. In: Yung, M., Dodis, Y., Kiayias, A., Malkin, T.G. (eds.) PKC 2006. LNCS, vol. 3958, pp. 257–273. Springer, Heidelberg (2006)
10. Libert, B., Quisquater, J.-J.: A new identity based signcryption scheme from pairings. In: Proceedings of the IEEE Information Theory Workshop, pp. 155–158 (2003)

11. Malone-Lee, J.: Identity-based signcryption. Cryptology ePrint Archive, Report 2002/098 (2002)
12. Mitomi, S., Miyaji, A.: A multisignature scheme with message flexibility, order flexibility and order verifiability. In: Clark, A., Boyd, C., Dawson, E.P. (eds.) ACISP 2000, vol. 1841, pp. 298–312. Springer, Heidelberg (2000)
13. Mu, Y., Susilo, W., Zhu, H.: Compact sequential aggregate signatures. In: Adams, C., Miri, A., Wiener, M. (eds.) SAC 2007. LNCS, vol. 4876, pp. 249–253. Springer, Heidelberg (2007)
14. Pang, X., Catania, B., Tan, K.-L.: Securing your data in agent-based p2p systems. In: DASFAA, p. 55. IEEE Computer Society, Los Alamitos (2003)
15. Sakai, R., Ohgishi, K., Kasahara, M.: Cryptosystems based on pairing. In: SCIS (2000)
16. Selvi, S.S.D., Vivek, S.S., Shriram, J., Kalaivani, S., Rangan, C.P.: Security analysis of aggregate signature and batch verification signature schemes. Cryptology ePrint Archive, Report 2009/290 (2009)
17. Selvi, S.S.D., Vivek, S.S., Rangan, C.P.: Breaking and fixing of an identity based multi-signcryption scheme. Cryptology ePrint Archive, Report 2009/235 (2009), http://eprint.iacr.org/
18. Seo, S.-H., Lee, S.-H.: A secure and flexible multi-signcryption scheme. In: Laganá, A., Gavrilova, M.L., Kumar, V., Mun, Y., Tan, C.J.K., Gervasi, O. (eds.) ICCSA 2004. LNCS, vol. 3046, pp. 689–697. Springer, Heidelberg (2004)
19. Shamir, A.: Identity-based cryptosystems and signature schemes. In: Blakely, G.R., Chaum, D. (eds.) CRYPTO 1984. LNCS, vol. 196, pp. 47–53. Springer, Heidelberg (1985)
20. Xu, J., Zhang, Z., Feng, D.: ID-based aggregate signatures from bilinear pairings. In: Desmedt, Y.G., Wang, H., Mu, Y., Li, Y. (eds.) CANS 2005. LNCS, vol. 3810, pp. 110–119. Springer, Heidelberg (2005)
21. Zhang, J., Mao, J.: A novel identity-based multi-signcryption scheme. Computer Communications 32(1), 14–18 (2009)
22. Zheng, Y.: Digital signcryption or how to achieve cost(signature & encryption) << cost(signature) + cost(encryption). In: Kaliski Jr., B.S. (ed.) CRYPTO 1997. LNCS, vol. 1294, pp. 165–179. Springer, Heidelberg (1997)

Round Efficient Unconditionally Secure MPC and Multiparty Set Intersection with Optimal Resilience

Arpita Patra[*], Ashish Choudhary[**], and C. Pandu Rangan[***]

Dept of Computer Science and Engineering
IIT Madras, Chennai India 600036
arpitapatra10@gmail.com, partho_31@yahoo.co.in, prangan55@gmail.com

Abstract. In information theoretic model, unconditionally secure multiparty computation (UMPC) allows a set of n parties to securely compute an agreed function f, even upto $t < n/2$ parties are under the control of an *active adversary* having *unbounded computing power*. The bound on the resilience/fault tolerance (i.e $t < n/2$) is *optimal*, as long as each party is connected with every other party by a secure channel and a common physical broadcast channel is available to the parties and a negligible error probability of $2^{-\Omega(\kappa)}$ (for some security parameter κ) is allowed in the computation. Any UMPC protocol designed under the above settings is called as *optimally resilient UMPC protocol*. In this paper, we propose an optimally resilient UMPC protocol with $n = 2t + 1$, which requires only $\mathcal{O}(\mathcal{D})$ rounds, where $\mathcal{D}$ is the multiplicative depth of the arithmetic circuit representing f. To the best of our knowledge, our protocol is the first UMPC protocol with optimal resilience, to attain a round complexity that is independent of n. When $\mathcal{D}$ is constant, then our protocol requires only constant number of rounds. Our protocol is to be compared with the most round efficient, optimally resilient, UMPC protocol of [16] that requires $\mathcal{O}(\log n + \mathcal{D})$ rounds in the same settings as ours.[1] Thus our UMPC significantly reduces the round complexity of [16]. Moreover, our UMPC protocol requires the same communication complexity as that of [16]. As a tool for designing our UMPC protocol, we propose a new and *robust* multiplication protocol to generate t-sharing of the product of two t-shared secrets.

As an interesting, practically-on-demand MPC problem, we present a protocol for unconditionally secure multiparty set intersection (UMPSI) with optimal resilience; i.e., with $n = 2t + 1$, having a negligible error probability in correctness. This protocol adapts the techniques used in our proposed general UMPC protocol. The protocol takes *constant number rounds*, incurs a private communication of $\mathcal{O}(m^2 n^4 \kappa)$ bits and

[*] Financial Support from Microsoft Research India Acknowledged.
[**] Financial Support from Infosys Technology India Acknowledged.
[***] Work Supported by Project No. CSE/05-06/076/DITX/CPAN on Protocols for Secure Communication and Computation Sponsored by Department of Information Technology, Government of India.

[1] see Theorem 1, page 198 of [16].

B. Roy and N. Sendrier (Eds.): INDOCRYPT 2009, LNCS 5922, pp. 398–417, 2009.
© Springer-Verlag Berlin Heidelberg 2009

broadcasts $\mathcal{O}((m^2n^4 + n^5)\kappa)$ bits, where each party has a set of size m. To the best of our knowledge, this is the first ever UMPSI protocol with $n = 2t + 1$. This solves an open problem posed in [15] and [17], urging to design an UMPSI protocol with $n = 2t + 1$. Our UMPSI protocol is to be compared with the best known UMPSI protocol of [17] with $n = 3t + 1$ (i.e., non-optimal resilience), which takes *constant number rounds*, incurs a private communication of $\mathcal{O}((m^2n^3 + n^4\kappa)\kappa)$ bits and broadcasts $\mathcal{O}((m^2n^3 + n^4\kappa)\kappa)$ bits. So even though the communication complexity of our UMPSI protocol is slightly larger than that of [17], our UMPSI protocol significantly improves the resilience of UMPSI protocol of [17]; i.e., from $t < n/3$ to $t < n/2$.

Keywords: Multiparty Computation, Information Theoretic Security, Error Probability.

1   Introduction

Secure Multiparty Computation (MPC): Secure multiparty computation (MPC) [19] allows a set of n parties $\mathcal{P} = \{P_1, \ldots, P_n\}$ to securely compute an agreed function f, even if some of the parties are under the control of a centralized adversary. More specifically, assume that f can be expressed as $f : \mathbb{F}^n \to \mathbb{F}^n$ and party P_i has input $x_i \in \mathbb{F}$, where $\mathbb{F}$ is a finite field. At the end of the computation of f, each honest P_i gets $y_i \in \mathbb{F}$, where $(y_1, \ldots, y_n) = f(x_1, \ldots, x_n)$, irrespective of the behavior of the corrupted parties (**correctness**). Moreover, the adversary should not get any information about the input and output of the honest parties, other than what can be inferred from the input and output of the corrupted parties (**secrecy**). MPC is one of the most important and fundamental problems in secure distributed computing and has been studied extensively in different settings (see [19,11,5,6,18,1,12,10,2,4,3,16] and their references). In any general MPC protocol, the function f is specified by an arithmetic circuit over $\mathbb{F}$, consisting of input, linear (e.g. addition), multiplication, random and output gates. We denote the number of gates of each type by c_I, c_A, c_M, c_R and c_O, respectively. *Among all the different types of gate, the evaluation of a multiplication gate requires the most communication complexity. So the communication complexity of any general MPC is usually given in terms of the communication complexity per multiplication gate* [4,3,2,16].

In this paper, we study MPC in the presence of a *threshold, adaptive, active* adversary $\mathcal{A}_t$, having *unbounded computing power* in *synchronous* network. The adversary $\mathcal{A}_t$ can actively corrupt at most t parties out of the n parties. To actively corrupt a party mean to take full control over the party and make it behave arbitrarily during any protocol execution. Moreover, $\mathcal{A}_t$ can corrupt parties during run time and the choice of the adversary (to corrupt a party) depends upon the data which is seen from the parties, currently under the control of $\mathcal{A}_t$ (with the restriction that total number of corrupted parties should not go beyond t). We assume that each party is directly connected to every other party by a secure channel and a common physical broadcast channel is available to all the parties. The broadcast channel allows any party to send some information identically to all other parties. Any protocol in such a network operates in a sequence of rounds. In each round, a party performs some computation, sends messages to neighbours over private channel, broadcasts information (if any) to everybody. After this, the party receives the information sent by the neighbours over private channel in this round and collect any information, which is broadcast in this round. We assume $\mathcal{A}_t$ to be *rushing* [8], who in a particular round first listens all the messages addressed to him, before sending/broadcasting his own message(s) for the current round.

It is known that *perfectly secure* MPC tolerating $\mathcal{A}_t$ is possible iff $n \geq 3t + 1$ and every two parties are directly connected by a secure channel [5]. Any perfectly secure MPC satisfies the **correctness** and **secrecy** condition, without any error. When a negligible error probability of $2^{-\Omega(\kappa)}$ (for a security parameter κ) is allowed in **correctness**, then we arrive at the notion of *unconditional MPC* (UMPC), which is also known as information theoretically secure MPC with statistical security. It is known that UMPC tolerating $\mathcal{A}_t$ is possible iff $n \geq 2t + 1$ and a common broadcast channel is available to all the parties (in addition to secure point to point channel between every two parties) [18]. Any UMPC designed in these settings (i.e., with a completely connected network of $n = 2t + 1$ parties, along with the presence of a physical broadcast channel and allowance of a negligible error probability in correctness) may be called as *optimally resilient* UMPC. In this paper, we investigate optimally resilient UMPC.

Our Motivation and Contribution: Round complexity and communication complexity are two important complexity measures of any distributed computing protocol. Looking at the recent trend in the literature of UMPC, we find that round complexity has been increased tremendously to reduce communication complexity [8,2]. If we every hope to practically implement UMPC protocols, then we should try to design a protocol, which tries to simultaneously optimize both round and communication complexity. Motivated by this, Patra et.al [16] have designed an optimally resilient UMPC protocol, which tries to *simultaneously optimize both round and communication complexity*. To the best of our knowledge, the UMPC protocol of [16] is the most round efficient optimally resilient UMPC protocol. In this paper, we further reduce the round complexity of the round efficient optimally resilient UMPC protocol of [16]. Moreover, our UMPC protocol has the same communication complexity as the UMPC protocol of [16]. In the following table, we compare our UMPC protocol with the best known optimally resilient UMPC protocols. *In the table, the communication complexity denotes the total number of field elements communicated to evaluate the multiplication gates in the circuit and $\mathcal{D}$ is the multiplicative depth of the circuit. Notice that the best known communication efficient optimally resilient UMPC protocol of [2] has a broadcast communication, which is independent of number of multiplication gates in the circuit.*

Reference	Communication Complexity		Round Complexity
[8]	Private: $\mathcal{O}(c_M n^5)$;	Broadcast: $\mathcal{O}(c_M n^5)$	$\mathcal{O}(n\mathcal{D})$
[2]	Private: $\mathcal{O}(c_M n^2)$;	Broadcast: $\mathcal{O}(n^3)$	$\mathcal{O}(n^2 + \mathcal{D})$
[16]	Private: $\mathcal{O}(c_M n^3)$;	Broadcast: $\mathcal{O}(c_M n^3)$	$\mathcal{O}(\log n + \mathcal{D})$
This Article	Private: $\mathcal{O}(c_M n^3)$;	Broadcast: $\mathcal{O}(c_M n^3)$	$\mathcal{O}(\mathcal{D})$

From the table, we find that our UMPC protocol has the best round complexity among the best known optimally resilient UMPC protocol. The round complexity of our protocol is independent of n (which may be huge in most of the practical situations). Though there exists *perfectly secure* MPC with $n = 3t + 1$, whose round complexity is independent of n (i.e., $\mathcal{O}(\mathcal{D})$) [5,13], to the best of our knowledge, our UMPC protocol is the first optimally resilient UMPC protocol with $n = 2t+1$, to provide the same. If $\mathcal{D}$ is constant, then our protocol requires only constant number of rounds.

As an interesting practically-on-demand MPC problem, we present a protocol for unconditionally secure multiparty set intersection (UMPSI) with optimal resilience; i.e., with $n = 2t+1$, having a negligible error probability in correctness. Informally in UMPSI problem, there are n parties, each with a private data set of m field elements. The goal is to design a protocol, such that at the end of the protocol, each honest party correctly gets the intersection of the n sets with very high probability. Moreover, this should hold in the presence of a computationally unbounded $\mathcal{A}_t$. Furthermore, $\mathcal{A}_t$ should not get any extra information, other than what can be computed from the data set of t corrupted parties and the intersection of the n sets. Our UMPSI protocol adapts the techniques used in our proposed general UMPC protocol and takes *constant number rounds*, incurs a private communication of $\mathcal{O}(m^2 n^4 \kappa)$ bits and broadcasts $\mathcal{O}((m^2 n^4 + n^5)\kappa)$ bits, where each party has a set of size m. To our knowledge, this is the first ever UMPSI protocol with $n = 2t + 1$. This solves an open problem posed in [15,17], urging to get an UMPSI protocol with $n = 2t + 1$.

Remark 1. We prefer to divide this article into two parts: the first part consisting of Section 2, Section 3 and Section 4 are related to our proposed UMPC protocol. The second part, comprising Section 5 describes the existing literature for multiparty set intersection and our proposed UMPSI protocol.

Notations: For a given security parameter κ, our protocols provide information theoretic security with a negligible error probability of $2^{-\Omega(\kappa)}$ in correctness. To bound the error probability by $2^{-\Omega(\kappa)}$, all our computation and communication are done over a finite field $\mathbb{F} = GF(2^\kappa)$. Thus each field element can be represented by $\mathcal{O}(\kappa)$ bits. Moreover, without loss of generality, we assume that $n = poly(\kappa)$. We also assume that the messages sent through the channels are from the specified domain. Thus if a party receives a message which is not from the specified domain (or no message at all), he replaces it with some pre-defined default message. Thus, we separately do not consider the case when no message or syntactically incorrect message is received by a party.

2   Overview of Our UMPC Protocol

Our UMPC protocol is a sequence of following three phases: preparation phase, input phase and computation phase. In the preparation phase, t-2D$^{(+)}$-sharing (the formal definition of t-2D$^{(+)}$-sharing will be given in Section 3.2) of $c_M + c_R$ random multiplication triples will be generated. A triple (a, b, c) is called random multiplication triple if a and b are random and $c = ab$ holds. Our preparation phase requires only constant number of rounds. Each multiplication gate and random gate of the circuit will be associated with a t-2D$^{(+)}$-sharing of random multiplication triple. In the input phase the parties t-2D$^{(+)}$-share their inputs. In the computation phase, based on the inputs of the parties, the actual circuit will be computed gate by gate, such that the outputs of the intermediate gates are always kept as secret and are properly t-2D$^{(+)}$-shared among the parties. Due to the linearity of the used t-2D$^{(+)}$-sharing, the parties can locally evaluate linear gates without doing any communication. Each multiplication gate will be evaluated with the help of the multiplication triple associated with it, using the so called Beaver's circuit randomization technique [1].

The input and computation phase of our protocol are exactly same as in [16] and takes $\mathcal{O}(\mathcal{D})$ rounds. However, our preparation phase is completely different from the preparation phase of [16]. Specifically, in [16], the preparation phase was divided into a sequence of $\lceil \log n \rceil$ segments, where each segment is responsible for generating t-2D$^{(+)}$-sharing of $\frac{c_M + c_R}{\lceil \log n \rceil}$ random multiplication triples. The computation of those segments were non-robust in the sense that the computation may be unsuccessful in case certain number of parties misbehave (the misbehaving parties are identified and removed for computations in subsequent segments). Specifically, their multiplication protocol used in each segment for generating multiplication triples was non-robust. They showed that there may be at most $\lceil \log n \rceil$ unsuccessful attempts for the segment computations; after which identities of all corrupted parties will be revealed and hence all segment computations will be successful thereafter. Clearly, the computation of their preparation phase require $\Theta(\log n)$ rounds as the segments were executed sequentially.

We replace the non-robust multiplication protocol of [16] by a robust protocol, which will be always successful, irrespective of the behavior of the corrupted parties. Moreover, we do not divide our preparation phase into segments. These two facts together lead to the efficient implementation of our preparation phase, which requires only *constant* number of rounds. Moreover, while doing so, we keep the communication complexity intact; i.e., the communication complexity of our round efficient preparation phase is same as that of [16]. It is this reduction in the number of rounds during preparation phase, which further allows our UMPC protocol to gain in number of rounds, in comparison to the UMPC protocol of [16]. We borrow all other sub-protocols used in [16] will minor modifications. Nevertheless, for the sake of completeness, we briefly recall all these sub-protocols, when ever they are appropriate.

3   Robust Generation of Multiplication Triples

Before presenting our robust multiplication protocol, we explain few sub-protocols, which will be used as a black-box. Some of these sub-protocols are borrowed from [16], while others are proposed by us for the first time.

3.1   Information Checking Protocol and IC Signatures

The Information Checking Protocol (ICP) is a tool for authenticating messages in the presence of computationally unbounded corrupted parties. The notion of ICP was first introduced by Rabin [18]. As described in [18,8], an ICP is executed among three parties: a dealer $D \in \mathcal{P}$, an intermediary $INT \in \mathcal{P}$ and a verifier $R \in \mathcal{P}$. The dealer D hands over a secret value $s \in \mathbb{F}$ to INT. At a later stage, INT is required to hand over s to R and convince R that s is indeed the value which INT received from D.

The basic definition of ICP involves only a *single* verifier R and deals with *only one* secret s [18,8]. In [16], this notion is extended to *multiple* verifiers, where entire set $\mathcal{P}$ acts as verifiers [16]. Moreover, ICP of [16] is extended to deal with *multiple* secrets, denoted by S, which contains $\ell \geq 1$ secret values. Thus, ICP of [16] is executed with respect to *multiple* verifiers and deals with *multiple* secrets concurrently (when appropriate). We rename their ICP as Multi-Verifier-ICP. Now similar to the ICP defined in [18,8], Multi-Verifier-ICP is a sequence of following three protocols:

1. Distr($D, INT, \mathcal{P}, S$): is initiated by D, who hands over secret $S = \{S^{(1)} \ldots S^{(\ell)}\}$, containing $\ell \geq 1$ elements from $\mathbb{F}$ to INT. In addition, D hands over some **authentication information** to INT and **verification information** to the individual parties (verifiers) in $\mathcal{P}$.

2. AuthVal($D, INT, \mathcal{P}, S$): is initiated by INT to ensure that in protocol Reveal-Val, secret S held by INT will be accepted by all the (honest) verifiers in $\mathcal{P}$.

3. RevealVal ($D, INT, \mathcal{P}, S$): is carried out by INT and the verifiers. Here INT produces S and **authentication information**, while individual verifiers produce **verification information**. Depending upon the values produced by INT and the verifiers, either S is accepted or rejected by all the (honest) verifiers.

The **authentication information**, along with S, held by INT at the end of AuthVal is called D's *IC signature* on S, denoted as $ICSig(D, INT, S)$. Multi-Verifier-ICP satisfies the following properties [16]:

1. If D and INT are *honest*, then S will be accepted in RevealVal by each honest verifier.
2. If INT is *honest*, then S held by INT at the end of AuthVal will be accepted in RevealVal by each honest verifier, except with probability $2^{-\Omega(\kappa)}$.
3. If D is *honest*, then every $S' \neq S$ produced by a corrupted INT will be rejected by each honest verifier, except with probability $2^{-\Omega(\kappa)}$.
4. If D and INT are *honest*, then at the end of AuthVal, $\mathcal{A}_t$ has no information about S.

Protocol Multi-Verifier-ICP of [16] with $n = 2t + 1$ is presented in next page.

Lemma 1 ([16]). *Protocol Multi-Verifier-ICP takes five rounds and correctly generates IC signature on ℓ field elements, by privately communicating $\mathcal{O}((\ell + n)\kappa)$ bits and broadcasting $\mathcal{O}((\ell + n)\kappa)$ bits. The protocol satisfies all the above properties, except with error probability of $2^{-\Omega(\kappa)}$.*

Notation 1. *In the rest of the paper, whenever we say that D hands over $ICSig$ (D, INT, S) to INT, we mean that Distr and AuthVal are executed in the background. Similarly, INT reveals $ICSig(D, INT, S)$ can be interpreted as INT, along with other parties, invoking RevealVal*

Multi-Verifier-ICP$(D, INT, \mathcal{P}, S = \{s^{(1)}, \ldots, s^{(\ell)}\})$

Distr$(D, INT, \mathcal{P}, S = \{s^{(1)}, \ldots, s^{(\ell)}\})$: **Round 1**: D selects a random $\ell + t - 1$ degree polynomial $F(x)$ over $\mathbb{F}$, whose lower order ℓ coefficients are $s^{(1)}, \ldots, s^{(\ell)}$. In addition, D selects another random $\ell + t - 1$ degree polynomial $R(x)$ over $\mathbb{F}$. D selects n distinct, random elements $\alpha_1, \alpha_2, \ldots, \alpha_n$ such that each $\alpha_i \in \mathbb{F} - \{0\}$. D privately gives $F(x)$ and $R(x)$ to INT. To verifier $P_i \in \mathcal{P}$, D privately gives α_i, v_i and r_i, where $v_i = F(\alpha_i)$ and $r_i = R(\alpha_i)$. The polynomial $R(x)$ is called **authentication information**, while for $1 \leq i \leq n$, the values α_i, v_i and r_i are called **verification information**.

AuthVal$(D, INT, \mathcal{P}, S = \{s^{(1)}, \ldots, s^{(\ell)}\})$: **Round 2**: INT chooses a random $d \in \mathbb{F} \backslash \{0\}$ and broadcasts $d, B(x) = dF(x) + R(x)$.

Round 3: For $1 \leq j \leq n$, D checks $dv_j + r_j \overset{?}{=} B(\alpha_j)$. If D finds any inconsistency, he broadcasts $F(x)$. Parallely, verifier P_i broadcasts "Accept" or "Reject", depending upon whether $dv_i + r_i = B(\alpha_i)$ or not.

Local Computation (by each party): IF $F(x)$ is broadcasted in **Round 3** then accept the lower order ℓ coefficients of $F(x)$ as D's secret and terminate the protocol. ELSE construct an n length bit vector V^{Sh}, where the $j^{th}, 1 \leq j \leq n$ bit is 1(0), if $P_j \in \mathcal{P}$ has broadcasted "Accept" ("Reject") during **Round 3**. The vector V^{Sh} is public, as it is constructed using broadcasted information. If V^{Sh} does not contain $n - t$ 1's, then conclude that D is corrupted and fails to give any signature to INT and IC protocol terminates here.

If $F(x)$ is not broadcasted during **Round 3** and the protocol has not terminated, then $(F(x), R(x))$ is called D's IC signature on $S = \{s^{(1)}, \ldots, s^{(\ell)}\}$ denoted by $ICSig(D, INT, S)$.

RevealVal$(D, INT, \mathcal{P}, S = \{s^{(1)}, \ldots, s^{(\ell)}\})$: (a) **Round 4**: INT broadcasts $F(x), R(x)$; (b) **Round 5**: P_i broadcasts α_i, v_i and r_i.

Local Computation (by each party): For the polynomial $F(x)$ broadcasted by INT, construct an n length vector $V_{F(x)}^{Rec}$ whose j^{th} bit contains 1 if $v_j = F(\alpha_j)$, else 0. Similarly, construct the vector $V_{R(x)}^{Rec}$ corresponding to $R(x)$. Finally compute $V_{FR}^{Rec} = V_{F(x)}^{Rec} \otimes V_{R(x)}^{Rec}$, where $\otimes$ denotes bit wise AND. If V_{FR}^{Rec} and V^{Sh} matches at least at $t + 1$ locations (irrespective of bit value at these locations), then accept the lower order ℓ coefficients of $F(x)$ as $S = \{s^{(1)}, \ldots, s^{(\ell)}\}$. In this case, INT is able to prove D's signature on S. Otherwise INT fails to prove D's signature on S.

Protocol Multi-Verifier-ICP satisfies *linearity* property as specified by the following lemma:

Lemma 2 (Linearity of Protocol Multi-Verifier-ICP [16]). *The IC signature generated by Multi-Verifier-ICP satisfies **linearity** property; i.e., INT can compute $ICSig(D, INT, ((r_1 s^{(1,1)} + r_2 s^{(2,1)}), \ldots, (r_1 s^{(1,\ell)} + r_2 s^{(2,\ell)})))$ from $ICSig$ $(D, INT, (s^{(1,1)}, s^{(1,2)} \ldots, s^{(1,\ell)}))$ and $ICSig(D, INT, (s^{(2,1)}, s^{(2,2)} \ldots, s^{(2,\ell)}))$*

and Verifiers can compute verification information corresponding to $ICSig$ $(D, INT, ((r_1 s^{(1,1)} + r_2 s^{(2,1)}), \ldots, (r_1 s^{(1,\ell)} + r_2 s^{(2,\ell)})))$, without any interaction, where r_1, r_2 are any two publicly known elements from $\mathbb{F}$.

3.2   Unconditional Verifiable Secret Sharing

We now recall the following definitions from [16].

Definition 1 (d-1D-Sharing [16]). *A value $s \in \mathbb{F}$ is d-1D-shared among the parties in $\mathcal{P}$ if there exists a degree-d polynomial $f(x)$ over $\mathbb{F}$ with $f(0) = s$ such that every honest $P_i \in \mathcal{P}$ is holding a share $s_i = f(i)$ of s. The vector $(s_1, s_2, \ldots, s_n)$ of shares is called a d-1D-sharing of s and is denoted by $[s]_d$. A set of shares/values is d-consistent if they lie on a unique degree-t polynomial.*

Definition 2 (t-1D$^{(+)}$-sharing [16]). *Let $D \in \mathcal{P}$ be a party called dealer, who has a value $s \in \mathbb{F}$. We say that s is correctly t-1D$^{(+)}$-shared among the parties in $\mathcal{P}$, denoted by $\langle s \rangle_t^D$, if there exists degree-t polynomial $f(x)$ held by D with $f(0) = s$ and every honest party $P_i \in \mathcal{P}$ holds a share $s_i = f(i)$ of s and IC signature $ICSig(D, P_i, s_i)$ of D on s_i.*

Definition 3 (t-1D$^{(+,\ell)}$-sharing [16]). *Let $S = \{s^{(1)}, \ldots, s^{(\ell)}\}$, where each $s^l \in \mathbb{F}$. We say that the values in S are correctly t-1D$^{(+,\ell)}$-shared among the parties in $\mathcal{P}$, denoted as $\langle s^1, \ldots, s^\ell \rangle_t^D$, if every secret $s^{(l)}$ is individually t-1D$^{(+)}$-shared. But now, instead of (honest) P_i holding separate IC-signatures $ICSig(D, P_i, s_i^{(1)}), \ldots, ICSig(D, P_i, s_i^{(\ell)})$ of D, party P_i holds a single IC signature $ICSig(D, P_i, s_i^{(1)}, \ldots, s_i^{(\ell)})$.*

Definition 4 (t-2D$^{(+)}$-sharing [2,16]). *A value $s \in \mathbb{F}$ is correctly t-2D$^{(+)}$-shared among the parties in $\mathcal{P}$, denoted as $\langle\langle s \rangle\rangle_t$, if there exists degree-t polynomials $f, f^1, f^2 \ldots, f^n$ with $f(0) = s$ and for $i = 1, \ldots, n$, $f^i(0) = f(i)$ such that every honest party $P_i \in \mathcal{P}$ holds a share $s_i = f(i)$ of s, the polynomial $f^i(x)$ for sharing s_i and a share-share $s_{ji} = f^j(i)$ of the share s_j of every honest $P_j \in \mathcal{P}$. In addition, every (honest) $P_i \in \mathcal{P}$ holds (honest) P_j's IC Signature on share-share $s_{ji} = f^j(i)$ of P_j's share s_j, i.e., $ICSig(P_j, P_i, s_{ji})$ for every honest $P_j \in \mathcal{P}$. Note that in [2], the authors called this sharing as 2D*-sharing.*

Definition 5 (t-2D$^{(+,\ell)}$-sharing [16]). *A set of values $s^{(1)}, \ldots, s^{(\ell)}$ are t-2D$^{(+,\ell)}$-shared among the parties in $\mathcal{P}$ if every secret $s^{(l)}$ is individually t-2D$^{(+)}$-shared. But now, instead of (honest) P_i holding separate IC-signatures $ICSig(P_j, P_i, s_{ji}^{(1)}), \ldots, ICSig(P_j, P_i, s_{ji}^{(\ell)})$ of (honest) P_j, party P_i holds a single IC signature $ICSig(P_j, P_i, s_{ji}^{(1)}, \ldots, s_{ji}^{(\ell)})$. The t-2D$^{(+,\ell)}$-sharing is denoted as $\langle\langle s^1, \ldots, s^\ell \rangle\rangle_t$.*

If s is t-2D$^{(+)}$-shared by a dealer $D \in \mathcal{P}$ (any party from $\mathcal{P}$ may perform the role of a dealer), then we denote it by $\langle\langle s \rangle\rangle_t^D$. Similarly if a set of ℓ secrets $s^{(1)}, \ldots, s^{(\ell)}$ are t-2D$^{(+,\ell)}$-shared by $D \in \mathcal{P}$, we denote it by $\langle\langle s^1, \ldots, s^\ell \rangle\rangle_t^D$.

Generating t-2D$^{(+,\ell)}$-sharing of ℓ secrets: In [16] a protocol called 2D$^{(+,\ell)}$ Share is given, which allows a dealer $D \in \mathcal{P}$ to t-2D$^{(+,\ell)}$-share secret $S = \{s^{(1)},$

$s^{(2)}, \ldots, s^{(\ell)}\}$. The protocol has the following properties: (a) If D is honest, then the protocol generates $\langle\langle s^{(1)}, \ldots, s^{(\ell)}\rangle\rangle_t^D$ with high probability, such that $s^{(1)}, \ldots, s^{(\ell)}$ remain secure from $\mathcal{A}_t$. (b) If D is corrupted and has not generated t-$2D^{(+,\ell)}$-sharing of secrets, then with high probability, D will be detected as corrupted during a public verification process. The protocol is given on next page

Lemma 3 ([16]). $2D^{(+,\ell)}$ *Share generates t-$2D^{(+,\ell)}$-sharing of ℓ field elements, except an error probability of $2^{-\Omega(\kappa)}$. The protocol takes ten rounds, privately communicates and broadcasts $\mathcal{O}((\ell n^2 + n^3)\kappa)$ bits.*

$$(\langle\langle s^{(1)}, \ldots, s^{(\ell)}\rangle\rangle)_t^D = 2D^{(+,\ell)}\mathsf{Share}(D, \mathcal{P}, t, S = \{s^{(1)}, \ldots, s^{(\ell)}\})$$

1. For every $l = 1, \ldots, \ell$, D picks a random bivariate polynomial $H^{(l)}(x, y)$ of degree t in both the variables, with $H^{(l)}(0,0) = s^{(l)}$. Let $f_i^{(l)}(x) = H^{(l)}(x, i)$ and $g_i^{(l)}(y) = H^{(l)}(i, y)$. For $i = 1, \ldots, n$, D hands over $ICSig(D, P_i, f_i^{(1)}(j), f_i^{(2)}(j), \ldots, f_i^{(\ell)}(j))$ and $ICSig(D, P_i, g_i^{(1)}(j), g_i^{(2)}(j), \ldots, g_i^{(\ell)}(j))$ to party P_i for all $j \in \{1, \ldots, n\}$.

2. For $l = 1, \ldots, \ell$, party P_i checks whether the values $f_i^{(l)}(1), \ldots, f_i^{(l)}(n)$ and $g_i^{(l)}(1), \ldots, g_i^{(l)}(n)$ are t-consistent. If the values are not t-consistent, for some $l \in \{1, \ldots, \ell\}$ then P_i reveals $ICSig(D, P_i, f_i^{(1)}(j), f_i^{(2)}(j), \ldots, f_i^{(\ell)}(j))$ and $ICSig(D, P_i, g_i^{(1)}(j), g_i^{(2)}(j), \ldots, g_i^{(\ell)}(j))$, for all $j \in \{1, \ldots, n\}$. If the signatures produced by P_i are valid and for some $l \in \{1, \ldots, \ell\}$, either $f_i^{(l)}(1), \ldots, f_i^{(l)}(n)$ or $g_i^{(l)}(1), \ldots, g_i^{(l)}(n)$ is not t-consistent, then everybody concludes that D is corrupted and the protocol terminates without generating desired output.

3. For every pair of parties (P_i, P_j) in $\mathcal{P}$, the following is executed:

  (a) P_i acting as a dealer and considering P_j as INT, hands over $ICSig(P_i, P_j, f_i^{(1)}(j), \ldots, f_i^{(\ell)}(j))$ to P_j. Upon receiving the signature, P_j checks whether $f_i^{(l)}(j) \stackrel{?}{=} g_j^{(l)}(i)$ for $l = 1, \ldots, \ell$. If there is an inconsistency then P_j raises a complaint by revealing $ICSig(D, P_j, g_j^{(1)}(i), g_j^{(2)}(i), \ldots, g_j^{(\ell)}(i))$ as INT.

  (b) If P_j has raised a complaint but fails to produce $ICSig(D, P_j, g_j^{(1)}(i), g_j^{(2)}(i), \ldots, g_j^{(\ell)}(i))$ as an INT in the previous step, then all the parties in $\mathcal{P}$ conclude that P_j is corrupted and ignore the IC signatures received from P_j as a dealer in the previous step. Otherwise, if P_j is able to produce $ICSig(D, P_j, g_j^{(1)}(i), g_j^{(2)}(i), \ldots, g_j^{(\ell)}(i))$, then $g_j^{(1)}(i), g_j^{(2)}(i), \ldots, g_j^{(\ell)}(i)$ become public. Using the public values P_i checks whether $f_i^{(l)}(j) \stackrel{?}{=} g_j^{(l)}(i)$ for $l = 1, \ldots, \ell$. If P_i finds any inconsistency, then P_i raises a complaint and reveals $ICSig(D, P_i, f_i^{(1)}(j), f_i^{(2)}(j), \ldots, f_i^{(\ell)}(j))$ as an INT.

  (c) If P_i has raised a complaint but fails to correctly produce $ICSig(D, P_i, f_i^{(1)}(j), f_i^{(2)}(j), \ldots, f_i^{(\ell)}(j))$ as an INT in previous step, then all the parties from $\mathcal{P}$ conclude that P_i is corrupted and ignore the IC signatures received from P_i as a dealer in step 3(a). Else if P_i is able to correctly produce $ICSig(D, P_i, f_i^{(1)}(j), f_i^{(2)}(j), \ldots, f_i^{(\ell)}(j))$, then the values $f_i^{(1)}(j), f_i^{(2)}(j), \ldots, f_i^{(\ell)}(j)$ become public. Every party then verifies $f_i^{(l)}(j) \stackrel{?}{=} g_j^{(l)}(i)$ for $l = 1, \ldots, \ell$. If $f_i^{(l)}(j) \neq g_j^{(l)}(i)$ for some $l \in \{1, \ldots, \ell\}$ then everybody concludes that D is corrupted and the protocol terminates without generating any output.

Notation 2. *We now define few notations which will be used heavily in the subsequent sections (these notations are also commonly used in the literature). By saying that the parties in $\mathcal{P}$ compute (locally) $([y^{(1)}]_t, \ldots, [y^{(\ell')}]_t) = \varphi([x^{(1)}]_t, \ldots, [x^{(\ell)}]_t)$ (for any function $\varphi : \mathbb{F}^\ell \to \mathbb{F}^{\ell'}$), we mean that each P_i computes $(y_i^{(1)}, \ldots, y_i^{(\ell')}) = \varphi(x_i^{(1)}, \ldots, x_i^{(\ell)})$, where $x^l(i)$ and $y^l(i)$ denotes the ith share of x^l and y^l respectively. Note that applying an affine (linear) function φ to a number of t-1D-sharings, we get t-1D-sharings of the outputs. So by adding two t-1D-sharings of secrets, we get t-1D-sharing of the sum of the secrets, i.e. $[a]_t + [b]_t = [a+b]_t$. However, by multiplying two t-1D-sharings of secrets, we get 2t-1D-sharing of the product of the secrets, i.e. $[a]_t[b]_t = [ab]_{2t}$.*

Since protocol $2D^{(+,\ell)}$Share is one of the important sub-protocols, which is going to be used in our multiplication protocol, we now briefly summarize the outcome of protocol $2D^{(+,\ell)}$Share. For proof, see [16].

Remark 2 (Outcome of Protocol $2D^{(+,\ell)}$ Share [16]). In protocol $2D^{(+,\ell)}$Share if D is not detected to be corrupted and $S = \{s^{(1)}, \ldots, s^{(\ell)}\}$ is t-$2D^{(+,\ell)}$-shared, then it implies the following with very high probability: none of the honest parties will be detected as corrupted. There exists bi-variate polynomials $H^1(x, y), \ldots, H^\ell(x, y)$ of degree t in both x and y, such that $H^l(0,0) = s^{(l)}, f_i^l(x) = H^l(x, i)$ and $g_i^l(y) = H^l(i, y)$ for $l = 1, \ldots, \ell$, where each honest P_i will hold the degree-t univariate polynomials $f_i^l(x)$ and $g_i^l(y)$. Moreover, $f_i^{(l)}(j) = g_j^{(l)}(i)$ for every two honest parties P_i, P_j.

For $l = 1, \ldots, \ell$, the secret $s^{(l)}$ is t-$1D$-shared using $f_0^l(x)$. Each honest P_i will hold the ith share $s_i^{(l)} = g_i^l(0) = f_0^l(i)$ and i^{th} share-share $s_{ji}^{(l)} = f_i^l(j) = g_j^l(i)$ corresponding to every other honest P_j's share $s_j^{(l)}$. Moreover, each P_i who is not detected to be corrupted will hold the IC signature $ICSig(P_j, P_i, f_j^1(i), \ldots, f_j^\ell(i))$ of every other party P_j, such that $f_i^l(j) = g_j^l(i)$, provided that P_j is not detected to be corrupted during the protocol. Furthermore, each honest P_i will also have $ICSig(D, P_i, f_i^1(j), \ldots, f_i^\ell(j))$ and $ICSig(D, P_i, g_i^1(j), \ldots, g_i^\ell(j))$. Thus protocol $2D^{(+,\ell)}$Share generates $\langle\langle s^{(1)}, \ldots, s^{(\ell)}\rangle\rangle_t^D$ as well as $\langle s_i^{(1)}, \ldots, s_i^{(\ell)}\rangle_t^D$, corresponding to each party P_i who is not detected to be corrupted. Moreover, it also generate $\langle s_j^{(1)}, \ldots, s_j^{(\ell)}\rangle_t^{P_j}$, corresponding to every party P_j, who is not detected to be corrupted.

Also note that given $\langle\langle a^{(1)}, \ldots, a^{(\ell)}\rangle\rangle_t$ and $\langle\langle b^{(1)}, \ldots, b^{(\ell)}\rangle\rangle_t$, which are generated by two separate instances of protocol $2D^{(+,\ell)}$Share, the parties in $\mathcal{P}$ can compute $\langle\langle c^{(1)}, \ldots, c^{(\ell)}\rangle\rangle_t$ without any interaction, where for $l = 1, \ldots, \ell$, $c^{(l)} = \mathcal{F}(a^{(l)}, b^{(l)})$ and $\mathcal{F}$ denotes any linear function. This follows from the previous notation and linearity of protocol Multi-Receiver-ICP. □

3.3 Public Reconstruction of t-$2D^{(+,\ell)}$-sharing of ℓ Values

Let $s^{(1)}, \ldots, s^{(\ell)}$ be ℓ values, which are t-$2D^{(+,\ell)}$-shared using protocol $2D^{(+,\ell)}$Share. We now present protocol Recon-t-$2D^{(+,\ell)}$-sharing, which publicly reconstruct

$s^{(1)}, \ldots, s^{(\ell)}$. Before reading the protocol, we request the reader to recall the outcome of protocol $2D^{(+,\ell)}$Share, as given in Remark 2.

Lemma 4. *Recon-t-$2D^{(+,\ell)}$-sharing correctly recovers each $s^{(l)}$, except with probability $2^{-\Omega(\kappa)}$. The protocol takes two rounds and broadcasts $\mathcal{O}((\ell n^2 + n^3)\kappa)$ bits.*

PROOF: From properties of $2D^{(+,\ell)}$Share given in Remark 2, each $P_i \in CORE$ is holding $ICSig(P_j, P_i, f_j^1(i), \ldots, f_j^\ell(i))$ corresponding to every $P_j \in CORE$. Moreover, each $f_j^l(i)$ will lie on a unique degree-t polynomial $g_i^l(y)$. In the worst case, there can be n parties in $CORE$ and hence there will be n^2 revelation of IC signatures. The rest follows from the properties of the ICP.   □

$$(s^{(1)}, \ldots, s^{(\ell)}) = \mathsf{Recon\text{-}}t\text{-}2D^{(+,\ell)}\text{-sharing}(\mathcal{P}, \langle\langle s^{(1)}, \ldots, s^{(\ell)}\rangle\rangle_t)$$

Let $CORE$ denote the set of parties which were not detected to be corrupted during the generation of $\langle\langle s^{(1)}, \ldots, s^{(\ell)}\rangle\rangle_t$ (see the description of $2D^{(+,\ell)}$Share). Only the parties in $CORE$ are allowed to participate.

1. Each $P_i \in CORE$ reveals $ICSig(P_j, P_i, f_j^1(i), \ldots, f_j^\ell(i))$, corresponding to each $P_j \in CORE$ (see Remark 2 for the description of $f_j^l(i)$).
2. Each party does the following local computation:
   (a) Let REC denote the set of all parties from $CORE$, who have successfully revealed all the signatures during previous step.
   (b) For each $P_i \in REC$, check whether the $f_j^l(i)$'s for $l = 1, \ldots, \ell$, produced by P_i during step 1 corresponding to P_j's in $CORE$ are t-consistent. If not, then remove P_i from REC.
   (c) Corresponding to $P_i \in REC$, let $g_i^l(y)$ be the degree-t polynomial passing through t-consistent $f_j^l(i)$'s, for $l = 1, \ldots, \ell$.
   (d) Interpolate $H^l(x, y)$ of degree t in x and y by using $g_i^l(y)$'s corresponding to P_i's in REC for $l = 1, \ldots, \ell$ and output $s^{(l)} = H^l(0, 0)$.

3.4   Public Reconstruction of t-$1D^{(+,\ell)}$-sharing of ℓ Values

Let $s^{(1)}, \ldots, s^{(\ell)}$ be ℓ be t-$1D^{(+,\ell)}$-shared by $D \in \mathcal{P}$; i.e., $\langle s^{(1)}, \ldots, s^{(\ell)}\rangle_t^D$. We present a protocol called Recon-t-$1D^{(+,\ell)}$-sharing that tries to reconstruct $s^{(1)}, \ldots, s^{(\ell)}$. The protocol has the following features: (a) If D is honest then with very high probability, the protocol will succeed to publicly reconstruct $s^{(1)}, \ldots, s^{(\ell)}$; (b) If the protocol fails to reconstruct the secrets then with very high probability D is corrupted, which every honest party will come to know.

$$(s^{(1)}, \ldots, s^{(\ell)}) = \mathsf{Recon\text{-}}t\text{-}1D^{(+,\ell)}\text{-sharing}(\mathcal{P}, \langle s^{(1)}, \ldots, s^{(\ell)}\rangle_t^D)$$

1. Given $\langle s^{(1)}, \ldots, s^{(\ell)}\rangle_t^D$, party P_i holds $ICSig(D, P_i, (s_i^{(1)}, \ldots, s_i^{(\ell)}))$, where $s_i^{(l)}$ denotes i^{th} share of $s^{(l)}$.
2. Each party P_i reveals $ICSig(D, P_i, (s_i^{(1)}, \ldots, s_i^{(\ell)}))$.
3. Each party P_j either reconstruct $s^{(l)}$ or decide that D is corrupted as follows:
   (a) For $l = 1, \ldots, \ell$, consider $s_i^{(l)}$ values corresponding to all P_i's, who are successful in producing the IC signature in step 2 and check whether they define a unique degree-t polynomial. If yes then the constant term of the degree-t polynomial is taken as $s^{(l)}$. Otherwise, D is decided to be corrupted.

Lemma 5. *In protocol Recon-t-1$D^{(+,\ell)}$-sharing if D is honest, then with very high probability the secrets $(s^{(1)}, \ldots, s^{(\ell)})$ will be reconstructed correctly. If the protocol fails to reconstruct the secrets then with very high probability, D is corrupted. The protocol takes two rounds and broadcasts $\mathcal{O}((\ell n + n^2)\kappa)$ bits.*

PROOF: Communication and round complexity is easy to analyze. If D is honest, then by property of IC signature, every P_i that succeeded to reveal $ICSig(D, P_i, (s_i^{(1)}, \ldots, s_i^{(\ell)}))$ has disclose correct $(s_i^{(1)}, \ldots, s_i^{(\ell)})$ with high probability. Hence the $s_i^{(l)}$ values will lie on degree-t polynomial and thus the secrets will be reconstructed correctly with high probability.

If the secrets are not reconstructed then there is some l, such that $s_i^{(l)}$ values do not lie on a degree-t polynomial. This is possible if D is corrupted and some corrupted party P_i forged corrupted D's IC signature on $(\overline{s_i^{(1)}}, \ldots, \overline{s_i^{(\ell)}})$ such that $\overline{s_i^{(l)}} \neq s_i^{(l)}$ for some l. □

3.5 Generating Random t-2$D^{(+,\ell)}$-sharing

The authors of [16] have presented a protocol called Random which allows the parties in $\mathcal{P}$ to jointly generate a random t-2$D^{(+,\ell)}$-sharing $\langle\langle r^{(1)}, \ldots, r^{(\ell)}\rangle\rangle_t$, about which $\mathcal{A}_t$ will have no information. The protocol is as follows:

$$\langle\langle r^{(1)}, \ldots, r^{(\ell)}\rangle\rangle_t = \mathsf{Random}(\mathcal{P}, t)$$

Each $P_i \in \mathcal{P}$ acts as a dealer and invokes $2D^{(+,\ell)}\mathsf{Share}(P_i, \mathcal{P}, t, r^{(1,P_i)}, \ldots, r^{(\ell,P_i)})$ to generate $\langle\langle r^{(1,P_i)}, \ldots, r^{(\ell,P_i)}\rangle\rangle_t^{P_i}$, where $r^{(1,P_i)}, \ldots, r^{(\ell,P_i)}$ are randomly selected from $\mathbb{F}$. Let $Pass$ denote the set of parties P_i in $\mathcal{P}$ such that t-$2D^{(+,\ell)}\mathsf{Share}(P_i, \mathcal{P}, t, r^{(1,P_i)}, \ldots, r^{(\ell,P_i)})$ is executed successfully. Now all the parties in $\mathcal{P}$ jointly compute $\langle\langle r^{(1)}, \ldots, r^{(\ell)}\rangle\rangle_t = \sum_{P_i \in Pass}\langle\langle r^{(1,P_i)}, \ldots, r^{(\ell,P_i)}\rangle\rangle_t^{P_i}$. Hence $r^{(l)} = \sum_{P_i \in Pass} r^{(l,P_i)}$, for $l = 1, \ldots, \ell$.

Lemma 6 ([16]). *With overwhelming probability, Random generates random $\langle\langle r^{(1)}, \ldots, r^{(\ell)}\rangle\rangle_t$ in ten rounds, such that $\mathcal{A}_t$ has no information about any $r^{(l)}$. The protocol privately communicates and broadcasts $\mathcal{O}((\ell n^3 + n^4)\kappa)$ bits.*

3.6 Proving $c = ab$

Let $D \in \mathcal{P}$ has already t-1$D^{(+,\ell)}$-shared $a^{(1)}, \ldots, a^{(\ell)}$ and $b^{(1)}, \ldots, b^{(\ell)}$ among the parties in $\mathcal{P}$. Now D wants to t-2$D^{(+,\ell)}$-share $c^{(1)}, \ldots, c^{(\ell)}$ without leaking any *additional* information about $a^{(l)}$, $b^{(l)}$ and $c^{(l)}$, such that every (honest) party knows that $c^{(l)} = a^{(l)}b^{(l)}$ for $l = 1, \ldots, \ell$. The authors of [16] have proposed a protocol called ProveCeqAB for this task. Due to space constraints we do not give the formal details of protocol ProveCeqAB and state only the following lemma. For complete details see [16].

Lemma 7 ([16]). *In ProveCeqAB, if D does not fail, then with overwhelming probability, every $(a^{(l)}, b^{(l)})$, $c^{(l)}$ satisfies $c^{(l)} = a^{(l)}b^{(l)}$. ProveCeqAB takes twenty six rounds, privately communicates and broadcasts $\mathcal{O}((\ell n^2 + n^4)\kappa)$ bits. Moreover, if D is honest then $a^{(l)}, b^{(l)}$ and $c^{(l)}$ are secure from $\mathcal{A}_t$.*

3.7 Robust Multiplication Protocol: Our Main Contribution

We now finally present our protocol called Mult, which allows the parties to generate $\langle\langle a^{(1)}, \ldots, a^{(\ell)}\rangle\rangle_t, \langle\langle b^{(1)}, \ldots, b^{(\ell)}\rangle\rangle_t$ and $\langle\langle c^{(1)}, \ldots, c^{(\ell)}\rangle\rangle_t$, where $a^{(l)}$'s and $b^{(l)}$'s are random and $c^{(l)} = a^{(l)}b^{(l)}$ for $l = 1, \ldots, \ell$. For simplicity, we first explain the idea of the protocol to generate $\langle\langle a\rangle\rangle_t, \langle\langle b\rangle\rangle_t$ and $\langle\langle c\rangle\rangle_t$.

To generate random $\langle\langle a\rangle\rangle_t$ and $\langle\langle b\rangle\rangle_t$, we invoke two parallel executions of protocol Random with $\ell = 1$. We call these executions as Random^a and Random^b respectively. Before proceeding further, let us closely look into Random^a and Random^b. In Random^a, each party P_i would have executed $2D^{(+,\ell)}$Share as a dealer with $\ell = 1$ to generate $\langle\langle a^{(P_i)}\rangle\rangle_t^{P_i}$, where $a^{(P_i)}$ is a random element from $\mathbb{F}$. Similarly, in Random^b, each party P_i would have executed $2D^{(+,\ell)}$Share as a dealer with $\ell = 1$ to generate $\langle\langle b^{(P_i)}\rangle\rangle_t^{P_i}$, where $b^{(P_i)}$ is a random element from $\mathbb{F}$. Let $Pass^a$ ($Pass^b$) denote the set of parties whose instance of $2D^{(+,\ell)}$Share as a dealer is successful in Random^a (Random^a). For the ease of presentation, let $Pass^a$ and $Pass^b$ contain all the n parties. Thus everyone has computed $\langle\langle a\rangle\rangle_t = \sum_{i=1}^n \langle\langle a^{(P_i)}\rangle\rangle_t^{P_i}$ and $\langle\langle b\rangle\rangle_t = \sum_{i=1}^n \langle\langle b^{(P_i)}\rangle\rangle_t^{P_i}$. This implies that each $a_i = \sum_{i=1}^n a_i^{(P_i)}$ and $b_i = \sum_{i=1}^n b_i^{(P_i)}$. Here a_i and b_i are the ith shares of a and b respectively. Moreover, the parties hold $\langle a_i^{(P_j)}\rangle_t^{P_j}$ and $\langle b_i^{(P_j)}\rangle_t^{P_j}$, for $i, j = 1, \ldots, n$. Furthermore, the parties hold $\langle a_i\rangle_t^{P_i}$ and $\langle a_i\rangle_t^{P_i}$ for $i = 1, \ldots, n$.

Now to generate $\langle\langle c\rangle\rangle_t$, we use the following idea from [8]: every party P_i computes $a_i b_i$ and generates $\langle\langle a_i b_i\rangle\rangle_t^{P_i}$ by executing ProveCeqAB. Notice that at most t corrupted parties may fail to generate $\langle\langle a_i b_i\rangle\rangle_t^{P_i}$. Since $a_1 b_1, \ldots, a_n b_n$ are n points on a $2t$ degree polynomial, say $C(x)$, whose constant term is c, by Lagrange interpolation formula [7], c can be computed as $c = \sum_{i=1}^n r_i(a_i b_i)$ where $r_i = \prod_{j=1, j\neq i}^n \frac{-j}{i-j}$. The vector $(r_1, \ldots, r_n)$ is called recombination vector [7] which is public and known to every party. So for shorthand notation, we write $c = Lagrange(a_1 b_1, \ldots, a_n b_n) = \sum_{i=1}^n r_i(a_i b_i)$. Now all parties can compute $\langle\langle c\rangle\rangle_t = Lagrange(\langle\langle a_1 b_1\rangle\rangle_t^{P_1}, \ldots, \langle\langle a_n b_n\rangle\rangle_t^{P_n}) = \sum_{i=1}^n r_i\langle\langle a_i b_i\rangle\rangle_t^{P_i}$, to obtain the desired output. Notice that since $C(x)$ is of degree $2t$, we need all the $n = 2t + 1$ P_i's to successfully generate $\langle\langle a_i b_i\rangle\rangle_t^{P_i}$ (a $2t$ degree polynomial requires $2t + 1$ points on it to be interpolated correctly) in order to successfully generate $\langle\langle c\rangle\rangle_t$ using the above mechanism. Even if a single corrupted party P_i fails to generate $\langle\langle a_i b_i\rangle\rangle_t^{P_i}$, protocol Mult fails to work. *In [16], the multiplication protocol was non-robust for this reason.* To make Mult robust, we reconstruct a_i and b_i publicly when P_i fails to generate $\langle\langle a_i b_i\rangle\rangle_t^{P_i}$ in ProveCeqAB. All the parties then assume default $\langle\langle a_i b_i\rangle\rangle_t^{P_i}$ and proceeds with the above mentioned computation.

So assume that a corrupted party P_i fails to generate $\langle\langle a_i b_i\rangle\rangle_t^{P_i}$ in ProveCeqAB. We then try to publicly reconstruct a_i and b_i as follows: as explained earlier, $a_i = \sum_{j=1}^n a_i^{(P_j)}$ and $b_i = \sum_{j=1}^n b_i^{(P_j)}$. Moreover, the parties hold $\langle a_i^{(P_j)}\rangle_t^{P_j}$ and $\langle b_i^{(P_j)}\rangle_t^{P_j}$. So we first try to publicly reconstruct $a_i^{P_j}$ and $b_i^{P_j}$ corresponding to every P_j, using $\langle a_i^{(P_j)}\rangle_t^{P_j}$ and $\langle b_i^{(P_j)}\rangle_t^{P_j}$. For this, we use protocol Recon-t-$1D^{(+,\ell)}$-sharing. From the properties of protocol Recon-t-$1D^{(+,\ell)}$-sharing, corresponding to every *honest* P_j, the values $a_i^{P_j}$ and $b_i^{P_j}$ will be reconstructed correctly. However, corresponding to a *corrupted* P_j, the protocol may not output $a_i^{P_j}$ and $b_i^{P_j}$, in which case, everybody will come to know that P_j is corrupted. Like this, there can be at most t corrupted P_j's, corresponding to which the protocol Recon-t-$1D^{(+,\ell)}$-sharing may fail to output $a_i^{P_j}$ and/or $b_i^{P_j}$. Let $\mathcal{C}$ be the set of such corrupted parties. Now corresponding to the parties in $\mathcal{C}$, everyone computes $\langle\langle\sum_{P_j \in \mathcal{C}} a^{(P_j)}\rangle\rangle_t$, $\langle\langle\sum_{P_j \in \mathcal{C}} b^{(P_j)}\rangle\rangle_t$ and use protocol Recon-t-$2D^{(+,\ell)}$-sharing to publicly reconstruct $\sum_{P_j \in \mathcal{C}} a^{(P_j)}$ and $\sum_{P_j \in \mathcal{C}} b^{(P_j)}$. Once $\sum_{P_j \in \mathcal{C}} a^{(P_j)}$ and $\sum_{P_j \in \mathcal{C}} b^{(P_j)}$ are known, the ith shares of these values, namely $\sum_{P_j \in \mathcal{C}} a_i^{(P_j)}$ and $\sum_{P_j \in \mathcal{C}} b_i^{(P_j)}$ are also publicly known. Now everyone computes $a_i = \sum_{P_j \in \mathcal{P} \backslash \mathcal{C}} a_i^{(P_j)} + \sum_{P_j \in \mathcal{C}} a_i^{(P_j)}$ and $b_i = \sum_{P_j \in \mathcal{P} \backslash \mathcal{C}} b_i^{(P_j)} + \sum_{P_j \in \mathcal{C}} b_i^{(P_j)}$. Our protocol Mult follows the above ideas for ℓ pairs concurrently.

$$\langle\langle a^{(1)}, \ldots, a^{(\ell)}\rangle\rangle_t, \langle\langle b^{(1)}, \ldots, b^{(\ell)}\rangle\rangle_t, \langle\langle c^{(1)}, \ldots, c^{(\ell)}\rangle\rangle_t = \mathsf{Mult}(\mathcal{P})$$

1. Invoke **Random**$(\mathcal{P}, t)$ twice in parallel to generate $\langle\langle a^{(1)}, \ldots, a^{(\ell)}\rangle\rangle_t$ and $\langle\langle b^{(1)}, \ldots, b^{(\ell)}\rangle\rangle_t$. Let in these two executions of **Random**, P_i try to generate $\langle\langle a^{(1,P_i)}, \ldots, a^{(\ell,P_i)}\rangle\rangle_t^{P_i}$ and $\langle\langle b^{(1,P_i)}, \ldots, a^{(\ell,P_i)}\rangle\rangle_t^{P_i}$ respectively. Moreover, without loss of generality, let all P_i's are successfully able to to do so. This implies that $a^{(l)} = \sum_{j=1}^n a^{(l,P_j)}$ and $b^{(l)} = \sum_{j=1}^n b^{(l,P_j)}$, for $l = 1, \ldots, \ell$. Let $a_i^{(l)}$ and $b_i^{(l)}$ denote the ith share of a^l and b^l respectively. Clearly $a_i^{(l)} = \sum_{j=1}^n a_i^{(l,P_j)}$ and $b_i^{(l)} = \sum_{j=1}^n b_i^{(l,P_j)}$, where $a_i^{(l,P_j)}$ and $b_i^{(l,P_j)}$ are i^{th} shares of $a^{(l,P_j)}$ and $b^{(l,P_j)}$.

2. Given $\langle\langle a^{(1)}, \ldots, a^{(\ell)}\rangle\rangle_t$ and $\langle\langle b^{(1)}, \ldots, b^{(\ell)}\rangle\rangle_t$, we have $\langle a_i^{(1)}, \ldots, a_i^{(\ell)}\rangle_t^{P_i}$ and $\langle b_i^{(1)}, \ldots, b_i^{(\ell)}\rangle_t^{P_i}$ for each $P_i \in \mathcal{P}$. So party P_i invokes **ProveCeqAB**$(P_i, \mathcal{P}, t, \langle a_i^{(1)}, \ldots, a_i^{(\ell)}\rangle_t^{P_i}, \langle b_i^{(1)}, \ldots, b_i^{(\ell)}\rangle_t^{P_i})$ to generate $\langle\langle c_i^{(1)}, \ldots, c_i^{(\ell)}\rangle\rangle_t^{P_i}$.

3. If party P_i fails during his instance of **ProveCeqAB**, then with high probability, P_i must be corrupted and hence we reconstruct $a_i^{(1)}, \ldots, a_i^{(\ell)}$ and $b_i^{(1)}, \ldots, b_i^{(\ell)}$ publicly by executing the following steps. We describe the steps with respect to $a_i^{(1)}, \ldots, a_i^{(\ell)}$ only. The same should be executed for $b_i^{(1)}, \ldots, b_i^{(\ell)}$.
   (a) First, we try to reconstruct $a_i^{(1,P_j)}, \ldots, a_i^{(\ell,P_j)}$ corresponding to each $P_j \in \mathcal{P}$ from $\langle a_i^{(1,P_j)}, \ldots, a_i^{(\ell,P_j)}\rangle_t^{P_j}$. Since P_j had generated $\langle\langle a^{(1,P_j)}, \ldots, a^{(\ell,P_j)}\rangle\rangle_t^{P_j}$ in Random, it implies that parties hold $\langle a_i^{(1,P_j)}, \ldots, a_i^{(\ell,P_j)}\rangle_t^{P_j}$. So parties execute Recon-t-$1D^{(+,\ell)}$-sharing$(\mathcal{P}, \langle a_i^{(1,P_j)}, \ldots, a_i^{(\ell,P_j)}\rangle_t^{P_j})$ corresponding to every $P_j \in \mathcal{P}$ to either publicly reconstruct $a_i^{(1,P_j)}, \ldots, a_i^{(\ell,P_j)}$ or detect P_j as corrupted.
   (b) If no P_j has been detected as corrupted then everybody get $a_i^{(l)} = \sum_{j=1}^n a_i^{(l,P_j)}$ for all $l = 1, \ldots, \ell$. Otherwise let $\mathcal{C}$ denotes the set of all P_j's which are detected as corrupted (i.e., all P_j's, corresponding to which, Recon-t-$1D^{(+,\ell)}$-sharing$(\mathcal{P}, \ell, \langle a_i^{(1,P_j)}, \ldots, a_i^{(\ell,P_j)}\rangle_t^{P_j})$ fails).
   (c) The parties execute Recon-t-$2D^{(+,\ell)}$-sharing$(\mathcal{P}, \langle\langle\sum_{P_j \in \mathcal{C}} a^{(1,P_j)}, \ldots, \sum_{P_j \in \mathcal{C}} a^{(\ell,P_j)}\rangle\rangle_t)$ to publicly reconstruct $\sum_{P_j \in \mathcal{C}} a^{(1,P_j)}, \ldots, \sum_{P_j \in \mathcal{C}} a^{(\ell,P_j)}$.
   (d) Finally every party computes $a_i^{(l)} = \sum_{P_j \in \mathcal{C}} a_i^{(l,P_j)} + \sum_{P_i \in \mathcal{P} \backslash \mathcal{C}} a_i^{(l,P_j)}$.
   (e) Every party finds $c_i^{(l)} = a_i^{(l)} b_i^{(l)}$ and assumes some default t-$2D^{(+,\ell)}$-sharing $\langle\langle c^{(1)}, \ldots, c^{(\ell)}\rangle\rangle_t^{P_i}$.

4. All the parties compute: $\langle\langle c^{(1)}, \ldots, c^{(\ell)}\rangle\rangle_t = \sum_{i=1}^{2t+1} r_i \langle\langle c_i^{(1)}, \ldots, c_i^{(\ell)}\rangle\rangle_t^{P_i}$, where $(r_1, \ldots, r_{2t+1})$ represents the recombination vector [7].

Lemma 8. *With overwhelming probability, protocol* **Mult** *produces* $\langle\langle a^{(1)}, \ldots, a^{(\ell)}\rangle\rangle_t, \langle\langle b^{(1)}, \ldots, b^{(\ell)}\rangle\rangle_t$ *and* $\langle\langle c^{(1)}, \ldots, c^{(\ell)}\rangle\rangle_t$, *where* $a^{(l)}$'s *and* $b^{(l)}$'s *are random and* $c^{(l)} = a^{(l)}b^{(l)}$ *for* $l = 1, \ldots, \ell$. *Moreover,* $\mathcal{A}_t$ *will have no information about* $a^{(l)}, b^{(l)}$ *and* $c^{(l)}$ *for* $l = 1, \ldots, \ell$. *The protocol takes forty rounds, privately communicates* $\mathcal{O}((\ell n^3 + n^5)\kappa)$ *bits and broadcasts* $\mathcal{O}((\ell n^3 + n^5)\kappa)$ *bits.*

PROOF: Round and communication complexity is easy to analyze. The randomness of $\langle\langle a^{(1)}, \ldots, a^{(\ell)}\rangle\rangle_t$ and $\langle\langle b^{(1)}, \ldots, b^{(\ell)}\rangle\rangle_t$ follows from the properties of protocol Random. The correctness follows from the protocol steps and the explanation given before the protocol. The secrecy follows from protocol steps and secrecy of protocol ProveCeqAB. □

4   Our Round Efficient UMPC Protocol

We now present our UMPC protocol. As in [16], our UMPC protocol is also divided into three phases. We now give the details of each of these phases.

4.1   Preparation Phase

The goal of this phase is to generate correct t-$2D^+$-sharing of $(c_M + c_R)$ secret multiplication triples. Due to space constraints, we only present the overall idea of the protocol for this phase. We first execute our robust protocol Mult with $\ell = c_M + c_R$ to generate $\langle\langle a^{(1)}, \ldots, a^{(c_M+c_R)}\rangle\rangle_t, \langle\langle b^{(1)}, \ldots, b^{(c_M+c_R)}\rangle\rangle_t$ and $\langle\langle c^{(1)}, \ldots, c^{(c_M+c_R)}\rangle\rangle_t$, where for $l = 1, \ldots, c_M + c_R$, $a^{(l)}, b^{(l)}$ are random and $c^l = a^l b^l$. Now to get $\langle\langle a^{(1)}\rangle\rangle_t, \ldots, \langle\langle a^{(c_M+c_R)}\rangle\rangle_t$ from $\langle\langle a^{(1)}, \ldots, a^{(c_M+c_R)}\rangle\rangle_t$, we use a protocol called Convert presented in [16]. Similarly, by using Convert, we get $\langle\langle b^{(1)}\rangle\rangle_t, \ldots, \langle\langle b^{(c_M+c_R)}\rangle\rangle_t$ and $\langle\langle c^{(1)}\rangle\rangle_t, \ldots, \langle\langle c^{(c_M+c_R)}\rangle\rangle_t$ from $\langle\langle b^{(1)}, \ldots, b^{(c_M+c_R)}\rangle\rangle_t$ and $\langle\langle c^{(1)}, \ldots, c^{(c_M+c_R)}\rangle\rangle_t$ respectively.

Protocol Convert [16]: Given $\langle\langle s^{(1)}, \ldots, s^{(\ell)}\rangle\rangle_t$ which is either generated using protocol $2D^{(+,\ell)}$Share or protocol Random, the authors of [16] have presented a protocol called Convert$2D^{(+,\ell)}$to$2D^+$ which produces the t-$2D^+$-sharing of the individual ℓ secrets, namely $\langle\langle s^{(l)}\rangle\rangle_t$ for $l = 1, \ldots, \ell$.

Lemma 9 ([16]). *Protocol* Convert$2D^{(+,\ell)}$to$2D^+$ *takes five rounds, privately communicates* $\mathcal{O}((\ell n^3 + n^4)\kappa)$ *bits and broadcasts* $\mathcal{O}((\ell n^3 + n^4)\kappa)$ *bits. Given* $\langle\langle s^{(1)}, \ldots, s^{(\ell)}\rangle\rangle_t$, *the protocol correctly produces* $\langle\langle s^{(l)}\rangle\rangle_t$ *for* $l = 1, \ldots, \ell$ *with very high probability.*

Lemma 10. *With overwhelming probability, protocol* Preparation Phase *produces correct* t-$2D^+$-*sharing of* $(c_M + c_R)$ *secret multiplication triples in forty five rounds, privately communicates* $\mathcal{O}((c_M+c_R)n^3 + n^5)\kappa$ *bits and broadcasts* $\mathcal{O}((c_M + c_R)n^3 + n^5)\kappa$ *bits.*

Remark 3 (Comparison with the Preparation Phase of [16]). The **Preparation Phase** of [16] has the same communication complexity as ours (see Lemma 11, page 196 of [16]). However, the **Preparation Phase** of [16] takes $\Theta(\log t)$ rounds, where as our **Preparation Phase** takes $\Theta(1)$ rounds. It is this reduction in the number of rounds, which finally contributes to the reduction in the number of rounds in our final UMPC protocol, in comparison to the UMPC of [16].

4.2   Input and Computation Phase

Once the **Preparation Phase** is over, the **Input** and **Computation Phase** are same as in [16]. Due to this similarity, we only recall the high level idea of these phases. For complete details see [16].

The goal of the **Input Phase** is to generate t-$2D^+$-sharing of the inputs (to the circuit representing function f) of each party. Assume that $P_i \in \mathcal{P}$ has c_i inputs. So total number of input gates $c_I = \sum_{i=1}^{n} c_i$. We stress that though some parties might have been detected to be corrupted during **Preparation Phase**, we still allow them to feed their input. In **Input Phase**, each P_i on having input $s^{(i,1)}, s^{(i,2)}, \ldots, s^{(i,c_i)}$, acts as a dealer and executes an instance of $2D^{(+,\ell)}$Share with $\ell = c_i$ to generate $\langle\langle s^{(i,1)}, \ldots, s^{(i,c_i)}\rangle\rangle_t$. If P_i is corrupted and fails in his instance of $2D^{(+,\ell)}$Share, then everybody accepts a default t-$2D^{(+,c_i)}$ sharing on behalf of P_i. After this, protocol Convert$2D^{(+,c_i)}$to$2D^+$ is called to generate $\langle\langle s^{(i,l)}\rangle\rangle_t$, for $l = 1, \ldots, c_i$ from $\langle\langle s^{(i,1)}, \ldots, s^{(i,c_i)}\rangle\rangle_t$.

Lemma 11. *With overwhelming probability, the protocol for* **Input Phase** *produces correct t-$2D^+$-sharing of c_I inputs in fifteen rounds by privately communicating $\mathcal{O}((c_I n^3 + n^5)\kappa)$ bits and broadcasting $\mathcal{O}((c_I n^3 + n^5)\kappa)$ bits. Moreover, $\mathcal{A}_t$ gets no information about the inputs of the honest parties.*

Once **Preparation Phase** and **Input Phase** are over, the computation of the circuit (of the agreed upon function f) proceeds gate-by-gate. First, to every random and every multiplication gate, a prepared t-$2D^+$-shared random multiplication triple (generated during **Preparation Phase**) is assigned. A gate (except output gate) g is said to be *computed* if a t-$2D^+$-sharing $\langle\langle x_g\rangle\rangle_t$ is computed for the gate. Note that all the random and input gates will be *computed* as soon as we assign t-$2D^+$-shared random triples (generated in **Preparation Phase**) and t-$2D^+$-shared inputs (generated in **Input Phase**) to them respectively. A gate is said to be in *ready state*, when all its input gates have been *computed*. In the **Computation Phase**, the circuit evaluation proceeds in rounds wherein each round all the ready gates will be computed parallely. Evaluation of input and random gates do not require any communication. Due to linearity of t-$2D^+$-sharing, linear gates can be computed without any communication.

For evaluating a multiplication gate, we use Beaver's *Circuit Randomization* technique [1]. Let x and y be input of a multiplication gate, such that parties hold $\langle\langle x\rangle\rangle_t$ and $\langle\langle y\rangle\rangle_t$. Moreover, let $(\langle\langle a\rangle\rangle_t, \langle\langle b\rangle\rangle_t, \langle\langle c\rangle\rangle_t)$ be the multiplication triple (generated during **Preparation Phase**), which is associated with the multiplication gate. Now the parties want to generate $\langle\langle z\rangle\rangle_t$, where $z = xy$. Moreover, if x and y are unknown to $\mathcal{A}_t$, then x, y and z should be still unknown to $\mathcal{A}_t$. This can be done using Beaver's *Circuit Randomization* technique as follows: notice that $xy = \{(x - a) + a\}\{(y - b) + b\}$. Let $\alpha = (x - a)$ and $\beta = (y - b)$. The parties compute $\langle\langle \alpha\rangle\rangle_t$ and $\langle\langle \beta\rangle\rangle_t$. Then the parties reconstruct α and β. For this the parties execute protocol $2D^+$Recons [2]. Once α and β are

---

[2] Given $\langle\langle s\rangle\rangle_t$, the authors in [16] have presented protocol $2D^+$Recons, which allows each party to *privately* reconstruct s with very high probability. The protocol takes takes one round and privately communicates $\mathcal{O}(n^3\kappa)$ bits.

known to every body, the parties compute $\langle\langle z\rangle\rangle_t = \alpha\beta + \alpha\langle\langle b\rangle\rangle_t + \beta\langle\langle a\rangle\rangle_t + \langle\langle c\rangle\rangle_t$. The secrecy of x, y and z follows from the fact a, b are completely random and unknown to $\mathcal{A}_t$ [1]. As soon as an output gate becomes ready, the input to the output gate is reconstructed by every party by executing protocol $2D^+$Recons. It is easy to see that protocol takes $\mathcal{O}(\mathcal{D})$ rounds of communication, where $\mathcal{D}$ is multiplicative depth of the circuit.

Lemma 12 ([16]). *Given t-$2D^+$-sharing of $(c_M + c_R)$ secret multiplication triples, the protocol for* **Computation Phase** *correctly evaluates the circuit gate-by-gate in a shared fashion and outputs the desired outputs with overwhelming probability. The protocol takes $\mathcal{O}(\mathcal{D})$ rounds and privately communicates $\mathcal{O}((c_M + c_O)n^3\kappa)$ bits, where $\mathcal{D}$ is the multiplication depth of the circuit.*

4.3 Our Final UMPC Protocol

Now our new UMPC protocol for evaluating function f is: (1). Invoke **Preparation Phase** (2). Invoke **Input Phase** (3). Invoke **Computation Phase**.

Theorem 1. *With overwhelming probability, our new UMPC protocol can evaluate an agreed upon function securely against an active adaptive rushing adversary $\mathcal{A}_t$ with $t < n/2$ and requires $\mathcal{O}(\mathcal{D})$ rounds, privately communicates $\mathcal{O}((c_I + c_R + c_M + c_O)n^3\kappa)$ bits and broadcasts $\mathcal{O}(((c_I + c_M + c_R)n^3 + n^5)\kappa)$ bits.*

5 Unconditionally Secure Multiparty Set Intersection

We now show how to use the ideas presented in our UMPC protocol to design an unconditionally secure multiparty set intersection (MPSI) protocol with $n = 2t + 1$. In MPSI problem, each party P_i has a private data set $S_i = \{e_i^{(1)}, e_i^{(2)}, \ldots, e_i^{(m)}\}$, containing m field elements. The goal is to design a protocol that can compute the intersection of these n sets, satisfying the following properties: (1) **Correctness:** At the end of the protocol, each honest party correctly gets the intersection of n sets, irrespective of the behavior of $\mathcal{A}_t$; (2) **Secrecy:** The protocol should not leak any *extra* information to $\mathcal{A}_t$, other than what is implied by the input of the corrupted parties (i.e., the data-sets possessed by corrupted parties) and the final output (i.e., the intersection of n data-sets).

Existing Literature on MPSI: The MPSI problem was first studied in *cryptographic* model in [9,14], under the assumption that $\mathcal{A}_t$ has *bounded computing power*. By representing the data-sets as polynomials, the set intersection problem is converted into the task of computing the common roots of n polynomials in [9,14] as follows: Let $S = \{s_1, s_2, \ldots, s_m\}$ be a set of size m, where $\forall i, s_i \in \mathbb{F}$. Now set S can be represented by a polynomial $f(x)$ of degree, m, where $f(x) = \prod_{i=1}^{m}(x - s_i) = a_0 + a_1 x + \ldots + a_m x^m$. It is obvious that if an element s is a root of $f(x)$, then s is a root of $r(x)f(x)$ too, where $r(x)$ is a *random* polynomial of degree-m over $\mathbb{F}$. Now for MPSI, party P_i represents his set S_i, by a degree-m polynomial $f^{(P_i)}(x)$ and supplies its $m + 1$ coefficients as his input, in a secure manner. Then all the parties jointly and securely compute

$$F(x) = (r^{(1)}(x)f^{(P_1)}(x) + r^{(2)}(x)f^{(P_2)}(x) + \ldots + r^{(n)}(x)f^{(P_n)}(x)) \quad (1)$$

where $r^{(1)}(x), \ldots r^{(n)}(x)$ are n secret random polynomials of degree-m over $\mathbb{F}$, jointly generated by the n parties. Note that $F(x)$ preserves all the common roots of $f^{(P_1)}(x), \ldots, f^{(P_n)}(x)$. Every element $s \in (S_1 \cap S_2 \cap \ldots \cap S_n)$ is a root of $F(x)$, i.e. $F(s) = 0$. Hence after computing $F(x)$ in a secure manner, it can be reconstructed by every party, who locally checks if $F(s) = 0$ for every s in his private set. All s's at which the evaluation of $F(x)$ is zero forms the intersection set $(S_1 \cap S_2 \cap \ldots \cap S_n)$. In [14], it has been proved formally that $F(x)$ does not reveal any *extra* information to the adversary, other than what is deduced from $(S_1 \cap S_2 \cap \ldots \cap S_n)$ and input set S_i of the corrupted parties.

Remark 4 ([17]). Even though every $s \in (S_1 \cap S_2 \cap \ldots \cap S_n)$ is a root of $F(x)$, there may exist some $s' \in \mathbb{F}$, such that $F(s') = 0$, even though $s' \notin (S_1 \cap S_2 \cap \ldots \cap S_n)$. This is possible if s' happens to be the common root of all $r^{(i)}(x)$'s. However, as stated in [14], the probability of this event is negligible.

In [15], the authors presented the first information theoretically secure protocol for MPSI, assuming $\mathcal{A}_t$ to be *computationally unbounded* and $n \geq 3t + 1$. Specifically, the authors have shown how to securely compute $F(x)$ in the presence of a computationally unbounded $\mathcal{A}_t$. *Notice that, although not explicitly stated in [15], the MPSI protocol of [15] involves a negligible error probability in* **Correctness**. *This is due to the argument given in Remark 4. Hence, the MPSI protocol of [15] is not perfectly secure. Thus the MPSI protocol of [15] is unconditionally secure, having a negligible error probability in* **Correctness**. From here onwards, we call *unconditionally secure multiparty set intersection* as UMPSI.

Recently in [17], Patra et.al have shown that the round complexity and communication complexity of the UMPSI protocol of [15] is much more than what is claimed in [15]. Specifically, in [17], it is shown that in the presence of a physical broadcast channel in the system (in addition to point to point secure channels between every two parties), the UMPSI protocol of [15] takes $\Omega(n)$ rounds, privately communicates $\Omega(n^5 m)$ field elements and broadcast $\Omega(n^5 m)$ field elements. In addition, Patra et.al [17] have given a new UMPSI protocol with $n = 3t + 1$, which takes $\Theta(1)$ rounds, privately communicates $\mathcal{O}((m^2 n^3 + n^4 log(|\mathbb{F}|))$ field elements and broadcasts $\mathcal{O}((m^2 n^3 + n^4 log(|\mathbb{F}|))$ field elements. In our context, $|\mathbb{F}| = 2^\kappa$. Thus, the UMPSI protocol of [17] privately communicates and broadcasts $\mathcal{O}((m^2 n^3 + n^4 \kappa)\kappa)$ bits, having a negligible error probability in correctness. To the best of our knowledge, the UMPSI protocol of [17] is the best known UMPSI protocol.

Our Results: Notice that the UMPSI protocol of [15] as well as [17] are *unconditional* and designed with $n = 3t + 1$ and thus have non-optimal resilience. In fact, in [15] and [17], the authors have left it as an open problem to design an UMPSI protocol with *optimal resilience*; i.e., with $n = 2t + 1$. In this article, we make a positive step towards solving this problem. Specifically, we design a new UMPSI protocol with $n = 2t + 1$. To design our UMPSI protocol, we use several ideas from our proposed UMPC protocol, specifically the new robust multiplication protocol Mult. Our UMPSI protocol takes $\Theta(1)$ rounds, privately communicates $\mathcal{O}(m^2 n^4 \kappa)$ bits and broadcasts $\mathcal{O}((m^2 n^4 + n^5)\kappa)$ bits. So even though the communication complexity of our UMPSI protocol is slightly larger than that of [17], it significantly improves the resilience of the UMPSI of [17].

As in [15,17], our UMPSI protocol tries to securely evaluate the function given in (1) and is divided into following three phases:

1. **Preparation Phase**: Let for $i = 1, \ldots, n$ polynomial $r^{(i)}(x)$ be expressed as $r^{(i)}(x) = b^{(0,i)} + b^{(1,i)}x + \ldots + b^{(m,i)}x^m$. Each of the random coefficients of $r^{(i)}(x)$ polynomials can be interpreted as a random gate. So there are $c_R = n(m+1)$ random gates (n polynomials $r^{(1)}, \ldots, r^{(n)}$ have in total $n(m+1)$ random co-efficients). Also there are $c_M = n(m+1)^2$ multiplication gates (computing $r^{(i)}(x)f^{(P_i)}(x)$ requires $(m+1)^2$ co-efficient multiplications). So in preparation phase we will generate t-$2D^+$-sharing of $c_R + c_M = n(m+1) + n(m+1)^2$ random multiplication triples following the protocol for **Preparation Phase** of our UMPC protocol. Now consider the first c_R triples generated in **Preparation Phase**. The first component of these triples can be directly interpreted as $\langle\langle b^{(0,i)} \rangle\rangle_t, \ldots, \langle\langle b^{(m,i)} \rangle\rangle_t$ for $i = 1, \ldots, n$.

Theorem 2. *With overwhelming probability, the protocol for* **Preparation Phase** *produces correct t-$2D^+$-sharing of $n(m+1) + n(m+1)^2$ secret multiplication triples in forty five rounds, privately communicates $\mathcal{O}((n^4m^2 + n^5)\kappa)$ bits and broadcasts $\mathcal{O}((n^4m^2 + n^5)\kappa)$ bits.*

2. **Input Phase**: Once **Preparation Phase** is over, the parties execute **Input Phase**. Here every $P_i \in \mathcal{P}$ represents his set $S_i = \{e_i^{(1)}, e_i^{(2)}, \ldots, e_i^{(m)}\}$ by polynomial $f^{(P_i)}(x) = (x - e_i^{(1)}) \ldots (x - e_i^{(m)}) = a^{(0,P_i)} + a^{(1,P_i)}x + \ldots + a^{(m,P_i)}x^m$. Since $a^{(m,P_i)} = 1$ always, every party in $\mathcal{P}$ assumes a predefined t-$2D^+$-sharing of 1, namely $\langle\langle 1 \rangle\rangle_t$ on behalf of $a^{(m,P_i)}$, for $i = 1, \ldots, n$. Now for $i = 1, \ldots, n$ and $j = 0, \ldots, m-1$, the parties generate $\langle\langle a^{(j,P_i)} \rangle\rangle_t$ by executing the protocol for **Input Phase** of our UMPC protocol, with $c_I = nm$.

Theorem 3. *The protocol for* **Input Phase** *allows party P_i to generate t-$2D^+$-sharings of all the coefficients of his polynomial $f^{(P_i)}(x)$ with overwhelming probability. The protocol takes fifteen rounds, privately communicates $\mathcal{O}((n^4m+n^5)\kappa)$ bits and broadcasts $\mathcal{O}((n^4m+n^5)\kappa)$ bits. Moreover, $\mathcal{A}_t$ gets no information about the inputs of the honest parties.*

3. **Computation and Output Phase**: After preparation and input phase, the parties jointly compute the coefficients of the polynomial $F(x) = \sum_{i=1}^{n} r^{(i)}f^{(P_i)}(x)$ in a shared manner. And finally the coefficients of $F(x)$ are reconstructed by each party. In the **Output Phase**, each party locally evaluates $F(x)$ at each element of his private set. All the elements at which $F(x) = 0$ belongs to the intersection of the n sets with very high probability.

Theorem 4. *The protocol for Computation and Output phase takes two rounds and privately communicates $\mathcal{O}(n^4m^2\kappa)$ bits.*

PROOF: Follows from Lemma 12 by substituting $c_M = \mathcal{O}(nm^2), c_O = \mathcal{O}(nm)$ and $\mathcal{D} = 1$. $\qquad\square$

Now our final UMPSI protocol is: (a) Invoke **Preparation Phase**; (b) Invoke **Input Phase**; and (c) Invoke **Computation and Output Phase**.

Theorem 5. *MPSI protocol with $2t+1$ parties takes sixty four rounds, privately communicates $\mathcal{O}(m^2 n^4 \kappa)$ bits and broadcasts $\mathcal{O}((m^2 n^4 + n^5)\kappa)$ bits.*

References

1. Beaver, D.: Efficient multiparty protocols using circuit randomization. In: Feigenbaum, J. (ed.) CRYPTO 1991. LNCS, vol. 576, pp. 420–432. Springer, Heidelberg (1992)
2. Beerliová-Trubíniová, Z., Hirt, M.: Efficient multi-party computation with dispute control. In: Halevi, S., Rabin, T. (eds.) TCC 2006. LNCS, vol. 3876, pp. 305–328. Springer, Heidelberg (2006)
3. Beerliová-Trubíniová, Z., Hirt, M.: Simple and efficient perfectly-secure asynchronous MPC. In: Kurosawa, K. (ed.) ASIACRYPT 2007. LNCS, vol. 4833, pp. 376–392. Springer, Heidelberg (2007)
4. Beerliová-Trubíniová, Z., Hirt, M.: Perfectly-secure MPC with linear communication complexity. In: Canetti, R. (ed.) TCC 2008. LNCS, vol. 4948, pp. 213–230. Springer, Heidelberg (2008)
5. Ben-Or, M., Goldwasser, S., Wigderson, A.: Completeness theorems for non-cryptographic fault-tolerant distributed computation. In: STOC, pp. 1–10 (1988)
6. Chaum, D., Crépeau, C., Damgård, I.: Multiparty unconditionally secure protocols (extended abstract). In: STOC, pp. 11–19 (1988)
7. Cramer, R., Damgård, I.: Multiparty Computation, an Introduction. In: Contemporary Cryptography, Birkhuser Basel (2005)
8. Cramer, R., Damgård, I., Dziembowski, S., Hirt, M., Rabin, T.: Efficient multiparty computations secure against an adaptive adversary. In: Stern, J. (ed.) EUROCRYPT 1999. LNCS, vol. 1592, pp. 311–326. Springer, Heidelberg (1999)
9. Freedman, M.J., Nissim, K., Pinkas, B.: Efficient private matching and set intersection. In: Cachin, C., Camenisch, J.L. (eds.) EUROCRYPT 2004. LNCS, vol. 3027, pp. 1–19. Springer, Heidelberg (2004)
10. Gennaro, R., Rabin, M.O., Rabin, T.: Simplified VSS and fact-track multiparty computations with applications to threshold cryptography. In: PODC, pp. 101–111 (1998)
11. Goldreich, O., Micali, S., Wigderson, A.: How to play any mental game. In: STOC, pp. 218–229 (1987)
12. Hirt, M., Maurer, U.M.: Complete characterization of adversaries tolerable in secure multi-party computation. In: PODC, pp. 25–34 (1997)
13. Katz, J., Koo, C.Y.: Round-efficient secure computation in point-to-point networks. In: Naor, M. (ed.) EUROCRYPT 2007. LNCS, vol. 4515, pp. 311–328. Springer, Heidelberg (2007)
14. Kissner, L., Song, D.: Privacy-preserving set operations. In: Shoup, V. (ed.) CRYPTO 2005. LNCS, vol. 3621, pp. 241–257. Springer, Heidelberg (2005)
15. Li, R., Wu, C.: An unconditionally secure protocol for multi-party set intersection. In: Katz, J., Yung, M. (eds.) ACNS 2007. LNCS, vol. 4521, pp. 226–236. Springer, Heidelberg (2007)
16. Patra, A., Choudhary, A., Rangan, C.P.: Round efficient unconditionally secure multiparty computation protocol. In: Chowdhury, D.R., Rijmen, V., Das, A. (eds.) INDOCRYPT 2008. LNCS, vol. 5365, pp. 185–199. Springer, Heidelberg (2008)
17. Patra, A., Choudhary, A., Pandu Rangan, C.: Information theoretically secure multi party set intersection re-visited. In: Jacobson Jr., M.J., Rijmen, V., Safavi-Naini, R. (eds.) SAC 2009. LNCS, vol. 5867, pp. 71–91. Springer, Heidelberg (2009)
18. Rabin, T.: Robust sharing of secrets when the dealer is honest or cheating. J. ACM 41(6), 1089–1109 (1994)
19. Yao, A.C.: Protocols for secure computations. In: FOCS, pp. 160–164 (1982)

Non-committing Encryptions Based on Oblivious Naor-Pinkas Cryptosystems

Huafei Zhu and Feng Bao

I^{2}R, A*STAR, Singapore

Abstract. Designing non-committing encryptions tolerating adaptive adversaries, who are able to corrupt parties on the fly in the course of computation has been a challenge task. In this paper, we make progress in this area. First, we introduce a new notion called oblivious Naor-Pinkas cryptosystems that benefits us to extract the randomness used to generate local public keys and thus enable us to construct corresponding simulator for a given adaptive adversary in a real-world protocol. We then give a simple construction of non-committing encryptions based on oblivious Naor-Pinkas cryptosystems. We show that the proposed non-committing encryption scheme is provably secure against an adaptive PPT adversary assuming that the decisional Diffie-Hellman problem is hard.

Keywords: adaptive security, non-committing encryption, oblivious Naor-Pinkas cryptosystem, Naor-Pinkas randomizer.

1 Introduction

Designing protocols securely computing any function dates back to the papers by Yao [18] and Goldreich, Micali and Wigderson [11]. Goldreich, Micali and Wigderson [12] have shown how to securely compute any function in the computational setting. Ben-Or, Goldwasser and Wigderson [3] and independently Chaum, Crépeau and Damgård [6] have shown how to securely compute any function in the secure channel setting. These constructions are secure in the presence of non-adaptive adversaries. In contrary to folklore believes, problems are encountered when attempting to prove security in the adaptive adversary setting. Consider the scenario where an honest sender S sends a ciphertext c to a receiver R in an insecure channel. All communications are seen by an adaptive adversary. As long as the adversary $\mathcal{A}$ obtains c, it corrupts the sender S. By the security definition, a simulator $\mathcal{S}$ has to generate a dummy ciphertext and sends it to the uncorrupted R since it has no prior knowledge about the sender's input. When the adversary corrupts the simulated sender S, it expects to see all of S's internal data including the random bits used for the encryption. Thus, it may be the case that the dummy ciphertext c was generated as an encryption of m_0, and the simulated sender S now needs to convince the adversary that the ciphertext c is in fact an encryption of m_1. This task is impossible if standard public-key encryption schemes are used since a classic public-key encryption is a committed encryption in essence.

B. Roy and N. Sendrier (Eds.): INDOCRYPT 2009, LNCS 5922, pp. 418–429, 2009.

1.1 The State-of-the-Art

At STOC'96, Canetti, Feige, Goldreich and Naor [4] introduced a new cryptographic primitive called non-committing encryptions to deal with adaptive adversary in the context of multi-party computation. A non-committing encryption scheme is a two-party function $f(m, \perp) = (\perp, m)$ for communicating a message m over an insecure channel. Nielsen [17] has shown that no non-interactive communication protocol can be adaptively secure in the asynchronous model.

The research on non-committing encryption problem date back to the paper by Beaver and Haber [2]. Beaver and Haber's protocol depends on the use of erasure. Canetti et al [4] proposed the first non-committing encryption protocol in the non-erasure model. To encrypt 1 bit, $\Theta(k^2)$ public key bits are communicated. Later, Beaver [1] and Damgård and Nielsen [7] proposed more efficient constructions such that for communicating 1 bit only $\Theta(k)$-bit are communicated. We stress that all mentioned non-committing encryption schemes are formalized and analyzed in the stand-alone framework.

1.2 This Work

This paper constructs non-committing encryptions from oblivious Naor-Pinkas cryptosystems in the computational setting where all communications among parties are seen by adversaries. An oblivious Naor-Pinkas cryptosystem, as its name indicates, is in turn constructed from an instance of Naor and Pinkas randomizer. We will give a simple construction of non-committing encryptions based on oblivious Naor-Pinkas cryptosystems and show that the proposed non-committing encryption scheme is provably secure against any PPT adaptive adversary in the computational setting assuming that the decisional Diffie-Hellman problem is hard.

The idea: The communication channel in our model is insecure and asynchronous. The adversary adaptively corrupts a party during an execution of a real world protocol. The idea of our constructions is sketched below (please refer to Section 4.1 for more details):

- Let G be a cyclic group with order q, where $p = 2q + 1$, p and q are prime numbers. To communicate a bit $m \in \{0, 1\}$, S first generates a Diffie-Hellman quadruple pk_α and a non-Diffie-Hellman quadruple $pk_{1-\alpha}$ in G independently, where $\alpha \in \{0, 1\}$ is chosen uniformly at random by the sender S.
- Upon receiving (pk_0, pk_1), a receiver R chooses a bit $\beta \in \{0, 1\}$ uniformly at random and then produces (u_0, v_0) and (u_1, v_1), where (u_β, v_β) is computed from Naor-Pinkas randomizer while $(u_{1-\beta}, v_{1-\beta})$ is chosen randomly from G^2.
- Upon receiving (u_0, v_0) and (u_1, v_1), S checks the relationship $\mathcal{R}(u_\alpha, v_\alpha)$ using its secret key sk_α. If $\mathcal{R} = 1$, S sends Success to R, otherwise sends Unsuccess to the receiver R. Once a bit γ ($= \alpha = \beta$) is communicated successfully, S sends a ciphertext c ($= m \oplus \gamma$) to R and R decrypts c to obtain the message m.

A crucial feature of Naor-Pinkas randomizer is that it can be transferred into an oblivious cryptosystem immediately. The resulting oblivious Naor-Pinkas cryptosystem benefits us to extract randomness that is used to generate Diffie-Hellman quadruples and thus enables us to construct corresponding simulator for a given adaptive adversary in the real world non-committing encryption protocol.

What's new? The novelty of our implementation relies on the Naor-Pinkas randomizer rather than oblivious public-key encryptions. The application of Naor-Pinkas randomizer enables us to define a global key generator and local key generator in a separate way. The global key of an oblivious Naor-Pinkas cryptosystem will be used by all parties involved in the real-world protocol execution. The local public keys are oblivious. Thus, to simulate an adaptive adversary's behavior, we need only to extract randomness used to generate local key pk_α or local key $pk_{1-\alpha}$ without predetermination of α (hence the proposed scheme is secure against an adaptive adversary). The separation of a global public key and a local key generation algorithm of oblivious Naor-Pinkas cryptosystem benefits us for efficient randomness extraction. This is the most significant feature of our implementation differing from the state-of-the-art solutions.

We remark that the randomness used to generate global public-key (say, a large prime number p for generating Z_p^* and a cyclic group $G \subseteq Z_q$) must be extracted in the state-of-the-art constructions for communicating a bit. For example, to extract a randomness r_p for p, Damgård and Nielsen [7] use the following approach: picking p by drawing random numbers in some interval until a number is tested to primality by some probabilistic test. The r_p is set to these bits p, and bits used to test p using the primality. The extraction of random strings for generating generators of G and random elements in G is chosen in a natural way.

Our contribution: This paper aims to construct non-committing encryption schemes securely against any PPT adaptive adversary. The contribution of this paper is two-fold:

- in the first fold, a new notion which we call oblivious Naor-Pinkas cryptosystems is introduced and formalized. The oblivious Naor-Pinkas cryptosystem captures the following intuition — we can generate public keys without knowing the corresponding secret keys and interpret an non-obliviously generated public-keys as obliviously generated one, i.e., the randomness used to generate public-key can be efficiently extracted. The oblivious Naor-Pinkas cryptosystem comprise a global key generation algorithm and a local key generation algorithm in our model. The separation of key generation algorithms benefits us to extract randomness in a more efficient way since we need not to extract the global randomness (it is sufficient for us to extract randomness used to generate local keys since no encryption algorithm and decryption algorithm is defined in the oblivious Naor-Pinkas cryptosystem).
- in the second fold, a new implementation of non-committing encryption schemes is described and analyzed. We show that the proposed scheme is secure against any PPT adaptive adversary assuming that the classic decisional Diffie-Hellman problem is hard in G. That is, the simulator S in our proof does not rewind the real-world adversary A and thus it reaches the universally composable security.

Efficiency: According to the protocol described in Section 4.1, for communicating a bit, we need to communicate total $12k$ bits, where $8k$ is sent by S and $4k$ by R in a Success execution and $12k$ bits are wasted in a Unsuccess execution, where k is a security parameter. Thus, for communicating 1 bit, the expected $24k$ bits are communicated. To communicate 1 bit by applying the best implementation (say, [7]), the expected $32k$ bits are communicated.

Road-map: The rest of this paper is organized as follows: In Section 2, oblivious Naor-Pinkas cryptosystem is introduced and formalized; The functionality and security definition for non-committing encryption protocol is presented in Section 3. Our implementation of non-committing encryption scheme is described and analyzed in Section 4. We conclude our work in Section 5.

2 Oblivious Naor-Pinkas Cryptosystems

Naor-Pinkas randomizer: Let p be a large safe prime number, i.e., $p=2q+1$, p and q are prime numbers and $G \subseteq Z_p^*$ be a cyclic group of order q. For any $0 \neq x \in Z_q$, we define $\mathsf{DLog}_G(x) = \{(g, g^x) : g \in G\}$. On input $(g_1, h_1) \in \mathsf{DLog}_G(x_1)$, and $(g_2, h_2) \in \mathsf{DLog}_G(x_2)$, a mapping ϕ which we call Naor-Pinkas randomizer is defined below:

$$\phi((g_1, g_2, h_1, h_2) \times (s, t)) = (g_1^s g_2^t \bmod p, h_1^s h_2^t \bmod p), \quad \text{where } s, t \in Z_q$$

Denote $u = g_1^s g_2^t \bmod p$ and $v = h_1^s h_2^t \bmod p$. Naor and Pinkas [14] have shown that

- if $x_1 = x_2$ $(=x)$, then (u, v) is uniformly random in $\mathsf{DLog}_G(x)$;
- if $x_1 \neq x_2$, then (u, v) is uniformly random in G^2.

The Naor-Pinkas randomizer is a useful tool not only in cryptography and but also in other application scenarios. For example, Peikert, Vaikuntanathan and Waters [15] have presented a framework for efficient and composable oblivious transfer based on Naor-Pinkas randomizer. Freedman et. al [9] used the Naor-Pinkas randomizer for constructing keyword search and oblivious pseudo-random functions. Pinkas [16], Lindell and Pinkas [13] and Freedman [9] have successfully applied the Naor-Pinkas randomizer to privacy preserving data mining.

Naor-Pinkas encryption scheme: Given an instance of Naor-Pinkas randomizer ϕ, an encryption scheme can be derived immediately (such a derived encryption scheme is called Naor-Pinkas encryption scheme inherently, denoted by Φ). The Naor-Pinkas encryption scheme, consists of the following PPT algorithms: a global public-key generation algorithm $\mathcal{K}_{gpk}$, a local key generation algorithm $\mathcal{K}$ (*simply abbreviated as a key generation algorithm throughout the paper*), an encryption $\mathcal{E}$ and a decryption algorithm $\mathcal{D}$. More precisely,

- global public-key $\mathcal{K}_{gpk}$: on input a security parameter 1^k, $(G, p, q) \leftarrow \mathcal{K}_{gpk}(1^k)$, where $p = 2q + 1$, p and q are large prime numbers, and $G \subseteq Z_p^*$ is a cyclic group of order q; The global public-key gpk is (p, q, G).
- Encryption algorithm $\mathcal{E}$: on input gpk and a message $m \in G$, $\mathcal{E}$ invokes a local key generation algorithm $\mathcal{K}$ to generate two random generators g_1 and g_2 of G, and two elements h_1 and h_2 in G such that $(g_1, h_1) \in \mathsf{DLog}_G(x)$, and $(g_2, h_2) \in \mathsf{DLog}_G(x)$. The public key pk is $((g_1, h_1), (g_2, h_2))$, and the secret key sk is x. Let $(u, v) = \phi((g_1, g_2, h_1, h_2) \times (s, t))$, where $s, t \in_r Z_q$. The output of encryption algorithm is a ciphertext (u, mv);

- Decryption algorithm $\mathcal{D}$: on input a secret key x, gpk, pk and a ciphertext c $=(c_0, c_1)$, $\mathcal{D}$ outputs m by computing c_1/c_0^x.

Considering the following two distributions over $G \subseteq Z_p^*$ ($p=2q+1$, p, q are prime numbers and $< g > =G$ is a cyclic group with order q):

- Given a Diffie-Hellman quadruple g, g^x, g^y and g^{xy}, where $x, y \in Z_q$, are strings chosen uniformly at random;
- Given a random quadruple g, g^x, g^y and g^r, where $x, y, r \in Z_q$, are strings chosen uniformly at random.

An algorithm that solves the decisional Diffie-Hellman problem is a statistical test that can efficiently distinguish these two distributions. The decisional Diffie-Hellman assumption means that there is no such a polynomial statistical test. This assumption is believed to be true for many cyclic groups, such as the prime sub-group of the multiplicative group of finite fields. As an immediate application of Naor-Pinkas randomizer, we have the following claim

Lemma 1. *The derived Naor-Pinkas encryption scheme is semantically secure assuming that the decisional Diffie-Hellman problem is hard in G.*

Oblivious Naor-Pinkas cryptosystem: A simplified cryptosystem can be further derived from Naor-Pinkas encryption scheme. That is, we eliminate the encryption algorithm and decryption algorithm in Φ. Such a derived cryptosystem is called as an instance of oblivious Naor-Pinkas cryptosystem (see **Fig.1** for details). The interesting feature of oblivious Naor-Pinkas cryptosystem is that it allows us to generate public keys without knowing the corresponding secret keys and to explain a non-obliviously generated public-keys as one which is obliviously generated, i.e., the randomness used to generate public-key can be efficiently extracted.

Oblivious Naor-Pinkas Cryptosysems

Let $\mathcal{K}_{gpk}$ be a global public-key generator. Let $\mathcal{K}$ be a local key generation algorithm.

- on input a security parameter 1^k, $\mathcal{K}_{gpk}$ outputs a large safe prime number p ($p=2q+1$, q is also a prime number) and a cyclic group $G \subseteq Z_p^*$ of order q. The global key gpk is (p, q, G).
- on input $gpk=(p, q, G)$, $\mathcal{K}$ outputs two random generators g_1 and g_2 of G, and two elements h_1 and h_2 in G such that $h_i = g_i^x \bmod p$ ($i = 1, 2$). The public key pk is $((g_1, h_1), (g_2, h_2))$ and the secret key sk is $x \in Z_q$.

Naor-Pinkas Cryptosysems On input the public key pk ($=(g_1, h_1), (g_2, h_2)$), Naor-Pinkas randomizer ϕ outputs $\phi((g_1, g_2, h_1, h_2) \times (s, t)) = (g_1^s g_2^t \bmod p, h_1^s h_2^t \bmod p)$, where $s, t \in_r Z_q$. Let $u = g_1^s g_2^t \bmod p$ and $v = h_1^s h_2^t \bmod p$. The ciphertext (u, v) of oblivious Naor-Pinkas Cryptosysem can be viewed as a random ciphertext of the dummy message 1.

Fig. 1. Description of Oblivious Naor-Pinkas Cryptosystem

Definition 1. *Let $(\mathcal{K}_{gpk}, \mathcal{K}, \phi)$ be an instance of Naor-Pinkas cryptosystem with public-key generation algorithm $\mathcal{K}_{gpk}$, key generation algorithm $\mathcal{K}$ and randomizer ϕ. The Naor-Pinkas cryptosystem is called oblivious if there exists a PPT oblivious key generator $\mathcal{F}_k$ and a PPT oblivious output (or ciphertext) generator $\mathcal{F}_c$ such that the following conditions hold:*

- *oblivious key generator $\mathcal{F}_k$: Let $gpk \leftarrow \mathcal{K}_{gpk}(1^k)$, $(pk, sk) \leftarrow \mathcal{K}(1^k, gpk)$, and $pk' \leftarrow \mathcal{F}_k(1^k, gpk)$. The random variables pk and pk' are computationally indistinguishable;*
- *oblivious ciphertext generator $\mathcal{F}_c$: Let $gpk \leftarrow \mathcal{K}_{gpk}(1^k)$, $(pk, sk) \leftarrow \mathcal{K}(gpk)$, $c_1 \leftarrow \phi(gpk, pk)$ and $c_2 \leftarrow \mathcal{F}_c(gpk)$, the random variables (pk, c_1) and (pk, c_2) are computationally indistinguishable;*

Lemma 2. *The Naor-Pinkas cryptosystem is oblivious assuming that the decisional Diffie-Hellman problem is hard.*

Proof. On input gpk, $\mathcal{F}_k$ chooses (g_1', g_2', h_1', h_2') uniformly at random in G^4. Let (g_1, g_2, h_1, h_2) be a Diffie-Hellman quadruple generated by the genuine key generator $\mathcal{K}$ (recall that $\mathcal{K}$ is a Diffie-Hellman quadruple generator). As a result, assuming that the decisional Diffie-Hellman problem is hard over G, the random variables (g_1, g_2, h_1, h_2) and (g_1', g_2', h_1', h_2') are computationally indistinguishable.

Let (u, v) be an output (ie., a ciphertext) generated by Naor-Pinkas randomizer ϕ on input pk (recall that pk is a Diffie-Hellman quadruple generator over G). Let (u', v') be an element chosen uniformly at random in G^2. Let $c_1 \leftarrow (u, v)$ and $c_2 \leftarrow (u', v')$. As a result, (pk, c_1) and (pk, c_2), are computationally indistinguishable assuming that the decisional Diffie-Hellman problem is hard over G.

We remark that the idea for oblivious public key generation, i.e., generation of public-key without knowing the secret key, is not new. It seems to date back to De Santis and Persiano [8] in the context of non-interactive zero-knowledge proof.

3 Non-committing Encryptions: Functionality and Security Definition

The universally composable framework was proposed by Canetti for defining the security and composition of protocols [5]. In this framework one first defines an ideal functionality of a protocol and then proves that a particular implementation of this protocol operating in a given environment securely realized this functionality. The basic entities involved are n players, an adversary $\mathcal{A}$ and an environment $\mathcal{Z}$. The environment has access only to the inputs and outputs of the parties of π. It does not have direct access to the communication among the parties, nor to the inputs and outputs of the subroutines of π. The task of $\mathcal{Z}$ is to distinguish between two executions sketched below.

In the real world execution, the environment $\mathcal{Z}$ is activated first, generating particular inputs to the other players. Then the protocol π proceeds by having $\mathcal{A}$ exchange messages with the players and the environment. At the end of the protocol execution, the environment $\mathcal{Z}$ outputs a bit.

In the ideal world, the players are replaced by dummy parties, who do not communicate with each other. All dummy parties interact with an ideal functionality $\mathcal{F}$. When a dummy party is activated, it forwards its input to $\mathcal{F}$ and receives the output from the functionality $\mathcal{F}$. In addition, $\mathcal{F}$ may receives messages directly from the ideal world adversary $\mathcal{S}$ and may contain instructions to send message to $\mathcal{S}$. At the end of the ideal world execution, the environment $\mathcal{Z}$ outputs a bit.

Let $\mathrm{REAL}_{\pi,\mathcal{A},\mathcal{Z}}$ be $\mathcal{Z}$'s output after interacting with adversary $\mathcal{A}$ and players running protocol π; Let $\mathrm{IDEAL}_{\mathcal{F},\mathcal{S},\mathcal{Z}}$ be $\mathcal{Z}$'s output after interacting with $\mathcal{S}$ and $\mathcal{F}$ in the ideal execution. A protocol π securely realizes an ideal functionality $\mathcal{F}$ if $\mathrm{REAL}_{\pi,\mathcal{A},\mathcal{Z}}$ and $\mathrm{IDEAL}_{\mathcal{F},\mathcal{S},\mathcal{Z}}$ are computationally indistinguishable. For further details on the universally composable framework, please refer to [5].

The notion of non-committing encryption scheme introduced in [4] is a protocol used to realize secure channel in the presence of an adaptive adversary. In particular, this means that a simulator can build a fake transcript to the environment $\mathcal{Z}$, in such a way that the simulator can open this transcript to the actual inputs, that the simulator receives from the functionality when the parties get corrupted.

Let $\mathcal{N}$ be a non-information oracle which is a PPT Turing machine that captures the information leaked to the adversary in the ideal-world. That is, $\mathcal{N}$ is the oracle which takes $(\mathsf{Send}, sid, P, m)$ as input and outputs $(\mathsf{Send}, sid, P, |m|)$. Let ChSetup be a channel setup command which on inputs $(\mathsf{ChSetup}, sid, S)$ produces no output and (Corrupt be a corruption command which takes $(\mathsf{Corrupt}, sid, P)$ produces no output. The functionality of non-committing encryption secure channels defined below is due to Garay, Wichs and Zhou [10].

The ideal functionality $\mathcal{F}_{\mathrm{SC}}^{\mathcal{N}}$

Channel setup: upon receiving an input $(\mathsf{ChSetup}, sid, S)$ from party S, initialize the machine $\mathcal{N}$ and record the tuple $(sid, \mathcal{N})$. Pass the message $(\mathsf{ChSetup}, S)$ to R. In addition, pass this message to $\mathcal{N}$ and forward its output to $\mathcal{S}$;

Message transfer: Upon receiving an input $(\mathsf{Send}, sid, P, m)$ from party P, where $P \in \{S, R\}$, find a tuple $(sid, \mathcal{N})$, and if none exists, ignore the message. Otherwise, send the message $(\mathsf{Send}, sid, P, m)$ to the other party $\overline{P} = \{S, R\} \setminus \{P\}$. In addition, invoke N with $(\mathsf{Send}, sid, P, m)$ and forwards its output $(\mathsf{Send}, sid, P, |m|)$ to the adversary $\mathcal{S}$.

Corruption: Upon receiving a message $(\mathsf{Corrupt}, sid, P)$ from the adversary $\mathcal{S}$, send $(\mathsf{Corrupt}, sid, P)$ to $\mathcal{N}$ and forward its output to the adversary. After the first corruption, stop execution of $\mathcal{N}$ and give the adversary $\mathcal{S}$ complete control over the functionality.

Definition 2. *(due to [10]) We call the functionality $\mathcal{F}_{\mathrm{SC}}^{\mathcal{N}}$ a non-committing encryption secure channel. A real-world protocol π which realizes $\mathcal{F}_{\mathrm{SC}}^{\mathcal{N}}$ is called a non-committing encryption scheme.*

4 Non-committing Encryptions from Oblivious Naor-Pinkas Cryptosystems

In this section, we first describe an implementation of non-committing encryptions from oblivious Naor-Pinkas Cryptosystems. We then prove that the proposed non-committing scheme is secure against any PPT adaptive adversary in the standard computation complexity model assuming that the classic decisional Diffie-Hellman problem is hard in G.

4.1 Description of Non-committing Protocol

We sketch the idea for implementing non-committing encryptions based on oblivious Naor-Pinkas cryptosystems. A sender S with a bit $m \in \{0, 1\}$ first generates a Diffie-Hellman quadruple pk_α and a non-Diffie-Hellman quadruple $pk_{1-\alpha}$ independently, where $\alpha \in \{0, 1\}$ is chosen uniformly at random. Upon receiving (pk_0, pk_1), a receiver R chooses a bit $\beta \in \{0, 1\}$ uniformly at random and then produces (u_0, v_0) and (u_1, v_1), where (u_β, v_β) is computed from Naor-Pinkas randomizer while $(u_{1-\beta}, v_{1-\beta})$ is chosen randomly from G^2. Upon receiving (u_0, v_0) and (u_1, v_1), S checks the relationship $\mathcal{R}(u_\alpha, v_\alpha)$ using its secret key. If $\mathcal{R} = 1$, S sends Success to R, otherwise sends Unsuccess to the receiver R. Once a bit γ ($= \alpha = \beta$) is communicated successfully, S sends a ciphertext c ($= m \oplus \gamma$) to R and R decrypts c to obtain m. The details of the protocol is depicted below:

Step 1: S chooses a bit $\alpha \in \{0, 1\}$ uniformly at random and then performs the following computations (running an instance of Naor-Pinkas oblivious cryptosystems described in Section 2):

- on input a security parameter 1^k, S runs a global public-key generator $\mathcal{K}_{gpk}$. Let $(p, q, G) \leftarrow \mathcal{K}_{gpk}(1^k)$ and $gpk = (p, q, G)$, where p is a large safe prime number (i.e., $p=2q + 1$, q is a prime number) and G is a cyclic group with order q. We assume that the discrete logarithm problem over G is hard;
- on input gpk, a key generator algorithm $\mathcal{K}$ outputs (pk_α, sk_α), where $pk_\alpha = (g_1, g_2, h_1, h_2)$, g_1 and g_2 are two random generators of G, and h_1 and h_2 are two elements in G such that $(g_1, h_1) \in \mathsf{DLog}_G(x_\alpha)$, and $(g_2, h_2) \in \mathsf{DLog}_G(x_\alpha)$. $sk_\alpha = x_\alpha \in Z_q$;
- on input a security parameter gpk and $\alpha \in \{0, 1\}$, an oblivious key generator $\mathcal{F}_k$ outputs (g'_1, g'_2, h'_1, h'_2) which is chosen uniformly at random in G^4. Let $pk_{1-\alpha} = (g'_1, g'_2, h'_1, h'_2)$;
- S keeps the secret key sk_α, and sends (pk_0, pk_1) to R;

Step 2: Upon receiving (pk_0, pk_1), R chooses a bit $\beta \in \{0, 1\}$ uniformly at random and then performs the following computations:

- R chooses a random string $r_\beta = (s_\beta, t_\beta) \in (Z_q)^2$ and runs Naor-Pinkas randomizer ϕ on pk_β; Let $(u_\beta, v_\beta) = \phi(pk_\beta, r_\beta)$;
- R also chooses $(u_{1-\beta}, v_{1-\beta}) \in G^2$ uniformly at random;
- R then sends (u_0, v_0) and (u_1, v_1) to S.

Step 3: Upon receiving (u_0, v_0) and (u_1, v_1), S checks $v_\alpha \stackrel{?}{=} u_\alpha^{x_\alpha}$. If the equation is valid, then S outputs an index $\sigma = 1$ and sends σ to R indicating **Success** of 1-bit exchange (in case of **Success**, $\beta = \alpha$); Otherwise, S outputs an index $\sigma = 0$ and sends σ to R indicating **Unsuccess** of 1-bit exchange. S then goes back to **Step 1** and starts a new session with R;

Step 4: In case of **Success**, S sends a ciphertext c of a message $m \in \{0, 1\}$ by computing $c = m \oplus \alpha$;

Step 5: Upon receiving a ciphertext c, R obtains m by computing $c \oplus \beta$;

This ends the description of non-committing protocol.

4.2   The Proof of Security

Theorem 1. *The non-committing encryption scheme described in Section 4.1 is secure against any PPT adaptive adversary assuming that the decisional Diffie-Hellman problem is hard in G.*

Proof. There are four cases defined in the following proof, depending on when the real world adversary $\mathcal{A}$ makes its first corruption request:

- Case 1: the real world adversary $\mathcal{A}$ makes its first corruption request after a secure channel has been set up successfully;
- Case 2: the real world adversary $\mathcal{A}$ makes its first corruption request after the sender S has received R's first message;
- Case 3: the real world adversary $\mathcal{A}$ makes its first corruption request after S has generated its first message, but before S receives R's first message;
- Case 4: the real world adversary $\mathcal{A}$ makes its first corruption request before any messages are generated.

We show that in each case above there exists an ideal-world adversary S such that no environment $\mathcal{Z}$, on any input, can tell with non-negligible probability whether it is interacting with $\mathcal{A}$ and players running π, or with S and $\mathcal{F}_{SC}^{\mathcal{N}}$ in the ideal execution if the decisional Diffie-Hellman assumption holds.

To simplify the description of a simulator, we omit the explicit description of the non-information oracle $\mathcal{N}$ here and what follows since the non-commitment encryption scheme described in this paper is a well-structured protocol (informally, a well-structured protocol requires the message sizes and the number of rounds are completely determined by the protocol and are independent of the input values or random coins of the parties. For the details definition of well-structured protocol, please refer to [10]). We here and what follows, also omit the explicit checks that the simulator has seen the previous steps of the protocol.

Case 1: the real world adversary $\mathcal{A}$ makes its first corruption request after a secure channel has been set up successfully; The corresponding simulator S is defined below:

- The simulator S runs $\mathcal{K}_{gpk}$ to generate an instance of global public-key gpk, where $gpk = (p, q, G)$.

- Let $P_i \in \{S, R\}$ be the first corrupted party. The simulator corrupts the corresponding dummy party $\widetilde{P}_i$ in the ideal world and learns a message $m \in \{0, 1\}$ from the non-committing encryption functionality. Let $\gamma \leftarrow c \oplus m$. Since $\sigma = 1$, it follows that $\alpha = \beta = \gamma$, and thus this value is consistent with values $c = m \oplus \alpha$ and $m = c \oplus \beta$. Let γ denote the common value of α and β. S runs $\mathcal{K}$ independently to generate (pk_γ, sk_γ) and $(pk_{1-\gamma}, sk_{1-\gamma})$, where $pk_\gamma = (g_1, g_2, h_1, h_2)$ and $pk_{1-\gamma} = (g_1', g_2', h_1', h_2')$ such that $h_1 = g_1^{x_\gamma}$, $h_2 = g_2^{x_\gamma}$ and $h_1' = g_1'^{x_{1-\gamma}}$, $h_2' = g_2'^{x_{1-\gamma}}$, $sk_\gamma = x_\gamma$ and $sk_{1-\gamma} = x_{1-\gamma}$.
- on input Diffie-Hellman quadruples pk_γ and $pk_{1-\gamma}$, S runs Naor-Pinkas randomizer as honest parties to generate (u_γ, v_γ) and $(u_{1-\gamma}, v_{1-\gamma})$.

Given $(pk_{1-\gamma}, (u_{1-\gamma}, v_{1-\gamma}))$, the task of simulator S now is to convince the adversary $\mathcal{A}$ that pk_γ is a Diffie-Hellman quadruple and (u_γ, v_γ) is a random element in $\mathsf{DLog}_G(x_\gamma)$ while $pk_{1-\gamma}$ is a random quadruple and $(u_{1-\gamma}, v_{1-\gamma})$ is a random element in G^2.

To convince the adversary $\mathcal{A}$ that pk_γ is a Diffie-Hellman quadruple and (u_γ, v_γ) is a random element in $\mathsf{DLog}_G(x_\gamma)$, the simulator provides x_γ to $\mathcal{A}$. To convince the adversary $\mathcal{A}$ that $pk_{1-\gamma}$ is a random quadruple and $u_{1-\gamma}, v_{1-\gamma}$ is a random element in G^2, S will extract the random string $r_{1-\gamma}$ that has been used for generating $(pk_{1-\gamma}, (u_{1-\gamma}, v_{1-\gamma}))$ and show the existence of an oblivious key generation algorithm $\mathcal{F}_k$ such that the random variables $\mathcal{F}_k(r_{1-\gamma})$ and $(pk_{1-\gamma}, u_{1-\gamma}, v_{1-\gamma})$ are computationally indistinguishable.

To extract a random string from $pk_{1-\gamma}$, $(u_{1-\gamma}, v_{1-\gamma})$, we define a random string $r_{g_1'}$ that is a binary representation of g_1' in Z_p^*. Similarly, we define the string $r_{g_2'}$ representing for g_2', $r_{h_1'}$ for h_1', $r_{h_2'}$ for h_2', and $r_{u_{1-\gamma}}$ for $u_{1-\gamma}$ and $r_{v_{1-\gamma}}$ for $v_{1-\gamma}$. Let $r_{1-\gamma} = (r_{g_1'}, r_{g_2'}, r_{h_1'}, r_{h_2'}, r_{u_{1-\gamma}}, r_{v_{1-\gamma}})$. Let $(g_1', g_2', h_1', h_2', u_{1-\gamma}, v_{1-\gamma}) \leftarrow \mathcal{F}_k(r_{1-\gamma})$ (i.e., $\mathcal{F}_k$ is defined as an inverse mapping of the binary representation). It follows that the random variables $\mathcal{F}_k(r_{1-\gamma})$ and $(pk_{1-\gamma}, u_{1-\gamma}, v_{1-\gamma})$ are computationally indistinguishable assuming that the decisional Diffie-Hellman problem is hard. Consequently, the output simulator S is computationally indistinguishable from that of the real world execution. An earlier corruption in the course of a Success execution can be simulated similarly.

Case 2: a party is corrupted after $\sigma = 0$ is communicated in the course of a Unsuccess execution.

To simulate a party is corrupted after $\sigma = 0$ is communicated, we must construct a simulator S such that S outputs a bit α while R outputs a bit β $(= 1-\alpha)$. The detailed description of simulator S is described as below:

- S runs $\mathcal{K}_{gpk}$ to generate an instance of global public-key gpk, where $gpk = (p, q, G)$.
- S chooses a bit $\alpha \in \{0, 1\}$ uniformly at random (for the output of S in case that $\sigma = 0$). S runs $\mathcal{K}$ independently to generate (pk_α, sk_α) and $(pk_{1-\alpha}, sk_{1-\alpha})$, where $pk_\alpha = (g_1, g_2, h_1, h_2)$ and $pk_{1-\alpha} = (g_1', g_2', h_1', h_2')$ such that $h_1 = g_1^{x_\alpha}$, $h_2 = g_2^{x_\alpha}$ and $h_1' = g_1'^{x_{1-\alpha}}$, $h_2' = g_2'^{x_{1-\alpha}}$, $sk_\alpha = x_\alpha$ and $sk_{1-\alpha} = x_{1-\alpha}$.
- on input Diffie-Hellman quadruples pk_α and $pk_{1-\alpha}$, S runs Naor-Pinkas randomizer ϕ on input pk_α to generate (u_α, v_α) and chooses $(u_{1-\alpha}, v_{1-\alpha}) \in G^2$ uniformly at random.

Our task now is to show that the randomness used by the simulator $\mathcal{S}$ to generate $pk_{1-\alpha}$ and $(u_{1-\alpha}, v_{1-\alpha})$ can be extracted. This is an easy task since the same technique presented in **Case 1** can be applied here.

Using the same technique above, we can construct the corresponding simulator in **Case 3** and **Case 4**. Under the decisional Diffie-Hellman assumption is hard, no environment $\mathcal{Z}$, on any input, can tell with non-negligible probability whether it is interacting with $\mathcal{A}$ and players running π, or with $\mathcal{S}$ and $\mathcal{F}_{SC}^{\mathcal{N}}$ in the ideal execution.

5 Conclusion

In this paper, we have introduced and formalized a new notion called oblivious Naor-Pinkas cryptosystems which in turn, is constructed from Naor-Pinkas randomizer and proposed a novel implementation of non-committing encryptions based on oblivious Naor-Pinkas cryptosystems. The Naor-Pinkas oblivious cryptosystem benefits us to extract the randomness used to generate Diffie-Hellman quadruples and thus enables us to construct corresponding simulator for a given adaptive adversary in the real-world protocol execution. We have shown that the proposed non-committing encryption scheme is provably secure against an adaptive PPT adversary assuming that the decisional Diffie-Hellman problem is hard.

References

1. Beaver, D.: Plug and Play Encryption. In: Kaliski Jr., B.S. (ed.) CRYPTO 1997. LNCS, vol. 1294, pp. 75–89. Springer, Heidelberg (1997)
2. Beaver, D., Haber, S.: Cryptographic Protocols Provably Secure Against Dynamic Adversaries. In: Rueppel, R.A. (ed.) EUROCRYPT 1992. LNCS, vol. 658, pp. 307–323. Springer, Heidelberg (1993)
3. Ben-Or, M., Goldwasser, S., Wigderson, A.: Completeness Theorems for Non-Cryptographic Fault-Tolerant Distributed Computation (Extended Abstract). In: STOC 1988, pp. 1–10 (1998)
4. Canetti, R., Feige, U., Goldreich, O., Naor, M.: Adaptively Secure Multi-Party Computation. In: STOC 1996, pp. 639–648 (1996)
5. Canetti, R.: A new paradigm for cryptographic protocols. In: FOCS 2001, pp. 136–145 (2001)
6. Chaum, D., Crépeau, C., Damgård, I.: Multiparty Unconditionally Secure Protocols (Abstract). In: Pomerance, C. (ed.) CRYPTO 1987. LNCS, vol. 293, p. 462. Springer, Heidelberg (1988)
7. Damgård, I.B., Nielsen, J.B.: Improved non-committing encryption schemes based on a general complexity assumption. In: Bellare, M. (ed.) CRYPTO 2000. LNCS, vol. 1880, pp. 432–450. Springer, Heidelberg (2000)
8. De Santis, A., Persiano, G.: Zero-Knowledge Proofs of Knowledge Without Interaction (Extended Abstract). In: FOCS 1992, pp. 427–436 (1992)
9. Freedman, M.J., Ishai, Y., Pinkas, B., Reingold, O.: Keyword search and oblivious pseudorandom functions. In: Kilian, J. (ed.) TCC 2005. LNCS, vol. 3378, pp. 303–324. Springer, Heidelberg (2005)
10. Garay, J., Wichs, D., Zhou, H.-S.: Somewhat Non-Committing Encryption and Efficient Adaptively Secure Oblivious Transfer. In: Halevi, S. (ed.) CRYPTO 2009. LNCS, vol. 5677, pp. 231–249. Springer, Heidelberg (2009)

11. Goldreich, O., Micali, S., Wigderson, A.: Proofs that Yield Nothing But their Validity and a Methodology of Cryptographic Protocol Design (Extended Abstract). In: FOCS 1986, pp. 174–187 (1986)

12. Goldreich, O., Micali, S., Wigderson, A.: How to Play any Mental Game or A Completeness Theorem for Protocols with Honest Majority. In: STOC 1987, pp. 218–229 (1987)

13. Lindell, Y., Pinkas, B.: Privacy Preserving Data Mining. J. Cryptology 15(3), 177–206 (2002)

14. Naor, M., Pinkas, B.: Efficient oblivious transfer protocols. In: SODA 2001, pp. 448–457 (2001)

15. Peikert, C., Vaikuntanathan, V., Waters, B.: A framework for efficient and composable oblivious transfer. In: Wagner, D. (ed.) CRYPTO 2008. LNCS, vol. 5157, pp. 554–571. Springer, Heidelberg (2008)

16. Pinkas, B.: Cryptographic Techniques for Privacy-Preserving Data Mining. SIGKDD Explorations 4(2), 12–19 (2002)

17. Nielsen, J.B.: Separating random oracle proofs from complexity theoretic proofs: The non-committing encryption case. In: Yung, M. (ed.) CRYPTO 2002. LNCS, vol. 2442, pp. 111–126. Springer, Heidelberg (2002)

18. Yao, A.C.-C.: Protocols for Secure Computations (Extended Abstract). In: FOCS 1982, pp. 160–164 (1982)

Oblivious Multi-variate Polynomial Evaluation

Gérald Gavin[1] and Marine Minier[2]

[1] ERIC laboratory, Université Lyon 1 (UCBL)
43 bd du 11 nov 1918 - 69622 Villeurbanne - France
`gerald.gavin@univ-lyon1.fr`
[2] Lyon University - CITI Laboratory - INSA de Lyon
6, avenue des arts, 69621 Villeurbanne Cedex - France
`marine.minier@insa-lyon.fr`

Abstract. In this paper, we propose a protocol for Oblivious Polynomial Evaluation (OPE) considering a multi-variate polynomial. There are two parties, Alice who has a secret multi-variate polynomial f and Bob who has an input $x = (x_1, ..., x_T)$. Thus, Bob wants to compute $f(x)$ without any information leakage: Alice learns nothing about x and Bob learns only what can be inferred from $f(x)$. In [4], the authors proposed a solution for this problem using Oblivious Transfer (OT) protocol only. In this paper, we propose efficient OPE protocols for the multi-variate case based upon additive and multiplicative homomorphic encryption schemes defined on the same domain. Our protocol only reveals the number of monomials.

Keywords: Homomorphic encryption schemes, Oblivious Polynomial Evaluation (OPE), semantic security.

1 Introduction

Multi-Party computation (MPC) has been widely studied in the last few decades in the cryptographic community. It refers to a game where several players $P_1, \cdots P_n$ knowing respectively private values $(x_1, \cdots, x_n)$ want to evaluate the value $f(x_1, \cdots, x_n)$ where f is some publicly known function with n variables. Each player does not learn anything about the private inputs of the other players, except what is implied by the output result $f(x_1, \cdots, x_n)$.

The basic block of MPC is Oblivious Transfer (OT) introduced by Rabin in [17] and widely studied by Even, Goldreich et Lempel in [7]. In this last paper, a 1-out-2 OT protocol is proposed. It involves two parties, a sender, Alice, whose inputs are 2 secret values x_0 and x_1 and a receiver, Bob, whose input is a value $b \in \{0, 1\}$. At the execution end of the protocol Bob receives x_b without knowing x_{1-b} and Alice does not know b. The generalization of this problem known under the name of MPC was solved by Yao in [19] for every function f with finite domain and finite image in a constant-round protocol. This result was improved in [10] with weaker assumptions (i.e. the existence of OT is sufficient for general oblivious function evaluation). In [13], the authors improved the Yao result. They proposed efficient interactive evaluation of generic functions in a constant

B. Roy and N. Sendrier (Eds.): INDOCRYPT 2009, LNCS 5922, pp. 430–442, 2009.
© Springer-Verlag Berlin Heidelberg 2009

set of rounds in the presence of malicious adversaries. However, according to the authors, these general protocols "can not compete with protocols that are constructed for specific tasks".

Among the MPC problems, a particular one concerns Oblivious Polynomial Evaluation (OPE) first introduced by Naor and Pinkas in [14] and by Kiayias and Yung in [12]. In this case, one player possesses a polynomial P ($P(x) \in F[x]$ where F is a finite field) and the other player has a value $a \in F$. The second player wants to evaluate $P(a)$ without learning anything on P whereas the first player learns nothing about a. In [14] and in [1], the authors solve this problem describing three particular protocols based on two intractability assumptions: the polynomial reconstruction problem and the polynomial list reconstruction problem. The proposed protocols rely on hiding first the polynomial P in a bivariate polynomial and the value a in an univariate polynomial. In the multi-variate case, using this technique leads to an exponential complexity (all monomials of degree less than d should be considered in the circuit[1]). Moreover, in most of existing protocols, the degree d of P must be publicly known. In [6], Cramer and al. propose secure protocols to evaluate arithmetical circuits. They can be used to build OPE protocols. The protocols used to evaluate the multiplication gates are interactive. Thus, the computational complexity is really high.

In this paper, we focus on the multivariate version of OPE, i.e. the input a becomes a vector of T components $a = (a_1, \cdots, a_T)$ belonging to a same set F (most of times a finite field). In this case, f becomes a multi-variate polynomial from F^T into F. Two particular cases could be considered: the non-interactive case which is a really hard problem solved in [18] and the interactive one where the two parties interact as proposed in [4], [16] or in [1].

In this paper, we develop an OPE protocol for the multi-variate case (denoted by OMPE) revealing only m the number of monomials; where the set F is the group Z_n^* where n is the product of two large primes. The main idea is to use here two homomorphic encryption functions defined over the same domain. The first homomorphic encryption function is an additive semantically secure one defined over Z_n (denoted by E_0) and the second one defined over Z_n^* is multiplicatively homomorphic (denoted by E_1). As noticed in [18], homomorphic encryption schemes are closely related to and useful in secure circuit evaluation and the existence of a fully homomorphic function will solve the problem of a non-interactive OMPE protocol secure in the malicious model. Such a "perfect" function has been recently proposed by C. Gentry in [9] using ideal lattices.

This paper is organized as follows. Section 2 introduces classical homomorphic schemes and the underlying security notions used in public key cryptography. Section 3 deals with the modified versions of some homomorphic public key encryption schemes and especially introduces a new multiplicative semantically secure homomorphic encryption scheme defined over Z_n^*. In Section 4, we present our OMPE protocol based upon the previous homomorphic functions E_0 and E_1 and proved secure in the semi-honest model. It is also shown that parties don't

---

[1] The number of monomials of degree d is equal to C_{T+d-1}^d where T is the variables number.

get any advantage by deviating from the protocol. Moreover, in Section 4.3, we compare our protocol with the existing ones before concluding in Section 5.

2   Homomorphic Encryption Schemes

Several encryption schemes have been shown homomorphic. Concretely, this means that $Dec(Enc(x_1) \otimes Enc(x_2)) = x_2 \odot x_2$.

If $\odot$ is the addition (resp. multiplication), the encryption scheme is additively (resp. multiplicatively) homomorphic. Such homomorphic property is willing as soon as computations over encrypted data are requested. As far as we know, there does not exist a secure encryption scheme either multiplicatively and additively homomorphic. Finding such a protocol is very challenging and this paper can be interpreted in this sense. Indeed, we propose to build an interactive multiplicatively and additively homomorphic encryption scheme by considering homomorphic encryption schemes defined over the same domain Z_n^*. Generally, additive homomorphic encryption schemes are defined over Z_n while multiplicative ones are defined over Z_n^*. Furthermore, in order to ensure security, these encryption schemes should be semantically secure. This security notion is based on the well-known notion of indistinguishability between random variables families.

Definition 1. (*Semantic security*) *We say that a Public Key Encryption scheme $S = (Gen, Enc, Dec)$ is semantically secure if for every p.p.t algorithm A, for every M (such that for any public key pk, $M(pk) \in D_{pk}^2$ with D_{pk} the definition domain of Enc_{pk}) and for every polynomial p, for all k sufficiently large,*

$$P\left[\begin{array}{l} A(1^k, pk, x_0, x_1, c) = x | (pk, sk) \leftarrow Gen(1^k); \\ \{x_0, x_1\} \leftarrow M(pk); x \leftarrow \{x_0, x_1\}; c \leftarrow Enc_{pk}(x) \end{array} \right] \leq \frac{1}{2} + \frac{1}{p(k)}.$$

In other words, finding two messages x_0, x_1 such that a polynomial time algorithm can distinguish between $c \in Enc_{pk}(x_0)$ and $c \in Enc_{pk}(x_1)$ is impossible. We have to notice that any semantically secure encryption scheme should be probabilist. The above definition is based on indistinguishability of the distribution of ciphertexts created by encrypting two different values. Stronger security notions have been defined. However, this notion is sufficient to prove the security of the protocols of this paper. Let us now shortly describe the main famous homomorphic schemes.

Paillier's encryption scheme [15]. The public key pk is a k-bit RSA modulus $n = pq$ chosen at random and an element $g \in Z_{n^2}^*$ of order divisible by n. The secret key sk is $\lambda(n) = (p-1)(q-1)$. A value $x \in Z_n$ is encrypted by $Enc_{pk}(x) \in Z_{n^2}^*$ as follows: $Enc_{pk}(x) = g^x r^n \mod n^2$ where r is an integer randomly chosen in Z_n^* For a given cipher c, the encrypted value can be recovered with the following function Dec_{sk}

$$Dec_{sk}(c) = \frac{L(c^{\lambda(n)} \mod n^2)}{L(g^{\lambda(n)} \mod n^2)} \mod n$$

with $L(u) = \frac{u-1}{n}$ and $\lambda(n)$ the Carmicharel function. This scheme is additively homomorphic. This encryption scheme has been shown semantically secure under the DCRA assumption.

Goldwasser-Micali encryption scheme [11]. This scheme encrypts a bit $b \in \{0,1\}$. let $n = pq$, with p and q unknown large prime numbers. The private key is (p, q) and the public key (n, y) such that $y \in J_n$ and $y \notin QR(n)$. Then, b is encrypted as follows: $Enc_{pk}(b) = y^b x_i^2$ where x_i randomly chosen in J_n.

The decryption function consists in noticing that $(Enc_{sk}(b) \in QR(n)) \Leftrightarrow (b = 0)$. This encryption scheme is additively (boolean addition) homomorphic and semantically secure under the DQRA assumption.

El Gamal's encryption scheme [8]. Let G be a cyclic group, u a generator of G, s a number randomly chosen in $\{1, \cdots, |G|\}$ and $v = u^s$. The public key is (u, v) and the private key is s. For all $x \in G$, the encryption process is: $Enc_{pk}(x) = (u^r, v^r x)$ where r is randomly chosen in $\{1, \cdots, |G|\}$. The decryption function consists in computing $v^r = (u^s)^r = (u^r)^s$. Then, by inverting v^r, the encrypted value is given by $Dec_{sk}(c_1, c_2) = c_2 c_1^{-s}$.

This encryption scheme is multiplicatively homomorphic and semantically secure if and only if the DDH assumption holds for G. However, DDH assumption is not satisfied for $G = Z_n^*$ [5].

3   El Gamal's Encryption Scheme over Z_n^*

As seen previously, El Gamal is secure if the underlying group G satisfies the DDH property. It is well-known that groups Z_n^* do not satisfy this property. In this section, by assuming that subgroups of Z_n^* satisfy this property, new encryption schemes based on the DDH problem are proposed. Those schemes are proved to be multiplicatively homomorphic and semantically secure.

3.1   Domains Z_p^*

In this section, let p be a large strong prime number and J_p is the set of $x \in Z_p^*$ having a Jacobi symbol equal to $+1$. In this case, -1 has a Jacobi symbol equal to -1 (as p is a strong prime number, $(p-1)/2$ is odd). Thus, if $x \in J_p$ then $-x \notin J_p$. El Gamal's encryption scheme defined over the cyclic group $G = Z_p^*$ is not semantically secure. Indeed, 2 encrypted values with different Jacobi symbol can be distinguished (see [5]). We propose to extend El Gamal's encryption scheme over Z_p^*.

Assumption. DDH property holds over J_p.

According to this assumption, El Gamal's encryption scheme defined over J_p is semantically secure. As we have seen in the previous section, it consists in choosing a generator $u \in J_p$ and to encrypt a value $x \in J_p$ by $(u^r, v^r x)$ where $v = u^s$ for a secret $s \in \{1, \cdots, |J_p|\}$ and r a number randomly chosen in $\{1, \cdots, |J_p|\}$. The challenge is to extend the domain from J_p to Z_p^*. To achieve this, bx, instead of x, is encrypted with the previous encryption function where b is a random bit. The random bit b is encrypted with the homomorphic Goldwasser-Micali encryption function. The following definition precises it.

Definition 2. Let $S_{EGZ} = (Gen, Enc, Dec)$ be the encryption scheme defined by,

- $Gen(1^k) = (pk, sk)$ with $pk = (pk_1, p, u, v)$ and $sk = (sk_1, s)$ where s is randomly chosen $\{1, \cdots, (p-1)/2\}$, u a generator of J_p, $v = u^s$ and (pk_1, sk_1) generated by Goldwasser-Micali cryptosystem.
- for $x \in Z_p^*$, $Enc_{pk}(x) = (u^r, (-1)^b v^r x, Enc_{pk_1}(b))$ where r is randomly chosen in $\{1, \cdots, (p-1)/2\}$ and b randomly chosen in $\{0, 1\}$.
- Let (c_1, c_2, c_3) a cipher. $Dec_{sk} = (-1)^{Dec_{sk_1}(c_3)} c_1^{-s} c_2$

First, the correctness of this scheme is straightforward. The encryption scheme is also homomorphic: let $x, x' \in Z_p^*$ and $((c_1, c_2, c_3), (c'_1, c'_2, c'_3)) = (Enc_{pk}(x), Enc_{pk}(x'))$. By using homomorphic properties of El Gamal's and Goldwasser-Micali's encryption schemes we state the homomorphic property

$$Dec_{sk}(c_1 c'_1, c_2 c'_2, c_3 c'_3) = (-1)^{Dec_{sk_1}(c_3 c'_3)} (u^r u^{r'})^{-s} v^r v^{r'} (-1)^b x (-1)^{b'} x'$$
$$= (-1)^{b \oplus b'} u^{-s(r+r')} u^{s(r+r')} (-1)^{b+b'} xx'$$
$$= xx'$$

The security of this encryption scheme can be reduced to the security of the Goldwasser-Micali encryption scheme and to the DDH assumption over J_p.

Theorem 1. If Goldwasser-Micali encryption scheme is semantically secure and if DDH holds over J_p then S_{EGZ} is semantically secure.

Proof. The proof is given in Appendix A.

3.2   Domains Z_{pq}^*

This encryption scheme can be extended to domain Z_n^* with $n = pq$, with p and q large strong prime numbers. We denote by $QR(n)$ the cyclic group of quadratic residues (this group is cyclic because p and q are strong prime numbers). The following assumption is made.

Assumption. DDH property holds over $QR(n)$.

Let u be a generator of $QR(n)$, s a secret number randomly chosen in $\{1, \cdots, (p-1)(q-1)/4\}$, and $v = u^s$. Let's consider a square root unit β which does not belong to J_n. As p and q are strong primes, $-1 \in J_n$. Thus $\beta \neq -1$. As before, the idea consists in encrypting $x(-1)^{b_1}\beta^{b_2}$ (instead of x) where b_1 and b_2 are random bits. Encrypting the two bits b_1 and b_2 with the Micali-Golwasser scheme ensures homomorphic properties:

Definition 3. *Let $S_{GZ} = (Gen, Enc, Dec)$ be the encryption scheme defined by,*

- *$Gen(1^k) = (pk, sk)$ with $pk = (pk_1, n = pq, u, v)$ and $sk = (sk_1, s)$ where s is randomly chosen $\{1, \cdots, (p-1)(q-1)/4\}$, u a generator of $QR(n)$, $v = u^s$, p and q strong prime numbers of size k and (pk_1, sk_1) public and private key generated by the Goldwasser-Micali cryptosystem.*
- *for $x \in Z_n^*$, $Enc_{pk}(x) = (u^r, v^r(-1)^{b_1}\beta^{b_2}x, Enc_{pk_1}(b_1), Enc_{pk_1}(b_2))$ where r is randomly chosen in $\{1, \cdots, (p-1)(q-1)/4\}$ and b_1, b_2 randomly chosen in $\{0, 1\}$.*
- *Let (c_1, c_2, c_3, c_4) a cipher.*
  $Dec_{sk}(c_1, c_2, c_3, c_4) = \beta^{Dec_{sk_1}(c_4)}(-1)^{Dec_{sk_1}(c_3)}c_1^{-s}c_2$

Theorem 2. *Assuming DDH over $QR(n)$ and assuming the semantic security of Goldwasser-Micali's encryption scheme, S_{GZ} is multiplicatively homomorphic and semantically secure.*

Proof. (Sketch) First, we prove that the encryption scheme is secure over J_n by arguing in the same way than in the proof of theorem 1. Then, by considering the square root unit β, the security over Z_n^* can be proven by the same way. $\square$

Remark 1. Let's notice that the factorization of n is neither public nor private. If the factorization of n is unknown then $|QR(n)| = (p-1)(q-1)/4$ is also unknown. However, to encrypt a value, it is needed to randomly choose an integer r such that $r \mod |QR(n)|$ is uniform over $\{0, .., |QR(n)| - 1\}$. It suffices to notice that $r \mod |QR(n)|$ is indistinguishable to the uniform distribution when r is randomly chosen in $\{1, ..., n^2\}$.

4 Oblivious Multivariate Polynomial Evaluation (*OMPE*)

In this section, we will describe an *OMPE* protocol based on two homomorphic public key encryption schemes defined on the same domain. For instance, we could consider the domain Z_n where n is a RSA modulus. Over such a domain, Paillier's scheme is an additively homomorphic encryption scheme and El Gamal's encryption scheme (adapted in the previous section) is multiplicatively homomorphic. Now, let us see how to use those two schemes to build an OMPE secure protocol.

So first, Alice has a multi-variate polynomial function $f : Z_n^{*T} \to Z_n$ and Bob has a vector $x = (x_i)_{i=1..T} \in Z_n^*$. Alice's polynomial f is written as a sum of monomials m_j.

$$m_j(x_1, \cdots, x_T) = a_j \prod_{k=1}^{d_j} x_{i_{jk}} \text{ and } f(x_1, \cdots, x_T) = \sum_{j=1}^{m} m_j(x_1, \cdots, x_T)$$

where d_j is the degree of the monomial m_j and m is the monomials number. In our protocol, m is revealed while the coefficients a_i, the degree d of the polynomial and the variables belonging to each monomial $(m_j)_{j=1...m}$ are kept secret.

Bob generates an additively homomorphic encryption function E_0 and a multiplicatively homomorphic one E_1 defined over Z_n^*. Alice has an encryption $E_1(x)$ for an unknown value $x \in Z_n^*$. The protocol *Mult2Add* allows Alice to get $E_0(x)$ while nothing is leaked about x.

4.1   The Protocol *Mult2Add*

Algorithm 1. *Mult2Add* protocol

Require: Let k be a security parameter. Alice has an encrypted value $E_1(x)$ of an unknown value $x \in Z_n^*$

  Alice generates a k-uplet of random bits $(a_i)_{i=1..k}$ such that $\exists i_0 \in \{1, ..., k\}, a_{i_0} = 1$ and a k-uplet of random numbers $(r_i, s_i)_{i=1..k}$ with $r_i, s_i \in Z_n^*$. Let A be the set defined as $A = \{i = 1...k | a_i = 1\}$

  Alice sends $Y_i = E_1(r_i x^{a_i})$ for $i = 1...k$

  Bob sends $S_i = E_0(D_1(Y_i))$ for $i = 1...k$

  Alice outputs $Y = S_{i_0}^{r_{i_0}^{-1}} \prod_{i \notin A}(S_i E_0(-r_i))^{s_i} \prod_{i \in A \setminus \{i_0\}}((S_{i_0}^{r_{i_0}^{-1}})^{-1} S_i^{r_i^{-1}})^{s_i}$

It is easy to check the correctness of the protocol in the semi-honest model. Furthermore, if Bob sends a wrong vector S then the output is an (encrypted) random number with a high probability. Bob should guess the a_i values: if there exists $i \notin A$ such that $S_i \neq E_0(r_i)$ or $i \in A$ such that S_i and S_{i_0} does not encrypt the same values then the output Y encrypts a random value. The probability to guess if $a_i = 0$ or 1 for all $i = 1...k$ exponentially decreases with k.

Proposition 1. *Mult2Add satisfies the following properties:*

1. *It is secure in the semi-honest model.*
2. *If Bob does not follow the protocol then Alice (assumed honest) outputs a random encrypted value with probability closed to 1.*

Proof. Let's prove the two assertions.

1. The correctness can be deduced by homomorphic properties. Indeed, $S_{i_0}^{r_{i_0}^{-1}} =$
   $E_0(r_{i_0}^{-1} r_{i_0} x) = E_0(x)$
   $\forall i \notin A,\ S_i E_0(-r_i))^{s_i} = (E_0(r_i - r_i))^{s_i} = E_0(0)$
   $\forall i \in A \setminus \{i_0\},\ ((S_{i_0}^{r_{i_0}^{-1}})^{-1} S_i^{r_i^{-1}})^{s_i} = ((E_0(x))^{-1} E_0(x))^{-s_i}$
   $= E_0(0)^{s_i} = E_0(0)$
   Bob receives k random values and Alice k encryptions. As the homomorphic encryption schemes are assumed semantically secure, Alice's view and Bob's view can be simulated by generating k random numbers.

2. Let's suppose that Bob does not follow the protocol by sending invalid encryptions. In this case, Alice stops the protocol. The second way to not follow the protocol is to send valid encryptions of wrong values. Let's denote by v_i the encrypted value by S_i, i.e $D_0(S_i) = v_i$ and let's suppose there is $i' \in \{1, \cdots, k\}$ such that $v_{i'} \neq r_{i'} x^{a_{i'}}$. We can distinguish two cases:

   - *First case :* $i' \notin A$. Thus, $S_{i'} E_0(-r_{i'}))^{s_{i'}} = E_0(v_{i'} - r_{i'}))^{s_{i'}} = E_0(s_{i'}(v_{i'} - r_{i'})))$ is a random number (because $s_{i'}$ was chosen randomly). So the output Y encrypts a random value.
   - *Second case :* $i' \in A$. If there is $j \in A$ such that $v_i = r_i x^{a_i}$ then $((S_{i_0}^{r_{i_0}^{-1}})^{-1} S_{i'}^{r_{i'}^{-1}})^{s_{i'}}$ or $((S_{i_0}^{r_{i_0}^{-1}})^{-1} S_j^{r_j^{-1}})^{s_j}$ is a randomly drawn over Z_n^*. The output Y encrypts a random value.

Thus, in order to not output a random value without following the protocol, Bob should encrypt the correct value for each $i \notin A$ and an incorrect value for each $i \in A$. So, Bob should guess if $i \in A$ or $i \notin A$ for all $i = 1..k$. As Alice chooses A secretly and Bob only receives encrypted random values independent of A, the probability to achieves this is equal to $(2^k - 1)^{-1}$ because there are $2^k - 1$ non-empty sets $A \subseteq \{1, \cdots, k\}$.   □

4.2 The Complete *OMPE* Protocol

The *OMPE* protocol (described in Alg. 2) could thus be directly deduced from the *Mult2Add* protocol. Using homomorphic properties of E_1, Alice computes the encryption $E_1(m_j(x_1, \cdots, x_T))$ for all monomial values $(m_j)_{j=1...m}$. Then, she executes *Mult2Add* to get $E_0(m_j(x_1, \cdots, x_T))$. Thus, she can compute $E_0(f(x_1, \cdots, x_T))$ by using homomorphic properties. The *Mult2Add* executions number is equal to the number of monomials. This number is learnt and outputted by Bob.

Algorithm 2. *OMPE* protocol

Require: Alice has a polynomial function $f(x_1, \cdots, x_T) = \sum_{j=1}^m m_j(x_1, \cdots, x_T)$
   where m_j is a monomial function of degree d_j, i.e. $m_j = a_j \prod_{k=1}^{d_j} x_{i_{jk}}$.
Require: Bob has a vector $x = (x_i)_{i=1...T}$
   Bob sends $E_1(x_i)$ for all $i = 1..T$
   Alice computes $E_1(m_j(x_1, \cdots, x_T)) = \prod_{k=1}^{d_j} E_1(x_{i_{jk}})$ for all $j = 1...m$
   Alice and Bob execute *Mult2Add* on the input $E_1(m_j(x_1, \cdots, x_T))$ for all $j = 1...m$

   Alice computes $E_0(f(x)) = \prod_{j=1}^m (E_0(m_j(x_1, \cdots, x_T)))^{a_j}$ and sends it.
   Bob outputs $D_0(E_0(f(x)))$ and m.

Theorem 3. *OMPE satisfies the following properties.*

1. *It is secure in the semi-honest model.*
2. *It is private against any adversary controlling Alice.*
3. *It is secure against any adversary controlling Bob.*

Proof. Let's prove the three assertions.

1. The security in the semi-honest model is implied by the security of *Mult2Add* (see proposition 1). Knowing the output m and $f(x)$, the simulation of Bob's view simply consists in generating km random numbers. As encryptions schemes are assumed semantically secure, encryptions are indistinguishable from random values. So, the simulation of Alice's view consists in generating $T + km$ random numbers.

2. Let A be an adversary controlling Alice. It does not learn anything in protocol *OMPE* because it only receives encrypted values. The semantic security of the encryption schemes ensures privacy.

3. Let A be an adversary controlling Bob. The only way to deviate from the protocol is to send wrong values in protocol *Mult2Add*. By doing this, according to proposition 1, the last received encryption encrypts a random values. Consequently, as the km previous ones are also random, A received only random values. As Alice (the honest party) does not outputs anything, the protocol is secure against A (the simulation of the protocol simply consists in generating $km + 1$ random values to A).   □

Remark 2. The protocol is private but not secure against an adversary A controlling Alice. Indeed, in each execution of *Mult2Add*, A can compute k monomial values. So f can be a polynomial with km monomials (instead of m). As A can choose f arbitrarily (f is not committed), this advantage is not relevant is many applications.

Remark 3. To be rigorous, Bob should prove to Alice that n is an RSA modulus. Zero-knowledge proofs based on Boneh's test [2] can be built. In few words, Bob sends an encryption (with an additively homomorphic encryption function defined over a large domain, e.g. Z_{6n}) of p and q. By using the protocol *Multiplication* in [6], Alice gets encryptions of $n = pq$ and $\lambda(n) = (p - 1)(q - 1)$. Then, she checks that the first encryption encrypts (she asks to Bob to decrypt it) n, chooses $\alpha \in \{n^2, ..., n^2 + n\}$ and shares $\alpha\lambda(n)$, i.e. Alice chooses a random values in $s_1 \in \{0, ..., \alpha\lambda(n)\} \equiv^s \{0, ..., n^3\}$ and Bob gets a random value s_2 such that $s_1 + s_2 = \alpha\lambda(n)$. Then, Alice and Bob randomly choose basis $a \in Z_n$ and respectively compute $v_1 = g^{s_1} \mod n$ and $v_2 = g^{s_2} \mod n$. Alice is convinced that n is a RSA modulus if $v_1 v_2 = 1 \mod n$ for several basis a.

4.3   Complexity Analysis

The complexity of the proposed protocol is $O(Tm \log d)$. To encrypt all monomial values, Alice makes $O(Tm \log d)$ modular multiplications. The number of encryptions/decryptions/exponentiations made in *Mult2Add* is bounded by $T + 5mk$ (k being the security parameter of *Mult2Add*[2]).

---

[2] Note that if the monomial number m is large, Mult2Add can be modified in order reduce the constant k by computing all the encryptions $E_0(m_j/a_j)$ in the same time.

When compared to the other approaches, this protocol is still efficient. Oblivious evaluation of polynomials was initially proposed by Naor and Pinkas in [14]. They proposed efficient OPE protocols based on polynomial reconstruction. This approach has been extended to multivariate case by Ben-Ya'akov in [1]. The computational complexity of this last protocol is about $O\left(C_{d+T}^T T^3\right)$ elementary operations without taking into account the OT evaluations.

Other approaches deal with homomorphic encryptions schemes. Several interactive protocols as the one described in [6] have been built to securely evaluate arithmetical circuits. Addition gates evaluation are directly ensured by homomorphic properties. Multiplication gates are evaluated by using an interactive protocol. Thus, the multiplicative gates number is revealed while our protocol reveals the additive gates number. So these protocols can not be directly compared. In [6], a multiplication gate requires 6 modular exponentiations. So the modular exponentiations number is $O(T + \sum_{j=1}^{m}(d_j - 1))$ where d_j is the degree of the monomial m_j whereas our protocol requires $O(m + T)$ modular exponentiations.

4.4   Extension over Z_n^T

The *OMPE* protocol can be extended to polynomials $f : Z_n^T \to Z_n$ by decomposing an input $x_i = \alpha + x_i'$ where $\alpha \in Z_n^*$ is a random value ensuring that $x_i' \neq 0$ for all $i = 1...T$. The polynomial f can be expressed as a sum of monomials defined over the variables $\alpha, x_1', \cdots, x_T'$. The problem is that the monomial numbers exponentially grows with respect to the degree d of f. So only small degree polynomials $f : Z_n^T \to Z_n$ can be considered.

5   Conclusion and Future Work

In this paper, we have proposed an interactive *OMPE* protocol for the multivariate case. Its complexity is linear with the variable numbers. So, it could be considered as relatively efficient and it is proved to be secure in the malicious case even if many SFE, OPE and OMPE schemes could be modified to be proved secure in the malicious case as shown in [13].

The simple fundamental idea used in this paper is to combine an additively homomorphic semantically secure encryption scheme and a multiplicatively one defined over the same domain Z_n^*. We thus simply extend El Gamal's in order to get a secure multiplicatively homomorphic encryption over Z_n^*, with n being a RSA modulus.

As specified in the introduction, fully homomorphic encryption schemes (encryption scheme that allow both addition and multiplication) would provide noninteractive OPE protocol. Boneh, Goh and Nissim propose in [3] an encryption scheme for quadratic formulas. Obtaining an efficient additive and multiplicative homomorphic encryption scheme (fully homomorphic) has for long been known to be the perfect way to obtain OPE protocols, and a long-standing open problem until Gentry proposed a solution [9]. However, this cryptosystem is not still practical: according to the author, making the full scheme practical remains an open problem. Furthermore, its semantic security is based on new hardness assumptions. However, this is a very promising step for practical applications.

In further works, we are interested in finding a way to not reveal the monomials number and to see how the Gentry function could be used in our case. Moreover, we will compare our protocol with more existing works. Finally, our protocol only works with polynomials defined on Z_n. In many applications, floating numbers are required. It is very challenging to build protocols dealing with floating numbers.

Acknowledgments

The authors would like to thank anonymous referees for their helpful comments.

References

1. Ben-Ya'akov, Y.: Evaluation of multivariate polynomials and applications, M.Sc. degree in Computer Science, The Open University of Israel (2007)
2. Boneh, D., Franklin, M.: Efficient generation of shared rsa keys. In: Fumy, W. (ed.) EUROCRYPT 1997. LNCS, vol. 1233, pp. 425–439. Springer, Heidelberg (1997)
3. Boneh, D., Goh, E.-J., Nissim, K.: Evaluating 2-dnf formulas on ciphertexts. In: Kilian, J. (ed.) TCC 2005. LNCS, vol. 3378, pp. 325–341. Springer, Heidelberg (2005)
4. Chang, Y.-C., Lu, C.-J.: Oblivious polynomial evaluation and oblivious neural learning. In: Boyd, C. (ed.) ASIACRYPT 2001. LNCS, vol. 2248, pp. 369–384. Springer, Heidelberg (2001)
5. Chevallier-Mames, B., Paillier, P., Pointcheval, D.: Encoding-free elgamal encryption without random oracles. In: Yung, M., Dodis, Y., Kiayias, A., Malkin, T.G. (eds.) PKC 2006. LNCS, vol. 3958, pp. 91–104. Springer, Heidelberg (2006)
6. Cramer, R., Damgard, I., Nielsen, J.B.: Multiparty computation from threshold homomorphic encryption. In: Pfitzmann, B. (ed.) EUROCRYPT 2001. LNCS, vol. 2045, pp. 280–299. Springer, Heidelberg (2001)
7. Even, S., Goldreich, O., Lempel, A.: A randomized protocol for signing contracts. In: CRYPTO, pp. 205–210 (1982)
8. El Gamal, T.: A public key cryptosystem and a signature scheme based on discrete logarithms. IEEE Transactions on Information Theory 31(4), 469–472 (1985)
9. Gentry, C.: Fully homomorphic encryption using ideal lattices. In: Mitzenmacher, M. (ed.) STOC, pp. 169–178. ACM, New York (2009)
10. Goldreich, O., Vainish, R.: How to solve any protocol problem - an efficiency improvement. In: Pomerance, C. (ed.) CRYPTO 1987. LNCS, vol. 293, pp. 73–86. Springer, Heidelberg (1988)
11. Goldwasser, S., Micali, S.: Probabilistic encryption and how to play mental poker keeping secret all partial information. In: STOC, pp. 365–377. ACM, New York (1982)
12. Kiayias, A., Yung, M.: Secure games with polynomial expressions. In: Orejas, F., Spirakis, P.G., van Leeuwen, J. (eds.) ICALP 2001. LNCS, vol. 2076, pp. 939–950. Springer, Heidelberg (2001)

13. Lindell, Y., Pinkas, B.: An efficient protocol for secure two-party computation in the presence of malicious adversaries. In: Naor, M. (ed.) EUROCRYPT 2007. LNCS, vol. 4515, pp. 52–78. Springer, Heidelberg (2007)
14. Naor, M., Pinkas, B.: Oblivious transfer and polynomial evaluation. In: STOC, pp. 245–254 (1999)
15. Paillier, P.: Public-key cryptosystems based on composite degree residuosity classes. In: Stern, J. (ed.) EUROCRYPT 1999. LNCS, vol. 1592, pp. 223–238. Springer, Heidelberg (1999)
16. Freedman, M.J., Ishai, Y., Pinkas, B., Reingold, O.: Keyword search and oblivious pseudorandom functions. In: Kilian, J. (ed.) TCC 2005. LNCS, vol. 3378, pp. 303–324. Springer, Heidelberg (2005)
17. Rabin, M.O.: How to exchange secrets by oblivious transfer, Tech. Memo TR-81, Aiken Computation Laboratory (1981)
18. Sander, T., Young, A., Yung, M.: Non-interactive cryptocomputing for nc^1. In: FOCS, pp. 554–567 (1999)
19. Yao, A.C.-C.: How to generate and exchange secrets (extended abstract). In: FOCS, pp. 162–167. IEEE, Los Alamitos (1986)

A   Proof (schetch) of Theorem 1

Proof. (sketch). Let $k \in \mathbb{N}$ be a security parameter. In the following, we will denote by E, E_1, E_2, E_3 the sets of p.p.t algorithms M such that respectively $M(pk) \in Z_p^{*2}$, $M(pk) \in J_p^2$, $M(pk) \in (Z_p^* \setminus J_p) \times (Z_p^* \setminus J_p)$ and $M(pk) \in J_p \times (Z_p^* \setminus J_p) \cup (Z_p^* \setminus J_p) \times J_p$.

Let $M \in E$ be a p.p.t algorithm and $\{x, y\} = M(pk)$. To prove the security of the encryption scheme (see Definition 1) we have to prove that the two random variables families $X_{M,k} = (1^k, pk, x, y, Enc_{pk}(x))$ and $Y_{M,k} = (1^k, pk, x, y, Enc_{pk}(y))$ indexed by $k \in \mathbb{N}$ are computationally indistinguishable for any $M \in E$. In the following, in order to reduce notations, we consider that any distinguisher implicitly knows k, pk, x, y (thus, $X_{M,k} = Enc_{pk}(x)$ and $Y_{M,k} = Enc_{pk}(y)$). First, let's prove the indistinguishability between $Enc_{pk}(x)$ and $Enc_{pk}(y)$ for $M \in E_1$, $M \in E_2$, $M \in E_3$.

- $M \in E_1$ $(x, y \in J_p)$. Assuming that DDH property holds for J_p, El Gamal's encryption scheme is semantically secure over J_p. It means $(u^r, v^r x) \equiv^c (u^r, v^r y)$ which implies that $(u^r, -v^r x) \equiv^c (u^r, -v^r y)$.

  It implies that $(u^r, bv^r x + (b-1)v^r x) \equiv^c (u^r, bv^r y + (b-1)v^r y)$ where b is a random bit. As, $Enc_{pk}(x) = (u^r, bv^r x + (b-1)v^r x, Enc_{pk_1}(b))$ (idem for y), we state that

$$Enc_{pk}(x) \equiv^c Enc_{pk}(y) \tag{1}$$

- $M \in E_2$ $(x, y \notin J_p)$. By arguing in the same way than previously, we prove that

$$Enc_{pk}(x) \equiv^c Enc_{pk}(y) \tag{2}$$

- $M \in E_3$ $(x \notin J_p, y \in J_p$ or $x \in J_p, y \notin J_p)$. Let's assume $x \notin J_p$. First let's prove that $Enc_{pk}(x)$ and $Enc_{pk}(-x)$ are indistinguishable. Let b a random bit. By definition, $Enc_{pk}(-x)$ is equal to

$$(u^r, bv^r(-x) + (b-1)v^r(-x), Enc_{pk_1}(b))$$
$$= (u^r, (1-b)v^r x + ((1-b)-1)v^r x, Enc_{pk_1}(b))$$

The semantically security of Goldwasser-Micali encryption scheme ensures that $Enc_{pk_1}(b) \equiv^c Enc_{pk_1}(1-b)$. By noticing that $1-b$ is a random bit, the 2 previous assertions implies that $Enc_{pk}(x) \equiv^c Enc_{pk}(-x)$.

As $-x \in J_p$, by using (1), we can state that $Enc_{pk}(-x) \equiv^c Enc_{pk}(y)$, thus

$$Enc_{pk}(x) \equiv^c Enc_{pk}(y) \tag{3}$$

To conclude, we have to consider any $M \in E$. We could show that there exists $M_1 \in E_1$, $M_2 \in E_2$ and $M_3 \in E_3$ and an (polynomial or not) algorithm C with $C(pk) = (p_1, p_2, p_3)$ be a probability vector such that M can be simulated by an (polynomial or not) algorithm M' (meaning that M and M' (indexed by pk) are statistically indistinguishable $M' \equiv^s M$) defined by : $M'(pk) = M_i(pk)$ with a probability $p_i = C_i(pk)$.[3]

We notice that $M' \equiv^s M$ implies $X_{M',k} \equiv^s X_{M,k}$ and $Y_{M',k} \equiv^s Y_{M,k}$. We conclude by remarking that if there is a polynomial distinguisher between $X_{M,k}$ and $Y_{M,k}$ then there is a polynomial distinguisher between $X_{M',k}$ and $Y_{M',k}$ then there is a polynomial distinguisher between $X_{M_1,k}$ and $Y_{M_1,k}$ or between $X_{M_2,k}$ and $Y_{M_2,k}$ or between $X_{M_3,k}$ and $Y_{M_3,k}$. This contradicts (1), (2) or (3).   □

---

[3] Straightforwardly, C estimates the probability that $M(pk) \in J_p^2$, $M(pk) \in J_p \times (Z_p^* \setminus J_p) \cup (Z_p^* \setminus J_p) \times J_p$ or $M(pk) \in (Z_p^* \setminus J_p)^2$ by executing M sufficiently (C is not required to be polynomial). M_1 (resp. M_2, M_3) consists in executing $M(pk)$ a number of rounds upper bounded by polynomial $|pk|$ until $M(pk)$ belongs to J_p^2 (resp. $(Z_p^* \setminus J_p)^2$, $J_p \times (Z_p^* \setminus J_p) \cup (Z_p^* \setminus J_p) \times J_p$) (return random values otherwise). As deciding if $x \in J_p$ or not can be decided by a p.p.t algorithm, M_i is a p.p.t algorithm.

Author Index